KU-740-761

THE PRACTICE OF PUBLIC RELATIONS

6TH EDITION

FRASER P. SEITEL

Senior Counselor, Burson-Marsteller
Managing Partner, Emerald Partners

Prentice Hall, Englewood Cliffs, New Jersey 07632

**To Helen Seitel, The Mother of All Mothers—
Like the Energizer Bunny, She Keeps on Going!**

Library of Congress Cataloging-in-Publication Data
Seitel, Fraser P.
The practice of public relations / Fraser P. Seitel.—6th ed.
p. cm.
Includes bibliographical references (p.) and index.
ISBN 0-02-408840-4
1. Public relations—United States. I. Title.
HM263.S42 1995 94-6766
659.2—dc20 CIP

Acquisitions Editor: David Borkowsky
Assistant Editor: Melissa Steffens
Editorial Assistant: Aviva Rosenberg
Copy Editor: Helen Greenberg
Cover Designer: Andrea Miles/Menagerie Design & Publishing
In-house Project Liaison: Alana Zdinak
Manufacturing Buyer: Paul Smolinski
Production Management: Thomas E. Dorsaneo/Publishing Consultants

Cover Photo: Jon Levy/Gamma/Liaison Network

Printed in the United States of America

10 9 8 7 6 5 4 3

ISBN 0-20-408840-4

Prentice-Hall International (UK) Limited, *London*
Prentice-Hall of Australia Pty. Limited, *Sydney*
Prentice-Hall Canada Inc., *Toronto*
Prentice-Hall Hispanoamericana, S.A., *Mexico*
Prentice-Hall of India Private Limited, *New Delhi*
Prentice-Hall of Japan, Inc., *Tokyo*
Simon & Schuster Asia Pte. Ltd., *Singapore*
Editora Prentice-Hall do Brasil, Ltda., *Rio de Janeiro*

CONTENTS

APPENDIXES

FORWARD

Any effective executive today will spend a significant part of his or her time on public relations. Underlying all credible public relations is responsible and thoughtful action. But even with this correct background, there is often faulty communications between executives and their internal and external audiences.

In this Sixth Edition of *The Practice of Public Relations,* Fraser Seitel has built upon the foundation of one of the most widely-used public relations texts in America to incorporate new sections on video, integrated marketing, and multi-cultural communications. These new sections, along with the proven material from previous editions, make this an essential text for university communications students.

Fraser Seitel brings to each discussion of the tactics of public relations the insights of a practitioner in the field—at its highest level. A long-time corporate vice president and consultant, he not only knows what should work, he knows from personal experience what *will* work. For students seeking to enter this exciting field, or for others who want to gain more practical knowledge about public relations, there is no better mentor than Fraser Seitel and the Sixth Edition of *The Practice of Public Relations.*

Ralph L. Lowenstein
Dean
College of Journalism and Communications
University of Florida

PREFACE

Public relations is among the most *dynamic* professions in society.

At its epicenter are real-life situations—cases—that alter the communications landscape and redefine how we assess and handle communications challenges. The cases that dominate public relations discussion are the same ones that dominate the news of the day.

Whitewater. Waco. Watergate. Pepsi-Cola and its syringe scare. General Motors and NBC's exploding trucks. O.J. Simpson. Tonya Harding. Howard Stern. Ice T. Beavis and Butt-Head. All play a part in public relations lore and learning. To understand the public relations implications of each requires the development of technical skill, experience, and judgment.

That's what this book is all about.

The Practice of Public Relations, 6th edition is different from other introductory texts in the field. Its premise is that public relations is a brutally practical, constantly changing, thoroughly fascinating field. And while other texts may steer clear of the cases, the "how to" counsel, and the public relations conundrums that force students to think, this book confronts them all. It is, if you'll forgive the vernacular, an "in-your-face" textbook for an "in-your-face" profession.

Part One deals with the philosophical underpinnings of public relations practice, including the importance of management and planning, ethics and research, communications and public opinion. **Part Two** explores the practical communications applications of the field, including the emergence of video and the integration of public relations, marketing, and advertising into the study of communications cross-training. **Part Three** discusses the myriad publics with which the field deals, including multicultural communities. **Part Four** dissects emerging trends, including crisis management and the law.

The 40 case studies included here confront the reader with the most prominent and perplexing public relations problems—Pepsi, Exxon, Tylenol, United Way, Domino's Pizza, Jack-in-the-Box and contaminated burgers, AT&T and Monkeygate, O. J. Simpson's murder trial, and many more.

Beyond this, a number of unique elements set this book apart:

- The prominence of ethics in the practice of public relations is highlighted with "A Question of Ethics" cases in every chapter.
- "Between the Lines" features complement the text with provocative examples of what's right and what's wrong about public relations practice.
- Chapter Summaries and Discussion Starter questions highlight the key messages delivered in each chapter.
- Updated Suggested Readings and "Top-of-the-Shelf" book reviews supplement the text with the field's most current literature.
- Tips from the Top spotlights prominent professionals—from President Clinton's White House press secretary to the architect of General Motors' NBC defense to the public relations spokesman for the Pope.

Finally, fittingly, *The Practice of Public Relations*, 6th edition is produced in a full-color format to underscore the liveliness, vitality, and relevance of the practice of public relations.

Fraser P. Seitel

Acknowledgments

The 6th edition of *The Practice of Public Relations* is, in every sense of the word, a major revision.

With three new chapters, nine new interviews, and numerous new case studies, my ruthless editor, Dave Borkowsky, allowed precious little time to dawdle. He is a tough man but fair. And I am grateful to him as well as to Tom Dorsaneo, who skillfully edited from the deck of his San Rafael chateau.

I was also assisted in this effort by a crew of valiant citizens.

- First, Melanie Eisenberg arrived at the eleventh hour to ensure that this project stayed on course. Her organizational and administrative talents are without equal, and I am most grateful to her. Earlier on, my friend Diane Broschart stepped in heroically to keep the effort moving.
- The updated Suggested Readings in this volume are largely the work of Florida's own Gloria Devoto, whose early efforts on my behalf were magnificent. Bill Adams trained her well.
- I am indebted as well to the willing and well-known experts in the field who provided "Tips from the Top" interviews—Archbishop John Foley, Dee Dee Myers, Harry Pearce, Terrie Williams, Harold Burson, Ed Bernays, and all the others. I appreciate their participation very much.
- I am also most grateful to John Ward, one of the field's preeminent technological experts, who contributed the "Public Relations and Technology" feature in Chapter 20.
- In addition, Pepsi's Rebecca Maderia and Anne Ward and General Motors' Ed Lechtzin were too kind in their sharing of insights, written materials, and video tapes surrounding the landmark public relations cases with which they were directly involved.
- I also thank the public relations teachers whose insightful suggestions aided this 6th edition: William C. Adams, School of Journalism and Mass Communications, Florida International University; John Butler; Rachel L. Holloway, Department of Communications Studies, Virginia Polytechnic Institute and State University; Diana Harney, Department of Communication and Theater, Pacific

Lutheran University; Cornelius Pratt, Department of Advertising, Communications, and Public Relations, Michigan State University; Robert Cole, Pace University; Janice Sherline Jenny, College of Business, Herkimer County Community College, and Craig Kelly, School of Business, California State University, Sacramento.

- The constructive critiques of the other editions of the book by colleagues at leading universities helped make this sixth edition an all-around better book: Lyle J. Barker, Ohio State University; William G. Briggs, San Jose State University; E. Brody, Memphis State University; John S. Detweiler, University of Florida; Jim Eiseman, University of Louisville; Sandy Grossbart, University of Nebraska; Marjorie Nadler, Miami University; Sharon Smith, Middle Tennessee State University; Robert Wilson, Franklin University; Paul Brennan, Nassau Community College; Carol L. Hills, Boston University; George Laposky, Miami-Dade Community College; Mack Palmer, University of Oklahoma; Judy VanSlyke Turk, Louisiana State University; Roger B. Wadsworth, Miami-Dade Community College; James E. Grunig, University of Maryland; Robert T. Reilly, University of Nebraska at Omaha; Kenneth Rowe, Arizona State University; Dennis L. Wilcox, San Jose State University; Albert Walker, Northern Illinois University; Stanley E. Smith, Arizona State University; Dr. Jan Quarles, University of Georgia; Pamela J. Creedon, Ohio State University; Joel P. Bowman, Western Michigan University; Thomas H. Bivins, University of Oregon; Joseph T. Nolan, University of North Florida; Frankie A. Hammond, University of Florida; Bruce Joffe, George Mason University; Larissa Grunig, University of Maryland; Maria P. Russell, Syracuse University; and Melvin L. Sharpe, Ball State University.

Last but not least, the real reason we continue to push ahead with new and better editions of this tome—aside, of course, from the never-ending quest for higher scholarship—is that the Seitel brain trust—Rosemary, Raina, and David—keep cracking that whip!

It is indeed my pleasure to comply.

Fraser P. Seitel

About the Author

Fraser P. Seitel is a veteran of more than two decades in the practice of public relations.

In 1992, after serving for a decade as senior vice president and director of public affairs for Chase Manhattan Bank, Mr. Seitel formed Emerald Partners, a management and communications consultancy, and also became senior counselor at the world's largest public affairs firm, Burson-Marsteller. In his practice, Mr. Seitel continues to counsel in the areas for which he had responsibility at Chase—media relations, speechwriting consumer relations, employee communications, financial communications, philanthropic activities, and strategic management consulting.

Mr. Seitel has supplemented his professional public relations career with steady teaching assignments at Fairleigh Dickinson University, Pace University, New York's Professional Development Institute, Chicago's Ragan Report Workshops, and Colorado's Estes Park Institute. After studying and examining many texts in public relations, he concluded that none of them "was exactly right." Therefore, in 1980, he wrote the first edition of *The Practice of Public Relations* "to give students a feel for how stimulating this field really is."

In more than a decade of use at hundreds of colleges and universities, Mr. Seitel's book has introduced thousands of students to the excitement, challenge, and uniqueness of the practice of public relations.

The New York Times

Public Relations Has Potent Image

At Journalism Schools, It Now Ranks Ahead of Newspapers

By TRIP GABRIEL

The twice-monthly meeting of the New York University public relations club will now come to order. The topic of tonight's workshop, attended by half a dozen undergraduates who aspire to careers in the field, is that indispensable skill of our day: how to spin a news story.

But first a bit of old business. Neither Joyce Hauser, a former television talk show host who is the club's faculty adviser, nor Luis Perez, a practicing p.r. man who is tonight's invited guest, cares for the term spinning. Before getting down to cases, they want to put a spin on spin.

"We spin every day," said Ms. Hauser, looking down a table in the Loeb Student Center at club members picking at slices of mushroom pizza. "When we go out to find a boyfriend or girlfriend, we spin, don't we? 'Love me. I'm not going to show you my warts.' "

Yes, yes, the future spokespersons nod.

The students in the N.Y.U. club — its full membership is near 50, but attendance was low because of midterms — are representative of the widespread interest in a career in image-making among young people. The Public Relations Student Society of America, a pre-professional group, counts 179 chapters nationwide, including the one at N.Y.U. At America's journalism and mass communications schools, there are more students majoring in public relations today than in print reporting and editing.

"They've grown up seeing public relations spokespersons in front of the cameras," said Roberta Elins, an independent publicist who teaches the subject part-time at the Fashion Institute of Technology in Manhattan. "As opposed to when I started in the field in 1976, and you were never supposed to be in front of the camera. In its own way, it's become a much more glamorous job. I hate that word, but that's how they see it."

If the recent past saw the apotheosis of the corporate lawyer, the movie executive and the Wall Street banker, the 90's may turn out to be the decade of the spokesperson as culture hero.

Stars Begetting Stars

In a tough presidential campaign, it is George Stephanopoulos, mouthpiece for Bill Clinton, who, as depicted in the documentary "The War Room," manfully debates a slew of radio talk-show hosts. When Tom Cruise is scrutinized for his faith in Scientology, it is über-publicist Pat Kingsley who relays the words of the press-shy Mr. Cruise for a Q. & A. in Premiere magazine.

It's no surprise that members of the most media-besotted generation in history would fixate on the players shaping the

(Continued on next page)

stories, rather than on those whom the stories are actually about.

"A lot of the stories you see on the news are generated by public relations people," says Michael McHenry, a 21-year-old member of the N.Y.U. club. "I'm interested in politics or entertainment p.r. The spokespeople are in the public eye a lot."

Another club member, Erica McKeon, says that as a high school basketball player she resented that she had no alternative but to idolize the male players of the National Basketball Association. Now she wants to get into public relations to raise the profile of women athletes.

Ms. McKeon, who is 20, embodies a generation gap in levels of media savvy. "My parents always say why not coach a team?" she says. "They don't understand p.r. P.r. is where it starts."

Neal Gabler, a social critic who researched the history of public relations for a forthcoming book about the columnist Walter Winchell, said the prestige the field enjoys among students today is "spooky for what it says about the culture." But, he added, "one can't begrudge them the knowledge that this is the way it works now."

"I think the difference is we see and appreciate the mechanics of celebrity-making in a way previous generations did not. Then the whole idea was to hide the hand. Today there's a certain pride of authorship — Pat Kingsley's pride of authorship in Tom Cruise. We are so aware of the process. Almost everyone knows the process, so that it becomes a kind of performance art."

A Recent Boom

The popularity of public relations as a career goal has increased notably over the last six or seven years. During the image-conscious 1980's, independent public relations companies expanded rapidly, and at the same time some corporations welcomed their in-house p.r. people into top management juntas. Where the field once recruited from the ranks of burned-out or underpaid journalists, increasingly students with writing and communications skills go straight to public relations.

"A lot of it is market driven," says Jan Elliott, an associate professor at the School of Journalism and Mass Communication at the University of North Carolina, where the most popular major is advertising, followed by the news and editorial major, then public relations. "Back in the late 80's there was a shortage of newspaper jobs. Students found public relations was a job where they could get a lot of satisfaction and there were good opportunities for promotions, so they went after it. And schools have had to respond."

Susanne Shaw, a journalism professor at the University of Kansas, says, "If I have two or three students out of 15 or 20 in a basic reporting class today who want to be reporters, that's good." Most of the others, she says, are headed for public relations.

Nationwide there were 16,750 students majoring in print reporting and editing, compared with 18,220 majoring in public relations in the fall of 1992, according to a census of 413 higher-education programs conducted by Lee Becker of Ohio State University. The numbers have not fluctuated significantly since Mr. Becker began his annual survey in 1988. Though no hard figures exist for previous years, public relations and journalism professors agree the big surge of interest began in the mid- to late-80's.

Jobs Being Sliced

But many of today's aspiring public relations practitioners may be in for rough times when they hit the marketplace, where corporate downsizing has led to sharp cutbacks in the field. According to figures published this week in Jack O'Dwyer's Newsletter, an industry tip sheet, the top 10 public relations companies cut their payrolls by an average 7.5 percent in 1993. Mr. O'Dwyer says the growth areas are in health care, high-tech fields, and food and beverages — not exactly what some students may have in mind.

Hope Ewing, the 21-year-old president of the N.Y.U. club, says part of her role is to disabuse students of their glamorous image of public relations. High-visibility spokespeople in entertainment and politics are a tiny minority; most careers involve grinding out annual reports, newsletters and press releases for products and services.

But Ms. Ewing's warnings often fall on deaf ears. "If you had to pick one person who embodies what most of them want to be," she says, "it would be Warren Cowan," the pioneering Hollywood press agent befriended by clients from Rita Hayworth to Sylvester Stallone.

One of Mr. Cowan's latter-day counterparts, Lois Smith, who has represented Robert Redford since 1963 and more recently Michelle Pfeiffer and Sean Penn, says it's not all riding in limos. "I have an instinctive distrust of someone who wants to be a publicist," she says. "You're basically a salesman, except what you're selling is a person, not a table or chair." But the demurrals of Ms. Smith, who had just come from the set of "The Crossing Guard," starring Jack Nicholson and Anjelica Huston, when she was reached by phone in Los Angeles, may not have been entirely convincing to the N.Y.U. club members.

Their adviser, Ms. Hauser, told them public relations people had no reason to apologize for their profession, which can trace its roots in America all the way to Samuel Adams, the revolutionary patriot and newspaper essayist. What was the Boston Tea Party, which Adams helped plan, but a publicity stunt? How about the way he hyped the shooting of a handful of colonists by labeling it the Boston Massacre?

"Talk about spinning!" said Ms. Hauser, a peppy woman who used to be a guest host for a daytime talk show on Channel 5 in New York and is now an assistant professor. "He took something he believed in — the colonies — and said, 'How am I going to convince the media?' "

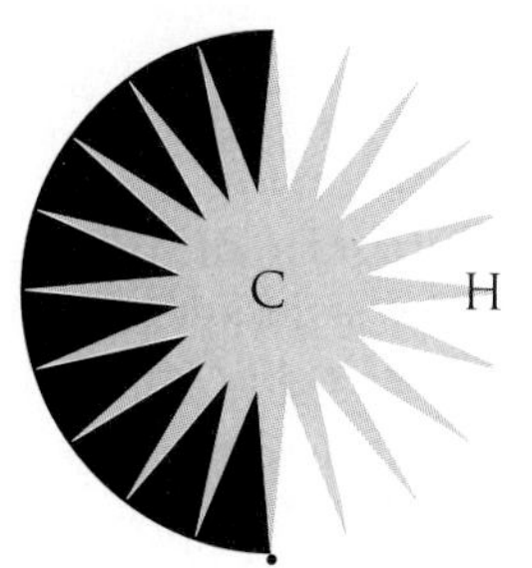

CHAPTER 1

*W*HAT IS PUBLIC RELATIONS?

AS THE PRACTICE OF PUBLIC RELATIONS PROCEEDS GINGERLY toward the year 2000, it is faced—with apologies to Charles Dickens—with "the best of times and the worst of times." On the one hand, the field has never been stronger or more respected.

Consider the following:

- The president of the United States, William Jefferson Clinton, who rode into office by deftly using the 1990s public relations techniques of town meetings, satellite press conferences, and message-rebuttal swat teams, considered the communications function so important that in the first seven months of his administration, he replaced his closest long-term adviser with a Republican—horror of horrors!—who also was a skilled public relations professional, to run the White House communications function.

- Meanwhile, Clinton's most irksome competitor, H. Ross Perot, miraculously won 30 percent of the popular vote, largely through public relations techniques such as using television talk shows to speak directly to the American public. Indeed, even after Clinton became president, Perot maintained his status as official thorn in the president's side by appearing regularly on Cable News Network's (CNN's) *Larry King Live* talk show (Figure 1–1).
- In the business world, Louis Gerstner, the new chairman of IBM, recruited in 1993 to resuscitate the once great computer company, made his first official move the replacement of IBM's long-time vice president of communications. Gerstner deemed the public relations function so important that he insisted it be staffed immediately by his own person.
- Salaries for public relations executives continued to rise in the 1990s, with the remuneration of the chief public relations officer at Time-Warner totaling in excess of $1 million annually.
- In the nonprofit world, America's largest charity, United Way, was stunned by a public relations scandal that led to the firing of the organization's highest official.

The prominence of public relations has never been greater.

On the other hand, the wave of downsizings, layoffs, mergers, and outright firings across America and the world has taken its toll on the public relations profession. The pervasive retrenchment of organizations has weighed heavily on public relations professionals. Many have lost their jobs, and the environment for the public relations people who remain employed has become decidedly less enjoyable or secure.

So the conundrum for public relations as the century draws to a close is that, on the one hand, the field has never been more accepted, respected, or high-paying but, on the other hand, jobs are less plentiful, less predictable, and certainly less pleasant.

GROWTH OF PUBLIC RELATIONS

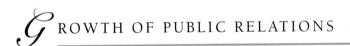

Despite the setbacks in the U.S. and world economies and the consequent layoffs of public relations people, the role and influence of public relations continue to grow. To wit:

- In the United States alone, public relations is a multi-billion-dollar business practiced by nearly 200,000 professionals, according to the U.S. Bureau of Labor Statistics.
- In a study of the chief executive officers of 200 organizations in the United States, Canada, and the United Kingdom, communications in general and the practice of public relations in particular were valued highly.[1]
- Approximately 200 colleges and universities in the United States and many more overseas offer a public relations sequence or degree program. Many more offer public relations courses. In the vast majority of college journalism programs, public relations sequences rank first or second in enrollment.
- By the end of the century, public relations is predicted to experience phenomenal growth, accounting for as many as 1 million jobs.[2]
- The U.S. government has 9,000 communications workers employed by the United States Information Agency alone. Another 1,000 communications spe-

Figure 1–1 The meteoric rise as a viable political candidate of slightly offbeat Texas billionaire H. Ross Perot was largely the result of Perot's frequent appearances on the nationwide Cable News Network's *Larry King Live*. Perot launched his independent campaign for president on this show and singlehandedly established the talk show as the campaign medium of choice for the 1990s. (*Courtesy Turner Broadcasting System*)

cialists work in the Department of Defense. The 20 largest public relations agencies generate more than $1 billion in fee income annually.[3]

The field's strength stems from its roots: "a democratic society where people have freedom to debate and to make decisions—in the community, the marketplace, the home, the workplace, and the voting booth. Private and public organizations depend on good relations with groups and individuals whose opinions, decisions, and actions affect their vitality and survival."[4]

So pervasive has the influence of public relations become in our society that some even fear it as a pernicious force; they worry about "the power of public relations to exercise a kind of thought control over the American public."[5]

All of this is quite remarkable when you consider that only a decade ago, public relations was still a maligned and misunderstood business, more renowned for the three-martini lunch than for almost anything else.

How times have changed! The practice of public relations has acquired new respect. Indeed, in an era of unrelenting questioning by the media and the public, an organization must not only be sensitive to but also highly considerate of its many publics.

A primary vehicle through which an organization shows its public sensitivity and consideration is its public relations professionals. Accordingly, the practice of public relations has shed its old misconceptions, acquired new responsibilities, and inherited an increasing amount of power, prestige, and pay.

However, along with its new stature, the practice of public relations is faced with unprecedented pressure.

- The most difficult pressure on public relations professionals is the new job insecurity that has afflicted the field in the 1990s. Just as public relations salaries have increased in the 1990s, so has the reality of decreasing job security.
- The very name *public relations* is being challenged by such euphemisms as *public affairs, corporate communications, integrated marketing, public information,* and a variety of other terms.
- As public relations positions have achieved greater credibility and heightened stature, competition from other fields has become more intense. Today the profession finds itself vulnerable to encroachment by people with a public relations background, such as lawyers, marketers, and general managers of every stripe. Ironically, the most prominent public relations person in America in the 1990s is the chief lawyer of General Motors, Harry Pearce, who took on the powerful NBC Network and won (see Chapter 18).
- The lack of leadership among public relations professionals continues to plague the field. Few practitioners are seen as leaders. No wonder cries of "PR for PR" are heard constantly.
- Many in public relations also are concerned about the preponderance of women in the field, the lack of equal pay for equal work among these women, and the paucity of minority practitioners.
- Finally, public relations continues to be hampered by a general lack of understanding, among senior managers, of its purpose and value. Even in the mid-1990s, many in management still don't understand what public relations is all about.[6]

Despite its considerable problems—in attaining leadership status, in finding its proper role in society, in earning enduring respect—the practice of public relations has never been more prominent. After less than 100 years as a formal, integrated, strategic thinking process, public relations has become part of the fabric of modern society.

DEFINING PUBLIC RELATIONS

The CEO who thunders, "I don't *need* public relations!" is a fool. He or she doesn't have a choice. Every organization has public relations, whether it wants it or not. The trick is to establish *good* public relations. That's what this book is all about—professional public relations, the kind you must work at.

Public relations affects almost everyone who has contact with other human beings. All of us, in one way or another, practice public relations daily. For an organization, every phone call, every letter, every face-to-face encounter is a public relations event.

To be sure, public relations is not yet a profession like law, accounting, or medicine, in which practitioners are trained, licensed, and supervised. Nothing prevents someone with little or no formal training from hanging out a shingle as a public relations specialist. Such frauds embarrass professionals in the field and, thankfully, are becoming harder and harder to find.

BETWEEN THE LINES

SO LONG, GEORGE

No event in the mid-1990s signaled the growing support of public relations more than the White House demotion of George Stephanopoulos in 1993.

When Bill Clinton became president, no adviser was a closer FOB (friend of Bill) than Stephanopoulos. As director of communications for the Clinton–Gore campaign, Stephanopoulos was rewarded when the president named him White House communications director, charged with improving the administration's relations with the news media.

From the start, Stephanopoulos was a disaster in the role.

His first act was to close off to reporters the corridor outside his office. Reporters complained of a lack of access to the president. Stephanopoulos's press briefings developed an air of tension and mistrust. By June, well aware of the critical nature of the chief White House public relations person, President Clinton reluctantly replaced his friend with, of all things, a Ronald Reagan Republican.

David Gergen, a former Reagan communications director and speech writer for presidents Nixon and Ford, was recruited to undo the damage Stephanopoulos had done. Within a month, under the watchful eye of Gergen, President Clinton's relations with the media improved and reporters' access to the President increased. Within months, the early image of a bumbling president was replaced by that of a man in control of the budget, health care, and other domestic issues. Gergen's in-depth, yet invisible public relations hand paid off remarkably well, and the corridor outside the communications director's office was reopened to one and all.

As the field has increased in prominence, it has grown in professional stature. The International Association of Business Communicators, a broad-based group that started with an internal communications focus, has 11,500 members. The Public Relations Society of America, with a national membership of 15,156, has accredited about one-third of its members through a standardized examination. The society has also investigated legal licensing—similar to that of the accounting and legal professions—for public relations practitioners.

The society's main objective is to increase the field's professionalism. It has a code of standards (see Appendix A), which focuses strongly on the practitioner's ethical responsibilities.

Whereas marketing and sales have as their primary objective selling an organization's products, public relations attempts to sell the organization itself. Central to its concern is the public interest.

Advertising also generally aims to sell products through paid means. Good public relations, on the other hand, cannot be bought; it must be earned. The credibility derived from sound public relations work may far exceed that gained through paid advertising.

The earliest college teachers of public relations exhorted students to

> learn new ways of using knowledge you already have—a different viewpoint, as if you moved to one side and looked at everything from unfamiliar angles. Project yourself into the minds of people you are trying to reach, and see things the way they do. Use everything you've learned elsewhere—English, economics, sociology, science, history—you name it.[7]

Two decades later, it is still widely thought that a broad background is essential to manage public issues effectively. Although specific definitions of public relations may differ, most who practice it agree that good public relations requires a firm base of theoretical knowledge, a strong sense of ethical judgment, solid communication skills, and, most of all, an uncompromising attitude of professionalism.

What, then, is public relations? Many people seem to have a pretty good idea, but few seem to agree. American historian Robert Heilbroner describes the field as "a brotherhood of some 100,000, whose common bond is its profession and whose common woe is that no two of them can ever quite agree on what that profession is."[8]

The reason for the confusion is understandable. On the one hand, the scope of activities taken on by public relations professionals is limitless. The duties of a practitioner in one organization may be completely different from those of a colleague in another organization. Yet both are engaged in the practice of public relations. Beyond this, because public relations is such an amorphous, loosely defined field, it is vulnerable to entry to anyone self-styled as a "public relations professional."

In 1923, Edward Bernays described the function of his fledgling public relations counseling business as one of providing "information given to the public, persuasion directed at the public to modify attitudes and actions, and efforts to integrate attitudes and actions of an institution with its publics and of publics with those of that institution."[9]

Today, although a generally accepted definition of public relations still eludes practitioners, there is a clearer understanding of the field. One of the most ambitious searches for a universal definition was commissioned in 1975 by the Foundation for Public Relations Research and Education. Sixty-five public relations leaders participated in the study, which analyzed 472 different definitions and offered the following 88-word sentence:

> Public relations is a distinctive management function which helps establish and maintain mutual lines of communications, understanding, acceptance, and cooperation between an organization and its publics; involves the management of problems or issues; helps management to keep informed on and responsive to public opinion; defines and emphasizes the responsibility of management to serve the public interest; helps management keep abreast of and effectively utilize change, serving as an early warning system to help anticipate trends; and uses research and sound and ethical communication techniques as its principal tools.[10]

In 1980, the Task Force on the Stature and Role of Public Relations, chartered by the Public Relations Society of America (PRSA), offered two definitions that project an image of the field at the highest policymaking level and encompass all its functions and specialties:

> Public relations helps an organization and its publics adapt mutually to each other.
> Public relations is an organization's efforts to win the cooperation of groups of people.[11]

DEFINING BY FUNCTIONS

Communications professor John Marston suggested that public relations be defined in terms of four specific functions: (1) research, (2) action, (3) communication, and (4) evaluation.[12] Applying the R-A-C-E approach involves researching attitudes on a particular issue, identifying action programs of the organization that speak to that issue, communicating those programs to gain understanding and acceptance, and evaluating the effect of the communication efforts on the public.

This formula is similar to one of the most widely repeated definitions of public relations, developed by Denny Griswold of *Public Relations News*, a leading newsletter for practitioners:

> Public relations is the management function which evaluates public attitudes, identifies the policies and procedures of an individual or an organization with the public interest, and plans and executes a program of action to earn public understanding and acceptance.[13]

The key words in this definition are two: *management* and *action.*

Public relations, if it is to serve the organization properly, must report to top management. Public relations must serve as an honest broker to management, unimpeded by any other group. For public relations to work, its advice to management must be unfiltered, uncensored, and unexpurgated. This can only be achieved if the public relations department reports to the CEO. While marketing promotes a specific product, public relations promotes the entire institution.

Nor can proper public relations take place without appropriate action. No amount of communications—regardless of its persuasive content—can save an organization whose performance is substandard. Performance—that is, action—must precede publicity. Indeed, in 1993, when Pepsi Cola was accused of allowing syringes to be placed in its cans, the company was so certain of the integrity of its manufacturing process that it "cried foul" immediately and was promptly vindicated. Pepsi could never have responded so quickly or triumphed so convincingly if its performance had been at all suspect.

Public relations, then, boils down to a process, as educator Melvin Sharpe has put it, that "harmonizes" long-term relationships among individuals and organizations in society.[14] Professor Sharpe applies five principles to this process:

1. Honest communication for credibility
2. Openness and consistency of actions for confidence
3. Fairness of actions for reciprocity and goodwill
4. Continuous two-way communication to prevent alienation and build relationships
5. Environmental research and evaluation to determine the actions or adjustments needed for social harmony

Stated yet another way, the profession is described by public relations professor Janice Sherline Jenny as "the management of communications between an organization and all entities that have a direct or indirect relationship with the organization, i.e. its publics."

The goal of effective public relations, then, is to harmonize internal and external relationships so that an organization can enjoy not only the goodwill of all of its publics, but also stability and long life.

INTERPRETING MANAGEMENT TO THE PUBLIC

Public relations practitioners are basically interpreters. On the one hand, they must interpret the philosophies, policies, programs, and practices of their management to the public; on the other hand, they must convey the attitudes of the public to their management.

To accomplish these tasks accurately and truthfully, practitioners must gain attention, understanding, acceptance, and, ultimately, action from target publics. But first, they have to know what management is thinking.

Good public relations can't be practiced in a vacuum. No matter what the size of the organization, a public relations department is only as good as its access to management. For example, it's useless for a senator's press secretary to explain the reasoning behind an important decision without first knowing what the senator had in mind. So, too, an organization's public relations staff is impotent without firsthand knowledge of the reasons for management's decisions and the rationale for organizational policy.

The public relations department in a profit-making or nonprofit enterprise can counsel management. It can advise management. It can even exhort management to take action. But management must call the shots on organizational policy. Practitioners must fully understand the whys and wherefores of policy and communicate these ideas accurately and candidly to the public. Anything less can lead to major problems.

INTERPRETING THE PUBLIC TO MANAGEMENT

The flip side of the coin is interpreting the public to management. Simply stated, this task means finding out what the public really thinks about the firm and letting management know. Regrettably, recent history is filled with examples of public relations departments failing to anticipate the true sentiments of the public.

In the 1960s, General Motors paid little attention to an unknown consumer activist named Ralph Nader, who spread the message that GM's Corvair was unsafe at any speed. When Nader's assault began to be believed, the automaker assigned private detectives to trail him. In short order, General Motors was forced to acknowledge its act of paranoia and the Corvair was eventually sacked, at great expense to the company.

In the 1970s, as both the price of gasoline and oil company profits rose rapidly, the oil companies were besieged by an irate gas-consuming public. When at the height of the criticism Mobil Oil purchased the parent of the Montgomery Ward department store chain, the company was publicly battered.

In 1980, Ronald Reagan rode to power on the strength of his ability to interpret what was on the minds of his countrymen. To his critics, President Reagan was a man of mediocre intellect and limited concentration. But to his supporters, Reagan was the "great communicator" who led the nation to eight years of unprecedented worldwide acclaim.

Reagan's successor in the White House, George Bush, turned out to be a less skillful communicator. Despite an overwhelming Gulf War victory and unprecedented popularity, President Bush suffered a stunning electoral defeat in 1992 at the hands of another savvy communicator, Governor Bill Clinton of Arkansas. While Bush stumbled, Clinton kept his candidacy focused on one single, unwavering message: "It's the economy, stupid." Candidate Clinton became President Clinton largely on the strength of correctly interpreting to the American public the importance of that key theme.

The savviest institutions in the 1990s—be they government, corporate or nonprofit—understand the importance of effectively interpreting their management and organizational philosophy, policies and practices to the public and, even more important, interpreting back to management how the public views their organization.

THE PUBLICS OF PUBLIC RELATIONS

The term *public relations* is really a misnomer. *Public relations,* or *relations with the publics,* would be more to the point. Practitioners must communicate with many different publics—not just the general public—each having its own special needs and requiring different types of communication. Often the lines that divide these publics are thin, and the potential overlap is significant. Therefore, priorities, according to organizational needs, must always be reconciled (Figure 1–2).

Technological change, in particular, has brought greater interdependence to people and organizations, and there is growing concern in organizations today about managing extensive webs of interrelationships. Indeed, managers have become interrelationship conscious.

Internally, managers must deal directly with various levels of subordinates, as well as with cross-relationships that arise when subordinates interact with one another. Externally, managers must deal with a system that includes government regulatory agencies, labor unions, subcontractors, consumer groups, and many other independent—but often related—organizations. The public relations challenge in all of this is to manage effectively the communications between managers and the various publics, which often pull organizations in different directions.

Definitions differ on precisely what constitutes a public. One time-honored definition states that a public arises when a group of people (1) face a similar indeterminate situation; (2) recognize what is indeterminate and problematic in that situation; and (3) organize to do something about the problem.[15]

Publics can also be classified into several overlapping categories:

1. **Internal and external** Internal publics are inside the organization: supervisors, clerks, managers, stockholders, and the board of directors. External publics are those not directly connected with the organization: the press, government, educators, customers, the community, and suppliers.

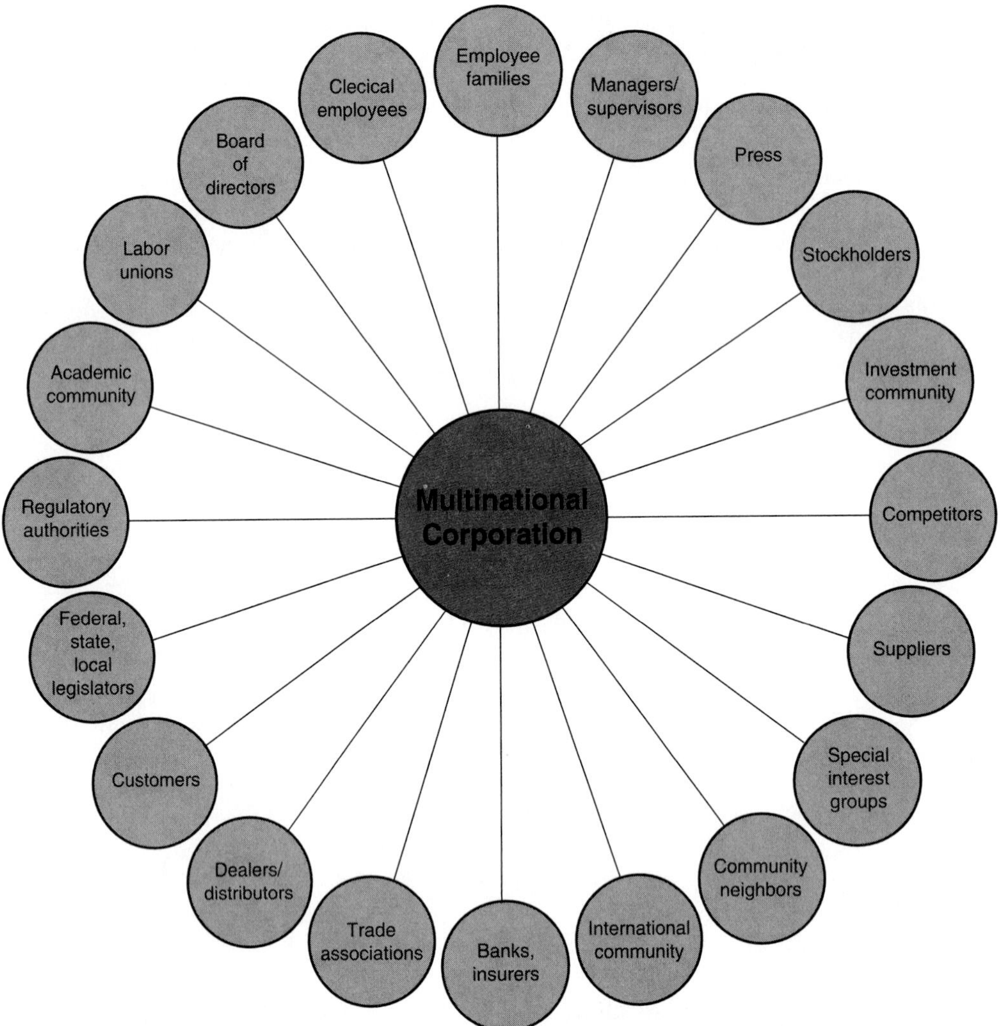

Figure 1–2 Twenty key publics of a typical multinational corporation. *(Art by Lou Braun)*

2. **Primary, secondary, and marginal** Primary publics can most help—or hinder—the organization's efforts. Secondary publics are less important, and marginal publics are the least important of all. For example, members of the Federal Reserve Board of Governors, who regulate banks, would be the primary public for a bank awaiting a regulatory ruling, whereas legislators and the general public would be secondary.
3. **Traditional and future** Employees and current customers are traditional publics; students and potential customers are future ones. No organization can afford to become complacent in dealing with its changing publics. Today, a firm's publics range from women to minorities to senior citizens to homosexuals. Each might be important to the future success of the organization.
4. **Proponents, opponents, and uncommitted** An institution must deal differently with those who support it and those who oppose it. For supporters, communications that reinforce beliefs may be in order. But changing the opinions of

skeptics calls for strong, persuasive communications. Often, particularly in politics, the uncommitted public is crucial. Many a campaign has been decided because the swing vote was won over by one of the candidates.

The typical organization is faced with a myriad of critical publics with whom it must communicate on a frequent and direct basis. It must be sensitive to the self-interests, desires, and concerns of each public. It must understand that self-interest groups today are themselves more complex. Therefore, the harmonizing actions necessary to win and maintain support among such groups should be arrived at in terms of public relations consequences.[16] And while management must always speak with one voice, its communications inflection, delivery, and emphasis should be sensitive to all its constituent publics.

Drawing the Line on Questionable Clients

In the 1990s, the essence of public relations practice—with management, journalists, and colleagues—comes down to one word: *integrity*. Once a public relations professional has lost that quality, he or she has lost the game.[17]

Ethical choices in public relations must be made daily.

On the one side are those who believe, like former PRSA President John Paluszek, that "Everybody is entitled to present a point of view and is entitled to professional assistance" in public relations.[18] On the other side are those who suggest that "If the trend continues of public relations people becoming image mercenaries, accepting any client regardless of character or conscience, as long as he or she pays the freight, then all of us will lose."[19]

One lightning rod for this issue of ethics in the 1990s was the huge public relations firm Hill & Knowlton. Early in the decade, Hill & Knowlton found itself under fire for deciding to accept such clients as the controversial Church of Scientology, the restrictive nation of China, and the antiabortion United States Conference of Catholic Bishops.

Hill & Knowlton attracted the greatest controversy when it represented Citizens For Free Kuwait in the fall of 1990. Hill & Knowlton's job was to stimulate U.S. public support for the war against Iraq. As part of its initiative, the firm distributed a video news release of a young Kuwaiti woman's testimony before Congress. The woman told of unspeakable Iraqi army atrocities, including the "dumping" of babies from incubators in Kuwaiti hospitals. The testimony of the woman, identified only as "Naryah," was riveting. The videotape was aired on stations throughout the country, and public support for the Kuwaiti plight was achieved.

Months later, it was revealed that Naryah was actually the daughter of the Kuwaiti ambassador. She had, in fact, never witnessed the Iraqi atrocities of which she spoke. Indeed, she hadn't been in Kuwait at the time.

The subsequent controversy over Naryah's videotaped testimony raised the question of public relations counsel representing issues and individuals of questionable veracity.

Stated another way, *Are there clients whom public relations people shouldn't represent? Where do you draw the line?*

UMMARY

Ethics, truth, credibility—these values are what good public relations is all about. Coverup, distortion, and subterfuge are the antitheses of good public relations.

Much more than customers for their products, managers today desperately need constituents for their beliefs and values. In the 1990s, the role of public relations is much more to guide management in framing its ideas and making its commitments. The counsel that management will need must come from advisers who understand public attitudes, public moods, public needs, and public aspirations.

Winning this elusive goodwill takes time and effort. Credibility can't be won overnight, nor can it be bought. If management policies aren't in the public's best interest, no amount of public relations can obscure that reality. Public relations is not effective as a temporary defensive measure to compensate for management misjudgment. (See the Exxon Case Study at the end of Chapter 3.) If management errs seriously, the best—and only—public relations advice must be to get the story out immediately.

One public relations professional who probably summed up the opinion of many colleagues about exactly what it is he does for a living was Peter F. Jeff, a Michigan practitioner who wrote to a local editor:

> A public relations professional is a bridge builder, not a drum beater—building long-term relationships between a company or organization and its publics based on two-way communication (i.e., listening and speaking). A public relations professional serves as an interpreter, helping the company adapt and adjust to the political, social, and economic climate . . . and assisting the public in more fully understanding the company.[20]

No less an authority than Abraham Lincoln once said, "Public sentiment is everything . . . with public sentiment nothing can fail. Without it, nothing can succeed. He who molds public sentiment goes deeper than he who executes statutes or pronounces decisions. He makes statutes or decisions possible or impossible to execute."

Stated another way, no matter how you define it, the practice of public relations has become an essential element in the conduct of relationships in the 1990s.

DISCUSSION STARTERS

1. Why has the practice of public relations become so pervasive in the 1990s?
2. Why are others—lawyers, accountants, general managers, and so on—interested in doing public relations?
3. Why is the practice of public relations generally misunderstood by the public?

4. Why isn't there one all-encompassing definition of the field?
5. Explain the approach toward defining public relations by the nature of its functions.
6. Explain the approach toward defining public relations as a harmonizing process.
7. Why is a public relations professional fundamentally an interpreter?
8. What are the four overlapping categories of publics?
9. What is the essence of proper public relations practice?
10. Has public relations truly rid itself of charlatan practitioners? Will it ever?

NOTES

1. James G. Grunig, "IABC Study Shows CEO Value PR," *IABC Communication World* (August 1990): 5.
2. John V. Pavlik, *Public Relations: What Research Tells Us* (Newbury Park, CA: Sage Publications, 1987), 85.
3. Jack O'Dwyer, "1992 PR Fee Income of 50 Firms," *O'Dwyer's PR Services Report* (May 1993): 18.
4. "The Design for Undergraduate Public Relations Education," a study cosponsored by the public relations division of the Association for Education and Journalism and Mass Communication, the Public Relations Society of America, and the educators' section of PRSA, 1987, 1.
5. Jeff Blyskal and Marie Blyskal, *PR: How the Public Relations Industry Writes the News* (New York: William Morrow, 1985), 61.
6. Philip Lesly, "Public Relations Numbers Are Up But Stature Down," *Public Relations Review* (Winter 1988): 3.
7. Berton J. Ballard, lecture at San Jose State University, San Jose, CA, 1948. Cited in Pearce Davies, "Twenty-Five Years Old and Still Growing," *Public Relations Journal* (October 1977): 22–23.
8. Cited in Scott M. Cutlip and Allen H. Center, *Effective Public Relations,* 6th ed. (Englewood Cliffs, NJ: Prentice-Hall, 1985), 5.
9. Edward L. Bernays, *Crystallizing Public Opinion* (New York: Liveright, 1961), LV.
10. Rex F. Harlow, "Building a Public Relations Definition," *Public Relations Review* 2, no. 4 (Winter 1976): 36.
11. Philip Lesly, "Report and Recommendations: Task Force on Stature and Role of Public Relations," *Public Relations Journal* (March 1981): 32.
12. John E. Marston, *The Nature of Public Relations* (New York: McGraw-Hill, 1963), 161.
13. Denny Griswold, *Public Relations News,* International Public Relations Weekly for Executives, 127 East 80th Street, New York, NY 10021.
14. This definition was developed by Dr. Melvin L. Sharpe, professor and coordinator of the Public Relations Sequence, Department of Journalism, Ball State University, Muncie, IN 47306.
15. John Dewey, *The Public and Its Problems* (Chicago: Swallow Press, 1927).
16. Sharpe, loc. cit.
17. "Leaders Not Lap Dogs, Needed to Ensure PR's Future," *O'Dwyer's PR Services Report,* January 1993, 17–18.
18. Stuart Elliott, "Public Relations Conference Is Devoted to Ethical Topics," *The New York Times,* November 4, 1991, D 10.

19. Fraser P. Seitel, "Walking the Public Relations High Wire in the 90's," speech delivered to the Raymond Simon Institute for Public Relations, Utica College–Syracuse University, April 1, 1992.
20. Peter F. Jeff, "Dissent! Public Relations," *Grand Rapids Press,* March 2, 1990.

TOP OF THE SHELF

Doug Newsom, Alan Scott, and Judy Van Slyke Turk,
This Is PR: The Realities of Public Relations, 5th ed.,
Belmont, CA: Wadsworth, 1993.

This Is PR offers a comprehensive and detailed view of the public relations field, emphasizing the larger social, economic, and political environment in which public relations plays a pivotal part.

The book's strength lies in its theoretical orientation; tracing the field through its origins and evolution; emphasizing the importance of research for backgrounding and planning; detailing research processes, procedures, and techniques; and highlighting the importance of persuasion communications theories, as well as problem-solving strategies that assist in public relations work.

A particular highlight is the extensive glossary of public relations–related terms, from *acetate transparencies* to *non-probability samples* to *synchronization rights.* The latter portion of the text is concerned with public relations tactics and techniques, including campaigns, case studies and crises.

This Is PR, with 615 pages and 15 chapters, is written by three veteran public relations educators. Its comprehensive coverage makes it a worthwhile public relations resource.

SUGGESTED READINGS

Albrecht, Karl. *At America's Service,* Homewood, IL: Dow Jones, 1988.

Baskin, Otis W., and Craig E. Aronoff. *Public Relations: The Profession and the Practice,* 2nd ed. Dubuque, IA: Wm. C. Brown, 1988.

Brody, E. W. *The Business of Public Relations.* New York: Praeger, 1987.

Cantor, Bill (Chester Burger, ed.). *Experts in Action: Inside Public Relations,* 2nd ed. White Plains, NY: Longman, 1989.

Center, Allen H., and Patrick Jackson. *Public Relations Practices: Managerial Case Studies and Problems,* 4th ed. Englewood Cliffs, NJ: Prentice-Hall, 1990.

Dilenschneider, Robert L., and Dan J. Forrestal. *Dartnell Public Relations Handbook,* 3rd ed. Chicago: Dartnell, 1987.

Dwyer, Thomas. *Simply Public Relations: Public Relations Made Challenging, Complete and Concise.* Stillwater, OK: New Forums, 1992.

Haberman, David, and Harry Dolphin. *Public Relations: The Necessary Art.* Iowa City: Iowa State University Press, 1988.

Hausman, Carl, and Phillip Benoit. *Positive Public Relations.* Blue Ridge Summit, PA: Tab Books, 1989.

Hiebert, Ray Eldon, editor. *Precision Public Relations.* White Plains, NY: Longman, 1988.
Jefkins, Frank. *Public Relations,* 4th ed. Philadelphia: Trans-Atlantic, 1992.
Lesly, Philip. *Bonanzas and Fool's Gold Treasures and Dross from the Nuggetizing of Our Lives.* Chicago: Lesly Co., 1987.
Newsom, Doug, Alan Scott, and Judy Van Slyke Turk. *This Is PR: The Realities of Public Relations,* 5th ed. Belmont, CA: Wadsworth, 1993.
Reilly, Robert T. *Public Relations in Action,* 2nd ed. Englewood Cliffs, NJ: Prentice-Hall, 1987.
Saffir, Leonard. *Power Public Relations: How to Get PR to Work for You.* Lincolnwood, IL: NTC Business, 1992.
Sullivan, Michael. *Management Audit for Public Relations Firms.* Doylestown, PA: Sullivan Associates (P.O. Box 229), 1987.
Wood, Robert J. *Confessions of a PR Man.* Scarborough, Ontario: New American Library of Canada, Ltd., 1989.
Wragg, David. *Public Relations Handbook.* Colchester, VT: Blackwell Business, 1992.

Case Study

Pepsi Punctures the Great Syringe Soda Scare

Pepsi-Cola's worst nightmare began inauspiciously enough on June 10, 1993, when an elderly Fircrest, Washington, couple claimed that they had discovered a syringe floating inside a can of Diet Pepsi.

For the next two weeks, the 50,000 people of Pepsi-Cola—from CEO and corporate communications staff to independent bottlers—worked round the clock to mount a massive public relations offensive that effectively thwarted a potential business disaster for its 95-year-old trademark.

The Pepsi case is a tribute to sound communications thinking and rapid, decisive public relations action in the face of imminent corporate catastrophe.

The day after the Fircrest complaint, a nearby Tacoma woman reported finding another hypodermic needle in a can of Diet Pepsi. The story of the two tampered cans—initially labeled "some sort of sabotage" by the local Pepsi bottler—ran on the Associated Press wire nationwide and sent shock waves throughout the country.

Pepsi, while immediately forming a crisis management team, headed by its president and CEO, Craig Weatherup, nonetheless chose to "hold its powder" publicly while first assessing all pertinent facts about the two incidents and devoting attention to the Seattle plant. Pepsi's perceived reluctance to confront the problem in a dramatic way—while it worked "behind the scenes"—drew initial fire from so-called crisis experts. One management communications professor warned, "They are underestimating the potential for rumors to feed off one another." Another crisis management counselor said, "This will be a terrible mistake if it turns out they should have acted in light of later events."

On June 13, the commissioner of the Food and Drug Administration (FDA), Dr. David A. Kessler, warned consumers in Washington, Oregon, Alaska, Hawaii, and Guam "to inspect closely cans of Diet Pepsi for signs of tampering and to pour the contents into a glass or cup before drinking."

In the face of criticism and with copycat tamperings accelerating, Pepsi held its ground. While critics urged the company to recall its products, the company continued to insist that its cans were virtually tamperproof. "We are 99% sure that you cannot open one and reseal it without its being obvious," the company assured its customers. Since there was "no health risk to either of the two consumers who filed the complaints or to the general public," Pepsi urged its bottlers and general managers *not* to remove the product from shelves.

On June 14, Pepsi issued an internal "consumer advisory" to its bottlers and general managers, reporting the results of its initial research on the reported claims:

> The syringes that were found are those commonly used by diabetics for insulin. We do not have syringes of this type in any of our production facilities.
>
> All cans used for Pepsi-Cola products are new packages. They are not reused or refilled at any time. There are two visual inspections during production: the first before cans are filled, the second while cans are on the filling line. The cans are then sealed.

Pepsi's strong inference was that first, the speed and security of its bottling production process made it extremely unlikely that any foreign object could appear in an unopened Pepsi container and second, what was being inserted wasn't being put into cans at the factory.

By June 14, the nation was awash in copycat Pepsi-Cola tamperings. Pepsi was barraged with reports of syringes in its cans from Louisiana to New York, from Missouri to Wyoming, from Pennsylvania to Southern California. Adding to Pepsi's nightmare was a media feeding frenzy the likes of which the company had never before encountered.

- "A 'Scared' Firm Fights to Save Its Good Name"—*New York Post*
- "FDA Warns Diet-Pepsi Drinkers"—*Associated Press*
- "Diet Pepsi Drinkers Warned of Debris"—*USA Today*
- "No Program for a Recall of Diet Pepsi"—*The New York Times*

Pepsi tampering stories dominated the national media, leading the evening news and network morning programs for three days. Local crews throughout the nation positioned themselves at local Pepsi bottling plants. Pepsi-Cola's president and six-person public relations staff put in 20-hour days in the company's Somers, New York, headquarters, each fielding 80 to 100 inquiries daily. The company was besieged by syringe-tampering mania.

Late on the evening of June 15, Pepsi received its first break.

A man in central Pennsylvania was arrested on the charge that he had fraudulently reported finding a syringe in a can of Pepsi.

With the first arrest made, Pepsi seized the offensive.

MEDIA RELATIONS

Pepsi's media strategy centered on one medium—television. Downplaying traditional print media— "the press conference is a dinosaur"—Pepsi-Cola's communications executives launched daily satellite feeds to the nation's electronic media to get out Pepsi's side of the tampering allegations.

- An initial video news release (VNR) picturing the high-speed can-filling lines, with voice-over narration by a plant manager, conveyed the message of a manufacturing process built on speed, safety, and integrity, in which tampering with products would be highly unlikely. The goal was to show that the canning process was safe. The initial VNR was seen by 187 million viewers (more than watched the 1993 Super Bowl) on 399 stations in 178 markets across the United States.
- A second VNR, picturing Pepsi President Weatherup and additional production footage, reported the first arrest for a false claim of tampering. It made four critical points: (1) complaints of syringes reported to be found in Diet Pepsi cans in other cities are unrelated; (2) tampering appears to be hap-

Figure 1–3 The subject of Pepsi's first VNR to reassure the public about its processing speed and safety was this rapid glimpse of a Pepsi bottling plant. (*Courtesy of Pepsi-Cola*)

pening *after* cans are opened; (3) the soft drink can is one of the safest packages for consumer food products; and (4) a recall is not warranted. This Pepsi-produced VNR was seen by 70 million viewers on 238 stations in 136 markets.

- A third VNR, narrated by President Weatherup, presented a segment from a convenience store surveillance video in which a woman was caught inserting a syringe into an open Diet Pepsi can. Weatherup thanked consumers for their support, reported additional arrests, and reaffirmed Pepsi's decision not to recall its product. This surveillance video was broadcast to 95 million viewers on 325 stations in 159 markets and, in effect, "broke the back" of the Pepsi syringe scare.
- In addition to the VNRs, Pepsi's media offensive included appearances by the company's president and a product safety expert on as many talk shows as could be fit into their schedules—each of the three major network evening newscasts, ABC's *Nightline,* CNN's *Larry King Live,* and so on.

Pepsi's was a video media blitz unparalleled in corporate public relations history.

GOVERNMENT RELATIONS

Meanwhile, Pepsi cooperated fully with Dr. Kessler and the FDA. While other consumer firms have adopted an adversarial position toward the watchdog agency, Pepsi embraced the FDA's investigation.

It was the FDA's Office of Criminal Investigation (OCI), in fact, that reported the breakthrough in the arrest of the man in central Pennsylvania. In addition to the FDA's "consumer alert" in the Pacific Northwest, Commissioner Kessler issued a statement on the tampering and the possibility of copycats. Later, Kessler appeared with Weatherup on *Nightline* and took the unprecedented step of declaring that "calm is in order . . . a recall is not necessary."

On June 17, Commissioner Kessler held a press conference in Washington, D.C. unequivocally characterizing the controversy as a hoax—the product of "misguided individual acts, magnified and multiplied by the attendant glare of the media, and a predictable outbreak of copycat behavior."

On June 21, Pepsi President Weatherup wrote to President Clinton, thanking him for the "excellent work" of Dr. Kessler and the FDA "in pursuing the recent product tampering hoax."

EMPLOYEE RELATIONS

In the area of employee relations—with its staff and bottlers—Pepsi adopted a policy of full and immediate disclosure as soon as it had discerned the pertinent facts.

Consumer advisories were dispatched at least once a day, usually twice or three times on each day of the crisis, letting bottlers and general managers in Pepsi's 400 field locations know what was going on, what had been reported, what the government was doing, and how the company was responding. Managers were advised on how to "communicate with

SCENES OF AN ALLEGED PRODUCT TAMPERING

FRAME: 08:32:15

An opened can of Diet Pepsi, held by a Colorado woman, appears to be lowered behind the counter of a convenience store, out of the clerk's line of sight.

FRAME: 08:32:27

The woman fumbles with her purse and pulls out wha appears to be a syringe.

FRAME: 08:32:34

The woman appears to place the syringe in the opened can of Diet Pepsi while keeping it behind the counter.

FRAME: 08:32:39

The woman places the can back on the counter then asks the clerk for a cup into which she pours the Diet Pepsi and allegedly discovers the syringe.

Figure 1–4 The evidence ending the Pepsi tampering hoax was this surveillance video of a woman caught stuffing a syringe into a Pepsi can. (*Courtesy of Pepsi-Cola*)

Pepsi is pleased to announce...

...nothing.

As America now knows, those stories about Diet Pepsi were a hoax. Plain and simple, not true. Hundreds of investigators have found no evidence to support a single claim.

As for the many, many thousands of people who work at Pepsi-Cola, we feel great that it's over. And we're ready to get on with making and bringing you what we believe is the best-tasting diet cola in America.

There's not much more we can say. Except that most importantly, we won't let this hoax change our exciting plans for this summer.

We've set up special offers so you can enjoy our great quality products at prices that will save you money all summer long. It all starts on July 4th weekend and we hope you'll stock up with a little extra, just to make up for what you might have missed last week.

That's it. Just one last word of thanks to the millions of you who have stood with us.

**Drink All The Diet Pepsi You Want.
Uh Huh.**

DIET PEPSI and UH-HUH are registered trademarks of PepsiCo, Inc

Figure 1–5 With its crisis proven to be a hoax, Pepsi triumphantly proclaimed its victory with this ad. (*Courtesy of Pepsi-Cola*)

employees and customers" in the form of "Product Tampering Guidelines," as well as procedures for reporting alleged tamperings.

President Weatherup also personally wrote to bottlers and general managers periodically during the crisis to keep them advised of breaking developments. When the surveillance video was found, Weatherup sent all Pepsi bottlers, by

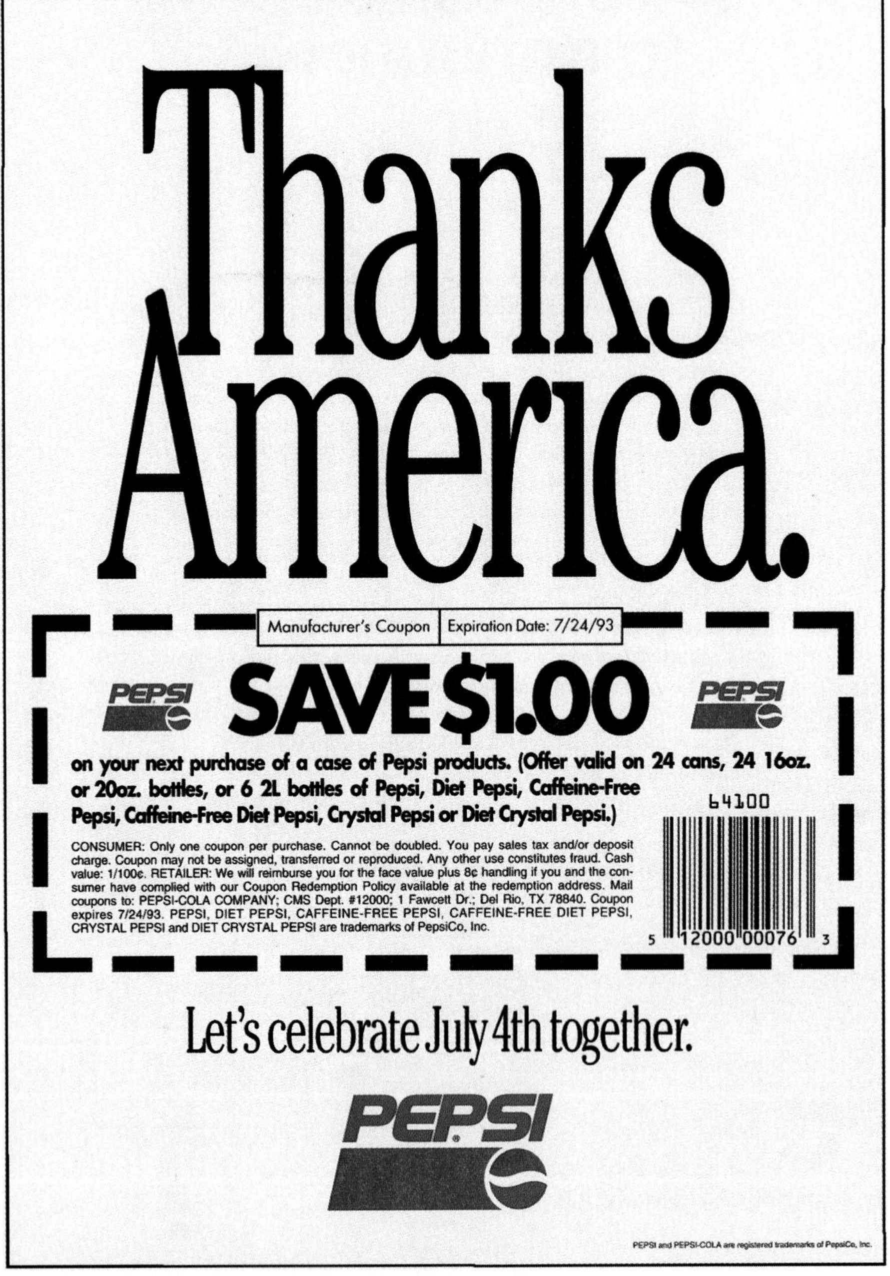

Figure 1–6 Case closed. Uh huh! (*Courtesy of Pepsi-Cola*)

overnight mail, a videotape of Commissioner Kessler's news conference, along with the surveillance footage.

"Please share it with your customers," the Pepsi president suggested.

By June 18, just one week—and what seemed like one millennium—after its product and reputation had been challenged, Pepsi declared victory in national ads:

> Pepsi is pleased to announce . . .
> . . . nothing.

What had begun as the worst kind of national nightmare, with critics and copycats threatening the company at every juncture, ended in a flurry of pervasive public praise. "Media-smart Pepsi" is how *Advertising Age* characterized the company's strategy. The *Milwaukee Sentinel*, in a rare journalistic admission of candor, labeled the media's leap to sensationalism on the Pepsi story "a mistake, a big mistake." *Business Week* credited the company for making "the right moves, Baby." The company was universally heralded for holding the line on a product recall and putting on the line its reputation and credibility.

Perhaps sweetest of all for Pepsi-Cola, after the FDA/OCI's arrest of 55 suspected hoaxers, was the bottom-line aftermath: Not only had Pepsi weathered the media storm and emerged with its credibility intact, but the impact on Pepsi's sales was negligible. President Weatherup reported that sales had fallen just 3 percent at the height of the crisis, approximately $30 million. By July and August, Pepsi sales were up 7%, the best summer in five years.

All in all, as one industry periodical put it, "Pepsi's response constituted nothing less than 'a textbook case' of how to come through a PR crisis."

QUESTIONS

1. Do you think Pepsi erred by not immediately volunteering to recall its product?
2. How would you assess Pepsi's overall public relations strategy?
3. How would you assess Pepsi's government relations strategy?
4. What were the pros and cons of ignoring print media and focusing instead on electronic media? Could this strategy backfire on Pepsi?
5. What were the pros and cons of using Pepsi's president as chief spokesperson?
6. What public relations lessons can be drawn from Pepsi's experience for handling future product tampering cases?

For further information about the Pepsi-Cola syringe scare case, see Claudia Carpenter, "A 'Scared' Firm Fights to Save Its Good Name," *New York Post*, June 17, 1993, 25; Gerry Hinckley, "'Big Mistake' Acknowledged on Syringe–Pepsi Story," *Milwaukee Sentinel*, June 21, 1993; Thomas K. Grose, "How Pepsico Overcame Syringe Challenge," *TJFR Business News Reporter*, July 1993, 1; Michael Janofsky, "Under Siege, Pepsi Mounts a TV Counter Offensive," *The New York Times*, June 17, 1993, D-1; Charles M. Madigan, "Recipe for National Scare: Pepsi, Media, Me-Too-Ism," *The Record*, June 21, 1993, D-1; Tom Mashberg, "Pepsi Puts Reputation on the Line," *The Boston Globe*, June 17, 1993, A-1; "Media-Smart Pepsi," *Advertising Age*, June 28, 1993, 26; "Public Relations Victory Sweep for Pepsi-Cola Officials," *Washington Post News Service*, June 20, 1993; Gary Strauss, "Scare Fails to Flatten Pepsi Sales," *USA Today*, June 23, 1993, B-1; Laura Zinn, "The Right Moves, Baby," *Business Week*, July 5, 1993, 30.

TIPS FROM THE TOP

JOSEPH T. NOLAN

Joseph T. Nolan is one of the world's foremost public relations practitioners. Dr. Nolan has spent the past decade teaching communications at the college level after a distinguished career in corporate public relations. He was vice president in charge of public and government relations and advertising at The Chase Manhattan Bank and later at the Monsanto chemical and pharmaceutical company. *Business Week* magazine cited him as one of the "top 10 executives in corporate public relations." Dr. Nolan has taught at the University of South Carolina, University of Florida, University of North Florida, and Flagler College in St. Augustine, where he now makes his home. His articles have appeared in the *Harvard Business Review, New York Times Magazine* and other publications.

What are the most significant challenges that confront the public relations profession?

Gaining management's confidence by providing high-quality advice and mature judgment, by focusing on results rather than on activities, and by being able to measure the results with greater precision than is now being done.

What do you see as the future of public relations education?

More emphasis on business management and on the social sciences, such as economics, social psychology, and sociology, and less on developing techniques and understanding gadgetry.

In order to get that first job, a student must be familiar with the carpentry of communications. But to advance on the job, he or she must demonstrate an ability to analyze, reason, and make judgments.

What do you see as the prospects for growth in employment in the public relations profession?
I think that employment will expand steadily, but not explosively, over the next decade or two, as more and more enterprises understand what public relations can do to help them.

What parts of the field do you see as growth areas in the 1990s?
Fund raising and investor and international relations are likely to increase, but I think that one of the biggest areas of growth will be in dealing with television in all of its aspects. Surveys show that perhaps 80 percent of the public gets its news through television, and yet most public relations departments suffer from a serious print bias.

What parts of the profession do you see as becoming more limited in available opportunities?
I suspect we've reached the saturation point in the placement area and in press agentry.

What are the greatest threats to the future of public relations?
Inept practitioners—men and women who don't understand thoroughly the enterprise they're trying to represent, or the most effective ways of carrying out that representation.

Do you envision that public relations practitioners will be called on to manage organizations in the future?
The best of the public relations practitioners will move up to top management roles, just as marketing and financial specialists, engineers, and lawyers have done in the past.

Will public relations ever attain the same stature as the professions of law and accounting?
If public relations keeps working at its accreditation procedure, improving it as it goes along, and does a better job of policing its ranks, it could very well eventually achieve a place alongside accounting, law, and the other professions. This would be an important development, but its importance should not be exaggerated. The only way to get this kind of stature is to merit it, and that must be done day by day.

What are the emerging trends you foresee in public relations over the next 20 years?
The most formidable challenge is likely to be managing the new business environment, both at home and abroad. The decisive issues will be external rather than internal, social and political rather than economic. The challenge will come primarily from the impact of laws and public opinion. Practitioners must understand how they are shaped, and how they can be changed.

By the year 2000, what do you predict will be the general state of the practice of public relations?

I predict that major organizations will have a public relations practitioner very near the top, and that they will weigh every major decision in light of its public relations impact, just as they do now with respect to its business and financial impact.

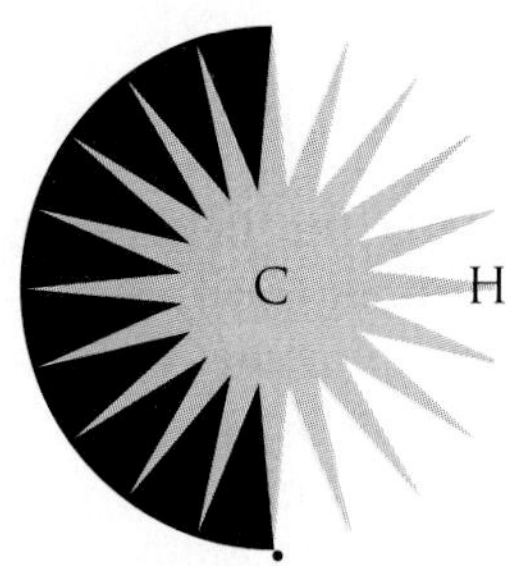

CHAPTER 2

THE EVOLUTION OF PUBLIC RELATIONS

THE STRENGTH OF THE PRACTICE OF PUBLIC RELATIONS today is based on the enduring commitment of the public to participate in a free and open democratic society. The bastion of public relations practice is America, where political participation is every individual's birthright and where democratic capitalism has forged an environment of competition in the marketplace of products and ideas.

Public relations as a modern American phenomenon—as we will note in this chapter—is less than 100 years old, much younger than other disciplines. The relative youthfulness of the practice means that the field is still evolving, and its status is improving daily. Indeed, the professionals entering the practice today are by and large superior in intellect, training, and even experience to their counterparts decades ago.

At least four trends are related to the evolution of public relations: (1) the growth of big institutions; (2) the increasing incidence of change, conflict, and confrontation in society; (3) the heightened awareness and sophistication of people everywhere as a result of technological innovations in communications; and (4) the increased importance of public opinion as democracy washes over the world in the 1990s (Figure 2–1).

- The bigness of today's society has played a significant role in the development of public relations. The days of the mom-and-pop grocery store, the tiny community college, and the small local bank are rapidly disappearing. In their places have emerged Wal-Marts, statewide community college systems with populous branches in several cities, and multibank, multistate banking networks. As institutions have grown larger, the public relations profession has evolved to interpret these large institutions to the publics they serve.

IN OTHER COUNTRIES IT TAKES COURAGE
TO STAND UP FOR THE RIGHT OF FREEDOM OF EXPRESSION.
IN AMERICA ALL IT TAKES IS A PHONE CALL.
Last year we watched Chinese students fight for freedom in Tiananmen Square. This year, freedom is being threatened again. But this time it's happening right here in America. This time we just can't sit back and watch.
For the past 25 years, the National Endowment for the Arts has provided support for over 80,000 cultural projects nationwide. But now Senator Jesse Helms and a small yet vocal minority are determined to restrict the Arts Endowment from funding anything that they consider to be "indecent or obscene."
While such censorship seems implausible in our society, this well-funded group of extremists has organized a massive campaign to pressure members of Congress to vote their way. And if we remain silent, that is exactly what will happen.
That's why it's so important for you to voice your opinion now.
To show that you strongly endorse freedom of expression, please call the toll-free number. When you do, two pre-written Western Union messages will be sent to Congress in your name.
As Americans, we take our right to freedom of expression for granted. But if we don't take a stand now, that right could be taken away.
People For The American Way
ACTION FUND
SEND A MESSAGE TO CONGRESS.
1-800-257-4900
OPERATOR 9681

Figure 2–1 The communications revolution sweeping the world was no more vividly illustrated than in 1989, when Chinese students, including this brave protestor, stood up for freedom in the face of military might. People for the American Way, a lobbying group, recalled this protest when, in 1990, U.S. Senator Jesse Helms threatened to censor government arts funding. (*Courtesy of People for the American Way*)

- The increasing incidence of change, conflict, and confrontation in society is yet another reason for the evolution of public relations. Women's rights, gay rights, animal rights, consumerism and environmental awareness, downsizings and layoffs, and unhappiness with large institutions have all contributed materially to the need for more and better communications and the existence of more and better communicators.
- A third factor in the development of public relations has been the heightened awareness of people everywhere. First came the invention of the printing press. Later it was the pervasiveness of mass communications: the print media, radio, and television. Then it was the development of cable, satellite, videotape, video discs, video typewriters, portable cameras, word processors, fax machines, and all the other communications technologies that have helped fragment audiences and create Marshall McLuhan's "global village."

  In a world where the image of a lone protestor blocking a line of tanks in Beijing's Tiananmen Square can be flashed around the world, to be seen on the evening news; when a war in Somalia can be witnessed in real time by people in their living rooms in Bangor, Maine; when a dictator in the Persian Gulf can be interviewed live by a reporter in Washington, there can be no doubt that the communications revolution has arrived.
- Finally, the outbreak of democracy in Latin America, Eastern Europe, the former Soviet Union, and South Africa has heightened the power of public opinion in the world. Just as increasing numbers of Americans made their voices heard through the civil rights movements, various consumer movements, the women's rights movement, and political movements throughout the ages, so too have oppressed peoples around the world risen up and spoken out. Accordingly, the practice of public relations, as a facilitator in understanding more clearly and managing more effectively in the midst of such democratic revolution, has increased in prominence.

ANCIENT BEGINNINGS

Although modern public relations is a twentieth-century phenomenon, its roots are ancient. Leaders in virtually every great society throughout history understood the importance of influencing public opinion through persuasion. For example, the Babylonians of 1800 B.C. hammered out their messages on stone tablets so that farmers could learn the latest techniques of harvesting, sowing, and irrigating.[1] The more food the farmers grew, the better the citizenry ate and the wealthier the country became—a good example of planned persuasion to reach a specific public for a particular purpose; in other words, public relations.

Later on, the Greeks put a high premium on communication skills. The best speakers, in fact, were generally elected to leadership positions. Occasionally, aspiring Greek politicians enlisted the aid of Sophists (individuals renowned for both their reasoning and their rhetoric) to help fight verbal battles. Sophists would gather in the amphitheaters of the day and extol the virtues of particular political candidates. Thus, the

Sophists set the stage for today's lobbyists, who attempt to influence legislation through effective communication techniques. From the time of the Sophists, the practice of public relations has been a battleground for questions of ethics. Should a Sophist or a lobbyist or a public relations professional "sell" his or her talents to the highest bidder, regardless of personal beliefs, values, and ideologies? When dyed-in-the-wool Republicans like David Gergen switch sides to join staunch Democrats like Bill Clinton, these ethical questions remain very much a focus of modern public relations.

The Romans, particularly Julius Caesar, were also masters of persuasive techniques. When faced with an upcoming battle, Caesar would rally public support through assorted publications and staged events. Similarly, during World War I, a special U.S. public information committee, the Creel Committee, was formed to channel the patriotic sentiments of Americans in support of the U.S. role in the war. Stealing a page from Caesar, the committee's massive verbal and written communications effort was successful in marshaling national pride behind the war effort. According to a young member of the Creel Committee, Edward L. Bernays (later considered by many to be the father of public relations), "This was the first time in our history that information was used as a weapon of war."[2]

Even the Catholic Church had a hand in the creation of public relations. In the 1600s, under the leadership of Pope Gregory XV, the Church established a college of propaganda to "help propagate the faith." In those days, the term *propaganda* did not have a negative connotation; the Church simply wanted to inform the public about the advantages of Catholicism. Today, the pope and other religious leaders maintain communications staffs to assist relations with the public. Indeed, the chief communications official in the Vatican maintains the rank of Archbishop of the Church. (See the interview in Chapter 3.)

EARLY AMERICAN EXPERIENCE

The American public relations experience dates back to the founding of the Republic. Influencing public opinion, managing communications, and persuading individuals at the highest levels were at the core of the American Revolution. The colonists tried to persuade King George III that they should be accorded the same rights as Englishmen. "Taxation without representation is tyranny!" became their public relations slogan to galvanize fellow countrymen.

When King George refused to accede to the colonists' demands, they combined the weaponry of sword and pen. Samuel Adams, for one, organized committees of correspondence as a kind of revolutionary Associated Press to disseminate speedily anti-British information throughout the colonies. He also staged events to build up revolutionary fervor, like the Boston Tea Party, where colonists, masquerading as Indians, boarded British ships in Boston Harbor and pitched chests of imported tea overboard—as impressive a media event as has ever been recorded *sans* television.

Thomas Paine, another early practitioner of public relations, wrote periodic pamphlets that urged the colonists to band together. In one issue of *Common Sense,* Paine wrote poetically, "These are the times that try men's souls. The summer soldier and the sunshine patriot will, in this crisis, shrink from the service of their country." The people listened, were persuaded, and took action—testifying to the power of early American communicators.

LATER AMERICAN EXPERIENCE

The creation of the most important document in our nation's history, the Constitution, also owed much to public relations. Federalists, who supported the Constitution, fought tooth and nail with anti-Federalists, who opposed it. Their battle was waged in newspaper articles, pamphlets, and other organs of persuasion in an attempt to influence public opinion. To advocate ratification of the Constitution, political leaders like Alexander Hamilton, James Madison, and John Jay banded together, under the pseudonym Publius, to write letters to leading newspapers. Today those letters are bound in a document called *The Federalist Papers* and are still used in the interpretation of the Constitution.

After ratification the constitutional debate continued, particularly over the document's apparent failure to protect individual liberties against government encroachment. Hailed as the Father of the Constitution, Madison framed the Bill of Rights in 1791, which ultimately became the first ten amendments to the Constitution. Fittingly, the first of those amendments safeguarded, among other things, the practice of public relations: "Congress shall make no law respecting an establishment of religion, or prohibiting the free exercise thereof; or abridging the freedom of speech, or of the press, or the rights of the people peaceably to assemble, and to petition the government for a redress of grievances." In other words, people were given the right to speak up for what they believed in and the freedom to try to influence the opinions of others. Thus was the practice of public relations ratified.[3]

INTO THE 1800s

The practice of public relations continued to percolate in the nineteenth century. Among the more prominent—yet negative—antecedents of modern public relations that took hold in the 1800s was press agentry. Two of the better-known—some would say notorious—practitioners of this art were Amos Kendall and Phineas T. Barnum.

In 1829, President Andrew Jackson selected Kendall, a writer and editor living in Kentucky, to serve in his administration. Within weeks, Kendall became a member of Old Hickory's "kitchen cabinet" and eventually became one of Jackson's most influential assistants.

Kendall performed just about every White House public relations task. He wrote speeches, state papers, and messages and turned out press releases. He even conducted basic opinion polls. Although Kendall is generally credited with being the first authentic presidential press secretary, his functions and role went far beyond that position.

Among Kendall's most successful ventures in Jackson's behalf was the development of the administration's own newspaper, the *Globe*. Although it was not uncommon for the governing administration to publish its own national house organ, Kendall's deft editorial touch refined the process to increase its effectiveness. Kendall would pen a Jackson news release, distribute it for publication to a local newspaper, and then reprint the press clipping in the *Globe* to underscore Jackson's nationwide popularity. Indeed, that popularity continued unabated throughout Jackson's years in office, with much of the credit going to the president's public relations adviser.*

Most public relations professionals would rather not talk about P. T. Barnum as an industry pioneer. Barnum was a huckster, pure and simple. His end was to make money, and his means included publicity. He remained undaunted even when the facts sometimes got in the way of his promotional ideas. "The public be fooled" might well have been his motto.

Like him or not, Barnum was a master publicist. In the 1800s, as owner of a major circus, Barnum generated article after article for his traveling show. He purposely gave his star performers short names—for instance, Tom Thumb, the midget, and Jenny Lind, the singer—so that they could easily fit into the headlines of narrow newspaper columns. Barnum also staged bizarre events, such as the legal marriage of the fat lady to the thin man, to drum up free newspaper exposure. And although today's practitioners scoff at Barnum's methods, some press agents still practice his techniques. Nonetheless, when today's public relations professionals bemoan the specter of shysters and hucksters that still overhangs their field, they inevitably place the blame squarely on the fertile mind and silver tongue of P. T. Barnum.

*Kendall was decidedly not cut from the same cloth as today's neat, trim, buttoned-down press secretaries. On the contrary, Jackson's man was described as "a puny, sickly looking man with a weak voice, a wheezing cough, narrow and stooping shoulders, a sallow complexion, silvery hair in his prime, slovenly dress, and a seedy appearance" (Fred F. Endres, "Public Relations in the Jackson White House," *Public Relations Review* 2, No. 3 [Fall 1976]: 5–12).

P. T. Barnum Revisited: The Rise of Howard Stern and the End of the World as We Know It

Although most public relations professionals disagree with the publicity-seeking antics attributed to P. T. Barnum, publicity for publicity's sake is still very much in vogue. In today's society of instantaneous mass communications, achieving the rank of celebrity, even if it is accomplished in a sleazy, Barnumesque way, can mean money—big money.

Behold the 1990s phenomenon of Howard Stern. New York City–based Stern is a foul-mouthed, venom-spouting, bathroom humor–mongering (and these are his good qualities!) host of a drive-time radio program. In 1993, as the nation rebelled against the outbreak of political correctness, Howard Stern suddenly, inexplicably, became hugely popular. His radio show was syndicated to multiple markets around the nation. Each morning, he and giggling sidekick Robin Quivers would shamelessly flog a variety of Howard Stern media properties for listeners to rush out and purchase.

Figure 2–2 Howard and sidekick, Robin, hucksters for the 90s. (*Photo courtesy of K-Rock 92.3 FM*)

And purchase they did. They subscribed to his cable television interview program. They dialed 800-52-STERN to buy his infantile videotapes—from the poignant "Butt Bongo Fiesta" to the pricier but more traditional "Miss Howard Stern 1994 New Year's Eve Pageant."

And ignominy of ignominies, Stern's book, *Private Parts*—published by Simon & Schuster, no less—rocketed into the number one spot on the best-seller lists in its first week out in 1993. Stern stood to realize more than $3.5 million from the book alone—not a bad investment for one summer's labors.

At least half of the American population finds Stern's humor gross and stupid, so they are dumbfounded as to why he is so popular. The reason is simple: The other half loves him! As Barnum himself might have phrased it, "The public"—or, at least in this case, half of it—"be fooled."

But the question remains: Is it right or proper to support such tasteless flotsam?

EMERGENCE OF THE ROBBER BARONS

The American Industrial Revolution ushered in many things at the turn of the century, not the least of which was the growth of public relations. The twentieth century began with small mills and shops, which served as the hub of the frontier economy, giving way to massive factories. Country hamlets, which had been the centers of commerce and trade, were replaced by sprawling cities. Limited transportation and communications facilities became nationwide railroad lines and communications wires. Big business took over, and the businessman was king.

The men who ran America's industries seemed more concerned with making a profit than with improving the lot of their fellow citizens. Railroad owners such as William Vanderbilt, bankers such as J. P. Morgan, oil magnates such as John D. Rockefeller, and steel impresarios such as Henry Clay Frick ruled the fortunes of thousands of others. Typical of the reputation acquired by this group of industrialists was the famous—and perhaps apocryphal—response of Vanderbilt when questioned about the public's reaction to his closing of the New York Central Railroad: "The public be damned!"

Little wonder that Americans cursed Vanderbilt and his ilk as robber barons who cared little for the rest of society. Although most who depended on these industrialists for their livelihood felt powerless to rebel, the seeds of discontent were being sown liberally throughout the culture. It was just a matter of time before the robber barons got their comeuppance.

ENTER THE MUCKRAKERS

When the ax fell on the robber barons, it came in the form of criticism from a feisty group of journalists dubbed *muckrakers*. The muck that these reporters and editors raked was dredged from the scandalous operations of America's business enterprises. Upton Sinclair's novel *The Jungle* attacked the deplorable conditions of the meat-packing industry. Ida Tarbell's *History of the Standard Oil Company* stripped away the public facade of the nation's leading petroleum firm. Magazines such as *McClure's* struck out systematically at one industry after another. The captains of industry, used to getting their own way and having to answer to no one, were wrenched from their peaceful passivity and rolled out on the public carpet to answer for their sins. Journalistic shock stories soon led to a wave of sentiment for legislative reform.

As journalists and the public became more anxious, the government got more involved. Congress began passing laws telling business leaders what they could and couldn't do. Trust busting then became the order of the day. Conflicts between employers and employees began to break out, and newly organized labor unions came to the fore. The Socialist and Communist movements began to take off. Ironically, it was "a period when free enterprise reached a peak in American history, and yet at that very climax, the tide of public opinion was swelling up against business freedom, primarily because of the breakdown in communications between the businessman and the public."[4]

For a time, these men of inordinate wealth and power found themselves limited in their ability to defend themselves and their activities against the tidal wave of public condemnation. They simply did not know how to get through to the public effectively. To tell their side of the story, the business barons first tried using the lure of advertising to silence journalistic critics; they tried to buy off critics by paying for ads in their papers. It didn't work. Next, they paid publicity people, or press agents, to present their companies' positions. Often, these hired guns painted over the real problems and presented their client's view in the best possible light. The public saw through this approach.

Clearly, another method had to be discovered to get the public to at least consider the business point of view. Business leaders were discovering that a corporation might have capital, labor, and natural resources, yet be doomed to fail if it lacked intelligent management, particularly in the area of influencing public opinion. The best way to influence public opinion, as it turned out, was through honesty and candor. This simple truth was the key to the accomplishments of American history's first successful public relations counselor, Ivy Lee.

 IVY LEE: A FATHER OF MODERN PUBLIC RELATIONS

Ivy Ledbetter Lee was a former Wall Street reporter who plunged into publicity work in 1903. Lee believed in neither Barnum's the-public-be-fooled approach nor Vanderbilt's the-public-be-damned philosophy. For Lee, the key to business acceptance and understanding was that the public be informed. Lee firmly believed that the only way business could answer its critics convincingly was to present its side honestly, accurately, and forcefully.[5] Instead of merely appeasing the public, Lee thought a company should strive to earn public confidence and good will. Sometimes this task meant looking further for mutual solutions. At other times, it even meant admitting that the company was wrong.* Hired by the anthracite coal industry in 1906, Lee set forth his beliefs in a Declaration of Principles to newspaper editors:

> This is not a secret press bureau. All our work is done in the open. We aim to supply news. This is not an advertising agency; if you think any of our matter ought properly to go to your business office, do not use it. Our matter is accurate. Further details on any subject treated will be supplied promptly, and any editor will be assisted most cheerfully in verifying any statement of fact. . . .
>
> In brief, our plan is frankly and openly, on behalf of business concerns and public institutions, to supply to the press and public of the United States prompt and accurate information concerning subjects which it is of value and interest to the public to know about.[6]

In 1914, John D. Rockefeller, Jr., who headed one of the most maligned and misunderstood of America's wealthy families, hired Lee. As Lee's biographer Ray Eldon Hiebert has pointed out, Lee did less to change the Rockefellers' policies than to give them a public hearing.[7] For example, when the family was censured scathingly for its role in breaking up a strike at the Rockefeller-owned Colorado Fuel and Iron Company, the family hired a labor relations expert (at Lee's recommendation) to determine the causes of an incident that had led to several deaths. The result of this effort was the formation of a joint labor–management board to mediate all workers' grievances on wages, hours, and working conditions. Years later, Rockefeller admitted that the public relations outcome of the Colorado strike "was one of the most important things that ever happened to the Rockefeller family."[8]

In working for the Rockefellers, Lee tried to humanize them, to feature them in real-life situations such as playing golf, attending church, and celebrating birthdays. Simply, Lee's goal was to present the Rockefellers in terms that every individual could

*Lee's dramatic influence on the standards of the emerging profession is obvious in an observation made in 1963 by Earl Newsom, a prominent public relations counselor who told a colleague, "The whole activity of which you and I are a part can probably be said to have had its beginning when Ivy Lee persuaded the directors of the Pennsylvania Railroad that the press should be given the facts on all railway accidents—even though the facts might place the blame on the railroad itself."

understand and appreciate. Years later, despite their critics, the family came to be known as one of the nation's outstanding sources of philanthropic support.

Ironically, even Ivy Lee could not escape the glare of public criticism. In the late 1920s, Lee was asked to serve as adviser to the parent company of the German Dye Trust, which, as it turned out, was an agent for the policies of Adolf Hitler. When Lee realized the nature of Hitler's intentions, he advised the Dye Trust cartel to work to alter Hitler's ill-conceived policies of restricting religious and press freedom. For his involvement with the Dye Trust, Lee was branded a traitor and dubbed "Poison Ivy" by members of Congress investigating un-American activities. The smears against him in the press rivaled the most vicious ones against the robber barons.

Despite his unfortunate involvement with the Dye Trust, Ivy Lee is recognized as the individual who brought honesty and candor to public relations. Lee, more than anyone before him, transformed the field from a questionable pursuit (that is, seeking positive publicity at any cost) into a professional discipline designed to win public confidence and trust through communications based on openness and truth.

THE GROWTH OF MODERN PUBLIC RELATIONS

Ivy Lee helped to open the gate. After he established the idea that firms have a responsibility to inform their publics, the practice began to grow in every sector of American society.

GOVERNMENT

During World War I, President Woodrow Wilson established the Creel Committee under journalist George Creel. It proved to be an effective force, mobilizing public opinion in support of the war effort and stimulating the sale of war bonds through Liberty Loan publicity drives. Not only did the war effort get a boost, but so did the field of public relations.

During World War II, the public relations field received an even bigger boost. With the Creel Committee as its precursor, the Office of War Information (OWI) was established to convey the message of the United States at home and abroad. Under the directorship of Elmer Davis, a veteran journalist, the OWI laid the foundations for the United States Information Agency as America's voice around the world.

World War II also saw a flurry of activity to sell war bonds, boost the morale of those at home, spur production in the nation's factories and offices, and, in general, support America's war effort as intensively as possible. By virtually every measure, this full-court public relations offensive was an unquestioned success.

The proliferation of public relations officers in World War II led to a growth in the number of practitioners during the peace that followed. This was probably a good thing, especially in light of the feisty, combative attitude of President Harry Truman toward many of the country's largest institutions. For example, in a memorable address over radio and television on April 8, 1952, President Truman announced that, as a result of a union wage dispute, "the government would take over the steel plants." The seizure of the steel mills touched off a series of historic events that reached into Congress and the Supreme Court and stimulated a massive public relations campaign, the likes of which had rarely been seen outside the government.[9]

COUNSELING

The nation's first public relations firm, the Publicity Bureau, was founded in Boston in 1900 and specialized in general press agentry. The first Washington, D.C., agency was begun in 1902 by William Wolff Smith, a former correspondent for the *New York Sun* and the *Cincinnati Inquirer.* Two years later, Ivy Lee joined with George Parker to begin a public relations agency that was later dissolved. Lee reestablished the agency in New York in 1919 and brought in T. J. Ross as a partner.

John W. Hill entered public relations in 1927 after a dozen years as a journalist. Together with William Knowlton, Hill founded Hill & Knowlton, Inc., in Cleveland. Hill soon moved east, and Knowlton dropped out of the firm. However, the agency quickly became one of the largest public relations operations in the world, with 1,050 employees in 20 countries and 20 U.S. cities. Hill stayed active in the firm for half a century and mused about the field's beginnings:

> In 1927, public relations was just in its infancy. Think of the contrast of the present with fifty years ago. Less than a handful of counseling firms anywhere in the world and barely a handful of practitioners tucked away and lost in the offices of a very few large corporations—far removed from the executive suite.[10]

In addition to Hill, Creel Committee Associate Chairman Carl Byoir launched his own public relations counseling firm in 1930. Ironically, 56 years later, Byoir's firm, Carl Byoir & Associates, merged with Hill & Knowlton to become the largest public relations company in the world.

Besides Byoir and Hill, Earl Newsom and Pendleton Dudley also founded early firms. Newsom, who began Newsom & Company in 1935, generally limited his public relations practice to counseling companies like Ford, General Motors, and Jersey Standard. In his otherwise critical treatment of public relations, *The Image Merchants,* author Irwin Ross paid tribute to Newsom's success:

> The goal of a good many public relations men is someday to attain the lonely eminence of Earl Newsom. His fees are high; his clients include some of the most august names in the corporate roster; and his work involves pure "consultation."[11]

Another early counselor, Harold Burson, emphasized marketing-oriented public relations, "primarily concerned with helping clients sell their goods and services, maintain a favorable market for their stock, and foster harmonious relations with employees."[12] Today, Burson-Marsteller ranks as the world's largest public relations agency.

In the early 1990s, the counseling business saw the emergence of international super agencies. Hill & Knowlton, Burson-Marsteller, and Shandwick all boasted worldwide networks with thousands of employees linked to serve clients with communications services throughout the world.

CORPORATIONS

Problems in the perception of corporations and their leaders dissipated in the United States after World War II. Opinion polls of that period ranked business as high in public esteem. People were back at work, and business was back in style.

Smart companies—General Electric, General Motors, American Telephone & Telegraph (AT&T), for example—worked hard to preserve their good names through both words and actions. Arthur W. Page became AT&T's first public relations vice-president in 1927. Page was a pacesetter, helping to maintain AT&T's reputation as a prudent and proper corporate citizen. Indeed, Page's five principles of successful corporate public relations are as relevant now as they were in the 1930s:

1. To make sure management thoughtfully analyzes its overall relation to the public
2. To create a system for informing all employees about the firm's general policies and practices
3. To create a system giving contact employees (those having direct dealings with the public) the knowledge needed to be reasonable and polite to the public
4. To create a system drawing employee and public questions and criticism back up through the organization to management
5. To ensure frankness in telling the public about the company's actions[13]

Paul Garrett was another person who felt the need to be responsive to the public's wishes. A former news reporter, he became the first director of public relations for General Motors in 1931. Garrett once reportedly explained that the essence of his job was to convince the public that the powerful auto company deserved trust, that is, "to make a billion-dollar company seem small."

EDUCATION

One public relations pioneer who began as a publicist in 1913 was Edward L. Bernays, nephew of Sigmund Freud and author of the landmark book *Crystallizing Public Opinion* (see page 46). Bernays was a true public relations scholar, teaching the first course in public relations in 1923. Bernays's seminal writings in the field were among the first to disassociate public relations from press agentry or publicity work. As Bernays wrote later:

> At first we called our activity "publicity direction." We intended to give advice to clients on how to direct their actions to get public visibility for them. But within a year we changed the service and its name to "counsel on public relations." We recognized that all actions of a client that impinged on the public needed counsel. Public visibility of a client for one action might be vitiated by another action not in the public interest.[14]

Historian Eric Goldman credited Bernays with "[moving] along with the most advanced trends in the public relations field, thinking with, around, and ahead of them."[15]

Bernays was also at least indirectly responsible for encouraging the development of another public relations phenomenon that would take on added impetus in the 1990s—the emergence of women in the field. Bernays's associate (and later, wife), Doris E. Fleischman, helped edit a leaflet, called *Contact,* that helped American leaders understand the underpinnings of the new profession Bernays represented. Fleischman's important assistance in spreading the Bernays doctrine was an early contribution to a field that, in the 1990s, showed women clearly in the majority among public relations professionals.

PUBLIC RELATIONS COMES OF AGE

As noted earlier, public relations really came of age as a result of the confluence of four general factors in our society: (1) the growth of large institutions and their sense of responsibility to the public; (2) the increased changes, conflicts, and confrontations among interest groups in society; (3) the heightened awareness of people everywhere brought about by increasingly sophisticated communications technology; and (4) the spread of global democracy.

GROWTH OF LARGE INSTITUTIONS

Ironically, the public relations profession received perhaps its most important thrust when business confidence suffered its most severe setback. The economic and social upheaval caused by the Great Depression of the 1930s provided the impetus for corporations to seek public support by telling their stories. Public relations departments sprang up in scores of major companies, among them Bendix, Borden, Eastman Kodak, Eli Lilly, Ford, General Motors, Standard Oil, Pan American, and U.S. Steel. The role that public relations played in helping regain post-Depression public trust in big business helped project the field into the relatively strong position it enjoyed during World War II.

The Truman years marked a challenging period for public relations, with government questioning the integrity of large business corporations. The ebbing and flowing conflict between government and business is unique to America. In other nations—Japan and Germany most prominently—government and business work more in concert to achieve common goals. In the United States, many businesses, both large and small, complain that government overregulation frustrates their ability to prosper. Businesses of every size have recognized that aggressively communicating corporate products and positions can help win public receptivity and support and ward off government intrusion.

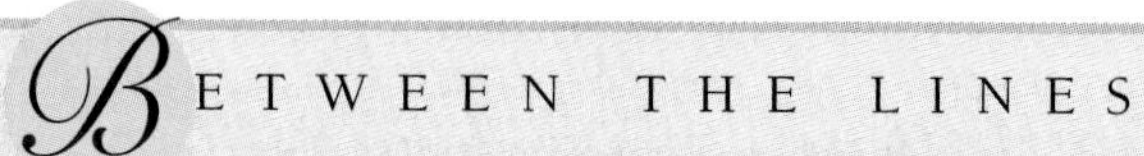

BETWEEN THE LINES

TERRORISM IN THE SATELLITE ERA

Nowhere has new communications technology been more striking than in its use as a persuasive tool in the politics of war—particularly by terrorists. Using the 1979 capture of American embassy employees as the linchpin, Iranian militants in Tehran launched a massive long-distance, nonstop media campaign to convince the world of their nation's mistreatment at the hands of the shah. Pictures of angry mobs of Iranian fanatics were beamed live and in blazing color to millions of Western homes on a nightly basis—serving to infuriate viewers and further harden anti-Iranian feelings.

In the summer of 1982, hopelessly surrounded in the suburbs of West Beirut, Lebanon, by the Israeli army, Palestinian Liberation Organization Chief Yasir Arafat also tried to use the world media to slip out of his predicament. When a U.S. congressional delegation with an accompanying television camera crew visited him, Arafat signed a document in his bunker—in full view of the television cameras—ostensibly recognizing Israel's right to exist. Within an hour of Arafat's televised encounter with the congressmen, authoritative Palestinians in the West rushed to clarify that what their leader really meant in signing the document was that "Israel would be recognized when we get an independent Palestinian state."

Three years later, when Palestinian gunmen hijacked a TWA jetliner, murdered an American passenger, and terrorized all aboard, they also gleefully posed for international television with a gun at the head of the plane's pilot.

In 1990, Iraq's president, Saddam Hussein, invited American journalists, including perpetual presidential candidate Jesse Jackson, to interview him, to show the world that, contrary to his global persona, Saddam was a kind and benevolent soul.* Hussein's shocking and bizarre attempt to manipulate the world's airwaves was the latest reminder of the importance that modern terrorists ascribe to manipulating the media.

*Evidently Reverend Jackson's producers at his syndicated *Inside Edition* TV show had second thoughts about their man's association with the bully of Baghdad. When asked later for a photo of Jackson and Hussein, *Inside Edition's* director of legal affairs told a certain textbook author, "I regret to inform you that we are not in a position to grant your request."

CHANGE, CONFLICT, AND CONFRONTATION

Disenchantment with big institutions peaked in the 1960s. The conflicts during the early part of the decade between private economic institutions—especially large corporations—and various disenfranchised elements of society arose from long-standing grievances. As one commentator put it, "Their rebellion was born out of the desperation of those who had nothing to lose. Issues were seen as black or white, groups as villainous or virtuous, causes as holy or satanic, and leaders as saints or charlatans."[16]

The social and political upheavals of the 1960s dramatically affected many areas, including the practice of public relations. The Vietnam War fractured society. Ralph Nader began to look pointedly at the inadequacies of the automobile industry. Women, long denied equal rights in the workplace and elsewhere, began to mobilize into activist groups such as the National Organization of Women (NOW). Environmentalists, worried about threats to the land and water by business expansion, began to support groups such as the Sierra Club. Minorities, particularly blacks and Hispanics, began to petition and protest for their rights. Homosexuals, senior citizens, birth control advocates, and social activists of every kind began to challenge the legitimacy of large institutions. Not since the days of the robber barons had large institutions so desperately needed professional communications help.

HEIGHTENED PUBLIC AWARENESS

The 1970s and 1980s brought a partial resolution of these problems. Many of the solutions came from the government in the form of affirmative action guidelines, senior citizen programs, consumer and environmental protection acts and agencies, aids to education, and myriad other laws and statutes.

Business began to contribute to charities. Managers began to consider community relations a first-line responsibility. The general policy of corporations confronting their adversaries was abandoned. In its place, most large companies adopted a policy of conciliation and compromise.

This new policy of social responsibility has continued into the 1990s. Corporations have come to realize that their reputations are a valuable asset to be protected, conserved, defended, nurtured, and enhanced at all times. In truth, institutions in the 1990s have had little choice but to get along with their publics.

By 1994, 93 million American homes had television, with 61% of U.S. homes wired for cable. The potential of two-way communications systems through cable, satellite, fax, computer, and video disc technologies promises to revolutionize further the information transmission and receiving process. As a result, publics have become much more segmented, specialized, and sophisticated. Public relations professionals have had to discard many of the traditional methods used to reach and influence these publics. Today companies face the new reality of instant communication through desktop video display terminals, instant file and retrieval through centralized data banks, and comprehensive management information systems.

SPREAD OF GLOBAL DEMOCRACY

As the world nears the end of the twentieth century, democracy has run rampant. The Berlin wall's destruction was transmitted live around the world. So was the dissolution of the Union of Soviet Socialist Republics. And in 1993, two longtime archenemies, Nelson Mandela and Nicholas DeKlerck, stood together to share the Nobel Peace Prize as free elections were held in South Africa. As the year 2000 approaches, with the world now truly "safe for democracy," the public relations challenge is growing in intensity.

PUBLIC RELATIONS EDUCATION

As the practice of public relations has developed, so too has the growth of public relations education. In 1951, 12 schools offered major programs in public relations. Today approximately 200 journalism or communication programs offer concentrated study in public relations, with nearly 300 others offering at least one course dealing with the profession. Although few data are available on public relations programs in business schools, the number is increasing, especially those related to marketing.[17]

As the debate continues about where public relations education should appropriately be housed—either in business or journalism schools—the best answer is that *both* should offer public relations courses. In business, the practice of public relations has become an integral part of the way companies operate. Therefore, business students should be exposed to the discipline's underpinnings and practical aspects before they enter the corporate world. In journalism, with about 60 percent of daily newspaper copy emanating from public relations–generated releases, journalists, too, should know what public relations is all about before they graduate. Wherever it is housed, the profession's role as an academic pursuit has continued to gain strength. This educational dimension has, in turn, contributed to the new respect accorded public relations in modern society.

SUMMARY

Today public relations is big business.

- The Public Relations Society of America, organized in 1947, boasts a growing membership of 15,000 in 107 chapters nationwide.
- The Public Relations Student Society of America, formed in 1968 to facilitate communications between students interested in the field and public relations professionals, has 5,000 student members at 180 colleges and universities.
- More than 5,400 U.S. companies have public relations departments.
- More than 5,080 public relations agencies exist in the United States, some billing hundreds of millions of dollars per year.
- More than 500 trade associations have public relations departments.
- Top communications executives at major companies and agencies draw six-figure salaries.

The scope of modern public relations practice is vast. Press relations, employee communications, public relations counseling and research, local community relations, audiovisual communications, contributions, and numerous other diverse activities fall under the public relations umbrella. Because of this broad range of functions, many public relations practitioners today seem preoccupied with the proper title for their calling—*public relations, external affairs, corporate communications, public affairs, corporate relations,* ad infinitum. They argue that the range of activities involved offers no hope that people will understand what the pursuit involves unless an umbrella term is used.[18]

Practitioners also worry that as public relations becomes more prominent, its function and those who purportedly practice it will be subject to increasingly intense public scrutiny.

Despite these concerns, the practice of public relations has emerged in the 1990s as a potent, persuasive force in society. Clearly, the public relations field today—whatever it is called and by whomever it is practiced—is in the spotlight. Its professionals command higher salaries. Its counselors command increased respect. And its practice is taught in increasing numbers, not only in American colleges and universities but around the world.

With upward of 155,000 men and women in the United States alone practicing public relations in some form, the field has become solidly entrenched as an important, influential, and professional component of our society.

DISCUSSION STARTERS

1. What societal factors have influenced the spread of public relations?
2. Why do public relations professionals think of P. T. Barnum as a mixed blessing?
3. What is the significance to the practice of public relations of American revolutionary hero Samuel Adams?
4. What did the robber barons and muckrakers have to do with the development of public relations?
5. Why are Ivy Lee and Edward Bernays considered two of the fathers of public relations?
6. What impact did the Creel Committee and the Office of War Information have on the development of public relations?
7. What was the significance of Arthur Page to the development of corporate public relations?
8. Identify and discuss the significance of some of the earliest public relations counselors.
9. What are some of the yardsticks indicating that public relations has arrived in the 1990s?
10. What are some of the issues that confront public relations in the 1990s?

NOTES

1. Scott M. Cutlip, Allen H. Center, and Glen M. Broom, *Effective Public Relations,* 6th ed. (Englewood Cliffs, NJ: Prentice-Hall, 1985), 23.
2. Edward L. Bernays, speech at the University of Florida Public Relations Symposium, Gainesville, FL, February 1, 1984.
3. Harold Burson, speech at Utica College of Syracuse University, Utica, NY, March 5, 1987.
4. Ray Eldon Hiebert, *Courtier to the Crowd: The Story of Ivy L. Lee and the Development of Public Relations* (Ames: Iowa State University Press, 1966).
5. Rex Harlow, "A Public Relations Historian Recalls the First Days," *Public Relations Review* (Summer 1981): 39–40.
6. Cited in Sherman Morse, "An Awakening in Wall Street," *American Magazine* 62 (September 1906): 460.
7. Hiebert, loc. cit.
8. Cited in Alvin Moscow, *The Rockefeller Inheritance* (Garden City, NY: Doubleday, 1977), 23.
9. John W. Hill, *The Making of a Public Relations Man* (New York: David McKay, 1963), 69.
10. John W. Hill, "The Future of Public Relations," speech delivered at the Seventh Public Relations World Congress, Boston, MA, August 14, 1976.
11. Irwin Ross, *The Image Merchants* (Garden City, NY: Doubleday, 1959), 85.
12. Burson, loc. cit.
13. Cited in Noel L. Griese, "The Employee Communications Philosophy of Arthur W. Page," *Public Relations Quarterly* (Winter 1977): 8–12.
14. Edward L. Bernays, "Bernays' 62 Years in Public Relations," *Public Relations Quarterly* (Fall 1981): 8.

15. David L. Lewis, "The Outstanding PR Professionals," *Public Relations Journal* (October 1970): 84.
16. S. Prakash Sethi, "Business and Social Challenge," *Public Relations Journal* (September 1981): 30.
17. James E. Grunig, "Teaching Public Relations in the Future," *Public Relations Review* (Spring 1989): 16.
18. "Diverse Titles Splinter Image of Field: Report of PRSA's Special Committee on Terminology," *Public Relations Reporter* (April 20, 1987): Tips & Tactics.
19. Marilyn Kern-Foxworth, "Status and Roles of Minority PR Practitioners," *Public Relations Review* (Fall 1989): 39.

TOP OF THE SHELF

Edward L. Bernays, *Crystallizing Public Opinion*, New York: Liveright Publishing Corp., 1961.

What *Casablanca* is to cinema, *Crystallizing Public Opinion* is to public relations literature—a classic. It defined for the first time public relations, principles, practices, and ethics and gave it recognition and professional status.

Ed Bernays's teachings are as relevant today as they were when he introduced them in 1923. His book covers the core aspects of the profession: the job of public relations counselors, the role of public opinion, and the techniques of public relations professionals. His writings on public opinion—"an ill-defined, mercurial, and changeable group of individual judgments"—are especially incisive. How are attitudes formed? How are they modified through persuasion? How does public opinion interact with forces like the media? Bernays examines these and related issues. Also of interest is a revised preface that Bernays wrote in 1961. In it, he takes readers through a detailed history of public relations, beginning when he and his late wife coined the term for the business they opened in 1919.

Bernays's experiences and insights in those formative years are preserved in *Crystallizing Public Opinion.* As the original book on public relations, Bernays's work is essential reading for all who are fascinated by this field.

SUGGESTED READINGS

Arnold, James E., and Consultants. *Issues and Trends in the 1990's*. PRSA Counselors Academy, 1992.

Bernays, Edward L. *The Later Years: PR Insights, 1956–1958*. Rhinebeck, NY: H & M, 1987 (44 W. Market St., P.O. Box 311 12572).

Burson, Harold. "A Decent Respect to the Opinion of Mankind." Speech delivered at the Raymond Simon Institute for Public Relations (Burson-Marsteller, 866 Third Ave., New York, NY 10022), March 5, 1987. This speech highlights public relations activities that have influenced the United States from colonial times to the present day.

International Encyclopedia of Communications (4 vols.). New York: Oxford University Press, 1989.

Newsom, Doug, Alan Scott, and Judy Van Slyke Turk. *This Is PR: The Realities of Public Relations,* 5th ed. Belmont, CA: Wadsworth, 1993.
Olasky, Marvin N. *Corporate Public Relations and American Public Enterprise.* Hillsdale, NJ: Erlbaum, 1987.
Poppe, Fred. *50 Rules to Keep a Client Happy.* New York: Harper & Row, 1987.
PR Reporter (P.O. Box 600, Exeter, NH 03833-0600). Weekly.
Public Relations Career Directory. Hawthorne, NJ: Career Press, 1987 (62 Beverly Rd., P.O. Box 34 17507).
Public Relations Journal (PRSA, 33 Irving Place, New York, NY 10003). Monthly.
Public Relations News (127 E. 80th St., New York, NY 10021). Weekly.
Public Relations Quarterly (P.O. Box 311, Rhinebeck, NY 12572).
Public Relations Review (10606 Mantz Rd., Silver Spring, MD 20903).
Rogers, Henry. *One-Hat Solution: Strategy for Creative Middle Management.* New York: St. Martin's Press, 1986.

CASE STUDY
WATERGATE

> I felt sure that it was just a public relations problem that only needed a public relations solution.
>
> Richard M. Nixon*

In 1972 Richard Nixon was elected president of the United States by a landslide. His opponent, Senator George McGovern, won only Massachusetts and the District of Columbia.

Two years later, on August 8, 1974, Nixon resigned in disgrace and humiliation. His administration had been tarnished by illegal wiretapping, illegal surveillance, burglary, and unlawful use of the law. The president and his men were toppled by the most profound political scandal in the nation's history, which grew out of a series of break-ins at the Democratic national headquarters in a Washington, D.C., building named Watergate.

One notion raised in the aftermath of Watergate was that the president and his advisers were too concerned about public relations—about covering up the facts—and that this concern led to their downfall. This castigation of public relations for its supposed role in Watergate is ironic. Had Nixon or his aides been able to comprehend the broad ramifications and deal with them honestly, they might have been judged with more compassion and spared their severe and precipitous fall. (Although the field of public relations took the heat for the Watergate scandal, most of Nixon's key public relations advisers came from the field of advertising.)

As excerpts from transcripts indicate, neither the president nor his advisers knew much about good public relations. By ignoring virtually every elementary public relations principle, they destroyed any chance that many Americans would understand and forgive them for their misjudgments.

Here are six of the more onerous miscalculations from the Watergate saga.

1. In late 1972, while rumors abounded that the administration was corrupt, the White House remained silent. As the president concluded in a conversation with top aides H. R. Haldeman and John Dean, "We take a few shots and it will be over. Don't worry." Evidently, Nixon felt the public would grow tired of the perpetual pounding on Watergate—thus his strategy, "Hang tough and ignore it."

*Richard Nixon, *RN: The Memoirs of Richard Nixon* (New York: Grosset & Dunlap, 1978), 773.

2. The spotlight on Watergate intensified, and the media refused to let up. Nixon ordered Dean to prepare an enemies list of journalists and others who opposed the administration, saying, "I want the most comprehensive notes on all those who tried to do us in." Evidently, Nixon felt that going directly after particular individuals would stifle their efforts. This step, according to Dean, involved using "available federal machinery to screw our political enemies."
3. In early 1973, the Senate's investigation dominated national news. The president and his aides were invited to testify, but they declined on the grounds of executive privilege.
4. Like *executive privilege,* the term *national security* received an extensive workout during the Watergate period. In March 1973, the president discussed with Haldeman and Dean the break-in at the office of the psychiatrist of Daniel Ellsberg, an administration enemy who had leaked secret Pentagon papers to the *New York Times.* Dean suggested that the break-in be defended as national security. The president agreed, saying, "We had to get information on national security grounds. We had to do it on a confidential basis. Neither [the FBI nor the CIA] could be trusted." Several years later, both Dean and Haldeman were imprisoned, primarily because of their roles in the break-in.
5. In October 1973, Nixon had had enough of Archibald Cox, the special prosecutor he had appointed to get to the bottom of the Watergate case. When Cox persisted in trying to secure the release of the president's confidential tapes, Nixon ordered Attorney General Elliot Richardson to fire him. Richardson refused and resigned. Deputy Attorney General William Ruckelshaus, next in line, also refused and was fired. Finally, Solicitor General Robert Bork, the third person in line, fired Cox. In one fell swoop, Nixon's Saturday Night Massacre became a new *cause célèbre,* and the Watergate fires were reignited.
6. The president's relations with the media steadily deteriorated. About a major report by Dean on Watergate, Nixon told an aide, "We've got to keep our eye on the Dean thing—just give them some of it, not all of it . . . just take the heat."

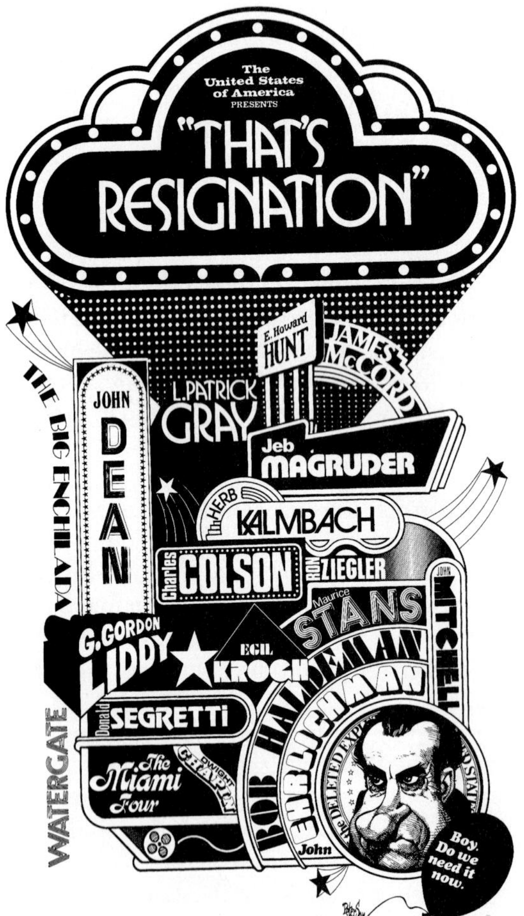

Figure 2–3 Watergate's dubious cast of characters stimulated this takeoff on the promotional work done for the movie, *That's Entertainment. (Courtesy of Frankfurt, Gips, Balkind)*

Facing an audience of several hundred newspaper editors in November 1973, the president rambled, "In all of my years of public life, I have never obstructed justice. And I think too that I could say that in my years of public life, that I welcome this kind of examination, because people have got to know whether or not their president is a crook. Well, I am not a crook."

Later on, the president instructed Press Secretary Ronald Ziegler how to respond to substantive press queries: "Just get out there and act like your usual cocky, confident self."

In 1994, in his last interviews before his death, Richard Nixon still recalled Watergate as his "most tragic mistake."*

*This case is adapted from one of the more significant analyses of Watergate as a study in public relations: Joseph T. Nolan, "Watergate: A Case Study in How Not to Handle Public Relations," *Public Relations Quarterly* (Summer 1975): 23–26. It is reprinted by permission. Also see Gladys Engle Lang and Kurt Lang, "Polling on Watergate: The Battle for Public Opinion," *Public Opinion Quarterly* 44 (Winter 1980): 530–547.

QUESTIONS

1. How sound was the early White House public relations strategy to hang tough in the midst of media flak?
2. Why didn't Watergate go away?
3. Why was the compilation of an enemies list a mistake?
4. Did the enemies list serve any purpose for Nixon?
5. Was invoking executive privilege justified in the administration's refusal to appear before the Senate Watergate Committee?
6. What were the public relations consequences of invoking executive privilege?
7. How would you have interpreted the Saturday Night Massacre if you were an objective observer?
8. What public relations/credibility problems might have been caused by the break-in at the office of Ellsberg's psychiatrist and the subsequent national security explanation defending it?
9. How would you assess Nixon's media relations philosophy?
10. If you had been Nixon's public relations counselor, what would you have recommended on learning the full story of Watergate?

Helpful hint for answering the questions: British statesman Edmund Burke once said, "It is not what a lawyer tells me I may do, but what humanity, reason, and justice tell me I ought to do.

TIPS FROM THE TOP

EDWARD L. BERNAYS

Edward L. Bernays is a public relations patriarch. A nephew of Sigmund Freud, Bernays, who celebrated his 102nd birthday in 1993, pioneered the application of the social sciences to public relations. In partnership with his late wife, he advised presidents of the United States, industrial leaders, and legendary figures from Enrico Caruso to Eleanor Roosevelt. Indeed, Edward Bernays himself is a legend in the field of public relations.

When you taught the first public relations class, did you ever envision the field growing to its present stature?
I gave the first course in public relations after *Crystallizing Public Opinion* was published in 1923. I decided that one way to give the term *counsel on public relations* status was to lecture at a university on the principles, practices, and ethics of the new vocation. New York University was willing to accept my offer to do so. But I never envisioned at that time that the vocation would spread throughout the United States and then throughout the free world.

What were the objectives of that first public relations course?
The objectives were to give status to the new vocation. Many people still believed the term *counsel on public relations* was a euphemism for publicity man, press agent, flack. Even H. L. Mencken, in his book on the American language, ranked it as such. But in his *Supplement to the American Language*, published some years later, he changed his viewpoint and used my definition of the term.

What are the most significant factors that have led to the rise in public relations practice?

The most significant factor is the rise in people power and its recognition by leaders. Theodore Roosevelt helped bring this about with his Square Deal. Woodrow Wilson helped with his New Freedom, and so did Franklin Delano Roosevelt with his New Deal. And this tradition was continued as time went on.

Do you have any gripes with the way public relations is practiced today?
I certainly do. The meanings of words in the United States have the stability of soap bubbles. Unless words are defined as to their meaning by law, as in the case of professions—for instance, law, medicine, architecture—they are in the public domain. Anyone can use them. Recently, I received a letter from a model agency offering to supply me with a "public relations representative" for my next trade fair at which we might exhibit our client's products. Today, any plumber or car salesman or unethical character can call himself or herself a public relations practitioner. Many who call themselves public relations practitioners have no education, training, or knowledge of what the field is. And the public equally has little understanding of the meaning of the two words. Until licensing and registration are introduced, this will continue to be the situation.*

What pleases you most about current public relations practice?
What pleases me most is that there are, indeed, practitioners who regard their activity as a profession, an art applied to a science, in which the public interest, and not pecuniary motivation, is the primary consideration; and also that outstanding leaders in society are grasping the meaning and significance of the activity.

What is the most significant problem that confronts the field?
The most significant problem confronting the field is this matter of definition by the state of what public relations is and does—defining it, registering and licensing practitioners through a board of examiners chosen from the field, and developing economic sanctions for those who break the code of ethics.

How would you compare the caliber of today's public relations practitioner with that of the practitioner of the past?
The practitioner today has more education in his subject. But, unfortunately, education for public relations varies with the institution where it is being conducted. This is due to the lack of a standard definition. Many institutions of higher learning think public relations activity consists of skillful writing of press releases and teach their students accordingly. This is, of course, not true. Public relations activity is applied social science to the social attitudes or actions of employers or clients.

Where do you think public relations will be twenty years from now?
It is difficult to appraise where public relations will be twenty years from now. I

*Ed. Note: The always gracious Mr. Bernays, in the winter of his ninety-eighth year, gently reminded the author that, as this response implies, "a profession is not a business." Thus, in this interview, Mr. Bernays pointedly defined the practice of public relations as a "vocation," not a "profession."

don't like the tendency of advertising agencies gobbling up large public relations organizations. That is like surgical instrument manufacturers gobbling up surgical medical colleges or law book publishers gobbling up law colleges. However, if licensing and registration take place, then the vocation is assured a long lifetime, as long as democracy's.

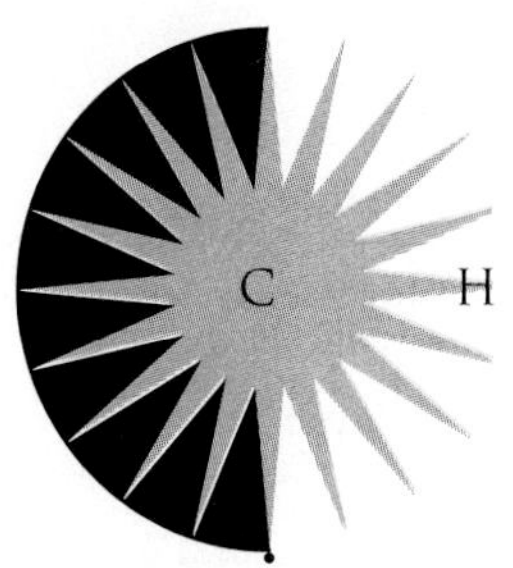

CHAPTER 3

PUBLIC OPINION

PUBLIC OPINION IS AN ELUSIVE AND FRAGILE COMMODITY. Consider the cases of Marge Schott and Michael Jordan.

- Ms. Schott, owner of baseball's Cincinnati Reds, developed a reputation as an outspoken and somewhat quirky executive. The folks in Cincinnati, used to her candid ways, rather liked the peculiar team owner. But in 1993, when a former employee reported that some of Ms. Schott's telephone rhetoric was decidedly racist, she was ostracized by the public and suspended from baseball. Her public opinion ratings hit rock bottom.
- Then there was the case of Michael Jordan. By the summer of 1993, the most widely recognized athlete in the world had begun to develop serious public opinion problems. After leading the U.S. Dream Team to an Olympic victory and then his Chicago

> Bulls to an unprecedented third straight National Basketball Association title, Jordan was the focus of nasty rumors regarding selfishness, aloofness, and serious gambling problems.
>
> Then, late in the summer of 1993, tragedy struck. Jordan's father, James, was found murdered in his car. The nation mourned with Michael. Scarcely two months later, in the midst of major league baseball's playoffs, Michael Jordan stunned the world by announcing his retirement from basketball. The news was so jarring that President Clinton even took time out to address a statement of support to Michael. In the space of one traumatic quarter of the year, Michael Jordan's public opinion ratings had rebounded from questionable to sky high[1] (Figure 3–1).

Such are the peculiarities of public opinion.

But the rapid change experienced by Ms. Schott and Mr. Jordan are the exception rather than the rule. Usually it's difficult to move people toward a strong opinion on anything. It's even harder to move them away from an opinion once they reach it. Recent research, in fact, indicates that mass media appeals may have little immediate effect on influencing public opinion.

Figure 3–1 No other individual in the 90s came close to rivaling the popular appeal of basketball star/marketing conglomerate Michael Jordan. When Jordan retired from basketball in 1993, people everywhere still yearned to "be like Mike." And corporate sponsors Nike, Kelloggs, and a host of others continued to support their superstar. (*Courtesy of Nike*)

Nonetheless, the heart of public relations work lies in attempting to affect the public opinion process. Most public relations programs are designed either to (1) *persuade* people to change their opinion on an issue, product, or organization, (2) *crystallize* uninformed or undeveloped opinions, or (3) *reinforce* existing opinions.

So public relations professionals must understand how public opinion is formed, how it evolves from people's attitudes, and how it is influenced by communication. This chapter discusses attitude formation and change and public opinion creation and persuasion.

WHAT IS PUBLIC OPINION?

Public opinion, like *public relations,* is not easily explained. Newspaper columnist Joseph Kraft called public opinion "the unknown god to which moderns burn incense." Edward Bernays called it "a term describing an ill-defined, mercurial, and changeable group of individual judgments."[2] And Princeton professor Harwood Childs, after coming up with no fewer than 40 different, yet viable definitions, concluded with a definition by Herman C. Boyle: "*Public opinion* is not the name of something, but the classification of a number of somethings."[3]

Splitting public opinion into its two components, *public* and *opinion,* is perhaps the best way to understand the concept. Simply defined, *public* signifies a group of people who share a common interest in a specific subject—stockholders, for example, or employees or community residents. Each group is concerned with a common issue—the price of the stock, the wages of the company, or the building of a new plant.

An *opinion* is the expression of an attitude on a particular topic. When attitudes become strong enough, they surface in the form of opinions. When opinions become strong enough, they lead to verbal or behavioral actions.

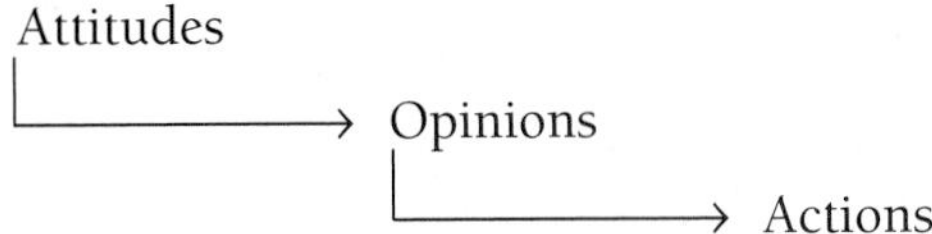

A corporate executive and an environmentalist from the Sierra Club might differ dramatically in their attitudes toward the relative importance of pollution control and continued industrial production. Their respective opinions on a piece of environmental legislation might also differ radically. In turn, how their organizations respond to that legislation—by picketing, petitioning, or lobbying—might also differ.

Public opinion, then, is the aggregate of many individual opinions on a particular issue that affects a group of people. Stated another way, public opinion represents a consensus. And that consensus, deriving as it does from many individual opinions, really begins with people's attitudes toward the issue in question. Trying to influence an individual's attitude—how he or she thinks on a given topic—is a primary focus of the practice of public relations.

WHAT ARE ATTITUDES?

If an opinion is an expression of an attitude on a particular topic, what then is an attitude? Unfortunately, that also is not an easy question to answer. It had been generally assumed that attitudes are predispositions to think in a certain way about a certain topic. But recent research has indicated that attitudes may more likely be evaluations people make about specific problems or issues. These conclusions are not necessarily connected to any broad attitude.[4] For example, an individual might favor a company's response to one issue but disagree vehemently with its response to another. Thus, that individual's attitude may differ from issue to issue.

Attitudes are based on a number of characteristics.

1. **Personal**—the physical and emotional ingredients of an individual, including size, age, and social status.
2. **Cultural**—the environment and lifestyle of a particular country or geographic area, such as Japan versus the United States or rural America versus urban America. National political candidates often tailor messages to appeal to the particular cultural complexions of specific regions of the country.
3. **Educational**—the level and quality of a person's education. To appeal to the increased number of college graduates in the United States today, public communication has become more sophisticated.
4. **Familial**—people's roots. Children acquire their parents' tastes, biases, political partisanships, and a host of other characteristics. Some pediatricians insist that children pick up most of their knowledge in the first seven years, and few would deny the family's strong role in helping to mold attitudes.
5. **Religious**—a system of beliefs about God or the supernatural. Religion is making a comeback. In the 1960s many young people turned away from formal religion. In the 1990s, even after several evangelical scandals, religious fervor has reemerged.
6. **Social class**—position within society. As people's social status changes, so do their attitudes. For example, college students, unconcerned with making a living, may dramatically change their attitudes about such concepts as big government, big business, wealth, and prosperity after entering the job market.
7. **Race**—ethnic origin, which today increasingly helps shape people's attitudes. The history of blacks and whites in America has been stormy, with peaceful coexistence often frustrated. Nonetheless, minorities in our society, as a group, continue to improve their standard of living. And in so doing, African-Americans, Latinos, Asians, and others have retained pride in and allegiance to their cultural heritage.

These characteristics help influence the formation of attitudes. So, too, do other factors, such as experience, economic class, and political and organizational memberships. Again, recent research has indicated that attitudes and behaviors are situational—influenced by specific issues in specific situations. Nonetheless, when others with similar attitudes reach similar opinions, a consensus, or public opinion, is born.

HOW ARE ATTITUDES INFLUENCED?

Strictly speaking, attitudes are positive, negative, or nonexistent. A person is for something, against it, or neutral. Studies show that for any one issue, most people don't care much one way or the other. A small percentage express strong support, and another small percentage express strong opposition. The vast majority are smack in the middle—passive, neutral, indifferent. Former Vice-President Spiro T. Agnew called them "the silent majority." In many instances—political campaigns being a prime example—this silent majority holds the key to success because they are the group most readily influenced by a communicator's message.

It's hard to change the mind of a person who is staunchly opposed to a particular issue or individual. Likewise, it's easy to reinforce the support of a person who is wholeheartedly in favor of an issue or an individual. Social scientist Leon Festinger discussed this concept when he talked about cognitive dissonance. He believed that individuals tend to avoid information that is dissonant or opposed to their own points of view and tend to seek out information that is consonant with, or in support of, their own attitudes.[5] An organization might attempt to remove dissonance to reach its goals. For example, a cigarette manufacturer, chastised by society for the products it produces, might try to mitigate this negative sentiment by supporting arts and educational endeavors.

As Festinger's theory intimates, the people whose attitudes can be influenced most readily are those who have not yet made up their minds. In politics this group is often referred to as the *swing vote.* Many elections have been won or lost on last-minute appeals to these politically undecided voters. In addition, it is possible to introduce information that may cause dissonance in the mind of a receiver.

Understanding this theory and its potential for influencing the silent majority is extremely important for the public relations practitioner, whose objective is to win support through clear, thoughtful, and persuasive communication. Moving a person from a latent state of attitude formation to a more aware state and finally to an active one becomes a matter of motivation.

MOTIVATING ATTITUDE CHANGE

People are motivated by different factors, and no two people respond exactly the same way to the same set of circumstances. Each of us is motivated by different drives and needs.

The most famous delineator of what motivates people was Dr. Abraham Maslow. His hierarchy of needs helps define the origins of motivation, which, in turn, help explain attitude change. Maslow postulated a five-level hierarchy:

1. The lowest order is physiological needs: a person's biological demands—food and water, sleep, health, bodily needs, exercise and rest, and sex.
2. The second level is safety needs: security, protection, comfort and peace, and orderly surroundings.
3. The third level is love needs: acceptance, belonging, love and affection, and membership in a group.
4. The fourth level is esteem: recognition and prestige, confidence and leadership opportunities, competence and strength, intelligence and success.
5. The highest order is self-actualization, or simply becoming what one is capable of becoming. Self-actualization involves self-fulfillment and achieving a goal for the purposes of challenge and accomplishment.[6]

According to Maslow, the needs of all five levels compose the fundamental motivating factors for any individual or public.

In the 1990s, as people once again get involved in causes—from abortion to animal rights to environmentalism—motivating attitude change becomes more important (Figure 3–2). Many activist groups, in fact, borrow heavily from psychological research on political activism to accomplish attitude change. Six cardinal precepts of political activism are instructive in attempting to change attitudes:

1. *Don't use graphic images unless they are accompanied by specific actions people can execute.* Many movements—the gay rights campaign, for one, and the antiabortion movement, for another—began by relying heavily on graphic images of death and destruction. But such images run the risk of pushing people away rather than drawing them in. Disturbing presentations rarely lead to a sustained attitude change.
2. *Go to the public instead of asking the public to come to you.* Most people will never become directly involved in an activist campaign. They will shy away. But

Press: D. McNally
(412)648-4832
ARISTA
GRATEFUL DEAD
1989
Grateful Dead Productions
Box 1073
San Rafael, CA 94915
Photo: Ken Friedman

Figure 3–2 As the Grateful Dead kept "truckin' along" through the 1990s, the group was so concerned with public opinion that it began mailing letters to fans asking them to "shape up or the band might have to ship out." The Dead, in its fourth decade of existence, was worried when thousands of people began showing up at its sold-out concerts without tickets. Clashes with police and public disorder became common. "We're running out of places to play, and we're running out of ways to say the obvious," wrote the Dead. The group beseeched its loyal Deadheads to leave "nothin' but footprints" in blazing a new, more refined image. *(Courtesy of Grateful Dead Productions)*

by recognizing the limits of public interest and involvement, you can develop realistic strategies to capitalize on public goodwill without demanding more than people are willing to give.

3. *Don't assume that attitude change is necessary for behavior change.* A large body of psychological research casts doubt on the proposition that the best way to change behavior is to begin by changing attitudes. Indeed, the relationship between attitudes and behavior is often quite weak. Therefore, informing smokers of the link between cigarettes and cancer is far easier than getting them to kick the habit.
4. *Use moral arguments as adjuncts, not as primary thrusts.* Moral views are difficult to change. It is much easier to gain support by stressing the practical advantages of your solution rather than the immorality of your opponent's. For example, it is easier to convert people to a meatless diet by discussing the health benefits of vegetables than by discussing whether the Bible gives people dominion over animals.
5. *Embrace the mainstream.* In any campaign, people from all walks of life are necessary to win widespread approval. No campaign can be won if it is dubbed "radical" or "faddish." That is why the involvement of *all* people must be encouraged in seeking attitude change.
6. *Don't offend the people you seek to change.* Research on persuasion shows that influence is usually strongest when people like the persuader and see the persuader as similar to themselves. It is impossible to persuade someone whom you have alienated. Or, as my mother used to say, "You can attract more flies with honey than you can with vinegar." The same applies to people.[7]

Power of Persuasion

Perhaps the most essential element in influencing public opinion is the principle of persuasion. Persuading is the goal of the vast majority of public relations programs. Persuasion theory has myriad explanations and interpretations. Basically, persuasion means getting another person to do something through advice, reasoning, or just plain arm twisting. Books have been written on the enormous power of advertising and public relations as persuasive tools.

Social scientists and communications scholars take issue with the view of many public relations practitioners that a story on network news or the front page of the *New York Times* has a tremendous persuasive effect. Scholars argue that the media have a limited effect on persuasion—doing more to reinforce existing attitudes than to persuade toward a new belief. There is little doubt, however, that the persuasiveness of a message can be increased when it arouses or is accompanied by a high level of personal involvement. In other words, an individual who cares about something and is in fundamental agreement with an organization's basic position will tend to be persuaded by a message supporting that view.

According to the persuasion theory of Michael Ray—the hierarchies of effects—there are at least three basic orderings of knowledge, attitude, and behavior relative to persuasion:

1. When personal involvement is low and little difference exists between behavioral alternatives, knowledge changes are likely to lead directly to behavioral changes.

2. When personal involvement is high but behavioral alternatives are indistinguishable, behavioral change is likely to be followed by attitudinal change, similar to Festinger's cognitive dissonance approach.
3. When personal involvement is high and clear differences exist among alternatives, people act in a more rational manner. First, they learn about the issue. Second, they evaluate the alternatives. Then they act in a manner consistent with their attitudes and knowledge.[8]

To these complex theories of persuasion is added the simpler, yet no less profound, notion of former Secretary of State Dean Rusk: "One of the best ways to persuade others is to listen to them." No matter how one characterizes persuasion, the goal of most communications programs is, in fact, to influence a receiver to take a desired action.

INFLUENCING PUBLIC OPINION

Public opinion is a lot easier to measure than it is to influence. However, a thoughtful public relations program can crystallize attitudes, reinforce beliefs, and occasionally change public opinion. First, the opinions to be changed or modified must be identified and understood. Second, target publics must be clear. Third, the public relations professional must have in sharp focus the "laws" that govern public opinion—as amorphous as they may be.

In that context, the 15 "Laws of Public Opinion," developed many years ago by social psychologist Hadley Cantril, remain pertinent:

1. Opinion is highly sensitive to important events.
2. Events of unusual magnitude are likely to swing public opinion temporarily from one extreme to another. Opinion doesn't become stabilized until the implications of events are seen in some perspective.
3. Opinion is generally determined more by events than by words—unless those words are themselves interpreted as an event.
4. Verbal statements and outlines of courses of action have maximum importance when opinion is unstructured and people are suggestible and seek some interpretation from a reliable source.
5. By and large, public opinion doesn't anticipate emergencies—it only reacts to them.
6. Opinion is basically determined by self-interest. Events, words, or any other stimuli affect opinion only insofar as their relationship to self-interest is apparent.
7. Opinion doesn't remain aroused for a long period of time unless people feel that their self-interest is acutely involved or unless opinion—aroused by words—is sustained by events.
8. Once self-interest is involved, opinions aren't easily changed.
9. When self-interest is involved, public opinion in a democracy is likely to be ahead of official policy.
10. When an opinion is held by a slight majority or when opinion is not solidly structured, an accomplished fact tends to shift opinion in the direction of acceptance.

11. At critical times, people become more sensitive to the adequacy of their leadership. If they have confidence in it, they are willing to assign more than usual responsibility to it; if they lack confidence in it, they are less tolerant than usual.
12. People are less reluctant to have critical decisions made by their leaders if they feel that somehow they themselves are taking part in the decision.
13. People have more opinions and are able to form opinions more easily on goals than on methods to reach those goals.
14. Public opinion, like individual opinion, is colored by desire. And when opinion is based chiefly on desire, rather than on information, it is likely to shift with events.
15. By and large, if people in a democracy are provided with educational opportunities and ready access to information, public opinion reveals a hard-headed common sense. The more enlightened people are to the implications of events and proposals for their own self-interest, the more likely they are to agree with the more objective opinions of realistic experts.[9]

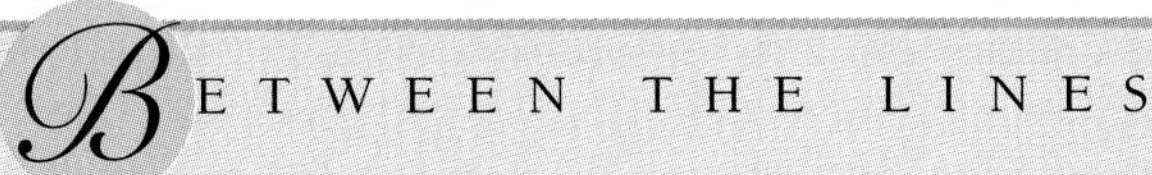

BETWEEN THE LINES

WHEN BARBIE TALKED, WOMEN WENT BONKERS

One of the quickest and savviest corporate reactions to negative public opinion came in late 1992 when Los Angeles-based Mattel Inc. reacted to criticism about its talking Barbie doll, which uttered the phrase "Math class is tough."

No sooner were the words out of Teen Talk Barbie's mouth than the American Association of University Women attacked the math comment as "sexist" in a report on how schools shortchange girls.

Mattel immediately announced that it was removing the offensive computer chip from the Barbie repertoire and offered to swap a new chip for anyone who bought an offending doll.

In a letter to the President of the Association, Mattel President Jill E. Barad said the company made a mistake.

"In hindsight, the phrase 'Math class is tough,' while correct for many students both male and female, should not have been included. We didn't fully consider the potentially negative implications of this phrase, nor were we aware of the findings of your organization's report."

Way 'ta go, Barbie![10]

POLISHING THE CORPORATE IMAGE

Most organizations today and the people who manage them are extremely sensitive to the way they are perceived by their critical publics. This represents a dramatic change in corporate attitude from years past. In the 1960s, 1970s, and well into the 1980s, only the most enlightened companies dared to maintain anything but a low profile. Management, frankly, was reluctant to step out publicly, "to stand up for what it stood for."

In the 1990s, however, organizations—particularly large ones—have had little choice but to go public.

Consider the following:

- Bedrock American companies, heretofore the symbols of pristine and silent management decorum, were crucified for lackluster executives, inefficient organizations, and, ultimately, falling profits. In rapid succession, the chairmen of General Motors, American Express, and IBM were beheaded in brutally public bloodlettings. So sensitive were big companies to public approval that some didn't wait to announce management problems. Early in 1993, the nation's 25th largest industrial company, Tenneco, announced that its high-profile chairman, Michael H. Walsh, was suffering from brain cancer. The announcement was made by Walsh himself.[11]
- Four days later, the board of directors of Brinker International convened a hastily called meeting to name and announce a new chairman and CEO to replace the company's well-known leader, Norman E. Brinker, who had been rendered unconscious in a jarring collision during a polo match.[12]
- Later that same year, when a Florida resident contended on *Larry King Live* that the brain cancer that killed his wife was due to her habitual use of a portable cellular telephone, the huge Motorola Company took the rare step of organizing a satellite teleconference to defend the safety of its cellular phones. What made this unprecedented event so remarkable was that Motorola's products weren't even mentioned in the original complaint.[13]

Most organizations today understand clearly that it takes a great deal of time to build a favorable image for a corporation but only one slip to create a negative public impression. In other words, the corporate image is a fragile commodity. Yet, most firms also believe that a positive corporate image is essential for continued long-term success.

As Ray D'Argenio, the former communications director of United Technologies, put it, "Corporate communications can't create a corporate character. A company already has a character, which communications can reinforce"[14](Figure 3–3).

BEWARE THE TRAPS OF PUBLIC OPINION

Analyzing public opinion is not as easy as it looks. Once a company wins favorable public opinion for a product or an idea, the trick is to maintain it (Figure 3–4). The worst thing to do is sit back and bask in the glory of a positive public image; that's a quick route to image deterioration (Figure 3–5).

Public opinion is changeable, and in assessing it, communicators are susceptible to a number of subtle yet lethal traps.

- **Cast in stone** This fallacy assumes that just because public opinion is well established on a certain issue, it isn't likely to change. Not true. Consider an issue such as women's liberation. In the early 1960s, people laughed at the hand-

Brighten Your Corner

Have you
noticed the
great difference
between the
people you
meet?
Some are as
sunshiny as
a handful of
forget-me-nots.
Others come on
like frozen mackerel.
A cheery, comforting
nurse can
help make a
hospital stay
bearable.
An upbeat secretary
makes visitors
glad they came
to see you.
Every corner of the
world has its clouds,
gripes, complainers,
and pains in the
neck—because many
people have
yet to
learn that
honey works better
than vinegar.
You're in control
of *your* small
corner of the
world.
Brighten it. . .
You *can*.

Figure 3–3 Although many companies attempted to construct a differentiable corporate image through advertising, few succeeded as well as United Technologies, which kept its messages succinct, savvy, and sparkling. *(Courtesy of United Technologies Corporation, Hartford, CT)*

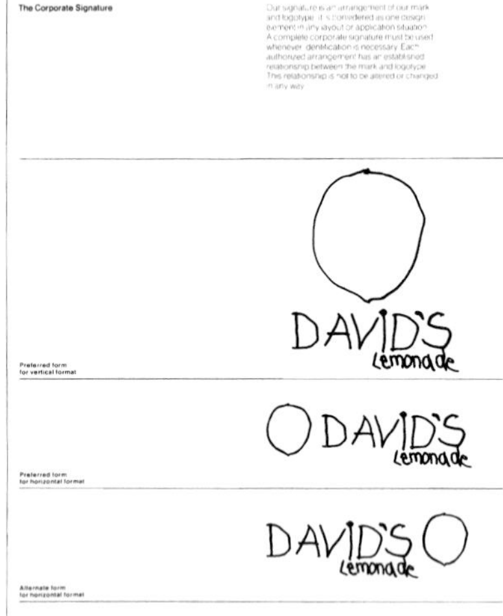

Figure 3–4 The key to a corporate image that gets through to people is a combination of simplicity, unity, and balance. These excerpts from the corporate identity manual of David's lemonade, the creation of Fulton + Partners, Inc., are examples of a clear corporate image. *(Courtesy of Sanders Printing Corporation)*

XEROX

Once a trademark, not always a trademark.

They were once proud trademarks, now they're just names. They failed to take precautions that would have helped them have a long and prosperous life.

We need your help to stay out of there. Whenever you use our name, please use it as a proper adjective in conjunction with our products and services: e.g., Xerox copiers or Xerox financial services. And never as a verb: "to Xerox" in place of "to copy," or as a noun: "Xeroxes" in place of "copies."

With your help and a precaution or two on our part, it's "Once the Xerox trademark, always the Xerox trademark."

Team Xerox. We document the world.

Figure 3–5 The Xerox Company has a unique name and logo problem. The Xerox name is so widely used that it must fight a continual battle to have the name treated as a proper adjective with a capital *X*, rather than a verb with a lowercase *x*—thus the frustration expressed in this ad. *(Courtesy of Xerox Corporation)*

ful of women raising a ruckus about equal rights, equal pay, and equal treatment. By the early 1970s, women's liberation pervaded every sector of our culture, and nobody laughed. In the space of a decade, public opinion about the importance of this issue had shifted substantially.

- **Gut reaction** This fallacy assumes that if management feels in its corporate gut that the public will lean strongly in a certain direction, then that must be the way to go. *Be careful.* Some managements are so cut off from the real world that their knee-jerk reactions to issues often turn out to be more jerk than anything else. One former auto company executive, perhaps overstating the case, described the problem this way: "There's no forward response to what the public wants today.

It's gotten to be a total insulation from the realities of the world." Certainly, management's instincts in dealing with the public may be questionable at times. Generally, gut-reaction judgments should be avoided in assessing public opinion.

- **General public** There may well be a public at large, but there's no such thing as the general public. Even the smallest public can be subdivided. No two people are alike, and messages to influence public opinion should be as pointed as possible rather than scattershot. Sometimes individuals may qualify as members of publics on both sides of an issue. In weighing the pros and cons of lower speed limits, for example, many people are both drivers and pedestrians. Categorizing them into one general group can be a mistake.
- **Words move mountains** Perhaps they do sometimes, but public opinion is usually influenced more by events than by words. For example, in 1979, nuclear power foes lacked a solid political base until an accident at Pennsylvania's Three Mile Island plant rallied public sentiment against the proponents of nuclear power.
- **Brother's keeper** It's true that most people will rise up indignantly if a fellow citizen has been wronged. But they'll get a lot more indignant if they feel they themselves have been wronged. In other words, self-interest often sparks public opinion. An organization wishing to influence public opinion might be well advised to ask initially, "What's in this for the people whose opinion we're trying to influence?"

LOVE THAT SARA LEE UNDERWEAR

Talk about clarifying the corporate image! Consolidated Foods Corporation learned that 98 percent of 800 people surveyed were aware of the products of its subsidiary, Sara Lee. At the same time, the company was unhappy that its own Consolidated Foods name didn't give consumers and investors an accurate picture of the broad range of the company's products—from foods to vacuum cleaners to underwear.

So, dismissing several alternative names recommended by consultants and defying all logic, corporation executives decided to rename the firm to take advantage of the high recognition level of the subsidiary responsible for only 8 percent of its products. Thus, the Sara Lee Corporation was born, complete with a line of underwear. As Yogi Berra said when they told him the people of Dublin had just elected a Jewish mayor, "Only in America!"

SARA LEE CORPORATION

Disney Cuts Its "Program"

In the 1990s, no company was more committed to maintaining an unimpeachable public image than the Walt Disney Company of Burbank, California. Disney, built into a multi-billion-dollar conglomerate on the goodwill of Mickey Mouse and Donald Duck, was most protective of its public opinion.

That's why, in the fall of 1993, Disney's management was confronted with a difficult ethical problem involving its hit movie *The Program.* In one sequence near the film's start, several drunken college football players lie prone in the middle of a busy road to prove their toughness.

Immediately after the film's release, a Pennsylvania teenager was killed when a pickup truck ran over him on a highway dividing line. Shortly thereafter, a Long Island teenager lying prone in the middle of a street also was run over. In rapid succession, two other teenagers were run over and hospitalized in critical condition, again after lying prone in the middle of busy thoroughfares. All the injured teenagers had one thing in common: They had just been to screenings of *The Program.*

Disney, in light of the public outcry, didn't hesitate. Said the film's writer and director, "While the scene in the movie in no way advocates this irresponsible activity, it is impossible for us to ignore that someone may have recklessly chosen to imitate it." In light of the reported incidents, Disney immediately deleted the scene from the movie.

At the time of the deletion, *The Program* was playing in more than 1,000 theaters and was the nation's 12th most popular release. Immediately after the offensive scene was removed, the film's attendance fell off precipitously, and Disney's profits plunged.

In light of the movie's early popularity and subsequent decline, did Disney act correctly in removing the controversial scene from its film?

SUMMARY

Influencing public opinion remains at the heart of professional public relations work. Perhaps the key to realizing this objective is anticipating or keeping ahead of trends in our society. Anticipating trends is no easy task. But in the 1990s, trend watching has developed into a veritable cottage industry. One self-styled prognosticator riding the crest of trend analysis was John Naisbitt, whose book *Megatrends 2000* claimed to predict the new directions that would influence American lives in the next decade. Among them are the following:

- Inflation and interest rates will be held in check.
- There will be a shift from welfare to workfare.
- There will be a shift from public housing to home ownership.
- There will be a shift from sports to the arts as the primary leisure preference.
- Consumers will demand more customized products.
- The media will amplify bad economic news.
- The rise of the Pacific Rim will be seen in terms of economic dominance. Asia will add 80 million more people.
- CEOs in a global economy will become more important and better known than political figures.[15]

Some might argue that there is nothing revolutionary in these megatrends (and they might well be right). Nonetheless, such trends deserve to be scrutinized, analyzed, and evaluated by organizations in order to deal more effectively with the future.

As public relations counselor Philip Lesly has pointed out, "The real problems faced by business today are in the outside world of intangibles and public attitudes."[16] To keep ahead of these intangibles, these public attitudes, and these kernels of future public opinion, managements will turn increasingly to professional public relations practitioners for guidance.

DISCUSSION STARTERS

1. What is public opinion?
2. What are attitudes, and on what characteristics are they based?
3. How are attitudes influenced?
4. What is Maslow's hierarchy of needs?
5. Explain the law of cognitive dissonance.
6. How difficult is it to change a person's behavior?
7. What are Cantril's Laws of Public Opinion?
8. How might an organization go about discovering its own corporate image?
9. What was the approach of Mobil Oil in terms of public opinion in the 1970s, and why is it significant?
10. What are the traps of public opinion?

NOTES

1. William C. Rhoden, "High Stakes: Low Sense of Values," *The New York Times,* July 21, 1993.
2. Cited in Edward L. Bernays, *Crystallizing Public Opinion* (New York: Liveright, 1961), 61.
3. Cited in Harwood L. Childs, *Public Opinion: Nature, Formation, and Role* (Princeton, NJ: Van Nostrand, 1965), 15.
4. James E. Grunig and Todd Hunt, *Managing Public Relations* (New York: Holt, Rinehart & Winston, 1984), 130.
5. Leon A. Festinger, *A Theory of Cognitive Dissonance* (New York: Harper & Row, 1957), 163.

6. Abraham Maslow, *Motivation and Personality* (New York: Harper & Row, 1954).
7. S. Plous, "Toward More Effective Activism," *The Animal's Agenda* (December 1989): 24–26.
8. John V. Pavlik, *Public Relations: What Research Tells Us* (Newbury Park, CA: Sage, 1987), 74.
9. Hadley Cantril, *Gauging Public Opinion* (Princeton, NJ: Princeton University Press, 1972), 226–230.
10. "Teen Talk Barbie Turns Silent on Math," *The New York Times*, October 20, 1992, p. 5.
11. Thomas C. Hayes, "Tenneco's Chief Has Brain Cancer," *New York Times*, January 21, 1993, D1, D20.
12. Thomas C. Hayes, "Brinker Names New Chief," *New York Times*, January 25, 1993, D1, D3.
13. Richard Ringer, "Motorola Defends the Safety of Cellular Phones," *New York Times*, January 26, 1993, D7.
14. Ray D'Argenio, speech at the Communications Executive of the Year Luncheon, sponsored by Corpcom Services, December 10, 1981.
15. John Naisbitt and Patricia Aburdene, *Megatrends 2000* (New York: Morrow, 1990).
16. Philip Lesly, "How the Future Will Shape Public Relations—and Vice Versa," *Public Relations Quarterly* (Winter 1981–82): 7.

SUGGESTED READINGS

A.R.3: The Complete Annual Report and Corporation Image Planning Book. New York: Macmillan, 1988.

Bennett, Amanda. "What Went Wrong: Experts Look at the Sudden Upheaval at Allegis," *The Wall Street Journal*, June 24, 1987, 29.

Creedon, Pamela J. *Women in Mass Communications: Challenging General Values*. Newbury Park, CA: Sage, 1989.

Garbett, Thomas F. *How to Build a Corporation's Identity and Project Its Image*. Lexington, MA: Lexington Books, 1988.

Gilbert, Dennis A. *Compendium of American Public Opinion*. New York: Facts on File, 1988.

Idea Bank for Annual Reports. New York: Corporate Shareholder Press, 1987.

Irvine, Robert B. *When You Are the Headline: Managing a News Story*. Homewood, IL: Dow Jones-Irwin, 1987.

Leff, Suzanne. "10 Dos and Don'ts of Naming. *Public Relations Journal* (December 1987): 37, 38. This checklist gives guidelines for coining memorable company or product names for effective promotion.

Lipset, Seymour Martin, and William Schneider. *The Confidence Gap: Business, Labor and Government in the Public*. New York: Free Press, 1988.

Lukaszewski, Jim. *Influencing Public Attitudes*. Leesburg, VA: Issue Action Publications, 1993.

McCombs, Maxwell, et al. *Contemporary Public Opinion: Issues and the News*. Hillsdale, NJ: Erlbaum, 1991.

McGill, Michael. *American Business and the Quick Fix*. New York: Holt & Co., 1988.

Mercer, Laurie, and Jennifer Singer. *Opportunity Knocks: Using PR*. Radnor, PA: Chilton, 1989.

Meyers, Gerald. *When It Hits the Fan.* Scarborough, Ontario: New American Library of Canada, Limited, 1987.

Nager, Norman, and Richard Truitt. *Strategic Public Relations Counseling.* White Plains, NY: Longman, 1987; University Press of America, 1991.

Napoles, Veronica. *Corporate Identity Design.* New York: Van Nostrand Reinhold, 1987.

Olasky, Marvin N. *Corporate Public Relations and American Public Enterprise.* Hillsdale, NJ: Erlbaum, 1987.

Paluszek, John. *Business and Society: 1976–2000.* Ann Arbor, MI: Books on Demand.

Pratkanis, Anthony, and Aronson, Elliot. *Age of Propaganda: The Everyday Use and Abuse of Persuasion.* New York: W. H. Freeman, 1992.

Sauerhaft, Stan, and Chris Atkins. *Image Wars.* New York: Wiley, 1989.

Selame, Elinor, and Joseph Selame. *The Company Image: Building Your Identity and Influence in the Marketplace.* New York: Wiley, 1988.

TOP OF THE SHELF

The New York Times. New York: The New York Times Company; and *The Wall Street Journal.* New York: Dow Jones & Company, Inc.

Public relations can be practiced only by understanding public opinion, and the best forums in which to study it are *The New York Times* and *The Wall Street Journal.* Their pages daily reveal the diverse views of pundits, politicians, and plain people.

Both papers, through their opinion pages and in-depth stories, express the attitudes of leaders in politics, business, science, education, journalism and the arts, on topics ranging from abortion rights to genetic engineering to race relations. Occasionally, *The Times* and *The Journal* supplement their usual coverage with public opinion polls to gauge attitudes and beliefs on particularly hot issues. *The Sunday Times,* with features that include the magazine section, "Week in Review" and "Business Forum," is an important resource for public relations professionals.

To influence public opinion, counselors must first understand it. Two excellent sources with which to begin the quest are *The New York Times* and *The Wall Street Journal.* Read these papers daily, and you'll keep abreast of popular thought on major issues and trends.

CASE STUDY

EXXON CORPORATION'S BAD GOOD FRIDAY

At 8:30 A.M. on March 24, 1989—Good Friday, no less—Lawrence G. Rawl, chairman and chief executive of the Exxon Corporation, one of the world's largest companies, was in his kitchen sipping coffee when the phone rang.

"What happened? Did it lose an engine? Break a rudder?" Rawl asked the caller.

"What happened" was that an Exxon tanker had run aground and was dumping gummy crude oil into the frigid waters of Prince William Sound, just outside the harbor of Valdez, Alaska.

What was about to happen to Mr. Rawl and his company—and to the environment—was arguably the worst environmental disaster in the history of the United States.

The facts, painfully portrayed in media across the country, were these: The *Exxon Valdez,* a 978-foot tanker, piloted by a captain who was later revealed to be legally drunk, ran aground on a reef 25 miles southwest of the port of Valdez. The resulting rupture caused a spill of 250,000 barrels, the largest spill ever in North America, affecting 1,300 square miles of water, damaging some 600 miles of coastline, and murdering as many as 4,000 Alaskan sea otters.

The disaster also enshrined the name of Exxon in the all-time Public Relations Hall of Shame.

Exxon's dilemma broke down roughly into five general categories.

TO GO OR NOT TO GO

The first problem that confronted Exxon and its top management after news of the Good Friday spill had broken was whether Chairman Rawl should personally fly to Prince William Sound to demonstrate the company's concern. This was what Union Carbide chairman, Warren Anderson, did when his company suffered a devastating industrial explosion in Bhopal, India. It was also what Ashland Oil's chairman, John R. Hall, did when his company suffered an oil spill earlier in 1989.

If Rawl went to Alaska, the reasoning went, he might have been able to reassure the public that the people who run Exxon acknowledged their misdeed and would make amends. What could be a better show of concern than the chairman flying to the local scene of the tragedy?

On the other hand, a consensus of executives around Rawl argued that he should remain in New York. "What are you going to do?" they asked. "We've already said we've done it, we're going to pay for it, and we're responsible for it." Rawl's more effective role, said these advisers, was right there at Exxon headquarters in Manhattan.

In the end, the latter view triumphed. Rawl didn't go to Alaska. He left the cleanup in "capable hands" and sent a succession of lower-ranking executives to Alaska to deal with the spill. As he summarized in an interview one year after the Prince William Sound nightmare, "We had concluded that there was simply too much for me to coordinate from New York. It wouldn't have made any difference if I showed up and made a speech in the town forum. I wasn't going to spend the summer there; I had other things to do."

Rawl's failure to fly immediately to Valdez struck some as shortsighted. Said one media consultant, "The chairman should have been up there walking in the oil and picking up dead birds."

WHERE TO ESTABLISH MEDIA CENTRAL

The second dilemma that confronted Exxon was where to establish its media center.

This decision started, correctly enough, with Exxon senior managers concluding that the impact of the spill was so great that news organizations should be kept informed as events unfolded. Exxon, correctly, wanted to take charge of the news flow and give the public, through the news media, a credible, concerned, and wholly committed corporate response.

It decided that the best place to do this would be in Valdez, Alaska, itself. "Just about every news organization worth its salt had representatives in Valdez," said Exxon's publicity chief. "But in retrospect, we should have sent live broadcasts of news conferences to several points around the country."

The problem was that Valdez was a remote Alaskan town with limited communications operations. This complicated the ability of Exxon to disseminate information quickly. As *Oil & Gas Journal* stated later, "Exxon did not update its media relations people elsewhere in the world. It told reporters it was Valdez or nothing."

Additionally, there was a 4-hour time difference between Valdez and New York. Consequently, "Exxon statements were erratic and contradictory," said the publisher of another oil bulletin. The phone lines to Valdez quickly became jammed, and even Rawl couldn't find a knowledgeable official to brief him. That left news organizations responsible for keeping the public informed cut off from Exxon information during the early part of the crisis. Because news conferences took place at unsuitable viewing hours for television networks and too late for many morning newspapers, predictable accusations of an Exxon "cover-up" resulted. Said one Exxon official about the decision to put the center in Valdez, "It didn't work."

RAPIDITY OF RESPONSE

A cardinal rule in any crisis is: Keep ahead of the information flow. Try not to let events get ahead of you. Keep in front of the information curve. Here Exxon had serious problems.

First, it took Chairman Rawl a full week to make any public comment on the spill. When he did, it was to blame others: the U.S. Coast Guard and Alaskan officials were "holding up" his company's efforts to clean up the spill. But Rawl's words were too little, too late. The impression persisted that, in light of the delay in admitting responsibility, Exxon was not responding vigorously enough.

A full 10 days after the crisis, Exxon placed an advertisement in 166 newspapers. To some readers, the ad seemed self-serving and failed to address the many pointed questions raised about Exxon's conduct.

"It seems the company was a bit too relaxed in its capabilities," offered the president of the Public Relations Society of America. Meanwhile, one group that wasn't relaxed was the Alaska state legislature, which enacted a tax increase on oil from the North Slope fields within weeks of the Exxon spill. Congressional committees in Washington moved just as quickly to increase liability limits and potential compensation for oil-spill damage and to increase the money available through the industry-financed Offshore Oil Pollution Compensation Fund.

When Exxon hesitated, its opponents seized the initiative. Concluded another public relations executive, "They lost the battle in the first 48 hours."

HOW HIGH THE PROFILE

Exxon's response in the face of this most challenging crisis in its history was, to put it mildly, muted.

From an operations and logistics viewpoint, Exxon did a good job. The company immediately set up animal rescue projects, launched a major cleanup effort, and agreed to pick up a substantial percentage of the cost. But it made the mistake of downplaying the crisis in public.

Exxon's public statements sometimes contradicted information from other sources. At one point, an Exxon spokesman said that damage from the oil spill would be minimal. Others watching the industry said the damage was likely to be substantial.

Chairman Rawl, an otherwise blunt and outspoken CEO, seemed defensive and argumentative in his public comments. In one particularly disastrous personal appearance on *CBS Morning News*, Rawl glared at interviewer Kathleen Sullivan and snapped, "I can't give you details of our cleanup plan. It's thick and complicated. And I haven't had a chance to read it yet. The CEO of a major company doesn't have time to read every plan."

Exxon's attempts to calm the public also were criticized. Its ad drew fire for not expressing enough concern. It hired an outside firm to do a series of video news releases to show how the company was cleaning up the spill. At an estimated cost of more than $3 million, a 13-minute tape was shown at the corporation's annual meeting. The video, called *Progress in Alaska*, attracted intense criticism from those attending the conference, as well as from the press. The film implied, argued *Boston Globe* reporter Robert Lenzner, that "The brutal scenes of damage to Alaskan waters seen nightly on television news programs were false." *USA Today* called the tape "Exxon's worst move of the day." When the consultant who devised the video wrote an op-ed article in *The New York Times* defending Exxon's approach in Alaska, the Alaskan representative to the National Wildlife Federation responded with a blistering letter to the editor, noting that the consultant omitted in his article that the spill had resulted in the death of more than 15,000 sea birds and numerous otters and eagles.

Exxon then added an environmental expert to its board of directors, but only after pension funds, which control a large chunk of its stock, demanded such a response.

DEALING WITH THE AFTERMATH

Finally, Exxon was forced to deal with all the implications of what its tanker had wrought in Valdez.

The company became embroiled in controversy when Exxon USA sent a $30,000 contribution to the Alaska Public Radio Network, which covered the crisis on a daily basis. The network, sniffing "conflict of interest," flatly turned down Exxon's attempted largesse. Subsequently, a special appropriations bill was introduced in the Alaskan legislature to forward an identical amount to Alaska Public Radio.

The accident and the company's reaction to it also had consequences for the oil industry. Plans to expand drilling into the Alaskan National Wildlife Refuge were shelved by Congress, and members called for new laws increasing federal involvement in oil spills.

The company's employees, too, felt confused, embarrassed, and betrayed. Summarizing the prevailing mood at the company, one Exxon worker said, "Whenever I travel now, I feel like I have a target painted on my chest."

In 1994, more than five years after the tanker ran aground, Exxon went to court in Anchorage to defend itself against $15 million in civil claims.

The lessons of the *Exxon Valdez*'s Good Friday oil spill would not soon be forgotten by corporate managers. The episode, predicted one, "will become a textbook example of what not to do when an unexpected crisis thrusts a company into the limelight." Said another, Exxon's response "is fast becoming the stuff of PR legend."

Reprinted by permission of UFS, Inc.

AN OPEN LETTER TO THE PUBLIC

On March 24, in the early morning hours, a disastrous accident happened in the waters of Prince William Sound, Alaska. By now you all know that our tanker, the Exxon Valdez, hit a submerged reef and lost 240,000 barrels of oil into the waters of the Sound.

We believe that Exxon has moved swiftly and competently to minimize the effect this oil will have on the environment, fish and other wildlife. Further, I hope that you know we have already committed several hundred people to work on the cleanup. We also will meet our obligations to all those who have suffered damage from the spill.

Finally, and most importantly, I want to tell you how sorry I am that this accident took place. We at Exxon are especially sympathetic to the residents of Valdez and the people of the State of Alaska. We cannot, of course, undo what has been done. But I can assure you that since March 24, the accident has been receiving our full attention and will continue to do so.

L. G. Rawl
Chairman

QUESTIONS

1. What would you have recommended Chairman Rawl do upon learning of the Prince William Sound oil spill?
2. How would you have handled the media in this case?
3. What would have been your "timing" in terms of public relations responses in this case?
4. What would be your overall public relations strategy—i.e., aggressive, low-key, etc.—if you were Exxon's public relations director?
5. Do you think this case will ever qualify as a "textbook example" of what not to do in a crisis?

For further information about the *Exxon Valdez* case, see Richard Behar, "Exxon Strikes Back," *Time* (26 March, 1990): 62–63: Claudia H. Deutsch, "The Giant with a Black Eye," *The New York Times*, 2 April 1989, B1–4; E. Bruce Harrison, with Tom Prugh, "Assessing the Damage," *Public Relations Journal* (October 1989): 40–45; John Holusha, "Exxon's Public-Relations Problem," *The New York Times*, 21 April 1989, D1–4; Peter Nulty, "Exxon's Problem: Not What You Think," *Fortune* (April 23, 1990): 202–204; James Lukaszewski, "How Vulnerable Are You? The Lessons from Valdez," *Public Relations Quarterly* (Fall 1989): 5–6; Phillip M. Perry, "Exxon Falters in PR Effort Following Alaskan Oil Spill," *O'Dwyer's PR Services Report*, (July 1989) 1,: 16–22; Allanna Sullivan, "Rawl Wishes He'd Visited Valdez Sooner," *The Wall Street Journal*, 30 June 1989, B7; and Paul Wiseman, "Firm Finds Valdez Oil Fowls Image," *USA Today*, (26 April 1990): B1.

TIPS FROM THE TOP

ARCHBISHOP JOHN P. FOLEY

John P. Foley was ordained as an archbishop and named president of the Pontifical Commission for Social Communications at the Vatican by Pope John Paul II in 1984. In this capacity, he is the highest-ranking public relations official in the Vatican. Archbishop Foley began his communications career writing radio plays as a teenager. He continued his writing, radio, and television work in secondary school. On being ordained to the priesthood, he was assigned to *The Catholic Standard and Times* newspaper. He became editor of the paper and later served as English language press secretary for Pope John Paul II's trip to Ireland and the United States in 1979.

What is the Church's attitude toward public relations?
The Church has always been interested in public relations in the wide sense of the term. Also, one can say that the Church has been involved in most communications media at the beginning—the first printed book was the Bible; Marconi himself developed Vatical Radio; among the first and still among the most widely transmitted satellite broadcasts are the papal ceremonies of Christmas, Holy Week, and Easter.

At the Vatican, press information that had previously been made available through *L'Osservatore Romano,* the Vatican daily, began to be made available through a special press office during the Second Vatican Council (1962–65). This press office of the Holy See has become a permanent fixture at the Vatican, and the director of the press office makes public the official statements of the Holy See. Contact with the electronic and film media is done through the Pontifical Council for Social Communications, which also makes arrangements for the satellite transmission of papal ceremonies. Naturally, there has been growing contact with the media over the years and an increased professionalism in such public relations contacts.

The Congregation for Catholic Education has also asked that all those preparing for the priesthood be trained in basic communications skills—for example, preparing press releases and responding to media queries.

What is the makup of the Vatican communications staff?
First, the 15 staff members of this Council authorize and provide technical assistance for about 1,500 audiovisual projects each year, promote Catholic communications work throughout the world, maintain contact with the three international Catholic communications organizations—one for press, one for radio-TV, and a third for cinema—maintain the Vatical film library, and prepare communications policy documents. There are also the more than 300 people of Vatican Radio, which broadcasts in more than 30 languages around the world; the somewhat smaller staff of *L'Osservatore Romano,* which publishes a daily newspaper in Italian and weekly editions in Italian, English, French, Spanish, German, and Portuguese and a monthly edition in Polish; the dozen staff members of the Vatican Television Center, a production facility that documents the public activity of the Pope and coproduces programs for TV stations and networks around the world; and the Press Office of the Holy See and Vatical Information Service, for contact with the media in Rome and elsewhere.

What is your normal working day?
Normal working day—Monday through Saturday: rise between 5:30 and 6 A.M. for prayer and Mass. Arrive at office at about 7:30 A.M. Review mail, in Italian, English, Spanish, French, Portuguese, German, and Dutch—someone else tells me what the German and Dutch correspondence says—and respond to letters; regular 9 A.M. meeting with top staff; appointments starting at 10 A.M. with communicators, bishops, ambassadors, technicians, etc., etc. Lunch: 2 P.M., often a working lunch. Afternoon—desk work and planning and meetings, in office or at home. Dinner—8 P.M., often a working dinner. Almost every day, it is necessary to speak four languages—Italian, English, Spanish, and French.

How active is the Pope in communications activity?
Pope John Paul II has a great interest in communications and is a natural communicator through his obvious authenticity and through his symbolic gestures. And he is, obviously, a major news maker. He does not, however, do anything specifically for the media, except the recording of an occasional radio or TV message before making a pastoral visit to a particular country. He is open to full coverage of all his public activity, however, and he does visit on the plane with journalists who accompany him on his international trips. He is most willing to meet with groups of communicators who come to Rome and to offer a specific message on the media. He is a very warm and expressive person, and this seems to be communicated well in the media, especially in television and in photos.

How active is the Pope's speaking schedule?
The Secretariat of State forms, among other things, a research staff for the Pope in gathering material for the preparation of speeches by the Pope. In the 15 years of his pontificate, during the 175 trips the Pope has made outside of Rome, the Pope

has made 2,728 speeches. The Pope generally makes between 20 and 25 speeches a week here in Rome.

What has been your most significant public relations challenge?
I would say that my biggest challenge is to get communicators to take *seriously* the religious and spiritual dimension of human life. These aspects of life—the validity and effectiveness, and indeed the importance, of spiritual and religious motivation in human activity—seem foreign to secular journalists. Without acceptance of the reality of such spiritual and religious motivation, how do you account for those who suffered for their faith under Communist oppression—and indeed, the thirst for religious livery, which was in part responsible for the collapse of Communism?

Allied to this is a certain amount of frustration in getting news people to recognize "good news"—as when the media, until the last minute, virtually ignored the presence of 250,000 young people for the World Day of Youth in Denver in August 1993 and focused on dissent and problems in the Church. I do not say that dissent and problems should not be covered; I do say that there is a story behind the presence of 250,000 enthusiastic and generous young people from around the world in Denver, which should not be overlooked or ignored. The reporting of such good news can also contribute to an improvement in social morale and can offer encouragement and models for imitation to others. I do not say that bad news should be covered up; I do say that good news is indeed news and should not be ignored.

Thus, my biggest challenge is to get people to accept the importance or reality of the spiritual and religious dimension of human life and to convince them not to ignore the good news—what the Baptist evangelist and educator Russell Conwell called the "acres of diamonds" in our own backyard.

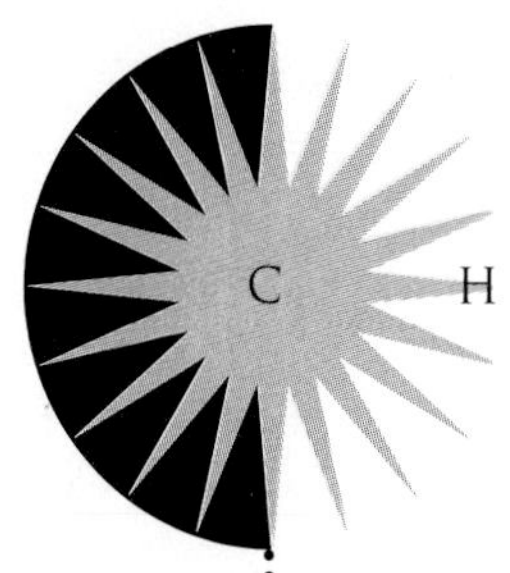

CHAPTER 4

RESEARCH

EVERY PUBLIC RELATIONS PROGRAM OR SOLUTION SHOULD begin with research. Most don't, which is a shame.

The four-step R-A-C-E approach to public relations problem solving, alluded to in Chapter 1, starts with research. Since public relations is still a misunderstood and amorphous function to many, public relations recommendations must be grounded in hard data whenever possible. In other words, before recommending a course of action, public relations professionals must analyze audiences, assess alternatives, and generally do their homework. In other words, most clients are less interested in what their public relations advisors think than in what they know. And the only way to know what to do is by researching first. Indeed, research has become the essential first step in the practice of modern public relations.

Instinct, intuition, and gut feelings all remain important in the conduct of public relations work; but management today demands more—measurement, analysis, and evaluation at every stage of the public relations process. In an era of scarce resources, management wants facts and statistics from public relations professionals, to show that their efforts contribute not only to overall organizational effectiveness but also to the bottom line. Why should we introduce a new employee newspaper? What should it say and cost? How will we know it's working? Questions like these must be answered through research.

Research should be applied in public relations work both at the initial stage, prior to planning a campaign, and at the final stage, to evaluate a program's effectiveness. Early research helps to determine the current situation, prevalent attitudes, and difficulties that the program faces. Later research examines the program's success, along with what else still needs to be done. Research at both points in the process is critical.

Even though research does not necessarily provide unequivocal proof of a program's effectiveness, it does allow public relations professionals to support their own intuition. It's little wonder, then, that the idea of measuring public relations work has steadily gained acceptance.[1]

Figure 4–1 An early research effort, albeit a futile one, was the return of the biblical scouts sent by Moses to reconnoiter the land of Canaan. They disagreed in their reports, and the Israelites believed the gloomier versions. This failure to interpret the data correctly caused them to wander another 40 years in the wilderness. (An even earlier research effort was Noah's sending the dove to search for dry ground.) *(Courtesy of Trout & Ries)*

WHAT IS RESEARCH?

Research is the systematic collection and interpretation of information to increase understanding (Figure 4–1).[2] Most people associate public relations with *conveying* information; although that association is accurate, research must be the obligatory first step in any project. A firm must acquire enough accurate, relevant data about its publics, products, and programs to answer these questions:

- How can we identify and define our constituent groups?
- How does this knowledge relate to the design of our messages?
- How does it relate to the design of our programs?
- How does it relate to the media we use to convey our messages?
- How does it relate to the schedule we adopt in using our media?
- How does it relate to the ultimate implementation tactics of our program?

It is difficult to delve into the minds of others, whose backgrounds and points of view may be quite different from one's own, with the purpose of understanding why they think as they do. Research skills are partly intuitive, partly an outgrowth of individual temperament, and partly a function of acquired knowledge. There is nothing mystifying about them. Although we tend to think of research in terms of impersonal test scores, interviews, or questionnaires, they are only a small part of the process. The real challenge lies in using research—knowing when to do what, with whom, and for what purpose.

TYPES OF PUBLIC RELATIONS RESEARCH

In general, research is conducted to do three things: (1) describe a process, situation, or phenomenon; (2) explain why something is happening, what its causes are, and what effect it will have; and (3) predict what probably will happen if we do or don't take action. Most research in public relations is either theoretical or applied. Applied research solves practical problems; theoretical research aids understanding of a public relations process.

APPLIED RESEARCH

In public relations work, applied research can be either strategic or evaluative. Both applications are designed to answer specific practical questions.

- **Strategic research** is used primarily in program development to determine program objectives, develop message strategies, or establish benchmarks. It often examines the tools and techniques of public relations. For example, a firm that wants to know how employees rate its candor in internal publications would first conduct strategic research to find out where it stands.

- **Evaluative research**, sometimes called *summative research*, is conducted primarily to determine whether a public relations program has accomplished its goals and objectives. For example, if changes are made in the internal communications program to increase candor, evaluative research can determine whether the goals have been met. *Formative research*, a variant of evaluation, can be applied during a program to monitor progress and indicate where modifications might make sense.

THEORETICAL RESEARCH

Theoretical research is more abstract and conceptual than applied research. It helps build theories in public relations work in areas such as why people communicate, how public opinion is formed, and how a public is created. Knowledge of theoretical research is important as a framework for persuasion and as a base for understanding why people do what they do.

Some knowledge of theoretical research in public relations and mass communications is essential for enabling practitioners to understand the limitations of communication as a persuasive tool. Attitude and behavior change have been the traditional goals in public relations programs, yet theoretical research indicates that such goals may be difficult or impossible to achieve through persuasive efforts. According to such research, other factors are always getting in the way.

Researchers have found that communication is most persuasive when it comes from multiple sources of high credibility. Credibility itself is a multidimensional concept that includes trustworthiness, expertise, and power. Others have found that a message generally is more effective when it is simple because it is easier to understand, localize, and make personally relevant. According to still other research, the persuasiveness of a message can be increased when it arouses or is accompanied by a high level of personal involvement in the issue at hand. The point here is that knowledge of theoretical research can help practitioners not only understand the basis of applied research findings, but also temper management's expectations of attitude and behavioral change resulting from public relations programs.

METHODS OF PUBLIC RELATIONS RESEARCH

Observation is the foundation of modern social science. Scientists, social psychologists, and anthropologists make observations, develop theories, and, hopefully, increase understanding of human behavior. Public relations research, too, is founded on observation. Three primary forms of public relations research dominate the field.

- **Surveys** are designed to reveal attitudes and opinions—what people think about certain subjects.
- **Communication audits** often reveal disparities between real and perceived communications between management and target audiences. Management may make certain assumptions about its methods, media, materials, and messages, whereas its targets may confirm or refute those assumptions.

- **Unobtrusive measures**—such as fact finding, content analysis, and readability studies—enable the study of a subject or object without involving the researcher or the research as an intruder.

Each method of public relations research offers specific benefits and should be understood and used by the modern practitioner.

SURVEYS

Survey research is one of the most frequently used research methods in public relations. Surveys can be applied to broad societal issues, such as determining public opinion about a political candidate, or to the most minute organizational problem, such as whether shareholders like the quarterly report (Figure 4–2). Surveys come in two types.

1. **Descriptive surveys** offer a snapshot of a current situation or condition. They are the research equivalent of a balance sheet, capturing reality at a specific point in time. A typical public opinion poll is a prime example.
2. **Explanatory surveys** are concerned with cause and effect. Their purpose is to help explain why a current situation or condition exists and to offer explanations for opinions and attitudes. Frequently, such explanatory or analytical surveys are designed to answer the question "Why?" Why are our philanthropic dollars not being appreciated in the community? Why are employees not believing management's messages? Why is our credibility being questioned?

Surveys generally consist of four elements: (1) the sample, (2) the questionnaire, (3) the interview, and (4) the analysis of results. (Direct mail surveys, of course, eliminate the interview step.) Because survey research is so critical in public relations, we will examine each survey element in some detail.

THE SAMPLE

The sample, or selected target group, must be representative of the total public whose views are sought. Once a survey population has been determined, a researcher must select the appropriate sample or group of respondents from whom to collect information. Sampling is tricky. A researcher must be aware of the hidden pitfalls in choosing a representative sample, not the least of which is the perishable nature of most data. Survey findings are rapidly outdated because of population mobility and changes in the political and socioeconomic environment. Consequently, sampling should be completed quickly.

Two cross-sectional approaches are used in obtaining a sample: random sampling and nonrandom sampling. The former is more scientific, the latter more informal.

Take a moment to tell us about your smoking preferences.

Please take a moment to fill out the postage-paid survey below and drop it in the mail today.

Your answers will help us to better understand the preferences of today's smokers. And you could be eligible for future offers of special interest to smokers.

Print corrections below.

5070100336789930

Mr. Fraser Seitel
12 King Place
Closter, NJ 07624-2936

By responding to this survey and signing below, I certify that I am a cigarette smoker 21 years of age or older. I am also willing to receive free samples of cigarettes and incentive items in the mail, subject to applicable state and federal law.

Signature (required) X ____________________ **Birthdate** (required) ___/___/___ Mo. Day Yr.

1. What is your regular brand of cigarettes–that is, the brand you smoke most often?
   ____________________ (brand)
2. Is your regular brand...? *(Check one.)*
   ☐ Regular/King Size, ☐ 100's or ☐ 120's
3. Is your regular brand...? *(Check one.)*
   ☐ Menthol or ☐ Non-Menthol
4. Is your regular brand...? *(Check one.)*
   ☐ Filter or ☐ Non-Filter
5. Is your regular brand...? *(Check one.)*
   ☐ Lowest/1 mg Tar ☐ Medium
   ☐ Ultra/Extra Low Tar ☐ Full Flavor
   ☐ Light/Mild
6. Do you usually buy it by the ...?
   ☐ Pack ☐ Carton ☐ Both Ways
7. How long have you smoked this brand?
   ☐ Less than 1 year ☐ 2 to 3 years
   ☐ 1 to 2 years ☐ 3 to 5 years
   ☐ Over 5 years
8. What, if any, was your previous brand?
   ____________________ (brand)
9. The next time you go to the store, if your regular brand were not available, what would you do? *(Check one.)*
   ☐ Go to another store to buy my regular brand.
   ☐ Buy another type or length of my regular brand.
   ☐ Wait until the store has my regular brand.
   ☐ Buy a different brand entirely.
10. Which of the following statements best describes the way you use cigarette coupons? *(Check one.)*
    ☐ I use almost any cigarette coupon I get.
    ☐ I occasionally use coupons for cigarettes, even if they are not for my regular brand.
    ☐ I only use coupons if they are for my regular brand.
    ☐ I never use coupons to buy cigarettes.
11. How often do you use special in-store cigarette offers, such as a free gift with purchase, a 2-for-1, or special prices?

	Frequently	*Occasionally*	*Never*
I look for special offers for my *regular brand*...	☐	☐	☐
I take advantage of special offers for brands *other than my regular brand*...	☐	☐	☐

12. If your regular brand were not available, what other brands would you consider buying? *(Check all that apply.)*

☐ Alpine	☐ Doral	☐ Now
☐ Basic	☐ GPC	☐ Parliament
☐ Benson & Hedges	☐ Kent	☐ Pyramid
☐ Best Buy	☐ Kool	☐ Raleigh Extra
☐ Best Value	☐ Magna	☐ Salem
☐ Bristol	☐ Marlboro	☐ Store Brand/Generic
☐ Bucks	☐ Merit	☐ Superslims
☐ Cambridge	☐ Misty	☐ True
☐ Camel	☐ Monarch	☐ Vantage
☐ Capri	☐ Montclair	☐ Viceroy
☐ Carlton	☐ More	☐ Virginia Slims
	☐ Newport	☐ Winston

☐ Other ____________________ (brand)
☐ None

13. Please list *all* the brands of cigarettes you smoked at least one pack of in the past two weeks. How many packs did you smoke of each brand? *(Use as many lines as you need. Write in exact number of packs for each brand below. Note: 1 carton=10 packs.)*
    ____________________ (brand) # of Packs____
    ____________________ # of Packs____
    ____________________ # of Packs____
    ____________________ # of Packs____
14. Which of the following best describes you? *(Check one.)*
    ☐ White ☐ Asian
    ☐ African-American ☐ American Indian
    ☐ Hispanic ☐ Other ________
15. Is there another smoker in your household 21 years of age or older? Please print full name, birthdate and regular brand.
    First Name ____ M.I. ____ Last Name ____
    Birthdate ___/___/___ Regular Brand ____
16. Would you be interested in receiving information about issues that affect smokers?
    ☐ Yes ☐ No
17. Would you be interested in joining a smokers' group to help protect your right to smoke?
    ☐ Yes ☐ No

Moisten here to seal before mailing.

If the store where you buy cigarettes hasn't heard about the change in Marlboro brand pricing, please leave this friendly calling card letting them know how to get details.

And thanks for your patience.

ANNOUNCING
NEW VALUE PRICING
ON PHILIP MORRIS BRANDS.

See retailer message other side.

Figure 4–2 In the mid-1990s, with cigarette companies faced with increasing pressure from nonsmoking advocates, smart companies like Philip Morris continually surveyed customers, not only to reveal smoking preferences but also to determine their willingness to assist in the battle to protect smokers' rights. (*Courtesy of Philip Morris*)

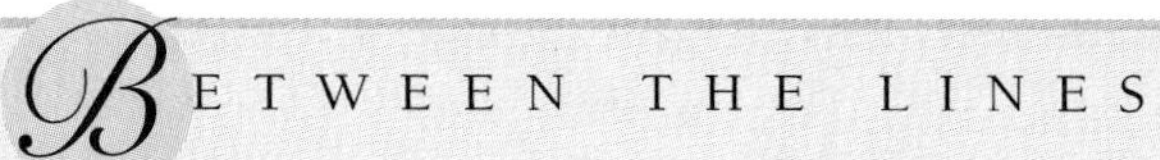

PAY ATTENTION TO WHAT I DO, NOT WHAT I SAY

Public relations professionals must always keep in mind that, as most research has shown, attitudes are not a reliable predictor of behavior. In other words, people often talk one way but act another—a phenomenon that researcher James Grunig has labeled *hedging/wedging*.*

- Ask American adults whether they're satisfied with their jobs, and 88 percent will answer yes. But only 30 percent of those adults expect to have the same job in 5 years. Another 31 percent of them plan to quit their jobs, and 25 percent don't know where they will be working in 5 years.
- A whopping 76 percent of American adults vow that they exercise regularly, and 33 percent will tell you that they exercise strenuously three or more times a week. But when those self-proclaimed fitness fans waddle over to the scales, the truth comes out. Fully 59 percent of all U.S. adults—about 105 million people—are overweight.
- Another 65 percent of adults claim they are making a real effort to eat more brussels sprouts and cauliflower; 59 percent try hard to eat enough fiber; 56 percent claim they avoid eating too much fat; 57 percent say they are cutting down on salt; and 46 percent say that they steer clear of high-cholesterol foods. But the number of adults who would like to see more all-you-can-eat specials in restaurants increased from 30 to 37 percent during the last decade. By contrast, the number who want more dieter's specials declined from 18 to 16 percent over the same period.

What's the point? People sometimes tell you what they think you want to hear rather than what they really believe. So, be wary of even the most buttoned-up research.

*Joe Schwartz, "Do as I Say," *U.S. Demographics* (April 1988).

RANDOM SAMPLING In random sampling, each member of a population has a known chance of being selected. Random sampling is based on a mathematical criterion that allows generalizations from the sample to be made to the total population. There are four types of random or probability samples.

1. **Simple random** sampling gives all members of the population an equal chance of being selected. First, all members of the population are identified, and then as many subjects as are needed are randomly selected—usually with the help of a computer. Election polling uses a random approach;

although millions of Americans vote, only a few thousand are ever polled on their election preferences. The Nielson national television sample, for example, consists of 4,000 homes. The Census Bureau uses a sample of 72,000 out of 93 million households to obtain estimates of employment and other population characteristics.

How large should a random sample be? The answer depends on a number of factors, one of which is the size of the population. In addition, the more similar the population elements are in regard to the characteristics being studied, the smaller the sample required. In most random samples, the following population-to-sample ratios apply, with a 5 percent margin of error:

Population	*Sample*
1,000	278
2,000	322
3,000	341
5,000	355
10,000	370
50,000	381
100,000	383
500,000	383
Infinity	384

Random sampling owes its accuracy to the laws of probability, which are best explained by the example of a barrel filled with 10,000 marbles—5,000 green ones and 5,000 red ones. If a blindfolded person selects a certain number of marbles from the barrel—say, 400—the laws of probability suggest that the most frequently drawn combination will be 200 red and 200 green. These laws further suggest that with certain margins of error, a very few marbles can represent the whole barrel, which can correspond to any size—city, state, or nation.

2. **Systematic random** sampling is closely related to simple random sampling, but it uses a random starting point in the sample list. From then on, the researcher selects every *n*th person in the list. Because each member of the population does not have an equal probability of being selected, this type of sampling is less reliable than simple random sampling. It is also cheaper and easier to perform.
3. **Stratified random** sampling is used to survey different segments or strata of the population. For example, if an organization wants to determine the relationship between years of service and attitudes toward the company, it may stratify the sample to ensure that the breakdown of respondents accurately reflects the makeup of the population. In other words, if more than half of the employees have been with the company more than 10 years, more than half of those polled should also reflect that level of service. By stratifying the sample, the organization's objective can be achieved.
4. **Cluster** sampling involves first breaking the population down into small heterogeneous subsets, or clusters, and then selecting the potential sample from the individual clusters or groups. A cluster may often be defined as a geographic area, such as an election district.

NONRANDOM SAMPLING Nonrandom samples come in three types, convenience, quota, and volunteer.

1. **Convenience** samples, also known as *accidental, chunk* or *opportunity* samples, are relatively unstructured, rather unsystematic, and designed to elicit ideas and points of view. Journalists use convenience samples when they conduct person-on-the-street interviews. The most common type of convenience sample in public relations research is the focus group. Focus groups generally consist of 8 to 12 people, with a moderator encouraging in-depth discussion of a specific topic. Focus groups generate concepts and ideas rather than validate hypotheses.
2. **Quota** samples permit a researcher to choose subjects on the basis of certain characteristics. For example, the attitudes of a certain number of women, men, blacks, whites, rich, or poor may need to be known. Quotas are imposed in proportion to each group's percentage of the population. The advantage of quota sampling is that it increases the homogeneity of a sample population, thus enhancing the validity of a study. However, it is hard to classify interviewees by one or two discrete demographic characteristics. For example, a particular interviewee may be black, Catholic, female, under 25, and a member of a labor union all at the same time, making the lines of demographic demarcation pretty blurry. (A derivative of quota sampling is called *purposive sampling.*)
3. **Volunteer** samples utilize willing participants who agree voluntarily to respond to concepts and hypotheses for research purposes.[3]

THE QUESTIONNAIRE

Before creating a questionnaire, a researcher must consider his or her objective in doing the study. What you seek to find out should influence the specific publics you ask, the questions you raise, and the research method you choose. After determining what you're after, consider the particular questionnaire design. Specifically, researchers should observe the following in designing their questionnaire:

1. Keep it short, probably under 20 questions. It's terrific if the questionnaire can be answered in 5 minutes.
2. Use structured, not open-ended, questions. People would rather check a box or circle a number than write an essay. But leave room at the bottom for general comments or "Other." Also, start with simple, nonthreatening questions before getting to the more difficult, sensitive ones. This approach will build respondent trust as well as commitment to finishing the questionnaire.
3. Measure intensity of feelings. Let respondents check "very satisfied," "satisfied," "dissatisfied," or "very dissatisfied" rather than "yes" or "no." One popular approach is the semantic differential technique shown in Figure 4–3.
4. Don't use fancy words or words that have more than one meaning. If you must use big words, make the context clear.
5. Don't ask loaded questions. "Is management doing all it can to communicate with you?" is a terrible question. The answer is always no.

Dictaphone

1	2	3	4	5
High price				Low price
1	2	3	4	5
Not reliable				Reliable
1	2	3	4	5
Bulky				Compact
1	2	3	4	5
Inconvenient				Convenient
1	2	3	4	5
Bad service				Good service
1	2	3	4	5
Not likely to buy				Likely to buy

Stowe

1	2	3	4	5	6	7	8	9	10
Hard to get to									Easy to get to
1	2	3	4	5	6	7	8	9	10
Severe weather									Moderate weather
1	2	3	4	5	6	7	8	9	10
Few levels of skiing									Many levels of skiing
1	2	3	4	5	6	7	8	9	10
Relatively easy trails									Very difficult trails
1	2	3	4	5	6	7	8	9	10
Poor trail grooming									Excellent trail grooming
1	2	3	4	5	6	7	8	9	10
Long liftlines									Short liftlines
1	2	3	4	5	6	7	8	9	10
Few apres-ski activities									Many apres-ski activities
1	2	3	4	5	6	7	8	9	10
Poor lodging facilities									Excellent lodging facilities
1	2	3	4	5	6	7	8	9	10
Poor overall resort value									Excellent overall resort value

Figure 4–3 In questionnaires, one common device to measure intensity of feelings is the semantic differential technique, which gives respondents a scale of choices from the worst to the best. These semantic differential scales for portable dictating equipment and for ski lodges are typical. *(Courtesy of Trout & Ries)*

6. Don't ask double-barreled questions. "Would you like management meetings once a month, or are bimonthly meetings enough?" is another terrible question.
7. Pretest. Send your questionnaire to a few colleagues and listen to their suggestions.
8. Attach a letter explaining how important the respondents' answers are, and let recipients know they will remain anonymous. Respondents will feel better if they think the study is significant and their identities are protected. Also, specify how and where the data will be used.
9. Hand-stamp the envelopes, preferably with unique commemorative stamps. Metering an envelope indicates assembly-line research, and researchers have found that the more expensive the postage, the higher the response rate. People like to feel special.
10. Follow up your first mailing. Send a reminder postcard 3 days after the original questionnaire. Then wait a few weeks and send a second questionnaire, just in case recipients have lost the first.
11. Send out more questionnaires than you think necessary. The major weakness of most mail surveys is the unmeasurable error introduced by nonresponders. You're shooting for a 50 percent response rate; anything less tends to be suspect.
12. Enclose a reward. There's nothing like a token gift of merchandise or money—a $2 bill works beautifully—to make a recipient feel guilty for not returning a questionnaire.[4]

Appendix B gives an example of a survey questionnaire.

THE INTERVIEW

Interviews can provide a more personal, firsthand feel for public opinion. Interview panels can range from focus groups of randomly selected average people to Delphi panels of so-called opinion leaders. Interviews can be conducted in a number of ways, including face to face, telephone, mail, and drop-off techniques.

FOCUS GROUPS This approach is probably the most common form of research in public relations today. Such interviews can be conducted one-to-one or through survey panels. These panels can be used, for example, to measure buying habits or the impact of public relations programs on a community or organizational group. They can also be used to assess general attitudes toward certain subjects, such as new products or advertising.

With the focus group technique, a well-drilled moderator leads a group through a discussion of opinions on a particular product, organization, or idea. Participants represent the socioeconomic level desired by the research sponsor—from college students to office workers to millionaires. Almost always, focus group participants are paid for their efforts. Sessions are frequently videotaped and then analyzed, often in preparation for more formal and specific research questionnaires.

Focus groups should be organized with the following guidelines in mind:

1. **Define your objectives and audience.** The more tightly you define your goals and your target audience, the more likely you are to gather relevant information. In other words, don't conduct a focus group with friends and family members, hoping to get a quick and inexpensive read. Nothing of value will result.
2. **Recruit your groups.** Recruiting participants takes several weeks, depending on the difficulty of contacting the target audience. Contact is usually made by phone, with a series of questions to weed out those who don't fit specifications, competitors' employees, and members of the news media (to keep the focus group from becoming a news story). Persons who have participated in a group in the past year should also be screened out; they may be more interested in the money than in helping you find what you're looking for.
3. **Choose the right moderator.** Staff people who may be excellent conversationalists are not necessarily the best focus group moderators. The gift of gab is not enough. Professional moderators know how to establish rapport quickly, how and when to probe beyond the obvious, how to draw comments from reluctant participants, how to keep a group on task, and how to interpret results validly.
4. **Conduct enough focus groups.** One or two focus groups are usually not enough. Four to six are better to uncover the full range of relevant ideas and opinions. Regardless of the number of groups, however, you must resist the temptation to add up responses; that practice gives the focus group more analytical worth than it deserves.
5. **Use a discussion guide.** This is a basic outline of what you want to investigate. It will lead the moderator through the discussion and keep the group on track.
6. **Choose proper facilities.** The discussion room should be comfortable, with participants sitting around a table that affords observers a good view of all members. Observers can use closed-circuit TV and one-way mirrors, but participants should always be told when they are being observed.

7. **Keep a tight rein on observers.** Observers should rarely be in the same room with participants; the two groups should ordinarily be separated. Observers should view the proceedings seriously; this is not "dinner and a show."
8. **Consider using outside help.** Setting up focus groups can be time-consuming and complicated. Often the best advice is to hire a firm recommended by the American Marketing Association or the Marketing Research Association so that the process, the moderator, and the evaluation are as professional as possible.[5]

TELEPHONE INTERVIEWS In contrast to personal interviews, telephone interviews suffer from a high refusal rate. Many people just don't want to be bothered. Such interviews may also introduce an upper-income bias because lower-income earners may lack telephones. However, the increasing use of unlisted numbers by upper-income people may serve to mitigate this bias. Telephone interviews must be carefully scripted so that interviewers know precisely what to ask, regardless of a respondent's answer. Calls should be made at less busy times of the day, such as early morning or late afternoon (Figure 4–4).

With both telephone and face-to-face interviews, it is important to establish rapport with the interview subject. It may make sense to begin the interview with nonthreatening questions, saving the tougher, more controversial ones—on income level or race, for example—until last. Another approach is to depersonalize the research by explaining that others have devised the survey and that the interviewer's job is simply to ask the questions.

MAIL INTERVIEWS This is the least expensive approach, but it often suffers from a low response rate. You are aiming for a 50 percent response rate. Frequently, people who return mail questionnaires are those with strong biases either in favor of or (usually) in opposition to the subject at hand. As noted, one way to generate a higher response from mail interviews is through the use of self-addressed, stamped envelopes or enclosed incentives such as dollar bills or free gifts.

DROP-OFF INTERVIEWS This approach combines face-to-face and mail interview techniques. An interviewer personally drops off a questionnaire at a household, usually after conducting a face-to-face interview. Because the interviewer has already established some rapport with the interviewee, the rate of return with this technique is considerably higher than it is for straight mail interviews.

DELPHI PANELS The Delphi technique is a more qualitative research tool that uses opinion leaders—local influential persons, national experts, and so on—often to help tailor the design of a general public research survey. Designed by the Rand Corporation in the 1950s, the Delphi method is a consensus-building approach that relies on repeated waves of questionnaires sent to the same select panel of experts. Delphi findings generate a wide range of responses and help set the agenda for more meaningful future research. Stated another way, Delphi panels offer a "research reality check."[6]

ANALYSIS

After selecting the sample, drawing up the questionnaire, and interviewing the respondents, the researcher must analyze the findings. Often a great deal of analysis is required to produce meaningful recommendations.

The objective of every sample is to come up with results that are valid and reliable. A margin of error explains how far off the prediction may be. A sample may be large

GUIDELINE RESEARCH CORPORATION
3 West 35th Street
New York, NY 10001

Job #C30-046

August, 1986

5-1

INTERNAL PUBLICATION SURVEY
- Screener -

SEX: (6)	LOCATION:
Male .... 1 Female 2	______________(7,8)

DIVISION: (9)
DOMESTIC
Corporate Industries 1
Domestic Inst. Banking 2
International (NY) 3
Investment (Capital Mkts.) ... 4
Tradings & Security 5
INTERNATIONAL
Asia 6
Europe 7
Latin America/Canada 8

RESPONDENT'S NAME: ______________

TELEPHONE #: ( ) ______________

INTERVIEWER: ______________ DATE: ______

ASK TO SPEAK WITH PERSON ON LIST.

A. Hello, my name is ______________ from Guideline Research Corporation, an independent market research firm in New York City. I would like to speak with (NAME OF PERSON ON LIST). (IF PERSON NO LONGER AT THAT NUMBER, TRY TO GET CONNECTED TO NEW NUMBER.)

TERMINATE Q. A: RESPONDENT NO LONGER AT THIS NUMBER ------------------ 1 2 3 4 5 6 7 8 9 (10)

B. (IF QUESTIONED BY SECRETARY ABOUT THE NATURE OF THE CALL, SAY:)
My company has been asked by Chase to conduct a survey among various bank officers throughout the world and (NAME OF OFFICER) has been selected as part of the study. (ONLY IF ASKED, SAY:) If you wish you can verify this by calling Mr. Fraser Seitel (Sy-Tell), head of Public Affairs and Internal Communications at 212-552-4503.

TERMINATE Q. B: RESPONDENT NOT AVAILABLE ----- 1 2 3 4 5 6 7 8 9 (11)

C. (IF LISTED RESPONDENT IS REACHED, SAY:)
Hello, my name is ______________ from Guideline Research Corporation, an independent market research firm in New York City. We have been asked by Chase to conduct a survey to get reactions to various employee publications. Your name has been randomly selected from a list of bank officers throughout the world. It will only take 15 minutes of your time and your cooperation will help Chase improve the quality of the information you receive in these publications.

(IF RESPONDENT REFUSES TO BE INTERVIEWED, TERMINATE AND TALLY BELOW.)

TERMINATE Q. C: REFUSED --------------------- 1 2 3 4 5 6 7 8 9 (12)

-2-

D. First, when thinking about publications that Chase publishes for its employees, which ones come to mind? (DO NOT READ LIST. RECORD "FIRST," AND THEN "ALL OTHER" MENTIONS APPROPRIATELY UNDER Q. D BELOW.) Any others?

(ASK Q. E FOR EACH PUBLICATION NOT MENTIONED IN Q. D. START AT X'D PUBLICATION OR FIRST PUBLICATION FOLLOWING THE "X".)

E. Have you ever heard of (FIRST PUBLICATION)? (RECORD UNDER Q. E BELOW.)

(IF "GLOBAL BANKER" NOT MENTIONED IN Q. D OR Q. E, TERMINATE, ERASE AND RECORD BELOW.)

TERMINATE Q. D/E: NOT AWARE ---------- 1 2 3 4 5 6 7 8 9 (13)

F. (ASK Q. F ONLY OF PRE-LISTED PUBLICATIONS THAT WERE MENTIONED IN Q. D OR Q. E.)
And, do you receive (FIRST PUBLICATION IN Q. D/Q.E)? (RECORD UNDER Q. F BELOW)

G. (ASK Q. G FOR EACH PRE-LISTED PUBLICATION MENTIONED IN Q. D OR Q. E.)
Have you ever read an issue of (FIRST PUBLICATION)? (REPEAT FOR EACH PRE-LISTED PUBLICATION IN Q. D OR Q. E. RECORD UNDER Q. G BELOW.)

H. (ASK Q. H FOR EACH PRE-LISTED PUBLICATION MENTIONED IN Q. G.)
Thinking about (FIRST PUBLICATION), how would you rate it overall on a scale of "1" to "5", with "5" meaning you like it very much and "1" meaning you don't like it at all. (REPEAT FOR EACH RESPONSE IN Q. G. RECORD RESPONSE UNDER Q. H BELOW.)

START HERE:		Q. D UNAIDED AWARENESS First Mention (14)	Q. D UNAIDED AWARENESS All Others (15)	Q.E Aided Awareness (16)	Q. F RECEIVE Yes	Q. F RECEIVE No	Q. F RECEIVE Don't Know	Q.G Ever Read (22)	Q. H Overall Rating
[X]	Chase Asia News	1	1	1	1	2	3 (17)	1	____(23)
[ ]	Chase Business	2	2	2	1	2	3 (18)	2	____(24)
[ ]	Chase Directions	3	3	3	1	2	3 (19)	3	____(25)
[ ]	Financial Outlook	4	4	4	1	2	3 (20)	4	____(26)
[ ]	Global Banker	5	5	5	1	2	3 (21)	5	____(27)
	Other (SPECIFY)								
	______________	0	0						
	______________	0	0						

I. (IF "GLOBAL BANKER" NOT MENTIONED IN Q. G, ASK Q. I. OTHERWISE, SKIP TO INSTRUCTIONS AFTER Q. I.)
What would you say are some of the reasons why you have not read Global Banker? (PROBE FULLY)

______________ 28-
______________ 29-
______________ 30-
______________ 31-
______________ 32-

- IF "GLOBAL BANKER" NOT READ IN Q. G, SKIP TO Q. 8 ON MAIN QUESTIONNAIRE. SAVE QUESTIONNAIRE. THIS DOES NOT COUNT TOWARDS COMPLETION QUOTA.
- IF "GLOBAL BANKER" READ IN Q. G, GO TO MAIN QUESTIONNAIRE -- Q. 1.

TERMINATE: QUALIFIED/REFUSED --------------- 1 2 3 4 5 6 7 8 9 (33)

Figure 4–4 Telephone interviewers must be guided by this kind of prepared script to ensure that appropriate responses are achieved for the whole questionnaire. *(Courtesy of Guideline Research Corporation)* enough to represent fairly the larger universe; yet, depending on the margin of sampling error, the results of the research may not be statistically significant. That is, the differences or distinctions detected by the survey may not be sizable enough to offset the margin of error. Thus, the margin of error must always be determined.

This concept is particularly critical in political polling, where pollsters are quick to acknowledge that their results may accurately represent the larger universe, but normally with a 2 or 3 percent margin of error. Thus, the results could be as much as 3 percent more or less for a certain candidate. Consequently, a pollster who says a candidate will win with 51 percent of the vote really means that the candidate could win with as much as 54 percent or lose with as little as 48 percent of the vote.

Political polls are fraught with problems. They cannot predict outcomes scientifically. Rather, they freeze attitudes at a certain point in time, and people's attitudes obviously change with the tide of events. Perhaps the most notorious political poll was that of the *Literary Digest* in 1936, which used a telephone polling technique to predict that Alf Landon would be the nation's next president. Landon thereupon suffered one of the worst drubbings in American electoral history at the hands of Franklin Roosevelt. It was probably of little solace to the *Literary Digest* that most of its telephone respondents, many of whom were Republicans wealthy enough to afford phones, did vote for Landon.

The point here is that in analyzing results, problems of validity, reliability, and levels of statistical significance associated with margins of error must be considered before recommendations based on survey data are offered.

COMMUNICATION AUDITS

An increasingly important method of research in public relations work is the communications audit. Such audits are used frequently by corporations, schools, hospitals, and other organizations to determine how the institution is perceived by its core constituents. Communications audits help public relations professionals understand more clearly the relationships between management actions and objectives, on the one hand, and communications methods to promote those objectives, on the other.

Communication audits are typically used to analyze the standing of a company with its employees or community neighbors; assess the readership of routine communication vehicles, such as annual reports and news releases; or examine an organization's performance as a corporate citizen. Communication audits often provide benchmarks against which future public relations programs can be applied and measured.

Communication audits typically are used to provide information on how to solve the following problems:

- Bottlenecked information flows.
- Uneven communication workloads.
- Employees working at cross-purposes.
- Hidden information within an organization that is not being used, to the detriment of the institution.
- Conflicting or nonexisting notions about what the organization is and does.[7]

The most effective communication audits start with a researcher who (1) is familiar with the public to be studied, (2) generally understands the attitudes of the target public toward the organization, (3) recognizes the issues of concern to the target public, and (4) understands the relative power of the target public vis-à-vis other publics (Figure 4–5).

The Credibility-Saving Audit

In 1993, a taxpayer-funded bank set up to aid Eastern Europe was rocked by scandal when it was revealed that the bank's president had spent millions of dollars of taxpayers' money on such "necessities" as shaded carpets, a marbled lobby, mirrored ceilings, and trips by private jet to exotic places.

Embarrassing publicity plagued the new bank for about six months, until the board could take no more. It summarily fired President Jacques Attali and commissioned an audit to restore the bank's credibility. Auditors Coopers & Lybrand revealed a president who spared no expense either in furnishing his bank or in feathering his nest. The audit revealed hundreds of millions of dollars on extravagances, such as special gray glass for conference rooms, a specially designed ceiling, and 57 presidential flights over a 2-year period that had cost the bank—and the taxpayers—nearly $2 million. Often, the auditors found, a private jet based in Paris flew empty to London for the sole purpose of picking up President Attali.

The audit report, in a word, was devastating, but bank directors seemed ambivalent. Said one, "The audit report has to bring credibility back to the board."

Is this a reasonable expectation for a single piece of research?

For further information, see Janet Guyon, "European Aid Bank Hopes Audit Chief's Departure Will End Chaos," *The Wall Street Journal*, July 19, 1993.

UNOBTRUSIVE METHODS

Of the various unobtrusive methods of data collection available to public relations researchers, probably the most widely used is simple fact finding. Facts are the bricks and mortar of public relations work; no action can be taken unless the facts are known, and the fact-finding process is continuous.

Each organization must keep a fact file of the most essential data with which it is involved. For example, such items as key organization statistics, publications, management biographies and photos, press clippings, media lists, competitive literature, pending legislation, organizational charters and bylaws should be kept on file and updated. Even better, computerized listings of such facts offer easier access when research is called for in these areas.

Another unobtrusive method is content analysis, the primary purpose of which is to describe a message or set of messages. For example, an organization with news releases that are used frequently by local newspapers can't be certain, without research, whether the image conveyed by its releases is what the organization seeks. By analyzing the news coverage, the firm can get a much clearer idea of

BANZAI HOSPITAL AUDIT
January 5, 1990

GUIDELINES

1. All interviews are confidential. Assure those you interview that their statements will be held in confidence so that the source of their remarks will not be identifiable.
2. Copy all of your interview notes within 24 hours after each interview is completed, to protect against possible loss of your notes.
3. Use an informal interview style, referring to the question sheets as little as possible. Have the questions in mind before the interview so that they can come up during conversation.
4. Type up your notes, using direct quotes as much as possible.

INTERVIEW CATEGORIES

Board members
Executive staff
Medical staff
Volunteers
Community leaders
Residents and tenants
Families of residents and tenants
Financial supporters
Business leaders
News media
General public

BANZAI COMMUNICATION AUDIT

Board members

1. How did you become involved with Banzai?
2. How do you perceive your role with Banzai? Are your assignments and responsibilities clear?
3. What are the strengths of Banzai today? weaknesses?
4. If it was in your power to do so, what would you change about Banzai?

Medical staff

1. How would you describe your relationship with the institution?
2. Is communications a factor in your relationship? How? Is there a need for improvement? What suggestions do you have?
3. How do you think the institution is perceived in the community? Why? Any suggestions for community programs that should be undertaken?
4. Do you believe this institution provides adequate patient information?

Volunteers

1. How do you get information about what is happening in the institution? What are your best sources? Do you think you get enough information? If not, what else would you like to know?
2. Is there an effective way for you to communicate upward? Do you take advantage of it? What type of information do you pass along?
3. How do you think the institution is perceived in the community? Why?

Community leaders

1. What do you know about the institution?
2. What are your sources of information? Which do you consider the most reliable?
3. How do you value the institution? Does the community perceive the institution in the same light?
4. What recommendations do you have that would help the institution respond to community needs?

BUDGET

The audit will take approximately 120 days. Budget will be kept to the lowest possible figure but will be in the $12,000 to $15,000 range for professional services and about $5,000 for out-of-pocket expenses.

PROCEDURE

A preliminary audit report will be prepared following completion of the interviews. This draft will be reviewed with appropriate members of Banzai staff to uncover possible misconceptions, misinterpretations, or errors. A final audit report will follow in 15 days.

Figure 4–5 A typical communication audit will gather subjective information on how an organization is perceived by its major constituencies. It determines which communications systems are being used, which are the most effective, and whether the information being transmitted is regarded as sufficient by recipients.

the effectiveness of its communications. Such content analysis might be organized according to the following specific criteria:

- **Frequency of coverage** How many releases were used?
- **Placement within the paper** Did releases appear more frequently on page 1 or 71?
- **People reached** What was the circulation of the publications in which the releases appeared?
- **Messages conveyed** Did the releases used express the goals of the organization, or were they simply informational in content?
- **Editing of releases** How much did the newspaper edit the copy submitted? Were desired meanings materially changed?
- **Attitude conveyed** Was the reference to the organization positive, negative, or neutral?

Another unobtrusive method, the readability study, helps a communicator determine whether messages are written at the right educational level for the audience. Typical measures include the Flesch Formula, the FOG Index, and the SMOG Index—all based on the concept that the greater the number of syllables in a passage, the more difficult and less readable the text.[8]

Clearly, there is nothing particularly mysterious or difficult about unobtrusive methods of research. Such methods are relatively simple to apply, yet they are essential for arriving at appropriate modifications for an ongoing public relations program.

EVALUATION

No matter what type of public relations research is used, results of the research and the research project itself should always be evaluated. In evaluating after the fact, researchers can learn how to improve future efforts. Were the target audiences surveyed the right ones? Were the research assumptions applied to those audiences correct? Were questions from research tools left unanswered?

Research results can be evaluated in a number of ways. Perhaps the most common in public relations is a seat-of-the-pants evaluation, in which anecdotal observation and practitioner judgment are used to estimate the effectiveness of the public relations program. Such evaluation might be based on feedback from members of a key public, personal media contacts, or colleagues, but the practitioner alone evaluates the success of the program with subjective observation.

More scientific evaluation results from public relations opinion polls and surveys and fact-finding research, such as content analysis, in which the numerical tabulation of results is evaluated and often combined with seat-of-the-pants observation. One of the most effective evaluative techniques to determine the success of a program is to pretest target audiences prior to the implementation of the public relations program and then posttest after the program's completion. A comparison of the results of the two tests enables a more scientific assessment of the program's success.

An ongoing system for monitoring public relations activities is yet another way to evaluate programs. Monitoring a public relations campaign, for example, may indicate necessary changes in direction, reallocation of resources, or redefinition of priorities. Another way to evaluate is to dissect public programs after the fact. Such postmortem

BETWEEN THE LINES

FIGURES AND FACES—LIE

If you don't believe the old maxim that "figures lie and liars figure," consider the following: In often repeated research, randomly selected participants are shown the following two faces and asked, "Which woman is lovelier?"

Faces *(Courtesy of Rivkin & Associates)*

Invariably, the answer is split 50-50.

However, when each woman is named—one "Jennifer" and the other "Gertrude"—respondents overwhelming vote for Jennifer as the more beautiful woman. The antibeauty bias against the name Gertrude is that pervasive. (Sorry, all you Gertrudes out there!)

The point is that audiences and researchers can't help but introduce their own biases. This factor always should be taken into account in evaluating public relations research.

evaluation can provide objective analysis when a program is still fresh in one's mind. This can be extremely helpful in modifying the program for future use.

USING OUTSIDE RESEARCH HELP

Despite its occasional rough spots, public relations research has made substantial gains in recent years in quantifying the results of public relations activities. Counseling firms have even organized separate departments to conduct attitude and opinion surveys, as well as other types of research projects.

Ketchum Public Relations, for example, has devised a computer-based measurement system that evaluates public relations results on both a quantitative and qualitative basis. The Ketchum system focuses on the differences in placement of publicity—that is, where in a periodical publicity has a better chance of being noticed. Although the Ketchum system cannot predict attitudinal or behavioral change, it is a step forward in providing practitioners with a mechanism to assess the extent to which their publicity has been seen.

It often makes sense to use outside counsel for research assistance. Once a firm is hired, public relations professionals should avoid the temptation of writing the questions or influencing the methodology. The best contribution a public relations practitioner can make to an outside-directed research endeavor is to state the objectives of the project clearly and then stand back and let the pros do the job.[9]

Often, before turning to outside consultants, the best first step is to determine whether research has already been done on your topic. Because research assistance is expensive, it makes little sense to reinvent the wheel. It is much wiser to piggyback on existing research.

SUMMARY

Research is a means of both defining problems and evaluating solutions. The day of the seat-of-the-pants practitioner is over. Even though intuitive judgment remains a coveted and important skill, management must see measurable results.

Nonetheless, informed managements recognize that public relations may never reach a point where its results can be fully quantified. Management confidence is still a prerequisite for active and unencumbered programs. However, such confidence can only be enhanced as practitioners become more adept in using research.

DISCUSSION STARTERS

1. Why is research important in public relations work?
2. What are several methods of public relations research?
3. What are the four elements of a survey?
4. What is the difference between random and stratified sampling?
5. What are the keys to designing an effective questionnaire?
6. What are the several rules of thumb in organizing focus groups?
7. What is a communication audit?

8. What is the most widely used unobtrusive method of public relations research?
9. Why is evaluation important in public relations research?
10. How essential do you think research will be in the future for public relations practice?

NOTES

1. Lisa Richter and Steve Drake, "Apply Measurement Mindset to Programs," *Public Relations Journal* (January 1993): 32.
2. John V. Pavlik, *Public Relations: What Research Tells Us* (Newbury Park, CA: Sage, 1987), 16.
3. Walter K. Lindenmann, "Opinion Research: How It Works; How to Use It," *Public Relations Journal* (January 1977): 13.
4. Walter K. Lindenmann, *Attitude and Opinion Research: Why You Need It/How to Do It*, 3d ed. (Washington, DC: Council for Advancement and Support of Education, 1983), 35–38.
5. David L. Nasser, "How to Run a Focus Group," *Public Relations Journal* (March 1988): 33–34.
6. "The Delphi: A Forecasting Methodology You Can Use to Generate Expert Opinion on Any Subject," *PR Reporter* (June 29, 1992): 3.
7. Seymour Hamilton, "Selling the CEO on a Communication Audit," *IABC Communication World* (May 1988): 33.
8. Pavlik, op. cit., 39.
9. Andrea L. Simpson, "Ten Rules of Research," *Public Relations Quarterly* (Summer 1992): 27–28.

TOP OF THE SHELF

Glen M. Broom and David M. Dozier, *Using Research in Public Relations: Applications to Program Management*. Englewood Cliffs, NJ: Prentice-Hall, 1990. John V. Pavlik, *Public Relations: What Research Tells Us*. Newbury Park, CA: Sage, 1987.

Research is an essential component of any communications program. Two texts that contribute to the understanding of this important public relations function are *Using Research in Public Relations: Applications to Program Management* and *Public Relations: What Research Tells Us*.

In *Using Research in Public Relations*, Glen Broom and David Dozier, leading public relations researchers, explain the value of conducting basic quantitative and qualitative analyses to help achieve communications goals. Such research, they contend, can substantiate a practitioner's hunches and enhance the credibility of the profession. The authors also present the research methods counselors employ:

statistical inference, focus groups, sampling, and content analysis, among others. To show how these tools influence and enhance public relations work, Broom and Dozier use several case studies.

In similar fashion, John Pavlik, a communications professor at Penn State University, explores the uses of research in the profession, as well as common research techniques. He also examines what methodical research can reveal about the profession itself—that is, what scientific evidence discloses about the field and its effects on the journalism people consume. Pavlik discusses these and similar issues by citing numerous media studies.

Sound research can yield benefits to public relations strategies at all phases, from development to execution to evaluation. For expert instruction on the public relations–research relationship, read *Using Research in Public Relations* and *Public Relations: What Research Tells Us.*

SUGGESTED READINGS

Attitude and Opinion Research: Why You Need It/How to Do It, 3d ed. Washington, DC: Case (11 Dupont Circle, 20036), 1983.

Awards, Honors, Prizes. Detroit: Gale Research Co., 1990.

Barabba, V. P., and G. Zaltman. *Hearing the Voice of the Market: Competitive Advantage Through Creative Use of Market Information.* New York: McGraw-Hill, 1991.

Barzun, Jacques, and Henry F. Graff. *The Modern Researcher,* 5th ed. Ft. Worth, TX: HBJ College Publications, 1992.

Blakenship, A. B., and George Breen. *State of the Art Marketing Research.* Lincolnwood, IL: NTC Business, 1992.

Bradburn, Norman, and Seymour Sudman. *Polls and Surveys.* San Francisco: Jossey-Bass, 1988.

Breen, George, and A. B. Blakenship. *Do-It-Yourself Marketing Research,* 3d ed. New York: McGraw-Hill, 1991.

Brody, E. W., and Gerald C. Stone. *Public Relations Research.* New York: Praeger, 1989.

Broom, Glen M., and David M. Dozier. *Using Research in Public Relations: Applications to Program Management.* Englewood Cliffs, NJ: Prentice-Hall, 1990.

Crispell, Diane. *The Insider's Guide to Demographic Know-how.* Chicago: Probus, 1992.

Druck, Kalman B., Merton Fiur, and Don Bates. *New Technology in Public Relations.* New York: Foundation for Public Relations Research and Education, 1987.

Duro, Robert, and Bjorn Sandstro. *The Basic Principles of Marketing Warfare.* New York: Wiley, 1987.

Emmert, Philip, and Larry Baker. *Measurements of Communication Behavior.* White Plains, NY: Longman, 1989.

FORTUNE 500 Directory. New York: Time Life, yearly.

The Foundation Director. New York: The Foundation Center, 1988.

Francese, Peter. *Capturing Consumers.* Ithaca, NY: American Demographics, 1989 (P.O. Box 68 14851).

Fuld, Leonard. *Monitoring the Competition: Finding Out What's Really Going on Over There.* New York: Wiley, 1988.

Grunig, James, and Larissa Grunig. *Public Relations Research Annual.* Hillsdale, NJ: Earlbaum, 1989.

Hamilton, Seymour. "Selling the CEO on a Communication Audit." *Communication World* (May 1988): 33, 34.

Hardy, Hugh S., ed. *The Politz Papers: Science and Truth in Marketing Research.* Chicago: American Marketing Association, 1990.

How to Find Business Intelligence in Washington. Washington, DC: Researchers Publishing Co., 1988.

Lowery, Shearon, and Melvin DeFleur. *Milestones in Mass Communications Research,* 2nd ed. White Plains, NY: Longman, 1987.

Makower, J., and A. Green, eds. *Instant Information.* Englewood Cliffs, NJ: Prentice-Hall, 1987.

The Markets Directory. Dobbs Ferry, NY: Dobbs Directories, 1991.

Martel, Myles. *Mastering the Art of Q & A.* Homewood, IL: Dow Jones-Irwin, 1988.

Nasser, David L. "How to Run a Focus Group." *Public Relations Journal* (March 1988): 33, 34.

New Technology and Public Relations. New York: Institute for PR Research and Education, 1988.

Newsletter on Newsletters (P.O. Box 311, Rhinebeck, NY 12572). Weekly.

Palshaw, John L. "Full Service Research." *Palshaw Measurement* (September–October 1987).

Palshaw, John L. "The Planning of Research." Pebble Beach, CA: *Palshaw Measurement* (November–December 1987). The author points out those items that must be considered to make a research plan work.

Public Interest Profiles (250 activist groups). Washington, DC: Foundation for Public Affairs.

Shaw, Robert, and Merlin Stone. *Database Marketing.* New York: Wiley, 1989.

Soares, Eric. *Cost-Effective Marketing Research.* Westport, CT: Quorum, 1988.

Stempel, Guido, and Bruce Westley. *Research Methods in Mass Communication,* 2nd ed. New York: Prentice-Hall, 1989.

Television and Cable Factbook. 2 vols. Washington, DC: TV Digest,

Van Minden, J. J. *The Dictionary of Marketing Research.* Detroit: St. James Press, 1987.

CASE STUDY

RESEARCHING A POSITION FOR ALAN LOUIS GENERAL

The administrator at Alan Louis General Hospital confronted a problem that he hoped research could help solve. Alan Louis General, although a good hospital, was smaller than most of Bangor, Maine's, other hospitals and less well known. In its area alone, it competed with 20 other medical facilities. Alan Louis needed a "position" that it could call unique to attract patients to fill its beds.

For a long time, the Alan Louis administrator, Sven Rapcorn, had believed in the principle that truth will out. Build a better mousetrap, and the world will beat a path to your door. Erect a better hospital, and your beds will always be 98 percent filled. Unfortunately, Rapcorn learned, the real world seldom recognizes truth at first blush.

In the real world, more often than not, perception will triumph. And because people act on perceptions, those perceptions become reality. Successful positioning, Rapcorn learned, is based on recognizing and dealing with people's perceptions. And so, Rapcorn set out with research to build on existing perceptions about Alan Louis General.

As a first step, Rapcorn talked to his own doctors and trustees to gather data about their perceptions, not only of Alan Louis General but also of other hospitals in the community. From this effort, pictures of each major competitor began to emerge. For example, the University Health Center had something for everybody—exotic care, specialized care, and basic, bread-and-butter care. Bangor General was a huge, well-respected hospital whose reputation was so good that only a major tragedy could shake its standing in the community. Mercy Hospital was known for its trauma center. And so on. As for Alan Louis itself, doctors and trustees said that it was a great place to work, that excellent care was provided, and that the nursing staff was particularly friendly and good. The one problem, everyone agreed, was that "nobody knows about us."

The second step in Rapcorn's research project was to test attributes important in health care. Respondents were asked to rank eight factors in order of importance and tell Rapcorn and his staff how each of the surveyed hospitals rated on those factors. The research instrument used a semantic differential scale of 1 to 10, with 1 the worst and 10 the best possible score. Questionnaires were sent to two groups: 1,000 area residents and 500 former Alan Louis patients.

The third step in the research was to tabulate the results. Among area residents who responded, the eight attributes were ranked accordingly:

1. Surgical care—9.23
2. Medical equipment—9.20
3. Cardiac care—9.16
4. Emergency services—8.96
5. Range of medical services—8.63
6. Friendly nurses—8.62
7. Moderate costs—8.59
8. Location—7.94

After the attributes were ranked, the hospitals in the survey were ranked for each attribute. On advanced surgical care, the most important feature to area residents, Bangor General ranked first, with University Health Center a close second. Alan Louis was far down on the list. The same was true of virtually every other attribute. Indeed, on nursing care, an area in which its staff thought Alan Louis excelled, the hospital came in last in the minds of area residents. Rapcorn was not surprised. The largest hospitals in town scored well on most attributes; Alan Louis trailed the pack.

However, the ranking of hospital scores according to former Alan Louis patients revealed an entirely different story. On surgical care, for example, although Bangor General still ranked first, Alan Louis came in a close second. And its scores improved similarly on all other attributes. In fact, in nursing care, where Alan Louis came in last on the survey of area residents, among former patients its score was higher than that of any other hospital. It also ranked first in terms of convenient location and second in terms of costs, range of services, and emergency care.

The fourth step in Rapcorn's research project was to draw some conclusions. He reached three conclusions:

1. Bangor General was still number one in terms of area hospitals.
2. Alan Louis ranked at or near the top on most attributes, according to those who actually experienced care there.
3. Former Alan Louis patients rated the hospital significantly better than the general public did.

In other words, thought Rapcorn, most of those who try Alan Louis like it. The great need was to convince more people to try the hospital.

But how could this be accomplished with a hospital? Other marketers generate trial by sending free samples in the mail, offering cents-off coupons, holding free demonstrations, and the like. Hospitals are more limited in this area. Rapcorn's challenge was to launch a communications campaign to convince prospects to see other area hospitals in a different, less favorable light and/or to give people a specific reason to think about trying Alan Louis. In other words, he needed to come up with a communications strategy that clearly differentiated Alan Louis—admittedly, among the smallest hospitals in the area—from the bigger, less personal hospitals. Rapcorn was confident that the data he had gathered from the research project were all he needed to come up with a winning idea.

QUESTIONS

1. What kind of communications program would you launch to accomplish Rapcorn's objectives?
2. What would be the cornerstone—the theme—of your communications program?
3. What would be the specific elements of your program?
4. In launching the program, what specific steps would you follow—both inside and outside the hospital—to build support?

TIPS FROM THE TOP

WALTER K. LINDENMANN

Walter K. Lindenmann, senior vice-president and director of research at Ketchum Public Relations, is among the foremost authorities in public relations research. Mr. Lindenmann is a former manager of the New York office of Opinion Research Corporation and was president of Group Attitudes Corporation, the Hill & Knowlton survey research subsidiary. A sociologist by training, Dr. Lindenmann has supervised more than 750 marketing, public relations, and advertising research projects. He is a frequent lecturer on public opinion research and has been visiting adjunct professor at the Syracuse University Newhouse School for Public Communications.

How important is research in public relations practice?
Extremely important. Public relations cannot be carried out effectively without some type of research being conducted. Research is essential for public relations planning, for program development, and for evaluation. It also is quite crucial when an organization needs to obtain information quickly in order to deal with a crisis. If public relations activities are carried out without any research at all, then the public relations practitioner ends up operating in the dark, without any insights and without necessary background information.

What is the "state of play" in public relations research today?
Mixed. More practitioners are carrying out research today than ever before, yet there is still a sizable segment of the field that does either no research at all or does research at a very superficial level.

Can you really measure public relations success?
Most definitely, if you set clear and precise targeted goals and objectives in advance of a public relations project or activity. It is impossible to assess the success or

failure of anything unless you have something specific to measure that success or failure against. If a public relations practitioner were to set a vague goal of hoping to have people somehow become better informed about his or her organization, the success or failure of trying to achieve that is very hard to measure. However, if the practitioner knows—through research—that perhaps only 40 percent of a given audience segment is well informed about something related to his or her organization and wants to improve that "well-informed" portion to, say, 50 percent, then it *is* possible to measure the success or failure of reaching that specific objective.

It is not at all difficult to measure individual components of public relations, such as whether a publicity campaign has succeeded or failed; the effectiveness of a community relations program; or how well an investor relations activity or a speakers' program is working. If goals and objectives are well defined in advance and are spelled out as precisely as possible, then measurement of results is always possible.

How do you answer practitioners who challenge the necessity of research in public relations work?
I tell them that trying to carry out public relations activities without the benefit of research is a little like trying to walk down a crowded street blindfolded. How can you possibly do effective public relations if you cannot see precisely where you are heading, how you are proceeding, and where you have been? Relying on your instincts is, of course, of some value, but if that's all you rely on, if you don't obtain necessary facts and opinions about issues or topics important to you or your organization, eventually you are going to miss the mark, go astray, and end up with a disaster.

What is the future of research in public relations?
Extremely promising. As the field of public relations matures, as practitioners engage more and more in strategic planning activities, and as they seek to respond to pressures from senior management to be more accountable for what they do, research will grow in importance during the 1990s.

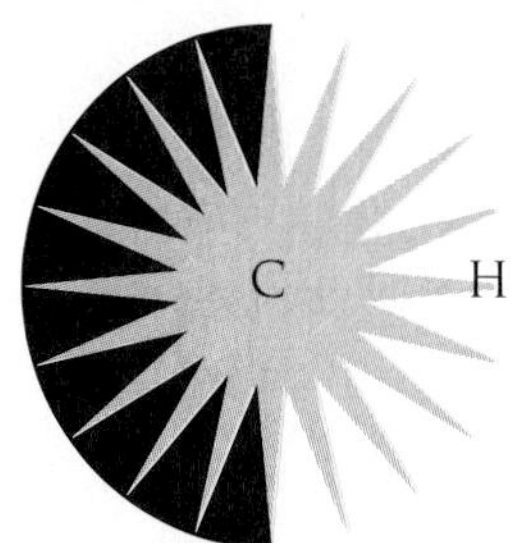

CHAPTER 5

COMMUNICATION

WALL STREET ACQUISITIONS EXPERT HENRY KRAVIS MAY BE one of the world's savviest financiers, but he had his head handed to him in the spring of 1990 when he tried to get cute with language. In a speech before a sold-out luncheon, sponsored by New York's Financial Women's Association, Kravis greeted his mostly female audience with an apology that his fashion-designer wife couldn't be there: "She could have gotten up and talked about what's probably of much more interest to you—fashion." The boos and hisses were unrelenting.[1] Kravis learned the hard way that, in the 1990s, communications must be handled with great care.

The public relations practitioner is a professional communicator. More than anyone else in an organization, the practitioner must know how to communicate. This knowledge sets the public relations professional apart from other employees.

Fundamentally, communication is a process of exchanging information, imparting ideas, and making oneself understood by others. Importantly, it also includes understanding others in return. Indeed, understanding is critical to the communications process. If one person sends a message to another, who disregards or misunderstands it, then communication hasn't taken place. But if the idea received is the one intended, then communication has occurred. Thus, a boss who sends subordinates dozens of memos isn't necessarily communicating with them. If the idea received is not the one intended, then the sender has done little more than convert personal thoughts to words—and there they lie.

Although all of us are endowed with some capacity for communicating, the public relations practitioner must be better at it than most. Indeed, the effectiveness of public relations professionals is determined by their own ability to communicate and to counsel others on how to communicate. Before public relations practitioners can earn the respect of management and become trusted advisers, they must demonstrate a mastery of many communications skills—writing, speaking, listening, promoting, and counseling. Just as the controller is expected to be an adept accountant and the legal counsel is expected to be an accomplished lawyer, the public relations professional is expected to be an expert communicator.

COMMUNICATIONS THEORY

Books have been written on the subject of communications theory. Consequently, we won't attempt to be all-encompassing here in discussing how people ensure that their messages get through to others. But, in its most basic sense, communication commences with a source, who sends a message through a medium to reach a receiver, who, we hope, responds.

One early theory of communication, the *two-step flow theory,* stated that an organization would beam a message first to the mass media, which would then deliver that message to the great mass of readers, listeners, and viewers for their response. This theory may have given the mass media too much credit. People today are influenced by a variety of factors, of which the media may be one but not necessarily the dominant one. Another theory, the *concentric-circle theory,* developed by pollster Elmo Roper, assumed that ideas evolve gradually to the public at large, moving in concentric circles from great thinkers to great disciples to great disseminators to lesser disseminators to the politically active to the politically inert. This theory suggests that people pick up and accept ideas from leaders, whose impact on public opinion may be greater than that of the mass media. The overall study of how communication is used for direction and control is called *cybernetics.*

Although there are numerous models of communication, one of the most fundamental is the S-M-R approach. This model suggests that the communication process begins with the source (S), who issues a message (M) to a receiver (R), who then decides what action to take, if any, relative to the communication. This element of receiver action, or feedback, underscores that good communication always involves dialogue between two or more parties.

The S-M-R model has been modified to include additional elements: (1) an encoding stage, in which the source's original message is translated and conveyed to the receiver, and (2) a decoding stage, in which the receiver interprets the encoded message and takes action. This evolution from the traditional model has resulted in the S-E-M-D-R method, which illustrates graphically the role of the public relations function in modern communications; both the encoding (E) and the decoding (D) stages are of critical importance in communicating any public relations message.

THE SOURCE

The source of a message is the central person or organization doing the communicating. The source could be a politician giving a campaign speech, a school announcing curriculum changes, or even, as one superior court judge in Seattle ruled, a topless go-go dancer in the midst of gyrating.

Although the source usually knows how it wants the message to be received, there is no guarantee that it will be understood that way by the receiver. In many cases—a public speech, for example—the speaker is relatively limited in ability to influence the interpretation of the message. Gestures, voice tone, and volume can be used to add special importance to certain remarks, but whether the audience understands what is intended may ultimately depend on other factors, particularly the encoder.

THE ENCODER

What the source wants to relate must be translated from an idea in the mind to a communication. In the case of a campaign speech, a politician's original message may be subject to translation or reinterpretation by at least three independent encoders.

1. The politician may consult a speech writer to help put ideas into words on paper. Speech writers become encoders in first attempting to understand the politician's message clearly and then translating that message effectively into language that an audience will understand and, hopefully, accept.
2. Once the speech is written, it may be further encoded into a news release. In this situation, the encoder—perhaps a different individual from the speech writer—selects what seem to be the most salient points of the speech and provides them to media editors in a fairly brief format.
3. A news editor may take the news release and retranslate it before reporting it to the voters, the ultimate audience for the politician's message.

Thus, the original message in the mind of the politician has been massaged three separate times before it ever reaches the intended receivers. Each time, in all likelihood, the particular encoder has added new subjective shadings to the politician's original message. The very act of encoding depends largely on the encoder's personal experience.

WORDS/SEMANTICS Words are among our most personal and potent weapons. Words can soothe us, bother us, or infuriate us. They can bring us together or drive us apart. They can even cause us to kill or be killed. Words mean different things to different people, depending on their backgrounds, occupations, education, or geographic locations. What one word means to you might be dramatically different from what that same word means to your neighbor. The study of what words really mean is called *semantics*, and the science of semantics is a peculiar one indeed.

Words are perpetually changing in our language. What's in today is out tomorrow. What a word denotes according to the dictionary may be thoroughly dissimilar to what it connotes in its more emotional or visceral sense. Even the simplest words—*liberal, conservative, profits, consumer activists*—can spark semantic skyrockets. Many times, without knowledge of the territory, the semantics of words may make no sense. Take the word *cool*. In American vernacular a person who is cool is good. A person who is "not so hot" is bad. So *cool* is the opposite of "not so hot." But wait a minute; "not so hot" must also be the opposite of *hot*. Therefore, in a strange and convoluted way, cool must equal hot.

In the 1990s, public relations professionals must constantly be alert to alterations in the language. In 1990, when the august New York Jockey Club restaurant offered a breakfast called the "Central Park Jogger"—a term widely used as the identification of a woman brutally attacked the year before in a well-publicized rape case—the menu was reprinted. On the other hand, when the term *couch potato* came into vogue to signify an inveterate television watcher, a Pennsylvania potato chip maker was quick to capitalize (Figure 5–1).

Words used in the encoding stage have a significant influence on the message conveyed to the ultimate receiver. Thus, the source must depend greatly on the ability of the encoder to accurately understand and effectively translate the true message—with all its semantic complications—to the receiver.

Figure 5–1 Pennsylvania snack food maker Snyder of Berlin was quick to take advantage of the pervasive use of the term *couch potato* by cooking up a "potato couch" for use in a promotion for Thunder Crunch, its newest line of potato chips. The spud sofa was a most "ap-peeling" promotion. (Sorry.) *(Courtesy of Marcus Public Relations)*

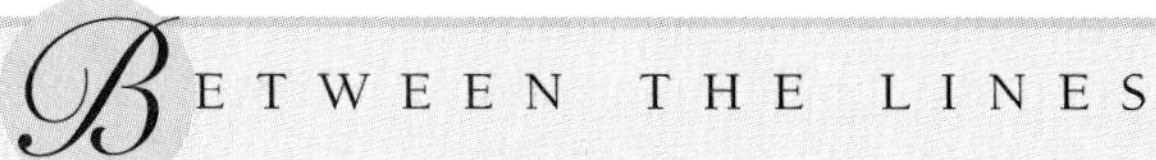

ARSENIOLOGY

While it's never been easy to understand the words and language of teenagers, in the 1990s it's downright impossible.

The "411" (latest news and information) is that the jargon of many younger Americans is far more complex than ever before. The offspring of rap music and hip-hop culture is a "slanguage" that is first picked up and promulgated by celebrity figures, such as Arsenio Hall, and then embraced by inner-city young people (homeys) and suburban teenagers (Bradys) alike.

Herewith a Guide to the Gab.

- *How ya livin?* How are you?
- *Livin large.* I'm doing well, thank you.
- *Sweat, that suit is dope.* Wow, what a nice outfit.
- *Looking for some "phat."* I'm hopeful that I might successfully ensnare a young lady.
- *She won't give up the digits.* The young lady isn't interested in providing her phone number.
- *Kicked to the curb.* It appears that I have been rejected in my attempts to win the young lady's favor.
- *I smell ya.* I know what you mean. (I, too, would abhor being "kicked to the curb.")
- *The posse's going back to the crib.* We're all planning to return home.
- *I've got to go to the J.O.* I've got to go to work.
- *I'm Audi 5000.* Goodbye, I'm leaving.

Where once such slang was confined to high school hallways, today companies from Pepsi to McDonald's regularly feature such slanguage in national commercials, demonstrating that even corporate "suits" can still be "fresh."

THE MESSAGE

Once an encoder has taken in the source's ideas and translated them into terms a receiver can understand, the ideas are then transmitted in the form of a message. The message may be carried in a variety of communications media: speeches, newspapers, news releases, press conferences, broadcast reports, and face-to-face meetings. Communications theorists differ on what exactly constitutes the message, but here are three of the more popular explanations.

1. **The content is the message.** According to this theory, which is far and away the most popular, the content of a communication—what it says—constitutes its

message. According to this view, the real importance of a communication—the message—lies in the meaning of an article or in the intent of a speech. Neither the medium through which the message is being communicated nor the individual doing the communicating is as important as the content.

2. **The medium is the message.** Other communications theorists—the late Canadian professor Marshall McLuhan being the best known—argue that the content of a communication is not the message at all. According to McLuhan, the content is less important than the vehicle of communication.

   McLuhan's argument stemmed largely from the fact that many people today watch television. He said that television is a "cool" medium—that is, someone can derive meaning from a TV message without working too hard. On the other hand, reading involves hard work to grasp an idea fully; thus, newspapers, magazines, and books are "hot" media. Furthermore, McLuhan argued, a television viewer can easily become part of that which is being viewed.

   One direct outgrowth of this medium-is-the-message theory was the development of the friendly-team style of local television news reporting. Often called the *eyewitness approach,* this format encouraged interaction among TV newscasters in order to involve viewers as part of the news team family.

   The medium of television has become particularly important to the president of the United States. Commencing with the cool, polished television demeanor of John F. Kennedy and proceeding through modern-day presidents, television has become the great differentiator in terms of presidential popularity. Ronald Reagan, a former movie actor and media spokesman for General Electric, was a magnificent master of the Teleprompter. Reagan's televised speeches were studies in proper use of the medium. George Bush, less good than his predecessor, nonetheless had his moments. And Bill Clinton, while not as polished as Reagan with prepared speeches, nonetheless is skilled in using the medium to suggest a committed, concerned, and undeniably human commander-in-chief.

3. **The person is the message.** Still other theorists argue that it is neither the content nor the medium that is the message, but rather the speaker. For example, Hitler was a master of persuasion. His minister of propaganda, Josef Goebbels, used to say, "Any man who thinks he can persuade, can persuade." Hitler practiced this self-fulfilling communications prophecy to the hilt. Feeding on the perceived desires of the German people, Hitler was concerned much less with the content of his remarks than with their delivery. His maniacal rantings and frantic gestures seized public sentiment and sent friendly crowds into a frenzy. In every way, Hitler himself was the primary message of his communications.

   Today, in a similar vein, we often refer to a leader's charisma. Frequently, the charismatic appeal of a political leader may be more important than what that individual says. President Clinton, for example, can move an audience by the very inflection of his words. Jesse Jackson can bring a group to its feet merely by shaking a fist or raising the pitch of his voice.

   Often people cannot distinguish between the words and the person who speaks them. The words, the face, the body, the eyes, the attitude, the timing, the wit, the presence—all form a composite that, as a whole, influences the listener. As communications consultant Roger Ailes has put it, it comes down to the "like" factor in communication. Ailes points out that some candidates get votes just because people like them. "They forget that you're short, or you're fat, or you're bald . . . they say 'I like that guy.'"[2] In such cases, the source of the communication becomes every bit as important as the message itself.

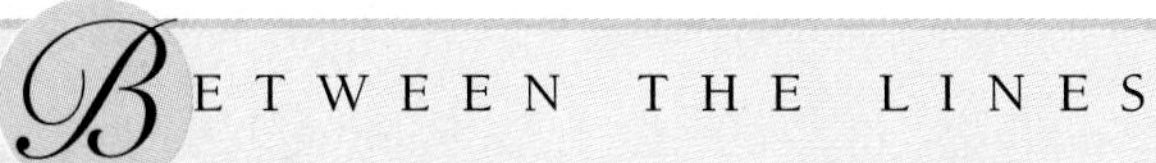

ARE YOU SURE YOU SAW WHAT YOU THOUGHT YOU SAW?

First read the sentence that follows:

FINISHED FILES ARE THE RESULT OF YEARS OF SCIENTIFIC STUDY COMBINED WITH THE EXPERIENCE OF MANY YEARS.

Now, count the *Fs* in the sentence. Count them only once, and do not go back and count them again.

QUESTION
How many *Fs* are there?

ANSWER
There are six *Fs*. However, because the capital *F* in *OF* sounds like a capital *V*, it seems to disappear. Most people perceive only three *Fs* in the sentence. Our conditioned, habitual patterns (mental blocks) restrict us from being as alert as we should be. Frequently, we fail to perceive things as they really are.

THE DECODER

After a message has been transmitted, it must be decoded by a receiver before action can be taken. This stage is like the encoding stage in that the receiver takes in the message and translates it into his or her own common terms. Obviously, language again plays a critical role. The decoder must fully understand the message before acting on it; if the message is unclear or the decoder is unsure of its intent, there's probably little chance that the action taken by the receiver will be the action desired by the source. Messages must be understood in common terms.

How a receiver decodes a message depends greatly on that person's own perception. How an individual looks at and comprehends a message is a key to effective communications (Figure 5–2). Remember that everyone is biased; no two people perceive a message identically. Personal biases are nurtured by many factors, including stereotypes, symbols, semantics, peer group pressures, and—especially in today's culture—the media.

BETWEEN THE LINES

DECODING LANGUAGE AT THE PENSION OFFICE

These 11 extracts supposedly emanate from genuine letters sent to the pensions office of some company, somewhere, sometime. Although crude, they were written in good faith by their authors. Try to decode them.

1. I can't get sick pay. I have six children. Can you tell me why this is?
2. This is my eighth child. What are you going to do about it?
3. Mrs. Morris has no clothes and has not had any for a year. The clergy have been visiting her.
4. Unless I get my husband's money quickly, I shall be forced to lead an immortal life.
5. I am sending you my marriage certificate and six children. I had seven and one died, which was baptized on a half sheet of paper by the Rev. Thomas.
6. In answer to your letter, I have given birth to a little boy weighing 10 pounds. Is this satisfactory?
7. You have changed my little girl into a little boy. Will this make any difference?
8. I have no children as my husband is a bus driver and works all day and night.
9. Milk is wanted for my baby as the father is unable to supply it.
10. I want money as quick as you can send it. I have been in bed with my doctor all week, and he does not seem to be doing me any good.
11. Sir, I am glad to say that my husband, reported missing, is now dead.

STEREOTYPES Everyone lives in a world of stereotypical figures. Ivy Leaguers, Midwesterners, feminists, bankers, blue-collar workers, PR types, and thousands of other characterizations cause people to think of certain specific images. Public figures, for example, are typecast regularly. The dumb blond, the bigoted right winger, and the shifty used-car salesman are the kinds of stereotypes our society—particularly television—perpetuates.

Like it or not, most of us are victims of such stereotypes. For example, research indicates that a lecture delivered by a person wearing glasses will be perceived as "significantly more believable" than the same lecture delivered before the same audience by the same lecturer without glasses. The stereotyped impression of people with glasses is that they are more trustworthy and more believable.

SYMBOLS The clenched-fist salute, the swastika, and the thumbs-up sign all leave distinct impressions on most people. Marshaled properly, symbols can be used as effective persuasive elements. The Statue of Liberty, the Red Cross, the Star of David, and many other symbols have been used traditionally for positive persuasion. Indeed,

What do you see: Fish or fowl?

Figure 5–2 Often what we see may not be what others see. (Hint: there are both white fish and black fowl.) *(Courtesy of Trout & Ries)*

in the Falkland Islands invasion by Argentina in 1982, England used the symbol of its queen—and the honor of the crown—to rally public sentiment behind the war effort to win the islands back. Later that same year, a disgruntled antinuclear activist tried to hold the Washington Monument hostage as a symbol of a threatened nation. In the Mideast in 1990, Iraqis burned the American flag as a symbol of the American "satan."

SEMANTICS Public relations professionals make their living largely by knowing how to use words effectively to communicate desired meanings. Occasionally, this is tricky because the same words may hold contrasting meanings for different people. Especially vulnerable are popular and politically sensitive phrases such as *capital punishment, law and order, liberal politician, right winger,* and on and on, until you reach the point where the Oakridge Mall in San Jose, California, demanded that the gourmet hamburger restaurant on its premises, with a logo depicting a smiling hamburger with a monocle and top hat, either change its "suggestive name" or leave the mall. The restaurant's name? Elegant Buns.

In the 1990s, the label *terrorists,* a misnomer that the media have bestowed on those who hijack planes and blow up buildings, may play right into the hands of those who attack innocent civilians. Behavioral science studies show that such people seek the aura of power. Labeling them as terrorists concedes that they are, in fact, achieving their aims.[3] The same can be argued about rap music artists, who preach a philosophy of violence and hate. Such gangster rappers claim that they are "telling it like it is" or "reporting what we see in the streets." But when reporters and record company executives give credence to such misguided rhetoric, they become just as guilty for the often unfortunate consequences that result.[4]

Semantics must be handled with extreme care because language and the meanings of words change constantly. Good communicators always consider the consequences of the words they plan to use *before* using them.

PEER GROUPS In one famous study, students were asked to point out, in progression, the shortest of three lines.

A ______________________

B _______________

C _________________

Although line B is obviously the shortest, each student in the class except one was told in advance to answer that line C was the shortest. The object of the test was to see whether the one student would agree with his peers. Results generally indicated that, to a statistically significant degree, all students, including the uncoached one, chose C. Peer pressure prevails.

MEDIA The power of the media—particularly as an agenda setter or reinforcement mechanism—is also substantial. A common complaint among lawyers is that their clients cannot receive fair trials because of pretrial publicity leading to preconceived verdicts among potential jurors who read newspapers and watch television.

In one famous case in North Carolina, army officer Jeffrey MacDonald was put on trial for the savage killing of his wife and two children. The officer claimed that he was innocent and that a band of hippies had stabbed him and killed his family. State newspapers publicized the case extensively, running photographs of the soldier and commentary about the circumstances of the murders. Neither the soldier nor his lawyer would talk to the press. A random telephone survey taken a week before the trial indicated that most people thought the soldier was guilty. Several weeks later, however, the army dropped the murder charges against him when it couldn't make a case. Ironically, 9 years later, the man was convicted of those murders, subsequently released, and then found guilty on appeal.

The point remains that people often base perceptions on what they read or hear, without bothering to dig further to elicit the facts. Although appearances are sometimes revealing, they are often deceiving.

THE RECEIVER

You really aren't communicating unless someone is at the other end to hear and understand what you're saying. This situation is analogous to the old mystery of the falling tree in the forest: Does it make a noise when it hits the ground if there's no one there to hear it? Regardless of the answer, communication doesn't take place if a message doesn't reach the intended receivers and exert the desired effect on those receivers.

Even if a communication is understood clearly, there is no guarantee that the motivated action will be the desired one. In fact, a message may trigger several different effects.

1. **It may change attitudes.** This result, however, is very difficult to achieve and rarely happens.
2. **It may crystallize attitudes.** This outcome is much more common. Often a message will influence receivers to take actions they might already have been thinking about taking but needed an extra push to accomplish. For example, a receiver might want to contribute to a certain charity, but seeing a child's photo on a contribution canister might crystallize the attitude sufficiently to trigger action.
3. **It might create a wedge of doubt.** Communication can sometimes force receivers to modify their points of view. A persuasive message can cause receivers to question their original thinking on an issue.
4. **It may do nothing.** Often communication results in no action at all. When the American Cancer Society waged an all-out campaign to cut into cigarette sales, the net impact of the communication campaign was hardly significant.

Feedback is critical to the process of communication. A communicator must get feedback from a receiver to know what messages are or are not getting through and how to structure future communications. Occasionally, feedback is ignored by professional communicators, but this is always a mistake.

Whether the objectives of a communication have been met can often be assessed by such things as the amount of sales, number of letters, or number of votes obtained. If individuals take no action after receiving a communication, feedback must still be sought. In certain cases, although receivers have taken no discernible action, they may have understood and even passed on the message to other individuals. This person-to-person relay of received messages creates a two-step flow of communications: (1) vertically from a particular source and (2) horizontally from interpersonal contact. The targeting of opinion leaders as primary receivers is based on the hope that they will distribute received messages horizontally within their own communities.

Time Warner Defends a "Cop Killer"

I got my black shirt on,
I got my black gloves on,
I got my ski mask on,
I'm 'bout to bust some shots off,
I'm 'bout to dust some cops off,
Die, die, die, pig, die.

Thus begins the ballad of "Cop Killer," part of the "Body Count" album recorded by the rap music artist Ice-T and distributed by Time Warner.

The song's release in the summer of 1992 and its subsequent defense on free-speech grounds by Time Warner triggered a predictable outcry among business-people and the general public alike. Philadelphia's municipal pension fund announced plans to sell $1.6 million of Time Warner stock to protest the company's decision to distribute the rapper's album. One corporate CEO said he found Time Warner's behavior "offensive as a corporation. I hope it kills them."

Equally vocal were those on the other side, who defended Time Warner's decision. "Everyone's voice must be heard," said the cofounder of Ben & Jerry's Ice Cream. Echoed a cable operator, "As a disseminator of information, it is not right for me to pull the plug."

Most of the media, though, seemed to side with the critics. *The Washington Post* reported in an editorial, "In recent months, Time Warner has emerged as the entertainment equivalent of a tobacco company: a manufacturer and merchant of toxic products." *The Wall Street Journal,* in a lead editorial headed "Schlock Shock," labeled the distributor of Ice-T, Madonna, and Prince as the nation's "undisputed schlockmeister."

Time Warner's public response was muted. Gerald Levin, the company's chairman, when asked what the firm's "standards of acceptability" were, answered with a prepared statement: "Time Warner is a home for journalists and artists who have significant messages to tell. They do it with journalistic and artistic integrity. Time Warner will finance, support and disseminate their work. That's what the company is."

Later, Mr. Levin defended Ice-T's album. "Rap," he said, "is the CNN of the streets."

Rap also was a substantial contributor to Time Warner's profits. Ironically, in 1990, at the time of the merger between Time and Warner, it was the same Mr. Levin who said, "Our good name is our basic asset. This company has a higher obligation than simply making money."

Does the dissemination of songs like Ice-T's "Cop Killer" help realize that "higher obligation"?

For further information about the Time Warner "Cop Killer" controversy, see Richard M. Clurman, "Pushing All the Hot Buttons," *The New York Times,* November 29, 1992, Arts & Leisure section, 16–17; Roger Salquist, "Time Warner's Hard Line Takes Hits," *The Wall Street Journal,* July 23, 1992, B-1, 8; Tom Unger, "In Defense of Free Speech," *Public Relations Journal,* August 1992, 6; Jonathan Yardley, "The Music Industry's Lame Song and Dance Over Free Speech," *The Washington Post,* July 27, 1992, B 6.

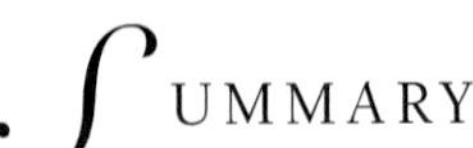

SUMMARY

As the year 2000 approaches, some communications consultants believe the future of communication may be a "step back in time." The advent of narrowcasting and communicating to more targeted, smaller audiences will mean a return to more direct communication between people. By combining the new technology—cable, videocassettes, telemarketing, floppy disks, CD-ROM, and all the rest—people will need the help of public relations professionals to communicate effectively.[5]

There is no trick to effective communication. Other than some facility with techniques, knowledge, hard work and common sense are the basic guiding principles.

Between the Lines

WHAAAT?

Extra credit for anyone who can decode the following sentence:

> We respectfully petition, request, and entreat that due and adequate provision be made, this day and the date herein after subscribed, for the satisfying of this petitioner's nutritional requirements and for the organizing of such methods as may be deemed necessary and proper to assure the reception by and for said petitioner of such quantities of baked products as shall, in the judgment of the aforesaid petitioner, constitute a sufficient supply thereof.*

Whaaat?

*Give us this day our daily bread.

Naturally, communication must follow performance; organizations must back up what they say with action. Slick brochures, engaging speeches, intelligent articles, and a good press may capture the public's attention, but in the final analysis, the only way to obtain continued public support is through proper performance.

DISCUSSION STARTERS

1. Above all else, the public relations practitioner is what?
2. Describe the process of communication.
3. Why do words like *liberal, conservative, profits*, and *consumer activist* spark semantic skyrockets?
4. What communications vehicle did President Reagan and President Bush use to maximum effectiveness?
5. Describe the S-E-M-D-R approach to communication.
6. Give an example of an encoder and a decoder.
7. How does perception influence a person's decoding?
8. Why is feedback critical to the communications process?
9. What common mistakes do people make when they communicate?
10. Why do some communications consultants believe that the future of communications may be a "step back in time"?

NOTES

1. Susan Antilla, "An Unfashionable Miscue by Kravis," *USA Today*, March 7, 1990, 2B.
2. "The 'Like Factor' in Communications," *Executive Communications* (February 1988): 1.
3. "Semantics Power," *Public Relations Reporter* (April 4, 1988): 4.

4. Brent Staples, "The Politics of Gangster Rap," *The New York Times,* August 27, 1993.
5. Communication May Step Back in Time '90s," *IABC Communication World* (February 1990): 9.

TOP OF THE SHELF

Roger Ailes and Jon Kraushar, *You Are the Message.* Homewood, IL: Dow Jones-Irwin, 1988.

Some rules to follow when speaking are: relax, think clearly, exhibit emotion, and, most important, be yourself. So advises *You Are the Message,* which builds on people's natural communications abilities to help them inform, persuade, and entertain.

Roger Ailes, a communications consultant whose clients have included U.S. presidents and Fortune 500 CEOs, shares his public speaking acumen in this useful book. Above all, he urges, play to your strengths when talking, whether you're at meetings, client presentations, or job interviews. That means cleverly employing facial expressions, body movement, vocal pitch, humor, tone, and volume. Once you've mastered these cues, Ailes suggests incorporating them into his "four essentials of a great communicator": be prepared, make others comfortable, be committed, and be interesting. Ailes says that if you consider these guidelines and are likeable—the "magic bullet"—you, too, can become a polished communicator. Your verbal and nonverbal skills will work together to produce crisp and lively speech.

Ailes suggests that communicating well counts more than on-the-job performance when it comes to moving up the corporate ladder. To help your climb, pay close attention to *You Are the Message.*

SUGGESTED READINGS

Agee, W. *Introduction to Mass Communication,* 9th ed. New York: Harper & Row, 1988.

Ailes, Roger, and Jon Kraushar. *You Are the Message.* Homewood, IL: Dow Jones-Irwin, 1988.

Bateman, David, and Norma Sigband. *Communicating in Business,* 3rd ed. Glenview, IL: Scott-Foreman, 1989.

Bittner, John. *Mass Communications,* 5th ed. Englewood Cliffs, NJ: Prentice-Hall, 1989.

Bovee, Courtland L., and John V. Thill. *Business Communication Today,* 3rd ed. New York: McGraw-Hill, 1992.

Brody, E. W. *Managing Communication Processes: From Planning to Crisis Response.* Westport, CT: Praeger, 1991.

Corman, Steven R., et al. *Foundations of Organization Communication.* White Plains, NY: Longman, 1990.

Diamant, Lincoln. *Broadcast Communications Dictionary,* 3rd ed. Lincolnwood, IL: NTC Business, 1991.

Dilenschneider, Robert L. *A Briefing for Leaders: Communication as the Ultimate Exercise of Power.* New York: Harper Business, 1992.

Fraser, Edith A. *Glossary of Common Acronyms and Terms of Modern Human Resource Management.* Orangeburg, NY: Implementation Support Associates,

Goldhaber, Gerald. *Organizational Communication,* 4th ed. Madison, WI: Brown and Benchmark, 1993.

Grazian, Frank. *Common Mistakes People Make When They Communicate.* Blackwood, NJ: Communication Briefings, August 1987. To help people identify areas that could be improved, the author brings some serious communication errors to light. This sheet is "must" reading.

Hamilton, Seymour. *A Communications Audit Handbook: Helping Organizations Communicate.* White Plains, NY: Longman, 1987.

International Encyclopedia of Communication, Vol. 4. New York: Oxford University Press, 1989.

Johnson, Hans. *Professional Communications—For a Change.* New York: Prentice-Hall, 1990.

Kreps, Gary L. *Organizational Communications,* 2nd ed. White Plains, NY: Longman, 1990.

Murphy, Kevin. *Effective Listening.* New York: Bantam, 1987.

Murphy, Kevin. *What Did You Say?* New York: Bantam, 1987.

Ragan Report. Chicago: Ragan Communications. Weekly.

Reardon, Kathleen. *Interpersonal Communication.* Belmont, CA: Wadsworth, 1987.

Severin, Werner, and James Tankard. *Communication Theories: Origins, Methods, Uses.* White Plains, NY: Longman, 1987.

Windahl, Sven, and Benno Signitzer. *Using Communications Theory: An Introduction to Planned Communications.* Newbury Park, CA: Sage, 1991.

CASE STUDY

BOXED IN AT JACK IN THE BOX

Food poisoning is a food company's worst nightmare. When hundreds of customers complain of symptoms and three children die, the firm faces communications and other problems that are severe. Thus in January 1993, when Jack in the Box, a subsidiary of Food Maker, Inc., was beseiged by customers in the Northwest who suddenly became ill after eating the company's hamburgers, the firm momentarily panicked.

Complaints began in Seattle and spiraled immediately. All told, some 800 people complained of food poisoning symptoms, with 477 infected by the painful—and occasionally deadly—*Escherichia coli* 0157:H7, a bacteria that damages the kidneys.

Of those who complained, 144 were hospitalized. A majority of the seriously ill were children, who had to undergo kidney dialysis for weeks. Three children died, but only one was directly linked to Jack in the Box.

Immediately upon being apprised of the situation, Jack in the Box voluntarily stopped selling all hamburger products in Washington State.

"Although this is an isolated case, we are taking every precaution to ensure that we meet and exceed health department standards," said the company's vice president in announcing the voluntary halt.

Three days later, as press reports of additional cases of bacterial infection emerged, Jack in the Box rushed its president to Seattle for a morning news conference. President Robert Nugent began the session by saying: "I would like to express my deepest sympathies to those who have been stricken—especially the children. I pray that they all have a speedy and complete recovery." President Nugent went on to describe the stellar historical record of Jack in the Box in Washington and then acknowledged that, "The problem is in fact due to contaminated hamburger."

However, the president suggested that the source of the contaminated hamburger wasn't Jack in the Box but rather a Northwest meat supplier with whom the company dealt. Further, said President Nugent, although Jack in the Box was accused of "violating the state's cooking procedures," the facts were the following: "Our cooking procedures were established to comply with all federal and state regulations and have been in use for over 30 years. . . . While the Washington State Health Department recently, and we think appropriately, upgraded their temperature regulations for hamburger, it is clear that Jack in the Box was not properly informed of this change."

At the height of the controversy, Food Maker, Inc., dismissed its long-time public relations firm, describing the breakup as "differences in strategic direction."

(Courtesy of Food Maker, Inc.)

In the ensuing weeks, Jack in the Box established an 800 number for the public to receive direct information about the bacteria outbreak. It announced the hiring of a new supplier of hamburger meat for its restaurants in the western United States. And Food Maker announced record first-quarter earnings, despite the Jack in the Box dilemma, to try to reassure the investment community.

The company's rebound was short-lived. A few weeks later, at Food Maker's annual meeting, President Nugent was obliged to make an embarrassing disclosure. He corrected his earlier statement that the company "hadn't received" new state food heating regulations from government officials. Rather, according to Nugent, the rules were "on file" at Food Maker's San Diego corpo-

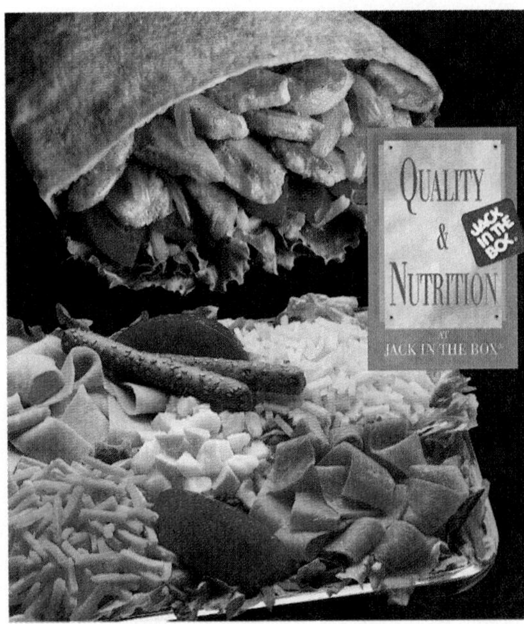

(*Courtesy of Food Maker, Inc.*)

rate headquarters. The Jack in the Box restaurant in Tacoma, Washington, site of the poisonings, also apparently had received a copy of the regulations in the mail.

Nugent said that a company vice president failed to alert top management of the new cooking regulations, which weren't adhered to. Had the new regulations, which required cooking hamburger patties at 155°F, been followed, the *E. coli* bacteria in the meat may have been killed.

As the gravity of the Jack in the Box situation began to sink in, Food Maker's stock plummeted and the company hit hard times. By June, 40 lawsuits in Washington, California, Idaho, and Nevada had been filed against Food Maker. The company immediately settled with the family of a 17-month-old boy whose death was attributed to a secondary infection picked up from another child, who had eaten at Jack in the Box.

Jack in the Box now sought to recover from its early missteps. It announced a program to pay the hospital costs of all customers hospitalized as a result of eating contaminated hamburgers. Said President Nugent, "We are committed to meeting all of our responsibilities in connection with this devastating situation. We are prepared to pay all hospital costs for our customers who have been affected by this tragedy."

As 1993 drew to a close, Food Maker and Jack in the Box aggressively sought to explain to customers, through ads and corporate literature, how the contamination had occurred and how the incidents were isolated. At the same time, the company continued to promote its program to pay the medical costs for all those sickened from eating at its restaurants.

Slowly, Jack in the Box began to reemerge from its nightmare, resigned to the long-term challenge of reassuring clients that its stores and its products were safe.

QUESTIONS

1. Was Jack in the Box's management right in reacting so quickly to the contamination problem?
2. How would you assess the strategy of spreading the blame for the contaminated hamburger?
3. How harmful to the Jack in the Box case was the inaccurate statement about the company's failure to receive new state hamburger cooking regulations?
4. What is your overall assessment of how Food Maker handled this communications challenge? What kinds of communications should the firm adopt in attempting to restore its credibility?

For further information about the Jack in the Box case, see "Jack in the Box's Worst Nightmare," *The New York Times*, February 6, 1993, 35, 37; "Last Patient Is Released in Jack in the Box Case," *The New York Times*, June 30, 1993, A14; and Calvin Sims, "Burger Chain Confronts Nightmare," *The New York Times*, July 16, 1993, 39, 51.

TIPS FROM THE TOP

FRANKIE A. HAMMOND

Frankie Hammond is associate professor and acting chair of the Department of Public Relations in the College of Journalism and Communications at the University of Florida, where she has taught since 1974. During a 5-year period as director of development and placement for the college, Professor Hammond helped more than 1,000 graduates launch their professional careers in public relations, advertising, journalism, and telecommunications. A former reporter and editor, Professor Hammond is a past president of the North Florida chapter of the Public Relations Society of America and served two terms on PRSA's Education Section Board.

How would you describe today's public relations students?
Today's students appear to be more career-driven than their earlier counterparts. They are ambitious and eager to join the workforce. But at the same time, they exhibit more altruism; they want to give something back to society. Current students' interests expand beyond the workplace, and money no longer seems to be a prime motivator.

What advice do you give those who want to become public relations practitioners?
Learn anything you can about everything you can. Then write. Rewrite. And rewrite some more. Sharpen your problem-solving capabilities. Get practical experience while you're in school and during the summers. Participate in the Public Relations Student Society of America. Take advantage of every opportunity to improve yourself and your skills.

Why should a student be interested in a career in public relations?
Public relations is such a multifaceted endeavor that any individual should be interested in it. The opportunities for personal and professional growth offer a lifetime of interesting work, interesting people, and a lot of enjoyment.

How does one land a job in the field?
Solid writing ability, common sense, and good judgment are always in demand. There are many entry-level jobs for well-rounded, enthusiastic, skilled, and persistent new graduates.

What distinguishes a good public relations practitioner?
Judgment and ethics, backed by communications skills and a familiarity with the social and behavioral forces that make people tick. An understanding of the public relations process and how it impacts on and is impacted by society is a must. The ability to view problems as opportunities and having a good sense of humor are also important.

What is the most significant challenge confronting public relations today?
The constant change in the environment in which public relations operates, and therefore the constant change in its practice, is undoubtedly the most significant challenge today. The successful practitioner must adapt to meet the societal, economic, and political changes in the world or become an anachronism.

If you had your career to start over again, what would you do?
Basically, I would do what I have done. I have had a variety of interesting experiences as the result of a willingness to take advantage of opportunities and new directions as they came up. It's added a broader perspective to my thinking, as well as being a lot of fun.

What will the state of public relations be like in the year 2000?
Virtually every organization will have a public relations effort because the organization's survival will depend on it. The need for and appreciation of public relations will increase as the field continues its shift from primarily communications toward more emphasis on counseling and advising. The number of practitioners in top-level jobs will increase by the turn of the century, with more and more CEOs named from the ranks of practitioners.

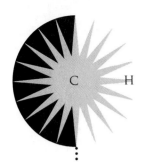

CHAPTER 6

Ethics

SEVERAL YEARS AGO, SOCIOLOGIST RAYMOND BAUMHART asked businesspeople, "What does ethics mean to you?" Among their replies:

> Ethics has to do with what my feelings tell me is right or wrong.
> Ethics has to do with my religious beliefs.
> Being ethical is doing what the law requires.
> Ethics consists of the standards of behavior our society accepts.
> I don't know what the word means.[1]

The meaning of *ethics* is hard to pin down, and the views many people have about ethics are uncertain. Nonetheless, ethical dilemmas are all around us. In many sectors of society in the 1990s, institutions are sending out mixed signals about the value of moral conduct.

Consider the following:

- In 1993, when Christine Todd Whitman won an upset victory in the New Jersey gubernatorial election, her campaign manager, Edward J. Rollins, Jr., claimed that victorious Republicans had paid to suppress the urban black vote in order to elect Ms. Whitman governor. Rollins quickly recanted his claim as a lie, but the damage was done, and Whitman's come-from-behind victory was tarnished.
- The American Express Company, among the world's largest and most prestigious corporations, contributed $8 million in 1990 to settle a dispute with a former top executive after acknowledging that the corporation had tried to discredit the man by linking him to illegal activities. (See the case study at the end of this chapter.)
- United Way of America, the nation's largest nonprofit group, was humiliated in 1992, when its president was found to be spending the organization's funds on lavish expenses and nepotism. (See the case study at the end of Chapter 7.)
- Wal-Mart, for years a proponent of a "Buy America" program, was exposed in late 1992 as hiring underage workers to produce garments in Bangladesh, slapping "Buy America" labels on the clothing, and shipping them to Wal-Mart's U.S. stores. (See the case study at the end of Chapter 15.)
- NBC-TV News, which prided itself as the model of objectivity and impartiality, was revealed to have rigged crash tests to ensure that a General Motors truck self-destructed on cue before rolling cameras. Only the tenacity of GM itself forced NBC to admit its abuse of investigative journalistic power. (See the case study at the end of Chapter 18.)

These incidents clearly step over the ethical line. Pollster Richard Wirthlin has discovered that "For most organizations, image is determined not only by what goods and services are provided, but also by the persona of the corporation. The first imperative of leadership is 'honesty.' "[2]

So, what constitutes ethics for an organization? Sadly, there is no one answer.

Ethical guidelines are just that—guidelines. They don't necessarily provide right answers, just educated guesses. And reasonable people can and do disagree about what is moral, ethical, and right in a given situation.

Nonetheless, when previously respected business, government, and religious leaders, as well as other members of society, are exposed as cheaters, con artists, and even crooks, those who would look up to and be influenced by such people are correctly appalled. Little wonder then that societal pressure in the area of ethics has never been more intense. In public relations no issue is more critical than ethics—of both the practice and the practitioner.

The bigness of most institutions in the 1990s—companies, schools, hospitals, associations, news organizations, and even professions like public relations—immediately makes them suspect. All have become concerned about their individual cultures—the values, ideals, principles, and aspirations that underlie their credibility and viability. As the internal conscience of many organizations, the public relations department has become a focal point for the institutionalization of ethical conduct. Increasingly, management has turned to public relations officers to lead the internal ethical charge, to be the keeper of the organizational ethic.

ETHICS IN SOCIETY

What exactly are ethics? Roughly translated, an individual's or organization's ethics come down to the standards that are followed in relationships with others—the real integrity of the individual or organization.

A discussion of the many classical theories of ethics lies beyond the scope of this book. Philosophers throughout the ages have debated the essence of ethics. To Aristotle, the *golden mean of moral virtue* could be found between two extreme points of view. Kant's *categorical imperative* recommended acting "on that maxim which you will to become a universal law." Mill's *principle of utility* recommended "seeking the greatest happiness for the greatest number." And the traditional Judeo-Christian ethic prescribes "loving your neighbor as yourself." Indeed, this *Golden Rule* makes great good sense in the practice of public relations.

Public relations people, in particular, must be ethical. They can't assume that ethics are strictly personal choices without relevance or related methodology for resolving moral quandaries. Rather, as the Code of Professional Standards of the Public Relations Society of America states (Appendix A), practitioners must be scrupulously honest and trustworthy, acting at all times in the public interest, which, by definition, also represents the best interests of individual organizations. Indeed, if the ultimate goal of the public relations professional is to enhance public trust of an organization, then only the highest ethical conduct is acceptable.

The essence of the PRSA Code of Standards and that of the International Association of Business Communicators (Figure 6–4) is that *honesty* and *fairness* lie at the heart of public relations practice. In light of the field's public nature, the PRSA code underscores the importance of members promoting and maintaining "high standards of public service and ethical conduct." Inherent in these standards of the profession is the understanding that ethics have changed and continue to change as society changes. Over time, views have changed on such areas as minority discrimination, double standards in the treatment of women, pollution of the environment, destruction of endangered species and natural resources, lack of concern for human rights, and on and on. Again, honesty and fairness are two critical components that will continue to determine the ethical behavior of public relations professionals.[3]

The first question that public relations must pose in any management discussion is "Are we doing the right thing?" Often the public relations professional will be the only member of management with the nerve to pose such a question. Sometimes this means saying "no" to what the boss wants to do. The bottom line for public relations professionals must always be what is in the best interests of the organization.

In the 1990s, this is easier said than done.

- Hill & Knowlton, one of the world's largest public relations firms, was embarrassed in recent years by taking on clients, such as the antiabortion National Conference of Catholic Bishops, the controversial Church of Scientology, and the criminal Bank of Credit and Commerce International.
- In 1993, one of the nation's best-known public relations counselors, Robert Dilenschneider, was slapped with a $50 million lawsuit for turning against a client and seizing control of his business.[4]

- That same year, legendary public relations figure Gershon Kekst was found to be representing both Paramount and Viacom in the latter's attempt to buy the former. What complicated the situation was that another hopeful acquirer, QVC, announced its willingness to pay more for Paramount than Viacom—thus compromising the integrity of the Kekst initiative.[5]

Examples like these point out the difficulty, in an increasingly competitive society, of maintaining high ethical standards in public relations practice specifically and in business in general.

ETHICS IN BUSINESS

For many people today, regrettably, the term *business ethics* is an oxymoron. Its mere mention stimulates thoughts of jailed financiers like Ivan Boesky and Michael Milken illegally raking in millions of dollars with insider stock tips or of companies like Rockwell International being indicted by a federal grand jury for defrauding the U.S. Air Force.

Fraud, price gouging, runaway pollution—all these allegations have made headlines in recent years. And American business, perhaps the most ethical business system in the world, has been shocked—so much so that in 1987 the former Securities and Exchange Commission chairman, John Shad, donated $23 million to begin a program at Harvard Business School to make the study of ethics an integral part of the curriculum.*

In one significant 1988 study, a leading business group, the Business Roundtable, pointed out the "crucial role of the chief executive officer and top managers in establishing a strong commitment to ethical conduct and in providing constant leadership in tending and reviewing the values of the organization."[6] The Roundtable study debunked the myth that there is an inherent contradiction between ethics and profits. On the contrary, it emphasized that there is a strong relationship between acting ethically, maintaining a good reputation for fair and honest business, and making money.

Another 1988 study of key business leaders, conducted by the accounting firm Touche Ross, corroborated the notion that a majority of business leaders—63 percent—"believe that a business enterprise actually 'strengthens' its competitive position by maintaining high ethical standards." Only 14 percent said that a company with high ethical standards was a "weaker competitor."[7] The Touche Ross research on more than 1,000 business leaders also turned up other interesting findings about the current state of business ethics:

- Intense concentration on short-term earnings is a major threat to American business ethics today. Respondents ranked this threat almost equal to that posed by decay in cultural and social institutions.

*Ironically Mr. Shad himself was the subject of an embarrassing ethical dilemma. He was called in to head Drexel Burnham Lambert after the firm was fined and discredited for junk bond indiscretions led by Milken. Shad was duly mortified when Drexel Burnham went belly up in 1989.

- Respondents ranked the United States as having higher standards of business ethics than any other country—noting high standards also in the United Kingdom, Canada, Switzerland, and Germany.
- Among industries, respondents ranked commercial banking, utilities, and drugs, pharmaceuticals, and cosmetics as the three most ethical.
- Among all professions, respondents ranked the clergy, teachers, engineers, and accountants as the four most ethical.[8]

CORPORATE CODES OF CONDUCT

Another manifestation of the increased attention to corporate ethics is the growth of internal codes of conduct. Codes of ethics, standards of conduct, and similar statements of corporate policies and values have proliferated in recent years.

The reasons corporations have adopted such codes vary from company to company.

- **To increase public confidence** The scandals concerning overseas bribery and domestic political campaign contributions during the 1970s led to a decline of public trust and confidence in business. Many firms responded with written codes of ethics.
- **To stem the tide of regulation** As public confidence declined, government regulation of business increased. Some estimated the cost to society of compliance with regulations at $100 billion per year. Corporate codes of conduct, it was hoped, would serve as a self-regulation mechanism.
- **To improve internal operations** As companies became larger and more decentralized, management needed consistent standards of conduct to ensure that employees were meeting the business objectives of the company in a legal and ethical manner.
- **To respond to transgressions** Frequently when a company itself was caught in the web of unethical behavior, it responded with its own code of ethics. For example, Fiat, Italy's biggest private company, sought to extricate itself in 1993 from a huge corruption scandal in the country by issuing the first Italian corporate code of ethical conduct for employees.[9]

Ralph Waldo Emerson once wrote that "an organization is the lengthened shadow of a man." By the 1990s, many corporate executives realized that just as an individual has certain responsibilities as a citizen, a corporate citizen has responsibilities to the society in which it is privileged to operate (Figure 6–1).

Corporate codes of conduct are not without their critics. Some ethics specialists say that what is contained in the codes doesn't really address ethics in general. A Washington State University study of ethical codes at 200 Fortune 500 companies found that while 75 percent failed to address the company's role in civic and community affairs, consumer relations, environmental safety, and product safety, more than 75 percent dealt with conflicts of interest—which can affect the bottom line.[10] Such skepticism notwithstanding, formal ethical codes, addressing such topics as confidentiality of corporate information, misappropriation of corporate assets, bribes and kickbacks, and political contributions, have become a corporate fact of life in the 1990s.

Our Guiding Principles

Over our long history we have evolved standards and values guiding the management of the company that comprise an unwritten creed. These beliefs are central to conducting our affairs responsibly in fulfilling our obligations to shareowners, employees, customers and the communities in which we work.

Two contemporary developments suggest that a more formal statement of the company's principles is in order. One, the substantial increase in the size and geographic breadth of the company, and, two, the growing interest of the public in the ethical practices and social commitments of business. To be responsive to these new needs, our Board of Directors two years ago approved a written declaration of the canons that have guided this company's operations for so many years.

Since these are not static rules to be filed, but active principles to be practiced, they have recently been reviewed and again endorsed.

Implicit in the responsible conduct of the affairs of the company is one fundamental consideration – our consistent compliance with all pertinent laws, regulations and ethical standards.

These principles are personal and important to us. Obviously, they are not unique. We share many of them with other responsible and successful members of the business community.

We set forth these guiding principles looking ahead to continued growth for our company, improvement in the quality of life of our people and continued constructive relationships with the communities closest to us.

T M Ford
Chairman and President

Figure 6–1 The principles enumerated here by the chief executive of the Emhart Corporation represent the obligations the company believes it has to its corporate community. *(Courtesy of Emhart Corporation)*

CORPORATE SOCIAL RESPONSIBILITY

Closely related to the ethical conduct of an organization is its social responsibility, which has been defined as a social norm. This norm holds that any social institution, including the smallest family unit and the largest corporation, is responsible for the behavior of its members and may be held accountable for their misdeeds.

In the late 1960s, when this idea was just emerging, initial responses were of the knee-jerk variety. A firm that was threatened by increasing legal or activist pressures and harassment would ordinarily change its policies in a hurry. Today, however, organizations and their social responsibility programs are much more sophisticated. Social responsibility is treated just like any other management discipline: Analyze the issues, evaluate performance, set priorities, allocate resources to those priorities, and implement programs that deal with issues within the constraints of the organization's resources. Many companies have created special committees to set the agenda and target the objectives.

Social responsibility touches practically every level of organizational activity, from marketing to hiring, from training to work standards. A partial list of social responsibility categories might include the following:

- **Product lines**—dangerous products, product performance and standards, packaging, and environmental impact
- **Marketing practices**—sales practices, consumer complaint policies, advertising content, and fair pricing
- **Employee services**—training, counseling and placement services, transfer procedures, and educational allowances
- **Corporate philanthropy**—contribution performance, encouragement of employee participation in social projects, and community development activities
- **Environmental activities**—pollution-control projects, adherence to federal standards, and evaluation procedures for new packages and products
- **External relations**—support of minority enterprises, investment practices, and government relations
- **Employment of minorities and women**—current hiring policies, advancement policies, specialized career counseling, and opportunities for special minorities such as the physically handicapped
- **Employee safety and health**—work environment policies, accident safeguards, and food and medical facilities

More often than not, organizations have incorporated social responsibility into the mainstream of their practice. Most firms recognize that social responsibility, far from being an add-on program, must be a corporate way of life. Beyond this, some studies have indicated that those organizations that practice social responsibility over time rank among the most profitable and successful firms in society.

ETHICS IN GOVERNMENT

Politics has never enjoyed an unblemished reputation when it comes to ethics. In the 1990s, American politics has developed a particularly sleazy reputation.

The 1993 Ed Rollins affair was symptomatic of the ethical problems afflicting politics. Rollins, a veteran of presidential political politics, should have known better than to talk about suppressing minority votes in the New Jersey governor's race. Also in 1993, Oregon Republican Senator Robert Packwood was the subject of embarrassing publicity regarding unseemly sexual advances that Packwood had made to women over decades in politics. On the other side of the political aisle, the president himself was dubbed "Slick Willy" during the campaign for refusing to be pinned down on specific programs.

The "sleaze factor" in government is, of course, nothing new. President Bush was plagued by skepticism about his role in secret Iran-Nicaraguan Contra negotiations. President Reagan suffered an embarrassing scandal in his Housing and Urban

Development Department and lobbying violations by several key assistants. Five U.S. senators in the winter of 1990 were accused of serious ethical violations in support of Charles Keating, a convicted savings and loan operator. Four years later, several of the "Keating Five" senators were gone from the Senate.

As the decade and the century draw to a close, the public seems less willing to tolerate such ethical violations from their elected officials. In the late 1990s, it is likely that ethics in government will become an even more important issue as fed-up voters insist on representatives who are honest, trustworthy, and ethical.

Sham or Shamu: The Push to Free Willy

In 1993, an increasing number of Americans opposed placing marine mammals in captivity. Helping to fuel the fire was a wildly successful and sympathetic movie, *Free Willy,* in which a young boy released a three-ton captive whale, as misty-eyed theatregoers cheered appreciatively.

On one side of the debate stood groups like the Fund for Animals and In Defense of Animals, who argued that dolphins and so-called killer whales or orcas weren't meant to swim in contained tanks in amusement parks. Rather, these groups argued, such unnatural treatment leads to an inordinate amount of dolphin and whale deaths.

Adding to the anti-captivity charge was the revelation that in the 1980s, theme park Sea World provided tour guides with an instruction package that read, in part, "If people ask you about a particular animal that you know has passed away, please say, 'I don't know.'"

Sea World answered critics by explaining that this practice was eliminated after Anheuser-Busch purchased Sea World in 1989.

Other aquariums around the nation, such as the Shedd Aquarium in Chicago, initiated public relations offensives to point out that "There is evidence that many species of dolphins live as long in aquariums as they do in the wild, if not longer." Nonetheless through the mid-90s, animal activists increased their protests, in communications such as the advertisement here, to keep the pressure on aqua exhibitors.

Indeed, in confronting an issue such as this, the question must be raised, What are the ethical implications in displaying dolphins in such unnatural habitats?*

*Gary Robbins, "Truth Unclear in Dolphin Debate," *The Sunday Record* (November 28, 1993): A-12.

Captive for 23 years, a gentle, intelligent orca at Anheuser-Busch's Sea World amusement park in San Diego should be returned home to her family before she dies. This is her real story. Read it with your children. They'll understand.

"Isn't It a *Shame* about *Shamu?*"

THIS IS A TRUE STORY about a 28-year-old orca, known as Corky, who performs at an amusement park under the stage name "Shamu."

When Corky was very young, just four or five years old, she was swimming with her family near Vancouver Island, Canada. It was just before Christmas. Fishermen who had been lying in wait ambushed Corky's family with nets and boats for the second time in two years. Corky and her mother were among those captured. Her mother managed to escape. Corky was trapped.

The fishermen sold Corky and the other orcas to companies that put on aquarium shows. Of the thirteen orcas they took in 1968 and 1969, only two, including Corky, are alive today.

AT THE AMUSEMENT PARK, people buy tickets to watch orcas do tricks, like jumping up in the air when trainers order them to. That's what Corky has been doing for the last 23 years — putting on shows. And the owners of the amusement park have gotten very rich because they've sold millions of tickets all those years.

THE TROUBLE IS, orcas don't live as long trapped in a tank of water as they do when they live wild and free in the ocean. Like a goldfish kept in a bowl that's too small, orcas in tanks get sick and die before their time.

A female orca like Corky might live as long as seventy years in the ocean. Corky's mother is 42 years old, for example, and is still frequently seen near Vancouver Island.

In orca families (called "pods") three or even four generations swim together all their lives: grandmothers, mothers, and their children. Every family has its own way of talking to each other and the only time they part is when they die or they're captured.

(Orcas, also known as killer whales, are the world's largest type of dolphin. Mammals like us, they breathe air, nurse their babies with milk, and live with their families all their long lives. Orcas are found in every ocean of the world, and they are the top predator wherever they live. Their only enemies are companies like Anheuser-Busch.)

CORKY IS CAPTIVE at an amusement park called Sea World, in San Diego. Most people don't even know her given name is Corky — all the orcas at every Sea World are called Shamu.

When one "Shamu" dies, the amusement park owners bring on another one, and the audience isn't supposed to know the difference.

And Shamus do die. A lot.

Eight orcas like Corky have died at Sea World aquariums since 1987. Three-quarters of all the wild-caught orcas ever kept at Sea Worlds around the country have died in their tanks. And they've died young.

ORCAS IN captivity are expected to live less than ten years. (In the ocean, remember, they can live up to seventy years.)

The fact is, at 28, Corky is the oldest captive orca in the world. And for 23 of those years, Corky has been jumping on command, ridden on by trainers, fed dead fish, and then been sent back to the holding tank, where she swims in circles, around and around, because there's no way out.

What is life like for Corky? She has been pregnant seven times, for a total of thirteen years. Yet something has always gone wrong.

Some of her babies died before they were born. Four of them died when they were just a few days or a few weeks old.

NOBODY REALLY KNOWS if this made Corky sad, or if she even feels emotion as we humans understand it. But her trainers do know that Corky isn't getting pregnant anymore (her own mother, in the wild, had a new baby in 1992). Her trainers also know that Corky is weakening. She's lost some of her teeth, and has other health problems.

SEND CORKY HOME

That's why so many people across America, including lots of children who have seen Corky in person, want Sea World to let Corky go home to her family (see photo).

SCIENTISTS WHO KNOW a great deal about orcas believe Corky can and should be released. Other kinds of dolphins held captive for years have been successfully returned to their ocean homes.

Corky still has a family to go back to. She still "talks" her family's special language of calls, clicks, and other sounds, so she'd be able to communicate with them — that's important because they can recognize her and accept her back.

The plan is to go slowly... make sure Corky can learn to catch her own fish again, and teach her to swim back to a boat so scientists and animal doctors can give her medical check-ups.

IF THE PLAN WORKS, Corky will be allowed to swim free. She'll see her mother again and be part of a family again — a family known to marine biologists as the A5 pod, part of a flourishing community of orcas along the Pacific coast between Alaska and Vancouver Island.

So why isn't Corky being set free? The company that owns Sea World won't even consider the idea.

Performing as "Shamu," Corky helps sell millions of dollars worth of tickets every year. That's so much money, the company would rather keep Corky until she dies than let her go home to her family.

CAN YOU IMAGINE how much money Corky has already made for this company while she's been at Sea World? And think of how soon she will die unless she goes home. It's just not fair.

To help send Corky home, your family can mail the messages at the bottom of the page — to Sea World's owner Anheuser-Busch, to Congress, and to us.

Orcas are much larger than human beings. But human beings will decide their fate. Let's work together as well as orcas do, to make sure stories like Corky's have a happy ending. — *Thank you!*

Call 1-800-950-5867* to tell Anheuser-Busch to let Corky go home...now!

AUGUST A. BUSCH III, PRES. AND CEO
Anheuser-Busch
1 Busch Plaza
St. Louis, Missouri 63118

Sea World and your company, Anheuser-Busch, have made money off Corky long enough. Please...send her home to her family in the wild before it's too late.

NAME

ADDRESS

CONGRESSMAN GERRY STUDDS
Merchant Marine & Fisheries Committee
U.S. House of Representatives
Washington, D.C. 20515

Taking dolphins and whales from the wild is wrong. I urge you to strengthen the Marine Mammal Protection Act to halt new captures and encourage release programs.

NAME

ADDRESS

FREE CORKY PROJECT
c/o In Defense of Animals
816 West Francisco Blvd.
San Rafael, California 94901

Make a REAL splash. FREE CORKY!

We want to help Corky go free. Please send a _ Free Corky! Action Kit _ Kids Action Kit _ Teachers Kit (send $5). Enclosed is my tax-deductible donation to help spread the word nationwide: __$25 __$50 __$100 __$250 __$500 or $_______.

NAME

ADDRESS

Prepared by Public Media Center

The campaign to free Corky is endorsed by: Action For Animals, Animal Welfare Institute, Citizens for Marine Mammal Protection, Coalition Against U.S. Exporting Dolphins, The Dolphin Project, Earth Island Institute, Environmental Investigations Agency, Fund for Animals, In Defense of Animals, Marine Mammal Fund, Midwest Whale Protection, NEAVS, Northern Lights Expeditions, Pacific Orca Society, People for the Ethical Treatment of Animals, Progressive Animal Welfare Society, Save the Whales, South Carolina Association for Marine Mammal Protection, Zoo Check Canada.

* Toll free. For $7.95 (charged to your credit card) letters will be sent in your name to the addresses listed above.

(Courtesy of *In Defense of Animals*)

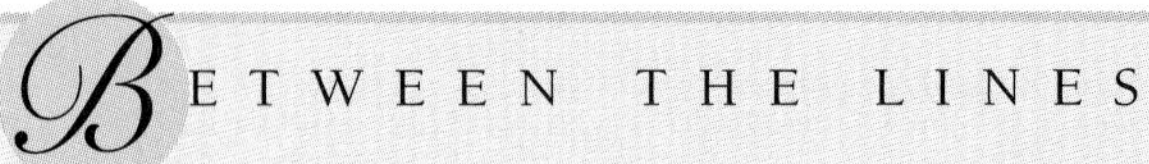

LARRY SPEAKES NO MORE

The sad saga of former White House press secretary Larry Speakes is as pointed an example of an ethical dilemma as any in recent public relations history. By all accounts, Speakes served President Ronald Reagan as an able and respected spokesperson. His credo seemed to be to tell the truth, regardless of the consequences. Indeed, Speakes was interviewed for the third edition of *The Practice of Public Relations* shortly after leaving the White House and offered the following observations:

> *What is the biggest problem of the president's press secretary?*
> It is impossible to identify something as the "biggest" problem. One of the greatest frustrations of the job was the fact that most reporters automatically assumed the government was lying. This was the aftermath of Watergate, but it was inappropriately and unfairly applied to the Reagan administration. We told the truth; I was always a bit disadvantaged when I was forced to convince people I was doing so.
>
> *What is the overriding objective of the president's chief spokesman?*
> My overriding objective as the president's chief spokesman was to tell the truth.
>
> *What advice would you give to the public relations practitioners of the future?*
> I would advise practitioners to do two things: (1) tell the truth, and (2) understand that journalists have a job to do and be as considerate of their professional needs as you expect them to be of yours.*

Such words would come back to haunt the former press secretary. In mid-1988, having become communications director of Merrill Lynch, Speakes revealed in his book *Speaking Out* that he had manufactured quotes and had attributed them to President Reagan. For example, when Reagan and Soviet leader Mikhail Gorbachev held their historic first meeting in Geneva in 1985, according to Speakes, White House officials found Mr. Gorbachev to be a master at handling the press, "while Reagan was very tentative and stilted." Consequently, Speakes told reporters that the president had said, "There is much that divides us, but I believe the world breathes easier because we are talking together," and the quote was widely reported by American news organizations, even though the president hadn't really said it. In his book, Speakes conceded in retrospect that it was "clearly wrong to take such liberties," even though the president would not have disavowed the words—until Speakes's book came out, that is.

*Fraser P. Seitel, *The Practice of Public Relations,* 3d ed. (Columbus, OH: Merrill, 1987), 137.

In a ringing denunciation, Larry Speakes's successor at the White House, Marlin Fitzwater, characterized his predecessor's actions as a "damn outrage." Merrill Lynch wasn't particularly happy either, reportedly alarmed that Speakes's admissions might tarnish its new ad campaign, "A Tradition of Trust." Two weeks after his book's publication, Speakes resigned from his Merrill Lynch job.

And the lesson in all of this? Frankly, despite the self-righteous indignation of the media, the lesson isn't at all clear. Like it or not, public relations people do indeed fabricate statements for their employers—it goes with the territory. And if such statements are approved by employers in advance, ethical questions are less pertinent. However, public relations people rarely announce or even acknowledge that they have authored such statements. Ironically, then, in violating the confidence of the president by retrospectively telling the truth about the bogus quotes, Larry Speakes may have made his most costly misstep.

ETHICS IN JOURNALISM

The Society of Professional Journalists, Sigma Delta Chi, is quite explicit on the subject of ethics (Figure 6–2).

> Journalists at all times will show respect for the dignity, privacy, rights and well-being of people encountered in the course of gathering and presenting the news.

THE SOCIETY OF PROFESSIONAL JOURNALISTS, SIGMA DELTA CHI

Code of Ethics

THE SOCIETY of Professional Journalists, Sigma Delta Chi believes the duty of journalists is to serve the truth.

WE BELIEVE the agencies of mass communication are carriers of public discussion and information, acting on their Constitutional mandate and freedom to learn and report the facts.

WE BELIEVE in public enlightenment as the forerunner of justice, and in our Constitutional role to seek the truth as part of the public's right to know the truth.

WE BELIEVE those responsibilities carry obligations that require journalists to perform with intelligence, objectivity, accuracy and fairness.

To these ends, we declare acceptance of the standards of practice here set forth:

RESPONSIBILITY:

The public's right to know of events of public importance and interest is the overriding mission of the mass media. The purpose of distributing news and enlightened opinion is to serve the general welfare. Journalists who use their professional status as representatives of the public for selfish or other unworthy motives violate a high trust.

FREEDOM OF THE PRESS:

Freedom of the press is to be guarded as an inalienable right of people in a free society. It carries with it the freedom and the responsibility to discuss, question and challenge actions and utterances of our government and of our public and private institutions. Journalists uphold the right to speak unpopular opinions and the privilege to agree with the majority.

ETHICS:

Journalists must be free of obligation to any interest other than the public's right to know the truth.

1. Gifts, favors, free travel, special treatment or privileges can compromise the integrity of journalists and their employers. Nothing of value should be accepted.
2. Secondary employment, political involvement, holding public office and service in community organizations should be avoided if it compromises the integrity of journalists and their employers. Journalists and their employers should conduct their personal lives in a manner which protects them from conflict of interest, real or apparent. Their responsibilities to the public are paramount. That is the nature of their profession.
3. So-called news communications from private sources should not be published or broadcast without substantiation of their claims to news value.
4. Journalists will seek news that serves the public interest, despite the obstacles. They will make constant efforts to assure that the public's business is conducted in public and that public records are open to public inspection.
5. Journalists acknowledge the newsman's ethic of protecting confidential sources of information.

ACCURACY AND OBJECTIVITY:

Good faith with the public is the foundation of all worthy journalism.

1. Truth is our ultimate goal.
2. Objectivity in reporting the news is another goal, which serves as the mark of an experienced professional. It is a standard of performance toward which we strive. We honor those who achieve it.
3. There is no excuse for inaccuracies or lack of thoroughness.
4. Newspaper headlines should be fully warranted by the contents of the articles they accompany. Photographs and telecasts should give an accurate picture of an event and not highlight a minor incident out of context.
5. Sound practice makes clear distinction between news reports and expressions of opinion. News reports should be free of opinion or bias and represent all sides of an issue.
6. Partisanship in editorial comment which knowingly departs from the truth violates the spirit of American journalism.
7. Journalists recognize their responsibility for offering informed analysis, comment and editorial opinion on public events and issues. They accept the obligation to present such material by individuals whose competence, experience and judgment qualify them for it.
8. Special articles or presentations devoted to advocacy or the writer's own conclusions and interpretations should be labeled as such.

FAIR PLAY:

Journalists at all times will show respect for the dignity, privacy, rights and well-being of people encountered in the course of gathering and presenting the news.

1. The news media should not communicate unofficial charges affecting reputation or moral character without giving the accused a chance to reply.
2. The news media must guard against invading a person's right to privacy.
3. The media should not pander to morbid curiosity about details of vice and crime.
4. It is the duty of news media to make prompt and complete correction of their errors.
5. Journalists should be accountable to the public for their reports and the public should be encouraged to voice its grievances against the media. Open dialogue with our readers, viewers and listeners should be fostered.

PLEDGE:

Journalists should actively censure and try to prevent violations of these standards, and they should encourage their observance by all newspeople. Adherence to this code of ethics is intended to preserve the bond of mutual trust and respect between American journalists and the American people.

Figure 6–2 The Society of Professional Journalists, Sigma Delta Chi, has elaborated in some detail on the ethical guidelines that should govern reporters and editors.

1. The news media should not communicate unofficial charges affecting reputation or moral character without giving the accused a chance to reply.
2. The news media must guard against invading a person's right to privacy.
3. The media should not pander to morbid curiosity about details of vice and crime.

And so on.

Unfortunately, what is in the code often doesn't reflect what appears in print or on the air. More often than not, journalistic judgments run smack into ethical principles.

- In 1988, when a Steele County, Minnesota, woman's description of a bloody fight between two men was broadcast over the police radio band, she begged an *Owatonna People's Press* reporter not to use her name. She feared reprisal from either or both of the men. The next day's story reported her name, address, and an account of what she had seen. The following day one of the men was found stabbed to death, and the other was arrested not far from the woman's home.
- In 1990, the banking reporter and business editor of the *St. Petersburg* (Florida) *Times* resigned under pressure when it was disclosed that they dealt in the stocks of companies they wrote about. Because the *Times's* policy cautions reporters to "avoid even the appearance of a conflict and to ask their supervisors if they have doubts about an investment," the two men were let go.
- In 1993, the problems of NBC-TV News and, in particular, its *Dateline NBC* program tarnished the reputation of television news in general. *Dateline NBC's* bogus presentation of exploding General Motors trucks was but one example of the blurring of the distinction between news and entertainment. As titillating pseudo-journalistic endeavors such as *Geraldo, Inside Edition,* and *A Current Affair* proliferated and gained in popularity, the ethical standards and performance of more legitimate TV news shows continued to deteriorate (Figure 6–3).

The point is that a sense of ethics helps an individual make moral decisions, and journalists have to make their decisions with speed and certainty. They can't usually afford to say maybe, and they can never say, "We'll have time to get back to this when the dust settles." Their decisions must meet a deadline. Usually, the principles, values, and ideals that get reported depend largely on the individual doing the reporting.

ETHICS IN PUBLIC RELATIONS

In light of numerous misconceptions about what the practice of public relations is or isn't, it is imperative that practitioners emulate the highest standards of personal and professional ethics. Within an organization, public relations practitioners must be the standard bearers of corporate ethical initiatives. By the same token, public relations consultants must always counsel their clients in an ethical direction—toward accuracy and candor and away from lying and hiding the truth.

The Public Relations Society of America has been a leader in the effort to foster a strong sense of ethics among its membership. Its Code of Professional Standards is a model in the attempt to promulgate high standards of public service and ethical conduct. In recent years, the PRSA code has been tested on a variety of issues, ranging from

Once this man held a flaming torch...now he wants to hold office..

You're an editor. One of your reporters learns that a candidate for public office once was a member of the Ku Klux Klan. But, on further investigation, she finds out that the man was actually a federal informant.
To reveal his name could mean death for him and his family. Do you print the whole story? Part of it? Or suppress it?

As reported in FineLine, this real life ethical dilemma raises tough questions about the right of privacy and the public's right to know. If you've faced similar situations, FineLine would like you to share them with us and your colleagues.

And we'll pay you $500 for every accepted article.

For more information on how you can be a contributor or to subscribe contact ...

FineLine™

The Newsletter On Journalism Ethics

600 E. Main Street, Louisville, Kentucky 40202 • 502/584-8182 • Robin Hughes, Editor • Barry Bingham, Jr., Publisher

Figure 6–3 The topic of journalistic ethics in the 1990s has become such an important one that newsletters like this one have begun to emerge. *(Courtesy of Fine-Line)*

noncompetition agreements with the employees of a public relations firm, to the protection of public relations campaign proposals to prospective clients, to paying employees and consultants finder's fees to obtain new accounts.

In 1987, a study by the Foundation for Public Relations Research and Education, covering the years 1950 to 1985, revealed a strong adherence in the field to the ethical code originally adopted in 1950. During that period, 168 issues and complaints were registered and investigated. Articles of the code most frequently cited were these:

- A member shall deal fairly with clients or employers—past, present, and potential—with fellow practitioners, and with the general public.
- A member shall adhere to truth and accuracy and to generally accepted standards of good taste.
- A member shall conduct his or her professional life in accord with the public interest.
- A member shall not intentionally communicate false or misleading information and is obligated to use care to avoid communication of false or misleading information.
- A member shall not engage in any practice that tends to corrupt the channels of communication or the processes of government.

The foundation concluded that the code, with its enforcement provisions, is a good one: "It has been, can be, and will be improved. It is a vibrant, living document that depends, as our future and that of public relations depends, on constant understanding and application by the society's members."[11] Another such code of ethics was that adopted by the International Association of Business Communicators (Figure 6–4).

Among the general public, the relatively strong state of public relations ethics apparently is being recognized more. In a 1989 ethics survey of The Pinnacle Group, businesspersons ranked public relations practitioners fifth among occupations in terms of ethics. Public relations counselors ranked ahead of lawyers, funeral home operators, and advertising professionals. In the same survey, senior high school students ranked public relations professionals seventh in terms of ethics, with doctors, dentists, accountants, and yes, even lawyers, outpacing public relations people.[12]

SUMMARY

The success of public relations into the year 2000 and beyond will depend largely on how the field responds to the issue of ethical conduct. Public relations professionals must have credibility in order to practice. They must be respected by the various publics with whom they interact. To be credible and to achieve respect, public relations professionals must be ethical. It is that simple.

The final arbiter in assessing whether ethics is important is the public (Fig. 6–5). And above all, the public is concerned with the credibility of an organization and of those who serve it. For public relations practice in general and individual public relations professionals in particular, credibility in the next few years will depend on how scrupulously they observe and apply, in everything they do, the principles and practice of ethics.

IABC CODE OF ETHICS

The IABC Code of Ethics has been developed to provide IABC members and other communication professionals with guidelines of professional behavior and standards of ethical practice. The Code will be reviewed and revised as necessary by the Ethics Committee and the Executive Board.

Any IABC member who wishes advice and guidance regarding its interpretation and/or application may write or phone IABC headquarters. Questions will be routed to the Executive Board member responsible for the Code.

Communication and Information Dissemination

1. *Communication professionals will uphold the credibility and dignity of their profession by encouraging the practice of honest, candid and timely communication.*

The highest standards of professionalism will be upheld in all communication. Communicators should encourage frequent communication and messages that are honest in their content, candid, accurate and appropriate to the needs of the organization and its audiences.

2. *Professional communicators will not use any information that has been generated or appropriately acquired by a business for another business without permission. Further, communicators should attempt to identify the source of information to be used.*

When one is changing employers, information developed at the previous position will not be used without permission from that employer. Acts of plagiarism and copyright infringement are illegal acts; material in the public domain should have its source attributed, if possible. If an organization grants permission to use its information and requests public acknowledgment, it will be made in a place appropriate to the material used. The material will be used only for the purpose for which permission was granted.

Standards of Conduct

3. *Communication professionals will abide by the spirit and letter of all laws and regulations governing their professional activities.*

All international, national and local laws and regulations must be observed, with particular attention to those pertaining to communication, such as copyright law. Industry and organizational regulations will also be observed.

4. *Communication professionals will not condone any illegal or unethical act related to their professional activity, their organization and its business or the public environment in which it operates.*

It is the personal responsibility of professional communicators to act honestly, fairly and with integrity at all times in all professional activities. Looking the other way while others act illegally tacitly condones such acts whether or not the communicator has committed them. The communicator should speak with the individual involved, his or her supervisor or appropriate authorities – depending on the context of the situation and one's own ethical judgment.

Confidentiality/Disclosure

5. *Communication professionals will respect the confidentiality and right-to-privacy of all individuals, employers, clients and customers.*

Communicators must determine the ethical balance between right-to-privacy and need-to-know. Unless the situation involves illegal or grossly unethical acts, confidences should be maintained. If there is a conflict between right-to-privacy and need-to-know, a communicator should first talk with the source and negotiate the need for the information to be communicated.

6. *Communication professionals will not use any confidential information gained as a result of professional activity for personal benefit or for that of others.*

Confidential information can be used to give inside advantage to stock transactions, gain favors from outsiders, assist a competing company for whom one is going to work, assist companies in developing a marketing advantage, achieve a publishing advantage or otherwise act to the detriment of an organization. Such information must remain confidential during and after one's employment period.

Professionalism

7. *Communication professionals should uphold IABC's standards for ethical conduct in all professional activity, and should use IABC and its designation of accreditation (ABC) only for purposes that are authorized and fairly represent the organization and its professional standards.*

IABC recognizes the need for professional integrity within any organization, including the association. Members should acknowledge that their actions reflect on themselves, their organizations and their profession.

Printed with the assistance of the Mead Corporation and Brown & Kroger Printing, Dayton, OH

Figure 6–4 The International Association of Business Communicators adopted these seven tenets to guide the professional behavior of its members.

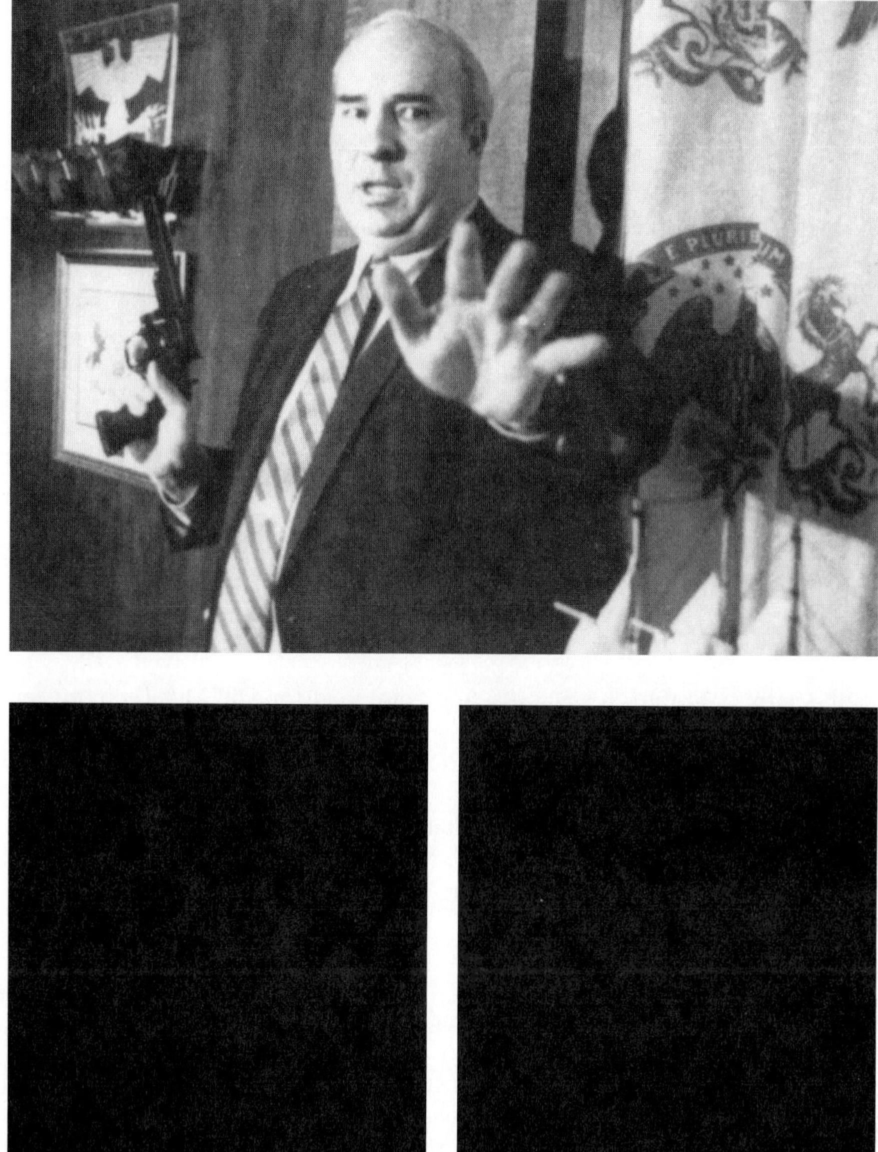

Figure 6–5 In 1987, a provocative series of three Associated Press photographs showed Pennsylvania treasurer R. Budd Dwyer motioning to reporters, putting a pistol in his mouth, and actually firing the shot that claimed his life. The first picture in the series is shown here; however, the other two are so graphic that ethical standards—not to mention good taste—precluded their presentation in this text. *(Courtesy AP/Wide World Photos)*

DISCUSSION STARTERS

1. How would you define *ethics?*
2. How would you describe the state of ethics in business, government, and journalism?
3. How important are ethics in the practice of public relations?
4. What two concepts underscore ethical conduct in public relations?
5. Compare the ethical codes of the Society of Professional Journalists and the Public Relations Society of America.
6. What is corporate social responsibility?
7. What are corporate codes of conduct?
8. What was the ethical dilemma in the case of Larry Speakes?
9. Is the public more or less tolerant of ethical violators today?
10. What is the significance, in terms of ethical practice, of Mike Milken,?

NOTES

1. "What Is Ethics?" *Issues in Ethics,* Center for Applied Ethics (October 1987): 2.
2. Fraser P. Seitel, "Ethics and Decency," *United States Banker* (April 1993): 58.
3. See Melvin L. Sharpe, "Exploring Questions of Media Morality," *Journal of Mass Media Ethics,* Vol. 4, No. 1 (1989): 113–115.
4. Paul Tharp, "'Double-crossing' PR Supremo Sued for $50 M," *The New York Post* (September 22, 1993): 33.
5. James Cox, "Kekst Under Fire in Paramount Fight," *USA Today* (October 12, 1993): B2.
6. "An Overview of a Landmark Roundtable Study of Corporate Ethics," *Roundtable Report* (February 1988): 1.
7. "Ethics in American Business," Touche Ross (January 1988).
8. Ibid.
9. Alan Cowell, "Fiat, in Scandal, Adopts Ethics Code," *The New York Times* (May 11, 1993).
10. Amanda Bennett, "Ethics Codes Spread Despite Skepticism," *The Wall Street Journal* (July 15, 1988): 18, 19.
11. Public Relations Society of America, study of ethical files, 1950–85, Foundation for Public Relations Research and Education, April 17, 1987, New York.
12. *Business Ethics Survey,* Minneapolis, MN.: The Pinnacle Group, Inc. (September 27, 1989).

SUGGESTED READINGS

Baker, Lee. *The Credibility Factor: Putting Ethics to Work in Public Relations.* Homewood, IL: Business One Irwin, 1992.

Beaucamp, Tom, and Norman E. Bowie, eds. *Ethical Theory and Business,* 3d ed. Englewood Cliffs, NJ: Prentice-Hall, 1988.

Behrman, Jack N. *Essays on Ethics in Business and the Professions.* Englewood Cliffs, NJ: Prentice-Hall, 1988.

TOP OF THE SHELF

Lee W. Baker, *The Credibility Factor: Putting Ethics to Work in Public Relations*. Homewood, Ill: Business One Irwin, 1992.

To Lee Baker, ethics is the foundation on which the mission of public relations rests. At the heart of public relations ethics, according to Baker, lies credibility.

In 319 pages, Baker takes on the leading ethical dilemmas in public relations—from the Reverend James Bakker to the Keating Five to Exxon and the *Valdez* to Union Carbide and Bhopal. In each case, Baker discusses the ethical issues involved and the ethical behavior—or lack thereof—that ensued.

In every case, Baker treats ethics as a practical problem rather than an intellectual exercise. The essence of his work, then, is a practical guide in dealing with ethical problems in public relations practice.

Since the subject of ethics is pivotal in any discussion of the practice of public relations, Lee Baker's contribution to the study of ethics—in particular, the critical element of credibility in public relations—is an important one that should be consulted.

Corporate Ethics: A Prime Business Asset. New York: Business Roundtable, February 1988. Members of TBR supplied information to develop this report on policy and practice in company conduct.

Dilenschneider, Robert L. *Power and Influence: Mastering the Art of Persuasion*. New York: Prentice-Hall, 1990.

Ethics in American Business. New York: Deloitte & Touche, January 1988. This report on ethical behavior is based on a poll of key business leaders.

Ferre, James. *Public Relations Ethics: A Bibliography*. Boston: G. K. Hall, 1991.

Fink, Conrad. *Media Ethics: In the Newsroom and Beyond*. New York: McGraw-Hill, 1988.

Foundation for Public Relations. New York, 1987.

Henderson, Verne E. *What's Ethical in Business*. New York: McGraw-Hill, 1992.

McElreath, Mark P. *Managing Systematic and Ethical Public Relations*. Dubuque, IA: Wm. C. Brown, 1993.

"An Overview of a Landmark Roundtable Study of Corporate Ethics." Roundtable Report. New York: Business Roundtable,

Posner, Ari. "The Culture of Plagiarism." *New Republic* (April 18, 1988): 19–24.

"PR Groups Combine on Code of Ethics." *Jack O'Dwyer's Newsletter* (May 18, 1988).

Sevareid, Eric. "Ethics and the Media." *Across the Board*. New York: Conference Board, May 1988: 12, 13.

Walton, Clarence. *The Moral Manager*. New York: Harper Business, 1990.

Ward, Gary. *Developing and Enforcing a Code of Business Ethics*. Babylon, NY: Pilot, 1989.

Weaver, Paul H. *The Suicidal Corporation*. New York: Simon & Schuster, 1988.

CASE STUDY

THE SAFRA SMEARS OF AMERICAN EXPRESS

Few companies were as well known for gold-plated integrity as the American Express Company. Chairman James Robinson cut a dashing swath in Washington, New York, and world capitals as a concerned, caring, and committed corporate leader.

The business community was therefore shocked to read, in a stunning disclosure in late 1989, that American Express admitted engaging in a covert campaign to ruin the reputation of a former colleague, Edmond Safra, by spreading rumors and stimulating articles in the international press. The company made a painful public apology for what its chairman called an "unauthorized and shameful effort," and paid $8 million to Mr. Safra and charities he selected. As part of the agreement, details of the "shameful effort" were to remain secret. Eventually, however, as inevitably happens to public citizens today, the events involving American Express and Mr. Safra became public.

American Express's problems with Mr. Safra began in the early 1980s, when it bought one of his former banks and hired Mr. Safra to manage it. But Mr. Safra soon tired of the corporate structure of American Express. He resigned as chairman and CEO of American Express International Banking Corporation at the end of 1984.

The international banker then turned his attention to his other principal holding, Republic New York Corporation, an American Express competitor. Accordingly, he began hiring international bankers away from American Express, ending up with as many as 23 American Express alumni over the next 4 years.

Apparently fearing that wealthy clients would abandon it, American Express formally opposed Mr. Safra's plans to seek a Swiss license and hired an investigator to gather information on its former colleague. Mr. Safra's successor at American Express allegedly put it this way, "If the son of a bitch competes with us, we'll turn him in to the IRS."

After Mr. Safra's Swiss license was approved in 1988, strange stories about him began appearing in the international press. One French newspaper linked him to the Mafia, South American drug traffickers, the CIA, and the Iran-Contra scandal.

And this was just the beginning. In the months that followed, articles appeared in papers throughout the world. One front-page profile from Peru linked Mr. Safra and his banks to drug-money laundering as the pawns of drug traffickers in New York.

The articles posed a potentially devastating attack on Safra's reputation for honesty and discretion. Private banking customers would be reluctant to deal with him. And just as Safra and his people debated what to do about the spate of nasty articles, a bombshell hit.

In Paris, a right wing, anti-Semitic newspaper charged that the Jewish Mr. Safra was actively involved with cocaine importers and the Mafia. "Billionaire of the White Stuff," the headline read.

Clearly, Mr. Safra concluded, there must be an organized campaign to destroy him. Mr. Safra had to find out who was behind it. So he sued the French paper.

As part of its documentation of Mr. Safra's underworld involvement, the paper produced a copy of a fax of an article dealing with the Mafia. Tiny lettering in one corner of the fax revealed that it had been sent from the corporate communications department of the American Express Company in New York.

Upon learning of American Express's involvement, Mr. Safra hired street-fighting New York attorney Stanley Arkin to get to the bottom of the smear campaign. And Arkin did.

Arkin accused the American Express director of communications, a close associate of Mr.

Robinson's for many years, of hiring a former ABC News investigative producer as a "secret weapon" against Safra. Her job, according to reports revealed later, was to influence the placement of anti-Safra articles in international publications.

By the spring of 1989, Safra had had enough. He met with Mr. Robinson, who reportedly said he would be "dumbfounded" if Safra's reports about an American Express smear campaign were true.

Arkin then turned up the heat on American Express. In his regular column for the *New York Law Journal,* he wrote a hypothetical story of a corporate executive who "cherishes his Boy Scout image" but whose "aides had spread rumors" that a competitor was involved in the drug business. "Spreading false or malicious rumors or flat-out lies may well amount to a criminal fraud," Arkin concluded.

Mr. Robinson got the message.

American Express lawyers began negotiating a settlement with Arkin. Soon thereafter, Robinson issued an apology to Safra on behalf of American Express and agreed to pay $8 million to Safra and to the charities he selected. Within a week of the apology, the American Express communications director announced his retirement and accepted "executive responsibility" for the campaign against Safra.

As a postscript to this unseemly affair, a year after its apology, American Express still denied that any of its employees knowingly spread false information. The company steadfastly declined to discuss details of the matter. Its attorney even went to the bizarre extreme of notifying *The Wall Street Journal* that he would "urge the company to sue" if it published defamatory statements about the anti-Safra campaign. The *Journal* responded with the longest article in its history, which dissected the whole sordid mess.

The *Journal* summarized, "For American Express, a company that has enjoyed a virtually unrivaled reputation for integrity, the Safra affair reveals a willingness to engage in unseemly corporate revenge when confronting a rival and, at the very least, a jarring lack of oversight on the part of top company officials."

As a postscript to the Safra affair, Robinson—for years an untouchable, "teflonesque" figure—was forced to step down from his post in 1993. While business reversals were the primary cause of Robinson's fall from grace, most observers also included as a contributing ingredient the hideous history of the smearing of Edmond Safra.

QUESTIONS

1. How would you describe the ethical implications of the American Express–Safra controversy?
2. How would you characterize the American Express settlement with Mr. Safra?
3. What is your view of the reaction of American Express and its lawyers to *The Wall Street Journal*'s 1990 inquiry of the case?
4. How does this case reflect on the ethics of the company, its chairman, and its communications department?

This case was largely based on Bryan Burrough, "How American Express Orchestrated a Smear of Rival Edmond Safra," *The Wall Street Journal*, September 24, 1990, A1, A27–28; Jeffrey A. Trachtenberg, "American Express Makes Apology to Safra," *The Wall Street Journal*, July 31, 1989, A3; and Jeffrey A. Trachtenberg, "Top American Express Official to Quit, Takes Responsibility for Safra Campaign," *The Wall Street Journal*, August 4, 1989, A3.

TIPS FROM THE TOP

BARBARA LEY TOFFLER

Barbara Ley Toffler is one of the nation's best-known authorities on the subject of ethics. A founding partner of Resources for Responsible Management in Boston, Toffler is a lecturer at the Yale School of Organization and Management. She served on the faculty of the Harvard Business School for eight years. She is the author of *Managers Talk Ethics: Making Tough Choices in a Competitive Business World*, published in 1991.

Are there any absolutes in dealing with ethics?
In the United States one has to start with the Judeo-Christian tradition. We believe that truth telling is an absolute. But, unfortunately, life today is a complicated exercise. For instance, what if telling the truth is harmful to someone else's sense of self-esteem? In most situations we're faced with competing claims—loyalty to an organization versus responsibility to the public, for example. Sometimes fulfilling one claim means having to compromise another. I dislike the negative implications of the term *situational ethics*, but, in reality, that's what usually applies.

What is the state of ethics in business?
Private industry clearly is struggling with ethical issues. Many companies are paying serious attention to creating an ethical environment in their firms and encouraging employees to act with integrity. The smart companies are those that take ethics seriously and realize that ethics can't be tacked on. It must be integrated into business goals, business practices, and the way that employees conduct themselves.

How do you solve an ethical problem in an organization?
First, you've got to talk to the key people, those who run the organization. Next, you must meet with other groups and elicit their views on issues and problems in

the organization. Then you must consider the environment in which the organization operates and what issues loom on the horizon. Then, like a doctor, you've got to diagnose the company and its problems so that you can both suggest preventive medicine and design and implement responses to existing conditions.

What is the state of ethics in government?
I wouldn't say the public sector is less ethical than others. But one of the most fascinating things I've noticed is that the public sector managers with whom I've dealt don't tend to think about ethics in terms of their own behavior. Rather, they think first about the constituencies they serve. A private sector manager, by contrast, focuses first on his or her behavior and is therefore more self-reflective. The reason that public sector people run into more difficulty in this area is not that they are less ethical, but rather they often don't know where to look.

What is the state of ethics in religion?
People who do pastoral counseling today struggle terribly with ethics and probably have the most difficulty in dealing successfully with ethical problems in complex situations. As professionals in religion, they feel obligated to enact that which is absolutely ethical. The stresses of dealing in a complex world make this particular charge difficult, if not impossible. A theologian might say, "I don't like any of the choices, so I won't decide." Well, often neither do we like our choices, but we *must* make a decision. A manager must always decide and act, and therein lies the ethical dilemma.

What is the state of ethics in public relations?
Public relations people have as difficult a job as anyone in society. Their role is to manage all of the boundaries between the organization and the outside world and within the organization itself. Consequently, they struggle mightily with difficult ethical problems all the time. If anything, they tend to err on the side of loyalty to and protection of the organization, which is their primary charge. Is that unethical? Again, it all depends.

How does one begin to act ethically?
First, spend time thinking about how others view the world. One critical word in ethics is *respect.* In fact, the Golden Rule falls a bit short. What it should say is, "Do unto others as you would have them do unto you—*if you were they.*" It takes empathy and understanding to settle conflicts. Another key word is *competence.* A manager can't be ethical unless he or she is also competent. Frankly, a great deal of unethical behavior in our society is attributable to incompetent people. Finally, because most ethical situations involve competing claims and complex situations where people can't simply apply what they believe, acting ethically also demands imagination. By imagination I don't mean creating stories to cover things up. Rather, I mean using an active, creative imagination to arrive at positive solutions that are also ethical.

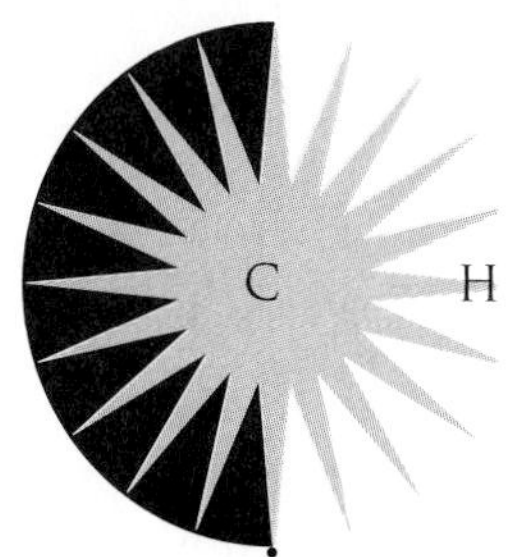

CHAPTER 7

MANAGEMENT

THE FIRST HALF OF THE 1990s WAS A PERIOD OF UNPRECEDENTED turbulence for the working class. Acquisitions, mergers, downsizings, layoffs, spinoffs, plant and company closings, and all the rest have had a great impact on the security of public relations positions. In a phrase, public relations positions are no longer secure.

Like most other organizational pursuits in an era of rising costs, shrinking resources, and increased competition, public relations must compete for its survival. As the year 2000 approaches, top management has begun to insist that public relations be run as a management process.

Like other management processes, professional public relations work emanates from clear strategies and bottom-line objectives that flow into specific tactics, each with its own budget, timetable, and allocation of resources. Stated another way, public relations today is much more a planned, persuasive social/managerial science than a knee-jerk, damage-control reaction to sudden flare-ups.

On the organizational level, as public relations has enhanced its overall stature, it has been brought increasingly into the general management structure of institutions. Indeed, the public relations function works most effectively when it reports directly to top management.

On the individual level, public relations practitioners are increasingly expected to have mastered a wide variety of technical communications skills, such as writing, editing, placement of articles, production of printed materials, and video programming. At the same time, by virtue of their relatively recent integration into the general management process, public relations professionals are expected to be fluent in management theory and technique. In other words, public relations practitioners themselves must be, in every sense of the word, managers.

REPORTING TO TOP MANAGEMENT

The public relations function, by definition, *must* report to top management. Often, alas, this is not the case, and public relations is subordinated to advertising or marketing or legal or human resources. This is a shame because, as noted in Chapter 1, public relations must be the interpreter of the organization—its philosophy, policy, and programs. These emanate from top management. Therefore, public relations must report to those who run the organization.

Increasingly, the public relations director reports directly to the CEO. The job of the public relations director consists of promoting the entire organization. If the public relations chief were to report to the director of marketing or advertising, the job would become one of promoting specific products. There's a big difference. The point is that if public relations is made subordinate to any other discipline—marketing, advertising, legal, administration, whatever—then its independence, credibility, and, ultimately, value as an objective, honest broker to management will be jeopardized.

Whereas the marketing and advertising groups must, by definition, be defenders of their specific products, the public relations department has no such mandated allegiance. Public relations, rightfully, should be the corporate conscience. An organization's public relations professionals should enjoy enough autonomy to deal openly and honestly with management. If an idea doesn't make sense, if a product is flawed, if the general institutional wisdom is wrong, it is the duty of the public relations professional to challenge the consensus.

This is not to say that advertising, marketing, and all other disciplines shouldn't enjoy a close partnership with public relations. Clearly, they must. All disciplines must work to maintain their own independence while building long-term, mutually beneficial relationships for the good of the organization. However, public relations should never shirk its overriding responsibility to enhance the organization's credibility by ensuring that corporate actions are in the public interest.

MANAGEMENT THEORY OF PUBLIC RELATIONS

In recent years, public relations has developed its own theoretical framework as a management system. The work of communications professors James Grunig and Todd Hunt, while not the only relevant management theory, nonetheless has done much to advance this development.[1] Grunig and Hunt suggest that public relations managers perform what organizational theorists call a *boundary role;* they function at the edge of an organization as a liaison between the organization and its external and internal publics. In other words, public relations managers have one foot inside the organization and one outside. Often, this unique position is not only lonely but also precarious.

As boundary managers, public relations people support their colleagues by helping them communicate across organizational lines both within and outside the organization. In this way, public relations professionals also become systems managers, knowledgeable about and able to deal with the complex relationships inherent in the organization.

- They must consider the relationship of the organization to its environment—the ties that unite business managers and operations support staff, for example, and the conflicts that separate them.
- They must work within organizational confines to develop innovative solutions to organizational problems. By definition, public relations managers deal in a different environment from that of their organizational colleagues. Public relations people deal with perceptions, attitudes, and public opinion. Other business managers deal in a more empirical, quantitative, concrete domain. Public relations managers, therefore, must be innovative, not only in proposing communications solutions, but also in making them understandable and acceptable to colleagues.
- They must think strategically. Public relations managers must demonstrate their knowledge of the organization's mission, objectives, and strategies. Their solutions must answer the real needs of the organization. They must reflect the big picture. Business managers will care little that the company's name was mentioned in the morning paper unless they can recognize the strategic rationale for the reference.
- Public relations managers must also be willing to measure their results. They must state clearly what they want to accomplish, systematically set out to accomplish it, and measure their success. This means using such accepted business school techniques as management by objectives (MBO), management by objectives and results (MOR), and program evaluation and research technique (PERT).
- Finally, as Grunig and Hunt point out, in managing an organization's public relations system, practitioners must demonstrate comfort with the various elements of the organization itself: (1) functions, the real jobs of organizational components; (2) structure, the organizational hierarchy of individuals and positions; (3) processes, the formal decision-making rules and procedures the organization follows; and (4) feedback, the formal and informal evaluative mechanisms of the organization.[2]

Such a theoretical overview is important to consider in properly situating the practice of public relations as a management system within an organization.

PLANNING FOR PUBLIC RELATIONS

Like research, planning in public relations is essential not only to know where a particular campaign is headed but also to win the support of top management. Indeed, one of the most frequent complaints about public relations is that it is too much a seat-of-the-pants activity, impossible to plan and difficult to measure. Clearly, planning in public relations must be given greater shrift. With proper planning, public relations professionals can indeed defend and account for their actions.

Before organizing for public relations work, practitioners must consider objectives and strategies, planning and budgets, and research and evaluation. The broad environment in which the organization operates must dictate overall business objectives. These, in turn, dictate specific public relations objectives and strategies. And once these have been defined, the task of organizing for a public relations program should flow naturally.

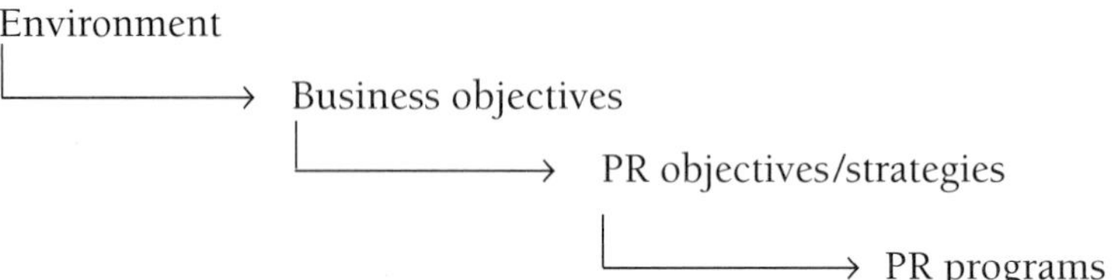

Setting objectives, formulating strategies, and planning are essential if the public relations function is to be considered equal in stature to other organizational components. Planning requires thinking. Planning a short-term public relations program to promote a new service may require less thought and time than planning a longer-term campaign to win support for a public policy issue. However, in each case, the public relations plan must include clear-cut objectives to achieve organizational goals, strategies to reach those objectives, tactics to implement the strategies, and measurement to determine whether the tactics worked.

Among the most important aspects of public relations practice is setting clear goals, objectives, and targets for the tactics applied. Public relations activities are meaningless unless designed to accomplish certain measurable goals.

For example, consider the following elementary public relations plan:

I. *Environment*

We need to increase product sales in the local market. Currently we are number three in the market, running close behind the second-place supplier but far behind the market leader.

II. *Business objectives*

Our goal is to build market share for our product in the local area. We seek to surpass the number-two provider and edge closer to number one.

III. *Public relations objectives*

- Confirm our company's solid commitment to local customers.
- Convince potential customers that our company offers the staff, expertise, products, and responsiveness that match their needs.
- Position our company as formidable competition to the two market leaders.

IV. *Public relations strategies*

Position our company as the expert in the market through company-sponsored surveys and research directed at local decision makers; media placement of company-related articles; speaking platforms of company executives; and company-sponsored seminars to demonstrate our expertise.

V. *Public relations programs/tactics*

- Seek media placements and bylined articles discussing company products for local media.
- Solicit profile features and interviews with company officials on an exclusive basis with leading trade publications.
- Sponsor a quarterly survey of local companies. Mail the survey to local decision makers, focus on a current topic of concern, and offer information and comment from the customer's view.
- Sponsor four seminars a year for emerging product-using companies in the local area. Tailor each seminar to particular audiences—women, minorities, small businesses, specific industries, not-for-profit groups, etc. Seminars should feature company experts and well-known outside speakers. Thus, they should reinforce our commitment to the local market and also stimulate publicity.
- Launch a company speakers bureau wherein company speakers address important groups throughout the area.

After the adoption of such public relations programs, the success or failure of the campaign must be evaluated. In devising the public relations plan along these lines, an organization is assured that public relations programs will reinforce and complement its overall business goals.

MANAGING BY PUBLIC RELATIONS OBJECTIVES

An organization's goals must define what its public relations goals will be, and the only good goals are ones that can be measured. Public relations objectives and the strategies that flow from them, like those in other business areas, must be results oriented. As the baseball pitcher Johnny Sain used to say, "Nobody wants to hear about the labor pains, but everyone wants to see the baby."

So, too, must public relations people think strategically. Strategies are the most crucial decisions of a public relations campaign. They answer the general question "How will we manage our resources to achieve our goals?" The specific answers then become the public relations tactics used to implement the strategies. Ideally, strategies and tactics should profit from pretesting.

As for objectives, good ones stand up to the following questions:

- Do they clearly describe the end result expected?
- Are they understandable to everyone in the organization?
- Do they list a firm completion date?
- Are they realistic, attainable, and measurable?
- Are they consistent with management's objectives?[3]

Increasingly, public relations professionals are managing by objectives, adopting MBO and MOR techniques to help quantify the value of public relations in an organization. The two questions most frequently asked by general managers of public relations practitioners are "How can we measure public relations results?" and "How do we know whether the public relations program is making progress?" MBO can provide public relations professionals with a powerful source of feedback. MBO and MOR tie public relations results to management's predetermined objectives. Even though procedures for implementing MBO programs differ, most programs share four points:

1. Specification of the organization's goals, with objective measures of the organization's performance.
2. Conferences between the superior and the subordinate to agree on achievable goals.

British Air's Image Shakeup

Early in 1992, British Airways announced several management changes, including the resignation of its popular chairman and its chief public relations officer. The latter reportedly had taken part in unethical practices to undermine the airline's primary competitor.

The trouble began when the flamboyant founder of Virgin Atlantic Airlines, Richard Branson, accused British Air of conducting a smear campaign against them and of using unethical and perhaps illegal measures to win away Virgin's customers and monitor the airline's activities. British Air's director of public affairs was named in numerous reports in the British press as a key participant in the campaign to win passengers away from Virgin.

In a campaign reminiscent of the American Express juggernaut to derail the reputation of Edmond Safra, British Air allegedly orchestrated scurrilous stories about Branson's character and activities. Ultimately, Branson sued.

To settle the matter, in 1993 British Airways paid Virgin and Branson $945,000 in damages and assumed $3,000,000 in legal expenses.

Shortly thereafter, British Air's Chairman Lord King, who had presided over the company for nearly 12 years and led it through its privatization by the government, was replaced by Sir Colin Marshall as the airline's CEO.

Lord King was replaced despite his protests that "lower-level employees," acting without the knowledge and approval of the board and top management, were responsible for the dirty tricks.

Shortly after seizing the reigns at British Air, Sir Colin adopted an aggressive, forthright, and personalized campaign to win public approval of British Air's proposed investment in US Air.

One presumes that the new management of British Air was hopeful that the new, more candid communications approach would help wash away the ethical stain that developed during the prior management's regime. Is such a strategy sensible?

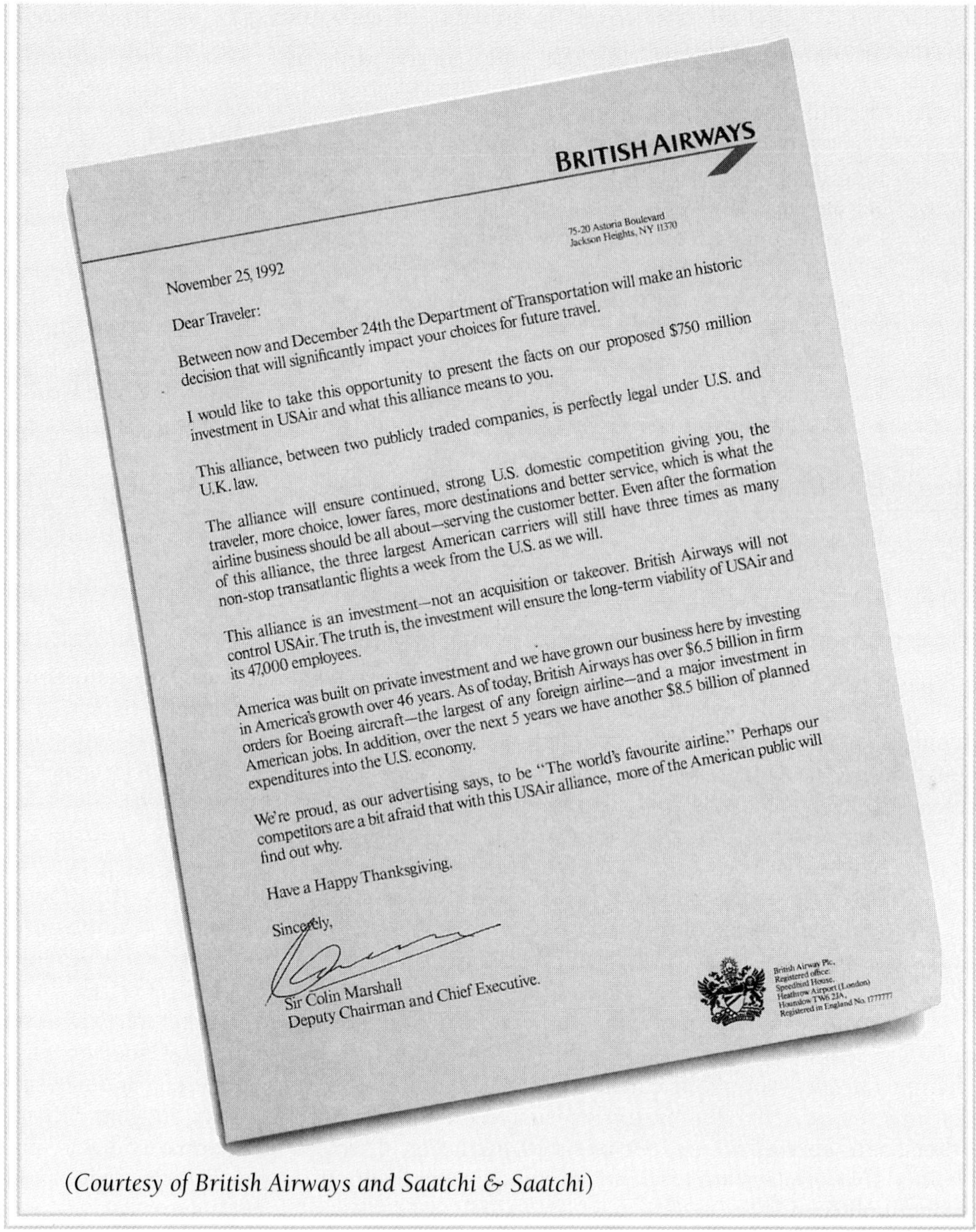

BRITISH AIRWAYS

75-20 Astoria Boulevard
Jackson Heights, NY 11370

November 25, 1992

Dear Traveler:

Between now and December 24th the Department of Transportation will make an historic decision that will significantly impact your choices for future travel.

I would like to take this opportunity to present the facts on our proposed $750 million investment in USAir and what this alliance means to you.

This alliance, between two publicly traded companies, is perfectly legal under U.S. and U.K. law.

The alliance will ensure continued, strong U.S. domestic competition giving you, the traveler, more choice, lower fares, more destinations and better service, which is what the airline business should be all about—serving the customer better. Even after the formation of this alliance, the three largest American carriers will still have three times as many non-stop transatlantic flights a week from the U.S. as we will.

This alliance is an investment—not an acquisition or takeover. British Airways will not control USAir. The truth is, the investment will ensure the long-term viability of USAir and its 47,000 employees.

America was built on private investment and we have grown our business here by investing in America's growth over 46 years. As of today, British Airways has over $6.5 billion in firm orders for Boeing aircraft—the largest of any foreign airline—and a major investment in American jobs. In addition, over the next 5 years we have another $8.5 billion of planned expenditures into the U.S. economy.

We're proud, as our advertising says, to be "The world's favourite airline." Perhaps our competitors are a bit afraid that with this USAir alliance, more of the American public will find out why.

Have a Happy Thanksgiving.

Sincerely,

Sir Colin Marshall
Deputy Chairman and Chief Executive.

British Airways Plc,
Registered office:
Speedbird House,
Heathrow Airport (London)
Hounslow TW6 2JA,
Registered in England No. 1777777

(Courtesy of British Airways and Saatchi & Saatchi)

3. Agreement between the superior and the subordinate on objectives consistent with the organization's goals.
4. Periodic reviews by the superior and the subordinate to assess progress toward achieving the goals.

Again, the key is to tie public relations goals to the goals of the organization and then to manage progress toward achieving those goals. The goals themselves should be clearly defined and specific, practical and attainable, and measurable.

The key to using MBO effectively in public relations work can be broken down into seven critical steps:

1. Defining the nature and mission of the work.
2. Determining key result areas in terms of time, effort, and personnel.
3. Identifying measurable factors on which objectives can be set.
4. Setting objectives/determining results to be achieved.
5. Preparing tactical plans to achieve specific objectives, including
    - Programming to establish a sequence of actions to follow.
    - Scheduling to set time requirements for each step.
    - Budgeting to assign the resources required to reach the goals.
    - Fixing individual accountability for the accomplishment of the objectives.
    - Reviewing and reconciling through a testing procedure to track progress.
6. Establishing rules and regulations to follow.
7. Establishing procedures to handle the work.[4]

UDGETING FOR PUBLIC RELATIONS

Like any other business activity, public relations programs must be based on sound budgeting. After identifying objectives and strategies, the public relations professional must detail the particular tactics that will help achieve those objectives. No organization can spend indiscriminately. And without a realistic budget, no organization can succeed. Likewise, public relations activities must be disciplined by budgetary realities.

The key to budgeting may lie in performing two steps: (1) estimating the extent of the resources—both personnel and purchases—needed to accomplish each activity and (2) estimating the cost and availability of those resources.[5] With this information in hand, the development of a budget and monthly cash flow for a public relations program becomes easier. Such data also provide the milestones necessary to audit program costs on a routine basis and to make adjustments well in advance of budget crises.

Most public relations programs operate on limited budgets. Therefore, whenever possible, adaptable programs—which can be readily recycled and redesigned to meet changing needs—should be considered. For example, television, magazine, and newspaper advertising generally are too expensive for most public relations budgets. On the other hand, special events, personalized literature, direct mail, personal contacts, and promotional displays are the kinds of inexpensive communications vehicles that can be easily duplicated.[6]

One way to ensure that budgets are adhered to is to practice the process of open bidding for public relations materials and suppliers. An open bidding process allows several vendors to demonstrate how they would fulfill the specifications enumerated for the job. These specifications should take into account programmatic considerations in terms of both quality and quantity. Public relations budgets should be reasonable—ordinarily, a fraction (10 percent or so)—of advertising budgets and flexible enough to withstand midcourse corrections and unexpected cost overruns.

Most public relations agencies treat client costs in a manner similar to that used by legal, accounting, and management consulting firms: The client pays only for services rendered, often against an established monthly minimum for staff time. Time records are kept by every employee—from chairperson to mail clerk—on a daily basis to be sure that agency clients know exactly what they are paying for.

REPARING THE PUBLIC RELATIONS CAMPAIGN PLAN

The public relations campaign puts all of the aspects of public relations planning—objectives, strategies, research, tactics, and evaluation—into one cohesive framework. The plan specifies a series of "whats" to be done and "hows" to get them done—whatever is necessary to reach the objectives.

Again, the public relations plan must track the strategies and objectives of the organization. Accordingly, the "blueprint" for the public relations campaign should be the R-A-C-E approach to public relations, defined in Chapter 1. Time should be taken in advance to determine what public relations approaches and activities are most likely to reach organizational goals. Every aspect of the public relations plan should be designed to be meaningful and valuable to the organization.

The skeleton of a typical public relations campaign plan resembles the following:

1. **Backgrounding the problem** This is the so-called situation analysis, background, or case statement that specifies the major aims of the campaign. It can be a general statement that refers to audiences, known research, the organization's positions, history, and the obstacles faced in reaching the desired goal. A public relations planner should divide the overriding goal into several subordinate objectives, which are the "whats" to be accomplished.
2. **Preparing a proposal** The second stage of the campaign plan sketches broad approaches to solve the problem at hand. It outlines the strategies—the "hows"—and the public relations tools to be used to fulfill the objectives. The elements of the public relations proposal may vary, depending on subject matter, but generally include the following:

   - *Situational analysis*—description of the challenge as it currently exists, including background on how the situation reached its present state.
   - *Scope of assignment*—description of the nature of the assignment: what the public relations program will attempt to do.
   - *Target audiences*—specific targets identified and divided into manageable groups.
   - *Research methods*—specific research approach to be used.
   - *Key messages*—specific selected appeals: What do we want to tell our audiences? How do we want them to feel about us? What do we want them to do?
   - *Communications vehicles*—tactical communications devices to be used.
   - *Project team*—key players who will participate in the program.
   - *Timing and fees*—a timetable with proposed costs identified.

   The specific elements of any proposal depend on the unique nature of the program itself. When an outside supplier submits a proposal, additional elements—such as cancellation clauses, confidentiality of work, and references—should also be included.

3. **Activating the plan** The third stage of a campaign plan details operating tactics. It may also contain a time chart specifying when each action will take place. Specific activities are defined, people are assigned to them, and deadlines are established. This stage forms the guts of the campaign plan.
4. **Evaluating the campaign** To find out whether the plan worked, evaluation methods should be spelled out here.

    - Did we implement the activities we proposed?
    - Did we receive appropriate public recognition for our efforts?
    - Did attitudes change—among the community, customers, management—as a result of our programs?

    Pretesting and posttesting of audience attitudes, quantitative analysis of event attendance, content analysis of media success, surveys, sales figures, staff reports, letters to management, and feedback from others—the specific method of evaluative testing is up to the practitioner. But the inclusion of a mechanism for evaluation is imperative.[7]

A public relations campaign plan should always be spelled out—in writing—so that planners can keep track of progress and management can assess results. And although planning in public relations is important and should be taken more seriously than it presently is by public relations professionals, the caveat of management gurus Thomas Peters and Robert Waterman must always be considered: "The problem is that the planning becomes an end in itself."[8] In public relations this cannot be allowed. No matter how important planning may be, public relations is assessed principally in terms of its action, performance, and practice.

PUBLIC RELATIONS TACTICS

The duties and responsibilities of public relations practitioners are as diverse as the publics with whom different institutions deal. For example, here is a partial list of potential public relations duties:

1. **Reaching the employees** through a variety of internal means, including newsletters, television, and meetings. Traditionally, this role has emphasized news-oriented communications rather than benefits-oriented ones, which are usually the province of personnel departments.
2. **Coordinating relationships with the print and electronic media**, which includes arranging and monitoring press interviews, writing news releases and related press materials, organizing press conferences, and answering media inquiries and requests. A good deal of media relations work consists of attempting to gain favorable news coverage for the firm.
3. **Coordinating activities with legislators** on local, state, and federal levels. This includes legislative research activities and public policy formation.
4. **Orchestrating interaction with the community**, perhaps including open houses, tours, and employee volunteer efforts designed to reflect the supportive nature of the organization to the community.

PR SALARIES GOING UP, UP, UP!

Public relations may once have been a corporate backwater, but at least in terms of executive salaries, it is a stepchild no longer.

By 1994, an increasing number of public relations executives around the country earned upwards of $200,000 in salary and bonus. At least one public relations professional approached the $1 million per year mark.

According to its 1992 proxy statement, Time Warner paid Communications Director Todd Hullin a salary and bonus of $906,250. In addition to his pay, Hullin was awarded stock options that, at the time, were worth nearly $2 million.

At Philip Morris, Corporate Affairs Vice President Craig L. Fuller, a former White House chief of staff, reportedly received a similar compensation package.

And public relations agency executives, whose remuneration wasn't available to the public, also received extremely high compensation. Of course, public relations salaries paled in comparison to those of the chief executives of America's largest corporations, led by the $34 million of Stephen A. Wynn of Mirage Resorts, $16 million of P. Roy Vagelos of Merck, and $15 million of John F. Welch of General Electric.

Nonetheless, by the mid-1990s, the compensation awarded to top public relations professionals was every bit as bountiful as that of other organizational executives.

5. **Managing relations with the investment community**, including the firm's present and potential stockholders. This task emphasizes personal contact with securities analysts, institutional investors, and private investors.
6. **Supporting activities with customers and potential customers**, with activities ranging from hard-sell product promotion activities to "soft" consumer advisory services.
7. **Coordinating the institution's printed voice with its publics** through reprints of speeches, annual reports, quarterly statements, and product and company brochures.
8. **Coordinating relationships with outside specialty groups**, such as suppliers, educators, students, nonprofit organizations, and competitors.
9. **Managing the institutional—or nonproduct—advertising image**, as well as being called on increasingly to assist in the management of more traditional product advertising.
10. **Coordinating the graphic and photographic services** of the organization. To do this task well requires knowledge of typography, layout, and art.
11. **Conducting opinion research**, which involves assisting in the public policy formation process through the coordination and interpretation of attitudinal studies of key publics.

12. **Managing the gift-giving apparatus**, which ordinarily consists of screening and evaluating philanthropic proposals and allocating the organization's available resources.
13. **Coordinating special events**, including travel for company management, corporate celebrations and exhibits, dinners, ground-breakings, and grand openings.
14. **Management counseling**, which involves advising administrators on alternative options and recommended choices in light of public responsibilities.

ORGANIZING THE PUBLIC RELATIONS DEPARTMENT

Once an organization has analyzed its environment, established its objectives, set up measurement standards, and thought about appropriate programs and budgets, it is ready to organize a public relations department. Departments range from one-person operations to those of firms such as General Motors, with a staff of more than 200 persons (half professionals and half support staff) responsible for relations with the press, investors, civic groups, employees, and governments around the world.

In the mid-90s, many corporate public relations departments suffered the ravages of downsizing and decentralization. The former has led to the shrinkage of once-large operations. The latter has led to the formation of decentralized, line-oriented departments to complement smaller central units. What's the best way to organize for public relations in an organization? There is no one answer. However, again, the strongest public relations department is one led by a communications executive who reports directly to the CEO. This is eminently preferable to reporting to a legal or financial or administrative executive, who may tend to "filter" top management messages.

In government, public relations professionals typically report directly to department heads. In universities, the public relations function is frequently coupled with fund-raising and development activities. In hospitals, public relations is typically tied to the marketing function.

As for the names of the departments in which public relations is housed, organizations use a wide variety of names for the function. Ironically, the trend in the 1990s seems to be away from use of the traditional term *public relations* and toward *corporate communications* (Figure 7–1). In one comprehensive analysis, about 30 percent of the organizations surveyed still used *public relations*, whereas *corporate communications* or just plain *communications* was used by nearly 20 percent. About 8 percent used *public affairs*, and another 8 percent used *advertising/public relations*. Among the other titles in use were *corporate relations* and *public information*.[9]

ORGANIZING THE PUBLIC RELATIONS AGENCY

The biggest difference between an external agency and an internal department is perspective. The former is outside looking in; the latter is inside looking out (often literally for itself). Sometimes the use of an agency is necessary to escape the tunnel-vision syndrome that afflicts some firms, in which a detached viewpoint is desperately needed. An

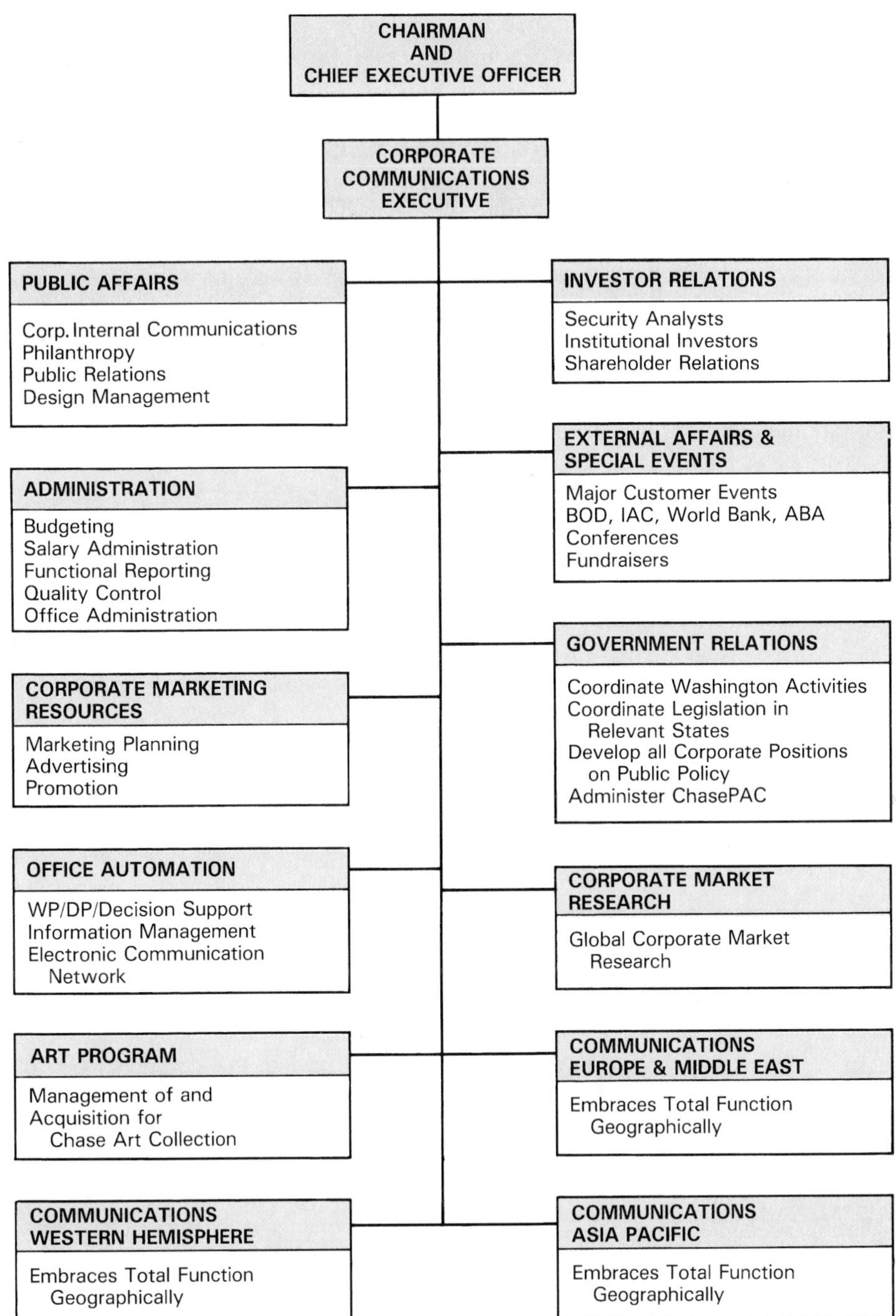

Figure 7–1 Chase Manhattan Bank's communications operation is headquartered in the Corporate Communications Group, reporting to the bank's CEO. Corporate Communications is composed of 100 professionals, who perform a variety of discrete functions. *(Courtesy of Chase Manhattan Bank)*

agency unfettered by internal corporate politics might be better trusted to present management with an objective reading of the concerns of its publics.

An agency has the added advantage of not being taken for granted by a firm's management. Unfortunately, management sometimes has a greater regard for an outside specialist than for an inside one. This attitude frequently defies logic but is nonetheless often true. Generally, if management is paying (sometimes quite handsomely) for outside counsel, it tends to listen carefully to the advice.

Agencies generally organize according to industry and account teams. Larger agencies are divided into such areas as health care, sports, fashion, technology, finance, and so on. Account teams are assigned specific clients. Team members bill clients on an hourly basis, with the intention of most firms being to retain as income two-thirds of each individual's hourly billing rate. In other words, if an account executive bills at a rate of $300 per hour—and many senior counselors do—the firm expects to retain $200 of that rate toward its profit. In recent years, as clients have begun to manage resources more rigorously, larger agencies have found it increasingly difficult to manage their overheads.[10] Adding to the problem, seven of the top 10 public relations agencies are owned by larger advertising agencies, intensely concerned about escalating public relations costs.

As a consequence, the leading gainers in recent years among public relations agencies have been independent firms, many of them smaller entrepreneurial ventures[11] (Table 7–1).

Public relations counsel is, by definition, a highly personalized service. A counselor's prescription for a client depends primarily on what the counselor thinks a client needs and how that assessment fits the client's own perception of those needs. Often an

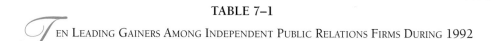

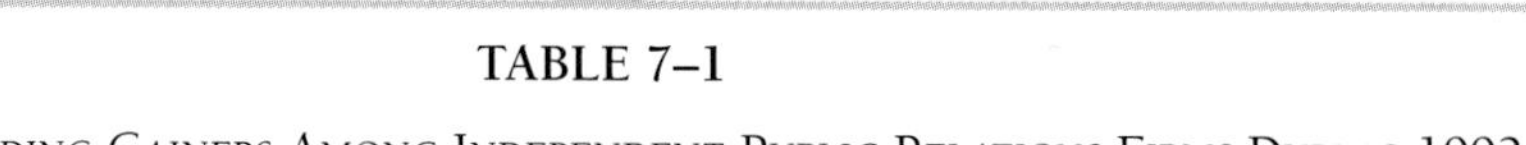

TABLE 7–1

TEN LEADING GAINERS AMONG INDEPENDENT PUBLIC RELATIONS FIRMS DURING 1992

	Firm	*1992 Fee Income*	*Percent Gain*
1.	Molino + Associates	$ 864,000	148
2.	Smith & Harroff	3,107,000	88
3.	Pacific/West Communications	3,819,000	60
4.	Noonan Russo Communications	2,290,000	59
5.	Pantin Partnership	570,000	55
6.	Morgen-Walke Associates	5,531,000	51
7.	Jefferson Group	7,383,000	50
8.	Patrice Tanaka & Co.	1,787,000	50
9.	Thomas Associates	1,187,000	45
10.	Morgan & Meyers	3,454,000	43

Source: O'Dwyers PR Services Report (May 1993): 25.

outsider's fresh point of view is helpful in focusing a client on particular problems and opportunities and on how best to conquer or capitalize on them.

On the other hand, because outside agencies are just that—outside—they are often unfamiliar about details affecting the situation of particular companies and with the idiosyncrasies of company management. The good external counselor must constantly work to overcome this barrier. The best client–agency relationships are those with free-flowing communications between internal and external public relations groups so that both resources are kept informed about corporate policies, strategies, and tactics. A well-oiled, complementary department–agency relationship can result in a more positive communications approach for an organization.

WHAT'S IT PAY?

Without question the communications function has increased in importance and clout. Top communications professionals in many large corporations today draw compensation packages well into six figures. Entry-level jobs for writers and editors generally fall into the $20,000–$30,000 range. Managers of public relations units, press relations, consumer relations, financial communications, and the like may earn anywhere from $40,000 to $100,000. Public relations directors may range in salary from $30,000 to upward of $300,000 (Table 7–2). Public relations agency salaries may be a bit higher in some cases than corporate staff salaries because account executives are on the line earning income for the firm (Table 7–3). But job security in an agency is usually less than that offered by a corporation, which also isn't what it used to be.

TABLE 7–2

COMPARISON OF 1989 AND 1988 MEDIAN SALARIES OF PUBLIC RELATIONS/PUBLIC AFFAIRS PRACTITIONERS IN THE UNITED STATES AND CANADA

					Median Salary	
Age Groups	*Percent of Total*	*Percent Men*	*Percent Women*	*Overall*	*Men*	*Women*
All (US and Canada)		44.4	55.6	$46,000	$54,000	$40,000
24 & under	0.1	0.0	100.0	____*	____*	____*
25–29	11.8	20.5	79.5	$30,000	$28,000	$30,000
30–34	14.0	29.5	69.9	$37,950	$42,750	$36,400
35–39	17.9	37.7	61.8	$45,000	$48,000	$43,000
40–49	32.7	50.8	48.9	$52,000	$59,500	$46,540
50–59	16.4	63.4	36.1	$60,000	$68,000	$50,000
60–64	4.4	64.6	35.4	$51,500	$60,750	$45,000
65+	1.5	47.1	52.9	$65,000	$70,000	$57,000
No Response	1.2	14.3	85.7			

Source: PR Reporter (October 1, 1990): 2.
*Sample size too small to compute valid median

TABLE 7–3

1993 PR FEE INCOME OF 50 FIRMS SUPPLYING DOCUMENTING FEES

(A) means ad agency related

		1993 Net Fees	*Employees*	*% Fee Change from 1992*
1.	Burson-Marsteller (A)	$192,491,000	1,739	−5.5
2.	Shandwick	151,800,000	1,808	−8.6
3.	Hill and Knowlton (A)	140,000,000	1,202	−5.0
4.	Omnicom PR Network (A)	85,852,418	1,157	+31.0
5.	Fleishman-Hillard	69,518,000	608	+18.5
6.	Edelman Public Relations Worldwide	63,351,064	745	+5.91
7.	Ketchum Public Relations (A)	50,100,000	432	+9.9
8.	The Rowland Co. (A)	38,000,000	391	−13.6
9.	Robinson Lake/Sawyer Miller/Bozell (A)	37,600,000	235	+14.0
10.	Manning, Selvage & Lee (A)	31,321,000	290	−0.3
11.	Ogilvy Adams & Rinehart (A)	30,105,000	285	−16.7
12.	Ruder Finn	27,162,219	256	+0.3
13.	GCI Group (A)	26,397,716	353	−6.0
14.	Cohn & Wolfe (A)	14,093,000	117	−0.89
15.	Financial Relations Board	12,485,452	141	+21.6
16.	Powell Tate	9,605,817	73	+9.2
17.	Gibbs & Soell	8,453,726	90	−4.3
18.	Stoorza, Ziegaus & Metzger	8,193,940	113	+15.7
19.	Cunningham Communication	8,086,970	84	+15.5
20.	Morgen-Walke Assocs.	7,485,958	71	+35.4
21.	The Jefferson Group	7,424,423	53	+0.5
22.	The Kamber Group	7,338,723	84	−1.0
23.	E. Bruce Harrison Co.	6,550,991	58	+12.4
24.	Dix & Eaton	6,478,338	57	+20.76
25.	Nelson Comms. Group & Nelson, Robb, DuVal & DeMenna	5,479,230	45	+40.4

SOURCE: 1994 O'Dwyer's Directory of PR Firms.

WHAT MANNER OF MAN/WOMAN?

What kind of individual does it take to become a competent public relations professional?

In order to make it, a public relations professional ought to possess a set of specific, technical skills, as well as an appreciation of the proper attitudinal approach to the job. On the technical side, these six skills are important:

TABLE 7–3 (CONTINUED)

1993 PR Fee Income of 50 Firms Supplying Documenting Fees

(A) means ad agency related

		1993 Net Fees	*Employees*	*% Fee Change from 1992*
26.	Earle Palmer Brown Cos. (A)	5,440,849	50	−27.4
27.	Pacific/West Communications Group	5,309,440	38	+39.0
28.	MWW/Strategic Communications	5,169,951	53	+59.5
29.	Dewe Rogerson	5,148,000	42	+38.0
30.	EvansGroup PR Division (A)	5,067,782	40	+70.0
31.	The Weber Group	5,005,570	63	+9.5
32.	Padilla Speer Beardsley	4,804,485	55	−6.0
33.	Copithorne & Bellows	4,683,875	35	+35.3
34.	S&S Public Relations	4,245,000	45	+5.3
35.	Anthony M. Franco	4,200,000	50	−16.8
36.	Makovsky & Co.	4,125,000	42	+35.8
37.	The Rockey Company	4,032,086	43	−16.2
38.	Cone Communications	4,012,011	37	+22.0
39.	Public Communications	3,855,327	44	−5.9
40.	Jasculca-Terman & Assocs.	3,818,128	36	−7.7
41.	Dye, Van Mol & Lawrence	3,803,700	64	+2.4
42.	Morgan & Meyers	3,748,718	59	+8.5
43.	Lobsenz-Stevens	3,698,450	43	+9.6
44.	Watt, Roop & Co.	3,628,779	24	+43.5
45.	KCSA PR	3,356,000	34	+0.3
46.	Dennis Davidson Assocs.	3,355,828	50	−7.0
47.	Bader Rutter & Assocs. (A)	3,353,600	43	+7.3
48.	Gross Townsend Frank Hoffman (A)	3,327,864	29	−2.0
49.	Taylor-Rafferty Assocs.	3,278,774	18	+15.0
50.	Edward Howard & Co.	3,193,190	35	−16.3

1. **Knowledge of the field**—the underpinnings of public relations, culture and history, philosophy, and social psychology
2. **Communications knowledge**—the media and the ways in which they work, communications research, and, most important, the writing process
3. **Knowledge of what's going on around you**—current events and factors that influence society: literature, language, politics, economics, and all the rest—from Bosnia to Somalia; from a unified Germany to a divided Lebanon; from Dr. Kevorkian to Dr. Dre; from John Major to Michael Jackson. A public relations professional must be, in the truest sense, a Renaissance man or woman.
4. **Business knowledge**—how business works, a bottom-line orientation, and a knowledge of one's company and industry

5. **Knowledge of bureaucracy**—how to get things done in a bureaucratic organization, how to use and gain power for the best advantage, and how to maneuver in a politically charged environment
6. **Management knowledge**—how public policy is shaped and the various pressures on and responsibilities of senior managers

In terms of attitude, public relations professionals ought to possess the following four characteristics:

1. **Communications orientation**—a bias toward disclosing rather than withholding information. Public relations professionals should *want* to communicate with the public. They should practice the belief that the public has a right to know.
2. **Advocacy**—a desire to be advocates for their employers. Public relations people must stand up for what their employers represent. Although they should never distort, lie, or hide facts, occasionally it may be in an organization's best interest to avoid comment on certain issues. If practitioners don't believe in the integrity and credibility of their employers, their most honorable course is to quit.
3. **Counseling orientation**—a compelling desire to advise senior managers. As noted, top executives are used to dealing in tangibles, such as balance sheets, costs per thousand, and cash flows. Public relations practitioners understand the intangibles, such as public opinion, media influence, and communications messages. Practitioners must be willing to support their beliefs—often in opposition to lawyers or personnel executives. They must even be willing to disagree with management at times. Far from being compliant, public relations practitioners must have the gumption to say "no."
4. **Personal confidence**—a strong sense of honesty and ethics, a willingness to take risks, and, not unimportant, a sense of humor. Public relations professionals must have the courage of their convictions and the personal confidence to represent proudly a curious—yet critical—role in any organization.

In recent years many more women have joined the public relations ranks. Women now account for just under half of all practitioners but still earn substantially less than men. For example, the median salary of public relations professionals, according to one survey, was $55,000 for men but only $39,000 for women.[12]

The issue of increased feminization, as noted, is a particularly thorny one for the practice of public relations. University public relations sequences across the country report a preponderance of female students, outnumbering males by as much as 80 percent. In public relations practice, too, women now outnumber men. However, the ranks of women executives in public relations, as opposed to their male counterparts, are still woefully thin. Hence the picture of, on the one hand, public relations becoming a "velvet ghetto" of women workers and, on the other hand, a profession in which women have not achieved upper-management status. This is a paramount concern to the profession.

In addition to gender gap problems, there is the issue of minority public relations professionals. According to the Bureau of Labor Statistics, only 7 percent of public relations professionals are minorities—one-third less than the national average for minorities in professional fields. To help more minorities enter the field, in 1990 the Public

Relations Society of America announced a program of scholarships and internships at public relations agencies for minority professionals.

SUMMARY

In recent years, the practice of public relations has become accepted not only as part of the marketing mix, but as part of the management process of any well-run organization.

Public relations objectives and goals, strategies, and tactics must flow directly from the organization's overall goals. Public relations strategies must reflect organizational strategies, and tactics must be designed to realize the organization's business objectives.

So, despite its stereotypes and demographic idiosyncrasies, public relations requires neither a false smile nor a glad hand. Rather, it demands a solid grounding in all aspects of professional communications, human relations, and judgmental and learning skills. Most of all, it takes hard work.

DISCUSSION STARTERS

1. Describe the elements of a public relations plan.
2. How does MBO relate to public relations?
3. How are public relations objectives derived?
4. What elements go into framing a public relations budget?
5. What are the four general steps in preparing a public relations campaign plan?
6. What activities are included in the scope of public relations practice?
7. What is the ideal reporting relationship for a director of public relations?
8. What are the technical skills that a public relations professional should possess?
9. What kinds of attitudinal characteristics should a public relations professional possess?
10. What is meant by the term *velvet ghetto*?

NOTES

1. James E. Grunig and Todd Hunt, *Managing Public Relations* (New York: Holt, Rinehart and Winston, 1984), 89–97.
2. Ibid.
3. Richard H. Truitt, "Wanted: Hard-Headed Objectives," *Public Relations Journal* (August 1969): 12, 13.
4. George L. Morrisey, *Management by Objectives and Results for Business and Industry,* 2d ed. (Reading, MA: Addison-Wesley, 1977), 9.
5. Jack Tucker, "Budgeting and Cost Control: Are You a Businessman or a Riverboat Gambler?" *Public Relations Journal* (March 1981): 15.
6. Donald T. Mogavero, "When the Funds Come Tumbling Down," *Public Relations Journal* (October 1981): 13.
7. Anthony Fulginiti, "How to Prepare a Public Relations Plan," *Communication Briefings* (May 1985): 8a, b.

8. Thomas J. Peters and Robert H. Waterman, Jr., *In Search of Excellence* (New York: Harper & Row, 1982), 40.
9. Jack O'Dwyer, *O'Dwyer's Directory of Corporate Communications* (New York: J. R. O'Dwyer, 1985), 2.
10. Cynthia Rigg, "A Giant Struggles to Overcome Size," *Crain's New York Business* (March 22, 1993): 17, 19.
11. "Six of Top Ten Independents Gained Ten Percent or More in 1992," *O'Dwyers PR Services Report* (May 1993): 20, 24–25.
12. "25th Annual Survey of the Profession, Part 1: Salaries and Demographics," *PR Reporter* (October 16, 1989): 1.

TOP OF THE SHELF

Jerry A. Hendrix, *Public Relations Cases, 2d ed.*
Belmont, CA: Wadsworth, 1992.

In this second edition of his case studies text, American University Professor Jerry Hendrix discusses 27 public relations case studies that test strategic thinking and public relations management skills. Examples include cases from the areas of media, community, public affairs, government, finance, consumer affairs, and crisis public relations.

Perhaps most significant, many cases discussed here are positive in nature—"The 100th Anniversary Celebration of the National Geographic Society," "Repositioning Cooper Tire's Investment Message," "Winning the Hearts of America's Dog Lovers," and the like. These cases test a student's skill in devising constructive solutions for public relations challenges.

The book also includes a number of negative case studies, such as "Amtrak's Worst Accident Ever" and "Phillips Petroleum's Explosion and Fire in Its Houston Chemical Complex."

As a construct for attacking such cases, the author offers an interactive process model that suggests confronting each case in terms of four criteria: research, objective setting, programming, and evaluation. All in all, a worthwhile book to test your public relations management acumen.

SUGGESTED READINGS

Block, Edward M. "Strategic Communications: Practicing What We Preach." Speech at the PRSA Annual Convention, November 8, 1987. New York: Burson Marsteller.

Brief, Arthur, and Gerald Tomlinson. *Managing Smart.* Lexington, MA: Lexington Books, 1987.

Brody, E. W. *Public Relations Programming and Production.* New York: Praeger, 1988.

Brody, E. W. *Professional Practice Development.* New York: Praeger, 1989.
Burson, Harold. *What Works for Me.* New York: Random House, 1987.
Careers in Public Relations. New York: PRSA,
Cluff, Susan. "The Changing Face of Corporate Communication." *Communication World* (May 1987): 27–31. (IABC, 870 Market St., San Francisco, CA 94102)
Fraser, Bruce W. "How to Be a Freelance Public Relations Professional . . . and Survive." *Tips and Tactics,* a supplement of *Public Relations Reporter* 25, no. 9 (June 22, 1987).
Grunig, James E. *Excellence in Public Relations and Communications Management.* Hillsdale, NJ: Erlbaum, 1992.
Hamilton, Seymour. *A Communications Audit Handbook: Helping Organizations Communicate.* White Plains, NY: Longman, 1987.
Harris, Thomas L. *Choosing and Working with Your Public Relations Firm.* Lincolnwood, IL: NTC Business, 1992.
Hart, Norman. *Effective Corporate Relations: Applying Public Relations in Business and Industry.* New York: McGraw-Hill, 1988.
Hendrix, Jerry A. *Public Relations Cases.* Belmont, CA: Wadsworth, 1988.
Hills, Curtis. *How to Save Your Clients from Themselves.* Phoenix, AZ: Olde & Oppenheim, 1988.
Jefkins, Frank. *P.R. Techniques.* Portsmouth, NH: William Heinemann, 1988.
Marsteller, William. *Creative Management.* Lincolnwood, IL: NTC Business, 1992.
Mitchell, Howard. *What Every Account Executive Should Know about Public Relations.* American Assn. of Advertising Agencies, 1989.
Monsanto Decentralizes and Downsizes Without Losing on Public Affairs. New York: Business International, October 19, 1987.
Nager, Norman R., and Allen T. Harrell. *Public Relations: Management by Objectives.* Lanham, MD: University Press of America, 1991.
Olins, Wally. *Corporate Identity.* Cambridge, MA: Harvard Business School Press, 1990.
Ross, Joel E. *Total Quality Management: Text, Cases and Readings.* Delray Beach, FL: St. Lucie Press, 1992.
Rukeyser, Louis, and John Cooney. *Louis Rukeyser's Business Almanac.* New York: Simon & Schuster, 1991.
Slater, Robert. *The New GE: How Jack Welch Revived an American Institution.* Homewood, IL.: Business One Irwin, 1992.
Thomsett, Michael C. *The Little Black Book of Product Management.* New York: AMACOM, 1990.
Tomasko, Robert M. *Downsizing: Reshaping the Corporation for the Future.* New York: AMACOM, 1990.
Weinstein, David A. *How to Protect Your Business, Professional and Brand Names.* New York: John Wiley, 1990.

CASE STUDY

WRONG WAY AT UNITED WAY

As Hill & Knowlton's Frank Mankiewicz recalls it, the media inquiries about top management's expense problems at United Way of America began in the winter of 1991.

Reporters from the *Washington Post* and Washington's *Regardie's* business magazine had heard rumors about profligate spending by the UWA president for travel, expenses, subsidiary commercial for-profit ventures, and personal nepotism. And the reporters wanted answers.

To accommodate them, United Way's board and President William Aramony authorized a private investigator to look into the charges. The investigator looked, gasped, and delivered the bad news: The allegations were all true.

Thereupon, the board and President Aramony slammed the lid on cooperating with the media. And United Way's troubles became a crisis.

When management closed off the public relations department to reporters, journalists looked to others within the organization for details. As United Way's vice president of corporate communications put it, "The building became a sieve of information."

By February 1992, Washington reporters had completed their investigations and reported the following:

- Aramony was paid more than any other charity leader, drawing pay and perks of $463,000 per year.
- Aramony spent freely on travel during his 21-year tenure as United Way's president, taking several trips on the supersonic Concorde and spending $20,000 for chauffeur services in New York City—in one year alone.
- Cronyism and nepotism flourished within both the national organization and five spinoff companies initially financed by United Way. Most striking, Aramony's son Robert worked for three spinoff companies and was the unpaid president of a fourth.
- One spinoff company created by United Way had purchased a plush condominium in New York City for Aramony's personal use.

What made the revelations even more tragic was that United Way, through its network of 2,100 autonomous local agencies, was arguably as worthwhile a nonprofit organization as any in the world. In 1991, United Way raised $3.1 billion, the vast majority of which supported 42,000 health and social service agencies affecting millions of people.

Immediately after the stories on Aramony broke, the president convened an emergency meeting of United Way's 14-member executive committee. The committee supported Aramony with a unanimous vote of confidence. Aramony and the committee members declined all interview requests.

A day later, the National Committee for Responsive Philanthropy called for Aramony to be placed on "administrative leave" until the comprehensive inquiry into the nature and activities of the spinoff firms could be completed. United Way officials responded that the spinoffs were "private, for-profit companies that would compromise competitiveness by opening their books." The spinoffs, they said, helped local agencies buy goods and services cheaply.

The fact that United Way's 37-member board of governors—which included such heavy-hitting corporate leaders as Microsoft Chairman William Gates, Johnson & Johnson Chairman Ralph Larsen, AT&T Chairman Robert Allen, and IBM Chairman John Akers—staunchly defended Aramony wasn't surprising. As United Way president, Aramony had been a master at mobilizing resources, mustering support among business leaders, and capitalizing on advertising and marketing—corraling $45 million in free advertising through the National Football League alone. Where Aramony fell down, however, was in the area of preserving his own and the organization's credibility through proper public relations practice.

In short order, despite management support and organizational stonewalling, Aramony's hold on United Way began to disintegrate. Millionaire Walter Annenberg, who a year earlier had donated $450,000 to United Way, called for Aramony to step down. "Think of all the little people who give $25 or $50 per year, who really have a hard time giving. This betrays them," Annenberg said.

United Way chapters, which underwrote the national organization's $29 million annual budget, announced that they would delay voluntary dues. Said the president of the Washington, D.C., chapter, "We are concerned that fund-raising will be adversely affected and people who need help in our society will go short."

How right he was.

- In response to the Aramony scandal, the 1992 United Way campaign suffered its sharpest donation decline in decades.
- The Justice Department began an investigation of the charity and of several spinoffs, preparing a total of 42 subpoenas to get to the bottom of the mess.
- United Way of America announced plans to reduce its staff, freeze salaries, and encourage workers to resign or go on extended leave.
- Finally, the man who started it all, William Aramony—still defending his salary and expenses as properly comparable to those of executives in private industry—was forced to resign.

By August 1992, United Way of America had named Elaine L. Chao, former director of the Peace Corps, as its new president. It was announced that Ms. Chao would be paid $195,000 a year, with no fringe benefits beyond those available to all employees.

The man she replaced, William Aramony, would be charged in 1994 with stealing more than $1 million from the organization he headed.

As part of the cleanup, United Way's board of governors was expanded from 37 to 45 members, and its membership included, for the first time, local United Way leaders. Six new board-level committees were added, including those on finance, budget, and ethics.

Ms. Chao was philosophical about the task of resurrecting United Way's image. "In the first year, if we are able to stabilize United Way of America, I would be happy. And then after that, I would hope to grow again."

Mucho
depende
de usted.

THE
UNITED
WAY

Figure 7–2 Even at the height of the Aramony turmoil, no one questioned the effectiveness of United Way's programs, such as those for the Hispanic community. *(Courtesy of United Way)*

QUESTIONS

1. What should have been United Way's public response after receiving the damaging investigative report about its president's finances?

2. How would you assess the board's refusal to discuss publicly the reasons for its vote of confidence of Aramony after the embarrassing disclosures?
3. In the wake of Aramony's disclosures, what strategy and tactics could local United Way agencies have adopted to distance themselves from United Way of America?
4. What overall public relations management philosophy would you suggest United Way embrace in the future?

For further information on the United Way case, see Felicity Barringer, "United Way Will Reduce Staff, Its President Says," *The New York Times* (June 3, 1992): 1; Felicity Barringer, "United Way Says Slump and Scandal May Bring Sharp Drop in Donations," *The New York Times* (November 20, 1992): A-14; Nannette Byrnes, "The Non-Profit 'Business,'" *Financial World* (August 3, 1993): 68; Desda Moss, "National United Way Under Fire," *USA Today* (February 27, 1992): A1, 3.

TIPS FROM THE TOP

HAROLD BURSON

Harold Burson is chairman of Burson-Marsteller, a worldwide public relations firm with 2,500 employees and 50 offices in 27 countries. He was CEO of Burson-Marsteller from its founding in 1953 until January 1988. Burson is a legendary public relations practitioner and lecturer, as well as the recipient of virtually every major honor awarded by the profession.

How has the business of public relations changed over time?
Public relations has, over time, become more relevant as a management function for all manner of institutions, public and private sector, profit and not-for-profit. CEOs increasingly recognize the need to communicate to achieve their organizational objectives. Similarly, they have come to recognize public relations as a necessary component in the decision-making process. This has enhanced the role of public relations both internally and for independent consultants.

How can a public relations firm influence public opinion?
The public relations function can be divided into two principal classes of activity: the strategic and the implementing. Public relations firms play a major role on behalf of clients in both areas. In the realm of the strategic, a public relations firm brings to a client an independent perspective based on broad organizational experience with a wide spectrum of clients and problems. The public relations firm is not encumbered with the many internal considerations that frequently enter into the corporate or institutional decision-making process. In implementing programs, the public relations firm has a broad range of resources, both functional and geographic, that can be brought to bear on a client's problem. Furthermore, the public relations firm can usually be held to more specific accountability—both in terms of results and costs.

What constitutes the ideal public relations man or woman?
Public relations today covers so broad a range of activity that it is difficult to establish a set of specifications for all the kinds of people wearing the public relations mantle. Generally, I feel four primary characteristics apply to just about every successful public relations person I know.

1. They're smart—bright, intelligent people; quick studies. They ask the right questions. They have that unique ability to establish credibility almost on sight.
2. They know how to get along with people. They work well with their bosses, their peers, their subordinates. They work well with their clients and with third parties like the press and suppliers. They are emotionally stable—even (especially) under pressure. They use the pronoun *we* more than *I*.
3. They are motivated, and part of that motivation involves an ability to develop creative solutions. No one needs to tell them what to do next; instinctively, they know. They don't fear starting with a blank sheet of paper. To them, the blank sheet of paper equates with challenge and opportunity.
4. They can write; they can articulate their thoughts in a persuasive manner.

How do ethics apply to the public relations function?
In a single word, pervasively. Ethical behavior is at the root of what we do as public relations professionals. We approach our calling with a commitment to serve the public interest, knowing full well that the public interest lacks a universal definition and knowing that one person's view of the public interest differs markedly from that of another. We must therefore be consistent in our personal definition of the public interest and be prepared to speak up for those actions we take.

How would you assess the future of public relations?
More so than ever before, those responsible for large institutions whose existence depends on public acceptance and support recognize the need for sound public relations input.

At all levels of society, public opinion has been brought to bear in the conduct of affairs both in the public and private sectors. A once-popular president failed in his reelection efforts; numerous CEOs of major corporations have been deposed following initiatives undertaken by the media, by public interest groups, by institutional stockholders—all representing failures that stemmed from a lack of sensitivity to public opinion.

Accordingly, my view is that public relations is playing and will continue to play a more pivotal role in the decision-making process than ever before.

The sources of public relations counsel may well become less structured and more diverse, simply because of the growing pervasive understanding that public tolerance has become so important in the achievement of any goals that have a recognizable impact on society.

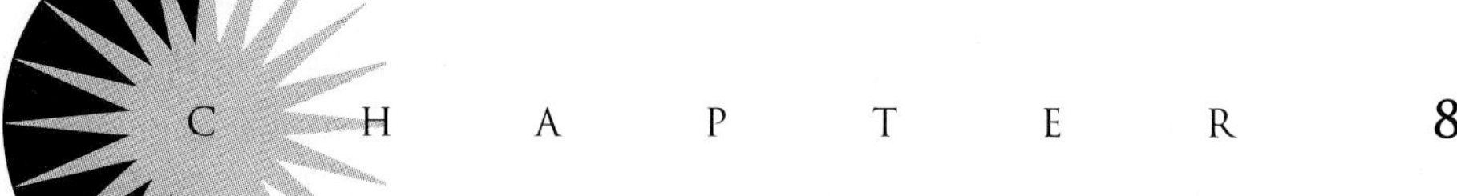

CHAPTER 8

PUBLIC RELATIONS WRITING

THE ABILITY TO WRITE EASILY, COHERENTLY, AND QUICKLY distinguishes the public relations professional from others in an organization. It's not that the skills of counseling and judgment aren't just as important; some experts argue that these skills are far more important than knowing how to write. Maybe. But not knowing how to write—how to express ideas on paper—may reduce the opportunities to ascend the public relations success ladder.

General managers usually have finance, legal, engineering, or sales backgrounds, where writing is not stressed. But when they reach the top, they are expected to write articles, speeches, memos, and testimony. They then need advisers, who are often their trusted public relations professionals. That's why it's imperative that public relations students know how to write. Even beginning public relations professionals are expected to have mastery over the written word. Chapters 8 and 9 focus on what public relations writing is all about.

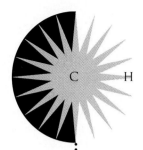

What does it take to be a public relations writer? For one thing, it takes a good knowledge of the basics. Although practitioners probably write for a wider range of purposes and use a greater number of communications methods than do other writers, the principles remain the same, whether writing an annual report or a case history, an employee newsletter or a public speech. This chapter and the next will explore the fundamentals of writing: (1) discussing public relations writing in general and news releases in particular; (2) reviewing writing for reading; and (3) discussing writing for listening.

WRITING FOR THE EYE AND THE EAR

Writing for a reader differs dramatically from writing for a listener. A reader has certain luxuries a listener does not have. For example, a reader can scan material, study printed words, dart ahead, and then review certain passages for better understanding. A reader can check up on a writer; if the facts are wrong, for instance, a reader can find out pretty easily. To be effective, writing for the eye must be able to withstand the most rigorous scrutiny.

On the other hand, a listener gets only one opportunity to hear and comprehend a message. If the message is missed the first time, there's usually no second chance. This situation poses a special challenge for the writer—to grab the listener quickly. A listener who tunes out early in a speech or a broadcast is difficult to draw back into the listening fold.

Public relations practitioners—and public relations students—should understand the differences between writing for the eye and the ear. Although it's unlikely that any beginning public relations professional would start by writing speeches, it's important to understand what constitutes a speech and how it's prepared and then be ready for the assignment when opportunity strikes. Because writing lies at the heart of the public relations equation, the more beginners know about writing, the better they will do. Any practitioner who doesn't know the basics of writing and doesn't know how to write is vulnerable and expendable.

FUNDAMENTALS OF WRITING

Few people are born writers. Like any other discipline, writing takes patience and hard work. The more you write, the better you should become, provided you have mastered the basics. Writing fundamentals do not change significantly from one form to another.

What are the basics? Here is a foolproof, three-part formula for writers, from the novice to the novelist.

1. **The idea must precede the expression.** Think before writing. Few people can observe an event, immediately grasp its meaning, and sit down to compose several pages of sharp, incisive prose. Writing requires ideas, and ideas require thought. Ideas must satisfy four criteria:

   - They must relate to the reader.
   - They must engage the reader's attention.
   - They must concern the reader.
   - They must be in the reader's interest.

Sometimes ideas come quickly. At other times, they don't come at all. But each new writing situation doesn't require a new idea. The trick in coming up with clever ideas lies more in *borrowing* old ones than in creating new ones. What's that, you say? Is your author encouraging "theft"? You bet! The old cliche, "Don't reinvent the wheel," is absolutely true when it comes to good writing. Never underestimate the importance of maintaining good files.[1]

2. **Don't be afraid of the draft.** After deciding on an idea and establishing the purpose of a communication, the writer should prepare a rough draft. This is a necessary and foolproof method for avoiding a mediocre, half-baked product.

   Writing, no matter how good, can usually be improved with a second look. The draft helps you organize ideas and plot their development before you commit them to a written test. Writing clarity is often enhanced if you know where you will stop before you start. Organization should be logical; it should lead a reader in a systematic way through the body of the text. Sometimes, especially on longer pieces, an outline should precede the draft.
3. **Simplify, clarify, aim.** In writing, the simpler the better. The more people who understand what you're trying to say, the better your chances for stimulating action. Shop talk, jargon, and "in" words should be avoided. Clear, normal English is all that's required to get an idea across. In practically every case, what makes sense is the simple rather than the complex, the familiar rather than the unconventional, and the concrete rather than the abstract.

   Clarity is another essential in writing. The key to clarity is tightness; that is, each word, each passage, each paragraph must belong. If a word is unnecessary, a passage redundant, a paragraph vague—get rid of it. Writing requires judicious editing; copy must always be reviewed with an eye toward cutting.

   Finally, writing must be aimed at a particular audience. The writer must have the target group in mind and tailor the message to reach them. To win the minds and deeds of a specific audience, one must be willing to sacrifice the understanding of certain others. Writers, like companies, can't expect to be all things to all people.

   Television journalist Bill Moyers offers this advice for good writing:

> Strike in the active voice. Aim straight for the enemy: imprecision, ambiguity, and those high words that bear semblance of worth, not substance. Offer no quarter to the tired phrase or overworn idiom. Empty your knapsack of all adjectives, adverbs, and clauses that slow your stride and weaken your pace. Travel light. Remember the most memorable sentences in the English language are also the shortest: "The King is dead" and "Jesus wept."[2]

FLESCH READABILITY FORMULA

Through a variety of writings, the late Dr. Rudolf Flesch staged a one-man battle against pomposity and murkiness in writing.* According to Flesch, anyone can become a writer. He suggested that people who write the way they talk will be able to write better.

*Among the more significant of Flesch's books are *Say What You Mean, The Art of Plain Talk, The Art of Readable Writing,* and *How to Be Brief: An Index to Simple Writing.*

In other words, if people were less inclined to obfuscate their writing with 25-cent words and more inclined to substitute simple words, then not only would communicators communicate better, but receivers would receive more clearly.

In responding to a letter, Flesch's approach in action would work as follows: "Thanks for your suggestion, Tom. I'll mull it over and get back to you as soon as I can." The opposite of the Flesch approach would read like this: "Your suggestion has been received; and after careful consideration we shall report our findings to you." See the difference?

There are countless examples of how Flesch's simple dictum works.

- Few would remember William Shakespeare if he had written sentences like "Should I act upon the urgings that I feel or remain passive and thus cease to exist?" Shakespeare's writing has stood the test of centuries because of sentences such as "To be or not to be?"
- A scientist, prone to scientific jargon, might be tempted to write, "The biota exhibited a 100 percent mortality response." But, oh, how much easier and infinitely more understandable to write, "All the fish died."
- One of President Franklin D. Roosevelt's speech writers once wrote, "We are endeavoring to construct a more inclusive society." FDR changed it to "We're going to make a country in which no one is left out."
- Even the most famous book of all, the Bible, opens with a simple sentence that could have been written by a twelve-year-old: "In the beginning, God created the heaven and the earth."

Flesch gave seven suggestions for making writing more readable.

1. Use contractions like *it's* or *doesn't.*
2. Leave out the word *that* whenever possible.
3. Use pronouns like *I, we, they,* and *you.*
4. When referring back to a noun, repeat the noun or use a pronoun. Don't create eloquent substitutions.
5. Use brief, clear sentences.
6. Cover only one item per paragraph.
7. Use language the reader understands.

To Flesch the key to all good writing was getting to the point.

Stated another way, public relations writers should remember their *A*'s and *B*'s:

- *A*void big words.
- *A*void extra words.
- *A*void cliches.
- *A*void Latin.
- *B*e specific.
- *B*e active.
- *B*e simple.
- *B*e short.
- *B*e organized.
- *B*e convincing.
- *B*e understandable.[3]

In addition to Flesch, a number of other communications specialists have concentrated on how to make writing more readable. Many have developed their own instruments to measure readability. The most prominent, the Gunning Fog Index, designed by Robert Gunning, measures reading ease in terms of the number of words and their difficulty, the number of complete thoughts, and the average sentence length in a piece of copy. The point is that good writing can't be confusing or unclear. It must be understandable.

THE SECRET OF THE INVERTED PYRAMID

Newspaper writing is the Flesch formula in action. Reporters learn that words are precious and are not to be wasted. In their stories every word counts. If readers lose interest early, they're not likely to be around at the end of the story.

That's where the inverted pyramid comes in. Newspaper story form is the opposite of that for a novel or short story. Whereas the climax of a novel comes at the end, the climax of a newspaper story comes at the beginning. A novel's important facts are rolled out as the plot thickens, but the critical facts in a newspaper story appear at the start. In this way, if readers decide to leave a news article early, they have already gained the basic ideas.

Generally, the first tier, or lead, of the inverted pyramid is the first one or two paragraphs, which include the most important facts. From there, paragraphs are written in descending order of importance, with progressively less important facts presented as the article continues—thus, the term *inverted pyramid.* (See Figure 8–1 for an exception to the inverted pyramid style.)

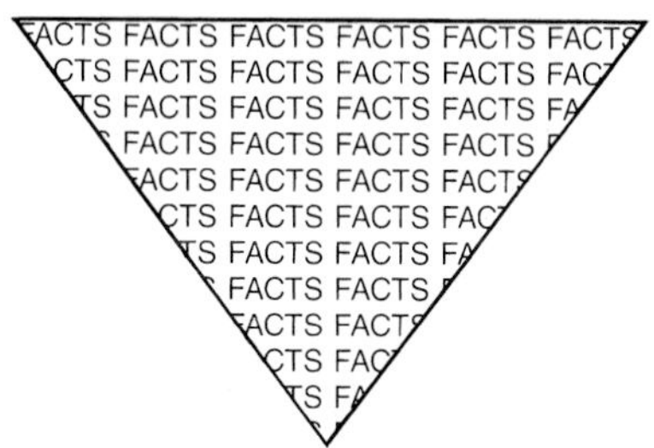

The lead is the most critical element, usually answering the questions concerning who, what, why, when, where, and occasionally how. For example, the following lead effectively answers most of the initial questions a reader might have about the subject of the news story.

> Magic Johnson announced yesterday in Hollywood that he is suffering from the AIDS virus and will retire from basketball.

That sentence tells it all; it answers the critical questions and highlights the pertinent facts. It gets to the point quickly without a lot of extra words. In only 19 words it captures and communicates the essence of what the reader needs to know.

This same style of easy, straightforward writing forms the basis for the most fundamental and ubiquitous of all public relations tools—the news release.

Palm Coast
ITT COMMUNITY DEVELOPMENT CORPORATION
CORPORATE RELATIONS
PALM COAST, FLORIDA 32051
(904) 445-5000

NEWS RELEASE
ITT

105**88 FOR IMMEDIATE HOLIDAY ENJOYMENT

CONTACT: CAL MASSEY 904/445-2653

Linda Chase and Family (Individual versions sent to media contacts)

TO ENJOY HAPPY HOLIDAY SEASON

PALM COAST, FL -- Palm Coast media relations guy Cal Massey introduced the world's first (possibly not) sing-along press release today, in order to wish Linda Chase and family happiness during the holidays and new year, and in order to embarrass himself and his profession for the fifth consecutive holiday season.

(Sung to the tune of "Jingle Bell Rock")

Writer's block/writer's block/writer's block rock...
The brain said goodbye/and left nothing but schlock...
Norm-al-ly you get/a witty release...
But this year/the PR guy's blocked!

Dum-de-dum-dum...

Writer's block/writer's block/writer's block rock...
Hope your holiday's fun/and you get more than socks...
Rhy-ming is tough/when there's nothing but -ock...
But this year/it's all that we've got!

A little as-son-ance...

Writer's block/writer's block/writer's block rock...
It's been a great year/with good news 'round the clock...
Palm Coast is growing/and not without thought...
Except for/the PR guy, BLOCKED!

Big finish, now...

Writer's block/writer's block/writer's block rock...
I'm taking a few days/so don't be too shocked...
If very soon/you receive in your mail...
Next year's/release in a box!

My brain's rested...

Dum-de-dum/dum-de-dum/dum-de-dum-dum...

The final refrain: I hope the media representatives I have had the pleasure of working with over the years enjoy a relaxing holiday and new year graced by a light touch --- Cal Massey/Manager, Media Services/ITT Community Development Corporation.

Figure 8–1 As a holiday exception to the inverted pyramid news release, Palm Coast Media Services manager Cal Massey dispatched this sing-along press release, tailored to each of his primary media contacts. *(Courtesy of ITT Community Development Corporation)*

HE NEWS RELEASE

The news release, a valuable but much-maligned device, is the granddaddy of public relations writing vehicles. Most public relations professionals swear by it. Some newspaper editors swear about it. But everyone uses the release as the basic interpretive mechanism to let people know what an organization is doing. That's why the news release deserves special attention as a public relations writing vehicle.

A news release may be written as the document of record to state an organization's official position—for example, in a court case or in announcing a price or rate increase. More frequently, however, releases have one overriding purpose: to influence a publication to write favorably about the material discussed. Each day, in fact, professionals send releases to editors in the hope of stimulating favorable stories about their organizations.

Most news releases are not used verbatim. Rather, they may stimulate editors to consider covering a story. In other words, the release becomes the point of departure for a newspaper, magazine, radio, or television story. Why then do some editors and others describe news releases as "worthless drivel"?[4] The answer, says researcher Linda Norton of the University of Oklahoma's Herbert School of Journalism, is threefold:

1. **Releases are poorly written.** Professor Norton found that most news releases are written in a more complicated and difficult-to-read style than most newspaper stories. "This could be the result of pressure from administrators as they review and critique press releases," she reasoned.
2. **Releases are rarely localized.** Newspapers focus largely on hometown or regional developments. The more localized a news release, the greater the chance it has of being used. However, according to Professor Norton, "Practitioners may not want to do the additional work that localization requires." This is a bad decision because research indicates that a news release is 10 times more likely to be used if it is localized.
3. **Releases are not newsworthy.** This is the grand dilemma. An editor will use a public relations release only if he or she considers it news. If it's not newsworthy, it won't be used. What determines whether something is news? Professor Norton suggests five requisites:
    - Impact
    - Oddity
    - Conflict
    - Known principal
    - Proximity

    Research indicates that the vast majority of public relations releases don't contain any of these elements, limiting their chances of "seeing the light of print."[5]

With these findings as backdrop, it is not surprising that research also indicates that only 3–8 percent of all news releases are published.[6] Nonetheless, each day's *Wall Street Journal, New York Times, USA Today,* and daily publications around the nation are filled with stories generated by public relations professionals.

So the fact is that the news release—despite the harsh reviews of some—remains the single most important public relations vehicle. The key challenge for public relations writers is to ensure that their news releases reflect news (Figure 8–2).

FORMAT

The format of a news release is important. Because the release is designed to be used in print, it must be structured for easy use by an editor. Certain mechanical rules of thumb should be followed (Figure 8–3):

- **Spacing** News releases should always be typed and double-spaced on 8½ by 11 inch paper. No editor wants to go rummaging through a handwritten release or a single-spaced, oversized piece of paper. Although most releases are typed on only one side, in these days of environmental concern releases typed on both sides of a page are acceptable.
- **Paper** Inexpensive paper stock should be used. Reporters win Pulitzer Prizes with stories written on plain copy paper. Nothing irritates an editor more than seeing an expensively embossed news release while watching newspapers die due to soaring newsprint costs.
- **Identification** The name, address, and telephone number of the release writer should appear in the upper part of the release in case an editor wants further information. It's a good idea to list two names, with office and home telephone numbers.
- **Release date** Releases should always be dated, either for immediate use or to be held until a certain later date, often referred to as an *embargoed date*. In this day of instant communication, however, newspapers frown on embargoes. And only in the most extreme cases—for example, proprietary or confidential medical or government data—will newspapers honor them. Frequently, a dateline is used on releases; it is the first line of the release and tells where the story originated.
- **Margins** Margins should be wide enough for editors to write in, usually about 1 to 1½ inches.
- **Length** A news release is not a book. It should be edited tightly so that it is no more than two to two and a half pages long. Words and sentences should be kept short.
- **Paragraphs** Paragraphs should also be short, no more than six lines at most. A single sentence can suffice as a paragraph. Because typographical composers may type exactly what they see, words should not be broken at the end of a line. Likewise, paragraphs should be completed before a new page is begun to ensure that a lost page in the news or composing room will not disrupt a particular thought in the release.
- **Slug lines** Journalistic shorthand, or slug lines, should appear on a release—such things as "more" at the bottom of a page when the release continues to another page and "30" or "###" to denote the end of the release. Page numbers and one-word descriptions of the topic of the release should appear on each page for quick editorial recognition.
- **Headlines** Headlines are a good idea. Often, headlines are avoided, and releases are begun one-third of the way down the page to allow editors to devise original headlines. Some practitioners prefer headlines to presell an editor on the gist of the news release that follows.

GLOBESET News

THE GLOBAL SETTLEMENT FUND, INC.

FOR IMMEDIATE RELEASE

Contact: Doff Meyer
212-222-3436

GLOBESET℠, WORLD'S FIRST ROUND-THE-CLOCK,
MULTI-CURRENCY PAYMENT SYSTEM, BEGINS OPERATION

The Global Settlement Fund, Inc. (GlobeSet℠), the world's first 24-hour-a-day, multi-currency payment system, has begun operation as a new form of margin collateral for futures trades. A mutual fund as well as a payment system, GlobeSet seeks to earn income for its shareholders.

Unlike traditional collateral management and payment systems, GlobeSet is the world's first system to offer the following features:

- Payments using GlobeSet shares are instantaneous and final.
- Payments using GlobeSet shares can be made 24 hours a day, every business day, 7 a.m. Monday, Tokyo time, through 8 p.m. Friday, New York time.
- GlobeSet is designed to accept payments in multiple currencies — initially United States Dollars, Japanese Yen and British Pound Sterling.

--- more ---

The New York Times

FRIDAY, NOVEMBER 27, 1992

A Fund-Shifting System That's Open All Night

By MICHAEL QUINT

The Global Settlement Fund may sound like a common money market fund, but behind that bland title is a novel 24-hour money transfer system that might some day be used by all kinds of businesses for sending payments to one another.

While securities and currencies are traded 24 hours a day in London, New York and Tokyo, there has not been any way for traders to send or receive payments outside of business hours in their local market.

The Bankers Trust Company, creator and manager of the new fund, began offering it earlier this month to members of the Chicago Mercantile Exchange. The exchange, whose 87 members include most of the nation's leading banks and securities firms, recently changed its rules so members can satisfy daily margin calls by sending the fund's shares to the exchange rather than cash or Treasury bills.

A 24-Hour Cash Exchange

Shares in the fund are the equivalent of money that can be transferred instantly to another shareholder, 24 hours a day, without a transaction fee.

The fund invests only in Treasury securities. Shares may only be bought by corporations and institutions that have the required computer connections with the fund's control room in New York. The minimum purchase is $100,000.

The rapidity of payment and round-the-clock access was important to the Chicago Merc, which started night-time trading of futures contracts in June. The exchange had been seeking a way to collect margin during hours that the banking system and Federal Reserve were closed.

"Right now, there are a lot of people on the sidelines waiting to see it work," said Robin B. Perlin, vice president of cash management at the Chicago Research and Trading Group, a Chicago Merc member firm that has decided to buy shares in the fund. "Hopefully, all the exchanges are going to approve the fund, which will give us a lot more flexibility to move funds between our accounts."

Designs Beyond Traders

Bankers Trust, which spent five years developing Global Settlement and obtaining the necessary approvals from banking and securities regu-

Growing Money Transfers

Estimated volume of transfers through the "Fed wire," the Federal Reserve's system for handling large payments between banks.

NUMBER OF TRANSFERS
70 million
60
50
40
30
20
10
0
'85 '87 '89 '91

DOLLAR VALUE
$200 billion
150
100
50
0
'85 '87 '89 '91

Source: Federal Reserve Bank of New York

Eileen Bedell, Bankers Trust director of global settlement services, expects the new fund to appeal to corporations that are tired of paying bank fees.

Figure 8–2 A news release is worthless unless it gets published. The key to getting published is to ensure that the release is newsworthy. This release of a revolutionary 24-hour-a-day payments system qualifies as news. (*Courtesy of Bankers Trust Company*)

ARM & HAMMER® Baking Soda  ...never stops being ~~new.~~ news!

FOR IMMEDIATE RELEASE

Contact: Benjamin Kessler
Burson-Marsteller
212-614-4948

BAKING SODA MOVING OUT OF THE KITCHEN
AS HOUSE-FULL OF NEW USES ARE FOUND

New York, N.Y. (August 30, 1993) Little yellow boxes are turning up in all kinds of places in American homes.

As more people become environmentally-conscious and economically-savvy, they're discovering it just makes good sense to use versatile products like ARM & HAMMER® Baking Soda to clean and deodorize every room in the house. Expanding from its humble beginnings as a baking ingredient or in the back of the refrigerator absorbing up odors, now baking soda is turning up everywhere.

So now the secret is out! Closets, bathrooms, dens, nurseries, kitchens--even the garage, are now likely places to find a box of baking soda discreetly at work neutralizing odors and standing ready to be used in the constant battle against dirt, grease and grime.

"I have utilized your baking soda to clean my bathroom and other soiled surfaces," wrote one consumer to Church & Dwight Co., Inc., which makes ARM & HAMMER® Baking Soda. "I am absolutely convinced that baking soda is the best for its cleaning ability and safety to the environment. I genuinely believe your product would be more readily used by the public if you sold a dispensing container," the consumer adds.

(more)

Figure 8–3 This Arm & Hammer release about "little yellow boxes" illustrates proper news release format, from spacing to identification, from margins to headlines, from slug lines to overall appearance. (*Courtesy of Arm & Hammer*)

- **Proofreading** Grammar, spelling, and typing must be perfect. Misspellings, grammatical errors, or typos are the quickest route to the editorial wastebasket.
- **Timing** News-release writers must be sensitive to editorial deadlines. Newspapers, magazines, and broadcast stations work under constant deadline pressure. Because stale news is no news, a release arriving even a little late may just as well never have been mailed.

STYLE

The style of a news release is almost as critical as its content. Sloppy style can break the back of any release and ruin its chances for publication. Style must also be flexible and evolve as language changes.

One element of style that has evolved over the years relates to sexism in writing. Dealing with gender has become more important for a writer and also more difficult. No matter how hard a writer tries to be evenhanded in treating men and women in print, he or she is bound to offend someone. The Washington Press Club has published guidelines for the elimination of sexual bias in the media. Among its highlights are these rules:

1. Terms referring to a specific gender should be avoided when an alternative term will do. Use *business executive* instead of *businessman* and *city council member* for *councilman.*
2. Where neither a gender-free term nor any term accurately designating gender is yet in common use, continue to employ the old terminology—for example, *Yeoman* First Class Betty Jones or Mary Smith, a telephone company *lineman.*
3. No occupational designation should include a description of the person's gender unless it is pertinent to the story. For example, don't use *woman lawyer* or *male nurse.*
4. Avoid terms like *man-made* for synthetic, *man on the street* for ordinary citizen, *manpower* for workforce, *man and wife* for husband and wife, and *co-ed* for student.

Despite such attempts to eliminate sexism in writing style, satisfying everyone is a nearly impossible task for any writer.

Most public relations operations follow the style practiced by major newspapers and magazines rather than that of book publishers. This news style is detailed in various guides published by such authorities as the Associated Press, United Press International, and the *New York Times.*

Because the press must constantly update its style to conform to changing societal concepts, news-release style is subjective and everchanging. However, a particular firm's style must be consistent from one release to the next. The following are examples of typical style rules:

- **Capitalization** Most leading publications use capital letters sparingly; so should you. Editors call this a *down style* because only the most important words begin with capital letters.
- **Abbreviations** Abbreviations present a many-faceted problem. For example, months, when used with dates, should be abbreviated, such as Sept. 2, 1995. But when the day of the month is not used, the month should be spelled out, such

as September 1995. Days of the week, on the other hand, should never be abbreviated. In addition, first mention of organizations and agencies should be spelled out, with the abbreviation in parentheses after the name, such as Securities and Exchange Commission (SEC).

- **Numbers** There are many guidelines for the spelling out of numbers, but a general rule is to spell out numbers through nine and use figures for 10 and up. Yet, figures are perfectly acceptable for such things as election returns, speeds and distances, percentages, temperatures, heights, ages, ratios, and sports scores.
- **Punctuation** The primary purpose of punctuation is to clarify the writer's thoughts, ensure exact interpretation, and make reading and understanding quicker and easier. Less punctuation rather than more should be the goal. The following are just some of the punctuation marks a public relations practitioner must use appropriately.

  1. The colon introduces listings, tabulations, and statements and takes the place of an implied "for instance."
  2. The comma is used in a variety of circumstances, including before connecting words, between two words or figures that might otherwise be misunderstood, and before and after nonrestrictive clauses.
  3. In general, exclamation points should be resisted in releases. They tend to be overkill!
  4. The hyphen is often abused and should be used carefully. A single hyphen can change the meaning of a sentence completely. For example, "The six-foot man eating tuna was killed" means the man was eating tuna; it should probably be punctuated "The six-foot, man-eating tuna was killed."
  5. Quoted matter is enclosed in double or single quotation marks. The double marks enclose the original quotation, whereas the single marks enclose a quotation within a quotation.

- **Spelling** Many words, from *adviser* to *zucchini,* are commonly misspelled. The best way to avoid misspellings is to have a dictionary always within reach. When two spellings are given in a dictionary, the first spelling is always preferred.

These are just a few of the stylistic stumbling blocks that writers must consider. In the news release, style should never be taken lightly. The style, as much as any other part of the release, lets an editor know the kind of organization that issued the release and the competence of the professional who wrote it.

CONTENT

Again, the cardinal rule in release content is that the end product be newsworthy. The release must be of interest to an editor and readers. Issuing a release that has little chance of being used by a publication serves only to crush the credibility of the writer.

When a release is newsworthy and of potential interest to an editor, it must be written clearly and concisely, in proper newspaper style. It must get to the facts early and answer the six key questions. From there it must follow inverted pyramid structure to its conclusion. For example, the following is not a proper lead for a release:

Leaking the Gleeful Disaster Memo

The best thing anyone can do after writing an internal memo is to avoid sending it unless absolutely necessary. Consider the case of Jeffrey W. Greenberg and Hurricane Andrew.

On August 24, 1992, Hurricane Andrew struck Florida with such vengeance that 17 people were killed and upward of $8 billion in damages was recorded. Hurricane Andrew, in fact, was arguably the most devastating storm in the nation's history.

Nonetheless, on the same day that Andrew hit Florida, Mr. Greenberg, executive vice-president of the insurance giant American International Group and the son of Chairman Maurice Greenberg, suggested in a memo to company presidents and regional vice presidents that they call their "underwriters together and explain the significance of the hurricane."

Greenberg the younger continued in his two-paragraph memo: "This may cause the industry the biggest storm loss ever. This is an opportunity to get price increases now. We must be the first."

While few could argue with the facts and reasoning suggested by Mr. Greenberg, several observers questioned (1) his choice of words and (2) his timing.

One such critic was Florida Insurance Commissioner Tom Gallagher, who, on reading about the leaked Greenberg memo, immediately issued an order freezing insurance rates and warning companies against "greed-motivated rate hikes" in the aftermath of Hurricane Andrew.

Gallagher said his department would reject any efforts by the insurance industry to "capitalize on the misfortune of Hurricane Andrew's victims. We have heard reports that some in the insurance business see Hurricane Andrew as an opportunity to raise rates unfairly." This practice, Gallagher warned, would not be tolerated.

AIG Chairman Greenberg blasted back that his son's memo had been taken out of context. He pointed out that commercial and industrial insurance rates "have been inadequate for some time." And he argued that the sense of the memo was correct—that rates should be higher so that insurance companies can remain financially strong to respond to future disasters.

Right or wrong, the errant memo's damage had been done. Had he to do it over again, might Mr. Greenberg have worded the memo differently?

For further information, see "Limits Are Urged on Insurers After Storm," *The New York Times* (September 8, 1992): D-4; and Thomas S. Mulligan, "Insurer Uses Hurricane to Promote Rate Hike," *Los Angeles Times* (September 5, 1992): D-1.

CLEVELAND, OHIO, MARCH 7, 1995—Chief Justice William Rehnquist will speak tomorrow in Cleveland. He will speak at 8 P.M. He will address the convention of the American Bar Association. His address will be a major one and will concern the topic of capital punishment.

Why would an editor discard this lead? In the first place, it does not get to the heart of the issue—the topic of the speech—until the very end. Second, it's wordy. If the editor decided to use it at all, he'd have to rewrite it. Here's what should have been submitted:

Chief Justice William Rehnquist will deliver a major address on capital punishment at 8 P.M. tomorrow in Cleveland before the American Bar Association convention.

Even though the second sample cut the verbiage in half, the pertinent questions still got answered: who (Chief Justice William Rehnquist), what (a major address on capital punishment), where (Cleveland), when (tomorrow at 8 P.M.), and why (American Bar Association is holding a convention). In this case, how is less important. But whether the reader chooses to delve further into the release or not, the story's gist has been successfully communicated in the lead.

To be newsworthy, news releases must be objective. All comments and editorial remarks must be *attributed* to organization officials. The news release can't be used as the private soapbox of the release writer. Rather, it must appear as a fair and accurate representation of the news that the organization wishes to be conveyed.

News releases can be written about almost anything. Three frequent subjects are product and institutional announcements, management changes, and management speeches.

THE ANNOUNCEMENT

Frequently, practitioners want to announce a new product or institutional development, such as construction plans, earnings, mergers, acquisitions, or company celebrations. The announcement release should have a catchy yet significant lead to stimulate an editor to capitalize on the practitioner's creative idea.

"Tennis whites," the traditional male court uniform, will yield to bright colors and fashion styling this spring as Jockey spearheads a new wave in tennis fashion with the introduction of a full line of tennis wear for men.

Typically in an announcement release, after the lead identifies the significant aspects of the product or development, a spokesperson is quoted for additional product information. Editors appreciate the quotes because they then do not have to interview a company official.

The new, lightweight plastic bottle for Coca-Cola began its national rollout today in Spartanburg, S.C. This two-liter package is the nation's first metric plastic bottle for soft drinks.

"We are very excited about this new package," said John H. Ogden, president, Coca-Cola U.S.A. "Our two-liter plastic bottle represents an important advancement. Its light weight, toughness, and environmental advantages offer a new standard of consumer benefits in soft drink packaging."

The subtle product "plug" included in this release is typical of such announcements. Clearly, the organization gains if the product's benefits are described in a news story. But editors are sensitive to product puffery, and the line between legitimate information and puffery is thin. One must always be sensitive to the needs and concerns of editors. A professional avoids letting the thin line of product information become a short plank of puffery.

THE MANAGEMENT CHANGE

Newspapers are often interested in management changes, but editors frequently reject releases that have no local angle. For example, the editor of the Valdosta, Georgia, *Citizen* has little reason to use this announcement:

> NEW YORK, NY, SEPT. 5, 1995—Jeffrey O. Schultz has been named manager of the hosiery department at Bloomingdale's Paramus, NJ, store.

On the other hand, the same release, amended for local appeal, would almost certainly be used by the *Citizen*.

> NEW YORK, NY, SEPT. 5, 1995—Jeffrey O. Schultz, son of Mr. and Mrs. Siegfried Schultz of 221 Starting Lane, Valdosta, has been named manager of the hosiery department at Bloomingdale's Paramus, NJ, store.

Sometimes one must dig for the local angle. For example, suppose Mr. Schultz was born in Valdosta but went to school in Americus, Georgia. With this knowledge, the writer might prepare the following release, which would have appeal in the newspapers of both Georgia cities.

> NEW YORK, NY, SEPT. 5, 1995—Jeffrey O. Schultz, son of Mr. and Mrs. Siegfried Schultz of 221 Starting Lane, Valdosta, and a 1976 graduate of Americus High School, was named manager of the hosiery department of Bloomingdale's Paramus, NJ, store.

Penetrating local publications with the management change release is relatively easy once the local angle has been identified, but achieving publication in a national newspaper or magazine is much harder. The *Wall Street Journal*, for example, will not use a management change announcement unless the individual has attained a certain level of responsibility, usually corporate vice-president or higher, in a major firm. In other words, if a release involves someone who has not attained senior executive status at a listed company, forget it, at least as far as the *Wall Street Journal* is concerned.

For national consumption it is the importance or uniqueness of the individual or company that should be emphasized. For example, an editor might not realize that the following management change is unique:

> WASHINGTON, DC, JUNE 6, 1995—Howie Barmad of Jersey City, NJ, today was promoted to the rank of admiral in the United States Navy.

However, the same release stands out clearly for its news value when the unique angle is played up.

WASHINGTON, DC, JUNE 6, 1995—Howie Barmad, born in Yugoslavia, today was named the first naturalized admiral in the history of the United States Navy.

One can never go wrong by being straightforward in a news release, but a local or unique angle to help sell the story to an editor should always be investigated.

THE MANAGEMENT SPEECH

Management speeches are another recurring source of news releases. The key to a speech news release is selecting the most significant portion of the talk for the lead. A good speech generally has a clear thesis, from which a lead naturally flows. Once the thesis is identified, the remainder of the release simply embellishes it.

BOONEVILLE, MO, OCT. 18, 1994—Booneville Mining Company is "on the verge of having several very profitable years," Booneville Mining President Dr. J. Kelenson said today.

Addressing the Booneville Chamber of Commerce, the Missouri mining company executive cited two reasons for the positive projections: the company's orders are at an all-time high, and its overseas facilities have "turned the corner" on profitability in the current year.

Normally, if the speech giver is not a famous person, the release should not begin with the speaker's name but rather with the substance of the remarks. If the speaker is a well-known individual, leading with the name is perfectly legitimate.

Federal Reserve Chairman Alan Greenspan called today for a "new attitude toward business investment and capital formation."

The body copy of a speech release should follow directly from the lead. Often, the major points of the speech must be paraphrased and consolidated to conform to a two-page release. In any event, it is frequently a significant challenge to convert the essence of a management speech to news-release form (Figure 8–4).

THE IMPORTANCE OF EDITING

Editing is the all-important final touch for the public relations writer. In a news release, a careful self-edit can save the deadliest prose. An editor must be judicious. Each word, phrase, sentence, and paragraph should be weighed carefully. Good editing will "punch up" dull passages and make them sparkle. For instance, "The satellite flies across the sky" is dead, but "The satellite roars across the sky" is alive.

In the same context, good editing will get rid of passive verbs. Invariably, this will produce shorter sentences. For example, "The cherry tree was chopped down by George Washington" is shorter and better as "George Washington chopped down the cherry tree."

A good editor must also be gutsy enough to use bold strokes—to chop, slice, and cut through verbiage, bad grammar, misspellings, incorrect punctuation, poorly constructed

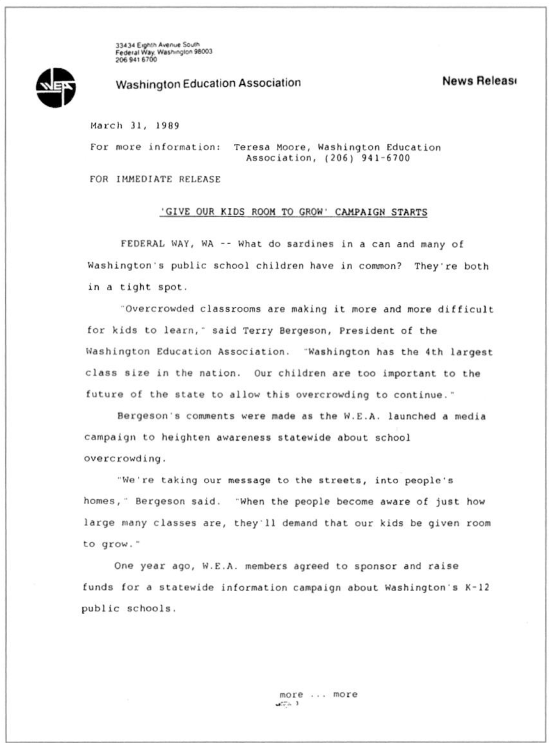

33434 Eighth Avenue South
Federal Way, Washington 98003
206 941 6700

Washington Education Association

News Releas

March 31, 1989

For more information: Teresa Moore, Washington Education Association, (206) 941-6700

FOR IMMEDIATE RELEASE

'GIVE OUR KIDS ROOM TO GROW' CAMPAIGN STARTS

FEDERAL WAY, WA -- What do sardines in a can and many of Washington's public school children have in common? They're both in a tight spot.

"Overcrowded classrooms are making it more and more difficult for kids to learn," said Terry Bergeson, President of the Washington Education Association. "Washington has the 4th largest class size in the nation. Our children are too important to the future of the state to allow this overcrowding to continue."

Bergeson's comments were made as the W.E.A. launched a media campaign to heighten awareness statewide about school overcrowding.

"We're taking our message to the streets, into people's homes," Bergeson said. "When the people become aware of just how large many classes are, they'll demand that our kids be given room to grow."

One year ago, W.E.A. members agreed to sponsor and raise funds for a statewide information campaign about Washington's K-12 public schools.

more ... more

Figure 8–4 A news release, derived from a speech by the president of the Washington Education Association on classroom overcrowding, was complemented by this provocative advertisement. *(Courtesy of Sharp Hartwig Communications)*

sentences, misused words, mixed metaphors, non sequiturs, cliches, redundancies, circumlocutions, and jargon. Sentences like "She is the widow of the late Marco Picardo" and "The present incumbent is running for reelection" are intolerable to a good editor.

Probably the two most significant writing and editing supports for a practitioner are a good unabridged dictionary and a thesaurus. To these might be added *Bartlett's Familiar Quotations,* the *World Almanac,* and an encyclopedia.

Editing should also concentrate on organizing copy. One release paragraph should flow naturally into the next. Transitions in writing are most important. Sometimes it takes only a single word to unite two adjoining paragraphs. Such is the case in the following example, which uses the word *size.*

> The machine works on a controlled mechanism, directed by a series of pulleys. It is much smaller than the normal motor, requiring less than half of a normal motor's components.
>
> Not only does the device differ in size from other motors, but it also differs in capacity.

Writing, like fine wine, should flow smoothly and stand up under the toughest scrutiny. Careful editing is a must.

BETWEEN THE LINES

DEOBFUSCATING OBFUSCATORY PROVERBS

Test your editing skills by tightening up these annoyingly verbose proverbs. (Answers are below. Don't cheat!)

1. Avian entities of identical plummage inevitably congregate.
2. Pulchritude possesses profundity of a merely cutaneous nature.
3. It is fruitless to become lachrymose over precipitately departed lacteal fluid.
4. It is inefficacious to indoctrinate a superannuated canine with innovative maneuvers.
5. Eschew the implement of correction and vitiate the scion.
6. Visible vapors that issue from ignited carbonaceous materials are a harbinger of simultaneous or imminent conflagration.
7. Lack of propinquity causes an effulgence of partiality in the cardiac area.
8. A revolving mass of lithic conglomerate does not accumulate a congery of small green bryophitic plants.
9. Presenter of the ultimate cachinnation thereby obtains the optimal cachinnation.
10. Ligneous or petrous projectiles may have the potential to fracture my osseous structure, but perjorative appellations remain eternally innocuous.

Answers

1. Birds of a feather flock together.
2. Beauty is only skin deep.
3. There's no use crying over spilt milk.
4. You can't teach an old dog new tricks.
5. Spare the rod and spoil the child.
6. Where there's smoke, there's fire.
7. Absence makes the heart grow fonder.
8. A rolling stone gathers no moss.
9. He who laughs last laughs best.
10. Sticks and stones may break my bones, but names can never hurt me.

SUMMARY

Writing is the essence of public relations practice. The public relations professional, if not the best writer in his or her organization, must at least be one of the best. Writing is the communications skill that differentiates public relations professionals from others.

Some writers are born. But writing can be learned by understanding the fundamentals of what makes interesting writing; by practicing different written forms; and by working constantly to improve, edit, and refine the written product.

When an executive needs something written well, one organizational resource should pop immediately into his or her mind—public relations.

DISCUSSION STARTERS

1. What is the difference between writing for the ear and for the eye?
2. What are several of the writing fundamentals one must consider?
3. What is the essence of the Flesch method of writing?
4. What is the inverted pyramid and why does it work?
5. What is the essential written communications vehicle used by public relations professionals?
6. Why is the format of a news release important to a public relations professional and the organization?
7. What are common purposes of news releases?
8. Should a news release writer try to work his own editorial opinion into the release?
9. What is the key to writing a release on a management speech?
10. What is the purpose of editing?

NOTES

1. Fraser P. Seitel, "Steal!" *United States Banker* (1992): 44.
2. Bill Moyers, "Watch Your Language," *The Professional Communicator* (August–September 1985): 6.
3. Fraser P. Seitel, "Getting It Write," *United States Banker* (December 1991): 54.
4. "J-Prof Says PR Releases Are 'Worthless,'" *Jack O'Dwyer's Newsletter* (July 14, 1993): 4.
5. "Researcher Finds Complaints Against Press Releases Are Justified," *Editor and Publisher* (May 8, 1993): 42, 52.
6. Linda P. Morton, "Producing Publishable Press Releases," *Public Relations Quarterly* (Winter 1992–1993): 9–11.

TOP OF THE SHELF

Merry Aronson and Donald E. Spetner, *The Public Relations Writer's Handbook*. New York: Lexington Books, 1993.

"While always acting as an advocate for the client or company and always having a specific point of view, the true professional does not exaggerate, equivocate, or misrepresent the facts."

Thus begins *The Public Relations Writer's Handbook*, which offers step-by-step advice on the wide range of writing required by public relations professionals. Using examples from successful public relations campaigns and hypothetical clients, the authors instruct readers on the ins and outs of writing effective public relations copy.

The authors, two contemporary public relations professionals, discuss such modern public relations challenges as attracting television and radio coverage, launching new products to the press, responding to unfavorable media coverage, writing management speeches, ensuring attendance at special events, creating press kits, and managing public relations projects.

Part of the appeal of this handbook is that the practical examples presented are relevant to today's public relations. Relatively little attention is paid to more anachronistic practices, such as arranging plant tours and preparing floats for the holiday parade. Whether writing for print or broadcast purposes, *The Public Relations Writer's Handbook* is a most useful guide for any professional.

SUGGESTED READINGS

Beach, Mark. *Editing Your Newsletter.* 3rd ed. Portland, OR: Coast to Coast Books, 1988 (2934 N.E. 16th Ave. 97130).

Bennett, David. *The Publication Marketing Plan.* Kirkwood, MO: Bennett Communications, 1988.

Berg, Karen, and Andrew Gilman. *Get to the Point.* New York: Bantam, 1989.

Bivins, Thomas. *Handbook for Public Relations Writing.* Lincolnwood, IL: National Textbook Company, 1991.

Bivins, Thomas, and William E. Ryan. *How to Produce Creative Publications: Traditional Techniques and Computer Applications.* Lincolnwood, IL: NTC Business, 1992.

Block, Mervin. *Writing Broadcast News—Shorter, Sharper, Stronger.* Chicago: NTC Business, 1992.

Cohen, Paula M. *A Public Relations Primer: Thinking and Writing in Context.* Engelwood Cliffs, NJ: Prentice-Hall, 1987.

Diving into Desktop Publishing. San Francisco: Gillian/Craig Associates (165 Eighth St.).

Iapoce, Michael. *A Funny Thing Happened on the Way to the Boardroom.* New York: Wiley, 1988.

MacDonald, R. H. *Broadcast News Manual of Style.* White Plains, NY: Longman, 1987.

Meyer, Herbert, and Jill Meyer. *How to Write.* Washington, DC: Storm King Press, 1991 (P.O. Box 3566 20007).

Newsome, Douglas, and Bob Carrell. *Public Relations Writing: Form and Style.* 2nd ed. Belmont, CA: Wadsworth, 1988.

Publishing Newsletters. Newsletter Clearinghouse (P.O. Box 311, Rhinebeck, NY 12572).

Rayfield, Robert., et al. *Public Relations Writing: Strategies and Skills.* Dubuque, IA: William C. Brown, 1991.

Standard Periodical Directory. New York: Oxbridge Communications, 1988.

Strunk, W., and E. B. White. *Elements of Style.* New York: Macmillan, 1979.

Success in Newsletter Publishing and Hotline. Newsletter Association (1341 G. St., NW, Washington, DC 20007). Biweekly.

Thomsett, Michael C. *The Little Black Book of Business Words.* New York: AMACOM, 1991.
Tilden, Scott, Anthony Fulginiti, and Jack Gillespie. *Harnessing Desktop Publishing.* Pennington, NJ: Scott Tilden, 1987 (4 West Franklin Ave. 08534-2211).
Video Monitor (10606 Mantz Road, Silver Spring, MD 20903). Monthly.
Wilcox, Dennis L., and Lawrence W. Nolte. *Public Relations Writing and Media Techniques.* New York: Harper College Press, 1990.
Williams, Patrick. *How to Create Winning Employee Publications.* Bartlesville, OK: Joe Williams Communications, 1990.

CASE STUDY

THE RAINA NEWS RELEASE

Background: The Raina, Inc., carborundum plant in Blackrock, Iowa, has been under pressure in recent months to remedy its pollution problem. Raina's plant is the largest in Blackrock, and even though the company has spent $1.3 million on improving its pollution-control equipment, black smoke still spews from the plant's smokestacks, and waste products are still allowed to filter into neighboring streams. Lately, the pressure on Raina has been intense.

- On September 7, Andrew Laskow, a private citizen, called to complain about the "noxious smoke" fouling the environment.
- On September 8, Mrs. Lizzy Ledger of the Blackrock Garden Club called to protest the "smoke problem" that was destroying the zinnias and other flowers in the area.
- On September 9, Clarence "Smoky" Salmon, president of the Blackrock Rod and Gun Club, called to report that 700 people had signed a petition against the Raina plant's pollution of Zeus Creek.
- On September 10, WERS Radio editorialized that "the time has come to force area plants to act on solving pollution problems."
- On September 11, the Blackrock City Council announced plans to enact an air and water pollution ordinance for the city. The council invited as its first witness before the public hearing Leslie Sludge, manager of the Raina carborundum Blackrock plant.

NEWS RELEASE DATA

1. Leslie Sludge, manager of Raina's carborundum Blackrock plant, appeared at the Blackrock City Council hearing on September 11.
2. Sludge said Raina had already spent $1.3 million on a program to clean up pollution at its Blackrock plant.
3. Raina received 500 complaint calls in the past three months protesting its pollution conditions.
4. Sludge said Raina was "concerned about environmental problems, but profits are still what keeps our company running."
5. Sludge announced that the company had decided to commit another $2 million for pollution-abatement facilities over the next three months.
6. Raina is the oldest plant in Blackrock and was built in 1900.
7. Raina's Blackrock plant employs 10,000 people, the largest single employer in Blackrock.
8. Raina originally scheduled its pollution-abatement program for 1995 but speeded it up because of public pressure in recent months.

9. Sludge said that the new pollution-abatement program would begin in October and that the company projected "real progress in terms of clean water and clean air" as early as June 1992.
10. In 1991, Raina, Inc., received a Presidential Award from the Environmental Protection Agency for its "concern for pollution abatement."
11. An internal Raina study indicated that Blackrock was the "most pollutant laden" of all Raina's plants nationwide.
12. Sludge formerly served as manager of Raina's Fetid Reservoir plant in Fetid Reservoir, New Hampshire. In two years as manager of Fetid Reservoir, Sludge was able to convert it from one of the most pollutant-laden plants in the system to the cleanest, as judged by the Environmental Protection Agency.
13. Sludge has been manager of Blackrock for two months.
14. Raina's new program will cost the company $2 million.
15. Raina will hire 100 extra workers especially for the pollution-abatement program.
16. Sludge, 35, is married to the former Polly Usion of Wheeling, West Virginia.
17. Sludge is author of the book *Fly Fishing Made Easy.*
18. The bulk of the money budgeted for the new pollution-abatement program will be spent on two globe refractors, which purify waste destined to be deposited in surrounding waterways, and four hyperventilation systems, which remove noxious particles dispersed into the air from smokestacks.
19. Sludge said, "Raina, Inc., has decided to move ahead with this program at this time because of its long-standing responsibility for keeping the Blackrock environment clean and in response to growing community concern over achieving the objective."
20. Former Blackrock plant manager Fowler Aire was fired by the company in July for his "flagrant disregard for the environment."
21. Aire also was found to be diverting Raina funds from company projects to his own pockets. In all, Aire took close to $10,000, for which the company was not reimbursed. At least part of the money was to be used for pollution control.
22. Aire, whose whereabouts are presently not known, is the brother of J. Derry Aire, Raina's vice-president for finance.
23. Raina's Blackrock plant has also recently installed ramps and other special apparatus to assist handicapped employees. Presently, 100 handicapped workers are employed in the Raina Blackrock plant.
24. Raina's Blackrock plant started as a converted garage, manufacturing plate glass. Only 13 people worked in the plant at that time.
25. Today the Blackrock plant employs 10,000, covers 14 acres of land, and is the largest single supplier of plate glass and commercial panes in the country.
26. The Blackrock plant was slated to be the subject of a critical report from the Private Environmental Stabilization Taskforce (PEST), a private environmental group. PEST's report, "The Foulers," was to discuss "the 10 largest manufacturing polluters in the nation."
27. Raina management has been aware of the PEST report for several months.

QUESTIONS

1. If you were assigned to draft a news release to accompany Sludge to the Blackrock City Council meeting on September 11, which items would you use in your lead (i.e., who, what, why, where, when, how)?
2. Which items would you avoid using in the news release?
3. If a reporter from the *Blackrock Bugle* called and wanted to know what happened to former Blackrock manager Fowler Aire, what would you tell him?

TIPS FROM THE TOP

WILLIAM C. ADAMS

William C. Adams is an associate professor in the School of Journalism and Mass Communication at Florida International University. Prior to joining FIU in 1990, Mr. Adams spent 25 years in corporate public relations, including management positions with Amoco Corporation, Phillips Petroleum Company, and ICI Americas. He has written and lectured extensively on all facets of organizational communications.

How important is writing in public relations?
Good writing is the essence of public relations. It's the lifeblood of our profession and is often what sets us apart from others in the organizations we serve. It's also a balancing act. By "good," I'm referring to well-thought-out, grammatically correct, targeted, purposeful, and effective writing. Writing to *communicate effectively* both inside and outside the organization is the most critical thing a student can learn when studying the many elements of public relations.

By "balancing act," I mean that public relations writers are both translators and interpreters of concepts and ideas, while also being the organization's advocate/persuader. It's skillfully achieving that fine balance between news and advocacy that gets your writing looked at and *read* by internal and external audiences alike.

What's the quality of today's public relations writing?
Unfortunately, much of it is not very good. And what *is* good—or even passable—is often mundane and perfunctory, devoid of even a whiff of humor or cleverness. News releases, for example, too often miss their target audiences, are loaded with jargon and legalese, aren't newsy and interesting, or offer nothing but hype. Many simply are not well written. (Ask any journalist.)

The same goes for other public relations communications tools, such as newsletters, brochures, memos, and even letters. I see too much sloppiness in sentence construction, a lack of smooth-flowing transition between paragraphs and thoughts, and an overall carelessness in editing and proofing (and don't blame Spell-Check!).

Are news releases still worthwhile?
It depends upon whom you ask. Some reporters and editors claim never to use news releases, while others find them indispensable for covering their beats. The trick, much like targeting audiences you wish to reach with your communications program, is to find out who prefers *what*. For example, one writer on a specific beat may prefer "fact sheets" or even a phone call, while another wants news releases.

Research has shown that the reasons most releases don't get used is because they have poor-quality writing, are full of hype, or are not newsy enough. A well-prepared, professional-appearing, and *targeted* release has an excellent chance of being used—or at least getting the reporter's or editor's attention.

A daily newspaper columnist once told one of my public relations writing classes not to "bother him" with "junk mail" (news releases) when they went out into the "real world." They were stunned until a reporter from that same newspaper followed by saying, "Don't believe him . . . he couldn't write his column without help from public relations people and their news releases."

So what's the key to writing an effective news release?
You and the reporters and editors should ask basically the same questions: "Is it *news?*" "Is it *timely?*" "Is it *localized?*" The newsperson asks a critical fourth question: "Is it *important* to my readers/listeners/viewers?" If the answer to all four of the questions is "yes," there's an excellent chance that your release will be used, or at least the basis from which a reporter will call you for further information.

Also important as a "use factor" is a well-crafted informational *lead* and the overall *quality* of the release itself, which includes grammar, punctuation, sentence structure, and style—free from jargon and hype.

What's the secret to effective public relations writing?
Clarity and *conciseness* are the keys to successful public relations writing (correct grammar goes without saying). You also must be able to grab a journalist's attention with a newsy and interesting opening statement (it *is* a "pitch," after all), followed with a *reason* that reporter should be interested in your story idea.

Does writing remain important throughout a public relations career?
The answer is a solid "yes." Even at the managerial level, writing remains a crucial part of the public relations profile.

First of all, to get to that level of success, public relations managers generally move through the "technician" stage, wherein they hone their communication skills, increasing their value to the organization.

Writing well is an art, however, and often scares young people just entering the profession. For example, once after speaking to a group of students, I was approached by a potential public relations major who asked, timidly: "If I go into PR, do I have to do all that *writing* stuff?" The answer remains "yes."

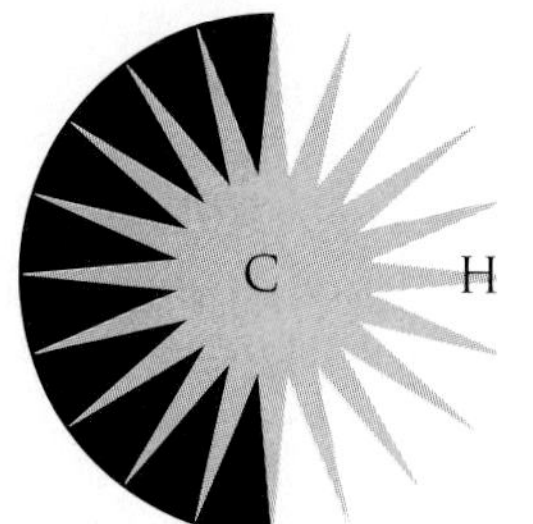

C H A P T E R 9

Writing for the Eye and Ear

WRITING FOR READING EMPHASIZES THE WRITTEN WORD. Writing for listening emphasizes the spoken word. The two differ significantly. Writing for the eye traditionally has ranked among the strongest areas for public relations professionals. Years ago, most practitioners entered public relations through print journalism. Accordingly, they were schooled in the techniques of writing for the eye, not the ear. Today, of course, a background in print journalism is not necessarily a prerequisite for public relations work. Just as important today is writing for the ear—writing for listening. The key to such writing is to write as if you are speaking. Use simple, short sentences, active verbs, contractions, and one- and two-syllable words. In brief, be brief.

This chapter will focus on two things: first, the most frequently used communication vehicles designed for the eye, beyond the news release; and second, the most widely used methods for communicating through the ear, particularly speeches and presentations. Communicating through the medium of video will be the focus of Chapter 10.

Today's public relations professional must be conversant in writing for both the eye and the ear.

THE MEDIA KIT

Beyond the news release, the most ubiquitous print vehicle in public relations work is the media or press kit. Press kits incorporate several communications vehicles for potential use by newspapers and magazines. A bare-bones media kit consists of a news release, backgrounder, biography, photo, and perhaps one or two other items. The kit is designed to answer all of the most likely questions that the media might ask about the organization's announcement. The kit is designed to be all the media need to understand and portray an announcement.

Media kits may also require fact sheets or Q&A (question-and-answer) sheets. The public relations professional must weigh carefully how much information is required in the media kit. Journalists don't appreciate being overwhelmed by too much copy and too many photos.

In preparing a media kit, public relations professionals must keep the following points in mind:

- Be sure the information is accurate and thorough and will answer a journalist's most fundamental questions.
- Provide sufficient background information material to allow the editor to select a story angle.
- Don't be too commercial. Offer balanced, objective information.
- Confine opinions and value judgments to quotes from credible sources.
- Never lie. That's tantamount to editorial suicide.
- Visually arresting graphics may mean the difference between finding the item in the next day's paper or in the same day's wastebasket.

Figure 9–1 shows the press kit used to launch the nationwide tour of one of our country's "most critical natural resources," the California Raisins.

THE BIOGRAPHY

Next to the news release, the most popular tool is the biography, often called the *biographical summary* or just plain *bio*. The bio recounts pertinent facts about a particular individual. Most organizations keep a file of bios covering all top officers. Major newspapers and wire services prepare standby bios on well-known people for immediate use on breaking news, such as sudden deaths.

STRAIGHT BIOS

The straight bio lists factual information in a straightforward fashion in descending order of importance, with company-oriented facts preceding more personal details.

FROM: KETCHUM PUBLIC RELATIONS
55 Union Street
San Francisco, CA 94111
Hilary Hanson
(415) 984-6385
David Emanuel
(415) 984-6326

FOR IMMEDIATE RELEASE

CELEBRATED CALIFORNIA DANCING RAISINS HIT THE ROAD THIS SUMMER
ON ACTION-PACKED SUMMER VACATION

FRESNO, Calif. -- Guess who's packing their bags for a summer vacation across America?

Rumor has it through the grapevine that it's not Chevy Chase filming a new sequel. . .It's the California Dancing Raisins -- those entertaining characters who have captured the hearts of Americans and become celebrities overnight since their top-rated commercials began airing two years ago. The Raisins are planning a whirlwind 6,500-mile road trip stopping in 27 U.S. cities this summer to visit America's favorite landmarks, receive keys to major cities, inform fans of their new national fan club and entertain young and old alike with their famous Grapevine dance.

(more)

55 Union Street • San Francisco, CA 94111

news from the grapevine...

FACT SHEET

CALIFORNIA RAISIN ADVISORY BOARD

The Ad Campaign

- The California Dancing Raisin campaign was voted the most popular television commercial in 1987 by consumers, according to research by Video Storyboard Tests, Inc.
- Three Claymation raisin commercials have been produced since 1986: "Lunch Box," "Late Show" and "Playing With Your Food." A fourth television ad will premiere this fall, airing nationwide beginning in October, starring Ray Charles and a hip new cast of Claymation Raisins.
- A 30-second commercial featuring the Claymation Raisin characters takes an average of three months to produce; it takes one full day of work to create one second of footage. Claymation is the process of creating animation with clay. Produced by Will Vinton, Claymation requires 25 frames of film or individual pictures to create one second of a commercial.

The Raisin Industry

- Approximately 350,000 tons of raisins are produced annually, generating $400 million dollars in sales.
- The California Raisin Advisory Board (CALRAB) represents the U.S. raisin industry, which is composed of 23 raisin packers and more than 5,000 raisin growers in the San Joaquin Valley.
- The California Raisin industry produces virtually the entire domestic supply and almost one-third of the world's supply of raisins.
- Raisins are harvested in late August. Skilled farm workers carefully hand-pick the grapes and place them on clean paper trays in the fields between the rows of vines. They are allowed to dry naturally for days in the sun. After about three weeks of exposure, the grapes become delicious and nutritious juicy raisins.

(more)

55 Union Street • San Francisco, CA 94111

Figure 9–1 When the California Raisin Advisory Board wanted to promote its product across the country, it launched a nationwide tour of the beloved California Raisins, announced via this media kit. *(Courtesy of Ketchum Public Relations)*

David Rockefeller became chairman of the board of directors and chief executive officer of the Chase Manhattan Bank, N.A. in New York on March 1, 1969, and of the Chase Manhattan Corporation upon its formation on June 4, 1969.

During his career with Chase Manhattan, Rockefeller gained a worldwide reputation as a leading banker and spokesman for the business community. He spearheaded the bank's expansion both internationally and throughout the metropolitan New York area and helped the bank play a significant role as a corporate citizen.

Rockefeller joined the Chase National Bank as an assistant manager in the foreign department in 1946. He was appointed an assistant cashier in 1947, second vice-president in 1948, and vice-president in 1949.

From 1950 to 1952, he was responsible for the supervision of Chase's business in Latin America, where, under his direction, new branches were opened in Cuba, Panama, and Puerto Rico, plus a representative office in Buenos Aires.

NARRATIVE BIOS

The narrative bio, on the other hand, is written in a breezier, more informal way. This style gives spark and vitality to the biography to make the individual come alive.

David Rockefeller, who has been described as a man possessed of "a peculiar blend of enterprise, prudence, knowledge, and dedication," was born in Manhattan on June 12, 1915. His mother was the former Abby Aldrich, daughter of Senator Nelson Aldrich of Rhode Island. She had met John D. Rockefeller, Jr., the shy son of multimillionaire John D. Rockefeller, when he was an undergraduate at Brown University in Providence.

John D. Rockefeller, Jr., was anxious that his children not be spoiled by the fortune his father had created and therefore put them on strict allowances. The household atmosphere was deeply religious, with one of the children reading the scriptures each morning before breakfast. Mrs. Rockefeller was an exceptional woman, with a strong interest in the arts. She and David were very close.

The narrative bio, in addition to bringing to life the individual discussed, doubles as a speech of introduction when the individual described serves as a featured speaker. In effect, the narrative bio becomes a speech.

THE BACKGROUNDER

Background pieces, or backgrounders, provide additional information to complement the shorter news release. Backgrounders can embellish the announcement, or can discuss the institution making the announcement, the system behind the announcement, or any other appropriate topic that will assist a journalist in writing the story (Figure 9–2).

Backgrounders are longer and more general in content than the news release. For example, a two-page release announcing the merger of two organizations may not permit much description of the companies involved. A four- or five-page backgrounder provides editors with more depth on the makeup, activities, and history of the merging firms. Backgrounders are usually not used in their entirety by the media but are excerpted.

Subject matter dictates backgrounder style. Some backgrounders are written like a news release, in a snappy and factual manner. Others take a more descriptive and narrative form.

EXAMPLE ONE: NEWS RELEASE STYLE

BACKGROUNDER—SWENSEN'S ICE CREAM COMPANY

The original Swensen's Ice Cream Shoppe was established in 1948 by Earle Swensen at the corner of Union and Hyde in San Francisco.

In 1963 Mr. Swensen licensed the company's predecessor, See Us-Freeze, Inc., later known as United Outlets, Inc., to use Swensen's trade names, trade secrets, recipes, and methods of operation as the basis for Swensen's franchise system. The license agreement was modified in June 1975 and permits the company to use the licensed property and franchise Swensen's shops in all areas of the world except the city and county of San Francisco.

EXAMPLE TWO: DESCRIPTIVE, NARRATIVE STYLE

BACKGROUNDER—SICKLE CELL DISEASE

The man was a West Indian black, a twenty-year-old student in a professional school in Illinois. One day in 1904, he came to James B. Herrick, an eminent Chicago cardiologist, with symptoms Herrick had never seen before and could not find in the literature. The patient had shortness of breath, a disinclination for exercise, palpitation, jaundice, cough, dizziness, headache, leg ulcers, scars from old leg ulcers, many palpable lymph nodes, pale mucous membranes, muscular rheumatism, severe upper abdominal pain, dark urine, and anemia. Blood smears showed many odd-shaped cells, but what arrested the eye was the presence of numerous sickle-shaped cells.

Herrick kept the patient under observation for many years. He did not suspect that he was looking at a disease that afflicted millions of people, including thousands of blacks in America.

In devising a backgrounder, a writer enjoys unlimited latitude. As long as the piece catches the interest of the reader/editor, any style is permissible.

THE FEATURE

Closely related to the backgrounder is the feature story. Features in magazines or newspapers are the opposite of news items. They're often light and humorous. One of the foremost sources of feature writing is the *Wall Street Journal*. Each business day the *Journal's* front page is dominated by three "leader" articles, most written in a time-tested

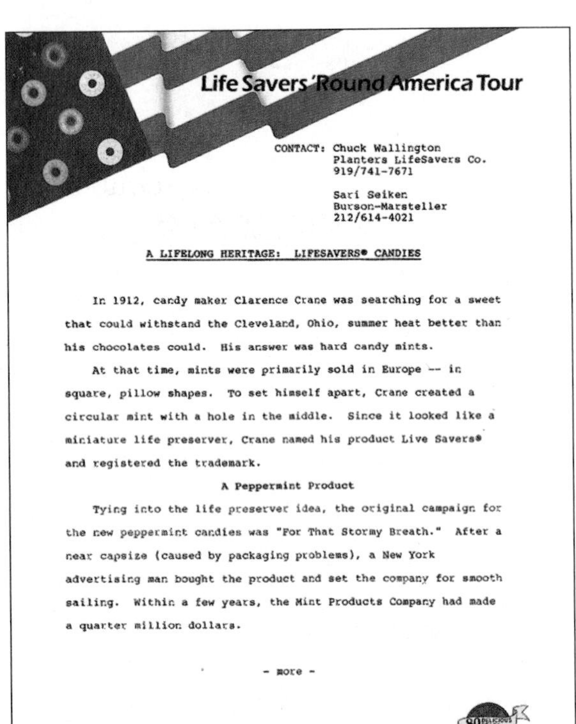

Life Savers 'Round America Tour

CONTACT: Chuck Wallington
Planters LifeSavers Co.
919/741-7671

Sari Seiken
Burson-Marsteller
212/614-4021

A LIFELONG HERITAGE: LIFESAVERS® CANDIES

In 1912, candy maker Clarence Crane was searching for a sweet that could withstand the Cleveland, Ohio, summer heat better than his chocolates could. His answer was hard candy mints.

At that time, mints were primarily sold in Europe -- in square, pillow shapes. To set himself apart, Crane created a circular mint with a hole in the middle. Since it looked like a miniature life preserver, Crane named his product Live Savers® and registered the trademark.

A Peppermint Product

Tying into the life preserver idea, the original campaign for the new peppermint candies was "For That Stormy Breath." After a near capsize (caused by packaging problems), a New York advertising man bought the product and set the company for smooth sailing. Within a few years, the Mint Products Company had made a quarter million dollars.

- more -

Life Savers Heritage/page 2 of 2

World War I put a temporary freeze on production and expansion but, a year after the war ended, mint sales increased more than 200 percent. In 1920, Wint-O-Green was introduced, to be followed by three other mint flavors.

In 1924, the company created fruit flavored drops, consisting of sugar syrups and flavor essences. Flavors included Lemon, Orange and Lime. Over the years, approximately 40 flavors have been launched, discontinued or revived according to consumer preference.

Today, all Life Savers candies are made in Holland, Michigan. The plant produced 568 million rolls of Life Savers in 1991 and expects to make 644 million rolls this year.

Company Expansion

Life Savers candies are made and marketed by the LifeSavers Division of the Nabisco Foods Group. With headquarters in Winston-Salem, N.C., the division's well-known brands include Life Savers® hard-roll candy, Life Savers® Holes, Bubble Yum®, Care*Free® and Fruit Stripe® gums.

# # #

Figure 9–2 This backgrounder accompanied the 80th birthday of Life Savers candies. It is written in a breezier, narrative style, to coincide with the subject matter—Laughin' Lemon, Outlandish Orange, Perky Pineapple, Looney Lime, and Wacky Wild Cherry. *(Courtesy of Planters LifeSavers Co.)*

feature-writing style. Basically, the *Journal* system separates each story into three distinct parts, sometimes labeled the *D-E-E system* (description, explanation, evaluation).

DESCRIPTION

The typical *Journal* story begins by describing an existing situation, often with a light or gripping touch, in such a way that readers are drawn directly into the story.

> When General Miguel Maza Marquez boarded a flight to his coastal hometown of Santa Marta not long ago, 17 fellow passengers abandoned the airplane and the pilot refused to take off. On a second flight, the flight engineer balked.
>
> The reason for the skittishness is that General Maza Marquez is the *good* guy, head of Colombia's equivalent of the Federal Bureau of Investigation—and Number One on the Medellin drug cartel's hit list. Few care to be nearby when somebody tries again to collect the cartel's $1.9 million bounty for killing him; too many bystanders already have perished in attempts on his life.[1]

EXPLANATION

The second part of the *Journal* feature explains how a situation, trend, or event came to be. It is often historical in nature, citing dates, places, and people from the past. It often relates how other factors (economic, sociopolitical, or environmental) may have come to bear on the topic.

> More than 500 people have died in Colombia's drug war in the past year. Gen. Maza Marquez, 51, a short, serene, powerfully built but pot-bellied policeman has been lucky to survive. Sixty-five people died and more than 600 were wounded last December when cartel hit men exploded an estimated 1,200 pieces of dynamite just outside the stark, cement high-rise that houses the DAS. "It was like an atomic bomb," says the general.[2]

EVALUATION

The final section of the *Journal* feature evaluates the meaning of what is contained in the first two parts. It often focuses on the future, frequently quoting sociologists, psychologists, or other experts on what is likely to happen to the subject discussed.

> As the general waits for his deadly duel with Mr. Escobar to resume, he draws some comfort from reports that Mr. Rodriguez Gacha, "the Mexican," in his last hunted days cursed his name. "The Mexican died a lonely man," the general says with satisfaction. As for the future, he is optimistic. "Come see me when you return to Colombia," he tells a visitor. "I should be alive." Then he disappears behind the heavy, bullet-proof metal doors of his office.[3]

In public relations the D-E-E approach often works in feature writing assignments.

HE CASE HISTORY

The case history is frequently used to tell about a customer's favorable use of a company's product or service. Generally, the case-history writer works for the company whose product or service is involved. Magazines, particularly trade journals, often welcome case histories, contending that one person's experience may be instructive to another.

Case-history articles generally follow a five-part formula:

1. They present a problem experienced by one company but applicable to many other firms.
2. They indicate how the dimensions of the problem were defined by the company using the product.
3. They indicate the solution adopted.
4. They explain the advantages of the adopted solution.
5. They detail the user company's experience after adopting the solution.

Incorporating the D-E-E approach into the case-history writing process may interest an editor in a particular product or service. Done skillfully, such a case history is soft sell at its best—beneficial to the company and interesting and informative to the editor and readers.

HE BY-LINER

The by-lined article, or by-liner, is a story signed and ostensibly authored by an officer of a particular firm. Often, however, the by-liner is ghostwritten by a public relations professional. In addition to carrying considerable prestige in certain publications, by-liners allow corporate spokespeople to express their views without being subject to major reinterpretation by the publication.

Perhaps the major advantage of a by-liner is that it positions executives as experts. The fact that an organization's officer has authored an informed article on a subject means that not only are the officer and the organization credible sources, but also, by inference, that they are perhaps more highly regarded on the issues at hand than their competitors. Indeed, the ultimate audience exposed to a by-liner may greatly exceed the circulation of the periodical in which the article appears. Organizations regularly use by-liner reprints as direct-mail pieces to enhance their image with key constituent groups.

HE MEMORANDUM

Humorist Art Buchwald tells of the child who visited his father's office. When asked what his dad did, the son replied, "He sends pieces of paper to other people, and other people send pieces of paper to him." Most people who work know a great deal about memoranda. In many organizations, the memo is the most popular form of communication. Memos are written for a multitude of purposes and take numerous forms. Even though almost everyone gets into the memo-writing act, writing memos correctly takes practice and hard work.

The key to writing good memos is clear thinking. Many memos reflect unclear thinking and are plagued by verbosity and fuzzy language. Inverted pyramid style is often a good way to compose a memo. More often, rewriting turns out to be the key.

Public relations people are expected to write good memos. This is no easy feat. The key is to keep in mind the six primary elements of a meaningful memo:

1. **State the issue.** Don't dilly dally. Memos don't require preambles. Get right to the issue at hand.
2. **Back it up with data.** Put the issue into a clear, snappy context so that the recipient understands your thought processes.
3. **Present alternatives.** List all the possibilities that must be considered before rendering a decision. Again, brevity is a virtue.
4. **Offer your solution/recommendation.** Be decisive. Stick your neck out. Suggest a clear course of action.
5. **Back it up with detail.** Explain, again briefly, why you believe the action you've recommended is justifiable.
6. **Call for the question.** Always end with a question that demands action. Don't leave things up in the air. Too often, memos end by drifting into space. Avoid this. Make the recipient get back to you by asking a question to which he or she must respond, such as "Do you agree with this? or "Can we move on this?"[4]

THE PITCH LETTER

The pitch letter is a sales letter, pure and simple. Its purpose is to interest an editor or reporter in a possible story, interview, or event. Figure 9–3 offers an example of two excellent pitch letters for the same product. Although letter styles run the gamut, the best are direct and to the point, while being catchy and evocative.

Some have questioned the utility of the pitch letter, replacing it with a straightforward "media alert" format to grab the attention of editors and news directors. The new format eschews the use of long paragraphs in favor of short, bulleted items highlighting the "5W's" used by journalists: who, what, when, where, and why. The premise of the media alert is that it "talks to the media in a language it has been trained to accept."[5]

Such criticism notwithstanding, a good pitch letter—especially one with a provocative lead—can hit a reader right between the eyes. For example, Father Bruce Ritter, the founder of Covenant House, who in 1989 met an ignominious fate due to allegations of financial mismanagement and sexual improprieties, nonetheless was responsible for legendary pitch letters. One of Father Bruce's letters began this way:

> *Please* read what I have to tell you.
> Children are being sold.
> Their bodies and spirits are being corrupted.
> They are forced into a life of abuse and degradation.
> Where?
> India? Uganda? Peru?

National Lampoon

This Is Your Last Chance . . .

Say good-bye, sweetheart. This is it! You can kiss the $7.95 one-year subscription to the *National Lampoon* good-bye just as you've said *au revoir* and *harry verderchi* to the fifty-cent gallon of gas, the ten-cent cigar, and the twenty-cent bus ride.

The price is going up and we're giving you fair warning. We're not saying exactly how much we're going to charge for the new one-year subscription but — it's less than the gross national product of Yugoslavia and more than a rubdown in a midget massage parlor.

The reasons for the increase in price are numerous in addition to greed:

1. The cost of paper has skyrocketed. All right, let's examine that. What does it mean to a magazine operation? Well, our editors drink a lot of coffee and this means an increase in the price of coffee cups. They throw paper airplanes around the room while trying to think of funny things to say. Up your cost of paper airplanes by 50 percent.
2. The cost of typewriters has increased. This doesn't affect us since no one on our staff knows how to type.
3. The cost of manufacturing has increased. This means that our editor in chief will be paying more for his Mercedes-Benz this year, and that means more for you to kick in. Would you ask the editor in chief of the world's most widely read adult humor magazine to drive around in last year's Mercedes-Benz?
4. The price of grain is spiraling. (We don't know what that means, but it is an exact quote from the *Wall Street Journal* so it must be important.)

O.K., put this all together and it means — raise the subscription prices. No more $7.95. So, this is it. This is your last chance. From here on in, it's clipsville. You pay more.

If you really want to save, take out a two- or three-year subscription. The savings are so big that we actually lose money every time you or anyone else subscribes for two or three years. We do it only because our subscription manager is insecure and he wants to know that he'll have at least a handful of people around for a long time.

No more message. If you want the latest in yocks, mirth, and lovable satire, subscribe today and subscribe at these pre-inflation prices.

Sincerely,

Herbert Hoover

Herbert Hoover
Subscription Manager

IF YOU EVER WANT TO SEE THE
LITTLE NATIONAL LAMPOON ALIVE
AGAIN IN YOUR CRUMMY MAILBOX,
YOU KNOW WHAT YOU HAVE TO DO!!!

YOU'VE BEEN WARNED.
DON'T PLAY CUTE.

Figure 9–3 Pitch letters should be enticing, catchy, and evocative. Even though these examples from the subscription department of the *National Lampoon* magazine may not qualify as garden-variety pitch letters, they certainly are enticing, catchy, and evocative. *(Courtesy of National Lampoon)*

No!
Right here in New York, the Big Apple, Fun City.
Covenant House began as a response to the needs of these children of the streets. Will you join with me in helping to carry out this work?

Such unbridled, heart-tugging language is typical of a good, compassionate pitch letter.

Pitch letters that sell generally contain several key elements. First, they open with a grabber, an interesting statement that impels the reader to read on. Next, they explain why the editor and/or publication should be interested in the pitch, or invitation. Finally, they are personally written to specific people, rather than being addressed to "editor" (which is the journalistic equivalent of "occupant").

OTHER TOOLS

Other public relations tools, such as the round-up article, the fact sheet, and the Q&A, may be helpful in certain infrequent situations.

THE ROUND-UP ARTICLE

Although many publications discourage publicity about a single company, they encourage articles that summarize, or round up, the experiences of several companies within an industry. These trend articles may be initiated by the publications themselves or at the suggestions of public relations people. Weaker or smaller companies, in particular, can benefit from being included in a round-up story with stronger, larger adversaries. Thoroughly researching and drafting round-up articles is a good way to secure articles that mention the practitioner's firm in favorable association with top competitors. *The Wall Street Journal* and *USA Today*, in particular, are regular users of round-ups.

THE FACT SHEET

Fact sheets are short documents that compactly profile an organization. They generally support the information in news releases and backgrounders. Editors find fact sheets helpful as a quick supply of resource material for articles.

Fact sheets are designed to provide an editor with a quick thumbnail sketch of an organization, individual, or event. For example, a typical one-page corporate fact sheet includes a brief description of the company and its product lines, the names of its top managers, its location, current sales figures, leading products, and a summary of its history. How is all this possible in a one-page sketch? Figure 9–4 shows how.

THE Q&A

The question-and-answer form, or Q&A, often substitutes for or complements a fact sheet in conveying easy-to-follow information. In the Q&A, the writer lists frequently asked questions about the subject and then provides appropriate answers. A skillfully written Q&A can often substitute for a personal interview between an editor and a company official.

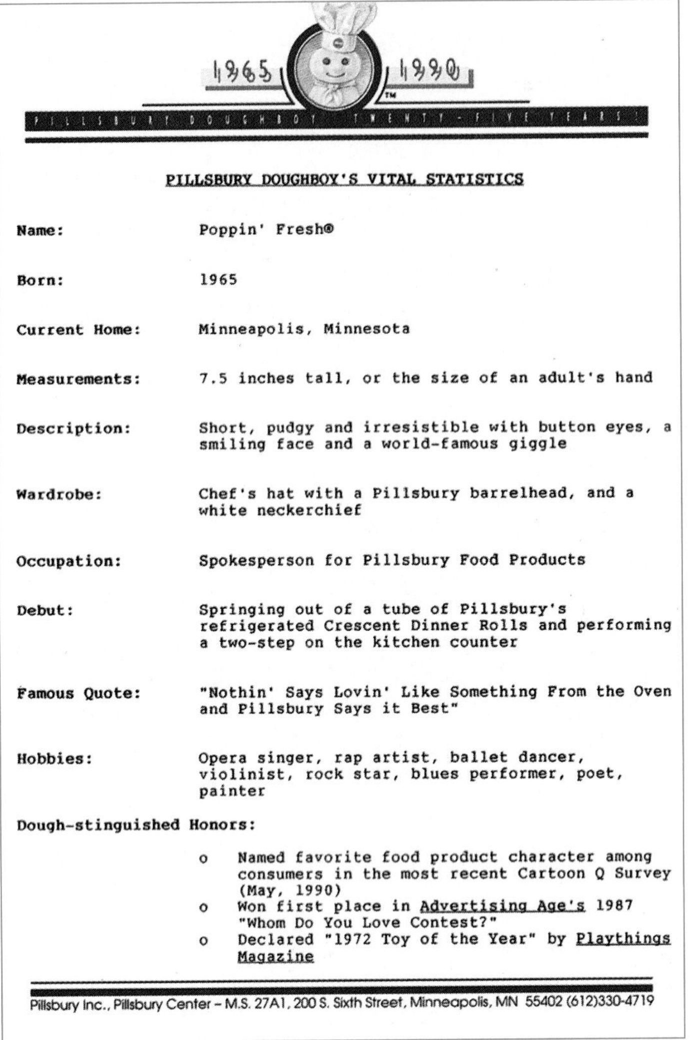

PILLSBURY DOUGHBOY'S VITAL STATISTICS

Name:	Poppin' Fresh®
Born:	1965
Current Home:	Minneapolis, Minnesota
Measurements:	7.5 inches tall, or the size of an adult's hand
Description:	Short, pudgy and irresistible with button eyes, a smiling face and a world-famous giggle
Wardrobe:	Chef's hat with a Pillsbury barrelhead, and a white neckerchief
Occupation:	Spokesperson for Pillsbury Food Products
Debut:	Springing out of a tube of Pillsbury's refrigerated Crescent Dinner Rolls and performing a two-step on the kitchen counter
Famous Quote:	"Nothin' Says Lovin' Like Something From the Oven and Pillsbury Says it Best"
Hobbies:	Opera singer, rap artist, ballet dancer, violinist, rock star, blues performer, poet, painter

Dough-stinguished Honors:

- Named favorite food product character among consumers in the most recent Cartoon Q Survey (May, 1990)
- Won first place in Advertising Age's 1987 "Whom Do You Love Contest?"
- Declared "1972 Toy of the Year" by Playthings Magazine

Pillsbury Inc., Pillsbury Center – M.S. 27A1, 200 S. Sixth Street, Minneapolis, MN 55402 (612)330-4719

Figure 9–4 Another variation on the fact sheet theme is this submission by Pillsbury in recognition of its Dough Boy's 25th birthday. *(Courtesy of Golin/Harris Communications)*

PHOTOGRAPHIC SUPPORTS

Photos, when used properly, enhance brochures, annual reports, and even news releases. Any practitioner involved with printed material should know the basics of photography. Although a detailed discussion of photographic terms and techniques is beyond the scope of this book, public relations practitioners should be relatively conversant with photographic terminology and able to recognize the attributes of good photos:

Figure 9–5 Occasionally a specially conceived photo will attract extensive publicity. In 1959, when Chase Manhattan Bank was in the midst of constructing its downtown New York City headquarters at One Chase Manhattan Plaza, photographer Robert Mottar asked the hundreds of workers to freeze for a moment so that this rare photo could be taken for posterity. It was also reported in many of New York City's daily newspapers, which acknowledged both the bank and its new location. (*Courtesy of Chase Manhattan Bank*)

1. Photos should be taken "live," in real environments with believable people, instead of in studios with stilted models (Figure 9–5).
2. They should focus clearly on the issue, product, image, or person that the organization wishes to emphasize, without irrelevant, visually distracting clutter in the foreground or background.
3. They should be eye-catching, using angles creatively—overhead, below, to the side—to suggest movement.
4. They must express a viewpoint—an underlying message.
5. Most of all, photos must make a visual impact. The best photos are those that remain in a person's mind long after written appeals to action have faded. These are the photos that are "worth 10,000 words."[6]

THE STANDBY STATEMENT

Organizations sometimes take actions or make announcements they know will lead to media inquiries or even public protests. In such cases, firms prepare concise statements to clarify their positions, should they be called to explain. Such standby statements generally are defensive. They should be brief and unambiguous so as not to raise more questions than they answer. Such events as executive firings, layoffs, price increases, and extraordinary losses are all subject to subsequent scrutiny by the media and are therefore proper candidates for standby statements.

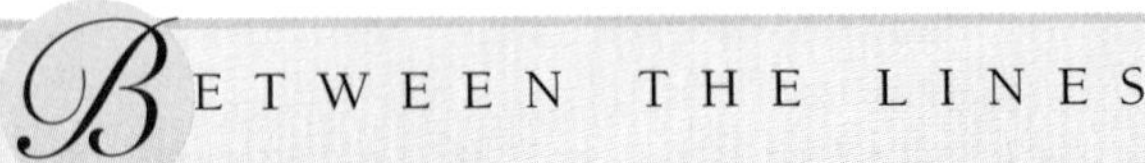

BETWEEN THE LINES

DON'T—REPEAT—DON'T USE "DO NOT"

In writing standby statements, public relations practitioners should keep in mind that publications sometimes mistakenly drop words in print. Invariably, the most important words are the ones dropped.

For example, the public relations officer of the labor union who issues the statement "We do not intend to strike" may have his quote appear in the next day's paper as "We do intend to strike"—the *not* having been inadvertently dropped by the paper. A slight yet significant change.

The remedy: Use contractions. It's pretty hard to drop a significant word or distort the intended meaning when the statement is "We don't intend to strike."

THE SPEECH

Speech writing has become one of the most coveted public relations skills. Increasingly, speech writers have used their access to management to move up the organizational ladder. The prominence they enjoy is due largely to the importance top executives place on making speeches. Today's executives are called on by government and special-interest groups to defend their policies, justify their prices, and explain their practices to a much greater degree than ever before. In this environment, a good speech writer becomes a valuable—and often highly paid—asset.

A speech possess five main characteristics:

1. **It is designed to be heard, not read.** The mistake of writing for the eye instead of the ear is the most common trap of bad speeches. Speeches needn't be literary gems, but they ought to sound good.
2. **It uses concrete language.** The ear dislikes generalities. It responds to clear images. Ideas must be expressed sharply for the audience to get the point.

3. **It demands a positive response.** Every word, every passage, every phrase should evoke a response from the audience. The speech should possess special vitality—and so, for that matter, should the speaker.
4. **It must have clear-cut objectives.** The speech and the speaker must have a point—a thesis. If there's no point, then it's not worth the speaker's or the audience's time to be there.
5. **It must be tailored to a specific audience.** An audience needs to feel that it is hearing something special. The most frequent complaint about organizational speeches is that they all seem interchangeable—they lack uniqueness. That's why speeches must be targeted to fit the needs of a specific audience.

Beyond adhering to these five principles and before putting words on paper, a speechwriter must have a clear idea of the process—the route—to follow in developing the speech.

THE SPEECHWRITING PROCESS

The speechwriting process breaks down into four components: (1) preparing, (2) interviewing, (3) researching, and (4) organizing and writing.

PREPARING

One easy way to prepare for a speech is to follow a 4W checklist. In other words, answer the questions who, what, where, and when.

- **Who** The who represents two critical elements: the speaker and the audience. A writer should know all about the speaker: manner of speech, use of humor, reaction to an audience, background, and personality. It's almost impossible to write a speech for someone you don't know.

  The writer should also know something about the audience. What does this audience think about this subject? What are its predispositions toward the subject and the speaker? What are the major points with which it might agree? The more familiar the writer is with the who of a speech, the easier the writing will be.
- **What** The what is the topic. The assigned subject must be clearly known and well defined by the writer before formal research is begun. If the writer fails to delineate the subject in advance, much of the research will be pointless.
- **Where** The where is the setting. A large hall requires a more formal talk than a roundtable forum. Often, the location of the speech—the city, state, or even a particular hall—bears historic or symbolic significance that can enhance a message.
- **When** The when is the time of the speech. People are more awake in the morning and get sleepier as the day progresses, so a dinner speech should be kept short. The when also refers to the time of year. A speech can always be linked to an upcoming holiday or special celebration.

INTERVIEWING

Interviewing speakers in advance is essential. Without that chance, the results can be dismal. A good interview with a speaker often means the difference between a strong speech and a poor one. Stated another way, the speechwriter is only as good as his or her access to the speaker.

In the interview the speechwriter gets some time—from as little as 15 minutes to over an hour—to observe the speaker firsthand and probe for the keys to the speech. The interview must accomplish at least three specific goals for the speech writer:

1. **Determine the object of the talk** The object is different from the subject. The subject is the topic, but the object is the purpose of the speech—that is, what exactly the speaker wants the audience to do after he or she is finished speaking. Does the speaker want them to storm City Hall? To love big business? To write their congressional representatives? The interviewer's essential question must be "What do you want to leave the audience with at the conclusion of your speech?" Once the speaker answers this question, the rest of the speech should fall into place.
2. **Determine the speaker's main points** Normally, an audience can grasp only a few points during a speech. These points, which should flow directly from the object, become touchstones around which the rest of the speech is woven. Again, the writer must determine the three or four main points during the interview.
3. **Capture the speaker's characteristics** Most of all, during the interview, the writer must observe the speaker. How comfortable is the speaker with humor? How informal or deliberate is he or she with words? What are the speaker's pet phrases and expressions? The writer must file these observations away, recall them during the writing process, and factor them into the speech.

RESEARCHING

Like any writer, a speechwriter sometimes develops writer's block: the inability to come up with anything on paper. One way around writer's block is to adopt a formalized research procedure.

1. Dig into all literature, books, pamphlets, articles, speeches, and other writings on the speech subject. Prior speeches by the speaker are also important documents to research. A stocked file cabinet is often the speechwriter's best friend.
2. Think about the subject. Bring personal thoughts to bear on the topic. Presumably, the speaker has already discussed the topic with the writer, so the writer can amplify the speaker's thoughts with his or her own.
3. Seek out the opinions of others on the topic. Perhaps the speaker isn't the most knowledgeable source within the organization about this specific subject. Economists, lawyers, accountants, doctors, and other technical experts may shed additional light on the topic. Outside sources, particularly politicians and business leaders, are often willing to share their ideas when requested.

ORGANIZING AND WRITING

Once preparation, interviewing, and research have been completed, the fun part begins. Writing a speech becomes easier if, again, the speech is organized into its four essential elements: introduction, thesis, body, and conclusion.

INTRODUCTION Writing a speech introduction is a lot like handling a bar of soap in the shower: the first thing to do is get control. An introduction must grab the audience and hold its interest. An audience is alert at the beginning of a talk and is with the speaker. The writer's job is to make sure the audience stays there.

The speechwriter must take full advantage of the early good nature of the audience by making the introduction snappy. Audience members need time to settle in their seats, and the speaker needs time to get his or her bearings on the podium. Often, the best way to win early trust and rapport with the audience is to ease into the speech with humor.

THESIS The thesis is the object of the speech—its purpose, or central idea. A good thesis statement lets an audience know in a simple sentence where a speech is going and how it will get there. For example, its purpose can be to persuade:

> The federal government must allow home football games to be televised.

Another thesis statement might be to reinforce or crystallize a belief:

> Sunday football viewing is among the most cherished of winter family home entertainments.

The purpose of yet another thesis statement might merely be to entertain:

> Football viewing in the living room can be a harrowing experience. Let me explain.

In each case, the thesis statement lets the audience know early what the point of the speech will be and leads listeners to the desired conclusion.

BODY The speech body is just that—the general body of evidence that supports the three or four main points. Although facts, statistics, and figures are important elements, writers should always attempt to use comparisons or contrasts for easier audience understanding. For example:

> In a single week, 272 million customers passed through the checkout counters of American supermarkets. That's equal to the combined populations of Spain, Mexico, Argentina, France, West Germany, Italy, Sweden, Switzerland, and Belgium.

Such comparisons dramatically hammer points home to a lazy audience.

CONCLUSION The best advice on wrapping up a speech is to do it quickly. As the old Texas bromide goes, "If you haven't struck oil in the first 20 minutes, stop boring."

Put another way, the conclusion must be blunt, short, and to the point. It may be a good idea to review orally the major points and thesis one last time and then stop.

THE SPOKEN WORD

Because speeches are meant to be heard, the writer should take advantage of tools that emphasize the special qualities of the spoken word. Such devices can add vitality to a speech, transcending the content of the words themselves. Used skillfully, these devices can elevate a mediocre speech into a memorable one.

Speeches are meant to be heard. Therefore, the speech writer should take advantage of tools—figures of speech—that emphasize the special qualities of the spoken word:

- *Alliteration,* the repetition of initial sounds in words.
- *Antithesis,* using sharply opposed or contrasting ideas in the same passage.
- *Metonomy,* substituting one term for another closely associated one to give a passage more figurative life.
- *Metaphor* and *simile,* which figuratively connect concepts that have little literal connection.
- *Personification,* which gives life to animals, inanimate objects, or ideas.
- *Repetition,* using the same words or phrases over and over again.
- *Humor* that is relevant, fresh, and in good taste.

The key to speech writing, as to any other kind of writing, is experience. With speech writing becoming a more competitive, highly paid, and sought-after pursuit in public relations, it has become increasingly difficult for an interested novice to break in. But don't be dismayed. Most political candidates or nonprofit community organizations are more than willing to allow beginners to try their hand at drafting speeches. While the pay for such endeavors may be limited—or nonexistent—such voluntary efforts are a good way to learn the ropes of speech writing.

Few other activities in public relations offer as much fulfillment—in both psychological and monetary rewards—as speech writing.

MAKING AN EFFECTIVE PRESENTATION

A business presentation is different from a speech. A presentation generally is designed to sell a product, service, or idea. Everyone, somewhere along the line, must deliver a presentation. Like any other speaking device, an effective presentation depends on following established guidelines. Here are 10 points worth pursuing prior to presenting:

1. **Get organized.** Before considering your presentation, consider the 4Ws of speechwriting: Who are you addressing? What are you trying to say? Where and when should something happen?
2. **Get to the point.** Know your thesis. What are you trying to prove? What is the central purpose of your presentation?

BETWEEN THE LINES

EVERY PICTURE TELLS A STORY

As executive speechmaking has become more important, a plethora of counseling firms have sprung up to advise executive speakers on how to create and deliver winning speeches. Communispond, Inc., developed one of the most novel concepts. Because most executives are neither comfortable at a podium nor confident in their ability to perform before a large audience, Communispond came up with the concept of drawing pictures to replace formal written speeches. Essentially, after gathering all available evidence and support material and outlining in words what they want to cover, Communispond-trained executives are encouraged to draw pictures, called *ideographs,* to reflect accurately the subject at hand. For example, a corporate speaker who wants to express the notion that the ship of American capitalism is still being fired on by entrenched socialist salvos around the world might sketch an ideograph similar to the one here.

In this way, Communispond-trained speakers are taught to use their nervousness to convey natural, human conviction. In other words, not constrained by lifeless written copy, an executive is free, as Communispond puts it, "to speak as well as you think."

Although not right for everyone, Communispond's unique approach, when mastered, allows for a much more extemporaneous and lively discourse than the average prepared text. Fortunately, however (at least as far as corporate speech writers are concerned), most executives still insist on the security blanket of a full written text.

3. **Be logical.** Organize the presentation with some logic in mind. Don't skip randomly from one thought to another. Lead from your objective to your strategies to the tactics you will use to achieve your goal.
4. **Write it out.** Don't wing it. If Johnny Carson and David Letterman write out their ad libs, so should you. Always have the words right in front of you.
5. **Anticipate the negatives.** Keep carping critics at bay. Anticipate their objections and defuse them by alluding yourself to vulnerabilities in the presentation.
6. **Speak, don't read.** Sound as if you know the information. Practice before the performance. Make the presentation part of you. Reading suggests uncertainty. Speaking asserts assurance.
7. **Be understandable.** Speak with clarity and concreteness so that people understand you. If you want to make the sale, you must be clear.
8. **Use graphics wisely.** Audiovisual supports should do just that—support the presentation. Graphics should be used more to tease than to provide full information. And graphics shouldn't be crammed with too much information. This will detract from the overall impact of the presentation. Because many audiovisual channels are available to a presenter (see Appendix D), it may be wise to seek professional help in devising compelling graphics for a presentation.
9. **Be convincing.** If you aren't enthusiastic about your presentation, no one else will be. Be animated. Be interesting. Be enthusiastic. Sound convinced that what you're presenting is an absolute necessity for the organization.
10. **STOP!** A short, buttoned-up presentation is much more effective than one that goes on and on. At his inaugural, U.S. President William Henry Harrison delivered a two-hour, 6,000-word address into a biting wind on Pennsylvania Avenue. A month later, he died of pneumonia. The lesson: when you've said it all, shut up!

Is learning how to make an effective presentation really worth it? Well, when General Norman Schwarzkopf retired after the Gulf War, he marched into the speaking world at $80,000 per speech.[7] That was $20,000 less than former President George Bush began charging when he ventured into the speech market in 1994. In the 1990s, in fact, about the only two celebrities not particularly interested in public speaking were golf champions Arnold Palmer and Jack Nicklaus. They each asked $45,000 per speech "because they really don't want to speak"—or, one presumes, need to do so.[8]

Beavis and Butt-Head Battle Backlash

Another indication that the world is coming to an end was the popularity in the mid-1990s of two inane MTV cartoon characters, the irrepressible Beavis and Butt-Head.

Artwork by Edison Lee

Each evening, millions of MTV viewers turned on *Beavis and Butt-Head* to hear their heroes repeat over and over again "Heh-heh-heh. Heh, heh, heh, cool." Or, if the contrary mood struck them, "Heh-heh-heh. Heh-heh-heh, sucks."

In October 1993, the two cartoon culprits came under attack after an Ohio mother blamed Beavis and Butt-Head's habit of lighting fires and saying "Fire is good" for causing the death of her two-year-old daughter after her five-year-old son set their trailer home ablaze.

The Senate Commerce Committee lambasted the cartoon duo and demanded that MTV take action.

MTV responded immediately. In a prepared statement, the network called the Ohio fire a "terrible tragedy" and promised to "reexamine issues regarding *Beavis and Butt-Head.*"

This "reexamination" led to an immediate shift by MTV of *Beavis and Butt-Head* to a later (10:30 P.M.) starting time. MTV added that it would seek "to come up with a different concept for new episodes of the series that could be on earlier."

In voluntarily moving the show to a later starting time, what was MTV admitting about *Beavis and Butt-Head?*

P.S.: So sensitive was the network about the two miscreants that when a certain author requested a photo of Beavis and Butt-Head for his textbook, MTV politely turned him down. (So, the author got one anyway from a talented high school artist. Heh, heh, heh, cool!)

SUMMARY

Skillful writing lies at the heart of public relations practice. Basically, public relations professionals are professional communicators. Ergo, each person engaged in public relations work must be adept at writing.

In today's overcommunicated society, everyone from newspaper editors to corporate presidents complains about getting too much paper. So, before a professional even thinks of putting thoughts on paper, he or she must answer the following questions:

1. **Will writing serve a practical purpose?** If you can't come up with a purpose, don't write.
2. **Is writing the most effective way to communicate?** Face-to-face or telephone communication may be better and more direct than writing.
3. **What is the risk?** Writing is always risky; just ask a lawyer. Once it's down in black and white, it's difficult or impossible to retract. So, think before you write.
4. **Are the timing and the person doing the writing right?** Timing is extremely important in writing. A message, like a joke, can fall flat if the timing is off. The individual doing the writing must also be considered. A writer should always ask whether he or she is the most appropriate person to write.

The pen—or, more likely, the personal computer—is a powerful weapon. Like any other weapon, writing must be used prudently and properly to achieve the desired result.

DISCUSSION STARTERS

1. What are the essential elements of a media kit?
2. What is the difference between a straight biography and a narrative biography?
3. What is a backgrounder?
4. What are the benefits of a round-up story?
5. When might an organization require a standby statement?
6. What are the essential characteristics of a speech?
7. What questions does one ask to begin the speech writing process?
8. What are the elements that constitute an effective presentation?
9. What is the purpose of using "figures of speech" in a presentation and what types are useful?
10. What are possible pitfalls that must be considered before writing anything?

NOTES

1. Jose de Cordoba, "Marked for Death, Colombia's Top Cop Is a Tough Target," *The Wall Street Journal* (October 2, 1990): A1.
2. Ibid.

3. Loc. cit.
4. Fraser P. Seitel, "Meaningful Memos," *United States Banker* (November 1993): 77.
5. "Farewell to the Pitch Letter," *Public Relations Journal* (July 1990): 13.
6. G. A. Marken, "Public Relations Photos . . Beyond the Written Word," *Public Relations Quarterly* (Summer 1993): 7–12.
7. Randall Poe, "Talk Isn't Cheap," *Across the Board* (September 1992): 19–24.
8. "One Speech Writer's Complaint," *The Effective Speech Writer's Newsletter* (October 6, 1989): 1.

SUGGESTED READINGS

Ailes, Roger, and John Krausher. *You Are the Message.* Homewood, IL: Dow Jones-Irwin, 1988.

Arrendondo, Lani. *How to Present Like a Pro.* New York: McGraw-Hill, 1991.

Detz, Joan. *How to Write and Give a Speech.* New York: St. Martin's Press, 1992.

Executive Speaker (P.O. Box 292437, Dayton, OH 45429). Newsletter.

Executive Speechmaker. New York: Institute for Public Relations Research and Education, 1980 (310 Madison Ave. 10017).

Fettig, Art. *How to Hold an Audience in the Hollow of Your Hand.* Battle Creek, MI: Growth Unlimited, 1988.

Gibbs, Ennis. *The Public Speaker's Emergency Repair Manual and Survival Kit.* Claremont, CA: Alert Publications, 1987.

Kaplan, Burton. *The Corporate Manager's Guide to Speechwriting.* New York: Free Press, 1988.

Radio Interview Guide. New York: Book Promotions, 1988 (26 E. 33rd St.).

Rafe, Stephen. *The Executive's Guide to Successful Presentations.* Warrentown, VA: S/RC, 1991.

Richardson, Linda. *Winning Group Sales Presentations.* Homewood, IL: Dow Jones-Irwin, 1991.

Robinson, James W. *Winning Them Over.* Rocklin, CA: Prima Publishing and Communications, 1987.

Roesch, Roberta. *Smart Talk.* New York: AMACOM, 1989.

Sarnoff, Dorothy. *Never Be Nervous Again.* New York: Crown, 1988.

Smith, Terry C. *Making Successful Presentations.* 2nd ed. New York: Wiley, 1991.

Speechwriter's Newsletter. (Available from Ragan Communications, 407 S. Dearborn, Chicago, IL 60605).

Thomserr, Michael C. *The Little Black Book of Business Speaking.* New York: AMACOM, 1989.

United Press International. *Broadcast Stylebook.* (Available from the author, 220 E. 42nd Street, New York, NY 10017.) This is not a rule book, but it suggests methods and treatment for properly preparing news copy, with examples of wire copy and brief comments on correct and incorrect methods of news wire copy preparation. It's designed to help people write the kind of copy used by an announcer.

Variety. (Available from 475 Park Ave. South, New York, NY 10016; published weekly on Wednesday.) This paper publishes news, features, and commentary each week on every aspect of show business, with extensive reviews of productions around the world.

TOP OF THE SHELF

Henry Ehrlich, *Writing Effective Speeches.* New York: Paragon House, 1992.

Henry Ehrlich, one of the nation's most gifted business speech writers, knows the difference between writing for the ear and the eye. This volume explains all a beginner needs to know about writing an effective speech.

Among the topics the author explores are the following:

- The difference between writing for yourself and for someone else.
- How to write a speech for a member of the opposite sex.
- New ways to begin a speech.
- Tackling an unfamiliar subject.
- Assessing an audience.
- Phrasing, coaching the speaker, typing the script, and adding visual cues.

Perhaps most appealing, the author confronts his subject with large doses of humor, developed over years of experience. He suggests effective ways to use humor and anecdotes, as well as how to organize lighter speeches, such as awards presentations, speaker introductions, and motivational talks.

All in all, Henry Ehrlich's contribution to speechwriting literature is as inspirational as it is instructive. (Besides, how can you dislike a guy who suggests to a bank president that he add a little levity to his speech by "imitating Marilyn Monroe"?)

ILLINOIS POWER'S REPLY

For three decades, no network news program rivaled the incredible impact of CBS-TV's *60 Minutes.* Watched each Sunday night by more than 20 million Americans, *60 Minutes* still ranks as one of the most popular programs in the nation and the show most feared by public relations professionals. When *60 Minutes* comes calling, scandal, or at least significant problems, can't be far behind.

Such was the thinking at Illinois Power Company (IP) in Decatur in the fall of 1979, when *60 Minutes* sent reporter Harry Reasoner to find out why the company's Clinton nuclear reactor project was behind schedule and over budget.

What followed—the exchange between Reasoner and IP—still ranks as history's most classic confrontation between television and corporate public relations professionals.

Because IP suspected that *60 Minutes* wanted to do a hatchet job, the company agreed to be interviewed only if it, too, videotaped the *60 Minutes* filming on its premises. In other words, IP would videotape the videotapers; it would report on the reporters; it would meet *60 Minutes* on its own terms. Reasoner and his producer reluctantly agreed to the arrangement.

And so in early October, IP's executive vice-president sat for an hour-and-a-half interview before the *60 Minutes*—and the IP—cameras. He answered Reasoner's questions straightforwardly and comprehensively. And he and his company prepared for the worst.

Which is precisely what they received.

On November 25, *60 Minutes* broadcast a 16-minute segment on the Clinton plant, charging IP with mismanagement, missed deadlines, and costly overruns that would be passed on to consumers. Viewers saw three former IP employees accuse the utility of making no effort to control costs, allowing slipshod internal reporting, and fabricating estimates of construction completion timetables. One of the accusers was shown in silhouette with a distorted voice because, as reporter Reasoner intoned, "He fears retribution." To add salt to the IP wound, the 90-minute interview with the company's executive vice-president merited less than 2 minutes of edited, misleading air time.

Worst of all, 24 million Americans viewed the crucifixion in their living rooms.

The day after the CBS story, IP's stock fell a full point on the New York Stock Exchange in the busiest trading day in the company's history. Rather than responding as most companies do—with bruised feelings, a scorched reputation, and feeble cries of "foul" to its stockholders—IP lashed back with barrels blazing. Within days of the broadcast, IP produced *60 Minutes/Our Reply*, a 44-minute film incorporating the entire *60 Minutes* segment, punctuated by insertions and narrative presenting the company's rebuttal.

The rebuttal included videotape of CBS film footage not included in the program, much of which raised serious questions about the integrity of the material CBS used. The rebuttal also documented the backgrounds and possible motives of the three former employees CBS quoted, all of whom had been fired for questionable performance. One of the former employees, in fact, was the leader of the local antinuclear group opposing IP.

Initially, the reply tape was aired to a relatively small audience: the company's employees, customers, shareholders, and investors. But word traveled quickly that IP had produced a riveting, broadcast-quality production, so true to the *60 Minutes* format—ticking stopwatch and all—that it could easily be mistaken for the original. Within a year, close to 2,500 copies of the devastating rebuttal had been distributed to legislators, corporate executives, journalists, and others. Excerpts were broadcast on television stations throughout the nation, and the IP production became legendary. As the *Wall Street Journal* put it, "The program focuses new attention on news accuracy. . . . Although even a telling, polished, counter-program like Illinois Power's can't reach the masses of a national broadcast, the reply tape has proven effective in reaching a significant 'thinking' audience."

Even CBS was impressed. The producer of the original *60 Minutes* segment called the rebuttal highly sophisticated, especially for a company that had first seemed to him to be a "down-home cracker barrel" outfit. The IP tape soon spawned imitators. Companies such as Chevron, Union Carbide, Commonwealth Edison, and many others began experimenting with defensive videotaping in dealing with television journalists.

Although *60 Minutes* admitted to some sloppiness in its reporting and to two minor factual inaccuracies, it essentially stood by its account. Complained CBS executive producer Don Hewitt, "We went in as a disinterested party and did a news report. They made a propaganda film for their side, using our reporting for their own purposes."

Perhaps. But one irrefutable result of the dramatic confrontation between the huge national network and the tiny local utility was that IP—by turning the television tables on the dreaded *60 Minutes*—had earned its place in public relations history.*

QUESTIONS

1. Do you agree with IP's original decision to let *60 Minutes* in despite the suspicion that the program would be a hatchet job? What might have happened if IP turned down the *60 Minutes* request?
2. If *60 Minutes* had turned down IP's request to videotape the Reasoner interviews, would you have still allowed the filming?
3. Presume that IP didn't tape the *60 Minutes* filming on its premises. What other communications options might the company have pursued to rebut the *60 Minutes* accusations?
4. Do you think IP did better by allowing *60 Minutes* in to film or would they have been better off keeping CBS out?

*Sandy Graham, "Illinois Utility Sparks Widespread Interest with Its Videotape," *The Wall Street Journal* (April 12, 1980): 23. For further information on the IP case, see *Punch, Counterpunch: "60 Minutes" vs. Illinois Power Company* (Washington, DC: Media Institute, 1981), and "Turning the Tables on '60 Minutes,'" *Columbia Journalism Review* (May–June 1980): 7–9.

TIPS FROM THE TOP

SHIRLEY CARTER

Dr. Shirley Staples Carter is professor and chairperson of the Department of Mass Communications and Journalism at Norfolk State University, Norfolk, VA. Prior to that, she was associate professor/director and former inaugural chairperson of the Department of Communications and Visual Arts at the University of North Florida. Dr. Carter directs the university's efforts to plan and develop new communications technologies, such as instructional television fixed-services delivery systems, other broadcast initiatives, and cable and community education. Dr. Carter's experience spans two decades in higher education administration and teaching. She is the first African-American female to serve as a department chairperson in journalism/mass communications at a mainstream university.

What does it take to become an effective print writer?
We need to return to the basics, which include reading, listening, and observing skills. As our society prepares for the explosion of the information superhighway, the effective print writer should incorporate visual elements into the writing task as well.

What does it take to become an effective writer for the spoken word?
The same, basically. We must be literate in terms of the environment, our society, political systems, and evolution. The broadcast writer must be able to stir the imagination of the listener if the medium is audio or evoke the desired response or emotion in the viewer if the medium is video.

How important is it for a public relations student to hone his or her writing skills?
It is extremely important. The most important tool for the public relations professional is writing. And perhaps one of the great challenges of the new information society is that writers must be versatile and knowledgeable about how to communicate with multicultural audiences or markets.

What is the caliber of public relations students today?
They are a diverse lot. Some are more mature, more focused, and tend to be highly specialized in their career aspirations, i.e., international relations, government relations, public affairs, sports marketing, political communications. They expect a tremendous technological impact on the industry and society in general, and they are beginning to understand, thanks to the global reach of CNN and other factors, that our world is getting smaller. Some have a great deal of potential, even if their notions about what public relations is (an easy job) and what public relations requires (a pretty smile) are erroneous. These qualities in our students make public relations education especially challenging and exciting.

What is the status of minorities in public relations?
There are still too few, as in other communications and related fields. Minorities account for less than 5 percent of mid-level jobs in mid-management; they are virtually invisible in senior management. We can do more at the grass-roots level to attract minorities to the public relations industry. University programs might focus as much on retention efforts as on recruitment and encourage minority student participation in organizations such as Public Relations Student Society of America and mainstream public relations internships. Professionals can take this one step further by mentoring and nurturing minorities interested in public relations careers. Now is the best time to prepare for the changes already taking shape in the workplace, the shifting demographics, the increasing black and Latino consumer markets, and expanding global opportunities.

What is the future for minorities in public relations?
I think the future is quite bright. The opportunities will definitely be there, but we need students who are fully prepared to take advantage of them. Education and awareness will be the key determinants. The responsibility of minority students is to develop essential skills such as writing, mastery of a foreign language, and appreciation of foreign cultures, and attain a strong liberal arts background and computer literacy. Minority students should also seek exposure to public relations career opportunities and be keenly aware of the possibilities open to them as a result of ethnic, global, and technological changes in our society.

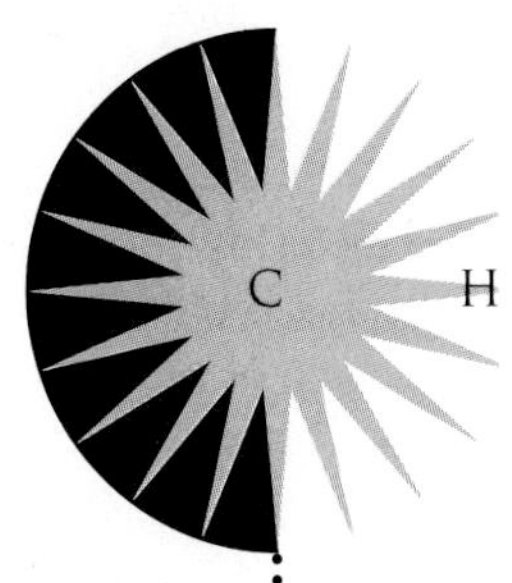

CHAPTER 10

VIDEO

THE WORD FOR THE 1990S IS *VIDEO*.

- When the Americans bombed Baghdad in 1991, television was there.
- When the Union of Soviet Socialist Republics was overthrown in 1992, television was there.
- When the government stormed a religious cult compound in Waco, Texas, in 1993 and scores of men, women, and children perished, television was there.
- When a Hitlerian onslaught murdered thousands of innocent victims in Bosnia-Herzogovena in 1994, television was there.

Television, in short, was everywhere.

According to a 1992 Roper Poll, at least 81 percent of all Americans received most of their news from television, and fully 54 percent received *all* of their news from television. Moreover, Americans reported that they were more likely to believe news received from television than from newspapers or other print media.[1] What makes this so disconcerting—some would say scary—is that the average 30-minute TV newscast would fill, in terms of words, only one-half of one page of the average daily newspaper!

Nonetheless, to many Americans, television *is* the news.

The growth of video in the United States has been astounding. In 1950, 3.8 million persons, or 9 percent of the population, possessed a television set. Twenty years later, the number had grown to 60 million, or 96 percent of the population. And by 1993, 93 million homes, or 98 percent, possessed televisions.

In 1950, the average number of channels receivable per U.S. TV home was about three. By 1970, seven channels were available. By 1992, the number was 35 channels, including cable (Figure 10–1). By the end of this decade, some predict that the information superhighway will usher in the era of 500-channel TV.[2]

Given the extent to which video dominates, it has become incumbent on public relations people to become more resourceful in accessing the electronic media.

TV NEWS PERVADES SOCIETY

Video news, in particular, has overwhelmed society.

In the 1990s, no situation comedy, ensemble drama, miniseries, movie, or documentary dominated American television the way news did.[3] From the Supreme Court confirmation hearings of Clarence Thomas to the resignation of Mikhail Gorbachev to the trials and travails of assorted sordid characters from Michael Jackson to Lorena Bobbitt to Tonya Harding, television news covered every gruesome detail.

The push toward information on television has spawned many imitators.

- News magazine programs such as *60 Minutes*, *20/20*, and *Dateline NBC*, which package scintillating news in entertainment formats.
- Talk shows such as *Oprah Winfrey*, *Phil Donahue*, and *Larry King Live*, which have become standard stomping grounds for politicians, authors, and anyone else seeking to sell a product or an issue (Figure 10–2).
- Reality-based shows such as *Unsolved Mysteries* and *Rescue 911*, which base reenactments on real-life events.
- Tabloid TV such as *Hard Copy*, *A Current Affair*, and *Inside Edition*, which try to outsleaze each other with lurid tales of agony and woe. The growth of tabloid television has helped blur the boundary of legitimate news programming. The 1993 attempt by *NBC Dateline* to rig an explosion of a General Motors truck was perhaps the worst example of TV journalism run amock. ABC's attempt in 1994 to pretend that a studio-based correspondent was reporting from in front of the Capitol Building was a less dramatic example.

One key factor in the rise of TV news around the world has been the growth of the Cable News Network (CNN). Entrepreneur Ted Turner's brainchild—which competitors mocked as "Chicken Noodle Network" when it began more than a decade ago—today boasts a domestic U.S. audience of upward of 60 million, international viewership in more than 7 million homes and 250,000 hotel rooms, news bureaus in 25 world capitals, and availability in more than 100 countries.[4]

AS SEEN IN
The New York Times
MARCH 25, 1992

AN OPEN LETTER ABOUT MAGIC JOHNSON, HIV, AND AIDS. FROM THE PRESIDENT OF NICKELODEON.

Dear Concerned Americans,

Tonight on Nickelodeon, Magic Johnson will join award-winning journalist Linda Ellerbee and a group of children and teens for an extraordinary candid discussion of HIV and AIDS. We want viewers to know that this program is powerful. Emotional. For some it may be unsettling. But it's real. Until a medical answer is found, the only solution to AIDS is education. That's what this show is all about.
As president of Nickelodeon, and a parent of two kids, I am constantly concerned about teaching our children to care about the world and the future.This program will help ensure that they have a future.

During *Nickelodeon Special Edition: A Conversation With Magic,* Linda and Magic begin a dialogue that we hope families will continue in their own living rooms. The important points of this conversation--about safe sex, talking to parents, postponing sex until later in life, and the need for compassion and straight talk about HIV/AIDS--will ring true to viewers of all ages.

Nickelodeon produced this half-hour special with Linda Ellerbee's Lucky Duck Productions, in cooperation with the NBA, the Nestlé Chocolate and Confection Company, The Magic Johnson Foundation and America's cable television operators. It airs tonight at 8:00 p.m. Of all the shows we've done in our 13 years as the kids' network, I am most proud of this program. It puts humanity back into this national health crisis, reminding us that behind the alarming statistics are human beings worth caring about. I believe it will have an enormous positive impact on the children and families who watch it.

Sincerely,

Geraldine Lay

Geraldine Laybourne
President, Nickelodeon

NICKELODEON®

1515 Broadway, New York, NY 10036

Figure 10–1 Video in the 1990s has become the dominant medium of news. After basketball star Magic Johnson stunned the world by announcing that he had contracted the AIDS virus, he chose a cable television venue to explain in detail what the disease was about. (*Courtesy of MTV Networks*)

Figure 10–2 In the 1990s, TV talk show hosts dominated the airways—from Oprah Winfrey to Geraldo Rivera, from Montel Williams to Larry King. Talk shows were eager to highlight the clients of public relations professionals. Among the most popular was *Donahue*. Host Phil Donahue interviewed people like public relations client Gary Himer of Group Health, Inc., who commented on topical health care issues. (*Courtesy of Padilla Spear Beardsley*)

Indeed, when Americans were trapped in Kuwait in the fall of 1990, they watched CNN to determine their next move. So did President Bush. And so, too, did Iraqi President Sadaam Hussein, who crafted statements especially for CNN to send back via satellite to American officials.

The growth of cable television in general and CNN in particular has created enormous new possibilities for publicity placement for public relations professionals.

Cable networks on the air or in the planning stages offer something for everyone—from the Food Channel to the Cable Health Club, from the Game Show Channel to the Military Channel, from the World African Network to National Empowerment Television.

The point is that dealing with such *narrow casting*—targeting one's message to a specific public—will become increasingly important as the new century approaches.[5]

HANDLING TV INTERVIEWS

As television has become a more potent channel of news, executives from all fields are being called on to appear on news and interview programs to air their views. For the uninitiated and the unprepared, a TV interview can be a harrowing experience. This is particularly true in the 1990s, when even television veterans like Dan Rather warn of "sleaze and glitz replacing quality and substance" on the airwaves.[6] To be effective on TV takes practice. Executives must accept guidance from public relations professionals on how to act appropriately in front of a camera that never blinks. The following dos and don'ts may help:

1. **Do prepare.** Preparation is the key to a successful broadcast appearance. Executives should know the main points they wish to make before the interview begins. They should know the audience. They should know who the reporter is and something about the reporter's beliefs. They should also rehearse answering tough hypothetical questions before entering the studio.
2. **Do be yourself.** Interviewees should appear relaxed. Smiles are appropriate. Nonverbal signs of tension (clenching fists, gripping the arms of a chair, or tightly holding one hand with the other) should be avoided. Gesturing with the palms opened, on the other hand, suggests relaxation and an eagerness to discuss issues. Giggling, smoking, or chewing gum should be avoided (unless you are ex-football coach Mike Ditka!). Proper posture also is important.
3. **Do be open and honest.** Television magnifies everything, especially phoniness. If facts are twisted, it will show. On TV, a half-truth becomes a half-lie. Credibility must be established early.
4. **Do be brief.** TV and radio have no time for beating around the bush. Main points must be summarized at the beginning of sentences. Language must be understandable. Neither the reporter nor the public is familiar with technical jargon, so avoid it.
5. **Do play it straight; be careful with humor.** An interviewee can't be giddy, vacuous, or irreverent. Attempts to be a comic may be interpreted as foolishness. Natural and relaxed use of appropriate humor may be a big plus in getting a point across. If humor doesn't come naturally, interviewees should play it straight. That way, they won't look stupid.
6. **Do dress for the occasion.** Bold patterns, checks, or pinstripes should be avoided; so should jewelry that shines or glitters. Skirts should fall easily below a woman's knees. Men's socks should be high enough to prevent a gap between socks and pants. Colors of shirts, socks, suits, and accessories generally should be muted.
7. **Don't assume the interviewer is out to get you.** Arguments and hostility come through clearly on TV. In a discussion on a controversial subject with a professional interviewer, the guest frequently comes out looking like the villain. Therefore, all questions, even naive ones, should be treated with respect and deference. If an interviewee becomes defensive, it will show.
8. **Don't think everything you say will be aired.** TV is a quick and imperfect medium. A guest might be interviewed for 45 minutes and appear as a 10-second segment on a newscast. That's why an interviewee must constantly hammer home his or her main points.
9. **Don't let the interviewer dominate.** Interviewees can control the interview by varying the length and content of their responses. If a question requires a complicated answer, the interviewee should state that before getting trapped in an incomplete and misleading response. If interviewees make mistakes, they should correct them and go on. If they don't understand the question, they should ask for clarification.
10. **Don't say "No comment."** "No comment" sounds evasive (Figure 10–3). If interviewees can't answer certain questions, they should clearly explain why.

Begging off for competitive or proprietary reasons is perfectly allowable as long as some explanation is offered.

11. **Do stop.** One common broadcast technique is to leave cameras running and microphones open even after an interviewee has responded to a question. Often the most revealing, misleading, and damaging statements are made by interviewees embarrassed by the silence. Don't fall for the bait. Silence can always be edited out later. Interviewers know this and interviewees should, too, especially before getting trapped.

These are just a few hints in dealing with what often becomes a difficult situation for the uninitiated. The best advice for a TV interviewee is to be natural, straightforward, and, most of all, prepared.

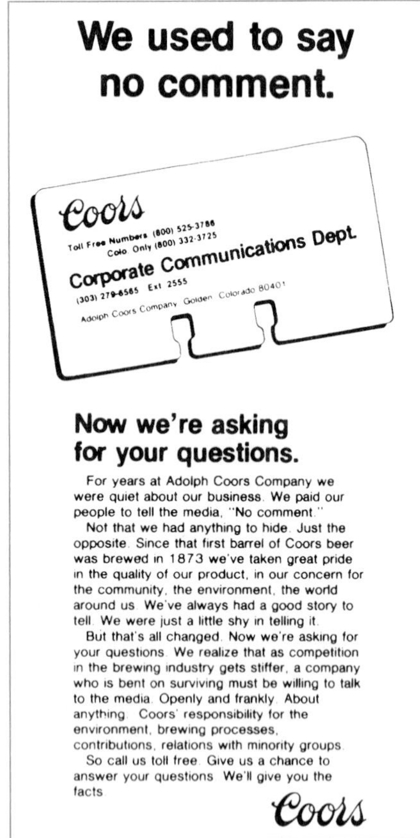

Figure 10–3 Typical of an enlightened attitude toward television and other media is this ad by Adolph Coors Company, a firm that once was criticized in the media for its traditional silence. (*Courtesy of Adolph Coors Co.*)

A QUESTION OF ETHICS

Live from Somalia: It's Tom, Ted, and Dan!

When U.S. troops landed at Mogadishu, Somalia, in the winter of 1992, they met an imposing sight as they jumped from their rubber boats onto the shore—the glare of television lights and cameras.

More than 75 reporters and camera crews were waiting on the beach with microphones on and cameras rolling as the military operation to fight the warlords in Somalia began. And boy was the U.S. military steamed!

"We're told they were not amused," reported NBC anchor Tom Brokaw, live from Somalia.

Said ABC newsman Ted Koppel, also in Somalia, "The most difficulty they had to face all day was having to face the cameras and the lights." And CBS anchor Dan Rather observed from the Mogadishu shore that the attack was "a sort of Hollywoodish, almost cartoonish situation on the beach. And if you're saying, well, this looks silly—in some ways it does, but remember, this is serious business for the U.S. military people."

So serious, in fact, that the Pentagon appealed to U.S. journalists to steer clear of the shore where the Marines were to land. The Pentagon admonished journalists that the situation was dangerous and that the night-vision goggles of the troops could be adversely affected by the television lights.

Journalists responded that the U.S. Defense Department had invited them to "cover the war," and they would set up where they pleased. The great Mogadishu debate ended in a standstill.

But the question remains in an age of around-the-clock, around-the-world video: Are any limits appropriate, even in the middle of a war?

*For additional information, see Michael R. Gordon, "TV Army on the Beach Took U.S. by Surprise," *The New York Times* (December 10, 1992): A18.

IMPORTANCE OF ORGANIZATIONAL VIDEO

Given the domination of the television culture today, organizational communicators must turn increasingly to video to communicate with a wide range of audiences, from employees to customers to shareholders to legislators.

Internally, an increasing number of companies are creating employee video magazines. Firms like NYNEX and Philip Morris find corporate videos useful to help a widely dispersed employee body understand corporate objectives, on the one hand, and individual department activities, on the other. Videos have the added benefit of accommodating group meetings to serve as a stimulus for interaction, response, and discussion among employees.

Externally, the use of video as a marketing and lobbying tool also is expanding. Many organizations create videos to introduce new products to potential clients. Videos also are used extensively to present issues to legislators. In addition, video annual reports have been used sporadically to give shareholders a more "lively" view of the organization. While video annual reports enjoyed fleeting popularity in the mid-1980s and then disappeared, some believe they will make a comeback in the years ahead, "coming through a modem to your computer terminal on demand."[7]

Although a variety of video vehicles are available to corporate public relations professionals, the most pervasive are video news releases, public service announcements, and satellite media tours.

VIDEO NEWS RELEASES

By far the most pervasive external video vehicle used by public relations professionals is the video news release (VNR). It is also the most controversial vehicle.

A VNR, simply stated, is a print news release put on video. Its aim is to achieve maximum exposure on television news. VNRs are designed to run from 30 to 90 seconds incorporated into local TV newscasts. VNRs have proliferated as a consequence of the growth of local news programming.

In the early 1980s, as news staffs were cut and air time for news programming was expanded with cable television, the golden age of VNRs began.[8] With news programs hungry for information, the companies sponsoring VNRs found they were used often. By the early 1990s, VNRs had become big business. In 1991, more than 4,000 were produced—10 for every day of the week. And today, as VNRs have proliferated, it has become increasingly difficult for organizations to place them on the air. Add to this the existence of upward of 150 video firms that produce VNRs, and the "hit rate" of VNR placements has declined measurably.

VNRs are not for everyone. In general, an organization should consider producing one when it has hard, visual news to promote. The best VNRs are those that cover breaking news stories, the kind broadcasters would cover for themselves if they had the resources. Timely stories with good visual impact are delivered by satellite directly to TV newsrooms. Satellite feeds of unedited footage—called *B-roll*—include a written preamble-story summary and *sound bites* from appropriate spokespersons. The TV stations then assemble the stories themselves, using as much or as little of the VNR footage as they see fit.

Such breaking news stories are superior to *evergreen* VNRs, which concern nonbreaking news features. In the "old days"—1990 and earlier—evergreen stories may well have been used by local stations (Figure 10–4). Today, with news stations better staffed and VNR competition increased, evergreens have decidedly less chance of being used.

In a general sense, an organization should consider producing a VNR in the following situations:

- It is involved in a legitimate medical, scientific, or industrial breakthrough.
- The video will clarify or provide a new perspective on issues in the news.
- The video will help a news department create a better story.

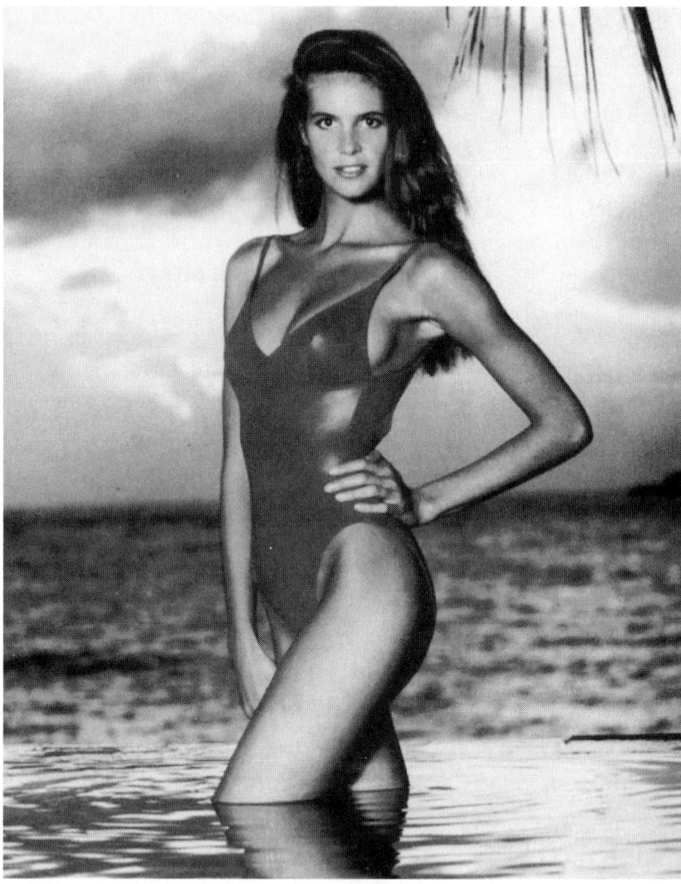

Figure 10–4 In 1989, HBO Video reached more than 45 million TV viewers with a VNR announcing its video of *Sports Illustrated*'s annual swimsuit issue featuring Elle McPherson. (*Courtesy of HWH Enterprises, Inc.*)

- The video can be used as background footage while a station's reporter discusses pertinent news copy.
- The organization can provide unusual visual footage that stations themselves can't get.
- The VNR provides an interview segment that stations, again, can't get on their own.[9]

VNR CAVEATS: EXPENSIVE AND CONTROVERSIAL

As noted, VNRs are not without risks.

For one thing, they are expensive. They must be created, produced, packaged, and distributed professionally. Budgets for VNRs can range from $5,000 to $100,000, depending on their complexity. In Pepsi-Cola's case in 1993, the substantial VNR expense to distribute videos defusing the tampering crisis was well worth it.

Nonetheless, before one creates a VNR—and since a good one is expensive—the following questions must be asked:

1. Is this VNR needed?
2. How much time do we have?
3. How much do we have to spend to make the VNR effective?
4. What obstacles must be considered, including bad weather, unavailability of key people, and so on?
5. Is video really the best way to communicate this story?

Then, too, there is the controversy surrounding VNRs in general. In 1992, *TV Guide,* angered primarily by the Kuwaiti VNR distributed by Hill & Knowlton to build support for the Desert Storm offensive, labeled video news releases "fake news—all the PR that news can use." *TV Guide*'s researchers reported that while broadcasters used elements from VNRs, rarely were they labeled so that viewers could know their sponsor's identity.

On the heels of the *TV Guide* controversy, the PR Service Council for VNR Producers issued a "Code of Good Practice" for VNRs, which called for putting the source of the material on every VNR issued. Still, the controversy persists.

Despite their problems, the fact remains that if an organization has a dramatic and visual story, using VNRs may be a most effective and compelling way to convey its message to millions of people.

PUBLIC SERVICE ANNOUNCEMENTS

The public service announcement (PSA) is a TV or radio commercial, usually 10 to 60 seconds long, that is broadcast at no cost to the sponsor. Nonprofit organizations, such as the Red Cross and United Way, are active users of PSAs (Figure 10–5). Commercial organizations, too, may take advantage of PSAs for their nonprofit activities, such as blood bank collections, voter registration drives, health testing, and the like. The spread of local cable television stations has expanded the opportunity for placing PSAs on the air. Nevertheless, radio PSAs are still far more widely used.

Unlike news releases, PSAs are generally written in advertising-copy style—punchy and pointed. The essential challenge in writing PSAs is to select the small amount of information to be used, discard extraneous information, and persuade the listener to take the desired action. The following is a typical 30-second PSA:

> The challenge of inflation has never been more serious than it is today.
>
> The need for strong national leadership has never been more pressing than it is today.
>
> Americans must tell their elected leaders to stop spending and regulating and start listening to the people.
>
> But they won't until you demand it.
>
> Until you demand that they stop overspending, stop crippling our economy with needless regulation, stop suffocating America with outrageous taxes.
>
> You can make a difference.
>
> This message brought to you by Hooter Valley National Bank.

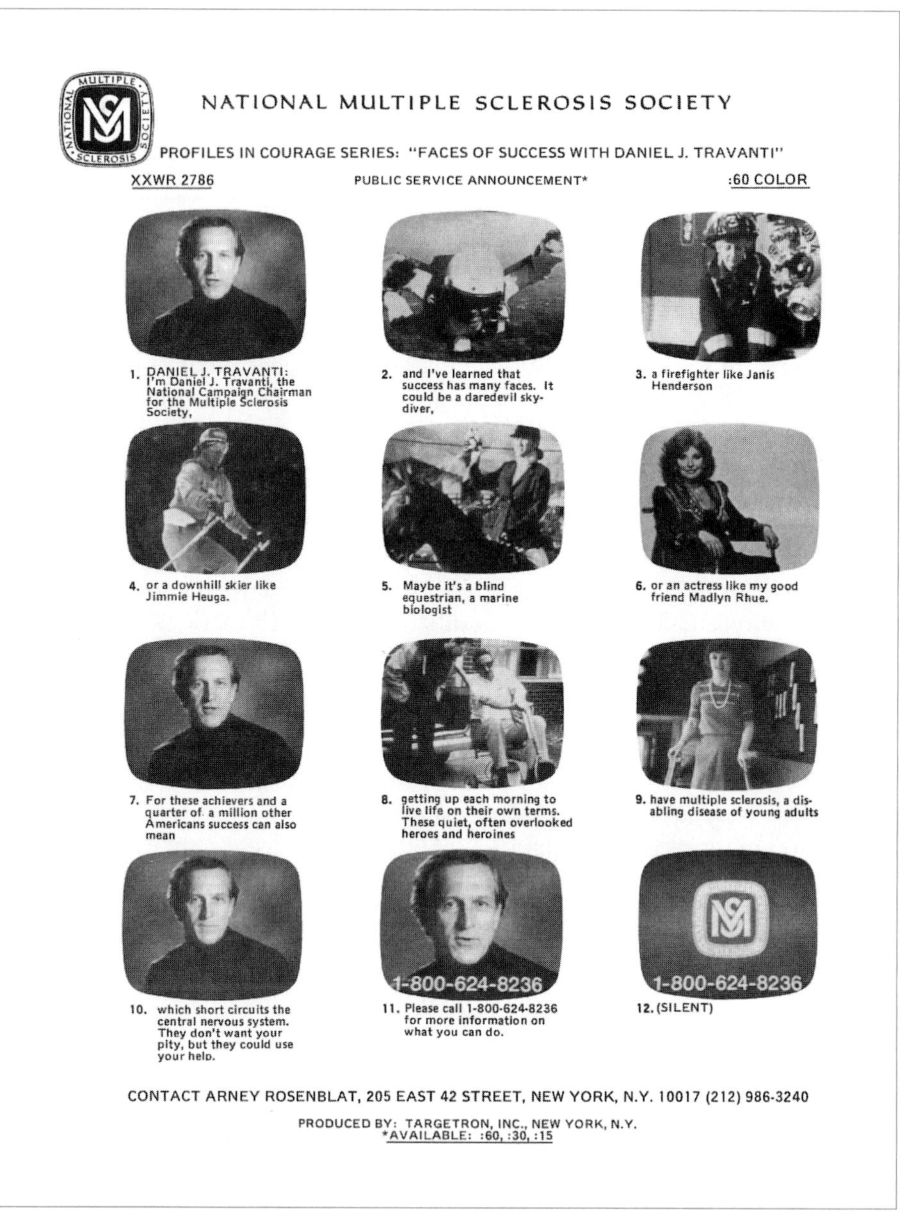

Figure 10–5 This is a typical PSA storyboard sent to TV stations. It enables station personnel to review the content of the Multiple Sclerosis Society's PSA before screening. (*Courtesy of the National Multiple Sclerosis Society*)

According to survey research, broadcasters use three primary criteria in determining which PSAs make the air: (1) sponsorship, (2) relevance of the message to the community, and (3) message design. In terms of sponsorship, the reputation of the sponsor for honesty and integrity is critical. As to the relevance of the message, urgent social problems, such as health and safety issues and education and training concerns, all rank high with broadcasters. In message design, the more imaginative, original, and exciting the message, the better the chance of its getting free play on the air.

SATELLITE MEDIA TOURS

The 1990s equivalent to the sit down, in-studio interview is the satellite media tour (SMT). An SMT is a series of preset interviews, conducted via satellite, between an organization's spokesperson and television station personalities across the nation or around the world.

An SMT originates with a subject speaking from one location, who is then whisked electronically from station to station where he or she enjoys on-air, one-on-one discussions. A derivative of the in-studio SMT is a remote SMT that originates on location from a site outside the studio.

A successful SMT relies on the immediate relevance of an organization's issue and message. Additionally, several steps must be taken to ensure the viability of an SMT:

1. **Defining objectives.** As in any public relations program, the organization's objectives must first be considered. What is the "news hook" required to interest stations? Who is the target audience? In which markets do we want interviews? What stations do we prefer? Within which programs on these stations will our interviews play best?
2. **Pitching the SMT.** Television producers must be contacted, first by letter and then by phone, about the availability of the organization's spokesperson. The key issue that must be stressed is news value. Press kits and background material should be sent to the stations at least two weeks in advance of the interview.
3. **Last-minute juggling preparation.** Stations often request time changes. Maintain contact with station personnel, even when placed on a waiting list, so that any scheduling "holes" can be filled if a station cancels an interview close to the SMT date.
4. **Satellite time.** Satellite time needs to be contracted for well in advance to ensure that the SMT is aired when the organization wants.
5. **B-roll.** Background footage—or B-roll video—should be available to further illustrate the topic and enhance the interest of stations.
6. **Availability of dedicated phone lines.** Several dedicated phone lines for communication with stations should be available, especially in case of interrupted feedback audio—in other words, static.
7. **Spokespeople briefing.** It is essential to brief spokespersons to avoid potential confusion regarding the names and locations of interviewers during an SMT. All names should be written out on a studio teleprompter or on large cue cards, to which the spokesperson should refer prior to the interview. The spokesperson also should become accustomed to the earpiece, as the director's voice can be initially distracting.
8. **Avoiding becoming too commercial.** Of course, the spokesperson is there to "plug" the organization or product, but don't overdo it or you won't be invited back.[10] SMTs can save time and streamline logistics for any organization. But they are expensive—costing $10,000 to $20,000 for a two-hour production.

VIDEO CONFERENCES

The latest phenomenon of the video revolution is the video conference, which connects audiences throughout the United States or around the world in a satellite-linked meeting.

While slow to catch on in the early 1990s, long-distance meetings via video conferences are now becoming much more popular. Analysts believe that the market for video conference equipment will approach $8 billion by 1997.[11] Video conferences may originate from hotel ballrooms or offshore oil platforms, from corporate headquarters or major trade shows. They can be used for information or motivation. All have the benefit of conveying a message—internally to employees or externally to the news media, investors, or consumers—instantly.

In considering a video conference, the following factors should be assessed:

- **Origination site.** Video conferences may originate from a broadcast studio. However, their impact can be increased by choosing a remote location that adds a sense of authenticity to the proceedings.
- **Visuals.** Since a video conference is a live television show, graphics to heighten the visual excitement of the presentation must be considered. In 1993, when General Motors exposed *Dateline NBC*'s fraudulent reporting of its trucks, the company used a host of visuals at its media video conference. GM not only made use of extensive video at the conference, it also displayed one of the actual trucks used in the bogus broadcast.
- **Interactivity.** A video conference also may be enhanced by allowing viewers to ask questions. Two-way audio link-ups are now common in video conferences. Again, these add a note of immediacy and spontaneity that enhances the interest in and impact of the video conference.

As the year 2000 approaches, video conference technology is being adopted by corporations, educational institutions, hospitals, and other organizations. In fact, classes broadcast by television have been a way of life on Alaska's North Slope for many years. So too around the world, the video conference has become a viable alternative for organizations wishing to convey information immediately with impact.

SUMMARY

The video revolution clearly has arrived. As generations weaned on television enter the public relations field, familiarity with broadcast methods will increase.

As cable television stations in particular proliferate, the need for additional programming—for more material to fill news and interview holes—also will expand. This will open the door to a new breed of public relations professional, comfortable with and proficient in the nuances of writing for, dealing with, and mastering the art of video. (See Appendix E, "Guide to Video/Satellite Terms.")

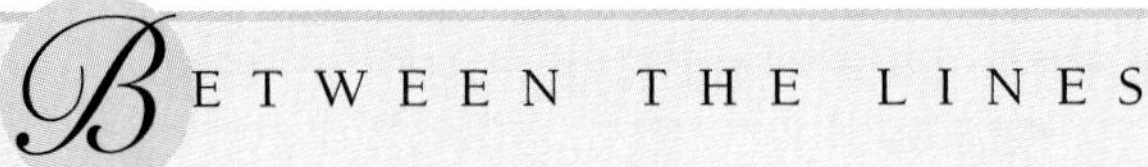

TURNING THE CAMERAS ON "OPEN MIKE"

No investigative video journalist has gained as fearsome a reputation for catching subjects off guard as television reporter Mike Wallace of CBS-TV's *60 Minutes*. Indeed, public relations professionals live in dread of the day when Mike Wallace appears at their door. That's why, in January 1982, many public relations practitioners may have felt a bit more chipper than usual when they read that Mike Wallace had been caught at his own game.

The story started when Wallace took his *60 Minutes* crew to the San Diego Federal Savings and Loan Company to interview a vice-president on the plight of low-income Californians—most of them either African-American or Hispanic, with minimal skills—who faced foreclosures after signing contracts for expensive air conditioners without realizing that their houses served as collateral. As a precondition of the interview, San Diego Federal insisted on filming the proceedings for its own use.

During a break in the filming, with the CBS camera off but the San Diego Federal camera still rolling, Wallace commented on the complex lien-sale bank contracts. "You bet your ______ they are hard to read," he said, "if you're reading them over the watermelon or over the tacos!" Thereupon, according to observers, Mike began to laugh uproariously—but not for long.

A few weeks, later Wallace learned that the San Diego Federal crew had videotaped his offhand remark, and he and CBS tried desperately to retrieve the offensive tape from the bank. They failed, and the story received nationwide coverage. Later, Wallace called the retrieval idea a "lame one," and he and CBS apologized for the racially disparaging remark.

Ironically, during a prior *60 Minutes* show about the behind-the-scenes workings of the broadcast, Wallace was asked how he would feel if a hidden camera one day captured some embarrassing material about him. "I wouldn't like it," he replied. Boy, was he right!

DISCUSSION STARTERS

1. Why has video become more important for public relations professionals?
2. How has the definition of *news* been expanded by video?
3. Is it a good idea for an executive to be spontaneous in a television interview?
4. How comprehensive should answers be on television?
5. When should an organization consider using a VNR?
6. Why are VNRs considered controversial?
7. What are the key facets of a PSA?
8. What are the key steps in creating an SMT?
9. What factors must be considered in arranging a video conference?
10. Why is narrow casting critical to public relations knowledge in the years ahead?

NOTES

1. "The Changing World of Corporate Video," *Inside PR* (June 1992): 13–16.
2. "The Hyperactive Highway," *Newsweek* (November 29, 1993): 56.
3. Bill Carter, "New Events Become Biggest Television Hits," *The New York Times* (December 30, 1991): 27.
4. Roxanne Roberts, "CNN on Top of the World," *The Washington Post* (August 21, 1990): C1, C10.
5. *Jack O'Dwyer's Newsletter* (January 26, 1994): 3.
6. "Rather to TV News Heads: Fight 'Sleaze and Glitz,'" *O'Dwyer's PR Services Report* (November 1993): 1, 22–26.
7. "The Changing World of Corporate Video."
8. Kevin E. Foley, "Ethics and Sigma Are in 'VNR Cartel,'" *O'Dwyer's PR Services Report* (April 1993): 13.
9. Michael M. Klepper, "Do-It-Yourself Evening News," *IABC Communication World* (July–August 1987): 62–63.
10. "Avoid Pitfalls and Reap Rewards of Remote SMT's," *O'Dwyer's PR Services Report* (April 1993): 16–17.
11. Andrew Kupfer, "Prime Time for Video Conferences," *Fortune* (December 28, 1992): 90–93.

SUGGESTED READINGS

Associated Press. *Broadcast News Stylebook.* (Available from the author, 50 Rockefeller Plaza, New York, 10020.) This has a more generalized style than that in the UPI style book. Suggestions of methods and treatment for the preparation of news copy and information pertinent to AP broadcast wire operations are given.

Block, Mervin. *Writing Broadcast News—Shorter, Sharper, Stronger.* Chicago: Bonus Books, 1987.

Broadcasting Publications. *Broadcasting.* (Available from the author, 1735 DeSales St., NW, Washington, DC 20036; published weekly on Monday.) This basic news magazine for the radio, television, and cable television industries reports all activities involved in the entire broadcasting field.

A Common Sense Guide to Making Business Videos. (Available from Creative Marketing Corporation, 285 S. 171 St., New Berlin, WI 53151–3511.) Anyone not familiar with business videos will benefit from this booklet, which zeros in on the planning needed to make a successful video.

Daily Variety. (Available from 1400 N. Cahuenga Blvd., Hollywood, CA 90028.) This trade paper for the entertainment industries is centered mainly in Los Angeles, with complete coverage of West Coast production activities; it includes reports from all world entertainment centers.

Green, Richard, and Denise Shapiro. "A Video News Release Primer." *Public Relations Quarterly* (Winter 1987–88): 10–13.

A Layperson's Guide to Satellite Broadcasting. O'Dwyer's PR Services Report (December 1987): 4 (271 Madison Ave., New York, NY 10016).

MacDonald, R. H. *Broadcast News Manual of Style.* White Plains, NY: Longman, 1987.

Stecki, Ed, and Frank Corrado. "How to Make a Video" (Part I). *Public Relations Journal* (February 1988): 33, 34.

Top of the Shelf

60 Minutes CBS Television News

For decades, the most widely-watched television program in the nation has been a Sunday night news magazine program which is the subject of fear and loathing of politicians, presidents and corporate potentates.

60 Minutes, as the saying goes, has been often imitated, never duplicated. The brainchild of news producer Don Hewitt, its correspondents—Mike Wallace, Morley Safer, Dan Rather, Diane Sawyer, the late Harry Reasoner, Ed Bradley, et. al—have become synonyms for investigative television journalism.

In its first decade, *60 minutes* was despised and avoided by most business organizations. They feared the consequences of a national TV skewering, and most refused to be interviewed. Invariably, this cost them, because *60 Minutes* correspondents ordinarily don't accept "not available" or "no comment" for an answer.

In recent, years smart organizations have realized that, in some cases, it makes sense to cooperate with *60 Minutes*, Coors Beer, and Johnson&Johnson, for example, found that 60 minutes treated them fairly in the midst of terrible crisis.

In the 90's with the plethora of *60 Minutes* copy cats—from respectable shows like ABC's 20-20 to more questionable shows like NBC's *Dateline* to downright unrespectable shows like *A Current Affair* and Hard Copy—it is incumbent on public relations students to make the viewing of *60 Minutes* a required Sunday evening ritual.

Case Study

They're Heeere!

Suppose you gave a party and *60 Minutes* showed up at the door. Would you let them in? Would you evict them? Would you commit hara-kiri?

Those were the choices that confronted The Chase Manhattan Bank at the American Bankers Association convention in 1988, when *60 Minutes* came to Honolulu to "get the bankers."

The banking industry at the time was taking its lumps. Profits were lagging. Loans to foreign governments weren't being repaid. And it was getting difficult for poor people to open bank accounts.

Understandably, few bankers at the Honolulu convention cared to share their thoughts on camera with *60 Minutes*. Some headed for cover when the cameras approached. Others barred the unwanted visitors from their receptions. In at least one case, a *60 Minutes* cameraman was physically removed from the hall. By the convention's third day, the *60 Minutes* team was decrying its treatment at the hands of the bankers as the "most vicious" it had ever been accorded.

By the third night, correspondent Morley Safer and his *60 Minutes* crew were steaming and itching for a confrontation.

And that's when *60 Minutes* showed up at our party.

For 10 years, with your author as its public affairs director, Chase Manhattan had sponsored a private convention reception for the media. It combined an informal cocktail party, where journalists and bankers could chat and munch hors d'oeuvres, with a more formal, 30-minute press conference with the bank's president. The press conference was on the record, no holds barred, and frequently generated news coverage by the wire services, newspapers, and magazines that regularly sent representatives. No TV cameras were permitted.

But when we arrived at Honolulu's scenic Pacific Club, there to greet us—unannounced and uninvited—were Morley and the men from *60 Minutes,* ready to do battle.

The ball was in our court. We faced five questions that demanded immediate answers.

- *First, should we let them in?*

What they wanted, said Safer, was to interview our president about "critical banking issues." He said they had been "hassled" all week and were "entitled" to attend our media reception.

But we hadn't invited them. And they hadn't had the courtesy to let us know they were coming. But it was true that they were members of the working press. And it was also true that our reception was intended to generate news.

So we had a dilemma.

- *Second, should we let them film the press conference?*

Chase's annual convention press conference had never before been filmed. TV cameras are bulky, noisy, and intrusive. They threatened to sabotage the normally convivial atmosphere of our party. Equally disconcerting would be the glaring TV lights that would have to be set up. The *60 Minutes* crew countered that their coverage was worthless without film. Theirs, after all, was a medium of pictures, and without pictures, there could be no story. As appetizing as this proposition sounded to us, we were worried that if we refused their cameras, what they might film instead would be us blocking the door at an otherwise open news conference.

So we had another problem.

- *Third, should we let them film the cocktail party?*

Like labor leader Samuel Gompers, television people are interested in only one thing: "More!" In the case of our reception, we weren't eager to have CBS film the cocktails and hors d'oeuvres part of our party. We were certain the journalists on hand would agree with us. After all, who wants to see themselves getting sloshed on national television when they're supposed to be working?

- *Fourth, should we let them film a separate interview with our president?*

Because few top people at the convention were willing to speak to CBS, *60 Minutes* was eager to question our president in as extensive and uninterrupted a format as possible. Safer wanted a separate interview before the formal press conference started.

So we also had to deal with the question of whether to expose our president to a lengthy, one-on-one, side-room interview with the most powerful—and potentially negative—television news program in the land.

- *Fifth, should we change our format?*

The annual media reception/press conference had always been an informal affair. Our executives joked with the journalists, shared self-deprecating asides, and generally relaxed. Thus, in light of the possible presence of *60 Minutes*, we wondered if we should alter this laid-back approach and adopt a more on-guard stance.

We had 10 minutes to make our decisions. We also had splitting headaches.

QUESTIONS

1. Would you let *60 Minutes* in?
2. Would you let them film the press conference?
3. Would you let them film the cocktail party?
4. Would you let them film a separate interview with the president?
5. Would you change the format of the party?

TIPS FROM THE TOP

MYRON KANDEL

Myron Kandel is one of the country's best-known financial writers and broadcasters. After serving as financial editor of three major newspapers, he switched to television in 1980 and helped start Cable News Network. He continues to serve as financial editor of CNN Business News and on-air economics commentator. Kandel lectures frequently and has taught journalism at Columbia University Graduate School of Journalism and City College of New York. He is the author of *How to Cash In On the Coming Stock Market Boom,* published in 1982.

What is the quality of business news coverage on television?
Business news, once the wasteland of television news coverage, has made great strides over a relatively short period of time. It was as recently as June 1980 that Cable News Network began broadcasting the first nightly half-hour business news program in the history of network television. Now, many other news organizations—on cable and public television and in syndication—are offering a wide assortment of business news programming. Up to now, however, the broadcast networks and local television stations have not devoted any real resources or time to such coverage.

What do journalists think of public relations people?
It once was conventional wisdom that journalists and public relations people were adversaries. I like to think of them, instead, as fellow communicators with different agendas. As long as each understands the other's goals, the relationship can be productive both ways. Some news people—a declining percentage, I think—still dismiss PR people as mere flacks, trying to foist untrue, misleading, or inappropriate facts or stories on the media. Although there may be some of those types still

around, that's an antiquated image. As PR people get more and more professional, that image will continue to diminish.

What kind of public relations person do you appreciate?
The PR person I like best is the one who knows what my news organization does, understands our needs, and is responsive to them. Conversely, those I like least don't know enough, or don't care enough, to relate to us specifically. This doesn't mean that a good PR person must necessarily grant our every request. But, first, he or she should know what we do, what kind of programming we're presenting, and who the relevant contacts are. They should understand our time constraints and deadlines and should get back to us accordingly, even if they can't provide a definitive answer. It's always a pleasure to find a PR person who anticipates a need and offers a way to meet it.

A spokesperson who is knowledgeable about his or her organization and has the necessary access to the top to get queries answered impresses me the most. The least impressive are those who obviously don't have the confidence of management to speak for the organization. I'm surprised at how often supposedly professional people are in that situation.

What problems have you encountered with public relations people?
I can't remember an occasion where a PR person lied to me deliberately, but there have been instances where they passed on incorrect information because they themselves were misinformed or were kept in the dark. That kind of situation undermines their credibility and sours any relationship that previously existed. Credibility and integrity are two attributes that any professional PR person must safeguard jealously.

Are most reporters hostile to organizations?
They often give that impression because they must be probing in their questioning and unwilling to accept statements they're given at face value. Rather than hostile or antiestablishment, they are nonestablishment, and that approach may seem hostile. Some news people do have biases that creep into their reports. As an editor, it's my responsibility to see that this does not happen. If a persistent pattern exists, I would welcome being informed about it. The principal goal of any news organization is to present the news fairly and objectively.

What is the status of the relationship between video journalists and public relations people?
I like to refer to the state of the video journalist-public relations relationship as an uneasy alliance, meaning that although they work together, each side may on occasion have a different objective. Nearly all the time, but not always, they share the goal of truth. They always share a desire for accuracy. The trend in recent years has been toward greater professionalism on both sides, and that means more respect and cooperation.

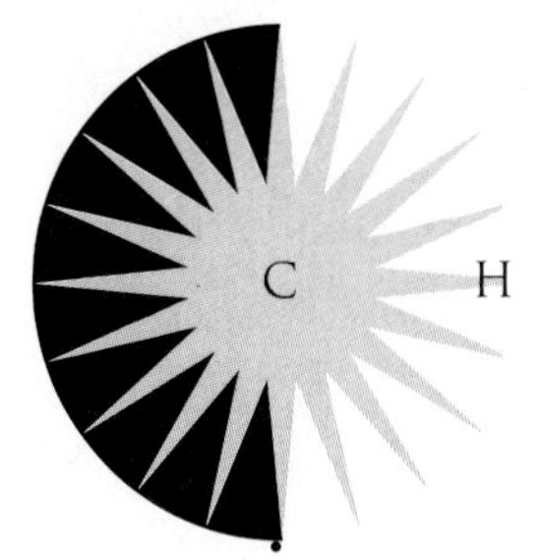

C H A P T E R 11

COMMUNICATIONS CROSS-TRAINING

MIDWAY THROUGH 1993, ONE COMMUNICATIONS WAG MADE the following observation:

> The practices of marketing, advertising and public relations, as we have known them, are dead.
>
> They died when automobile makers, consumer product firms, computer companies and many others began to realize that the world had changed. No longer was it possible to make money "the old-fashioned way."[1]

What this perhaps overzealous observer referred to was the irrepressible intertwining of the heretofore separate disciplines of advertising, marketing, sales promotion, and public relations into a sometimes "unholy alliance" to win consumer support. The symbiosis of these different disciplines was dubbed *integrated marketing communications*. One survey of 200 marketing executives named *integration* as the most important factor influencing the way marketing strategies would be set in the 1990s.[2]

As integrated marketing becomes more and more the rule in agencies and companies, the need for *communications cross-training* to become conversant in the skills of marketing, advertising, sales promotion, and public relations becomes a requirement for all communicators.

Integrated marketing basically means approaching communications issues from the customer's perspective. Consumers don't separate promotional material or newspaper advertising or community responsiveness into separate compartments. They lump everything together and make judgments about services and organizations based on total relationships.

Integrated marketing expert Mitch Kozikowski lists six "maxims" that can guide public relations professionals through the communications cross-training process:

1. **Integrated marketing communication is not about ads, direct mail pieces, or public relations projects. It is about understanding the consumer and what the consumer actually responds to.** In other words, behavioral change is the communicator's mission. If the customer doesn't act, the communicator—and the communication—have failed.
2. **Organizations can't succeed without good relationships with their publics.** Organizations need relationships with their customers that go beyond the pure selling of a product or service. They need to build relationships. Increasingly, as the world gets more competitive in everything from health care to auto repair, from selling insurance to selling cereal, relationship building becomes more critical.
3. **Integrated marketing communications requires collaboration on strategy, not just on execution.** This means that the entire communications function must be part of the launch of a product, service, campaign, or issue from its *inception*. In other words, communicators must participate in the *planning* of a campaign, not just in the implementation of communications vehicles.
4. **Strategic plans must be clear about the role that each discipline is to play in solving the problem.** The roles of advertising, marketing, and public relations are different. None can do everything by itself. Therefore, while advertising might control the message and marketing and while promotion might provide involvement, it is public relations that should be called on to provide credibility for the product and, even more important, for the organization.
5. **Public relations is about relationships. Public relations professionals can become proprietors of integrated marketing communications.** Since the essence of public relations is building relationships between an institution and its publics, public relations professionals, perhaps more than any other, should lead the integrated marketing initiative. Public relations professionals have long understood the importance of two-way communication that builds strong relationships with customers and others. Such an understanding is pivotal to the successful rendering of integrated marketing communications.
6. **To be players in integrated marketing communications, public relations professionals need to practice more than the craft of public relations.** Simply stated, public relations people must expand their horizons, increase their knowledge of other disciplines, and willingly seek out and participate in interdisciplinary skills building. In other words, public relations professionals must

approach their task, in the broadest terms, to enhance customer relationships through a strategy of total communications.[3]

Elements of public relations—among them product publicity, special events, spokesmanship, and similar activities—can enhance a marketing effort. A new discipline—marketing communications—has emerged that uses many of the techniques of public relations. While some may labor over the relative differences and merits of public relations versus advertising versus marketing versus sales promotion, the fact remains that a smart communicator must be knowledgeable about all of them.

PUBLIC RELATIONS VERSUS MARKETING

Marketing, literally defined, is the selling of a service or product through pricing, distribution, and promotion. *Public relations,* liberally defined, is the marketing of an organization. Most organizations now realize that public relations can play an expanded role in marketing. In some organizations, particularly service companies, hospitals, and nonprofit institutions, the selling of both individual products and the organization itself are inextricably intertwined.

Stated another way, while the practice of marketing creates and maintains a market for products and services and the practice of public relations creates and maintains a hospitable environment in which the organization may operate, marketing success can be nullified by the social and political forces public relations is designed to confront—thus the interrelationship of the two disciplines.[4]

In the past, marketers treated public relations as an ancillary part of the marketing mix. They were concerned primarily with making sure their products met the needs and desires of customers and were priced competitively, distributed widely, and promoted heavily through advertising and merchandising. Gradually, however, these traditional notions among marketers began to change for several reasons.

- Consumer protests about both product value and safety and government scrutiny of product demands began to shake historical views of marketing.
- Product recalls—from automobiles to tuna fish—generated recurring headlines.
- Ingredient scares began to occur regularly.
- Advertisers were asked to justify their messages in terms of social needs and civic responsibilities.
- Rumors about particular companies—from fast-food firms to pop rock manufacturers—spread in brushfire manner.
- General image problems of certain companies and industries—from oil to banking—were fanned by a continuous blaze of criticism in the media.

The net impact of all this was that, even though a company's products were still important, customers also began to consider a firm's policies and practices on everything from air and water pollution to minority hiring.

Beyond these social concerns, the effectiveness of advertising itself began to be questioned. The increased number of advertisements in newspapers and on the airwaves caused clutter and placed a significant burden on advertisers who were trying to make the public aware of their products. In the 1980s, the trend toward shorter TV advertising spots contributed to three times as many products being advertised on TV as there were in the 1970s. In the 1990s, the spread of cable TV has added yet another multichanneled outlet for product advertising. Against this backdrop, the potential of public relations as an added ingredient in the marketing mix has become increasingly credible.

Indeed, marketing guru Philip Kotler has suggested that to the traditional 4P's of marketing—product, price, place, and promotion—a fifth P, public relations, should be added. Kotler argues that a firm's success depends increasingly on carrying out effective marketing thinking in its relationships with 10 critical players: suppliers, distributors, end users, employees, financial firms, government, media, allies, competitors, and the general public. In other words, public relations.[5]

PRODUCT PUBLICITY

In light of the difficulty today of raising advertising awareness above the noise of so many competitive messages, marketers are turning increasingly to product publicity as an important adjunct to advertising. Although the public is generally unaware of it, a great deal of what it knows and believes about a wide variety of products comes through press coverage.

In certain circumstances, product publicity can be the most effective element in the marketing mix.[6] For example:

- **Introducing a revolutionary new product.** Product publicity can start introductory sales at a much higher level of demand by creating more awareness of the product.
- **Eliminating distribution problems with retail outlets.** Often, the way to get shelf space is to have consumers demand the product. Product publicity can be extremely effective in creating consumer demand.
- **Small budgets and strong competition.** Advertising is expensive. Product publicity is cheap. Often, publicity is the best way to tell the story.
- **A fine but complicated product.** Many products, their use, and their benefits are difficult to explain to mass audiences in a brief ad. Product publicity, through extended news columns, can be invaluable.
- **Generating new consumer excitement for an old product.** "Repackaging" an old product for the media can serve as a primary marketing impetus.
- **Tying the product to a unique representative.** "Morris the Cat" was one answer to consumer uninterest in cat food. Figure 11–1 illustrates yet another unique and memorable representative.

THIRD-PARTY ENDORSEMENT

Perhaps more than anything else, the lure of third-party endorsement is the primary reason smart organizations value product publicity as much as they do advertising. *Third-party endorsement* refers to the tacit support given a product by a newspaper, magazine, or broadcaster who mentions the product as news. Advertising often is perceived as self-serving. People know that the advertiser not only created the message but also paid for it. Publicity, on the other hand, which appears in news columns, carries no such stigma. When a message is sanctified by third-party editors, it is more persuasive than advertising messages, where the self-serving sponsor of the message is identified.

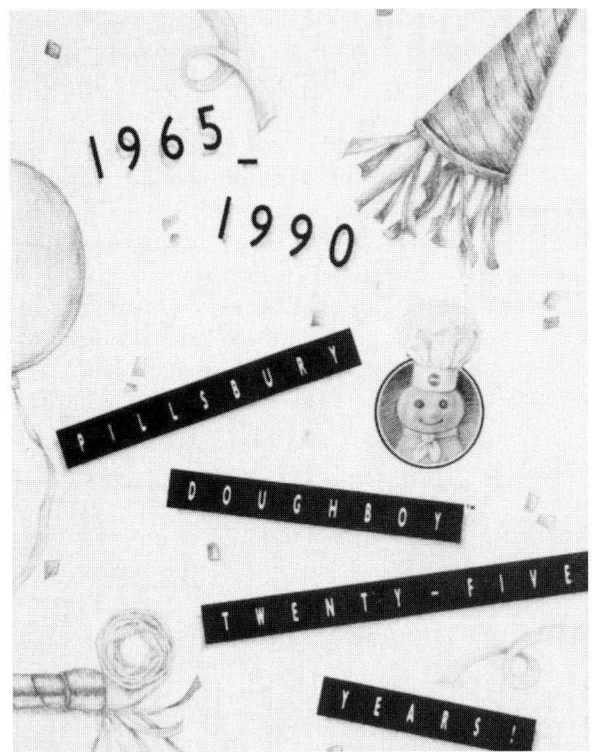

FOR IMMEDIATE RELEASE

CONTACT: Sally Garon/Diane Worton
Golin/Harris Communications
312/836-7100

OH BOY! PILLSBURY DOUGHBOY TURNS 25!

The Pillsbury Doughboy has grown up! America's most popular and adorable advertising symbol celebrates his 25th birthday this year.

In 1965, the Doughboy popped out of a tube of Pillsbury fresh, ready-to-bake dough for the first time. Soon, he became one of America's most loved and recognized characters and, 25 years later, he still tops the popularity charts. A contest conducted by Advertising Age magazine revealed the Doughboy is America's favorite character symbol.

What's his secret? "At 25, the Doughboy still has an almost magical relationship with consumers," says Michael Paxton, President, Pillsbury Bakery Products Division. "People tell us they trust him and believe in him. He makes the kitchen fun and festive. And, his giggle ... well, who can describe that giggle!

"When he 'popped' onto the scene a quarter century ago, we knew the Doughboy was someone special. He's done so much for us. Now it's our turn to salute him as he celebrates his 25th birthday," says Paxton.

- more -

Pillsbury Inc., Pillsbury Center – M.S. 27A1, 200 S. Sixth Street, Minneapolis, MN 55402 (612)330-4719

Figure 11–1 Among companies that chose unique representatives to earn product publicity as an enhanced marketing effort was food manufacturer Pillsbury. When the Pillsbury Dough Boy turned 25 in 1990, the company celebrated with national publicity-inducing events: cookbooks, recipes, and news releases featuring its cuddly and beloved Poppin' Fresh. *(Courtesy of Golin/Harris Communications)*

Editors have become sensitive to mentioning product names in print. Some, in fact, have a policy of deleting brand or company identifications in news columns. Public relations counselors argue that such a policy does a disservice to readers, many of whom are influenced by what they read and may desire the particular products discussed. Counselors further argue that journalists who accept and print public relations material for its intrinsic value and then remove the source of the information give the reader or viewer the false impression that the journalist generated the facts, ideas, or photography.

Equally reprehensible are the public relations practitioners who try to place sponsored features without disclosing promotional origins. In other words, some companies will distribute cartoons or stories—either directly or through mail-order services—without identifying the sponsor of the material. Obviously, such a practice raises ethical questions. Understandably, editors do not soon forgive firms that sponsor such anonymous articles.

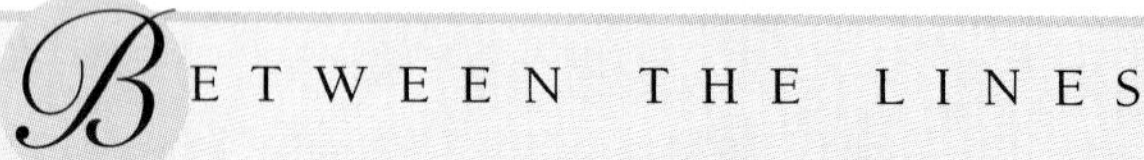

THE ULTIMATE THIRD-PARTY ENDORSERS

Third-party endorsement differed dramatically in the 1980s from that of the 1990s. Consider two of the top endorsers in the two decades.

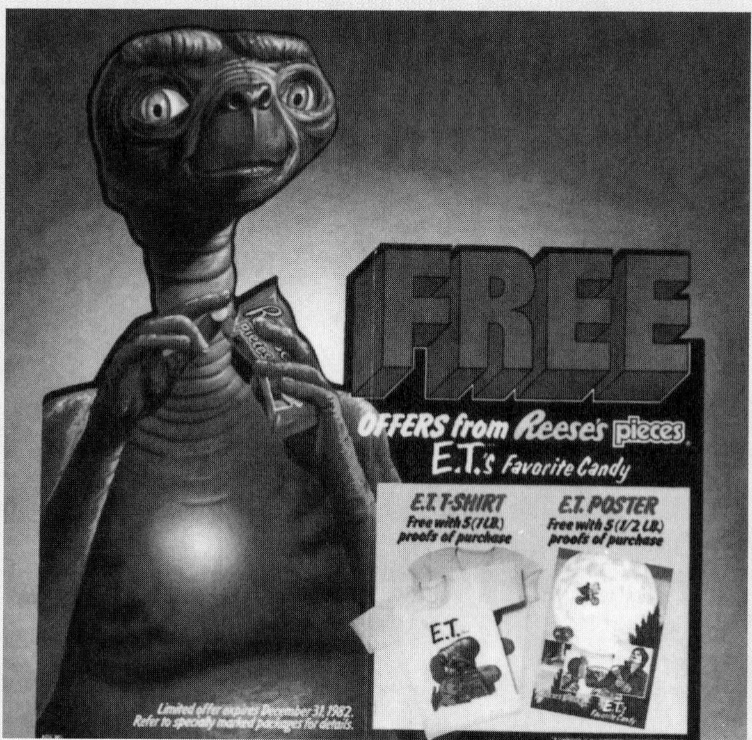

(Courtesy of Hershey Foods Corp.)

(*Courtesy of Berkheimer, Kline, Grolin/Harris Communications*)

- One of the most spectacular third-party endorsements of all time occurred in 1982, when Universal Pictures approached Hershey Foods Corporation for a promotional tie-in between Hershey's candy and the hero of a new Universal movie. Hershey, as it turned out, was Universal's second choice. Reportedly, the movie company's first choice, M&M/Mars, turned down the original offer to tie in its M&M candy. Hershey, however, accepted on behalf of its Reese's Pieces candy and, in a practice unheard of in Hollywood promotional deals, paid no money for the movie plug, so grateful were the filmmakers to land the candy company's endorsement. The rest, as they say, is Hollywood history. The movie was *E.T., The Extra-Terrestrial,* one of the biggest box-office draws in the history of moviedom. Early in the movie, a telltale trail of brown, yellow, and orange Reese's Pieces is followed to reveal one of the strangest, most unforgettable, most lovable creatures in the history of film.
- What a contrast when, in 1990, E.T.'s crown as the king of third-party endorsers was seized by a fresh-from-the-sewer, pizza-chomping, jive-talking band of Teenage Mutant Ninja Turtles, who endorsed everything from toys to theme parks to breakfast cereals—all eager to be associated with the turtles' magic marketing power.

PUBLIC RELATIONS MARKETING ACTIVITIES

In addition to product publicity, a number of other public relations activities are regularly used to help market products. These activities include article reprints, trade show participation, the use of spokespersons, and cause-related marketing.

ARTICLE REPRINTS

Once an organization has received product publicity in a newspaper or magazine, it should market the publicity further to achieve maximum sales punch. Marketing can be done through article reprints aimed at that part of a target audience—wholesalers, retailers, or consumers—that might not have seen the original article. Reprints also help reinforce the reactions of those who read the original article.

As in any other public relations activity, reprints should be approached systematically, with the following ground rules in mind:

1. **Plan ahead**, especially if an article has major significance to the organization. Ideally, reprints should be ordered before the periodical goes to press so that customers can receive them shortly after the article hits the newsstands.
2. **Select target publics** and address the recipients by name and title. This strategy will ensure that the reprint reaches the most important audience.
3. **Pinpoint the reprint's significance**, either by underlining pertinent information in the article, making marginal notes, or attaching a cover letter. In this way, the target audience will readily understand.
4. **Integrate the reprint** with other similar articles and information on the same or related subjects. Often, several reprints can be combined into a single mailing piece. Also, reprints can be integrated into press kits and displays.

TRADE SHOWS

Trade show participation enables an organization to display its products before important target audiences. The decision to participate should be considered with the following factors in mind:

1. **Analyze the show carefully.** Make sure the audience is one that can't be reached effectively through other promotional materials, such as article reprints or local publicity. Also, be sure the audience is essential to the sale of the product. For example, how responsible are the attendees for the actual purchase?
2. **Select a common theme.** Integrate public relations, publicity, advertising, and sales promotion. Unify all elements for the trade show and avoid, at all costs, any hint of interdepartmental rivalries.
3. **Make sure the products displayed are the right ones.** Decide well in advance exactly which products are the ones to be shown.

4. **Consider the trade books.** Often, trade magazines run special features in conjunction with trade shows, and editors need photos and publicity material. Always know what special editions are coming up, as well as their deadline schedules.
5. **Emphasize what's new.** Talk about the new model that's being displayed. Discuss the additional features, new uses, or recent performance data of the products displayed. Trade show exhibitions should reveal innovation, breakthrough, and newness.
6. **Consider local promotional efforts.** While in town during a trade show, an organization can enhance both the recognition of its product and the traffic at its booth by doing local promotions. This strategy involves visiting trade magazine editors and local media people to stir up publicity for the product during the show.

SPOKESPERSONS

In recent years, the use of spokespersons to promote products has increased. Spokespersons shouldn't disguise the fact that they are advocates for a particular product. Their purpose is to air their sponsor's viewpoint, which often means going to bat for a controversial product.

Spokespersons must be articulate, fast on their feet, and thoroughly knowledgeable about the subject. When these criteria are met, the use of spokespersons as an integrated marketing tool can be most effective.

In the 1990s, the use of spokespersons to promote products has become so crazed that professional basketball neophytes sign endorsement contracts first and concern themselves with making the team second.

Spokespersons come in a variety of sizes, shapes, and occupations. They range from corporate chairmen like Wendy's CEO Dave Thomas, who regularly hawks his hamburgers, to comedians Jay Leno for Doritos brand corn chips and Richard Lewis for Boku Fruit Drinks, to more controversial and even unknown spokespersons (Figure 11–2).

The most lucrative field for product spokespersons is sports. In 1992, the "10 Most Wanted Spokespersons List" read as follows:

1. Former basketball star and developing baseball player Michael Jordan, $13 million.
2. Golfer Jack Nicklaus, $10 million.
3. Golfer Arnold Palmer, $10 million.
4. Golfer Greg Norman, $8.5 million
5. Football player Joe Montana, $8.25 million
6. Hockey player Wayne Gretzky, $7.75 million.
7. Former tennis player Chris Everett, $7 million.
8. Tennis player Andre Agassi, $7 million.
9. Former basketball player Magic Johnson, $5 million.
10. Former tennis player Jimmy Connors, $4.5 million.[7]

Especially picky in marketing their images are rock stars. Indeed, when Prince, the diminutive Minnesota rocker with the risque lyrics who has since changed his name to

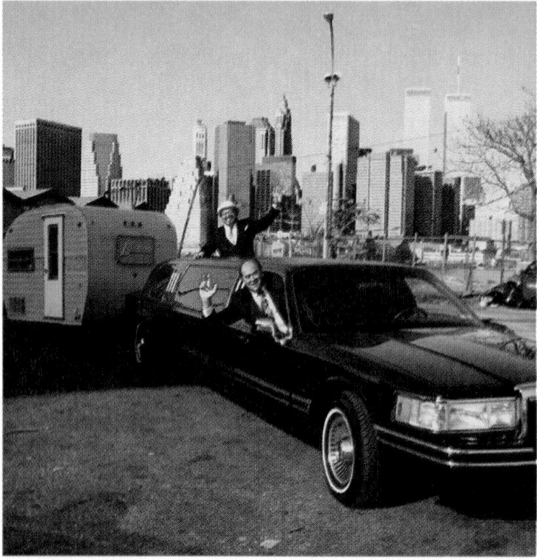

Figure 11–2 Celebrity spokespersons come in all sizes and shapes in the 1990s. Joe Montana, despite advancing age and frequent injuries, was a multi-million-dollar spokesman. So was new team owner Magic Johnson, despite his acknowledgment of being HIV positive. And when two obscure lottery players hit the jackpot, they were recruited by New York LOTTO to tour the state in a stretch limo to promote "the possibilities." *(Courtesy of the San Francisco 49ers, the Los Angeles Lakers, and Burson-Marsteller)*

an unpronounceable glyph, was asked for his photo for use in a certain public relations textbook, the author received the following warning from the decidedly unrocklike law firm of Manatt, Phelps, Rothenberg & Tunney.

> Please be advised that our client does not desire to grant you permission to use any picture or likeness of him in connection with your textbook.*
>
> So there.

CAUSE-RELATED MARKETING

Special public relations events also help to market products. Grand opening celebrations, for example, are a staple in the public relations arsenal. They present publicity opportunities and offer businesses a chance to meet customers face-to-face. With the cost of print and broadcast advertising going up each year, companies increasingly are turning to sponsorship of the arts, education, music, festivals, anniversaries, sports, and charitable causes for promotional and public relations purposes.

Such "cause-related marketing" is popular. Cause-related marketing brings together the fund-raising needs of nonprofit groups with the business objectives of sponsoring companies (Figure 11–3). Some companies have been called to task for using questionable tactics to promote their products by ostensibly doing good. Perhaps the most blatant example came in the winter of 1990, when Coca-Cola donated 20,000 cases of Coke to American troops in Saudi Arabia. It then promoted the gesture to the national media, which questioned the company's aggressive efforts to seek publicity. Later, Anheuser-Busch donated 22,000 cases of a nonalcoholic beer to the troops in Saudi Arabia and decided, in light of Coke's experience, to soft-pedal the announcement.[8]

Despite such false starts, cause-related marketing will continue to grow into the next century. Baby boomers are now middle-aged and more concerned about issues that affect their lives, like saving the rain forests and recycling household trash. This change in itself will drive the creation of events and decision-making by corporate sponsors.[9]

In planning special events and cause-related marketing activities, public relations people should first determine what area will best suit their organization's particular marketing objectives—culture, sports, community sponsorship, entertainment, and so on. Once the objectives are ascertained, cause-related marketing can significantly enhance the reception and overall sales of a product or institution.

PUBLIC RELATIONS ADVERTISING

Traditionally, organizations used advertising to sell products. In 1936, though, a company named Warner & Swasey initiated an ad campaign that stressed the power of America as a nation and the importance of American business in the nation's future. Warner & Swasey continued its ads after World War II, and thus was born a unique

*Letter from Jody Graham of Manatt, Phelps, Rothenberg & Tunney, Los Angeles, California, May 10, 1985.

Figure 11–3 In the summer of 1992, the public relations firm Cohn & Wolfe believed that a Barcelona Olympics tie-in would be ideal to generate new exposure for Cabbage Patch Kids dolls. The agency approached the U.S. Olympic Committee, which agreed to name the Kids the official mascots of the 1992 Olympic Team. Playing on the theme of the Games, "Friends for Life," Cabbage Patch Kids were distributed to sick children at Spain's largest children's hospital, thus winning not only support for the U.S. Olympians but great goodwill for the manufacturer of Cabbage Patch Kids.

type of advertising—the marketing of an image rather than a product. This technique became known variously as *institutional advertising, image advertising, public service advertising,* and ultimately *public relations advertising.*

In the 1970s, as the critics of American business proliferated, advertisers sought to create more responsible images for their firms in the face of harsh attacks (Figure 11–4).

BETWEEN THE LINES

MJ THE MERCHANDISING JUGGERNAUT

The undisputed king of 1990s spokespersons was Michael Jordan.

Despite retiring from professional basketball in 1993 at the ripe old age of 30, Michael Jordan's popularity as a corporate spokesman remained unsurpassed. When postbasketball Jordan took a fling at professional baseball in 1994, the Chicago White Sox's Florida spring training camp couldn't contain the sea of curious onlookers.

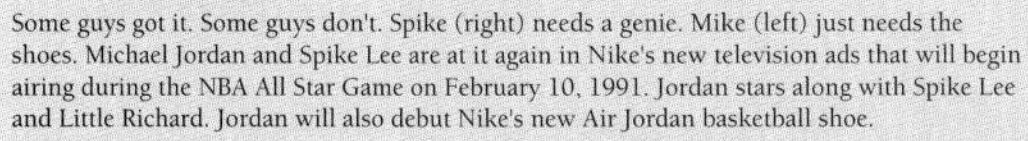

Some guys got it. Some guys don't. Spike (right) needs a genie. Mike (left) just needs the shoes. Michael Jordan and Spike Lee are at it again in Nike's new television ads that will begin airing during the NBA All Star Game on February 10, 1991. Jordan stars along with Spike Lee and Little Richard. Jordan will also debut Nike's new Air Jordan basketball shoe.

For more information call:
NIKE PUBLIC RELATIONS
(503)671-3071

(Courtesy of Nike, Inc.)

In his nine years as an NBA pro, MJ had taken endorsements to a new level. He pushed Wheaties for $1 million per year. He encouraged others to "Be Like Mike" for Gatorade, to the tune of $2 million per year. His signature sold nearly 15 million basketballs for Wilson Sporting Goods, at $1 million per year. And his munching for McDonald's and Hane's Ballpark Franks accounted for additional millions.

Jordan's most lucrative endorsement, and the one with which he was most identified, was that of sports shoe purveyor Nike. Some estimated that Jordan's annual take from Nike—where he was regularly featured with everyone from film director Spike Lee to cartoon hero Bugs Bunny—was upward of $20 million. Why not? Nike's Air Jordan brand was a $200 million enterprise, accounting for 5 percent of the firm's revenues.

While Jordan continued to profit as a spokesperson, even after retirement, another MJ wasn't as lucky.

In 1993, after he was accused of child molestation by a 13-year-old boy, singer Michael Jackson was unceremoniously dropped as a spokesperson for Pepsi-Cola. Less than a decade earlier, Pepsi began a lucrative alliance with the singer, reportedly making him the richest pitchman on earth. But once the Jackson name became synonymous with "less than refreshing" allusions, Pepsi ended his affiliation.

A QUESTION OF ETHICS

Supporting a Tormented Tonya

In the 1990s, no company was more controversial in terms of the celebrities it supported than Nike.

Nike's chairman, Philip H. Knight, was an iconoclast from the beginning. Most of corporate America went one way. Knight went the other.

When multisports star Bo Jackson stunned the sports world by revealing that he needed a hip replacement, Knight and Nike stayed with him in a multi-million-dollar advertising/endorsement campaign. (Jackson rewarded his benefactor when he returned to baseball and promptly hit a homerun in his first at bat!) Knight also was unflagging in his support of controversial sports heroes—from basketball

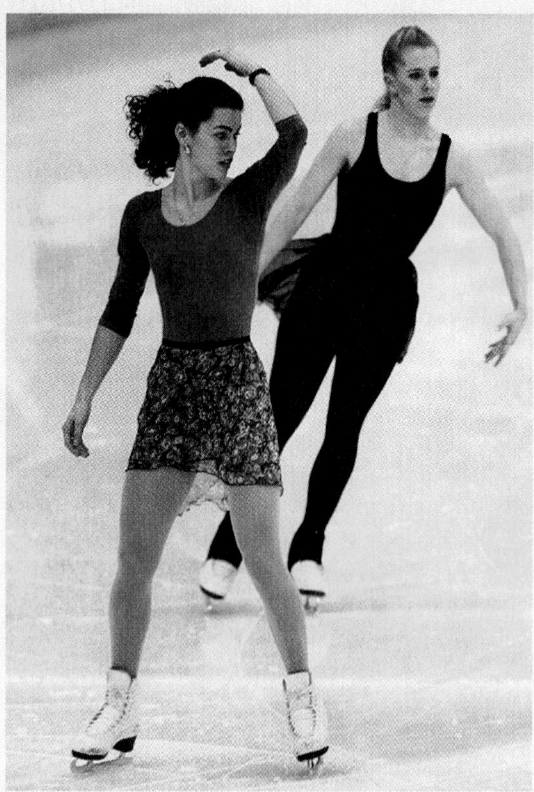

Arch skating rivals Tonya Harding (right) and Nancy Kerrigan. *(Courtesy of AP/Wide World Photos.)*

brawler Charles Barkley to tennis bad boy John McEnroe to baseball/football's unpredictable "Neon" Deion Sanders.

But clearly, Knight's most controversial support came in 1994, just prior to the Winter Olympics in Lillehammer, Norway, when associates of skater Tonya Harding admitted banging the knees of Harding's arch rival, Nancy Kerrigan, in an attempt to cripple her before the Olympics. While Harding was accused by her associates and suspected by many of having helped plan the attack, Philip Knight was the lone business figure to rise to her defense.

Nike contributed $25,000 in company funds to Harding to defend herself against the U.S. Olympic Committee, which was reconsidering her membership on the U.S. Olympic Team. Said Chairman Knight, "The U.S. Olympic Committee may try to circumvent the finest system of justice in the world and rush to judgment before that system has a chance to work."

Marketing experts were shocked at Nike's decision.

Said one, "If Harding is guilty, that doesn't reflect well on their side." Stated the spokesperson from rival shoemaker Reebok, "We really don't want to get into the controversy. It's a horrible commentary on what goes on in society."

But Knight, ever the iconoclast, held his ground. "She has virtually no endorsement value to us, now or in the future," he said. The firm's action was taken purely in the "cause of justice."

And while most scratched their heads at Nike's controversial contribution, at least one marketing professor thought favorably of their desire to support Tonya Harding. "Knight has a great skill in identifying people of enormous ability, and that's where the tragedy lies," he said. Defending Harding, he reasoned, was "consistent with their image of fair play."*

What do you think? Was Philip Knight right to rush to the defense of Tonya Harding? Was there "method in his madness"?

*Kathleen M. Berry, "Why Is Nike Publicly Backing Skater Tonya Harding?", *Investor's Business Daily* (February 3, 1994): 6.

These ads, which talked about social responsibility, equal employment hiring, minority assistance, and so on, were labeled *image advertising.*

In the 1980s, the logical extension of image advertising was *issues advertising,* which advocated positions from the sponsor's viewpoint. Often these concerned matters of some controversy. Organizations, led by the outspoken Mobil Oil, continued the practice of issue ads into the 1990s (Figure 11–5). Indeed, Mobil's practice of placing an issues ad on the Op-Ed page of *The New York Times* and other leading newspapers each Thursday continued into its fourth decade through the 1990s.

PURPOSES OF PUBLIC RELATIONS ADVERTISING

Traditional public relations, or nonproduct, advertising—as opposed to image or issue positioning—is still widely used. Such advertising can be appropriate for a number of mutually supportive activities:

This oil executive will go to bed hungry tonight.

Diana Church

HIS COMPANY earned almost two billion dollars in profits* last year, but that's not enough for him. Because he knows the world is running out of fossil fuels, and unless he can move in and monopolize a new power source, in the same way he's monopolized oil, he's going to be out of a job before very long.

That's why he says his company's astronomical profits aren't excessive—because he needs those profits to maintain his power. That's why he's asking for huge new handouts and tax incentives from the taxpayers—because he wants the government to pay the bills, and his company to reap the benefits.

If he doesn't get what he wants, he may not be able to go on collecting his $300,000 a year salary. He may not be able to go on manipulating the world energy market to the benefit of his stockholders and to the detriment of everyone else. He may be forced to give way to a system where the public controls the public resources for the public good.

If you think America's energy supply is too important to be left to a few huge multinational conglomerates, write your elected representatives and tell them that. The oil industry is making its voice heard in Washington. Isn't it time the shivering majority was heard from?

*

After-tax oil profits—1973

(millions of dollars)

	First nine months of 1973	Increase over 1972
Exxon	1,656	59.4%
Mobil	571	38.3%
Texaco	839	34.9%
Gulf	570	60.1%
Standard Calif.	560	39.7%
Standard Indiana	390	32.2%
Shell	253	40.6%
Continental	153	23.4%
Atlantic-Richfield	178	36.9%
Total all nine	5,170	**45.2%**
All oil companies	52,500	**30.3%**

Prepared by Public Interest Communications

ENERGY SHOULD BE EVERYBODY'S BUSINESS

Figure 11–4 This ad, critical of the nation's oil companies, was prepared by Public Interest Communications in the early 1970s and ran free of charge in several newspapers. *(Courtesy of Public Interest Communications)*

Where's the rip-off?

The sharp increase in gasoline prices has sparked thousands of words, most of them accusing the oil industry of reaping undeserved profits. Industry spokesmen have attempted to respond, with little apparent success.

So we decided to let the numbers do the talking.

West Texas Intermediate is a benchmark domestic crude oil. We've translated the price per barrel on the spot market to cents per gallon, and tracked the price movement from early July to last Tuesday. Gasoline also trades on the spot market, and we've shown the average spot price of regular unleaded across the U.S.

Finally, we've shown the average price we charged our dealers in 29 key cities for regular unleaded, along with the price for Mobil distributors. The dealers account for 70 percent and the distributors for about 30 percent of our gasoline business.

CRUDE/PRODUCT PRICES
JULY 3, AUGUST 7

(All numbers cents/gallon)	7/3/90	7/17/90	* 7/31/90	** 8/2/90	8/7/90	Increase 7/3-8/7
West Texas Intermediate Spot Market Crude	40.2	44.4	48.1	55.5	70.5	+30.3
†Regular Unleaded Spot Market Gasoline	60.4	63.7	62.8	68.9	85.1	+24.7
Average Mobil Price To Dealer Regular Unleaded	74.5	73.6	74.7	75.0	81.2	+ 6.7
Average Mobil Price To Distributor Regular Unleaded	67.8	68.0	69.6	69.8	78.3	+10.5

*OPEC Met July 26-27
**Iraq Invaded Kuwait August 2
†Platt's Low Weighted Average

The table shows that market prices for both crude oil and gasoline rose far more sharply than Mobil's.

One final observation: Much crude is now bought on terms specifying that the price is to be set by the spot market at the time of delivery. So the price of the gasoline you buy today was not set in concrete weeks ago.

Mobil®

Figure 11–5 In 1990, when gasoline prices rose quickly and the public once again castigated the oil industry, at least one petroleum firm was ready to answer back. *(Copyright © 1990 Mobil Corpora-*

1. **Mergers and diversifications.** When one company merges with another, the public needs to be told about the new business lines and divisions. Advertising provides a quick and effective way to convey this message.
2. **Personnel changes.** A firm's greatest asset is usually its managers, its salespeople, and its employees. Presenting staff members in advertising not only impresses a reader with the firm's pride in its workers, but also helps build confidence among employees themselves.
3. **Organizational resources.** A firm's investment in research and development implies that the organization is concerned about meeting the future intelligently, an asset that should be advertised. The scope of a company's services also says something positive about the organization.
4. **Manufacturing and service capabilities.** The ability to deliver quality goods on time is something customers cherish. A firm that can deliver should adver-

tise this capability. Likewise, a firm with a qualified and attentive servicing capability should let clients and potential clients know about it.

5. **Growth history.** A growing firm, one that has developed steadily over time and has taken advantage of its environment, is the kind of company with which people want to deal. It is also the kind of firm for which people will want to work. Growth history, therefore, is a worthwhile subject for nonproduct advertising.
6. **Financial strength and stability.** A picture of economic strength and stability is one that all companies like to project. Advertisements that highlight the company's financial position earn confidence and attract customers and investors.
7. **Company customers.** Customers can serve as a marketing tool, too. Well-known personalities who use a certain product may be enough to win additional customers. This strategy may be especially viable in advertising for higher-priced products, such as expensive automobiles or sports equipment.
8. **Organization name change.** Occasionally, firms change their names (Jersey Standard to Exxon, American Metal Climax to AMAX, First National City Corporation to Citicorp). To stick in people's minds, a name change must be well promoted and well advertised. Only through constant repetition will people become familiar with the new identity.
9. **Trademark protection.** Companies such as Xerox and Coca-Cola, whose products are household names, are legitimately concerned about the improper generic use of their trademarks in the public domain. Such companies run periodic ads to remind people of the proper status of their marks. In one such ad, a perplexed secretary reminds the boss, "If you had ordered 40 photocopies instead of 40 Xeroxes, we wouldn't have been stuck with all these machines!" (Figure 11–6).
10. **Corporate emergencies.** Occasionally, an emergency situation erupts—a labor strike, plant disaster, or service interruption. One quick way to explain the firm's position and procedures without fear of distortion or misinterpretation by editors or reporters is to buy advertising space. This tactic permits a full explanation of the reasons behind the problem and the steps the company plans to take to resolve the dilemma.

PUBLIC RELATIONS ADVERTISING IN THE 1990s

The 1990s have signaled a reemergence of public relations advertising. In a period of contraction and recession, profit-making organizations must justify their activities. Pressure on nonprofit organizations has intensified their need to prove why they, too, deserve contributions in a period of scarce resources. Hospitals, faced with unprecedented pressure from the public and the federal government to streamline their costs, also must position themselves in a manner that will allow them to stay in business. Public relations advertising is one way for organizations to position themselves in the mind of the public.

For the rest of the 1990s, then, institutions must keep in mind seven cardinal rules of public relations advertising:

XEROX

You can't Xerox a Xerox on a Xerox.

But we don't mind at all if you copy a copy on a Xerox copier.

In fact, we prefer it. Because the Xerox trademark should only identify products made by us. Like Xerox copiers and Xerox printing systems.

As a trademark, the term Xerox should always be used as an adjective, followed by a noun. And it's never used as a verb.

Of course, helping us protect our trademark also helps you. Because you'll continue to get what you're actually asking for.

And not an inferior copy.

XEROX
The Document Company

XEROX® is a trademark of XEROX Corporation.

Figure 11–6 Xerox throughout the 1990s continued to have a hard time identifying its name as a trademark of the Xerox Corporation. (*Courtesy of Xerox Corporation*)

1. **Ads must strengthen the bottom line.** The institution must keep in mind its own best long-term interest in its advertising. An organization pays for an ad for selfish reasons. For example, when Dresser Industries warned that "American jobs will be lost if Middle East–dependent firms, like Dresser, are subject to more boycott legislation," the bottom-line impact on Dresser and the country was apparent.
2. **Ads must be clear.** One purpose of public relations advertising is to promote understanding. If message and motives are cloudy, people simply won't understand, no matter how well conceived the ad is (Figure 11–7).
3. **Ads must be supported by top management.** The more controversial a public relations ad, the better it is. An ad that is watered down is one that is doomed to failure. Top management must be prepared to take the heat and support the advertising.
4. **Ads must persuade.** Again, this is the basis of advertising. Ads shouldn't just inform; they must be persuasive. When public interest groups opposed Judge Robert Bork's nomination to the Supreme Court in 1987, they initiated a public relations advertising campaign that said in part, "We're one vote away from losing our most fundamental rights . . . choosing between sterilization and job loss . . . declaring illegal the use of birth control . . . not being protected from sexual harassment." In other words, they used fear to persuade, and Bork's nomination was defeated.

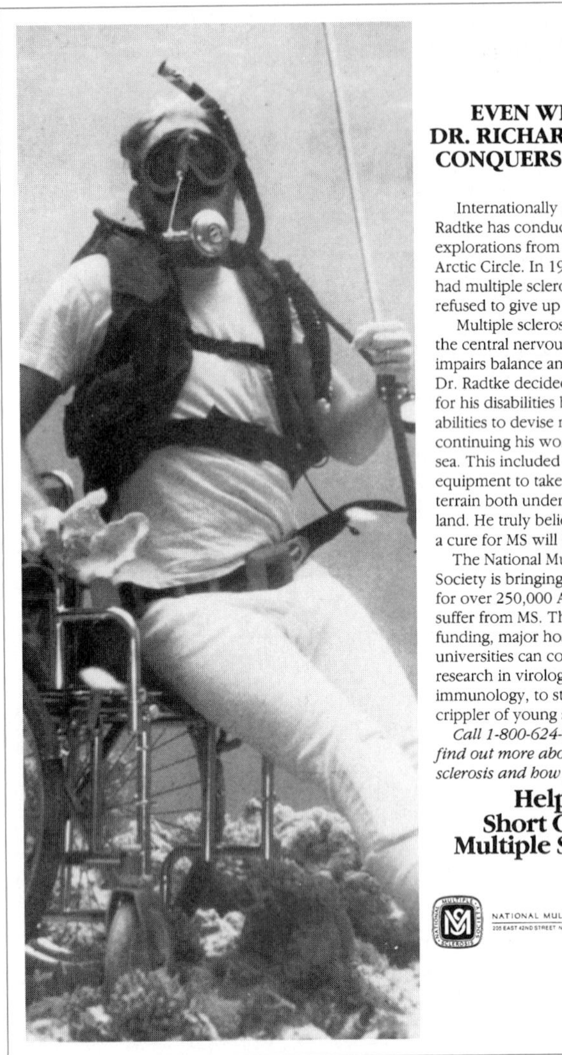

EVEN WITH MS,
DR. RICHARD RADTKE
CONQUERS THE DEEP
Internationally renowned, Dr. Radtke has conducted underwater explorations from Samoa to the Arctic Circle. In 1981 he learned he had multiple sclerosis, but he refused to give up his life's work.
Multiple sclerosis short circuits the central nervous system and impairs balance and coordination. Dr. Radtke decided to compensate for his disabilities by applying his abilities to devise new ways of continuing his work beneath the sea. This included creating special equipment to take him over rough terrain both under sea and over land. He truly believes that one day a cure for MS will be found.
The National Multiple Sclerosis Society is bringing that day closer for over 250,000 Americans who suffer from MS. Through its funding, major hospitals and universities can continue vital research in virology, genetics and immunology, to stop this great crippler of young adults.
Call 1-800-624-8236 today and find out more about multiple sclerosis and how you can help.
Help Us
Short Circuit
Multiple Sclerosis

Figure 11–7 The graphic photo and copy for this National Multiple Sclerosis Society ad was typical of a campaign that stated its message clearly. (*Courtesy of the National Multiple Sclerosis Society*)

5. **Ads must sell the persuaded.** All advertising, especially the public relations variety, must appeal to what the public wants—not what the organization wants. This is a subtle distinction that is often lost on public relations advertisers (Figure 11–8).
6. **Ads must be honest.** Any advertiser is suspect. All ads begin with a bias. If the organization is to be believed, the ad itself must be scrupulously straightforward and honest. Such was not the case when the head of the United Transportation Union in 1987 ostensibly paid for an ad in the *New York Times* appealing for support to fight a ban on smoking in commuter trains. Several

Figure 11–8 Husband and wife animal activists Kim Basinger and Alec Baldwin lent their show biz appeal to People for the Ethical Treatment of Animals for this provocative ad. (*Courtesy of People for the Ethical Treatment of Animals.*)

PEOPLE FOR THE ETHICAL TREATMENT OF ANIMALS
P.O. BOX 42516
WASHINGTON DC
20015-0516
(301) 770-7444
FAX (301) 770-8969

NEWS RELEASE

For Immediate Release:
February 9, 1994

Contacts:
Amanda Bate (301) 770-7382, ext. 372
Amy Bertsch (301) 770-7382, ext. 480
[after 2/13, (212) 581-8100]

KIM BASINGER TAKES IT ALL OFF FOR THE ANIMALS
Actor Unveils Anti-Fur Ad At N.Y. Party

New York -- Actor Kim Basinger has thrown her hat into the anti-fur ring -- and thrown her clothes off in the process.

Kim appears nude in the newest "Rather Go Naked Than Wear Fur" ad from People for the Ethical Treatment of Animals (PETA), which she will unveil with husband Alec Baldwin at the St. Regis Hotel (2 East 55th Street at Fifth Avenue) Monday, February 14 between 6:30 and 7:00 p.m. sharp in the Fontainebleau Suite.

Top fashion photographer Greg Gorman shot the ad with the heat turned way up in his Los Angeles studio. Both Gorman and Basinger donated their time and talents. "Beauty is not about wearing someone else's coat," reads the ad's headline.

The ad is set to run on billboards in major European cities and follows other "naked" poster campaigns featuring supermodels Christy Turlington and Naomi Campbell.

Note: To ensure that media requests are accommodated, please RSVP by 5:00 p.m. on Friday, February 11.

days later, it was revealed that the ad was secretly paid for by the Philip Morris Tobacco Company.

7. **A sense of humor helps.** Organizations, particularly big ones, can't take themselves too seriously, especially in public relations advertising. Humor disarms a skeptical populace, and a light touch can help to influence readers toward a particular viewpoint (Figure 11–9).

INTEGRATED MARKETING FOR THE 1990s

Beyond time-honored advertising, marketing, and public relations techniques, communications cross-training in the 1990s must keep pace with the ever-changing world of promotional innovations to help sell products and services. Specifically, communications professionals must be familiar with such new vehicles as infomercials, 900 numbers, and movie product placements.

INFOMERCIALS

Infomercials were greeted with universal catcalls in the 1980s when they were introduced as program-length commercials, shamelessly hawking products. Even today, the infomercial remains the Rodney Dangerfield of marketing, shunned and doubted for many reasons—state and federal investigations of infomercial producers, complaints about product performance, and, most important, the belief that a lengthy commercial disguised as a conventional program—like a talk show, complete with theme song and studio audience—unfairly masks what is nothing more than a failed spiel.[10]

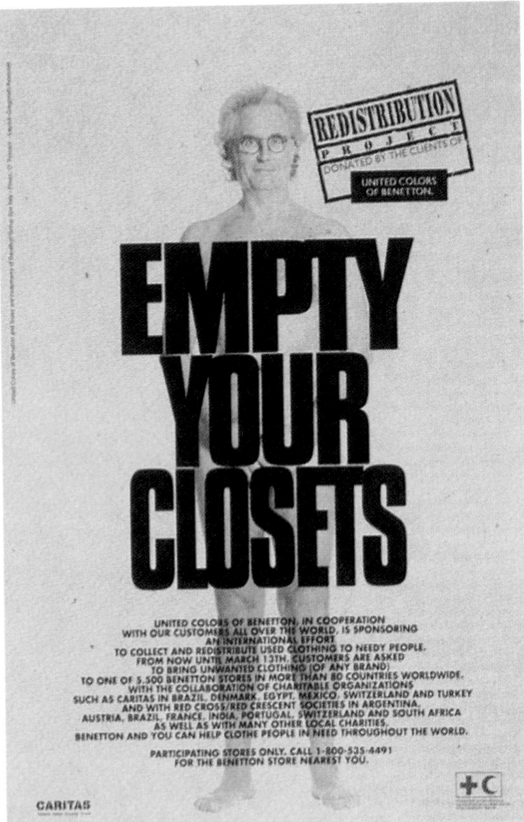

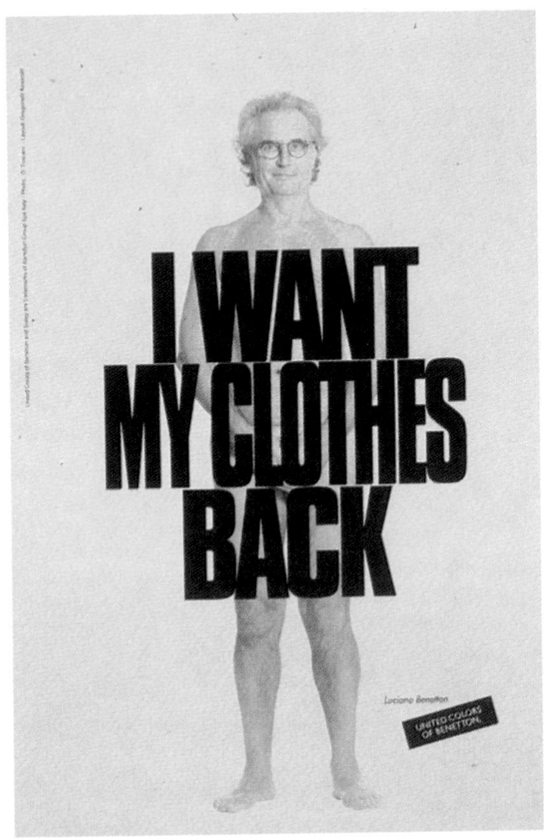

Figure 11–9 In 1993, the Benetton Company used this unique strategy to collect 500 tons of clothing for needy individuals around the world. *(Courtesy of United Colors of Benetton 1993 Spring/Summer Advertising Campaign; Photo: O Toscani)*

Nonetheless, infomercials are growing in popularity for one reason—they work. Between $1 and $2 billion worth of merchandise is sold each year as a result of infomercials. Today even the most well-established organizations—from General Motors to Time-Life—run infomercials. And movie stars like Cher, Martin Sheen, and Jane Fonda have joined the growing parade of infomercial pitchmen.

900 NUMBERS

Establishing a 900 telephone number is another way of publishing and selling information. Such numbers charge callers for the privilege of tuning in to current business news headlines, or stock quotes, or sports information. Just as infomercials were laughed at, 900 numbers were once associated more with parties and steamy adult sex than with mainstream marketing. In the 1990s, though, that situation has changed. Just as the government has cracked down on 900 phone services with increased regulations, Fortune 500 corporations, publishers, TV and movie companies, consumer products manufacturers, law firms, counseling services, nonprofit organizations, and even government agencies have joined the 900 marketing cavalcade. With 1996 revenue expected to approach $900 million, 900 numbers are here to stay.[11]

MOVIE PRODUCT PLACEMENTS

Product placements in films also are proliferating at a rapid rate. When Warner Brothers released *Demolition Man* in 1992, stars Sylvester Stallone and Wesley Snipes patrolled their 2032 terrain in a General Motors Oldsmobile. GM wanted to "send a subtle message to the public that it was alive and well in 2032."[12] Such product placements in films have become another integrated marketing resource that communicators, schooled in the ways of cross-training, should consider as part of their merchandising strategy.

SUMMARY

Marketing professor Philip Kotler has said that the days of traditional product marketing may be giving way to a more subtle, social, or public relations marketing. According to Kotler, companies must deal with dwindling resources, inflation that continues to limit buying power, consumers who are becoming more sophisticated, environmental and quality-of-life considerations, and government control.

In other words, what is needed now is an integrated approach to communications, combining the best of marketing, advertising, sales promotion, and public relations. Relationship building for organizations of every stripe is the name of the game as the year 2000 approaches. Building lasting relationships rather than selling to transactional customers must be the objective for any intelligent organization.

This implies the need for a communications professional knowledgeable about all aspects of the communications mix. Communications cross-training then becomes paramount in preparing public relations professionals for the next century.

DISCUSSION STARTERS

1. What is meant by communications cross-training?
2. Describe the differences among advertising, marketing, and public relations.
3. What is meant by third-party endorsement?
4. Discuss the phenomenon of the spokesperson.
5. Describe the pros and cons of using someone well known as a spokesperson.
6. What is cause-related marketing?
7. What is image advertising? Issues advertising?
8. What are the purposes of public relations advertising?
9. What has stimulated the reemergence of public relations advertising in the 1990s?
10. What are infomercials? 900 phone numbers?

NOTES

1. Fraser P. Seitel, "Communications Cross-Training," *United States Banker* (June 1993): 53.
2. Scot Hume, "Integrated Marketing: Who's in Charge Here?", *Advertising Age* (February 22, 1993): 1, 52.
3. Mitchell Kozikowski, "The Role of Public Relations in Integrated Marketing Public Relations," address presented to the National Conference of the Public Relations Society of America, November 15, 1993, Orlando, FL.
4. "Colloquium of Marketing and PR Spokespersons Agrees Organizations Suffer When Turf Wars Occur," *Public Relations Reporter* (February 13, 1989): 1.
5. Tom Harris, "Kotler's Total Marketing Embraces MPR," *MPR Update* (December 1992): 4.
6. "Marketing PR Can Outperform Advertising, Says Long-Time Counselor Dan Edelman," *Public Relations Reporter* (October 30, 1989): 3.
7. "Michael Jordan Stays on Top," *The New York Times* (May 22, 1992): D7.
8. Mark Landler and Seth Payne, "Publicity? Why, It Never Even Occurred to Us," *Business Week* (September 24, 1990): 46.
9. "Event Marketing: The Good, the Bad and the Ugly," address by David D'Alessandro at the International Events Group's Annual Event Marketing Conference, March 22, 1993, Chicago.
10. Stuart Elliot, "Some Big Marketers Join Audience for Infomercials," *The New York Times* (June 5, 1992): D9.
11. Sharon McDonald, "Laws Forcing 900 Numbers to Change Tone," *Crain's New York Business* (October 11, 1993): 26.
12. Stuart Elliot, "In 'Demolition Man' a Car Could Be Your Grandson's Oldsmobile," *The New York Times* (October 8, 1992): D10.

TOP OF THE SHELF

Regis McKenna, *Relationship Marketing*, Reading, MA: Addison-Wesley, 1991.

Regis McKenna has always been a public relations trailblazer. One of the first to consider his function more than publicity, McKenna has authored a book that centers on the public relations relationship with the consumer.

Relationship Marketing comes out squarely against advertising or public relations as the be-all and end-all of communications. Rather, McKenna sees integrated marketing communications as a necessity in the years ahead.

He writes that companies must win over and educate key members of the "industry infrastructure" before going to the media. He argues that since reporters will go first to customers, financial analysts, consultants, distributors, and resellers "to help them separate fact from fiction," smart public relations professionals must first work to build relationships with all of these constituencies rather than treating the press as superordinate.

The author suggests that to build lasting positions in the market, companies must first build strong relationships with these various publics. He points out that nobody buys a personal computer or an expensive sports car without obtaining favorable references from both users and other important third parties within the market-making structure.

McKenna advises public relations people to "broaden their focus" to gain involvement, understanding, and ultimately the "endorsement" of a much broader spectrum of constituent publics.

Such advice may not be traditional, but it's right. That's why reading McKenna's book *Relationship Marketing* is a must for all public relations professionals interested in making it to the year 2000.

SUGGESTED READINGS

Albrecht, Karl. *The Only Thing That Matters: Bring the Power of the Customers into the Center of Your Business.* New York: Harper Business, 1992.

Anderson, Walter. *Handbook of Business Communications.* (Available from P.O. Box 243, Lenox Hill Station, New York, NY 10021.)

Bennet, Peter. *Dictionary of Marketing Terms.* New York: AMACOM, 1989.

Benson, Richard. *Secrets of Successful Direct Mail.* Lincolnwood, IL: National Textbook, 1989.

The Changing World of Marketing: Conference Summary Report No. 92-112. Cambridge, MA: Marketing Science Institute, 1992.

Chestara, John A. *P.P.R. (Personal Public Relations): Using Public Relations Skills, Concepts, Techniques and Strategies in Your Business, Career, Family and Social Life.* Newbury Park, CA: Sage, 1988.

Communicators' Guide to Marketing. IABC, 1987 (870 Market St., San Francisco, CA 94102).

The Complete Guide to Creating Successful Brochures. Brentwood, NJ: Asher-Gallent Press, 1988 (131 Heartland Blvd. 11717).

Corporate Advertising Practices. New York: Association of National Advertisers, 1991.

Current Company Practices in the Use of Corporate Advertising. New York: Association of National Advertisers, 1988.

Davidson, Jeffrey. *Marketing on a Shoestring.* New York: Wiley, 1988.

Debelak, Don. *Total Marketing.* Homewood, IL: Dow Jones-Irwin, 1989.

Deran, Elizabeth. *Low-Cost Marketing Strategies: Field-Tested Techniques for Tight Budgets.* New York: Praeger, 1987.

Encyclopedia of Telemarketing. New York: Prentice-Hall, 1991.

Gross, Martin. *The Direct Marketer's Idea Book.* New York: AMACOM, 1989.

Haller, Robert T. *Creative Power! Grow Faster with New Proactive Tactics in Advertising and Public Relations.* New York: Leister & Sons, 1988.

Harris, Thomas L. *The Marketer's Guide to Public Relations.* New York: Wiley, 1993.

Hauman, David J. *The Capital Campaign Handbook: How to Maximize Your Fund-raising Campaign*. Rockville, MD: Taft Group, 1987 (12300 Twinbrook Parkway, Suite 450, 20852-9830).

How to Handle Public Relations for Your Advertising Agency. New York: American Association of Advertising Agencies, 1991.

How to Prepare and Write Your Employee Handbook. 2nd ed. New York: AMACOM, 1988.

Integrated Marketing Communications: A Survey of National Consumer Goods Advertisers. New York: American Association of Advertising Agencies, 1991.

Jefkins, Frank. *The Secrets of Successful Direct Response Marketing.* Portsmouth, NH: Heinemann, 1988.

Kaatz, Ron. *Advertising and Marketing Checklists.* Skokie, IL: NTC Business Books, 1988 (P.O. Box 554 60076).

Kern, Monague. *30-Second Politics: Political Advertising in the Eighties.* New York: Praeger, 1989.

Lazarus, George, and Bruce Wexler. *Marketing Immunity: Breaking Through Customer Resistance.* Homewood, IL: Dow Jones-Irwin, 1987.

Ljungren, Roy G. *Business to Business Direct Marketing Handbook.* New York: AMACOM, 1988.

Lyons, John. *Guts: Advertising from the Inside Out.* New York: AMACOM, 1989.

Magrath, Allan. *Six Imperatives of Marketing: Lessons from the World's Best Companies.* New York: AMACOM, 1992.

McGann, Anthony, and Thomas J. Russell. *Advertising Media.* Homewood, IL: Richard Irwin, 1987.

McNamara, Jay. *Advertising Agency Management.* Homewood, IL: Dow Jones-Irwin, 1990.

Miller, Peter G. *Media Marketing.* New York: Harper & Row, 1987.

Ogilvy, David. *Confessions of an Advertising Man.* New York: Macmillan, 1963.

Onkovist, Sak, and John Shaw. *Product Life Cycle and Product Management.* Westport, CT: Greenwood, 1989.

Ostrow, Rona, and Sweetman Smith. *The Dictionary of Marketing.* New York: Adweek Books, 1988.

Quelch, John A. *How to Market to Consumers.* New York: Wiley, 1989.

Ries, Al, and Jack Trout. *Bottom-up Marketing.* New York: McGraw-Hill, 1989.

Roberts, Mary, and Paul Berger. *Direct Marketing Management.* Englewood Cliffs, NJ: Prentice-Hall, 1989.

Robinson, Larry, and Roy Alder. *Marketing Megaworks: The Top 150 Books and Articles.* New York: Praeger, 1987.

Savidge, Jack. *Marketing Intelligence: Discover What Your Customers Really Want and What Your Competitors Are Up To.* Homewood, IL: Business One Irwin, 1992.

Schwartz, Gerald. "Planning Product Publicity Pays Off." *Nation's Business.* New York: G. S. Schwartz & Co.

Sethi, S. Prakash. *Handbook of Advocacy Advertising Concepts, Strategies, and Applications.* Cambridge, MA: Ballinger, 1987.

Shepard & Associates, David. *The New Direct Marketing . . . How to Implement a Profit Driven Database Marketing Strategy.* Homewood, IL: Dow Jones-Irwin, 1993.

Special Events Report (213 W. Institute Pl., Chicago, IL 60610). 24 per year.

Sports Marketing News (1771 Post East, Westport, CT 06880). Biweekly.

Stanley, Thomas J. *Marketing to the Affluent.* Homewood, IL: Dow Jones-Irwin, 1988.

Weiner, Richard. *Professional's Guide to Public Relations Services.* 6th ed. New York: AMACOM, 1988.

Weinrauch, Donald J., and Nancy Baker. *The Frugal Marketer: Smart Tips for Stretching Your Budget.* New York: AMACOM, 1989.

CASE STUDY

DOMINO'S CEASES TO DELIVER CONTROVERSIAL PIZZA POLICY

In the 1990s, Detroiter Thomas Monaghan epitomized the new breed of marketing-oriented CEO. Rising up from poverty, Monaghan had acquired a multi-million-dollar classic car collection, bought the Detroit Tigers baseball team, and spoke out in support of conservative causes.

He also founded and served as chairman of Domino's Pizza, the fastest-growing chain in a $13 billion market. From nowhere, Domino's, under Monaghan, became the nation's second fastest-growing franchise operation, with sales leaping from $179 million in 1981 to more than $2 billion at the beginning of 1990.

In a decade, the company grew from 300 outlets to about 5,000 owned and franchised stores, selling about 230 million pizzas per year.

Key to Domino's success, beyond the outspokenness and flamboyance of its owner, was a guarantee that if customers had to wait more than half an hour for their pizza, they'd get a $3 discount or a free pie.

Domino's Pizza's pledge also was the company's Achilles heel.

Employing between 70,000 and 80,000 drivers, Domino's became the target of critics who claimed that the company's 30-minute policy was causing reckless driving, accidents, and deaths. Through the latter part of 1989, the tension mounted.

- In June, a 17-year-old Indiana Domino's driver was killed when his small pickup truck skidded on a rain-slicked road and hit a utility pole. His mother said he was speeding and called Domino's guarantee "an invitation to break the law." In light of the death, Indiana Senator Richard Lugar wrote Domino's president, asking the company to review its 30-minute delivery policy.
- Later that month, after a Domino's delivery car hit a station wagon outside a Pittsburgh store, the driver of the hit car said that the Domino's manager rushed to the wreckage

"With our team, it only takes 12 minutes to make and bake a great pizza."

"Then I've got plenty of time to deliver safely."

A good system, and good people to run it. That's how we can deliver in 30 minutes or less. Our people are well trained and our kitchens are designed for efficiency. And we only deliver to neighborhoods that are within an average of two miles from the store. Our drivers don't have to hurry. So give us a call. We'll take care to be there.

©1989 Domino's Pizza, Inc.
Delivery area limited to ensure safe driving.

and demanded, "Let's get this pizza on the road." The driver subsequently filed a lawsuit against the company.

- In September, the Chicago-based National Safe Workplace Institute issued a report that at least 10 Domino's drivers, many of them students working part-time, were killed in the prior year, and that Domino's drivers were involved in about 100 traffic accidents that resulted in the deaths of 10 other people and many more serious injuries.

By the fourth quarter of 1989, it was clear that Domino's marketing publicity campaign of emphasizing the 30-minute delivery pledge had come back to haunt it.

Officials around the nation pleaded with Domino's to drop its speedy-delivery pledge. Insurance experts argued that the chain should scrap the guarantee because it pressured young drivers to speed. As the lawyer in the Pittsburgh case summarized, "People are being injured all over the country. These drivers are trying to deliver pizzas within 30 minutes, and sometimes it's just not physically possible. They may run a stop sign, go over speed limits, or make illegal turns."

Despite the ferocious national pressure, Domino's steadfastly refused to alter its 30-minute policy.

The company's position was that it had a "perception problem"—that the "speed" in the delivery process didn't occur on the highway but in the franchise outlet itself. Pizzas, Domino's said, were put together in a few minutes and relayed to drivers speedily enough to allow them adequate time to deliver the product safely. Besides, the company argued, Domino's "gain[ed] in customer goodwill what it may lose in income" each time the customer got a rebate.

Domino's backed up its defense with a massive integrated marketing effort to dispel the view that its policy endangered motorists. Its nationwide promotional campaign included the following elements:

1. A letter attached to millions of pizza boxes from the company's president, who wrote:

   Yes, a 30-minute delivery is important, but safe delivery is more important. The fact is, our entire delivery system is geared to give our drivers ample time to deliver.

   Since our delivery areas average two miles or less, this leaves our drivers nearly 18 minutes to make it to your home. After millions of safe deliveries, we know that's plenty of time.

2. A toll-free phone number, 1-800-DOMINOS for the public to register complaints against reckless delivery drivers.
3. Large posters plastered in Domino's Pizza stores with a photo of a stop sign and a listing of the toll-free number.
4. A publicity offensive, emphasizing safety. Domino's talked about how all drivers must complete an eight-hour, company-designed driving program. It announced the development of a new, more intensive driver-training program in selected locations. And it introduced a new requirement that all corporate-owned outlets—one-third of the chain's 5,000 stores—should terminate or reassign all drivers younger than 18.
5. A more candid approach in discussing its safety record. Domino's announced that its employees had been involved in accidents that resulted in 20 fatalities in a one-year period. This, it said, amounted to one fatality for every 11.5 million pizzas sold. It specified that not all of the accidents occurred during deliveries.

   It further specified that drivers were not penalized for failing to meet the 30-minute delivery guarantee—that the company, not the driver, paid the $3. It also publicly renounced the practice among some franchises of awarding "King of Lates" badges to delivery people making the most late deliveries.

   Domino's also announced plans to stop awarding its top driver an all-expenses-paid trip to the Indianapolis 500, where the company sponsored a race car. Instead, the firm would reward all drivers with at least 5,000 safe driving hours.
6. A print advertising campaign emphasizing the company's commitment to safety. The ads

featured delivery drivers, with the first focusing on a New York driver who administered cardiopulmonary resuscitation to a woman while he was delivering a pizza.

By the spring of 1990, the news for Domino's began to get better. For one thing, the steady drumbeat of negative publicity began to subside. Once again, owner Monaghan began to attract coverage—and controversy—but for projects other than the 30-minute guarantee. He announced Domino's intention to expand its one-item menu. He donated money to antiabortion groups. He announced development plans for a 35-story "Leaning Tower of Pizza" on a resort island in Michigan.

Regrettably for Domino's, in 1992 the "light at the end of the tunnel" turned out to be a locomotive.

In December, a jury in St. Louis awarded more than $78 million to a woman struck by a Domino's driver in 1989. Monaghan argued that what the jury decided was "shocking" and "out of line with the factual circumstances of the case." He said the company intended to appeal the verdict.

But Domino's president also announced that his company would no longer promise 30-minute delivery.

Marketing experts suggested that canceling the guarantee might send consumers to other pizza delivery companies. Securities analysts questioned whether Domino's sales might be severely hindered by the cessation of the guarantee. Said one, "With a major competitor like Pizza Hut, where the quality is very good, service becomes an important factor. With Domino's, the fact that they built their business by delivering in a timely fashion also is important. Now they will not be able to deliver so timely. In general, that could be a negative perception."

In the final analysis, Monaghan and Domino's were forced to "blink."

Summarized the embattled Monaghan, "Domino's has always been committed to safety. But there continues to be a perception—a perception I believe is not supported by the facts—that the guarantee is unsafe. We got that message loud and clear. So we are eliminating the element that creates that negative perception."

QUESTIONS

1. What were Domino's options when faced with the challenge to end the 30-minute delivery policy?
2. Would you have changed the policy initially? Why or why not?
3. How would you characterize Domino's publicity posture as part of its reactive promotional program?
4. What additional elements might Domino's have adopted as part of its promotional program?
5. Now that Domino's has relented and dropped its 30-minute guarantee, what can it do to restore its image?

For further information on the Domino's Pizza case, see Brian Dumaine, "How Managers Can Succeed Through Speed," *Time* (February 13, 1989): 54; Michael Janofsky, "Domino's Ends Fast Pizza Pledge After Big Award to Crash Victim," *The New York Times* (December 22, 1993): 1, D15; Patrick McMahon, "Publicity Forces Mistrial in Domino's Suit," *United Press International*, May 14, 1990; Bradley A. Stertz, "Domino's Beefs Up Menu to Keep Pace with Rivals," *Wall Street Journal* (April 21, 1989) B1–4; "That Quick Pizza Has Safety Costs," *Financial Times* (September 5, 1989): 6; Mark Hofmann, "Domino's Keeps Delivery Policy, Despite Deaths," *Crain's Detroit Business* (July 3, 1989): 29.

TIPS FROM THE TOP

STEVE RIVKIN

Steve Rivkin is president of his own communications counseling firm in Midland Park, New Jersey. Before forming Rivkin & Associates in 1989, he was executive vice-president of Trout & Ries, Inc., the prestigious marketing strategy firm known for its pioneering work in positioning. Before joining Trout & Ries, Rivkin worked in public affairs, advertising, and corporate identity for IU International Corporation, a Philadelphia-based conglomerate. He was previously associate editor of *Iron Age Magazine,* a weekly business publication. Rivkin speaks and lectures frequently on communications topics.

What is integrated communications?
Integrated communications is a new way of looking at the whole. Most of us only see parts—public relations, advertising, sales literature, employee communications, and so forth. Integrated communications is about realigning communications the way the customer sees it—as one flow of information.

Traditional communications is like going into a pharmacy to pick up some items—a package of publicity, a box of direct mail, a carton of advertising.

Integrated communications is more like going to see a team of doctors. Tell them where it hurts—what your communications problem is—and they'll prescribe comprehensive treatment—everything from a remedy through rehabilitation.

Why do today's business demands call for a new composition of communications functions?
Because the old lines are blurring. Today, consumers tend to lump all persuasive messages into something they may call *advertising*. They don't differentiate among messages from TV or magazines or an outdoor display. They don't even differentiate among various functional approaches marketers use, such as advertising, direct

mail, sales promotion, public relations, or even advertorials. These are all simply "advertising" or "product messages."

No matter where the message came from, or who created it, or where it appears, it stands for the brand, the company, or the organization.

What will happen to traditional practices of marketing, advertising and public relations?
They'll disappear over time. Specialists in these fields will become generalists in integrated marketing communications.

How do smart organizations approach the new realities of communications?
They're looking for synergy. They want the whole of communications to be greater than the sum of its parts.

When all the corporate and product messages are strategically coordinated, the effect is greater than when advertising, sales promotion, naming, PR, packaging, etc. are planned and executed independently. When each is independent, each area competes for budgets and power. And sometimes each area sends out conflicting messages.

What do you advise companies with traditional advertising and public relations departments to do?
To see the light. To let people out of their boxes.

What you've got now are people trained and then constrained. Their jobs should be to tackle your business problems. Instead, their jobs are to "do public relations" or "do advertising" or "do direct mail."

How should public relations students prepare for integrated communications?
Cross-train your brains. Don't turn up your nose at any one form of communication. What if the database turns out to be a more powerful communications tool than TV ever was?

And always consider communications from the customer's vantage point. That means you should ask (1) what media forms the customer or prospect uses, not simply what is most efficient for the marketer; (2) when your messages might be most relevant to the customer or prospect, not just when you'd prefer to schedule them; (3) when customers and prospects might be more receptive to your message, not simply when it might be most convenient to deliver that message.

What does integrated communications have to do with positioning an organization?
Positioning is a touchstone for integrated communications because it starts with the same "outside-in" orientation. Positioning an organization is actually thinking in reverse. Instead of starting with you or your company, you start with the prospect.

Positioning a company means getting into the mind of your prospect with a single, memorable concept or set of ideas about that company. The basic approach of positioning is not to create something new and different, but rather to manipulate what's already there, to retie the connections that already exist.

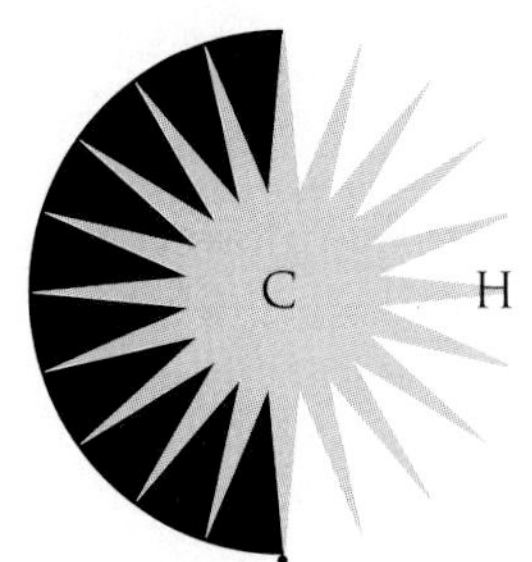

CHAPTER 12

MEDIA

THE MASS MEDIA COMPRISE THE PUBLIC THAT IS MOST associated with public relations. Most people believe that the term *public relations* is synonymous with *publicity.* It isn't. However, few are able to distinguish between securing favorable publicity for an organization and winning positive public relations.

Despite the fact that most public relations professionals use the mass media more than any other communications vehicle, research has indicated that with public relations becoming a more sophisticated profession, it should rely less on the mass media than in the past.[1] The mass media, according to this line of thought, are less pivotal in influencing public opinion in the 1990s.

Perhaps.

But the fact remains that securing positive publicity through the mass media is still a critical activity for most public relations professionals. Moreover, public relations professionals still regard the mass media as an institution of awesome power—and approach it with considerable caution. Consider the following:

- When Iran's Ayatollah Khomeini called for the death of author Salman Rushdie for his controversial book *The Satanic Verses,* the word to employees from Walden Books' headquarters was, "If anyone asks about the book, ask them if they're with the media. Do not answer any media inquiries and do not give your name. Just say, 'No comment.' This is our corporate statement."[2]
- After a New York public relations professional agreed to appear on NBC's *Today* show, she sued the program and its former co-host Jane Pauley for $2 million, charging the show falsely depicted her as a "financial illiterate."[3]
- Corporate public relations people were reported to be "minimizing" face-to-face contact with the media because, according to one reporter, "No one knows or trusts anyone anymore."[4]

This chapter focuses on coexisting with the media. That means working with the media to convey the most effective impression for an organization. And that means attracting *positive publicity.*

Since publicity, as we will see, is generally regarded as more *credible* than advertising, establishing a good working relationship with the media is essential for successful communications programs.

Dealing with the media traditionally has been a primary responsibility of public relations professionals. As noted, the practice of public relations has been most closely associated—for better or worse—with the function of media publicity. Accordingly, media relations has developed into a career specialty for many in the field.

When the media go to bat for an organization or individual, the rewards can be substantial. On the other hand, when the media take aim at a particular individual or institution, the results can be devastating.

Recent US history is studded with examples of people and organizations whose power and influence have been cut short as a result of attracting extensive and critical media attention.

- In 1991, when IBM Chairman John Akers fulminated in an internal memo that his troops were becoming "too damn comfortable . . . standing around the water cooler waiting to be told what to do," the word leaked to the press and the ensuing headlines weren't pleasant. A year later, Akers was shown the door by his board.[5]
- In 1993, two federal law enforcement agencies warned their agents that "loose and often uninformed comments to the press" would jeopardize their efforts to solve the bombing at the World Trade Center in New York City and the armed standoff at the Branch Davidian headquarters in Waco, Texas (see Case Study at end of this chapter). The directors of both agencies—the FBI at the World Trade Center and the Bureau of Alcohol, Tobacco, and Firearms in Waco—eventually were replaced.[6]
- In 1994, when a First Family friend and government attorney, Vincent Foster, was found dead and allegations of a cover-up in the financing of the Whitewater Development Corporation began to emerge, President Clinton's constant and vociferous denials couldn't shake the media from bird-dogging him and First Lady Hillary for months (see the Case Study in Chapter 16).

The vigilance of the media in exposing fraud, deception, and questionable practices in society is a tradition (Figure 12–1). The media's crowning achievement in this regard was the exposure of the Watergate break-in, which eventually led to the resignation of President Richard Nixon (see the case study in Chapter 2). The success of *The Washington Post* in getting to the bottom of Watergate encouraged journalists to focus on abuses of power in all areas of society. Over the years since Watergate, investigative reporting has gained a solid foothold, particularly on television, where one picture is worth a thousand words. The cream of the TV investigative crop, of course, is *60 Minutes,* among the nation's most widely watched shows for the better part of three decades. But even *60 Minutes* is not without its faults. According to CBS anchorman Dan Rather, "We make mistakes so often, violating the basics of accuracy, clarity, or fairness, that sometimes it shatters me. If with our budget and our staff and time we make so many mistakes in exposé material, what's it like under less luxurious circumstances?"[7]

What indeed? With the spate of gossip columnists and commentators in the 1990s—from Geraldo Rivera to Oprah Winfrey, from *A Current Affair* to *Entertainment Tonight,* from Liz Smith to the *National Enquirer*—the spread of tattletale journalism has put an added burden on public relations professionals, who, as the primary voice of management, seek fair and unbiased treatment of their organizations in the media.

WHAT RESEARCH TELLS US ABOUT THE MEDIA

The relationship between journalists and public relations people has never been an easy one. The former often accuse the latter of withholding information. The latter often accuse the former of left-leaning, one-sided reporting. Recent research corroborates an uneasy relationship between those who interview and those who are being interviewed. In one 1987 telephone survey of 100 top-level executives, 59 percent of those polled claimed that they "invariably get misquoted" by the press. "Journalistic ignorance" was cited by 39 percent, with 25 percent saying that journalists were guilty of an "overemphasis on the negative." Another 22 percent cited "sensationalist tendencies," and 12 percent cited clear-cut "bias" among members of the press.[8]

As to a liberal bias among journalists, a 1986 study of so-called elite journalists working for major news organs in Washington, D.C., and New York found evidence to support such a view. The authors concluded that evidence "does not imply a conspiracy to exclude conservative voices, but merely reflects the human tendency to turn more often to those you trust, and to trust most those who think most like you do." They suggest that when it comes time to find expert commentary on policy issues, it is the liberal left that most often provides that commentary. As proof, they cited investigations of articles on welfare reform, consumer protection, nuclear energy, and other issues for which liberal sources were quoted significantly more than conservative ones.[9]

Recent studies show that neither journalists nor public relations people hold the strongly negative views that may once have been common. According to several studies, there seems to be a fairly high level of mutual respect within the two camps: journalists tend to think that most public relations people do a good job and vice versa.

As for the general public, one 1985 study revealed that the public has a high level of confidence in the media.[10] This confidence is affected from time to time by controversial events, such as a debate between George Bush and Dan Rather in 1988. After his bout with Bush, Rather's favorability rating fell a monumental 18 points. His fall coincided

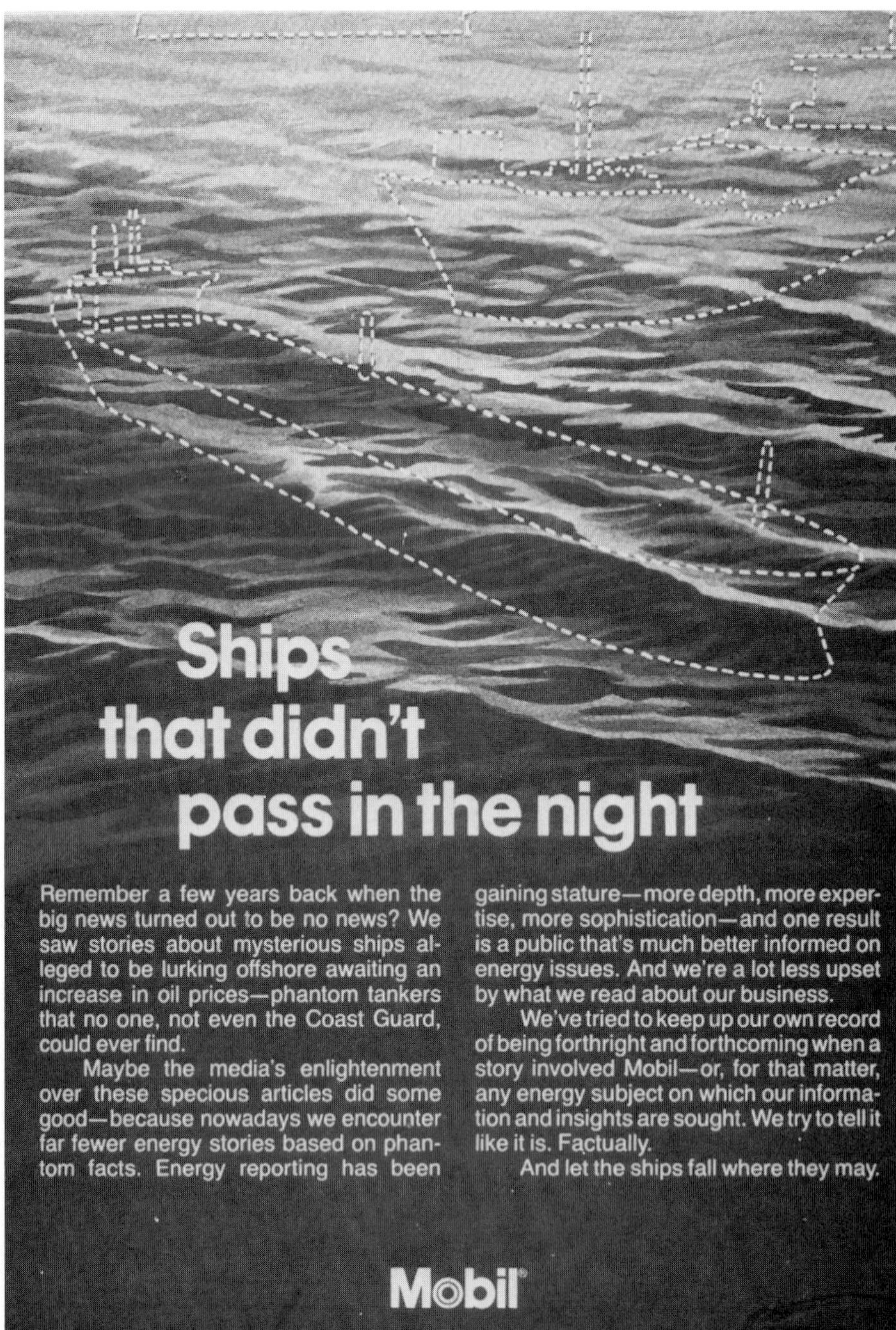

Figure 12–1 The oil companies have had their share of problems with investigative reporting. However, as this Mobil ad demonstrates, when the oil giants believe the media have learned from past mistakes, they occasionally duly acknowledge it. (*Courtesy of Mobil Oil Corporation*)

with a general weakening of support for news organizations in the late 1980s, particularly network news. Early in 1988, only 44 percent of the public believed that "news organizations get the facts straight," an 11-point drop in 2½ years.[11] Despite the decline, twice as many people still trusted Rather more than Bush to tell the truth.

OBJECTIVITY IN THE MEDIA

Total objectivity in reporting is unattainable; it would require complete neutrality and near-total detachment in reporting a story. Most people start with biases and preconceived notions about almost any subject. Reporting, then, is subjective. Nevertheless, scholars of journalism believe that reporters and editors should strive for maximum objectivity (Figure 12–2).

By virtue of their role, the media view officials, particularly business and government spokespersons, with a degree of skepticism. Reporters shouldn't be expected to accept on faith the party line. By the same token, once a business or government official effectively substantiates the official view and demonstrates its merit, the media should be willing to report this accurately, without editorial distortion.

Stated another way, the relationship between the media and the establishment should be one of healthy adversaries rather than bitter enemies. Unfortunately, this is not always the case. According to one network anchorman, the fault lies with the First Amendment, which discourages critical analysis of the press by the press. Says NBC's Tom Brokaw, "In American journalism, we generally are inclined to call attention to almost everyone's failings but our own. When criticism is directed at us, we are very likely to develop a glass jaw."[12] Author Janet Malcolm takes an even dimmer view: "Every journalist who is not too stupid or too full of himself to notice what is going on knows that what he does is morally indefensible. He is a kind of confidence man, preying on people's vanity, ignorance, or loneliness, gaining their trust and betraying them without remorse."[13] Whew!

Fortunately, such journalists are in the minority. Most want to get the facts from all sides, and they acknowledge and respect the public relations practitioner's role in the process. If they are dealt with fairly, they will reciprocate in kind. However, some executives fail to understand the essential difference between the media and their own organizations. The reporter wants to get all the information possible and interpret it as he or she sees fit, while the people in the organizations being covered want things to be presented in the best light. Because of this difference, some executives consider journalists to be adversaries, and they fear and distrust the media.

Thoughtful journalists, of course, abhor the enemy tag. They implore officials in business and government to continue to talk to the media, to explain complex issues so that the public can better understand them. According to Lewis H. Young, former editor-in-chief of *Business Week* magazine, "The chief executive officer has to learn to be comfortable with the press. And the only way to be comfortable with the press is to get to meet media people, to talk to them, to go out for lunch with them, go out to dinner with them, and get used to the kinds of things that they're going to ask about, what they're interested in."[14] Based on the deep-seated distrust that some business and government people reserve for the media, Young's wish is no easy task.

Most attitude studies about the media have been inconclusive. One by the America Society of Newspaper Editors concluded that 75 percent of U.S. adults "have some

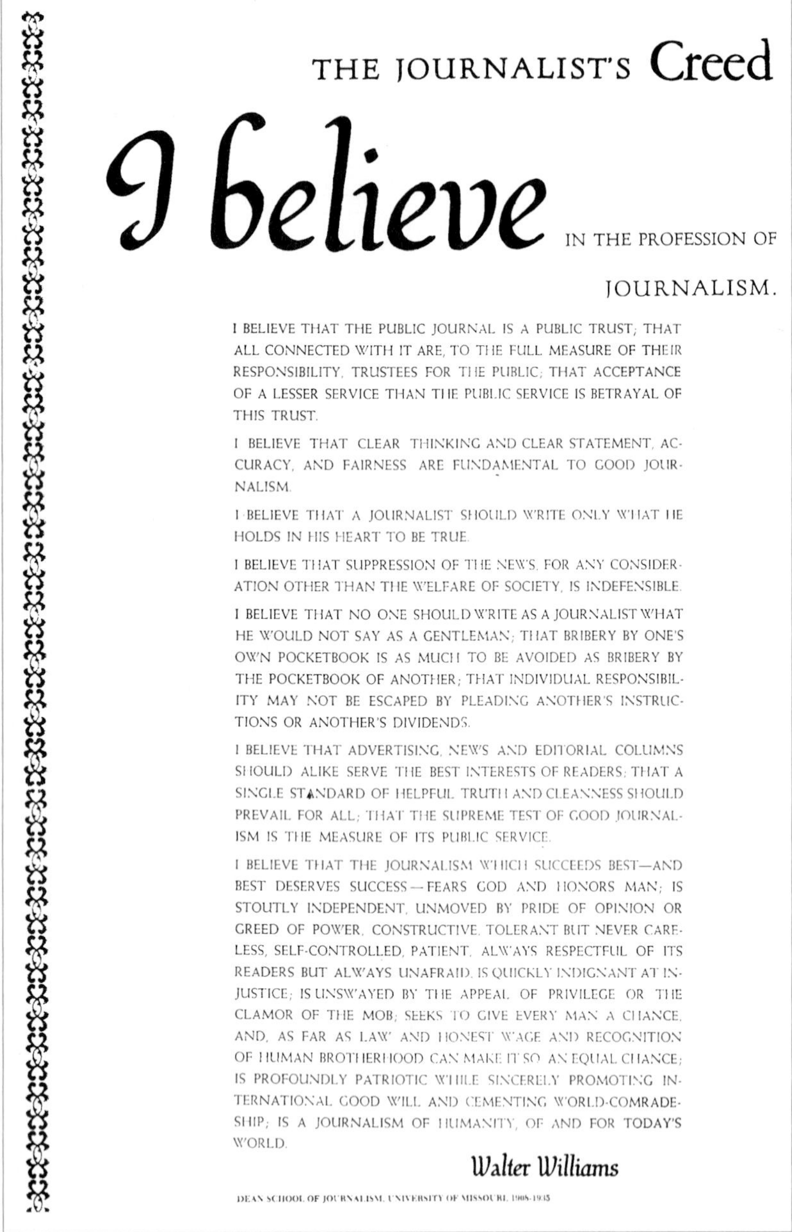

THE JOURNALIST'S Creed
I believe IN THE PROFESSION OF JOURNALISM.
I BELIEVE THAT THE PUBLIC JOURNAL IS A PUBLIC TRUST; THAT ALL CONNECTED WITH IT ARE, TO THE FULL MEASURE OF THEIR RESPONSIBILITY, TRUSTEES FOR THE PUBLIC; THAT ACCEPTANCE OF A LESSER SERVICE THAN THE PUBLIC SERVICE IS BETRAYAL OF THIS TRUST.
I BELIEVE THAT CLEAR THINKING AND CLEAR STATEMENT, ACCURACY, AND FAIRNESS ARE FUNDAMENTAL TO GOOD JOURNALISM.
I BELIEVE THAT A JOURNALIST SHOULD WRITE ONLY WHAT HE HOLDS IN HIS HEART TO BE TRUE.
I BELIEVE THAT SUPPRESSION OF THE NEWS, FOR ANY CONSIDERATION OTHER THAN THE WELFARE OF SOCIETY, IS INDEFENSIBLE.
I BELIEVE THAT NO ONE SHOULD WRITE AS A JOURNALIST WHAT HE WOULD NOT SAY AS A GENTLEMAN; THAT BRIBERY BY ONE'S OWN POCKETBOOK IS AS MUCH TO BE AVOIDED AS BRIBERY BY THE POCKETBOOK OF ANOTHER; THAT INDIVIDUAL RESPONSIBILITY MAY NOT BE ESCAPED BY PLEADING ANOTHER'S INSTRUCTIONS OR ANOTHER'S DIVIDENDS.
I BELIEVE THAT ADVERTISING, NEWS AND EDITORIAL COLUMNS SHOULD ALIKE SERVE THE BEST INTERESTS OF READERS; THAT A SINGLE STANDARD OF HELPFUL TRUTH AND CLEANNESS SHOULD PREVAIL FOR ALL; THAT THE SUPREME TEST OF GOOD JOURNALISM IS THE MEASURE OF ITS PUBLIC SERVICE.
I BELIEVE THAT THE JOURNALISM WHICH SUCCEEDS BEST—AND BEST DESERVES SUCCESS—FEARS GOD AND HONORS MAN; IS STOUTLY INDEPENDENT, UNMOVED BY PRIDE OF OPINION OR GREED OF POWER, CONSTRUCTIVE, TOLERANT BUT NEVER CARELESS, SELF-CONTROLLED, PATIENT, ALWAYS RESPECTFUL OF ITS READERS BUT ALWAYS UNAFRAID, IS QUICKLY INDIGNANT AT INJUSTICE; IS UNSWAYED BY THE APPEAL OF PRIVILEGE OR THE CLAMOR OF THE MOB; SEEKS TO GIVE EVERY MAN A CHANCE, AND, AS FAR AS LAW AND HONEST WAGE AND RECOGNITION OF HUMAN BROTHERHOOD CAN MAKE IT SO, AN EQUAL CHANCE; IS PROFOUNDLY PATRIOTIC WHILE SINCERELY PROMOTING INTERNATIONAL GOOD WILL AND CEMENTING WORLD-COMRADESHIP; IS A JOURNALISM OF HUMANITY, OF AND FOR TODAY'S WORLD.
Walter Williams
DEAN SCHOOL OF JOURNALISM, UNIVERSITY OF MISSOURI, 1908-1935

Figure 12–2 "The Journalist's Creed" was written after World War I by Dr. Walter Williams, dean of the School of Journalism at the University of Missouri. (*Courtesy of the University of Missouri School of Journalism*)

problem with media credibility." However, a later study commissioned for Times Mirror Company, the publisher of the *Los Angeles Times*, found that "there is no credibility crisis for the nation's news media." Among the findings from the 5,000 interviews were that 79 percent believe the media care about the quality of their work; 72 percent rated the media "highly professional"; and 55 percent said the media report accurately.[15]

In the 1990s, with the media and the public still on different philosophical wavelengths, the challenge for public relations professionals remains one of fostering a closer relationship between their organizations and those who present the news.

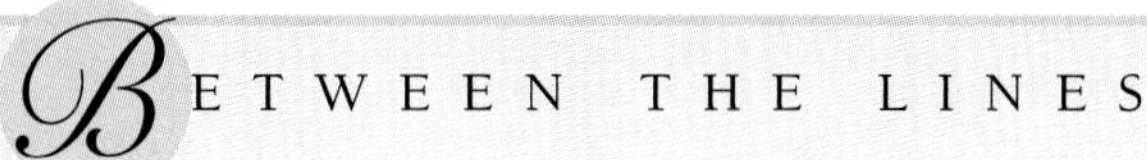

CONFESSIONS OF A MEDIA MAVEN

Dealing with the media for fun and profit, even for an experienced public relations hand, is a constant learning experience. Often, such learning is achieved the hard way.

By the spring of 1984, many of the nation's largest banks were a bit jittery about negative publicity about their loans to lesser developed countries. One of the most vociferous bank bashers was Patrick J. Buchanan, a syndicated columnist who later became President Reagan's communications director.

After one particularly venomous syndicated attack on the banks, a certain young and impetuous bank public affairs director wrote at the time directly to Buchanan's editor asking whether he couldn't "muzzle at least for a little while" his wild-eyed columnist. The letter's language, in retrospect, was perhaps a bit harsh.

Some weeks later, in a six-column article that ran throughout the nation, Mr. Buchanan wrote in part:

> Another sign that the banks are awaking to the reality of the nightmare is a screed that lately arrived at this writer's syndicate from one Fraser P. Seitel, vice-president of Chase Manhattan.
>
> Terming this writer's comments "wrong," "stupid," "inflammatory," and "the nonsensical ravings of a lunatic," Seitel nevertheless suggested that the syndicate "tone down" future writings, "at least 'til the frenetic financial markets get over the current hysteria."*

The columnist went on to describe the fallacy in bankers' arguments and ended by suggesting that banks begin immediately to cut unnecessary frills—such as directors of public affairs!

Moral: Never get into a shouting match with somebody who buys ink by the barrel.

Secondary moral: Just because you write a textbook doesn't mean you know everything!

*Patrick J. Buchanan, "The Banks Must Face Up to Losses on Third World Loans," *New York Post* (July 12, 1984): 35.

HANDLING THE MEDIA

It falls on public relations professionals to orchestrate the relationship between their organizations and the media. To be sure, the media can't ordinarily be manipulated in our society. They can, however, be confronted in an honest and interactive way to convey the organization's point of view in a manner that may merit being reported. First, an organization must establish a formal media relations policy (Figure 12–3). Second, an organization must establish a philosophy for dealing with the media, keeping in mind the following 10 principles:

1. **Flexibility is key.** Having a plan to deal with the media is fine. But an organization must remain flexible, dealing with media inquiries on a case-by-case basis and not being locked into an overly restrictive policy.
2. **Provide the media with only one voice.** The media prefer many spokespersons, but an organization should stick to one. He or she should be available to one and all in the press, and everyone in the organization should understand that it is this person's job alone to convey information to the outside world.
3. **Don't volunteer the chief as spokesperson.** The media insist on speaking to the top person. Sometimes this makes sense. Normally, though, exposing the chief executive to the media is the worst thing one can do. It is much better to offer a trained spokesperson, who is knowledgeable and experienced in dealing with the idiosyncracies of reporters and the media.
4. **Don't always take the lawyer's advice.** A lawyer's job is to protect the organization from challenge in a court of law. However, a lawyer's advice often may not be responsive to the likely perception of the institution in another critical court—the "court of public opinion." The smart manager always weighs legal advice against public relations advice.
5. **Don't wait until you've got all the facts.** If you wait for all the data, you may still be sitting after the public has branded you "guilty as charged." Often, it makes sense to launch a preemptive rebuttal to media charges. This shows the public that you're not going to accept unfounded accusations.
6. **Don't answer every question.** The fact that the media ask doesn't mean you have to answer. You have no obligation to answer every question. And you should answer only those questions you are prepared to handle.
7. **Squawk if you're wronged.** If the media print inaccuracies, blast them. Call the reporter and demand a correction. Correct the public record. If you don't, the inaccuracy will go uncorrected for so long that eventually it will become a "media fact."
8. **Don't keep journalists at arm's length.** As noted, a journalist's job is to get a story, whatever that entails. The public relations professional's role is to be an advocate for the institution. As long as both understand and respect each other's position, cooperating with a journalist can often be in an organization's best interest.
9. **Share information with allies.** Limiting information to those who need to know can be counterproductive. Employees, customers, and even stockholders can serve as valuable allies in dealing with the public and the media. They should be kept aware of the organization's position on issues of media interest.

Organization and Policy Guide

Unit with Primary Responsibility for Review Corporate Communications

It is frequently in Chase's best interest to take advantage of interest from the media to further the reputation and services of the bank. In dealing with the media, Chase officers must be careful to protect the best interests of the bank, particularly with regard to the area of customer confidence.

The following policies will serve as a guideline for media relationships. Specific questions regarding the media should be addressed to the Public Relations Division.

Inquiries from the Media

Most journalists call the Public Relations Division when they need information about the bank or wish to arrange an interview with a bank officer. Many times, public relations officers are able to handle inquiries directly. Occasionally, however, more complex questions require input from appropriate bank officers. In these cases, inasmuch as journalists are often under deadline pressures, it is important that bank officers cooperate as fully and respond as promptly as possible. Such cooperation enhances Chase's reputation for integrity with the news media.

Less frequently, reporter inquiries will go directly to line officers. In this case, either one of two responses may be appropriate:

1. If a journalist seeks simple, factual information such as Chase's current rate on a particular savings instrument or the factual details of a new bank service, officers may provide it directly.
2. If a reporter seeks Chase policy or official opinion on such subjects as trends in interest rates, legislation, etc., responses should be reviewed with the Public Relations Division. If an officer is unfamiliar with a particular policy or requires clarification of it, he or she should always check first with the Public Relations Division before committing the bank in print.

In talking with a reporter, it is normally assumed that whatever a bank officer says may be quoted and attributed directly to him or her by name as a spokesperson for the bank. An officer not wishing to be quoted must specify that desire to the journalist.

Most reporters with whom the bank deals will respect an officer's wishes to maintain anonymity. Most journalists recognize that it is as important for them to honor the wishes of their sources at the bank as it is for the bank to disseminate its comments and information to the public through the news media. Chase's policy toward the media should be one of mutual trust, understanding and benefit.

Interviews With the Media

In order to monitor the bank's relationships with journalists, all requests for interviews with bank officers by journalists must be routed through the Public Relations Division.

As a rule, public relations officers check the credentials of the journalist and determine the specific areas of inquiry to be examined. The public relations officer will then decide whether the interview is appropriate for the bank. When the decision is affirmative, the public relations officer will discuss subject matter with the recommended interviewee and together they will decide on a course of action and Chase objectives for the interview.

A member of the public relations staff is normally present during any face-to-face interview with an officer of the bank. The purpose of the public relations staffer's attendance is to provide assistance in handling the interview situation as well as to aid the reporter with follow-up material.

When a reporter calls an officer directly to request an interview, the officer should check with the Public Relations Division before making a commitment.

Authorized Spokespersons

Vice presidents and above are normally authorized to speak for the bank on matters in their own area of responsibility.

Normally, officers below the level of vice president are not authorized to speak for attribution on behalf of the bank except where they are specialists in a particular field, such as technical directors, economists, etc.

Exceptions may be made in special situations and in concert with the Public Relations Division.

Written Material for the Media

Chase articles bylined by officers may either be written by the officer approached or by a member of the public relations staff. If an officer decided to author his or her own article, the public relations division must be consulted for editing, photographic support and policy proofing.

Occasionally, customers or suppliers may wish to include Chase in an article or advertisement they are preparing. This material too must be routed through the Public Relations Division for review.

Figure 12–3 This press relations policy of Chase Manhattan Bank is typical of that found in many large organizations. Relationships with the media are generally encouraged, with the public relations division taking overall responsibility for all of the bank's relationships with journalists. (*Courtesy of Chase Manhattan Bank*)

10. **You can lose the media battle but still win the longer-term credibility war.** Sometimes, especially if you're wrong, the most sensible thing to do is admit it. Had Richard Nixon done this over Watergate, he might have served his full second term. There is nothing as refreshing as hearing an official admit, "We made a mistake. We'll make restitution. It won't happen again." That's how an organization retains its credibility.[16]

SECURING PUBLICITY

Publicity, through news releases and other methods, is designed to broaden knowledge and positive recognition of an organization, its personnel, and its activities. Publicity is most often gained by dealing directly with the media, either by initiating the communication or by reacting to inquiries. Publicity differs dramatically from advertising, despite the fact that most people confuse the two.

Advertising possesses the following characteristics:

1. You pay for it.
2. You control what is said.
3. You control how it is said.
4. You control to whom it is said.
5. To a degree, you control where it is put in a publication or on the air.
6. You control the frequency of its use.

Publicity, on the other hand, offers no such controls. Typically, publicity is subject to review by news editors, who may decide to use all of a story, some of it, or none of it. When it will run, who will see it, how often it will be used are all subject, to a large degree, to the whims of a news editor. However, even though publicity is by no means a sure thing, it does offer two overriding benefits that enhance its appeal, even beyond that of advertising:

- First, although not free, publicity costs only the time and effort expended by public relations personnel and management in attempting to place it in the media. Therefore, relatively speaking, its cost is minimal, especially when compared with the costs of advertising and assessed against potential returns.
- Second and more important, publicity, which appears in news rather than in advertising columns, carries the implicit endorsement of the publication in which it appears. In other words, publicity is perceived as objective news rather than self-serving promotion, which translates into the most sought-after commodity for an organization: credibility.

This is the true value of publicity over advertising.

VALUE OF PUBLICITY

Publicity has many values for an organization. In light of the implicit third-party endorsement that publicity carries, it is often regarded as news and therefore as more credible than advertising. For any organization, then, publicity makes great sense in the following areas:

- **Announcing a new product or service.** Because publicity can be regarded as news, it should be used *before* advertising commences. A new product or service is news only once. Once advertising appears, the product is no longer news. Therefore, one inflexible rule—that most organizations, alas, break—is that publicity should *precede* advertising.
- **Reenergizing an old product.** When a product has been around for a while, it's difficult to make people pay attention to advertising. Therefore, publicity techniques—staged events, sponsorships, and so on—may pay off to rejuvenate a mature product. The Sharps Beer Truck (Figure 12–4) is a good example.
- **Explaining a complicated product.** Often there isn't enough room in an advertisement to explain a complex product or service. Insurance companies, banks, mutual funds, and so on, all of which offer products that demand thoughtful explanation, may find advertising space too limiting. Publicity, on the other hand, allows enough room to tell the story.
- **Little or no budget.** Often, organizations don't have the budget to accommodate advertising. To make an impact, advertising requires frequency—the constant repetition of ads so that readers eventually see them and acknowledge the product. In the case of Samuel Adams Lager Beer, for example, the company lacked an advertising budget to promote its unique brew. So it used public relations techniques to spread the word about this different-tasting beer. Over time, primarily through publicity about its victories at beer-tasting competitions, Samuel Adams grew in popularity. Today, its advertising budget is robust. But the company's faith in publicity endures.

Figure 12–4 The Sharps Beer Truck, which traveled from town to town, attracting curious onlookers and plenty of publicity photos, proved an excellent way to reinvigorate a mature product. (*Courtesy of Miller Brewing Co.*)

- **Enhancing the organization's reputation.** Advertising is, at base, self-serving. When a company gives to charity or does a good deed in the community, taking out an ad is the *wrong way* to communicate its efforts. It is much better for the recipient organization to commend its benefactor in the daily news columns.
- **Crisis response.** In a crisis, publicity techniques are the fastest and most credible means of response. In 1993, when Pepsi-Cola suffered its tampering scare, the company launched an immediate publicity response. Only when the crisis was resolved and Pepsi had won did the company authorize ads thanking its employees and customers for their loyalty amid the turmoil.

These are just a few of the advantages of publicity over advertising. A smart organization therefore will always consider publicity as a vital component in its overall marketing plan.

AVENUES OF PUBLICITY

Many vehicles can be used for publicity purposes, from skywriting to *Pennysavers* to the bull horn at a political rally.

The vehicle that remains the most frequent target of public relations professionals is the newspaper. Even though the electronic media have become increasingly important, the news of the day is still dictated by daily newspapers. In fact, the first thing a TV news director does when he or she reaches the office in the morning is to check the daily paper to set the TV news agenda.

Newspapers provide more diversity and depth of coverage than television or radio. It may be for this reason that approximately 63 million copies of daily newspapers are sold each day. Newspapers range from giant dailies with circulations approaching 2 million to small weekly papers written, edited, and produced by a single individual. There are approximately 1,650 daily newspapers in the United States, most of which appear in the afternoon (Table 12–1).

In recent years, as operating costs have skyrocketed and many Americans have left central cities for the suburbs, some urban papers have folded. In such cities, traditional competition between morning and evening newspapers has diminished. Occasionally, the same publishing firm owns both papers. The huge Rochester-based Gannett chain, for example, owns 97 daily newspapers reaching 6 million readers, as well as 8 TV stations and 15 radio stations.

In 1982, Gannett launched its most ambitious project to date with the publication of *USA Today,* a truly national newspaper, transmitted from Rosslyn, Virginia, to major American cities via satellite. The paper costs Gannett upward of $50 million per year. The full-color newspaper lists daily news from all 50 states; offers national weather, sports, and business; and downplays international news. *USA Today* has become "America's hometown newspaper." Some critics still charge that *USA Today*'s abbreviated articles are fast-food journalism and derisively label the publication "McPaper." Nevertheless, its circulation has reached 1.83 million, second only to that of the *The Wall Street Journal*.

Despite the loss of journalistic competition in many cities, the newspaper is still a primary target for media relations activities. To practitioners and their managements, penetrating the daily with positive publicity is a critical challenge. To many corporate

TABLE 12–1

TOP 20 NEWSPAPERS BY CIRCULATION

Rank	Newspaper	Daily	Sunday
1	*Wall Street Journal*	1,852,967	none
2	*USA Today*	1,832,345	2,003,620
3	*New York Times*	1,230,461	1,812,458
4	*Los Angeles Times*	1,138,353	1,521,197
5	*Washington Post*	855,171	1,170,150
6	*New York Daily News*	769,801	997,599
7	*Newsday*	762,043	851,685
8	*Chicago Tribune*	691,941	1,117,816
9	*Detroit Free Press*	574,817	*
10	*San Francisco Chronicle*	564,374	715,299
11	*Chicago Sun-Times*	553,355	549,038
12	*Dallas Morning News*	527,816	834,035
13	*Boston Globe*	504,869	811,409
14	*Philadelphia Enquirer*	502,740	965,350
15	*Newark Star-Ledger*	483,012	728,579
16	*New York Post*	427,319	None
17	*Houston Chronicle*	423,256	608,429
18	*Miami Herald*	414,216	542,450
19	*Minneapolis-St. Paul Star Tribune*	413,603	695,710
20	*Cleveland Plain Dealer*	408,829	548,789

Source: Audit Bureau of Circulations, March 31, 1993.
*Sunday Circulation of the *Detroit News and Free Press* is 1,179,197.

managements, favorable publicity in *The New York Times* is a special achievement. To politicians, a complimentary story in the *Washington Post* is equally cherished. In other communities, a positive piece in the local daily is just as rewarding.

Not to be overlooked in media relations are the suburban newspapers, the small-city dailies, and the nearly 7,500 weekly newspapers. All are targets for news releases and story ideas. When an organization has a branch or plant in an area, these local media contacts can be of critical importance, particularly for consumer product publicity.

PLACING PUBLICITY

How does a public relations practitioner "place" a story in a newspaper? How does he or she convert publicity to news? After getting the release written, the following hints may help achieve placement:

1. **Know deadlines.** Time governs every newspaper. *The New York Times* has different deadlines for different sections of the paper, with its business section essentially closing down between 6:00 and 7:00 P.M. News events should be scheduled, whenever possible, to accommodate deadlines. An old and despised practice (at least by journalists) is to announce bad news close to deadline time on Friday afternoon, the premise being that newspaper journalists won't have time to follow up on the story and that few people will read Saturday's paper anyway. Although this technique may work on occasion, it leaves reporters and editors hostile.
2. **Generally write, don't call.** Reporters are barraged with deadlines. They are busiest close to deadline time, late afternoon for morning newspapers and morning for afternoon papers. Thus, it's preferable to mail or send news releases by messenger rather than try to explain them over the telephone. Also, follow-up calls to reporters to "make sure you got our release" should be avoided. If reporters are unclear on a certain point, they'll call to check.
3. **Direct the release to a specific person or editor.** Newspapers are divided into departments: business, sports, style, entertainment, and the like. The release directed to a specific person or editor has a greater chance of being read than one addressed simply to "editor." At smaller papers, one person may handle all financial news. At larger papers, the financial news section may have different editors for banking, chemicals, oil, electronics, and many other specialties. Public relations people should know who covers their beat and target releases accordingly.

   Public relations professionals should also know the differences in the functions of newspaper personnel. For example, the publisher is the person responsible for overall newspaper policy. The editorial editor is generally responsible for editorial page content, including the opinion-editorial (op-ed) section. The managing editor is responsible for overall news content. These three should rarely, if ever, be called to secure publicity. That leaves the various section editors and reporters as key contacts for public relations practitioners.
4. **Make personal contact.** Knowing a reporter may not result in an immediate story, but it can pay residual dividends. Those who know the local weekly editor or the daily city editor have an advantage over colleagues who don't. Also, when a reporter uses your story idea, follow up with a note of commendation—particularly on the story's accuracy.
5. **Don't badger.** Newspapers are generally fiercely independent about the copy they use. Even a major advertiser will usually fail to get a piece of puffery published. Badgering an editor about a certain story is bad form, as is complaining excessively about the treatment given a certain story. Worst of all, little is achieved by acting outraged when a newspaper chooses not to run a story. Editors are human beings, too. For every release they use, dozens get discarded. If a public relations person protests too much, editors will remember.
6. **Use exclusives sparingly.** Sometimes public relations people promise exclusive stories to particular newspapers. The exclusive promises one newspaper a scoop over its competitors. For example, practitioners frequently arrange to have a visiting executive interviewed by only one local newspaper. Although the chances of securing a story are heightened by the promise of an exclusive, there is a risk of alienating the other papers. Thus, the exclusive should be used sparingly.

Figure 12–5 The media are always looking for a visual angle. And that's just what Guinness World of Records and its public relations counselor, Dorf & Stanton, came up with in the spring of 1988 to publicize the opening of the renovated Guinness World of Records in New York City. Specifically, they had Bruce Block, holder of the record for cigar box balancing, demonstrate his talent. And the cameras rolled, reaching 15,470,000 viewers through television coverage. (*Courtesy of Guinness World of Records/Dorf & Stanton Communications*)

7. **When you call, do your own calling.** Reporters and editors generally don't have assistants. Most do not like to be kept waiting by a secretary calling for the boss. Public relations professionals should make their own initial and follow-up calls. Letting a secretary handle a journalist can alienate a good news contact. And above all, be pleasant and courteous.

Although cynics continue to predict "the end of reading as we know it," newspapers and magazines continue to endure. While some predicted a decline in the magazine business in the 1990s, in 1993 alone 679 magazines were started.[17] Today approximately 11,002 are published in the United States. They range from the mainstream *Time* and *Newsweek*, to the gossipy *People* and *Us*, to publications further afield, such as *Out*, catering to the upscale gay and lesbian market, and *Chile Pepper*, the bimonthly that covers peppers of all types.

The fact remains that dealing with the print media is among the most essential technical skills of the public relations professional. Ergo, anyone who practices public relations must know how to deal with the print press (Fig. 12–5).

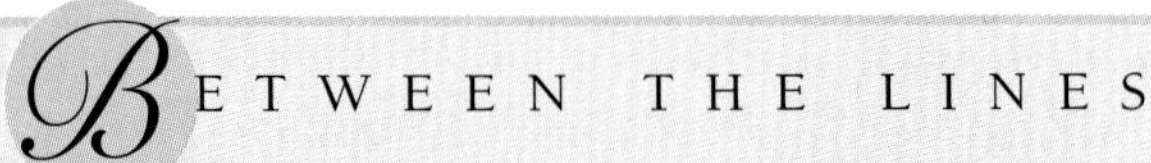

BETWEEN THE LINES

HANDLING THE MEDIA

How well would you do if asked to go toe to toe with a reporter? Take this yes-or-no quiz, borrowed from *Public Relations Reporter*, and find out. Answers are given on the next page.

1. When addressing a print reporter or electronic medium moderator, should you use his or her first name?
2. Should you ever challenge a reporter in a verbal duel?
3. Are reporters correct in thinking they can ask embarrassing questions of anyone in public office?
4. Should you answer a hypothetical question?
5. Should you ever say, "No comment"?
6. When a reporter calls on the telephone, should you assume that the conversation is being taped?
7. Do audiences remember most of the content of a TV interview 30 minutes after it is broadcast?
8. Should you ever admit you had professional training to handle the media?
9. If you don't know the correct answer to a reporter's question, should you try to answer it anyway?

Bonus Question:
What did Henry Kissinger say at the start of his press briefings as secretary of state?

Answers

1. Yes. In most cases, using first names is the best strategy. It makes the discussion much more conversational and less formal than using "Mr." or "Ms."
2. No. Most people should try to gain goodwill in an interview. This is rarely achieved by getting into an acrimonious debate.
3. Yes. Journalists must be suspicious of any claim by a public person that he or she is telling not only the truth, but the whole truth. Anyone in public office must be prepared to respond to such questions.
4. No. Avoid hypothetical questions. Rarely can you win by dealing with them.
5. No. It is tantamount to taking the Fifth Amendment against self-incrimination. You appear to be hiding something.
6. Yes. Many state laws no longer require the "beep" that signals a taped call. Always assume that everything you say is being recorded and will be used.
7. No. Studies have found that audiences remember only 60 percent of the content after 30 minutes. They remember 40 percent at the end of the day and 10 percent by the end of the week.
8. Yes. By all means. You should point out that good communication with the public is a hallmark of your organization and that you're proud it has such a high priority.
9. No. Don't be afraid to say, "I don't know." Offer to find the answer and get back to the interviewer. Don't dig yourself into a hole you can't get out of.

Bonus Answer:
"Does anyone have any questions . . . for my answers?"

WIRE SERVICES

Traditionally, two news-gathering organizations formed the backbone of the nation's news delivery system, supplying up-to-the-minute dispatches from around the world to both the print and electronic media. The Associated Press (AP) and United Press International (UPI) wire services traditionally have competed to deliver the most accurate news first. The AP serves more than 15,000 worldwide clients—newspapers, magazines, TV, and radio stations—through 220 bureaus around the country and the world. UPI, which has experienced financial problems, has far fewer subscribers. Both wire services report in a simple, readable, understandable style.

Staging an equally intense rivalry on the financial side are two business wires—Dow Jones and Reuters. These wires specialize in business-oriented news. Reuters, based in London, is a worldwide business service plus a general news service. Dow Jones, whose flagship publication is *The Wall Street Journal,* also has an international affiliate in AP-Dow Jones.

When a company releases news that may influence the decision of an investor to hold, sell, or buy the company's stock, it is required to release the information promptly to the broadcast group of investors. In this instance, Dow Jones, Reuters, and the local press are notified simultaneously. Dow Jones and Reuters news wires, like those of AP and UPI, are found in newspaper offices, brokerage firms, banks, investment houses, and many corporate offices throughout the country.

The most recent organization to compete with Dow Jones and Reuters is Bloomberg Financial News. Bloomberg, begun by former Wall Street broker Michael Bloomberg, has in just a few years become a formidable competitor. Bloomberg's on-line data are transmitted to media and corporate offices throughout America, and the Bloomberg Financial News Wire is used extensively by many leading daily newspapers (with the singular exception of *The Wall Street Journal!*).

Additionally, commercial wire services, such as PR News Wire and Business Wire, distribute public relations material to news outlets nationwide. Unlike AP and UPI, these commercial wires charge organizations a fee for running news release stories verbatim. Such commercial wires serve as an effective backup, ensuring that announcements at least reach news outlets.

Feature syndicates, such as North American Newspaper Alliance and King Features, are another source of editorial material for newspapers and magazines. They provide subscribing newspapers with a broad spectrum of material, ranging from business commentaries to comic strips to gossip columns. Some of their writers—such as Art Buchwald, Don Barry, and Jane Bryant Quinn—have built national reputations. Many such columnists depend heavily on source material provided by public relations personnel.

MEDIA DIRECTORIES

Another publicity support is the media directory, which describes in detail the various media.

1. *Gale's Directory of Publications* lists about 20,000 publications, including daily and weekly newspapers, as well as general circulation, trade, and special interest magazines. *Gale's* also includes the names, addresses, and phone numbers of publication editors.
2. *Bacon's Publicity Checker* provides data on almost 5,000 U.S. and Canadian trade and business publications organized in some 100 categories—from accounting and advertising to woolens and yachting. *Bacon's* includes editors' names, addresses, and phone numbers.
3. *Broadcasting Yearbook* contains information on radio and TV stations in the United States, Canada, and Latin America. It also lists key personnel, along with their addresses and telephones.
4. *Editor & Publisher Yearbook* lists newspapers across the United States (daily, weekly, national, black, college and university, foreign language) and their personnel.
5. *Working Press of the Nation* is a five-volume publication. It lists locations and editorial staff for the following media: newspapers, magazines, radio, television, feature writers, syndicates, and house magazines.
6. Specialized directories—from *Hudson's Washington News Media Directory* and *Congressional Staff Guide* to the *Anglo-Jewish Media List*—and various state media directories, published by state press or broadcasters' associations, are also excellent resources for publicity purposes. Appendix C offers a comprehensive list of leading media directories compiled from *O'Dwyer's PR Services Report*.

MEASUREMENT ASSISTANCE

After an organization has distributed its press materials, it needs an effective way to measure the results of its publicity. A variety of outside services can help.

PRESS CLIPPING BUREAUS

Some agencies monitor company mentions in the press. These press clipping bureaus can supply newspaper and magazine clippings on any subject and about any company. The two largest, Burrelle's and Luce, each receive hundreds of newspapers and magazines daily. Both services dispatch nearly 50,000 clippings to their clients each day. Burrelle's, for example, employs about 800 people and subscribes to about 1,700 daily newspapers, 8,300 weeklies, 6,300 consumer and trade magazines, and various other publications.

These bureaus may also be hired in certain regions to monitor local news or for certain projects that require special scrutiny. Most charge $200 monthly fees plus $1.00 per clipping. For a practitioner who must keep management informed of press reports on the firm, the expense is generally worthwhile.

BROADCAST TRANSCRIPTION SERVICES

Specialized transcription services have arisen to monitor broadcast stories. A handful of such broadcast transcription services exist in the country, the largest being Radio-TV Reports, with offices in several cities. This firm monitors all major radio and TV stations around the clock, checking for messages concerning client companies. After a client orders a particular segment of a broadcast program, Radio-TV Reports either prepares a typed transcript or secures an audiotape. Costs for transcripts are relatively high.

CONTENT ANALYSIS SERVICES

A more sophisticated analysis of results in the media is supplied by firms that evaluate the content of media mentions concerning clients. Firms such as Ketchum Public Relations and PR Data use computer analysis to find positive and negative mentions about organizations. Although this measurement technique is rough and somewhat subjective, it enables an organization to get a clearer idea of how it is being portrayed in the media. However, such press-clipping computer analysis stops short of being a true test of audience attitudes.

HANDLING INTERVIEWS

Public relations people coordinate interviews for both print and broadcast media. Most executives are neither familiar with nor comfortable in such interview situations. For one thing, reporters ask a lot of searching questions, some of which may seem impertinent. Executives aren't used to being put on the spot. Instinctively, they may resent it. So the counseling of executives for interviews has become an important and strategic task of the in-house practitioner, as well as a lucrative profession for media consultants.

The following 10 dos and don'ts are important in newspaper, magazine, or other print interviews:

1. **Do your homework in advance.** An interviewee must be thoroughly briefed—either verbally or in writing—before the interview. Know what the interviewer writes, for whom, and what his or her opinions are. Also, determine what the audience wants to know.
2. **Relax.** Remember that the interviewer is a person, too, and is just trying to do a good job. Building rapport will help the interview.
3. **Speak in personal terms.** People distrust large organizations. References to "the company" and "we believe" sound ominous. Use "I" instead. Speak as an individual, as a member of the public, rather than as a mouthpiece for an impersonal bureaucracy.
4. **Welcome the naive question.** If the question sounds simple, it should be answered anyway. It may be helpful to those who don't possess much knowledge of the organization or industry.
5. **Answer questions briefly and directly.** Avoid rambling. Be brief, concise, and to the point. An interviewee shouldn't get into subject areas about which he or she knows nothing. This situation can be dangerous and counterproductive when words are transcribed in print.
6. **Don't bluff.** If a reporter asks a question that you can't answer, admit it. If there are others in the organization more knowledgeable about a particular issue, the interviewee or the practitioner should point that out and get the answer.
7. **State facts and back up generalities.** Facts and examples always bolster an interview. An interviewee should come armed with specific data that support general statements. Again, the practitioner should furnish all the specifics.
8. **If the reporter is promised further information, provide it quickly.** Remember, reporters work under time pressures and need information quickly to meet deadlines. Anything promised in an interview should be granted soon. Conveniently forgetting to answer a request may return to haunt the organization when the interview is printed.
9. **There is no such thing as being off the record.** A person who doesn't want to see something in print shouldn't say it. It's that simple. Reporters may get confused as to what was off the record during the interview. And although most journalists will honor an off-the-record statement, some may not. Usually, it's not worthwhile to take the risk. Occasionally, reporters will agree not to attribute a statement to the interviewee but to use it as background. Mostly, though, interviewees should be willing to have whatever they say in the interview appear in print.
10. **Tell the truth.** Telling the truth is the cardinal rule. Journalists are generally perceptive; they can detect a fraud. So don't be evasive, don't cover up, and, most of all, don't lie. Be positive, but be truthful. Occasionally, an interviewee must decline to answer specific questions but should candidly explain why. This approach always wins in the long run.

Invading the Privacy of Arthur Ashe

Tennis star Arthur Ashe was one of the most respected athletes—and people—in the world. A proud yet soft-spoken African-American, Ashe was among the first of his race to penetrate the formerly all-white sport of tennis. His early experience with racial prejudice did nothing to deter Ashe from becoming a world hero and revered personality.

People were stunned in 1979 when Ashe, seemingly in prime physical condition, suffered a near-fatal heart attack. This attack, most surmised, caused Ashe to retire from tennis several years later. He adopted a less public lifestyle to spend more time with his wife and young daughter. In April 1992, Arthur Ashe, against his wishes, was thrust back into the spotlight in a most abrupt way.

USA Today's tennis writer Doug Smith—a long-time friend of Ashe—told the former tennis star that he planned to reveal that Ashe had contracted AIDS.

Ashe begged Smith not to write the story. He argued that he was no longer a public figure with public responsibilities. He said that an announcement of his condition would unnecessarily infringe on his family's right to privacy. Smith and his newspaper saw things differently.

Finally, when *USA Today* failed to relent, Arthur Ashe went public with his own news conference to announce the tragic news he had kept secret since September 1988.

Ashe summed up his tearful news conference with the following statement:

> The quality of one's life changes irrevocably when something like this becomes public. Reason and rational thought are too often waived out of fear, out of caution, or out of just plain ignorance. My family and I must now learn a new set of behavioral standards to function in the everyday world. And sadly, there really was no good reason for this to have happened now.

USA Today disagreed. Do you?

PRESS CONFERENCES

Press conferences, the convening of the media for a specific purpose, are generally not a good idea (Figure 12–6). Unless an organization has real news to communicate, press conferences can flop. Reporters don't have the time for meetings offering little news. Therefore, before attempting a conference, ask this question: Can this information be disseminated just as easily in a news release? If the answer is yes, the conference should be scratched.

Eventually, though, every organization must face the media in a conference—in connection with an annual meeting or a major announcement or a presentation to securities analysts. The same rules and guidelines hold true for dealing with the press in conference as in a one-on-one interview. Be honest, forthright, and fair. Follow these additional guidelines in a press conference:

1. **Don't play favorites; invite representatives from all major news outlets.** Normally, it makes sense to alert wire services, which in turn may have the resources to advise their print and broadcast subscribers. For example, the AP carries daily listings, called the *day book,* of news events in major cities.
2. **Notify the media by mail well in advance of the conference and follow up by phone.** Ordinarily, the memo announcing the event should be straightforward and to the point, listing the subject, date, time, and place, as well as the speaker and the public relations contact's name, title, and phone number. If possible, the memo should reach the editor's desk at least 7 to 10 days before the event. Also, the day before the event, a follow-up phone call reminder is wise.
3. **Schedule the conference early in the day.** Again, the earlier in the business day, the better, particularly for TV consumption.

"Just tell the press the Ambassador feels it would be inappropriate to comment until he's had time to study the complete text."

Figure 12–6 For some, "meeting the press" isn't a particularly pleasant prospect. *(Drawing by Lorenz; © 1979, Courtesy of The New Yorker Magazine, Inc.)*

4. **Hold the conference in a meeting room, not someone's office.** Office auditoriums and hotel meeting rooms are good places for news conferences. Chairs should be provided for all reporters, and space should be allowed for TV crews to set up cameras. The speaker at the conference should preside from either a table or a lectern so that microphones and tape recorders can be placed nearby.
5. **The time allotted for the conference should be stated in advance.** Reporters should be told at the beginning of the conference how much time they will have. Then no one can complain later.
6. **Keep the speaker away from the reporters before the conference.** Mingling prior to the conference will only give someone an edge. Keep all reporters on equal footing in their contact with the speaker.
7. **Prepare materials to complement the speaker's presentation.** The news conference is an apt place for a press kit, which should include all the pertinent information about the speaker, the subject, and the organization.
8. **Let the reporters know when the end has come.** Just before the stated time has elapsed, the practitioner should announce to the reporters that the next question will be the last one. After the final question, the speaker should thank the reporters for coming and should take no more questions. After the conference, some reporters (particularly broadcast journalists) may want to ask follow-up questions on an individual basis. Do so only if all reporters have an opportunity to share in the one-on-one format.

SUMMARY

As is true of any other specialty in public relations work, the key to securing publicity is professionalism. Because management relies on the practitioners for expertise in handling the media effectively, practitioners must not only know their own organization and management, but must also be conversant in and respectful of the role and practice of journalists.

Publicists, who charge clients for getting their names in print or on the air, are the latest innovation in the relationship between journalists and public relations people. One Mill Valley, California, practitioner received extensive publicity when he announced his publicity price list—$24,075 for a placement on *20/20,* $21,560 for a placement on *NBC Nightly News,* $21,400 for a placement in *The Wall Street Journal,* and $21,135 for a placement in *People* magazine. Such schemes, however, are in the minority.

The role of public relations professionals in the news-gathering process has become more respected by journalists. As Fred Andrews, the former business/finance editor of *The New York Times,* once said, "PR has gotten more professional. PR people can be a critical element for us. It makes a difference how efficiently they handle things, how complete the information is that they have at hand. We value that and understand all the work that goes into it."[18] Indeed, the best public relations–journalist relationship today—the only successful one over the long term—must be based on mutual understanding, trust, and respect.

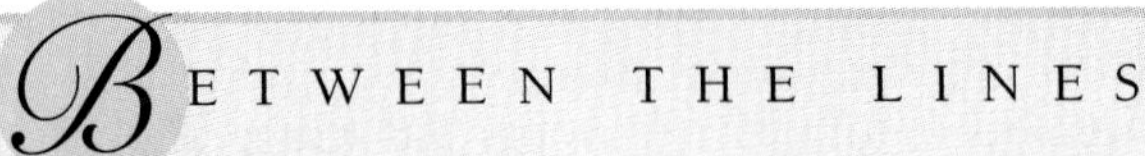

BETWEEN THE LINES

AW SHADDUP!

Nothing was sweeter in the 1990s than hearing about experienced journalists, who ought to know better, putting their proverbial feet in their proverbial mouths.

- In the winter of 1990, network interviewer and Miss America judge Larry King answered another interviewer's question by denouncing Miss Pennsylvania as the "ugliest contestant in the pageant." A devastated Miss Pennsylvania demanded an apology, which was quickly volunteered.

  Poor Larry was at it again some weeks later when he asked, on a national broadcast, if a certain pro football holdout had "a drug problem." The player didn't. But that didn't prevent him and his agent from blasting King for raising the question before 15 million viewers.
- Another cable commentator joined King in the "foot-in-mouth" derby for making what sounded suspiciously like anti-Semitic remarks about Israel's views on a possible war in the Middle East. The commentator, who was denounced by friend and foe alike, had earlier defended a Nazi gas chamber operator being prosecuted for war crimes. The bombastic broadcaster's name? Patrick J. Buchanan, the self-same journalist who once picked on a poor, defenseless public affairs director.

Moral: What goes around, comes around.

DISCUSSION STARTERS

1. What is the difference between advertising and publicity?
2. What is the current state of the newspaper industry?
3. Why should public relations professionals be familiar with newspaper deadlines?
4. Is magazine publishing likely to experience a renaissance in the 1990s?
5. What is the difference between public relations and publicity?
6. What are the general interest, financial, and commercial wire services?
7. How can public relations professionals keep track of the publicity they receive for their organizations?
8. What are the several dos and don'ts of interviews?
9. Are press conferences advisable in most cases?
10. What are five recommended ways to work with the media?

NOTES

1. James E. Grunig, "Theory and Practice of Interactive Media Relations," *Public Relations Quarterly* (Fall 1990): 18.
2. "Overheard," *Newsweek,* February 27, 1989, 13.

3. Linda Stevens, "'Today' Guest Sues—Says Tube Treated Her Like Boob," *New York Post* (March 16, 1990): 6.
4. Jack O'Dwyer, "Corp. PR People Minimize Face-to-Face Press Contact," *O'Dwyer's PR Services Report* (July 1989): 1–2.
5. Fraser P. Seitel, "Loose Lips," *U.S. Banker* (October 1991): 81.
6. Howard Kurtz, "Federal Agents Warned on Comments to Media," *The Washington Post* (March 10, 1993): A-12.
7. Kevin Goldman, "TV Network News Is Making Re-Creation a Form of Recreation," *The Wall Street Journal* (October 30, 1989): A4.
8. Judith A. Mapes, "Top Management and the Press—The Uneasy Relationship Revisited," *Corporate Issues Monitor,* Egon Zehnder International, vol. 11, no. 1 (1987): 2.
9. S. Robert Lichter, Stanley Rothman, and Linda S. Lichter, *The Media Elite: America's New Powerbrokers* (Bethesda, MD: Adler & Adler, 1986).
10. John V. Pavlik, *Public Relations: What Research Tells Us* (Newbury Park, CA: Sage, 1987), 59.
11. "Bush-Rather Debate Adds to Eroding Public Attitudes Toward News Media," *PR Reporter Purview* (May 9, 1988): 1.
12. "What's News?" *New York University Magazine* (Fall 1989): 16–17.
13. Janet Malcolm, "The Journalist and the Murderer," *The New Yorker* (March 13, 1989): 38.
14. Lewis H. Young, "The Media's View of Corporate Communications in the '80s," *Public Relations Quarterly* (Fall 1981): 10.
15. Jack Kelley, "An Absence of Malice," *USA Today* (January 16, 1986): 6A.
16. Fraser P. Seitel, "Confronting the Media," *United States Banker* (January 1989): 53.
17. Patrick M. Reilly, "As Magazine Industry Faces a Shakeout, Some Publishers Start to Close the Books," *The Wall Street Journal* (January 31, 1990): B3.
18. "Getting into the Times: How Andrews Views PR," *Across the Board* (August 1989): 21.

TOP OF THE SHELF

Joyce Nelson, *Sultans of Sleaze: Public Relations and the Media.* Monroe, ME: Common Courage Press, 1992.

A different—purists would say "jaundiced"—view of public relations and the media is revealed in this polemic, which covers the growth of public relations practice over the last two decades.

The author describes public relations practice "as a virtual 'gray eminence' behind the scenes, gliding in and out of troubled situations with the ease of a Cardinal Richelieu and the conscience of a mercenary."

The author argues that public relations wields enormous power in an unexamined and hidden way through the use of the media. She states that the role of public relations practice thoroughly scrambles our expected notions of "the news, of freedom of the press and of 'free world politics generally.' "

Furthermore, she says, public relations is so pervasive—yet "so unexamined and hidden"—that it is allowed to corrupt society without being scrutinized at all.

At the root of public relations practice, the author argues, is nothing short of "an attempt to transform the way people think about reality, especially as it is carried on through media relations." As proof, she offers several international examples.

Public relations, in other words, is capable of exerting unchecked power and influence—often for nefarious purposes.

While few public relations professionals will agree with her premise, Ms. Nelson's work should be consulted, if for no other reason than to keep apprised of how the other half thinks.

SUGGESTED READINGS

American Society of Journalists and Authors Directory (1501 Broadway, New York, NY 10036). Freelance writers.

Bacon's Media Alerts. Chicago: Bacon Publishing Co. (332 S. Michigan 60604). Bimonthly.

Barhydt, James D. *The Complete Book of Product Publicity.* New York: AMACOM, 1987.

Beals, Melba. *Expose Yourself: Using the Power of Public Relations to Promote Your Business and Yourself.* San Francisco: Chronicle, 1990.

Biagi, Shirley. *Media/Impact.* Belmont, CA: Wadsworth, 1988.

Blohowiak, Donald W. *No Comment! An Executive's Essential Guide to the News Media.* New York: Praeger, 1987.

Boot, William. "Capital Letter: The New Tattlers." *Columbia Journalism Review* (January–February 1988): 14–18. New York: Columbia University. This article discusses distinguishing between news and gossip.

Boyden, Donald P. *Gale Directory of Publications* (formerly *Ayer's Directory of Publications*). Detroit: Gale Research, 1989.

Chambers, Wicke, and Spring Asher. *TV PR: How to Promote Yourself, Your Product/Service or Your Organization on TV.* Rocklin, CA: Prima, 1987.

Cook, Timothy E. *Making Laws and Making News.* Washington, DC: The Brookings Institution, 1989.

Doty, Dorothy I. *Publicity and Public Relations.* Hauppauge, NY: Barron, 1990.

Electronic News Releases. Washington, DC: U.S. Newswire, 1988.

Engel, James F., et al. *Promotional Strategy: Managing the Marketing Communications Process.* Homewood, IL: Business One Irwin, 1990.

Evans, Fred J. *Managing the Media: Proactive Strategy for Better Business–Press Relations.* Westport, CT: Quorum Books, 1987.

"Funding the News. Nonprofits and the Media Elite." Organization Trends. Washington, DC: Capital Research Center (December 1987) (1612 K Street, NW Suite 605 20006).

Gannett Center Journal: Publicity. New York: Gannett Center for Media Studies and the Gannett Foundation, 1990 (Columbia University, 2950 Broadway).

Gottschalk, Jack A. *Promoting Your Professional Services.* Homewood, IL: Business One Irwin, 1991.

Goulden, Joseph C. *Fit to Print: A. M. Rosenthal and His Times.* Secaucus, NJ: Lyle Stuart, 1988.

Hart, Norman. *Practical Advertising and Publicity.* New York: McGraw-Hill, 1989.

Hiebert, Ray E., and Carol Ruess. *Impact of Mass Media.* 2nd ed. White Plains, NY: Longman, 1988.

Hiebert, Ray E., Donald F. Ungurait, and Thomas W. Bohn. *Mass Media VI.* White Plains, NY: Longman, 1991.

Hilton, Jack. *How to Meet the Press: A Survival Guide.* New York: Dodd, Mead, 1987.

Howard, Carol, and Wilma Mathews. *On Deadline: Managing Media Relations.* Prospect Heights, IL: Waveland, 1988.

International Directory of Special Events and Festivals. Chicago: Special Events Reports (213 W. Institute Place 60610).

Irvine, Robert B. *When You Are the Headline: Managing a Major News Story.* Homewood, IL: Dow Jones-Irwin, 1987.

Klein, Barry. *Guide to Free Product Publicity Sources.* West Nyack, NY: Todd Publications, 1992.

Kremer, John. *How to Make the News: A Step-By-Step Guide to National Publicity.* Fairfield, IA: Open Horizons, 1991.

Lavine, John, and Daniel Wackerman. *Managing Media Organizations.* White Plains, NY: Longman, 1987.

Lewis, Peter Y., and Jerry Booth. *The Invisible Medium: Commercial, Public and Community Radio.* Washington, DC: Howard University Press, 1990.

Martel, Myles. *Mastering the Art of Q&A.* Homewood, IL: Dow Jones-Irwin, 1989.

Martin, Dick. *Executive's Guide to Handling a Press Interview.* Babylon, NY: Pilot Books, 1985.

Media News Keys (40–29 27th St., Long Island City, NY 11101). Weekly.

Michels, Gloria. *How to Make Yourself (or Anyone Else) Famous: Secrets of a Professional Publicist.* New York: Cross Gates, 1988.

Miller, Peter G. *Media Marketing.* New York: Harper & Row, 1987.

Miller, Peter G. *Media Power: How Your Business Can Profit from the Media.* Chicago: Dearborn, 1991.

National Research Bureau. *Working Press of the Nation.* (Available from the author, 242 N. 3rd St, Burlington, IA 52601.) Each volume covers a different medium—newspapers, magazines, radio-TV, features writers, syndicates, and house organs.

Network Futures (Television Index, 40–29 27th St., Long Island City, New York 11101). Monthly.

Newsletter on Newsletters (P.O. Box 311, Rhinebeck, NY 12572). Weekly.

O'Dwyer, Jack, ed. *O'Dwyer's Directory of Corporation Communications.* New York: J. R. O'Dwyer, 1994. This guide provides a full listing of the public relations departments of nearly 3,000 companies and shows how the largest companies define public relations and staff and budget for it.

O'Dwyer, Jack, ed. *O'Dwyer's Directory of PR Firms.* New York: J. R. O'Dwyer, 1994. This directory has listings of 1,200 public relations firms. In addition to providing information on executives, accounts, types of agencies, and branch office locations, the guide offers a geographical index to firms and cross-indexes more than 8,000 clients.

Pasqua, Thomas M. *Mass Media in the Information Age.* New York: Prentice-Hall, 1989.

Perry, David. *Media How-To Guidebook.* San Francisco: Media Alliance, 1991.
Pollack, Martin. *Publicity: How To.* Ft. Lauderdale, FL: Alliance, 1989.
Power-Packed PR: Ideas That Work. Pitman, NJ: Communication Publications and Resources, 1988 (140 South Broadway 08071).
PR Aids' Party Line. (Available from 221 Park Ave. South, New York, NY 10003.) This information service weekly, published on Monday, lists editorial placement opportunities in all media, including network and local radio and TV.
Public Relations, Inc. (221 Park Ave. South, New York, NY 10003). A computerized media system lets a client select local broadcast media by market, type of programming, power of radio stations, network for TV, and department (news, program, women's interest, public service, etc.).
The Publicity Process. 3rd ed. Ames: Iowa State University Press, 1989.
Radio Interview Guide. New York: Macmillan, 1988.
Ramacitti, David F. *Do-It-Yourself Publicity.* New York: AMACOM, 1990.
Rein, Irving, Philip Kotler, and Martin Stoller. *High Visibility.* New York: Dodd, Mead, 1987.
Robinson, James W. *Winning Them Over.* Rocklin, CA: Prima, 1987.
Sellers, Jim. *Speaking Out.* New York: Macmillan, 1988.
Shimp, Terence. *Promotion Management and Marketing Communications.* Ft. Worth, TX: Dryden, 1990.
Sopow, Eli. *Taking Charge! A Survival Guide to Media Relations.* Canada: Media Scope, 1992.
Tharpe, Louis. *The Complete Manager's Guide to Promotional Merchandise.* Homewood, IL: Dow Jones-Irwin, 1989.
Veciana-Suarez, Ana. *Hispanic Media: Impact and Influence.* Washington, DC: The Media Institute, 1990.
Weiner, Richard. *Dictionary of Media and Communications.* New York: Simon & Schuster, 1990.
What to Do When the Media Contact You. (New York State Bar Association, Dept. of Communications and Public Affairs, One Elk St., Albany, NY 12207).
Yale, David. *The Publicity Handbook.* Lincolnwood, IA: NTC Business, 1991.

CASE STUDY

WACO

The first bona fide nightmare of the Clinton Administration arrived in February 1993 when four federal agents were killed in the line of duty, attempting to arrest the leader of an obscure religious sect, the Branch Davidians, in Waco, Texas.

Over the next two months, FBI and Bureau of Alcohol, Tobacco and Firearms (ATF) agents attempted to negotiate with Branch Davidian leader David Koresh to release the 86 individuals, including two dozen children, literally imprisoned behind the compound's walls.

For 51 days, television viewers around the world witnessed a standoff between the American government and the leader of the fringe religious group. Each day, spokesmen from the FBI or ATF would cryptically update the world on "progress."

On Monday, April 19, the showdown came to

(*Courtesy AP/Wide World Photos*)

a grim conclusion. At 12:05 p.m., the first wisps of smoke were seen coming from several windows of the compound. Until then armored vehicles had been battering the building's sides all morning, injecting tear gas through a long boom. Ultimately, a raging fire commenced.

At 12:13 p.m. the FBI called the Waco Fire Department for help. Two fire trucks were dispatched and arrived about 15 minutes later. It was another 21 minutes before the authorities allowed the fire trucks onto the compound. The reason for the delay, the FBI said, was that the Davidians were armed with automatic weapons.

When the firefighters were finally allowed to enter the compound, there was no one left to save. Thirty-mile-an-hour winds coupled with the flimsy wooden construction of compound buildings created a tinder box. All that remained at the grisly scene were charred bodies and skeletal remains of 86 people.

"The American people are shocked," said New York's Governor Mario M. Cuomo. "This is an awful tragedy and the American people want an explanation." In particular, the question that dominated the dialogue was, "Why did the children have to die?"

That question—and all others surrounding the debacle—were fielded by Attorney General Janet Reno, the appointed Waco spokesman for the Clinton Administration.

The Attorney General argued that "reports of child abuse inside the compound" had led her to order Federal authorities to act quickly. Reno also volunteered to one and all that she took "full responsibility" for the action on the cultist compound.

Indeed, during the first 24 hours after the Waco raid, President Clinton remained mysteriously unavailable. Reno said she had spoken with the President, who agreed with her decision.

Two days after the destruction, President Clinton reemerged to conduct a news conference on Waco. "Why," he was asked, did he choose to "distance himself for 24 hours?" The President replied that he was "bewildered" by the accusation. "The only reason I made no public statement yesterday," he said, "is that I had nothing to add to what was being said."

Later it was revealed that not only was there no proof of "child abuse within the compound," but also that the FBI, apparently unwilling to rotate a new force of agents to continue to monitor the stalemate with Koresh, decided to push the issue to a conclusion. Attorney General Reno, so the story went, willingly acquiesced.

News organizations rushed to "pick apart" the Administration's story on Waco. Where first Reno was hailed for "stepping up" to the responsibility of the raid, later she was ostracized. Journalists and others began openly to question the logic of her decision to raid the compound.

With the government steadfastly maintaining a "no other alternative" explanation, reporters began to quote law enforcement experts and others who questioned the timing and justification of the raid. "I think they haven't made the public case for the necessity to do what they did," argued one legal scholar in *The New York Times*.

Each day, it seemed, brought a new element of doubt about the necessity of the raid.

The situation for the Administration steadily deteriorated. Justice Department Spokesman Carl Stern, a former NBC newsman, acknowledged that while there had in fact been "accounts of child beatings" at the compound, he could recall no assertions that there had been any incidents of abuse. Later, it was disclosed that the FBI and ATF had squabbled over jurisdiction in the Waco matter. To heighten the controversy, Koresh's lawyer claimed that his client "would have been ready soon to give himself up if the government had just waited."

In the final analysis, Waco stood as one of the Clinton Administration's darkest hours. Summarized one law school professor, "The question is, could we have done anything differently? And the answer is, 'I would have exhausted all the alternatives before launching the fatal raid.' "

QUESTIONS

1. How would you assess the public relations handling of Waco?
2. What could have been done to avoid public squabbling between the FBI and ATF?
3. In a crisis like Waco, what media relations philosophy and approach should be used?
4. Do you agree with the decision to appoint Janet Reno as public relations focal point after the raid on Waco?
5. How would you characterize President Clinton's public performance after the raid?
6. Had you been the President's communications advisor, what strategy and tactics would you have suggested be adopted immediately after the raid on Waco?

TIPS FROM THE TOP

ANDREW S. EDSON

Andrew S. Edson is president and chief operating officer of Anreder & Company, a New York– and Los Angeles–based public relations agency. Formerly, Mr. Edson served as senior vice-president and managing director of the New York office of Padilla Speer Beardsley, Inc. His extensive background in public relations includes experience as a college teacher and frequent lecturer on public relations subjects.

How would you define public relations?
Advertising is what you pay for. Public relations is what you pray for.

How does one deal effectively with the media?
You must know the media you plan to deal with. Read the pertinent publications, listen to or watch the actual news program. Be inquisitive and do your homework beforehand. This will show when you write that first pitch letter or make the introductory call. Honesty also counts. Don't hide under a hundred platitudes once you've established a contact. If you cannot effectively answer a question or aid a journalist, be truthful and let that person know. It'll pay off in the long run.

How important are contacts in media relations?
Very. If you develop a good and continuous working relationship with members of the fourth estate, you, too, can engage in a game of "give and go." It's not imprudent to ask a favor or question a journalist. Basically, it's a two-way street. The newsperson wants your help when he or she needs it. Conversely, there will come a day when you will need a favor in return. Good media contacts are invaluable in practicing public relations.

What is the proper relationship between a journalist and a public relations practitioner?
Some say at "arm's distance," while others make it a habit of getting to know a journalist on an almost personal and social basis. There really isn't any concrete formula for setting the tone of a practitioner–journalist relationship. Common sense and adherence to a professional code of ethics, such as that of the Public Relations Society of America, more than anything else, constitute what is proper and improper.

What steps do you follow in publicizing a client?
I first try to put together a publicity plan that will help the client achieve his or her objectives through proven strategies and action programs. Sure, everyone would love to be in *The New York Times* or *Wall Street Journal* or on ABC's *Good Morning America* program, but it doesn't always happen. While your client may push for his or her appearance in a national book, the company and its products may be more appropriate for a series of by-lined articles in trade publications (not at all unlike hitting a few singles in baseball) before pitching a major book or program. Those "singles" will help advance your runners and build a better case for pitching your client before other target media.

Are clients understanding when they don't attract publicity?
Some are. Some aren't. If you make the client aware from the outset of the success/failure ratio and don't make any unnecessary promises, then you shouldn't get harmed. All too often, public relations practitioners get overzealous and almost guarantee that certain things will happen when they may not. Unlike advertising, we don't control what gets into print, or heard on the airwaves, or seen on the tube.

What special tips can you offer in dealing with the media?
Be honest, forthright, and cooperate with the media person in a professional manner. Don't forget to send a proper thank-you note when the occasion calls for it. Think of your relationship as a continuing, not a one-shot, deal. Stay in touch, even if you have nothing in particular to sell.

How can you stay current with an ever-expanding media universe?
While it may appear to be a difficult task, it requires good time management. Peruse new publications. Scan new television programs. This will give you a leg up on the competition and will enable you to counsel your organization or client from a stronger position. Not every publication or program will withstand the test of time, advertising, or ratings. Still, in order to be adept at your job, you must read, listen, and watch.

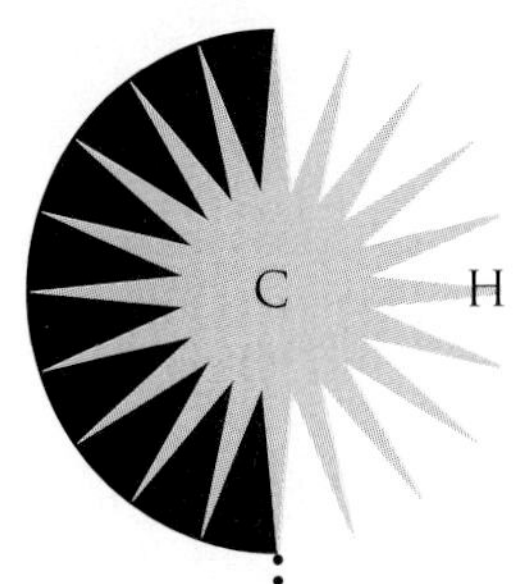

CHAPTER 13

EMPLOYEES

THE FUNCTION OF INTERNAL COMMUNICATIONS—OF COMMUNICATING with employees—has never been more challenging or more critical than it is today. Doubt that? Then consider the following:

In the spring of 1994, Fleet Financial Group of Providence, Rhode Island, one of the nation's healthiest financial institutions, announced plans to reduce its 21,000-employee roster by 5,500. That, in itself, wasn't startling. What was unusual was that the vast majority of the Fleet cuts emanated from the suggestions of Fleet employees themselves! In other words, in many cases, the company's employees presided over their own beheading.

Fleet decided to "tear up the bank," as the chairman put it, to get itself "fit" for the new business realities of the 1990s and beyond. Summarized one nervous employee, "Your life is on hold until they make decisions."[1]

And Fleet was not alone.

After the excesses of the 1980s, with increased competition from overseas and elsewhere making it more difficult to please shareholders, the 1990s continued as a period of downsizings, reorganizations, mergers, acquisitions, retrenchments, and all the other euphemisms that equate to *employee job loss*.

The days when an employee joined the phone company or the utility or the bank or the Fortune 500 manufacturer to guarantee job security and lifetime employment are gone forever. Employees who remain in such firms today are less secure, less confident, and therefore less loyal than their predecessors.

All of these changes pose a significant challenge for employee communicators.

Internal communications has become a "hot ticket" in public relations, particularly as organizations face the harsh realities of the 1990s. With fewer employees expected to do more work, staff members are calling for empowerment—for more of a voice in decision making. Although some managements are willing, others evidently are not. Resultant relations between employer and employee these days are not particularly good. Just about every researcher who keeps tabs on employee opinion finds evidence of a "trust gap" between management and rank-and-file workers.

Evidence of this trust gap was among the findings of an opinion study of employees in nearly 300 organizations conducted by the International Association of Business Communicators in conjunction with employee benefits consultant Towers, Perrin, Forster and Crosby. Among other findings were these:

- The majority of employees want face-to-face information from first-line supervisors as the preferred source of communication.
- First-line supervisors aren't communicating satisfactorily. Senior management remains invisible and out of touch.
- The companywide publication scores high marks from employees in many respects, yet it rates low as a preferred source of information. Although employees are more satisfied with the information they're getting, communications efforts are still not meeting their needs.
- Employees are intensely critical of management's unwillingness to listen to them or to act on their ideas.[2]

There is no such thing today as a single "employee public." The employee public is made up of numerous subgroups. Indeed, today the staff is generally younger, increasingly female, more ambitious and career-oriented, less complacent, and less loyal to the company than in the past. Today's more hard-nosed employee demands candor in communications. Internal communications, like external messages, must be targeted to reach specific subgroups of the employee public. Communications must be continuous to reinforce a consistent management message.

What distinguishes the communication effort at a "better place to work"? According to Milton Moskowitz, coauthor of the *100 Best Companies to Work For,* six criteria, in particular, are important:

1. **Willingness to express dissent** Employees, according to Moskowitz, want to be able to "feed back" to management their opinions and even dissent. They want access to management. They want critical letters to appear in internal publications. They want management to pay attention (Figure 13–1).

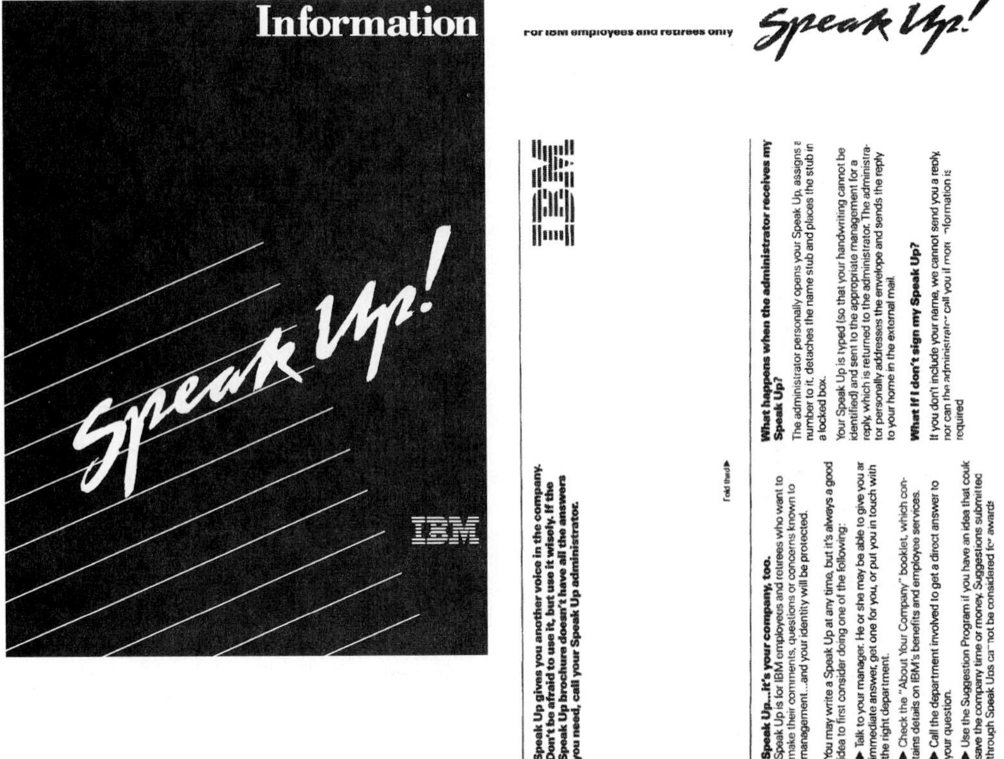

Figure 13–1 For more than three decades, IBM's "Speak Up" program has provided a two-way communication channel for employees around the world to speak directly to management. The program is managed by IBM's communications organization through 80 location, division, and country "Speak Up" administrators. "Speak Up" is anonymous. An employee can complain, compliment, or ask a question, and, in return, receive an answer from management without revealing his or her identity to anyone except the "Speak Up" administrator. Such programs are essential in the less trusting employee environment of the 1990s. (*Courtesy of IBM*)

2. **Visibility and proximity of upper management** Enlightened companies try to level rank distinctions, eliminating such status reminders as executive cafeterias and executive gymnasiums. They act against hierarchical separation, says Moskowitz. He adds that smart CEOs practice MBWA—"management by walking around."
3. **Priority of internal to external communication** The worst thing to happen to any organization is for employees to learn critical information about the company on the 10 o'clock news. Smart organizations *always* release pertinent information to employees first and consider internal communication primary.
4. **Attention to clarity** How many employees regularly read benefits booklets? The answer should be "many" because of the importance of benefit programs to the entire staff. Because most employees never open such booklets, good companies write them with clarity—to be readable for a general audience rather than for human resources specialists.

5. **Friendly tone** According to Moskowitz, the best companies "give a sense of family" in all that they communicate. One high-tech company, says Moskowitz, makes everyone wear a name tag with the *first* name in big block letters. These little things are most important, declares Moskowitz.
6. **Sense of humor** Most experts agree that in the 1990s organizational work is very serious. People are worried principally about keeping their jobs. Corporate life for many is grim. Moskowitz says this is disastrous. "It puts people in straightjackets, so they can't wait to get out at the end of the day."[3]

What internal communications comes down to—just like external communications—is the single word *credibility.* The task for management, at a disaffected and disloyal time, is to convince employees that it not only desires to communicate with them, but also wishes to do so in a truthful, frank, and direct manner. That is the overriding challenge that confronts today's internal communicator.

CREDIBILITY: THE KEY

The employee public is a savvy one. Employees can't be conned because they live with the organization every day. They generally know what's going on and whether management is being honest with them. That's why management must be truthful.

Evidently being truthful isn't easy for many managements. The days when management could say "Trust us, this is for your own good" are over. Research indicates that if organizations (1) communicated earlier and more frequently, (2) demonstrated trust in employees by sharing bad news as well as good, and (3) involved employees in the process by asking for their ideas and opinions, employees would substantially increase their trust in management.[4] The fact is, employees desperately want to know in what direction an organization is headed and what their own role is in getting it there.

In the 1990s, smart companies realize that well-informed employees are the organization's best goodwill ambassadors. Managements have become more candid in their communications with the staff. Gone are the days when all the news coming from the communications department was good. In today's environment, being candid means treating people with dignity and giving them the opportunity to understand the realities of the marketplace.[5]

IBM, for example, gutted its award-winning, four-color magazine, *Think,* with the arrival of new CEO Lou Gerstner in 1993. The new *Think* is smaller and more candid than its predecessor, discussing such formally taboo topics as "avoiding getting swallowed up in bureaucracy" and "working without the warmth of a corporate security blanket." The new *Think* is most successful.

So, too, is the no-holds-barred *The SPARK,* the monthly publication of Arco International (Figure 13–2). *The SPARK* pokes fun at the company, encourages blunt feedback from employees, and generally promotes an environment of candor and openness at Arco.

At AT&T, another frank, hard-hitting magazine, *Focus,* was introduced in 1990. As its editor explained, faith in the company had been "shaken," and an honest, straightforward magazine was designed to help restore that faith.[6] Ironically, in 1993, *Focus* became the focus of an embarrassing scandal involving a cartoon perceived as racially insensitive. AT&T subsequently terminated *Focus.* (See the Case Study in Chapter 14.)

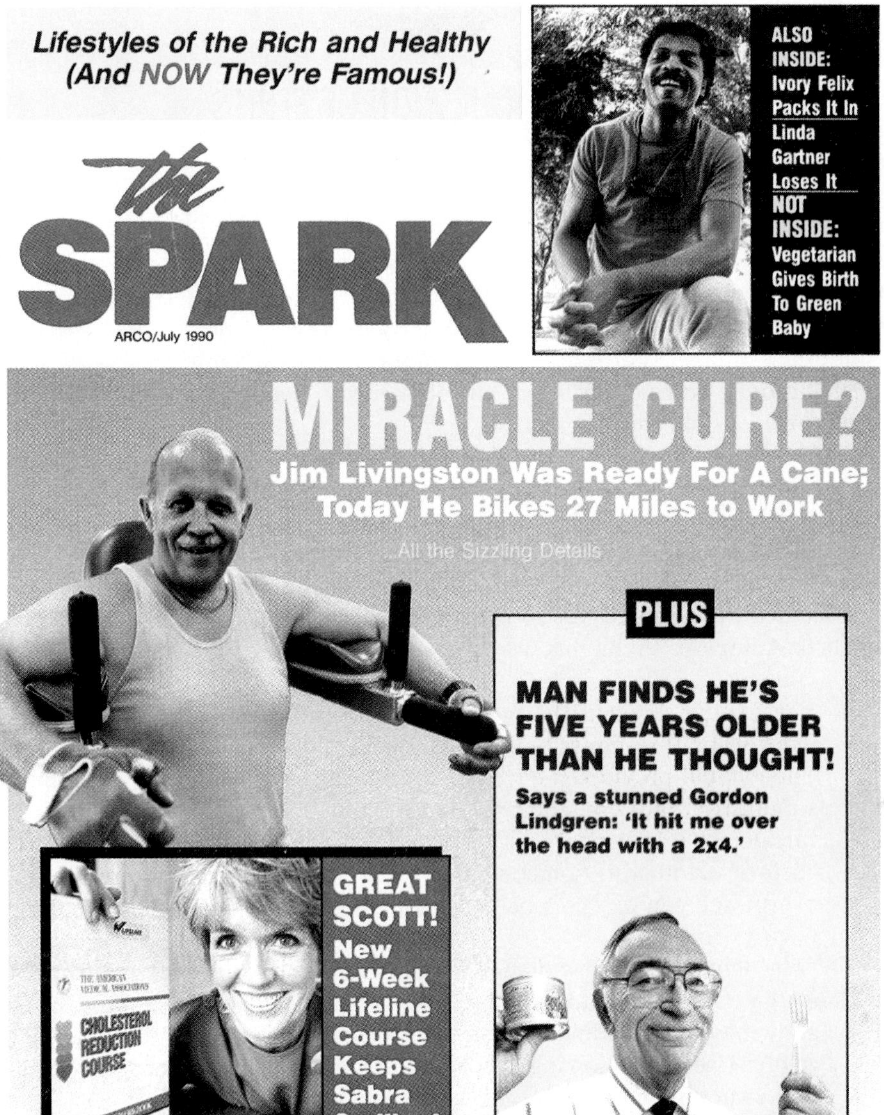

Figure 13–2 *The SPARK*, from Arco International, is perhaps the most well-known employee publication in America. Its candor and openness are legendary. Few similar publications would have the chutzpah to feature their own employees in a *National Enquirer* "Lifestyles of the Rich and Famous" motif. (*Courtesy of Arco*)

In any organization, employees must feel that they are appreciated. They want to be treated as important parts of an organization; they should not be taken for granted, nor should they be shielded from the truth. Thus, the most important ingredient of any internal communications program must be credibility.

Facilitating the PG&E Layoffs

When San Francisco's Pacific Gas and Electric Company decided to fire 3,000 workers in 1993, the cutbacks were the largest in the company's 88-year history. As in other similar companies, the restructuring was difficult because of a traditional corporate culture that stood for job security, generous benefits, and recruitment of relatives for employment.

The typical shock faced by employees given such news was exacerbated by the company's clumsy internal notification program.

"My boss read from a script and told me not to return to my office," griped one veteran employee. "It was incredible." Another complained that he learned about his fate through a posting on a department bulletin board. A PG&E guidebook handed out to managers to execute layoffs was leaked to the *San Francisco Chronicle*. Among its highlights were the following:

- The manual likened the possible reaction of a displaced worker to "the fight-or-flight response typical of animals under siege."
- The manual provided a checklist for terminating employees, including "be supportive, but not compromising," "Don't be apologetic," and "Don't threaten or traumatize."
- "Before terminating someone, determine whether that person could easily overpower you or has a belligerent nature. In that event, ensure that you have a witness."
- "The actual act of termination should occur within the first FIVE minutes of the termination interview. The remainder of this time should be spent allowing the individual to express his or her feelings and questions."
- (Note: Use the following according to individual situations.) "Under the new structure, your position has been eliminated as of today."

  OR

  "You have not been selected to fill your current position."

Employees, many of them long-time veterans of PG&E, were generally outraged at the impersonal manner in which the company chose to terminate them.

"At a time when the company needs friends, it has cultivated an army of enemies," groused one worker whose job was eliminated.

Might there have been a better way for PG&E to relay the unfortunate news without risking the loss of goodwill and morale among its workers?

EMPLOYEE COMMUNICATIONS STRATEGIES FOR THE '90s

Enhancing credibility, being candid, and winning trust must be the primary employee communications objectives in the 1990s. Earning employee trust may result in more committed and productive employees. But scraping away the scar tissue of distrust that exists in many organizations requires a strategic approach to employee communications. Five elements are key in any strategic program:

1. **Survey employees' attitudes regularly.** Ironically, it is organizations that audit their financial resources on a daily basis that regularly fail to take the temperature of their own employees. They "fly blind." Attitude surveys can identify problems before they become crises. Employees who are surveyed about their attitudes, consulted on what the surveys reveal, and then shown action as a result of the survey findings will be much more willing to accept management's policies.
2. **Be consistent.** Management that promises open and honest communications must practice it. An open door must *remain* open—not just be partly open part of the time. Communications must be consistent to be believed. That means conveying both good and bad news on a regular basis.
3. **Personalize communications.** One study found that 80 percent of corporate chief executives believed that "personally communicating with employees benefits the bottom line." But only 22 percent of them did it on a regular basis, however. Workers want personal attention from those for whom they work, particularly their immediate supervisor. In light of this finding, companies like Union Carbide conduct "town meetings," at which senior managers barnstorm around the nation to answer employees' questions.
4. **Be candid.** Employees in the 1990s are younger, less well educated, less loyal, and include more women, minorities, and immigrants than workers of the past. These new, more skeptical, less trusting employees demand honesty in everything management says.
5. **Be innovative.** New employees in the work force and increased skepticism in the workplace demand new communications solutions. This means resorting to the new technology—voice, video, data transmission on PCs, and so on—to reach workers. Today's work force, weaned on a daily diet of high-resolution, mind-numbing television, demands innovative solutions to counteract the "trust gap"[7] (Fig. 13–3).

EMPLOYEE COMMUNICATIONS TACTICS

Once objectives are set, a variety of techniques can be adopted to reach the staff. The initial tool again is research. Before any communications program can be implemented, communicators must have a good sense of staff attitudes. Perhaps the most beneficial form of research to lay the groundwork for effective employee communications is the internal communications audit. This consists essentially of old-fashioned personal, in-depth interviews to determine staff attitudes about their jobs, the organization, and its management, coupled with an analysis of existing communications techniques. The findings of such audits are often startling, always informative, and never easily ignored.

GRANTLAND®

Figure 13–3 One of the more innovative internal communications techniques of the 1990s is the use of tailored cartoons to reinforce employee communications. Producing humor to fit into the staid world of internal communications wasn't easy. But Grant Brownrigg's "Grantland" cartoons attracted more than 1,000 subscribers. (*Courtesy of Grantland Enterprises, Inc.*)

Once internal communications research is completed, the public relations practitioner has a clearer idea of the kinds of communications vehicles that make sense for the organization. Several of the more popular vehicles are discussed here.

NEWSLETTERS

By far the most heavily used medium to communicate with employees is print. The long-heralded revolution of pictures and electronics may be the wave of the future, but it is not yet a serious challenger to letters, bulletins, brochures, manuals, and particularly the oldest staple in the employee communications arsenal—the employee newsletter.[8]

The format and content of the employee newsletter vary from organization to organization. However, the broad concept of informing the staff through one major organizational publication has stood the test of time.

A traditional first job for an entry-level public relations professional is working on the employee newsletter. In approaching the writing or editing of an employee newsletter, the professional should ponder the following questions:

1. Who is this paper designed to reach?
2. What kinds of articles should be featured?
3. What is the budget for the newsletter?
4. What is the appropriate format for the newsletter?
5. How frequently should the newsletter be published?
6. What is the desired approval process for the newsletter?

The answers to these questions, of course, vary from one organization to another, but all should be tackled before approaching the assignment. Employee newsletters should appear regularly, on time, and with a consistent format. Employees should expect them and even look forward to them.

The employee newsletter serves as a first-line communications vehicle from management to explain the company's philosophy and policies. In the 1990s, it is becoming increasingly important that such newsletters provide two-way communications, expressing not only management wishes but staff concerns as well.

A typical employee newsletter editor must consider the following steps in approaching the task:

1. **Assigning stories.** Article assignments must focus on organizational strategies and management objectives. Job information—organizational changes, mergers, reasons behind decisions, and so on—should be stressed (Figure 13–4). Articles must reflect the diversity of the organization: different locations and departments, as well as the different kinds of people the organization employs. The editor must review with each writer the desired "thesis" conveyed by the article.
2. **Enforcing deadlines.** Employees respect a newsletter that comes out at a specific time—whether weekly, bimonthly, or monthly. An editor therefore must assign and enforce rigid copy deadlines. Deadline slippage can't be tolerated if the newsletter is to be respected.
3. **Assigning photos.** Many newsletters include photographs. Because internal publications compete with glossy, high-tech newspapers and magazines, organizational photos can't be dull. Editors must take pains to "think visually" by assigning visually arresting photos—the more provocative, the better (Figure 13–5).
4. **Editing copy.** An editor must be just that: a critic of sloppy writing, a student of forceful prose, a motivator to improve copy style. Employees must want to read about what's going on in the organization. Riveting writing must be the goal of a good newsletter.

All the News That Fits ... We Print"

THE BAGEL BUGLE

SPECIAL Lender/Kraft WEDDING EDITION

Published by Lender's Bagel Bakery, Inc.

WEDDING OF THE CENTURY

INNISBROOK, Florida — Lender's Bagels and Kraft Inc. tied the knot in a spectacular wedding celebration held here on Saturday, September 15.

The joining of the two dynamic food companies was symbolized in a colorful ceremony which included eight-foot-high replicas of Kraft and Lender's products marching down the aisle.

"This is the proudest moment of our lives," said Murray and Marvin Lender as they escorted Len, the groom.

The bride, Phyl, was given away by the president of Kraft's Retail Food Group, Keith Ridgway. Len and Phyl had been dating for 20 years.

The weekend was filled with much eating, drinking and merriment as a crowd of more than 250 people including brokers, wives and associates enjoyed the luxurious accommodations at Innisbrook, the world-famous resort hotel in Tampa.

Most guests gained at least five pounds.

Figure 13–4 One of the most unusual employee publications in recent years was this issue of the *Bagel Bugle,* published by Lender's Bagel Bakery of West Haven, Connecticut. Lender's commemorated its merger with Kraft, maker of Philadelphia cream cheese, with this special "wedding" edition. (*Courtesy of Lender's Bagel Bakery*)

Figure 13–5 People love to look at other people. Accordingly, when Days Inns of America wanted to celebrate National Tourism Awareness Day, the company assembled 300 corporate employees in the shape of the Days Inns' sunburst logo to provide this visually arresting photo. (*Courtesy of Days Inns of America; Michael Pugh/Atlanta*)

5. **Formatting copy.** An editor must also make the final decisions on the format of the newsletter: how long articles should run, where to put photos, how to crop artwork, what headlines should say, and so on. As desktop publishing becomes more pervasive, the task of formatting becomes more important for an editor.
6. **Ensuring on-time publication.** An editor's job doesn't stop when the newsletter is sent to the printer. It is the editor's responsibility to ensure that no last-minute glitches interfere with the on-time publication of the finished product.
7. **Critiquing.** After the publication hits the stands, the editor's job must continue. He or she must scrupulously review copy, photos, placement, content, philosophy, and all the other elements of the current product. The goal in critiquing, stated simply, is to make certain that the next edition will be even better. It is this challenge, in particular, that makes the task of a newsletter editor among the most rewarding in public relations work.

One organization devoted originally to internal communications, the International Association of Business Communicators (IABC), has in a relatively short time come to rival the much older Public Relations Society of America. With more than 11,500 members throughout the United States, and in 40 countries, the IABC helps set journalistic standards for communicators.[9]

MANAGEMENT PUBLICATIONS

Managerial employees must also know what's going on in the organization. The company needs their support. Continual, reliable communication is one way to ensure it. Many firms publish frequent bulletins for management with updates on personnel changes, office relocations, new telephone numbers, and revised company policies. Occasionally, special bulletins concerning new-product developments, breaking company news, or other matters of urgent interest are circulated.

More formal publications, such as management magazines, are often more technical and more confidential than related employee newspapers. For example, a firm may publicize its corporate mission to all employees through the employee newspaper but may reveal its business profitability objectives only in the management magazine. This element of confidentiality is always a sensitive one. Employees occasionally object that internal publications don't reveal enough pertinent details about corporate decisions and policy. One common complaint is that outside newspaper reporters "know more than we do about our own firm's activities." Although limitations may be necessary for certain issues, those who run the organization must try to be as candid as possible, in particular with fellow managers.

Because of the personal, vested interest of a manager in the organization, management publications are generally among the best read internal communications. They shouldn't be underestimated as a way to build confidence, enhance credibility, and promote team spirit.

EMPLOYEE ANNUAL REPORTS

It often makes sense to print a separate annual report just for employees. Frequently, the lure of this report—published in addition to the regular corporate shareholder annual report—is that it is written for, about, and by the employees.

Most employees do care about how their organization functions and what its management is thinking. The annual report to the staff is a good place to discuss such issues informally, yet candidly. The report can be both factual, explaining the performance of the organization during the year, and informational, reviewing organizational changes and significant milestones during the year. It can also be motivational in its implicit appeal to team spirit and pride.

Staff reports observe few hard-and-fast rules about concept and format. Staff annuals can be as complex as the shareholder annual report itself or as simple as a brief outline of the highlights of the year for the company. Typical features of the employee annual report include the following:

1. **Chief executive's letter** A special report to the staff reviewing the performance and highlights of the year and thanking employees for their help.
2. **Use-of-funds statement** Often a graphic chart describing how the organization used each dollar it took in.
3. **Financial condition** Frequently a chart describing the assets and liabilities of the corporation and the stockholders' equity.
4. **Description of the company** Simple, graphic explanation of what the organization is and where its facilities are located.
5. **Social responsibility highlights** Discussion of the organization's role in aiding society through monetary assistance and employee participation during the year.

6. **Staff financial highlights** General description, usually in chart form, of salaries, benefits, and other staff-related expense items.
7. **Organizational policy** Discussion of current issues about which management feels strongly and for which it seeks employee support.
8. **Emphasis on people** One general theme throughout the report is the importance of the people who make up the organization: in-depth profiles of people on the job, comments from people about their jobs, and/or pictorial essays on people at work (Figure 13–6).

Employees appreciate recognition. The special annual report is a measure of recognition that does not go unnoticed—or unread—by a firm's workers.

FOREWORD

Remembering John J. Martin

John J. Martin, the gregarious and outspoken Aetna executive and a 34 year veteran of the company, died June 7 after a 13-month battle with cancer. Martin, 57, was senior vice president, Marketing, at the time of his death.

In a memo to all employees announcing Martin's death, Aetna Chairman Ronald E. Compton said, "In his 34 years with Aetna, John consistently applied his superior expertise and management skills to improve the company and to provide the best products and services to Aetna's customers. He was critical to our efforts to become more responsive to consumers, and, at the same time, he dedicated himself to explaining Aetna's actions and positions. John was very proud to be a part of Aetna, and he took great pleasure in helping others in the company to develop their professional skills."

Calling Martin "the industry's most persuasive and engaging spokesperson," Compton said Martin was "Aetna's most energetic, entertaining and compelling advocate. Even after he was diagnosed with a brain tumor in May 1991, John continued to work hard to champion change at Aetna and to make absolutely certain that he and others were doing everything possible to make this company the very best it could be.

"He was a precious resource whose contributions to Aetna and the industry — along with his special wit — will not be forgotten," Compton said.

A 1958 graduate of the University of Massachusetts, Martin joined Aetna that same year as an underwriter, and spent his entire professional career with the company. After serving in various positions in the Group Division, he moved to the Casualty & Surety Division in 1969, serving as general manager in Denver for four years and then as general manager of the Hartford branch office for another four. Martin was named vice president, Corporate Communications, in 1978, and subsequently held key executive positions in the Personal Insurance Department and Personal Financial Security Division. He was named PFSD president in 1988 and assumed his most recent position as head of Marketing in 1990. In that capacity, Martin was responsible for the company's efforts to reengineer its product delivery and customer service systems. He also headed Aetna's Office of Consumer Issues.

Over the course of his career, Martin played a major role in numerous insurance industry organizations, including the Independent Insurance Agents of America; the Insurance Services Office; the Health Insurance Association of America, and the American Insurance Association of the American Council of Life Insurance. He also chaired, for two terms, the Insurance Information Institute Board of Directors.

In 1987, Martin was awarded a Special Presidential Citation by the Independent Insurance Agents of America. IIAA President Dwight Dillon called Martin "a diligent supporter of agent-company relationships."

Known nationally as a voice for the insurance industry, Martin spoke frequently on auto insurance issues in recent years. He debated politicians and consumer advocates, including Ralph Nader, on the auto insurance affordability problem. As spokesman for Aetna, Martin said, "We have to take a long, hard look at the auto insurance system, to find the fairest and fastest ways to compensate accident victims."

He also spoke about the industry in general. *The Hartford Courant* quoted from a speech Martin gave at a local conference on "Insurance Change." "Insurance bashing has become a popular sport to be covered in the press, and the rules are heavily slanted in favor of the bashers," Martin said.

The flip side of Martin's sharp commentary was his sharp wit. Examples of his well-known sense of humor abound.

He often used humor and knowledge to deflate Nader's criticisms of the insurance industry. In a debate between the two at the 1989 PIA National Convention, Nader commented on what he believed was an inordinate amount of power possessed by insurance executives. Martin responded off-handedly, "Well, you didn't exactly come here in a canoe yourself, you know."

At the 1986 Great Performers Executive Council meeting, Martin chose to forego his planned speech and respond directly to agents' concerns. In an illustration of both his wit and his close rapport with agents, Martin began what had become his familiar pitch to agents for more life business, saying, "I know you guys are sick of hearing me talk about life insurance, but let me take one more stab at it. ... It is more than just pure greed that forces us down this path to sell life insurance. Now, this may sound corny, but I'm absolutely convinced. I feel it in my bones. God wants us to have your life insurance. Otherwise we wouldn't call it universal life!"

Martin is survived by his wife, Carol, and their three children, John Jr., Christopher and Laurie. Memorial contributions in his memory may be sent to: The John Martin Cancer Fund, the Cancer Centers, St. Francis Hospital, 114 Woodland Street, Hartford, CT 06105. □

Art Sribanpot

AETNAIZER/2

Figure 13–6 Humanizing management is a continuing challenge for internal communicators in the 1990s. This poignant tribute to a beloved Aetna executive is illustrative of the new "people" emphasis of savvy internal communicators. (*Courtesy of Aetna Life & Casualty*)

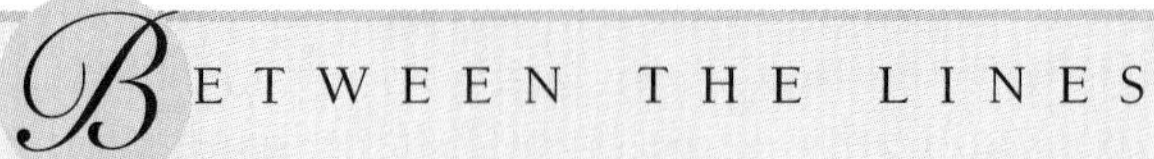

DESKTOP PUBLISHING EMERGES

In the 1990s, the advent of desktop publishing, in which a professional can produce a newsletter at his or her own desk, promises to revolutionize employee communications.

Introduced in 1985, desktop publishing allows an editor to write, lay out, and typeset a piece of copy. However, the term *desktop publishing* is a misnomer. *Desktop layout* or *desktop page layout* is more accurate. Desktop publishing requires a personal computer, a laser printer, and software for word processing, charts, and drawings, if desired, and publishing applications such as layout. Experts say that anything less than a $10,000 investment for a desktop publishing workstation and software may not be worth the aggravation.

Desktop publishing allows a user to control the typesetting process in house, provides faster turnaround for clients, and saves money on outside design.

The near-term future for desktop publishing includes scanning photos and drawings, incorporating those images into page layouts, using the computer to assign color in design elements, and, instead of printing camera-ready pages, producing entire color-separated pages of film from which a printer can create plates for printing.

To be sure, desktop publishing is still in its infancy for internal communicators. Most who have switched to desktop publishing to gain control and curb the costs of their printed materials combine the new high technology with more conventional editing methods. Some who have tried desktop publishing complain that it takes the human part of writing and editing out of newsletter production.

Nonetheless, with desktop video already being hailed as the next generation of desktop publishing, the continued improvement of the new technology will surely change the way public relations writers and editors approach employee communications in the 1990s.

BULLETIN BOARDS

Bulletin boards are making a comeback in corporations, hospitals, and other organizations. For years they were considered second-string information channels, generally relegated to the display of federally required information and policy data for such activities as fire drills and emergency procedures. Most employees rarely consulted them. But the bulletin board has experienced a renaissance and is now being used to improve productivity, cut waste, and reduce accidents on the job. Best of all, employees are taking notice.

How come? For one thing, yesterday's bulletin board has become today's news center. It has been repackaged into a more lively visual and graphically arresting medium. Using enlarged news pictures and texts, motivational messages, and other company announcements—all illustrated with a flair—the bulletin board has become a primary source of employee communications. Hospitals, in particular, have found that a strategically situated bulletin board outside a cafeteria is a good way to promote employee understanding and cooperation.

One key to stimulating readership is to keep boards current. One person in the public relations unit should be assigned to this weekly task.

INTERNAL VIDEO

Just as increasing numbers of people today are receiving their external news from television, television—more specifically, videotape—is becoming an internal medium of preference for many organizations. Faced with the fact that almost 80 percent of the public gets most of its news from television, major companies have headed to the tube to compete for their employees' attention.

Internal television can be demonstrably effective. A 10-minute videotape of an executive announcing a new corporate policy imparts hundreds of times more information than an audiotape of that same message, which, in turn, contains hundreds of times more information than a printed text of the same message.

In the 1990s, internal video, like desktop publishing, appears ready to take off.

- Burger King in Miami produces video in an in-house studio and sound stage to train workers in its 5,000 restaurants. All Burger King restaurants have playback equipment. Key messages and philosophies are distributed to run for 20 minutes or less.
- Miller Brewing Company produces a 20-minute video magazine, distributed every three months to all company locations. It features new company commercials, brand promotions, happenings at Miller plants, and employee human interest stories. Miller's reasoning is that its top executives can talk more easily on a five-minute video than in person to its far-flung locations.[10]
- The Ford Motor Company has taken the unprecedented step of stopping work on assembly lines to show videotapes to workers. In one celebrated incident, Ford showed a quality-improvement videotape at 35 plants employing 100,000 workers. By doing so, Ford underscored the importance of the message conveyed in its tapes, as well as the new prominence of internal video.[11]
- Wal-Mart stores began in the late 1980s to turn founder Sam Walton's store visits into simultaneous video meetings with thousands of stores. Using the technology of very small aperture terminals (VSATs), Wal-Mart remains a frequent user of business television.[12]

Notwithstanding its power, internal video is a medium that must be approached with caution. Specifically, a public relations professional must raise at least a dozen questions before embarking on an internal video excursion:

1. Why are we doing this video?
2. Whom are we trying to reach with this video?
3. What's the point of the video?
4. What do we want viewers to do after seeing the video?

5. How good is our video script?
6. How sophisticated is the quality of our broadcast?
7. How innovative and creative is the broadcast? Does it measure up to regular television?
8. How competent is our talent?
9. How proficient is our crew?
10. Where will our viewers screen the video?
11. With what communications vehicles will we supplement the video?
12. How much money can we spend?[13]

The keys to any internal video production are, first, to examine internal needs; then to plan thoughtfully before using the medium; and, finally, to reach target publics through the highest-quality programming possible. Broadcast quality is a tough standard to meet. If an organization can't afford high-quality video, it shouldn't get involved.

SUPERVISORY COMMUNICATIONS

First and foremost, employees want information from their supervisors. Supervisors, in fact, are the preferred source for 90 percent of employees, making them the top choice by far. In 1980, about two-thirds of employees surveyed said that their supervisors discussed job performance at least once a year. Today that proportion has jumped to almost 90 percent.[14]

That's the good news.

The bad news is that while 55 percent of employees in 1980 said their supervisor was a good source of information, that percentage hasn't changed in more than a decade. While employees today are somewhat more likely to think that their supervisors are being kept informed by higher management, they are not reaping the benefits any more than they did in the 1980s. Thus, while most employees vastly prefer information from their supervisor over what they learn through rumors, many still rely on the grapevine as a primary source of information.

What can public relations departments do to combat this trend?

Some departments formalize the meeting process by mixing management and staff in a variety of formats, from gripe sessions to marketing/planning meetings. Many organizations embrace the concept of skip-level meetings, in which top-level managers meet periodically with employees at levels several notches below them in the organizational hierarchy. As with any other form of communication, the value of meetings lies in their substance, their regularity, and the candor managers bring to face-to-face sessions.

DEALING WITH THE GRAPEVINE

In many organizations, the company grapevine is one of the most powerful means of communications. But the rumor mill can be devastating. As one employee publication described the grapevine:

> It's faster than a public address announcement and more powerful than a general instruction. It's able to leap from L.A. to San Francisco in a single bound. And its credibility is almost beyond Walter Cronkite's.

Rumors, once they pick up steam, are difficult to stop. Consequently, an organization must work to correct rumors as soon as possible because employees tend to distort future events to conform to a rumor.

Identifying the source of a rumor is often difficult, if not impossible—and it's usually not worth the time. However, dispelling the rumor quickly and frankly is another story. Often a bad-news rumor—about layoffs, closings, and so on—can be dealt with most effectively through forthright communication. Generally, an organization makes a difficult decision after a thorough review of many alternatives. The final decision is often a compromise, reflecting the needs of the firm and its various publics, including, importantly, the work force. However, in presenting a final decision to employees, management often overlooks the value of explaining how it reached its decision. By comparing alternative solutions so that employees can understand more clearly the rationale behind management decisions, an organization may make bad news more palatable.

As demonic as the grapevine can become, it shouldn't necessarily be treated as the enemy in effective communications with employees. A company grapevine can be as much a communications vehicle as internal publications or employee meetings. It may even be more valuable because it is believed, and everyone seems to tap into it.

UMMARY

The best defense against damaging grapevine rumors is a strong and candid communications system. Employee communications may be the most neglected strategic opportunity in corporate America. Organizations build massive marketing plans to sell products but often fail to apply that same knowledge and energy to communicating with their own employees.

In the 1990s, organizations have no choice but to build rapport with and morale among employees. Public relations professionals must seize this initiative to foster the open climate that employees want and the two-way communications that organizations need. If public relations people don't rise to this challenge, the employee communications function is likely to fall to the management of human resources professionals.

It is up to public relations professionals to suggest appropriate vehicles, tone, and content to ensure meaningful and effective communication with employees.

DISCUSSION STARTERS

1. According to recent research, are employees satisfied with the level and content of the communications they receive from management?
2. What one element is the key to organizational communication?
3. What characteristics constitute the best employee communicators in the 1990s?
4. What method of employee communications is making a comeback in many organizations?
5. What are the primary tasks of an employee newsletter's editor?
6. What are the typical features of an employee annual report?
7. What questions should be raised before communicating through internal video?
8. What is the preferred channel of communications among most employees?
9. What is the best way to combat the grapevine?
10. What function has challenged public relations in the management of employee communications?

NOTES

1. G. Bruce Knecht and Suzanne Alexander Ryan, "Fleet Financial's Plan to Reduce Its Payroll Involved Long Process," *The Wall Street Journal* (March 10, 1994): A1, A8.
2. Julie Foehrenbach and Steve Goldfarb, "Employee Communications in the 90s: Greater Expectations," *IABC Communication World* (May–June 1990): 101.
3. "An Employee's-Eye View of Business," *Ragan Report* (November 25, 1991): 1, 2.
4. Ibid.
5. "On Communicating with the 'Free Agent Employee,'" *Ragan Report* (January 10, 1994): 3.
6. "Focus' Strives for Credibility Through Candor," *Ragan Report* (October 1, 1990): 3.
7. Fraser P. Seitel, "Leaping the 'Trust Gap,'" *United States Banker* (November 1990): 61.
8. "The Winner and Champeen Is: Print," *Ragan Report* (January 16, 1989): 1.
9. For further information about the International Association of Business Communicators, write to IABC, One Hallidie Plaza, Suite 600, San Francisco, CA 94102.
10. "Trends in Non-Print Employee Communications," *Ragan Report* (May 8, 1989): 3.
11. John Holusha, "Live, from Detroit, the Big Three on TV," *The New York Times* (November 14, 1988): D3.
12. Chuck Wheat, "Video Demand or Supply: Which Came First, the Chicken or the Egg?" *IABC Communication World* (March 1994): 31.
13. Fraser P. Seitel, "In-House Video: Think Before You Tape," *United States Banker* (December 1989): 60–61.
14. Foehrenbach and Goldfarb, op. cit., 104.

TOP OF THE SHELF

Alvie L. Smith, *Innovative Employee Communication.* Englewood Cliffs, NJ: Prentice-Hall, 1991.

Alvie Smith says an informed employee is a more productive and satisfied employee. This belief is the heart of *Innovative Employee Communication,* Smith's complete guide to internal communications.

A former director of corporate communications for General Motors, Alvie Smith provides the essentials for planning, organizing, and conducting employee communications programs that help generate enthusiasm, commitment, teamwork, and better performance. He counsels communicators to use a variety of media—publications, video, face-to-face meetings—to provide workers with meaningful information consistent with management's objectives. Smith also promotes research, which he says should be used not only to help plot future communications programs but also to gauge the success of current ones. He accentuates his instruction with meaty case studies featuring corporate titans like AT&T, General Electric, and Union Carbide.

Smith says that "winning back the loyalty and commitment of employees" will be the paramount challenge facing communicators in the 1990s. If that's true, then reading *Innovative Employee Communication* is the first step toward victory.

SUGGESTED READINGS

Anderson, Walter. *Handbook of Business Communications.* (Available from P.O. Box 243, Lenox Hill Station, New York, NY 10021.)

Corbett, William. "The Bottom Line in Internal Communications: The Human Factor." *Tips & Tactics* (May 30, 1988). (Supplement to *PR Reporter.*) The writer stresses how important informed, motivated staffers are to their firms. He goes on to describe various channels of company communications.

Hartley, Jean F., and Geoffrey M. Stephenson. *Employment Relations: The Psychology of Influence and Control at Work.* Colchester, VT: Blackwell Business, 1992.

How to Prepare and Write Your Employee Handbook, 2nd ed. New York: AMACOM, 1988.

Marchington, Mick. *Managing the Team: A Guide to Successful Employee Involvement.* Colchester, VT: Blackwell Business, 1992.

Case Study

HILL & KNOWLTON'S EMPLOYEE RELATIONS SNAFU

As the nation's largest public relations counseling firm, Hill & Knowlton is used to helping its customers deal with crises. But in the spring of 1990, H&K created a knotty public relations problem for itself, particularly with its own employees, by agreeing to promote the antiabortion views of the Bishop's Pro-Life Committee of the U.S. Catholic Conference. The new account, which reportedly would generate $5 million over five years, drew intense criticism both within and outside the firm.

The issue actually began in 1989, when the Supreme Court agreed to address once again the issue of legalized abortion, originally addressed in the landmark case *Roe v. Wade.* The National Conference of Catholic Bishops and the U.S. Catholic Conference decided at a conference in Washington, D.C. that "the rights of the unborn child is the fundamental human rights issue of our time." They decided that they had lost ground to pro-choice advocates and needed to reframe the debate, hence the decision to hire a public relations firm to help them.

In early 1990, the bishops reportedly approached Burson-Marsteller, the second largest public relations firm, and were turned down. Then they turned to H&K.

H&K's president, Bob Dilenschneider, didn't hesitate. "Ever since John W. Hill founded the firm, Hill & Knowlton has recognized that every legitimate organization or cause has the constitutional right to self-expression," Dilenschneider said. "When considering an offer from the Catholic bishops, we were clearly aware that our acceptance would subject us to criticism and possible vilification."

Including, most stingingly, from the H&K staff.

An estimated 65 percent of H&K employees were women. When word of the new account spread, more than a third of the headquarters staff signed a petition of protest. Dozens of employees in Washington and New York refused to work on the project. Many were outraged, especially at the way management made known its acceptance of the account.

Indeed, the first many staffers knew about it was when syndicated columnists Rowland Evans and Robert Novak reported that H&K had been retained by the U.S. Catholic Conference to represent the group in its fight against abortion rights. Said one H&K executive, "Everyone was wandering around in a daze, asking, 'Do you know anything about this? What is going on here?'" Incredibly, H&K had been blindsided by the press—the very consequence it makes a living counseling others to avoid.

Ultimately, a memo, citing the First Amendment right of free speech, was sent to employees. The memo noted that anyone who didn't want to work on the account would not be compelled to do so. But because the memo was given to department heads, with no explicit instructions to circulate it, most employees reportedly never saw it. Those who did took the memo for what it seemed to be: a news release rather than a sincere attempt at personal communication.

Some employees felt betrayed. Said one, "I don't want to know that the person I work with 10 hours a day doesn't believe a woman has a right to do what she wants with her body."

Eventually, a month after the Evans and Novak column, a meeting was called in the New York office and an attempt made to put the controversy to rest.

Said Dilenschneider, "An important part of our business is helping clients deal with controversial issues. In this sense, we are advocates. But whenever a cause we agree to represent goes against the grain of an employee or employees, they are automatically exempted from working on it. We have had people, for instance, who refused to work on cigarette accounts and alcoholic beverages. We have always respected their scruples. We always will."

Nonetheless, according to reports, H&K women staffers remained "apoplectic" about the firm's new client. Reports circulated about "regular meetings in the ladies' room." Some suspected that the source of negative media accounts about the bishops' account was H&K employees themselves.

Many in the field rose to H&K's defense. Said one public relations scholar, "H&K's representation of pro-life does not automatically mean that all H&K employees support this position. A PR firm that takes a controversial account is showing that it believes the account has the right to be heard in a meaningful way. The true PR professional at H&K, for instance, could disagree with the pro-life position but still feel pro-life is entitled to a full and fair public hearing. If the PR person does not believe that all legitimate positions are entitled to such a hearing, he or she should get out of the practice."

The real problem for many H&K staffers seemed to lie in the belief that the firm was implicitly attempting to change the law on abortion. Said one 23-year H&K veteran about her company's participation in the issue, "It will ultimately lead to legislation that will interfere with a woman's right to choose what she does with her body . . . legislation that will be, in effect, a form of coercion. And I don't think Hill & Knowlton should be in the business of coercion."

Throughout his most grueling employee communications crisis, Dilenschneider stood his ground. "Our agreement with the Catholic Conference specifies that we will not engage in lobbying. But as an agency that helps the Church voice and project its opinion on the subject, we are doing work that is unquestionably legitimate and, in fact, that millions of Americans agree with.

"To those who criticize us for accepting this assignment, there is no other answer."

QUESTIONS

1. When should H&K have informed employees about the bishops' account?
2. What do you think of the memorandum H&K sent to employees about the account? How might the memo have been refined?
3. What would you have advised H&K management upon receiving the petition of protest from employees?
4. Should H&K have accepted the U.S. Catholic Conference account?

For further information, see James N. Baker with Eleanor Clift, "The Bishops Under Fire," *Newsweek* (April 23, 1990): 24; Jeffrey Goodell, "What Hill & Knowlton Can Do for You," *The New York Times Magazine* (September 9, 1990): 44, 74–75, 102–104; Kevin McCauley, "H&K Keeps Pro-Life Account Despite Heavy Opposition," *O'Dwyer's PR Services Report* (June 1990): 1, 8, 31–35; Barbara W. Selvin, "Abortion Battle at Hill & Knowlton, *Newsday* (April 5, 1990): 51, 54; Peter M. Stevenson, "Hill & Knowlton's Big PR Problem," *Manhattan, Inc.* (July 1990): 61–68; and Harold W. Suckenik, "H&K's Pro-Life Account Is Example of Professionalism," *O'Dwyer's Services Report* (July 1990): 43.

TIPS FROM THE TOP

ROBERT S. COLE

Robert S. Cole is vice president and manager of external relations for Canadian Imperial Bank of Commerce in the United States. A former reporter for the *New York Daily News,* he teaches public relations at St. John's University in New York City and marketing at Pace University in Pleasantville, New York, and is the author of *The Practical Handbook of Public Relations.* Mr. Cole also serves as a director of the New York chapter of the Public Relations Society of America.

What are the fundamental principles in dealing with employees?
Management must be honest with employees, maintain a two-way flow of communications, and be willing to share bad as well as good news. Most of all, management has to demonstrate through verbal, print, and electronic communications that it genuinely cares about getting information to and from its staff.

How can employee communications influence morale?
Very simply, informed workers are better workers—hence, happier and more productive. They know how their work fits into the overall operations of an organization, and they are better able to shape career goals. A well-managed internal communications program can convince employees that they'll be told what they need to know to maximize their value to the organization and that they are welcome to contribute ideas and opinions.

Should certain information (e.g., layoffs, losses, lawsuits, etc.) be kept from employees?
Never and yes. Never on layoffs, losses, lawsuits, or the like because these are important stories that must be shared with employees, who have a right and a

need to know about them. Moreover, these stories will be covered in the media and through the grapevine anyway. If employees, on learning of such incidents, don't believe they'll get the real facts through internal communications, the company has a credibility problem—probably a morale problem, too. Yes, however, on the small number of details that violate employee or customer confidentiality. But employees should then be told why they can't have all the facts.

What are the most effective ways to communicate to employees?
It's hard to generalize. Some people prefer to get their information in print; others like video; others remember it better if they are told verbally by their boss or their boss's boss. Honesty, timeliness, thoroughness, and a willingness to receive as well as dispense information have to be parts of the process, regardless of how the message is conveyed. Also, a certain degree of targeting is in order. We can't expect one internal vehicle to meet the needs of all employee groups. While the overall messages remain constant, there *is* merit in the "different strokes for different folks" adage.

Is the employee newsletter an outmoded concept?
I hope not. Some of the nicer people I know are newsletter editors. More important, people are used to (and receptive to) receiving information in printed form at regular intervals. Additionally, the permanence of words on paper provides a valuable historic perspective. The concept of a newsletter serving as the beginning and end of employee communications is outdated. There are too many other written, electronic, and verbal vehicles at our disposal. And speaking of "electronic," it would be wise for *all* internal communicators to learn and master desktop publishing. Additionally, they should prepare themselves for video house organs—a medium that didn't live up to its early 1970s promise but one that seems ready to advance in the '90s.

What are the characteristics that distinguish good employee communicators from mediocre ones?
The ability to (1) educate in an entertaining manner; (2) show how jobs and processes fit into the overall operation; (3) explain how what happens outside the organization can affect the bottom line; (4) find interesting, work-related ways to get the clerical staff (as opposed to officers only) into company publications; (5) generate ideas and feedback from employees so that the internal communications process is a two-way street; and (6) convince employees that management considers them at least as important as shareholders, customers, and other publics. Finally, smart employee communicators recognize that employees and their families are potential goodwill ambassadors.

How important is top management involvement in employee communications?
Very. Top management must recognize (via budget and staff allocations) the importance of employee communications. They must also participate in the process as spokespeople and listeners, and they must encourage middle management to do the same.

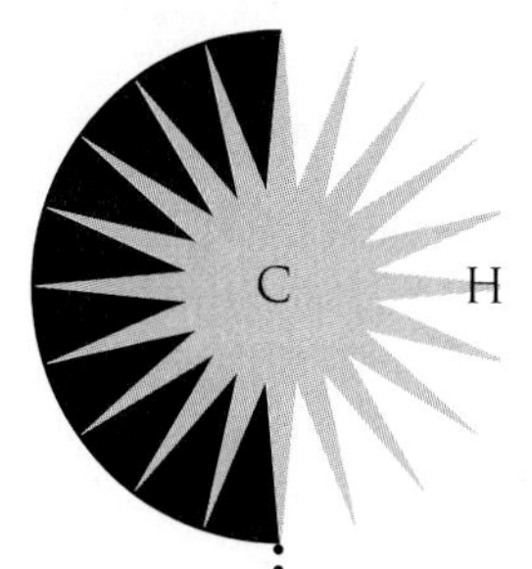

CHAPTER 14

MULTICULTURAL COMMUNITIES

AMERICA HAS ALWAYS BEEN A MELTING POT, ATTRACTING freedom-seeking immigrants from countries throughout the world. Never has this been more true than today, as America's face continues to change. Consider the following:

- In 1990, the U.S. population was 76 percent Anglo, 12 percent African-American, 9 percent Latino, and 3 percent Asian. By the year 2050, the breakdown is projected to be 52 percent Anglo, 16 percent African-American, 22 percent Latino, and 10 percent Asian. Today ethnic minorities spend $600 billion a year out of a total U.S. consumer economy of $4.4 trillion. This amount is certain to increase substantially.[1]
- In 1940, 70 percent of U.S. immigrants came from Europe. In 1992, 15 percent of immigrants came from Europe, 37 percent from Asia, and 44 percent from Latin America and the Caribbean.

- In 1976, there were 67 Spanish-language radio stations in the United States. Today there are 311, plus 3 Spanish-language TV networks and 350 Spanish-language newspapers.
- In New York City alone, 12 percent of the population under 18 is foreign-born, and that percentage continues to increase.

Such is the multicultural diversity enjoyed today by America and the world. The implications for organizations are profound. Almost two-thirds of the new entrants into the work force between now and the year 2000 will be women. People of color will make up 29 percent of these new entrants over the same period. For the first time since World War I, immigrants will represent the largest share of the increase in the population and the work force.[2]

In light of the increasing diversity of U.S. society, profit-making and nonprofit organizations alike must themselves become more diverse and learn to deal and communicate with those who differ in work background, education, age, gender, race, ethnic origin, physical abilities, religious beliefs, sexual orientation, and other perceived differences.

Those organizations that waver in responding to the new multicultural communities do so at their own peril. To wit:

- Denny's restaurant chain agreed to pay more than $54 million in 1994 to settle lawsuits filed by thousands of black customers who had been refused service, forced to wait longer, or pay more than white customers. This marked the largest settlement in history under federal laws to end segregation in restaurants and other places that serve the public.
- The chief of the Los Angeles Police Department was forced to step down and police officers were jailed after an African-American motorist, Rodney King, was beaten after a high-speed chase in 1992. The King beating triggered a massive riot and focused attention on the department's problems in dealing with minorities (Figure 14–1).
- AT&T, a company traditionally sensitive to multicultural issues, was threatened with a boycott by African-American activists late in 1993 after an in-house magazine published a racially offensive cartoon. (See the case study at the end of this chapter.)

As the arbiters of communications in their organizations, public relations people must be sensitive to society's new multicultural realities. Dealing in an enlightened manner with multicultural diversity and being sensitive to nuances in language and differences in style is a logical extension of the concept of social responsibility that has been an accepted part of American organizational life since the 1960s.

SOCIAL RESPONSIBILITY IN THE COMMUNITY

More and more, companies and other organizations acknowledge their responsibilities to the community: helping to maintain clean air and water, providing jobs for minorities, and, in general, enhancing everyone's quality of life. This concept of social responsibility has become widely accepted among enlightened organizations. For example, most companies today donate a percentage of their profits to nonprofit organizations—schools, hospitals, social welfare institutions, and the like. Employee volunteer pro-

THE RIOTS OF '92

CRISIS BRINGS OUT EDISON'S BEST

When civil disturbances erupted in the south-central metropolitan area last Wednesday evening, April 29, no one could guess the material and emotional devastation that would result.

Throughout the next two long, fiery days and an uneasy weekend, Edison employees responded with courage, dedication and a sense of community.

This special issue of SCE NEWS is a salute to Edison's 18,000 employees who worked together to handle problems as they arose and who are continuing to work to heal the wounds and build a community of pride.

Stories on last week's civil disturbances were researched and written by Lynda Baker, Charles Beal, Sandy Doubleday and Ken Perry. Photos are by Mitch Kaufman and Greg O'Loughlin.

EDISON LOSSES TOTAL $150,000

Damage to Edison facilities from civil unrest after the Rodney King trial totaled $150,000. No Edison employees were injured.

At press time, most of the damage had occurred in the Southern Region, Edison officials said, with nine circuit interruptions affecting 10,500 customers. Eight of the circuits were in the Compton district.

Disturbances delayed repairs, with some outages lasting up to 35 hours. Multiple local outages affecting service to 1,500 customers were the result of secondary conductors destroyed by structure fires. Eight poles, three transformers and 130 services were removed in the Region.

Often escorted by police, Southern Region crews conducted repairs during daylight hours over the weekend. A regional command center was established at the Compton Service Center to coordinate repairs. In Long Beach, an unused Edison building was damaged by fire.

In other regions, the Perris Service Center reopened Monday after being vacated the previous Thursday. Normal field activities in remaining regions resumed and all local offices were open Monday morning.

ON OUR COVER

Edison crews braved fires and looters to restore power to affected areas.

Above, smoke from unused Edison building blackens Long Beach sky Friday. Left, the fire left only a shell of the building.

Figure 14–1 Los Angeles was sorely tested in the spring of 1992, when the Rodney King beating led to riots. Southern California Edison published a special issue of its *SCE News* to report on the company's response to the disturbances and to salute employees who worked through the crisis. The issue was called "Time to Heal." (*Courtesy of Southern California Edison*)

grams to assist local charitable groups are also common. In the 1990s, social responsibility is no longer the exception but the rule among organizations.

This enlightened self-interest among executives has taken time to develop. The social and political upheavals of the 1960s forced organizations to confront the real or perceived injustices inflicted on certain social groups. The 1970s brought a partial resolution of those problems as government and the courts moved together to compensate for past inequities, outlaw current abuses, and prevent future injustice.

In the 1980s, the conflict between organizations and society became one of setting priorities—of deciding which community group deserved to be the beneficiary of corporate involvement. Today most organizations accept their role as an agent for social change in the community. For an organization to coexist peacefully in its community in the 1990s requires three skills in particular: (1) determining what the community knows and thinks about the organization, (2) informing the community of the organization's point of view, and (3) negotiating or mediating between the organization and the community and its constituents, should there be a significant discrepancy.

Basically, every organization wants to foster positive reactions in its community. This becomes increasingly difficult in the face of protests from and disagreements with community activists. Community relations, therefore—to analyze the community, help understand its makeup and expectations, and communicate the organization's story in an understandable and uninterrupted way—is critical in the 1990s.

COMMUNITY RELATIONS EXPECTATIONS

The community of an organization can vary widely, depending on the size and nature of the business. The mom-and-pop grocery store may have a community of only a few city blocks; the community of a Buick assembly plant may be the city where the plant is located; and the community of a multinational corporation may embrace much of the world.

WHAT THE COMMUNITY EXPECTS

Communities expect from resident organizations such tangible commodities as wages, employment, and taxes. But communities have come to expect intangible contributions, too.

- **Appearance** The community hopes that the firm will contribute positively to life in the area. It expects facilities to be attractive, with care spent on the grounds and the plant. Increasingly, community neighbors object to plants that belch smoke and pollute water and air. Occasionally, neighbors organize to oppose the entrance of factories, coal mines, oil wells, drug treatment centers, and other facilities suspected of being harmful to the community's environment. Government, too, is acting more vigorously to punish offenders and to make sure that organizations comply with zoning, environmental, and safety regulations.
- **Participation** As a citizen of the community, an organization is expected to participate responsibly in community affairs, such as civic functions, park and recreational activities, education, welfare, and support of religious institutions. Organizations generally cannot shirk such participation by blaming headquarters' policy.
- **Stability** A business that fluctuates sharply in volume of business, number of employees, and taxes paid can adversely affect the community through its impact on municipal services, school loads, public facilities, and tax revenues. Communities prefer stable organizations that will grow with the area. Conversely, they want to keep out short-term operations that could create temporary boom conditions and leave ghost towns in their wake.
- **Pride** Any organization that can help put the community on the map simply by being there is usually a valuable addition. Communities want firms that are proud to be residents. For instance, to most Americans, Battle Creek, Michigan, means cereal; Hershey, Pennsylvania, means chocolate; and Armonk, New York, means IBM. Organizations that help make the town usually become symbols of pride.

WHAT THE ORGANIZATION EXPECTS

Organizations expect to be provided with adequate municipal services, fair taxation, good living conditions for employees, a good labor supply, and a reasonable degree of support for the business and its products. When some of these requirements are missing, organizations may move to communities where such benefits are more readily available.

New York City, for example, experienced a substantial exodus of corporations during the 1970s, when firms fled to neighboring Connecticut and New Jersey, as well as to the Sun Belt states of the Southeast and Southwest. These became commercial centers because of tax moratoriums, lower labor costs, and business incentives. New York's state and city legislators responded to the challenge by working more closely with business residents on such issues as corporate taxation. By the 1990s, not only had the corporate flight to the Sun Belt been arrested, but some firms decided that they agreed with the "I Love New York" ad campaign and returned to the state.

The issue for most urban areas faced with steadily eroding tax bases is to find a formula that meets the concerns of business corporations while accommodating the needs of other members of the community.

COMMUNITY RELATIONS OBJECTIVES

Research into community relations indicates that winning community support for an organization is no easy task. One study suggested that the goal of compatibility between organization and community "is quite unrealistic in many situations." Researchers found that conflict often exists between a community and an agency or corporation that is controlled elsewhere.[3] Additional community relations research has shown that a high level of public communication does not always lead to increased support for a newly introduced community relations program.

Such studies indicate something of the difficulty in achieving rapport with community neighbors. One device that is helpful is a written community relations policy. A community relations policy must clearly define the philosophy of management as it views its obligation to the community. Employees, in particular, must understand and exemplify their firm's community relations policy; to many in the community, the workers *are* the company.

Typical community relations objectives may include the following:

1. To tell the community about the operations of the firm: its products, number of employees, size of the payroll, tax payments, employee benefits, growth, and support of community projects.
2. To correct misunderstandings, reply to criticism, and remove any disaffection that may exist among community neighbors.
3. To gain the favorable opinion of the community, particularly during strikes and periods of labor unrest, by stating the company's position on the issues involved.
4. To inform employees and their families about company activities and developments, so that they can tell their friends and neighbors about the company and favorably influence opinions of the organization.
5. To inform people in local government about the firm's contributions to community welfare and to obtain support for legislation that will favorably affect the business climate of the community.
6. To find out what residents think about the company, why they like or dislike its policies and practices, and how much they know of its policy, operations, and problems.
7. To establish a personal relationship between management and community leaders by inviting leaders to visit the plant and offices, meet management, and see employees at work.

8. To support health programs through contributions of both funds and employee services to local campaigns.
9. To contribute to culture by providing funds for art exhibits, concerts, and drama festivals and by promoting attendance at such affairs.
10. To aid youth and adult education by cooperating with administrators and teachers in providing student vocational guidance, plant tours, speakers, films, and teaching aids and by giving financial support to higher education (Figure 14–2).
11. To encourage sports and recreational activities by providing athletic fields, swimming pools, golf courses, and/or tennis courts for use by community residents and by sponsoring teams and sports events.

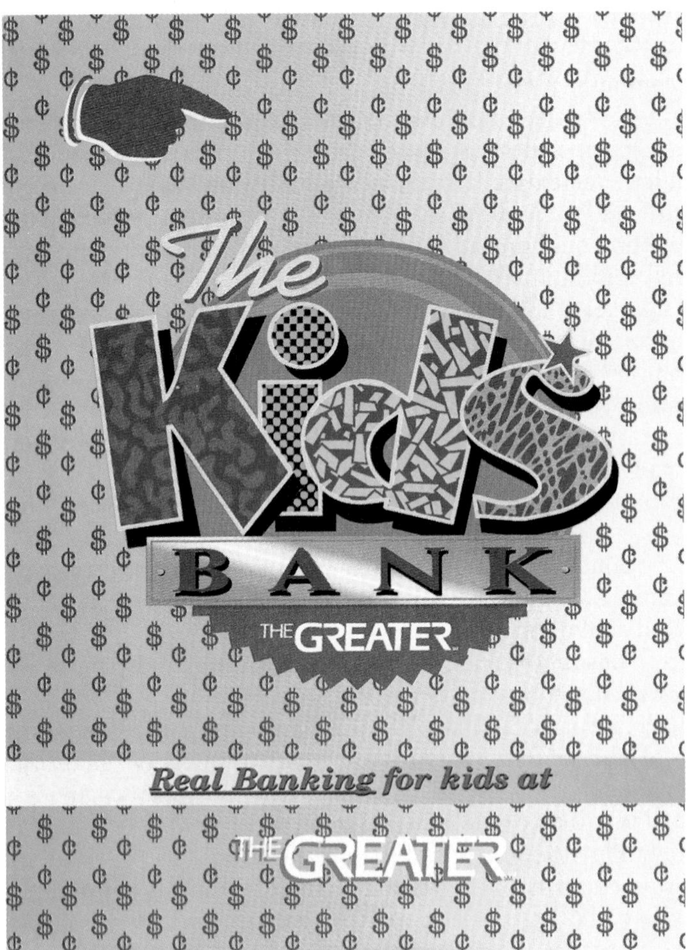

Figure 14–2 The Greater New York Savings Bank, a Brooklyn-based institution with strong roots in the community, began its Kid's Bank in 1994 to attract no-fee deposits from fourth graders. Within three months, the bank had 1,600 new customers depositing in excess of $200,000. Not bad for 10-year olds! (*Courtesy of The Greater New York Savings Bank*)

12. To promote better local and county government by encouraging employees to run for public office or volunteer to serve on administrative boards; lending company executives to community agencies or to local government to give specialized advice and assistance on municipal problems; and making company facilities and equipment available to the community in times of emergency.
13. To assist the economy of the community by purchasing operating supplies and equipment from local merchants and manufacturers whenever possible.
14. To operate a profitable business to provide jobs and to pay competitive wages that increase the community's purchasing power and strengthen its economy.
15. To cooperate with other local businesses in advancing economic and social welfare through joint community relations programs financed and directed by the participating organizations.

ERVING MULTICULTURAL COMMUNITIES

What were once referred to as minorities are rapidly becoming the majority today.

A revision of the U.S. Census Bureau's long-term population projections, announced at the end of 1992, estimated that by the year 2050 Asians, Latinos, and African-Americans will represent as much as 47 percent of the total population of the United States compared to less than 25 percent today.

Latinos will overtake African-Americans as the largest minority group early in the next century, according to the Census Bureau, but the fastest-growing segment of that population will be Asians and Pacific Islanders, whose numbers will increase fivefold.[4]

For many years, women were considered a minority by public relations professionals. This is no longer the case; women now dominate not only the public relations field but also many service industries. Women, African-Americans, Latinos, Asians, gays, and a variety of other groups have become not only important members of the labor force but also important sources of discretionary income. Public relations professionals must be sensitive to the demands of all for equal pay, promotional opportunities, equal rights in the workplace, and so on.

Communicating effectively in light of the multicultural diversity of society has become an important public relations challenge.

WOMEN

Amid all the breakthroughs and backlashes, "Mommy tracks" and "Mommy wars," glass ceilings and pink-collar ghettos, the fact remains that women were big economic winners in the 1980s. And their gains are likely to keep coming in the 1990s.[5] While the median annual salary for men slid 8 percent after inflation between 1979 and 1990—to $28,843 from $31,315—the comparable salary for women rose 10 percent to $20,656 from $18,683.

So, while it's still true that women, by and large, earn less than men, the gap has narrowed dramatically: For each dollar of men's earnings, women's earnings rose to a record 72 cents in 1990.

Things look even better for young women aged 24 to 35. They now earn 80 cents for every dollar earned by men of the same age, up from 69 cents in 1980.

In public relations, where women clearly rank as a majority, the glass ceiling is still a significant hurdle. While many more women have graduated into middle-management public relations positions, relatively few are yet included in department or agency top management.[6] Nonetheless, with increasing numbers of women entering the public relations field and others slowly but surely graduating into the higher reaches of government, as well as profit-making and nonprofit organizations, it is only a matter of time before women assume their rightful place in the executive leadership of the public relations profession.

AFRICAN-AMERICANS

Today, 25 of the nation's largest cities—including Chicago, Detroit, and Los Angeles—have a majority population of African-Americans, Latinos and Asians. The socioeconomic status of African-Americans also has improved markedly over the past decade. African-Americans have increased their disposable income fivefold over the past decade.[7] Indeed, as one publication put it:

> A new breed of Black American has emerged who is impacting upon decisions and implementing policies at every level of American life. They are more willing to contribute economically to our future in America, more apt to reject the status quo, more assertive and aggressive, ready to seize every opportunity available and willing to create opportunities where none exist.[8]

Despite their continuing evolution in the white-dominated workplace, African-Americans can still be reached effectively through special media. Magazines such as *Ebony, Jet, Black Enterprise,* and *Essence* are natural vehicles. *Ebony,* the largest African-American-oriented publication in the world, has a circulation of 1.3 million. Newspapers such as the *Amsterdam News* in New York City and the *Daily Defender* in Chicago also are targeted to African-Americans. Such newspapers are controlled by active owners whose personal viewpoints dominate editorial policy. All should be included in the normal media relations functions of any organization.

Companies in recent years have made a concerted push to reach African-Americans. Occasionally, these attempts have been controversial. In 1990, for example, R. J. Reynolds Tobacco Company announced a promotional campaign to target its "Uptown" cigarette toward African-Americans. Reminiscent of the protests against Aunt Jemima in an earlier era, African-Americans outspokenly opposed the campaign. Reynolds was forced to drop its product after spending $10 million to develop it.[9] African-American leaders, including U.S. Secretary of Health and Human Services Louis Sullivan, condemned the proliferation of advertisements for cigarettes and alcohol in African-American neighborhoods. Other leaders, like civil rights activist Benjamin Hooks, condemned the condemnation as a form of paternalism. "Buried in this line of thinking," he said, "is the rationale that Blacks are not capable of making their own free choices."[10] At the root of Hooks' comments was the realization that tobacco companies donated huge sums to support African-American causes, ranging from jazz festivals to the United Negro College Fund.

The practice of public relations also has come in for criticism with respect to African-American practitioners. In recent years, the field has been frustrated in its efforts to recruit African-Americans. Surveys indicate that minorities represent a little more than 7 percent of all practitioners, with African-Americans reflecting just a small fraction of that percentage.[11] Public relations leaders agree that minority professionals

Mucho
depende
de usted.
THE
UNITED
WAY

Figure 14–3 Latinos have become an increasingly important constituent public, not only as consumers of goods but also as donors of funds. As this United Way ad suggests, "much depends" on the Latino community. (*Courtesy of United Way*)

are not adequately represented in the public relations industry, and that one challenge that confronts the industry is to recruit more minorities, especially African-Americans.

LATINOS

Latinos, like African-Americans, make up a growing proportion of the labor and consumer markets in major American cities. There are 20 million Latinos in the United States, with a median family income of more than $16,000. More than 70 percent of all U.S. Latinos reside in California, Texas, New York, and Florida. The majority of U.S. Latinos—62 percent—are of Mexican origin. About 13 percent are of Puerto Rican origin, and 5 percent are of Cuban origin. In Los Angeles, Latino kindergarten enrollment is 66 percent and rising. The Anglo enrollment is 15 percent and falling.

Because 75 percent of Latinos communicate primarily in Spanish, smart organizations can readily identify and target this public—and increase their retail sales—simply by communicating in the Spanish language (Figure 14–3). In an attempt to reach Latinos, advertisers spent $550 million in 1988, with the overwhelming percentage going to television.[12] In addition, radio stations and newspapers that communicate in Spanish, such as New York City's *El Diario* and *La Prensa,* are prominent voices in reaching this increasingly important community.

Beyond Latinos, other ethnic groups—particularly Asians—have increased their importance in the American marketplace. Japanese, Chinese, Koreans, Vietnamese, and others have gained new prominence as consumers and constituents. In California, the 1992 formation of the Asian American Advertising and Public Relations Alliance underscored the increasing prominence of Asian Americans in the public relations profession.

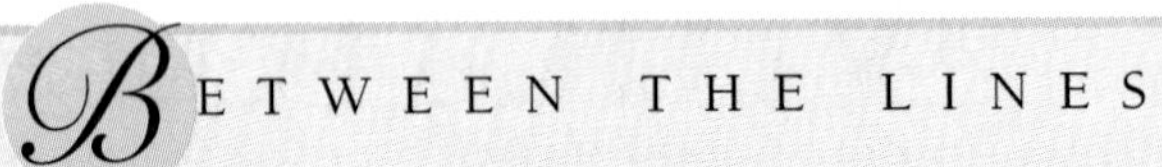

"LATINO," NOT "HISPANIC"

One problem in dealing with society's new multicultural diversity is mastering the lingo. Specifically, the preferred identity of a particular minority is often unclear.

The following is excerpted from a 1993 memo from the Mexican Empowerment Committee:

> *TO: News Media, Government, Business, and "Hispanic Organizations"*
>
> This is to notify you that the term "Hispanic" is unacceptable when referring to the 18-million-plus Mexican and Mexican-American population in the United States. Hispanic refers to the people, language, and culture of Spain.
>
> It is insulting to include us, Mexicans and Mexican-Americans, when you use this term that denies us our native Mexican (non-European) roots. We are over 92% of the so-called Hispanics in the Southwest and over 70% in the U.S.
>
> We, the activists and proud Mexican and Mexican-Americans, are launching a campaign to defend our identity, culture, history and honor.
>
> When referring to the general Spanish-speaking population and those of Mexican descent, who are over 90% of the so-called "Hispanics" in California, please use the following terms: "Mexican/Latino population"; "Mexicans and other Latinos of California"; "Mexican and Latino population of the U.S."; or "Latino" if you must.
>
> But please—NEVER HISPANIC!

GAYS, SENIORS, AND OTHERS

The 1990s have introduced a diverse assortment of special communities into the mainstream of American commerce.

One such group is the gay market (Figure 14–4). While "homosexuality may remain a legitimate target of political opprobrium" for many, it also has become big business.[13] The gay market—20 million people, average age 36, household income six times higher than the national average, three times more likely to be college graduates than the national average, with more discretionary income than the average, 86 percent

Mr. President...

"I believe patriotic Americans should have the right to serve the country as a member of the armed forces, without regard to sexual or affectional orientation."

February, 1992

"I want to make this very clear. This is a very narrow issue. It is whether a person, in the absence of any other disqualifying conduct, can simply say that he or she is homosexual and stay in the military."

January, 1993

Your words. Our lives.

Human Rights
CAMPAIGN FUND
Tim McFeeley, Executive Director
P.O. Box 1396, Washington, DC 20077

Figure 14–4 When President Bill Clinton wavered on his campaign pledge in 1993 to allow acknowledged homosexuals to remain in the armed forces, he attracted an outpouring of outrage from a well-organized gay community. (*Courtesy of the Human Rights Campaign Fund*)

of whom say they would purchase products specifically marketed to them—has become extremely attractive to all kinds of marketers.

- In 1994, the First National Gay and Lesbian Business Expo in New Jersey drew companies from Perrier to Xerox to AT&T.
- In 1994, Wainwright Bank and Trust Company of Boston launched a special credit card for gay men and women.
- That same year, the first Gay Games were held in New York City, attracting athletes—and sponsors—from around the world.

In addition to gay men and women, senior citizens also have become an important community for public relations professionals and the organizations they represent. The baby-boomer generation is approaching 50 years of age. Together, the over-50 crowd controls more than 50 percent of America's discretionary income. By the year 2000, 13 percent of the population will be older than 65.[14] As the American population grows older, the importance of senior citizens will increase. Public relations professionals must be sensitive to that reality, as well as to the fact that other special communities in the society will increasingly demand specialized treatment and targeted communications.

NONPROFIT PUBLIC RELATIONS

Among the most important organizations in any community are those represented in the nonprofit sector. Nonprofit organizations serve the social, educational, religious, and cultural needs of the community around them. So important is the role of public relations in nonprofit organizations that this sector is a primary source of employment for public relations graduates.

The nonprofit sector is characterized by a panoply of institutions: hospitals, schools, social welfare agencies, religious institutions, cultural organizations, and the like. The general goals of nonprofit agencies are not dissimilar to those of corporations. Nonprofits seek to win public support of their mission and programs through active and open communications. Unlike corporations though, nonprofits also seek to broaden volunteer participation in their efforts.

Because America is a nation of joiners and belongers, nonprofit organizations in our society are encouraged to proliferate. As the number of nonprofit agencies has grown, it has become increasingly difficult to find funding sources. Most nonprofits depend on a combination of government funding and private support. In 1989, total corporate giving to all causes rose to an estimated $6.5 billion, a little over 2 percent of pretax corporate profits. The largest portion of that money—about $2.8 billion—went to educational institutions.[15] In 1990, as resources have become more scarce, the competition among nonprofits to attract funding has become more intense. One Conference Board study showed a 2.5 percent decline in charitable giving among leading corporate donors, with half of the major contributors—those donating more than $10 million annually—cutting back to 78 percent.[16]

All of this suggests that public relations professionals at nonprofits, in addition to writing speeches, dealing with the media, communicating with employees, and counseling managements, must be prepared to devote increased efforts to one activity that corporate communicators ordinarily aren't involved in—fund-raising.

FUND-RAISING

Fund-raising—the need to raise money to support operations—lies at the heart of every nonprofit institution (Figure 14–5). Schools, hospitals, churches, and organizations—from the mighty United Way to the smallest block association—can't exist without a constant source of private funds. Frequently, the fund-raising assignment becomes the province of public relations professionals. Like other aspects of public relations work, fund-raising must be accomplished in a planned and programmatic way.

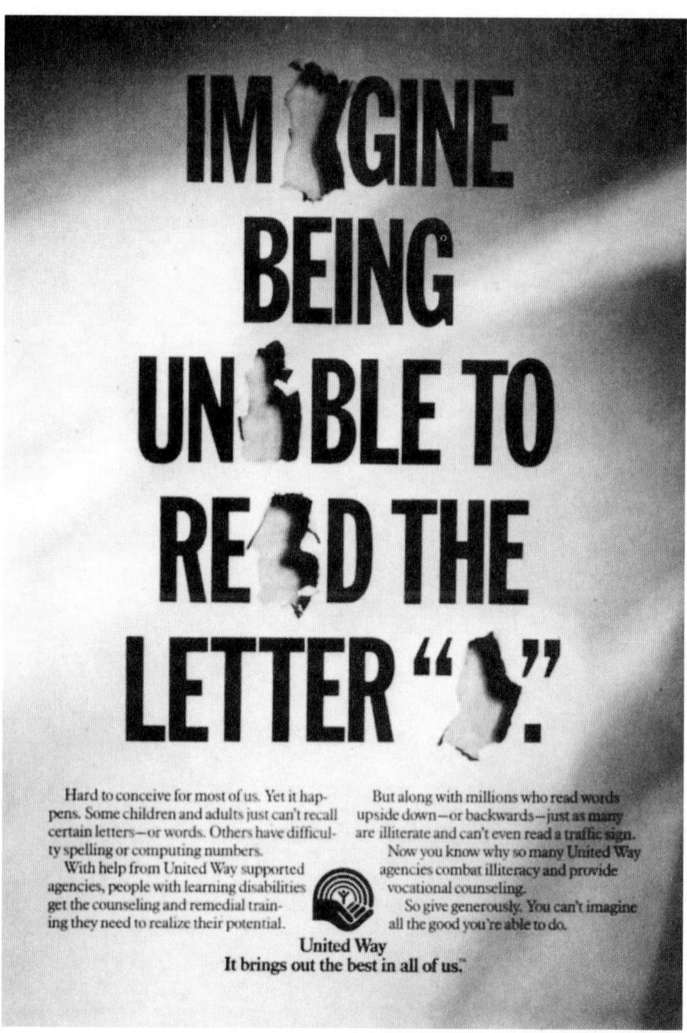

Figure 14–5 The granddaddy of all fund raisers is the United Way, which uses provocative advertising like this to raise the enormous sums necessary to fund thousands of community nonprofits. (*Courtesy of United Way*)

A successful fund-raising campaign should include the following basic steps:

1. **Identify campaign plans and objectives.** Broad financial targets should be set. A goal should be announced. Specific sectors of the community, from which funds might be extracted, should be targeted in advance.
2. **Organize fact finding.** Relevant trends that might affect giving should be noted. Relations with various elements of the community should be defined. The national and local economies should be considered, as should current attitudes toward charitable contributions.
3. **Recruit leaders.** The best fund-raising campaigns are ones with strong leadership. A hallmark of local United Way campaigns, for example, is the recruitment of strong business leaders to spearhead contribution efforts. Leaders should be designated to coordinate the various targets of opportunity defined in the fund-raising program. United Way designates leaders in each industry group to tap potential funding sources.
4. **Plan and implement strong communications activities.** The best fund-raising campaigns are also the most visible. Publicity and promotion must be stressed. Special events should be organized, particularly featuring national and local celebrities to support the drive. Updates on fund-raising progress should be communicated, particularly to volunteers and contributors. Unique communications vehicles—from direct mail to raffles to bazaars to the sale of stamps and seals—should be considered. All help get out the word and increase campaign coffers.
5. **Periodically review and evaluate.** Review the fund-raising program as it progresses. Make mid-course corrections when activities succeed or fail beyond expectations. Evaluate program achievements against program targets. Revise strategies constantly as the goal becomes nearer.

Because many public relations graduates enter the nonprofit realm, a knowledge of fund-raising strategies and techniques is especially important. Beginning practitioners, once hired in the public relations office of a college, hospital, charitable organization, or other nonprofit organization, are soon confronted with questions about how public relations can help raise money for the organization.

SUMMARY

The increasing cultural diversity of society as the year 2000 approaches has spawned a wave of "political correctness," particularly in the United States. Predictably, many have questioned whether sensitivity to women, people of color, the physically challenged, seniors, and other groups has gone too far. One thing, however, is certain. The makeup of society—of consumers, employees, political constituents, and so on—has been altered inexorably. The number of discrete communities with which organizations must be concerned will continue to increase as the new century approaches.

Intelligent organizations in our society must be responsive to the needs and desires of their communities. Positive community relations in the 1990s must begin with a clear understanding of community concerns, an open door for community leaders, an open and honest flow of information from the organization, and an ongoing sense of continuous involvement and interaction with community publics.

Abandoning the Boy Scouts

In 1992, when "family values" became a catch phrase, San Francisco's huge Bankamerica Corporation touched off a political firestorm when it first abandoned and then returned to support the Boy Scouts of America.

Earlier, the bank had cut off its charitable contributions to the Scouts because of their policy of prohibiting homosexuals from becoming members or troop leaders. But after an outright attack from Christian conservatives, the bank reversed its stand.

The flip-flop, especially in a city where gays hold considerable political power, led to threats of retaliation from the city government and a boycott by homosexuals.

Bankamerica tried to defend its reversal by claiming that the change reflected a refinement in the Boy Scouts' policy. The group, the bank said, had issued a "clarification" that affirmed that it was open to "all boys who subscribed to the Boy Scout oath and law."

The Scouts, however, begged to differ. "We've never changed," said their spokesman. "A homosexual lifestyle does not allow a person to be a member or a leader."

Gay activists in San Francisco claimed that Bankamerica bowed to pressure from television evangelist Pat Robertson, among others, who called for a boycott of the bank. Demonstrators upholding traditional values met outside Bankamerica's headquarters to burn deposit books and rip up credit cards.

For its part, Bankamerica steadfastly refused to respond to questions on the matter, which received wide coverage in the local press. Said one lesbian member of San Francisco's Board of Supervisors, "The bank yielded to pressure." Indeed, the Board of Supervisors considered a resolution to withdraw funds from the bank, while gay activists called for a total boycott of the company.

Said a writer for a San Francisco gay newspaper, "They should have admitted they were being pressured. Wouldn't that have been more honest?"

Community relations is only as effective as the support it receives from top management. Once that support is clear, it becomes the responsibility of the public relations professional to ensure that the relationship between the organization and all of its multicultural communities is one of mutual trust, understanding, and support.

DISCUSSION STARTERS

1. How is the atmosphere for community relations different in the 1990s than it was in the 1960s?
2. What is meant by the term *multicultural diversity?*

3. In general terms, what does a community expect from a resident organization?
4. What are typical community relations objectives for an organization?
5. What are some of the multicultural communities with which organizations must be concerned?
6. What are the key steps in mounting a sound fund-raising program?
7. Why should organizations care about the gay community in the 1990s?
8. What communications vehicles should be used in appealing to Latinos?
9. What is meant by the term *corporate social responsibility?*
10. What internal factor does community relations most depend on?

NOTES

1. Bob Weinstein, "Ethnic Marketing: The New Numbers Game," *Profiles* (May 1994): 51–52.
2. Paul Holmes, "Viva la Difference," *Inside PR* (March 1994): 13–14.
3. John V. Pavlik, *Public Relations: What Research Tells Us* (Newbury Park, CA: Sage, 1987), 109.
4. "The First Black Face I Ever Saw in Public Relations was in the Mirror," *Inside PR* (March 1993): 25.
5. Sylvia, Nassar, "Women's Progress Stalled? Just Not So," *The New York Times* (October 18, 1992): D1.
6. Glenn, M. Broom and David M. Dozier, "Advancement for Public Relations Role Models," *Public Relations Review* (Spring 1986): 37.
7. Marilyn Kern-Foxworth, "Status and Roles of Minority Public Relations Practitioners," *Public Relations Review* (Fall 1989): 39.
8. "As Minorities Grow in Number and Influence, They Will Become Vital Publics," *Public Relations Reporter* (February 11, 1985): 1.
9 Marilyn Kern-Foxworth, "Plantation Kitchen to American Icon: Aunt Jemima," *Public Relations Review* (Fall 1990): 64.
10. Michael Quinn, "Don't Aim That Pack at Us," *Time* (January 29, 1990): 60.
11. *Employment and Earnings* (Washington, DC: U.S. Department of Labor, Bureau of Statistics), 1991.
12. Anna Veciana-Suarez, "Hispanic Media: Impact and Influence," (Washington, DC: The Media Institute, 1990): 15.
13. "Gay Market Gaining Acceptance," *Inside PR* (September 1992): 6.
14. Peter Kreysa, "You Can Improve Your Bank's Service to Older Customers," *Hoosier Banker* (November 1990): 48.
15. Fraser P. Seitel, "Giving Wisely," *United States Banker* (April 1989): 64.
16. "Corporate Giving to Rise 5% in 1990, Survey Says," *The Wall Street Journal* (August 8, 1990): A2.

Top of the Shelf

Saul D. Alinsky. *Rules for Radicals.*
New York: Vintage Books, 1971.

Alinsky's *Rules for Radicals* is *the* classic handbook for those bent on organizing communities, rattling the status quo, and effecting social and political change, as well as for those who wish to learn from a legendary master.

Alinsky, a veteran community activist who fought on behalf of the poor from New York to California, provides strategies for building coalitions and for using communication, conflict, and confrontation advantageously. In "Of Means and Ends," Alinsky lists 11 rules of ethics that define the uses of radical power. His discussion of tactics suggests 13 ways to help organizers defeat their foes. Rule Three, for instance, tells activists to go outside the experience of their enemy to "cause confusion, fear, and retreat."

Alinsky supports his principles with numerous examples, the most colorful of which occurred when he wanted to draw attention to a particular cause in Rochester, New York. To do so, Alinsky and his group attended a Rochester Symphony performance—after a meal of nothing but beans. The results were hilarious.

Alinsky died in 1972, but his lessons endure in this offbeat guide to seizing power. Whether your goal is to fluster the establishment or defend it, *Rules for Radicals* is must reading.

SUGGESTED READINGS

Brion, Denis J. *Essential Industry and the NIMBY Phenomenon.* Westport, CT: Quorum, 1991.

Brown, Peter C. *The Complete Guide to Money Making Ventures for Nonprofit Organizations.* Washington, DC: The Taft Group, 1987 (5130 MacArthur Blvd. NW 20016).

Community Relations Report (P.O. Box X, Bartlesville, OK 74005). *Corporate 500 Directory of Corporate Philanthropy.* Detroit: Gale Research, 1988 (835 Penobscot Bldg. 48226).

Corporate Giving Watch. Washington, DC: The Taft Group.

Effective Public Relations for Colleges. Washington, DC: Case, (11 Dupont Circle 20036).

Foster, Lawrence G. *A Company That Cares: Johnson & Johnson.* New Brunswick, NJ: Johnson & Johnson, 1989.

Harris, April. *Special Events: Planning for Success.* Washington, DC: Case, 1988.

Kruckeberg, Dean, and Kenneth Stark. *Public Relations and Community: A Reconstructed Theory.* New York: Praeger, 1988.

Making Community Relations Pay Off. Washington, DC: Public Affairs Counsel, 1987.

National Conference of State Legislatures. *Building Communities That Work: Community Economic Development.* Denver, CO: NCSL, 1991.

The 1992 Community Relations Idea Book. Bartlesville, OK: Joe Williams Communications, 1992.

Religious Public Relations Handbook for Local Congregations. Gladwyne, PA: RPRC, 1988 (P.O. Box 315 19035).

CASE STUDY

MONKEYGATE

For three years, AT&Ts full-color monthly publication, *Focus*, was as good as internal communications gets. It was candid and straightforward and allowed employees to be heard. *Focus* was the envy of the internal communications profession.

All the admiration, however, came to a crashing halt in September 1993, when *Focus* published a cartoon on its "Fun 'N Games" page depicting people around the globe using telephones, except in Africa, where the phone-using individual depicted was a gorilla.

First, AT&T officials handled the incident as an internal matter, but at least some of the 315,000 AT&T employees worldwide who received *Focus* were angered by the illustration. Evidently one offended staffer provided a tip to an Associated Press reporter in Raleigh, North Carolina, that the September issue contained an offensive illustration.

The AP story was carried in several newspapers across the country, and AT&T sprang into action.

First, AT&T communicators tried to defuse the controversy by telling reporters that a staff member had made a proofing error. The staffer, it was argued, approved the illustration using a "fax of a fax," making it difficult to see the sketch, which allowed it to go by unnoticed. AT&T also notified the media that the artist, a freelancer, had been told he could no longer do any work for AT&T.

Local 1058 of the Communications Workers of America, which represented 4,000 AT&T employees and criticized AT&T's failure to catch the illustration, used the incident to attack AT&T's use of nonunion outside contractors.

Formal apologies to the staff trailed the illustration by several days. AT&T's senior vice president for public relations expressed her regrets to all employees in a letter in mid-September. "The offensive cartoon . . . was the result of a serious breakdown in editorial procedures. There is no excuse for it, and we have sincerely apologized for publishing such insulting material," she wrote in part. AT&T's CEO, Robert E. Allen, also took the lead in a letter that acknowledged "the hurt people feel" and promised a redoubling of efforts to drive any vestiges of racism from the company.

The Rev. Jesse Jackson entered the fray by leading a protest in front of AT&T's New York headquarters. And Joseph Lowery, president of the Southern Christian Leadership Conference (SCLC), held a similar protest rally on the steps of AT&T's regional headquarters in Atlanta.

CEO Allen and AT&T, whose domestic work force was almost 15 percent African-American—far higher than that of the 10 percent national workplace average—now had a real problem.

Allen immediately met with several groups, including African-American engineers and managers at AT&T, the Congressional Black Caucus, the SCLC, and the National Association for the Advancement of Colored People (NAACP).

After the meetings, the African-American leaders appeared mollified. For example, after a meeting with the NAACP's executive director, Benjamin F. Chavis, AT&T agreed to work together on minority recruitment, scholarships for African-American students, promotion goals, use of black financial institutions, and senior executive programs. Allen also appointed five

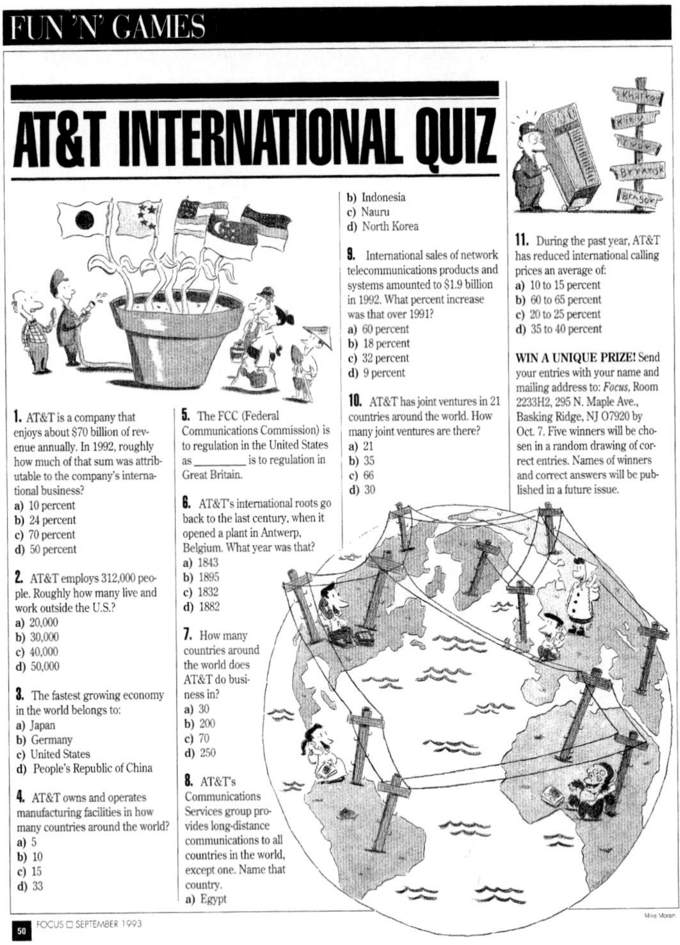

FUN 'N' GAMES

AT&T INTERNATIONAL QUIZ

1. AT&T is a company that enjoys about $70 billion of revenue annually. In 1992, roughly how much of that sum was attributable to the company's international business?
a) 10 percent
b) 24 percent
c) 70 percent
d) 50 percent

2. AT&T employs 312,000 people. Roughly how many live and work outside the U.S.?
a) 20,000
b) 30,000
c) 40,000
d) 50,000

3. The fastest growing economy in the world belongs to:
a) Japan
b) Germany
c) United States
d) People's Republic of China

4. AT&T owns and operates manufacturing facilities in how many countries around the world?
a) 5
b) 10
c) 15
d) 33

5. The FCC (Federal Communications Commission) is to regulation in the United States as _________ is to regulation in Great Britain.

6. AT&T's international roots go back to the last century, when it opened a plant in Antwerp, Belgium. What year was that?
a) 1843
b) 1895
c) 1832
d) 1882

7. How many countries around the world does AT&T do business in?
a) 30
b) 200
c) 70
d) 250

8. AT&T's Communications Services group provides long-distance communications to all countries in the world, except one. Name that country.
a) Egypt
b) Indonesia
c) Nauru
d) North Korea

9. International sales of network telecommunications products and systems amounted to $1.9 billion in 1992. What percent increase was that over 1991?
a) 60 percent
b) 18 percent
c) 32 percent
d) 9 percent

10. AT&T has joint ventures in 21 countries around the world. How many joint ventures are there?
a) 21
b) 35
c) 66
d) 30

11. During the past year, AT&T has reduced international calling prices an average of:
a) 10 to 15 percent
b) 60 to 65 percent
c) 20 to 25 percent
d) 35 to 40 percent

WIN A UNIQUE PRIZE! Send your entries with your name and mailing address to: *Focus*, Room 2233H2, 295 N. Maple Ave., Basking Ridge, NJ 07920 by Oct. 7. Five winners will be chosen in a random drawing of correct entries. Names of winners and correct answers will be published in a future issue.

50 FOCUS □ SEPTEMBER 1993

This offensive cartoon from AT&T's *Focus* was drawn by a freelancer who said he was a "King Kong fan and used gorillas frequently in his illustrations as a humorous signature." Although he said he had "not meant to offend anyone," he was let go and *Focus* was terminated. (*Courtesy of AT&T*)

senior corporate executives to lead a new "diversity" team of culturally diverse employees to recommend internal communications changes.

A day after the appointment of the diversity team, AT&T's public relations director announced that the two senior editors for *Focus* had been reassigned and the design firm responsible for the magazine terminated. She also announced AT&T's decision to eliminate *Focus* magazine.

To its credit, AT&T, its CEO, communications director, and communications staff remained accessible throughout the crisis. No one could accuse the company of ducking the "Monkeygate" controversy.

In the aftermath of the *Focus* shutdown, AT&T initiated a "Don't Hate—Communicate" public relations campaign. In early 1994, the company recruited black TV talk show host Montel Williams to moderate a public forum on racial intolerance. Forums were scheduled in Atlanta, Chicago, Dallas, Detroit, and New York.

In the spring of 1994, AT&T announced that

three new employee publications would be adopted to replace *Focus*.

Summarized a sadder but wiser public relations chief, "Our employee publications—especially *Focus*—have always reflected an openness and a level of candor unique in industry. I believe they contributed to the development of a more responsive, customer-focused culture at AT&T. I will always be proud of them and of the people who introduced them."

QUESTIONS

1. How well do you think AT&T handled Monkeygate?
2. Should the company have killed *Focus?*
3. How do you feel about the company's decision to reassign or replace those responsible for *Focus?*
4. Was it a good idea to impanel a task force of culturally diverse employees to recommend internal communications changes?
5. How should AT&T restore its credibility with its employees?

For further information on Monkeygate, see Duane Stoltzfus, "Wake Up Call at AT&T," *The Sunday Record* (September 7, 1993): B1, B3; Jerry Walker, "AT&T Introduces New Employee Publications," *Jack O'Dwyer's Newsletter* (March 23, 1994): 3; and Jerry Walker, "AT&T Repairs Damage Caused by Cartoon," *O'Dwyer's PR Services Report* (November 1993): 16, 17.

TIPS FROM THE TOP

TERRIE M. WILLIAMS

Terrie M. Williams is president of The Terrie Williams Agency, called by *New York* magazine "the most powerful black [owned] public relations firm in the country." Ms. Williams graduated from social worker to adviser to the stars when she landed her first client, Eddie Murphy, in 1988. She has been featured in many national magazines, is a sought-after lecturer on self-development topics, and is author of *The Personal Touch: What You Really Need to Succeed in Today's Fast-Paced Business World.*

How did you get started in public relations?
I am a strong believer in destiny. I was a practicing medical social worker at New York Hospital and was very deeply affected by my inability to really change a lot of people's circumstances. It was just very, very depressing. I saw an advertisement in the *Amsterdam News,* New York's largest black-owned newspaper, and there was a one-paragraph article about a public relations course being taught at the Y on Lexington and 51st. And the idea of it just seemed intriguing. I didn't know anyone in the field, but it sounded like something I should check out. I did. And that was really it.

How would you characterize entertainment public relations?
Extremely grueling. You have to put in a full day's work, which, of course, does not end at five. And then you have a movie premiere or a benefit dinner or a concert. And oftentimes, you don't get home till very late, 12 or 1 in the morning. And then you have to be ahead of the game the next morning, to see what's in the papers, to get items in the papers, *and* to have to function as if you've had a good

night's rest when, in fact, you're running on empty. So, I would say that it's not nearly as glamorous and as exciting as it's cracked up to be.

What's been your most difficult challenge?
Running a business. It's one thing to be good at what you do and quite another to run a business. It's also hard to find good strong, talented, intelligent, creative people who have a strong, strong work ethic and integrity. That, I think, is very challenging.

How does a college graduate get started in entertainment public relations?
Be adventurous, creative, not afraid to introduce yourself to people and ask for what you want. If you're not able to get a job immediately in the PR business, reach out to people and volunteer, do an internship. Be two steps ahead of people you want to do business with. Keep an eye on all of the trade publications, all the general consumer interest magazines. Get a good, solid feel for who is being written about, who's doing what with whom, what the trend stories are, who's writing what kinds of pieces. All of that information is key.

What is the future of public relations practice for minorities?
We have a long way to go. But we're making progress. People need to understand the importance of stretching themselves, to do business and interact with people with whom you're not most comfortable. That's probably the single biggest reason why our numbers are not great. It really blows me away when I hear mainstream PR firms and executives say, "There are not qualified minorities out there." I receive two or three resumes a day and an equal number of phone calls, which range from experienced practitioners to entry-level candidates. Many mainstream firms overlook the fact that minority PR professionals bring a much more well-rounded perspective to the table. As a member of an ethnic group, the ability to operate effectively with both majority and minority publics is second nature. Majority practitioners often are without the benefit of being exposed to an ethnically diverse population. We, on the other hand, have to know how to make it, how to be conversant and survive in our own world and the world of the majority. We've got to be culturally aware and sensitive. It's a matter of necessity. And if the numbers are low now—and they are—it's really because nobody has made a real effort to reach out to this segment of PR professionals. And we make it a priority here at our agency that anybody who wants to get into it, or wants to change careers or whatever, has an opportunity to work with us. They hang out with us for a day or assist us in the evening on an event. That's the only way that we are going to increase our numbers in this business.

What's the secret of individual success in public relations?
I don't believe in using race or sex or anything of any kind as an obstacle or a barrier to being able to accomplish great things. If you perfect your craft, treat people correctly, have a strong work ethic, believe in passing it on and giving it back to the community, if you're detail oriented, do the things you say you're going to do, there's no way you can lose. You will, in fact, excel.

TIPS FROM THE TOP

RAY DURAZO

Ray Durazo is president of Los Angeles–based Durazo Communications and a nationally recognized authority on Latino public relations. Prior to forming his own firm, Mr. Durazo was a partner in the Latino public relations firm of Moya, Villanueva & Durazo. Earlier, he headed the Los Angeles office of Ketchum Public Relations. Before returning to his native Southern California, Mr. Durazo headed Ketchum's Washington, DC, office.

How important is the ethnic market in the United States?
The United States receives two-thirds of the world's immigrants. Two-thirds of those immigrants will settle in California and Texas. By the year 2000, "minorities" will be the "majority" in Los Angeles, Dallas, Denver, Houston, and 23 other major U.S. cities. In Los Angeles, the Latino kindergarten enrollment is 66 percent and rising; Anglo enrollment is 15 percent and falling. Latino, Asians, and African-Americans constitute more than half the population of Los Angeles County. In short, the U.S. ethnic market has become too large to ignore.

What about communicating with Latinos and Asians?
Within these two major categories, there are differences, much of it having to do with the length of time the person has been in the United States and has become "acculturated" or to use a nonscientific term, "Americanized."

- Among *Latinos,* for instance, there are demographic and psychographic differences between a second-generation Mexican-American and a recently arrived immigrant from, say, Guatemala. The first was educated in the United States, speaks fluent English, and has adopted a mainstream

American lifestyle. The new immigrant speaks mostly Spanish, may not have progressed beyond an elementary school education, and maintains a lifestyle very similar to the one he/she practiced in Guatemala.

- Among *Asians,* the equation may be even more complex. Many Koreans, for example, arrive in this country with extensive education and experience as businesspeople. They tend to be entrepreneurial, aggressive, and ambitious. In contrast, many newly arrived immigrants from war-torn countries such as Vietnam, Cambodia, Thailand, and others are relatively uneducated and sometimes illiterate even in their own languages.

Why deal specially with ethnic markets?
Addressing ethnic audiences is simply another form of market segmentation, a recognition that the lifestyles, the life experiences, the attitudes and outlooks of ethnic persons may influence their receptivity to certain messages, to the way in which products and ideas are presented to them. As to why it's worth doing, all you have to do is look at the numbers, the buying power, the proportion of the population made up by ethnics, and you conclude that it's worth the effort.

What should a practitioner do to become conversant with the ethnic market?
The market isn't going to come to you. You have to go out and find it, experience it, learn it. And it isn't hard. Next time there's a Cinco de Mayo festival, or a Chinese New Year celebration, or an African-American heritage celebration, or any other ethnic event in your community, get out of your home or office, get in your car, drive over there, and *participate!*

What is the future of minority-oriented public relations?
The world is becoming a more competitive place every day. Recent history has shown that only the strong, the smart, the courageous, will survive in this new international arena. If you are too timid even to venture into your own backyard to reach important new audiences, I hate to think what will happen to you in the future! Aggressive, progressive companies have already concluded that the U.S. ethnic audience is too big to ignore. They are already out there, communicating and marketing effectively, with the growth in market share that is the ultimate benefit of such efforts. It isn't about being politically correct. It isn't about being touchy-feely. It's about the bottom line, about profits, about market share, about *winning.*

Wake up and smell el cafe!

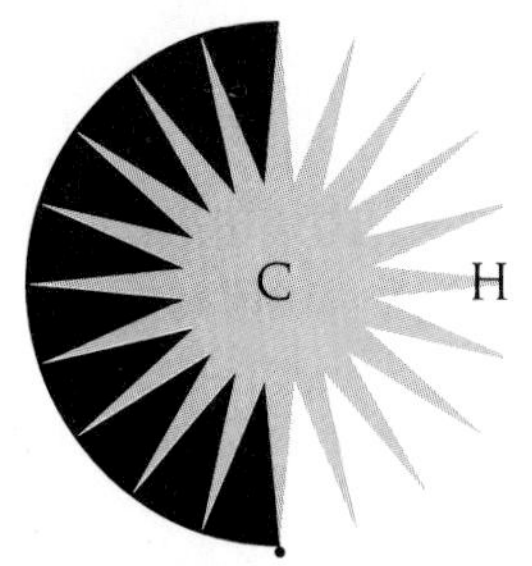

CHAPTER 15

CONSUMERS

FOR MOST PERSONS WHO WORK FOR A LIVING, THE 1990s WILL forever be known as the decade of downsizing and restructuring, layoffs and cutbacks, consolidations and terminations. In public relations, as in most other lines of work, jobs—or more specifically, *keeping* one's job—has become the primary order of the day.

In the wake of massive reconfigurations of companies, hospitals, schools, and the like, the "battle cry" that dominates the institutions that have emerged is summarized in two words: "customer service."

At the start of the decade, "quality" was king. The creation by Congress in 1987 of the Malcolm Baldridge National Quality Award focused business, in particular, on the importance of providing reliable products and service.

The latter half of the decade has taken the quality concept one step further. In addition to providing quality products, organizations, in order to remain viable, have to serve their customers in a more efficient and effective manner. Customer service, then—the response to the demands of the consumer—has become an overriding priority for most organizations.

In the 1990s, consumers simply won't tolerate defective merchandise, misleading advertising, packaging and labeling abuses, quality and safety failures, inadequate service and repair, diffident corporate complaint handlers, incomprehensible or inadequate guarantees and warranties, or slow settlements when products don't live up to advance claims.[1]

Whether or not today's "consumer" is king, he or she *demands* quality service. Organizations, locked in an increasingly competitive battle for consumer loyalty, must be responsive to consumer demands. Thus, the practice of consumer relations has increased in importance among business organizations.

GROWTH OF THE CONSUMER MOVEMENT

Although consumerism is considered to be a relatively recent concept, legislation to protect consumers first emerged in the United States in 1872, when Congress enacted the Criminal Fraud Statute to protect consumers against corporate abuses. In 1887, Congress established the Interstate Commerce Commission to curb freewheeling railroad tycoons.

However, the first real consumer movement came right after the turn of the century when journalistic muckrakers encouraged legislation to protect the consumer. Upton Sinclair's novel *The Jungle* revealed scandalous conditions in the meat-packing industry and helped establish federal meat inspection standards as Congress passed the Food and Drug Act and the Trade Commission Act. In the second wave of the movement, from 1927 to 1938, consumers were safeguarded from the abuses of manufacturers, advertisers, and retailers of well-known brands of commercial products. During this time, Congress passed the Food, Drug, and Cosmetic Act.

By the early 1960s, the movement had become stronger and more unified. President John F. Kennedy, in fact, proposed that consumers have their own Bill of Rights, containing four basic principles:

1. **The right to safety**—to be protected against the marketing of goods hazardous to health or life.
2. **The right to be informed**—to be protected against fraudulent, deceitful, or grossly misleading information, advertising, labeling, or other practices and to be given the facts needed to make an informed choice.
3. **The right to choose**—to be assured access, whenever possible, to a variety of products and services at competitive prices.
4. **The right to be heard**—to be assured that consumer interests will receive full and sympathetic consideration in the formulation of government policy.

Subsequent American presidents have continued to emphasize consumer rights and protection. Labeling, packaging, product safety, and a variety of other issues continue to concern government overseers of consumer interests.

FEDERAL CONSUMER AGENCIES

Today a massive government bureaucracy attempts to protect the consumer against abuse: upward of 900 different programs, administered by more than 400 federal entities. Key agencies include the Justice Department, Federal Trade Commission, Food and Drug Administration, Consumer Product Safety Commission, and Office of Consumer Affairs.

- **Justice Department** The Justice Department has had a consumer affairs section in its antitrust division since 1970. Its responsibilities include the enforcement of such consumer protection measures as the Truth in Lending Act and the Product Safety Act.
- **Federal Trade Commission** The FTC, perhaps more than any other agency, has vigorously enforced consumer protection. Its national advertising division covers television and radio advertising, with special emphasis on foods, drugs, and cosmetics. Its general litigation division covers areas not included by national advertising, such as magazine subscription agencies, door-to-door sales, and income tax services. Its consumer credit and special programs division deals with such areas as fair credit reporting and truth in packaging.
- **Food and Drug Administration** The FDA is responsible for protecting consumers from hazardous items: foods, drugs, cosmetics, therapeutic and radiological devices, food additives, and serums and vaccines.
- **Consumer Product Safety Commission** This bureau is responsible for overseeing product safety and standards.
- **Office of Consumer Affairs** This agency, the central point of consumer activities in the government, publishes literature to inform the public of recent developments in consumer affairs.

In the 1990s, national office seekers have campaigned on a platform of getting government out of the lives of the citizenry. Nonetheless, under President Clinton, federal regulators continue to occupy positions of great importance to most industry groups. For example, in recent years, the FDA, whether attacking the cigarette companies for the perils of smoking or the pharmaceutical firms for exorbitant prices, has been extremely aggressive. The reality, as the nation approaches the year 2000, is that public companies—from utilities to banks to consumer products firms to cable TV purveyors—must communicate directly and frequently with their regulators in Washington. Often the best policy is to keep regulators advised of corporate developments and to work at winning their understanding and support.

CONSUMER ACTIVISTS

The consumerist movement has attracted a host of activists in recent years. Private testing organizations, which evaluate products and inform consumers about potential dangers, have proliferated. Perhaps the best known, Consumers Union, was formed in 1936 to test products across a wide spectrum of industries. It publishes the results in a monthly magazine, *Consumer Reports,* which reaches about 3.5 million readers.

Often an evaluation in *Consumer Reports*, either pro or con, greatly affects how customers view particular products. Consumers Union also produces books, a travel newsletter, a column for 450 newspapers, and monthly features for network television. It has an annual budget of $70 million.

Consumers also have begun taking a more active role in their own affairs. The Consumer Federation of America was formed in 1967 to unify lobbying efforts for proconsumer legislation. Today the federation consists of 200 national, state, and local consumer groups, labor unions, electric cooperatives, and other organizations with consumer interests.

Although companies often find activists' criticism annoying, the emergence of the consumer watchdog movement has generally been a positive development for consumers. Ralph Nader and others have forced organizations to consider, even more than usual, the downside of the products and services they offer. Smart companies have come to take seriously the pronouncements of consumer activists.

BUSINESS GETS THE MESSAGE

Obviously, few organizations can afford to shirk their responsibilities to consumers. Consumer relations divisions have sprung up, either as separate entities or as part of public relations departments. The title of vice president for consumer relations is showing up with more frequency on corporate organization charts.

In many companies, consumer relations began strictly as a way to handle complaints, an area to which all unanswerable complaints were sent. Such units have frequently provided an alert to management. In recent years, some companies have broadened the consumer relations function to encompass such activities as developing guidelines to evaluate services and products for management, developing consumer programs that meet consumer needs and increase sales, developing field-training programs, evaluating service approaches, and evaluating company effectiveness in demonstrating concern for customers.

The investment in consumer service apparently pays off. Marketers of consumer products say that most customer criticism can be mollified with a prompt, personalized reply (Figure 15–1)—and a couple of coupons. Failing to answer a question, satisfy a complaint, or solve a problem, however, can result in a blitz of bad word-of-mouth advertising.[2] More typical of the increased concern shown today by most business organizations are the following:

- When Alamo Rent-A-Car experienced a shortage of vehicles in a busy vacation season at certain locations, it eagerly reimbursed customers for the difference between their reserved Alamo rate and the one they were forced to pay.
- When the Swingline Company received numerous complaints about its Tot stapler, it reconstituted the product and sent new models, free of charge, to people who complained.
- When Newman's Own Microwave Popcorn received complaints that its bags were leaking, it hired a technical consulting organization to reevaluate the bag sealing system. It also refunded the cost of the purchase.
- In 1994, when mutual funds were criticized for failing to explain their risks to the public, Fidelity Investments, the largest U.S. mutual funds company, became

COMMAND AIRWAYS INC.
DUTCHESS COUNTY AIRPORT
WAPPINGERS FALLS, NEW YORK 12590 (914) 462-6100 TELEX: 289371 COMD UR

January 21, 1985

Mr. David Kemp
176 West 87th Street
New York, NY 10024

Dear Mr. Kemp:

Clearly we screwed up. Please accept our apologies.

Attached is a check for $168.00, which represents a full refund.

Again, please accept our apologies.

Sincerely,

Kingsley G. Morse,
President

KGM:nj
Encl.

Figure 15–1 Here's a classic response, from the CEO, no less, that was guaranteed to restore consumer confidence in Command Airways. (*Courtesy of Command Airways*)

the first investment house to produce its own half-hour infomercial to explain the risks and rewards of mutual fund investing.

In adopting a more activist consumerist philosophy, firms like these have found that consumer relations need not take a defensive posture. Consumer relations people can't afford to be simple complaint handlers. Rather, they must be activist in the very best sense to make certain that consumers understand the benefits and realities of using their products (Figure 15–2).

Nutritional Information for HERSHEY'S Grocery Products on a Per Serving Basis

HERSHEY'S Grocery Products	Serving Size (oz)	Cal-ories	Protein (g)	Carbohydrate Total (g)	Carbohydrate Sugar (g)	Carbohydrate Other (g)	Fat (g)	Cho-lesterol (mg)	So-dium (mg)	Percentage of U.S. Recommended Daily Allowances (U.S. RDA) Pro-tein	Vit. A	Vit. C	Thia-min	Ribo-flavin	Niacin	Cal-cium	Iron
HERSHEY'S Chocolate Flavored Syrup	1.4 (approx. 2 Tbsp.)	110	1**	25	21	4	<1	0	20	*	*	*	*	2	*	*	2
HERSHEY'S Chocolate Fudge Topping[b]	1.2 (approx. 2 Tbsp.)	120	2	17	N.A.	N.A.	5	5	40	2	*	*	*	4	*	4	4
HERSHEY'S Chocolate Milk (2% Low Fat)[b]	8.0 fl. oz. (1 Cup)	190	8	29	N.A.	N.A.	5	20	130	20	10	4	6	25	*	30	*
HERSHEY'S Chocolate Milk Mix	0.83 (3 Heaping Tsp.)	90	<1**	22	N.A.	N.A.	<1	0	40	*	*	*	*	*	*	*	*
HERSHEY'S Chocolate Milk (3.5% Fat)[b]	8.0 fl. oz. (1 Cup)	210	7	28	N.A.	N.A.	8	N.A.	120	15	4	4	6	25	*	30	*
HERSHEY'S Genuine Chocolate Flavored Drink[a]	8.0 fl. oz.	150	5	28	N.A.	N.A.	2	N.A.	85	10	*	*	4	10	*	20	*
HERSHEY'S Cocoa[a]	1.0 (approx. ⅓ Cup)	110	8**	12	0	12	3	0	25	*	*	*	2	4	4	4	15
HERSHEY'S European Style Cocoa[a]	1.0 (approx. ⅓ Cup)	90	7**	8	1	7	3	0	15	*	*	*	*	4	4	4	50
HERSHEY'S Milk Chocolate Chips	1.5 (approx. ¼ Cup)	220	2	27	26	1	12	10	55	2	*	*	*	4	*	6	2
HERSHEY'S Milk Chocolate Chunks	1.0 (approx. 12 Pieces)	160	2	16	15	1	9	10	25	2	*	*	*	6	*	6	*
HERSHEY'S Mint Chocolate Chips[b]	1.5 (approx. ¼ Cup)	230	2**	28	N.A.	N.A.	12	N.A.	0	*	N.A.	N.A.	N.A.	N.A.	N.A.	*	6
REESE'S Peanut Butter Flavored Chips[a]	1.5 (approx. ¼ Cup)	230	9	19	18	1	13	5	90	15	*	*	*	6	20	4	4
HERSHEY'S Premium Baking Bar Semi-Sweet Chocolate[b]	1.0	140	1**	16	N.A.	N.A.	8	N.A.	N.A.	*	N.A.	N.A.	N.A.	N.A.	N.A.	N.A.	N.A.
HERSHEY'S Semi-Sweet Chocolate Chips (regular & miniature)[b]	1.5 (approx. ¼ Cup)	220	2**	27	N.A.	N.A.	12	0	0	*	*	*	*	4	*	*	6
HERSHEY'S Semi-Sweet Chunks[b]	1.0 (approx. 12 Pieces)	140	1**	15	N.A.	N.A.	8	N.A.	N.A.	*	N.A.	N.A.	N.A.	N.A.	N.A.	N.A.	N.A.
HERSHEY'S Premium Baking Bar Unsweetened Chocolate[a]	1.0	190	4**	7	N.A.	N.A.	16	0	5	*	*	*	*	8	2	2	10
HERSHEY'S Vanilla Milk Chips[b]	1.5 (approx. ¼ Cup)	220	1	25	22	3	13	N.A.	100	*	*	*	*	4	*	2	*

N.A. – Data not available at present
* – Less than 2% of U.S. RDA
** – Not a significant source of protein
a – These nutrient values are based on limited laboratory analyses
b – This nutrient information is based on calculated values
< – "Less than" symbol

Figure 15–2 Hershey foods produced this *Nutritional Information Guide* to inform consumers about the realities of chocolate. (*Courtesy of Hershey Foods Corporation*)

CONSUMERIST PHILOSOPHY

Most companies begin with the premise that customers, if they are to remain customers, deserve to be treated fairly and honestly. Historically, the companies that initiated their own activist consumer affairs units have been those to escape the wrath of outside activists.

The Grand Union Company, the second oldest food chain in the nation, began a consumer affairs department two decades ago and drew up its own Consumer Bill of Rights. Its example has been followed by numerous companies in a variety of industries. Typical is Chrysler Motors "Car Buyer's Bill of Rights":

1. Every American has the right to quality.
2. Every American has the right to long-term protection.
3. Every American has the right to friendly treatment, honest service, and competent repairs.

4. Every American has the right to a safe vehicle.
5. Every American has the right to address grievances.
6. Every American has the right to satisfaction.

Chrysler, like other companies, backed up its Bill of Rights with a customer arbitration board to deal with warranty-related problems and commissioned a research organization to survey car owners periodically on customer satisfaction.

Such an enlightened approach to customer relations was typical of businesses in the 1990s (Figure 15–3).

CONSUMERIST OBJECTIVES

Building sales is the primary consumer relations objective. A satisfied customer may return; an unhappy customer may not. Here are some typical goals:

- **Keeping old customers** Most sales are made to established customers. Consumer relations efforts should be made to keep these customers happy. Pains should be taken to respond to customers' concerns. For example, when the San Francisco earthquake struck on October 17, 1989, AT&T suspended normal practice and asked operators to make three and even four attempts to complete calls. AT&T operators worked throughout the night handling 253,000 calls—double the normal volume.
- **Attracting new customers** Every business must work constantly to develop new customers. In many industries, the prices and quality of competing products are similar. In choosing among brands, customers may base decisions on how they have been treated.
- **Marketing new items or services** Customer relations techniques can influence the sale of new products. Thousands of new products flood the market each year, and the vast array of information about these products can confuse the consumer. When General Electric's research revealed that consumers want personalized service and more information on new products, it established the GE Answer Center, a national toll-free, 24-hour service that informed consumers about new GE products and services. Building such company and product loyalty lies at the heart of a solid consumer relations effort.
- **Expediting complaint handling** Few companies are free of complaints. Customers protest when appliances don't work, errors are made in billing, or deliveries aren't made on time. Many large firms have established response procedures. Often a company ombudsman can salvage a customer relationship with a speedy and satisfactory answer to a complaint.
- **Reducing costs** To most companies, an educated consumer is the best consumer. Uninformed buyers cost a company time and money—when goods are returned, service calls are made, and instructions are misunderstood. Many firms have adopted programs to educate customers about many topics (Figure 15–4): what to look for in choosing fruits and vegetables, how to shop for durable goods, how to use credit wisely, and how to conserve electricity.

A Customer's Bill Of Rights

1. *A customer has the right to courteous, considerate treatment at all times by all members of the seller organization.*

2. *A customer has the right to receive accurate information about features, applications, prices and availability of products or services which are offered for sale.*

3. *A customer has the right to have his or her expectations met that quality, price and delivery of the product or service will be as represented prior to having made the purchase.*

4. *A customer has the right to be served by skilled, knowledgeable personnel dedicated to representing his or her best interests with other departments in the seller organization.*

5. *A customer has the right to be promptly and fully informed when the seller's commitment cannot be met as originally stated.*

6. *A customer has the right to complain—and to receive prompt, fair handling and resolution of the complaint on its merits.*

7. *A customer has the right to expect extra effort by the seller's personnel in genuine emergencies, regardless of their cause.*

8. *A customer has the right to expect honesty and integrity at all levels in the seller organization, and assurance that all legal requirements have been met and rights observed.*

9. *A customer has the right to expect teamwork from the seller—and never to hear the expression: "That's not my department!"*

10. *A customer has the right to expect appreciation from everybody in the seller organization with which he or she does business, appreciation for business already given as well as for business to be given in the future . . . provided this Customer's Bill of Rights continues to be observed by the seller organization.*

Figure 15–3 The Customer Service Institute lived up to its name with the publication of this manifesto, which summarizes what a customer ought to be entitled to. (*Courtesy of the Customer Service Institute*)

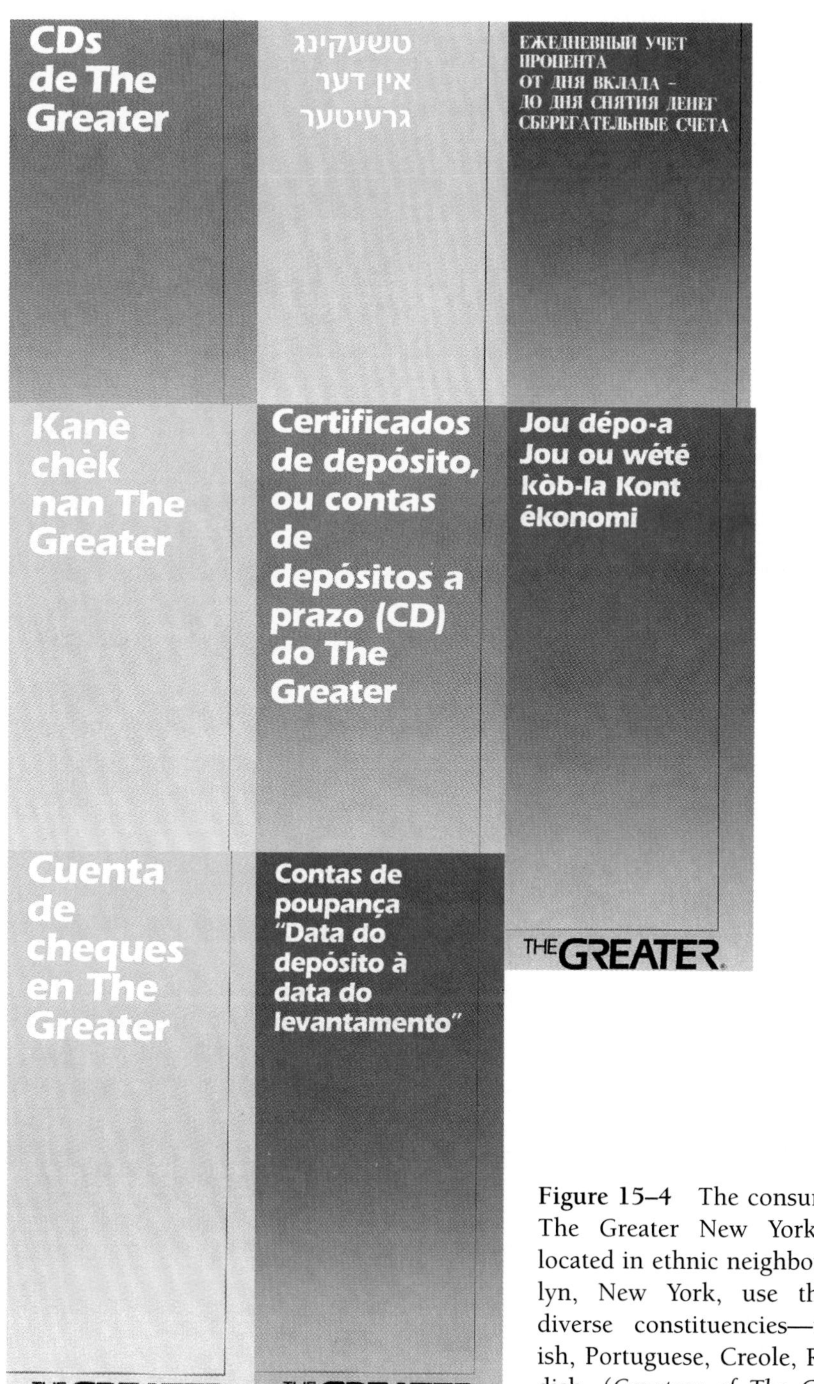

Figure 15–4 The consumer brochures of The Greater New York Savings Bank, located in ethnic neighborhoods in Brooklyn, New York, use the languages of diverse constituencies—including Spanish, Portuguese, Creole, Russian, and Yiddish. (*Courtesy of The Greater New York Savings Bank*)

A QUESTION OF ETHICS

Glass in the Baby Food

For Gerber Products, a company that keeps a stash of teddy bears and cookies to welcome children to the lobby of its Michigan headquarters, the events of February 1986 were unsettling. Specifically, a jar of Gerber's baby food in Schenectady, New York, was reported to have glass in it. Tests at a Gerber laboratory showed that there was no glass in the jar turned in, and the supermarket reporting the incident said it had lost the fragment the customer had turned in and therefore couldn't prove the existence of the glass.

Nonetheless, the action triggered a wave of similar complaints about glass in Gerber baby food across the nation. Gerber, rejecting the conciliatory posture adopted by other companies in crisis situations, decided to shed its cuddly image and get tough. "We feel strongly we're being had," the company's CEO said. He noted that the Food and Drug Administration tested 40,000 unopened jars of Gerber baby food and concluded there was no public health problem.

The company refused to knuckle under to nationwide consumer groups that urged a recall. It denounced the Brooklyn, New York, district attorney's announcement that she was opening a criminal investigation of the matter. When the governor of Maryland ordered Gerber's strained peaches off his state's supermarket shelves, the company filed a $150 million lawsuit against Maryland officials, asserting that the action had injured its 58-year reputation for integrity and quality.

Gerber officials argued that it was virtually impossible that the chunks of glass consumers were reporting could have come from its jars. They said that each year Gerber produces about a billion jars of baby food under tight technical controls, using advanced glass-washing equipment and screens designed to filter out any particle larger than four-thousandths of an inch. The company added that it kept X-ray machines in factories to check for breakage along the fast-moving production line.

Gerber officials further noted that in special tests, where chunks of glass were crammed into its jars, special jar washers successfully flushed out every last fragment. Said Gerber's director of corporate communications. "We feel this is a lynch mob" and added that the company's objective was "not to get panicked." So, in the face of 227 complaints to the Food and Drug Administration about Gerber baby food jars, the nation's largest manufacturer of baby food continued to hang tough.

What do you think of Gerber's public relations strategy?

OFFICE OF THE OMBUDS OFFICER

One classic research project for the White House Office on Consumer Affairs revealed the following:

- Only 4 of 100 dissatisfied customers will complain.
- For every complainer, there are 24 with the same complaint who never say anything.
- About 13 percent of dissatisfied customers will tell 20 people about it.
- Almost 90 percent of dissatisfied customers don't repurchase from the offending company, compared to 54 to 70 percent who remain loyal when complaints are satisfactorily handled.[3]

In the old days, a frequent response to complaint letters was to dust off the so-called bed bug letter. This stemmed from occasional letters to the railroads complaining about bed bugs in the sleeper cars. To save time, railroad consumer relations personnel simply dispatched a prewritten "bed bug" letter in response. Today, although an occasional bed bug letter still appears from time to time (Figure 15–5), most organizations handle consumer relations with more care (Figure 15–6).

At many companies the most immediate response to complaints has been the establishment of ombudsman offices. The term *ombudsman* originally described a government official—in Sweden and New Zealand, for example—appointed to investigate complaints against abuses of public officials. In most firms, the office of the ombuds officer investigates complaints made against the company and its managers. Such an office generally provides a central location that customers can call to seek redress of grievances.

A five-year study of consumer complaint handling commissioned by the U.S. Office of Consumer Affairs suggested two important caveats for suppliers of consumer goods and services:

1. Consumers who do not complain when they are dissatisfied are often unhappy enough to switch product brands, companies, or both.
2. Because marketing costs are extremely high, it may be less expensive to resolve the complaints of existing customers than to win new ones.[4]

Typically, the ombuds officer monitors the difficulties customers are having with products. Often, he or she can anticipate product or performance deficiencies. Ombuds officers are in business to inspire customer confidence and to influence an organization's behavior toward improved service. They accomplish this by responding more often than not, in the following manner:

- "We'll take care of that for you."
- "We'll take full responsibility for that defect."
- "We want your business."
- "Thank you for thinking of us."
- "Consider it done."[5]

Such "magic words" should be heard more often in many organizations. Courteous, knowledgeable, and skilled complaint-handling ombuds officers—cheerful, positive,

12 King Place
Closter, New Jersey
07624
June 2, 1993

President Clinton
The White House
Washington, D.C. 205000

Dear President Clinton:

My name is David Seitel, and I am a sixth grader. I'm writing about a very important topic. This topic is SMOKING. Our tobacco companies in the U.S. are setting a bad example for us kids today. They are going to other countries, and encouraging people in their teens especial my age, to smoke.

Please, won't you try to help stop American tobacco companies from addicting the world's children. Thank you.

Sincerely,
David Seitel

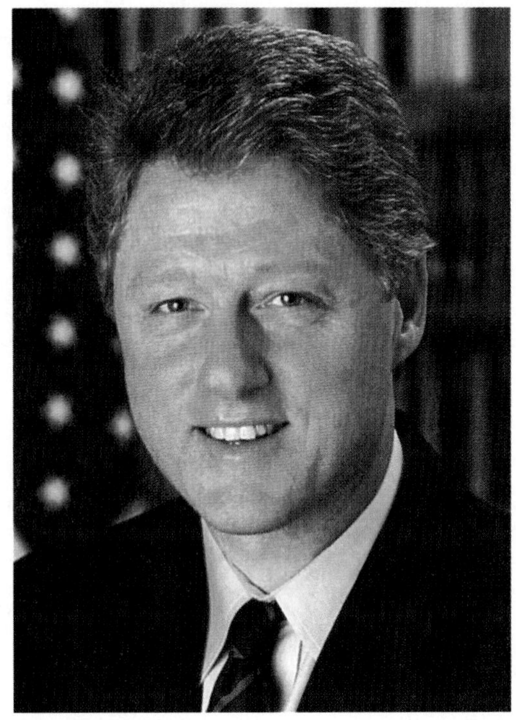

Thank you for writing to me. I enjoy hearing from young people because you are the future of our country. I am honored to be your President.

Bill Clinton

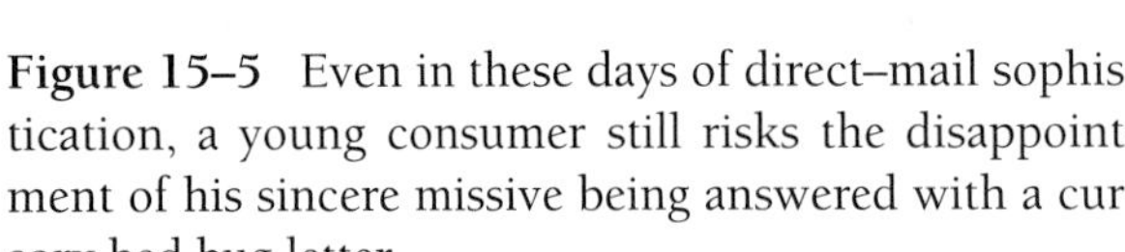

Figure 15–5 Even in these days of direct–mail sophistication, a young consumer still risks the disappointment of his sincere missive being answered with a cursory bed bug letter.

and genuinely concerned with solving a customer's problems—can keep clients happy and loyal for many years.

SUMMARY

Despite periodic legislative setbacks and shifting consumerist leadership, the cause of consumerism seems destined to remain strong. The increasing use of seat belts, increased environmental concerns about packaging and pollution, rising outrage about secondhand smoke, and numerous other causes indicate that the push for product safety and quality will likely increase in the years ahead.

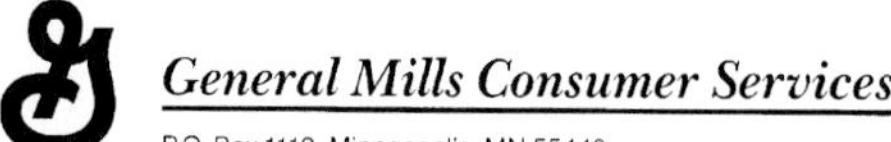

General Mills Consumer Services
P.O. Box 1113, Minneapolis, MN 55440

November 22, 1993

David Seitel
12 King Place
Closter, NJ 07624

Dear Mr. Seitel:

Thank you for telling us our product was not of its usual quality. We are sorry to learn of your disappointment with your purchase of Pop Secret butter microwave popcorn.

Occasionally, the Pop Secret bags can be damaged so slightly that a hole in the bag is not noticed. If this happens, (or if the vent hole is completely sealed) the volume of popped corn will be less because the combination of heat and steam necessary to pop the corn will not occur. In addition, some of the popcorn may scorch.

You are right to expect high-quality products, and we appreciate your bringing the matter to our attention. Please be assured this will be carefully reviewed with the appropriate personnel.

An adjustment is enclosed for your purchase. We hope you continue to use and enjoy General Mills' products.

Sincerely,

Jan Ecklund

VJP/0031931119

General Offices at Number One General Mills Boulevard

Figure 15–6 In the end, even a young consumer who remains vigilant will triumph in winning the day—or, in this case, the microwave popcorn. (*Courtesy of General Mills*)

Business will not sit idly by. Indeed, the consumer affairs function continues to grow in stature. In 1987, the Society of Consumer Affairs Professionals had 600 companies among its members. By 1990, the society boasted 1,400 members.

With the election of a Democratic president, public interest groups see a greater opportunity to help set the nation's agenda into the year 2000.

The likely reemergence of activism in the 1990s means that businesses must respond with an even greater sense of consumerism. In 1990, when Star Kist Tuna received thousands of letters from schoolchildren protesting the killing of dolphins in the hunt for tuna, the company changed its tuna-fishing policy. As a result of Star Kist's

BETWEEN THE LINES

A DAY IN THE LIFE OF THE OMBUDS OFFICER

So you want to handle consumer complaints? Here is a random selection of complaints received by the consumer affairs division of a local bank. How would you have handled them?

1. A businessman carrying an attaché case made a deposit at a midtown branch before going to his office. Inadvertently, he left his case on the main banking floor. By the time he discovered that it was missing, the police bomb squad had smashed the innocent case and cordoned off the area. The owner asked the bank for a replacement. Would you have given it to him?
2. After making a deposit and leaving the bank, a woman reported that a huge icicle fell from the bank's roof and nearly hit her. She complained bitterly to consumer affairs. How would you appease her?
3. A young installment-loan customer claimed that his car had been removed for reclamation because of delinquent loan payments. He claimed that he had paid the loan on time and objected to the illegal seizure. On checking, it was determined that several loan payments were, in fact, delinquent. Nevertheless, the car was returned, in a very damaged condition. The young man sought reimbursement for repairs. What would you recommend?
4. A customer complained that she had received no response to her numerous letters and memos concerning the hostile treatment accorded her at the local branch. After investigation, it was learned that the woman was a nuisance to branch officers, yet kept a very healthy balance in her savings account. Furthermore, all the correspondence to which she referred was written on the backs of checks she submitted in loan payments. How would you handle this problem?
5. The executor of an estate complained that his deceased client, who had been a bank customer, had received a card reading "Best wishes in your new residence." What remedial action would you recommend?

action to refit boats and retrain fishermen, fewer dolphin died and the company was hailed as a hero.[6]

That same year, the Walt Disney Company pulled a controversial "Steve the Tramp" doll off the market, after homeless rights groups complained. Although "Steve the Tramp" was one of 14 Disney action figures of criminals and gangsters inspired by the hit *Dick Tracy* movie, Disney didn't hesitate to yank the doll and lose thousands of dollars in the face of a nationwide firestorm.[7]

Similarly, any organization in the 1990s interested in muffling activist protests and ensuring a reputation for integrity must meet the consumerist challenge by establishing safety, performance, and service standards that demonstrate good faith and public interest. In the long run, the firm that lives by a proconsumer philosophy will prosper. The firm that ignores the irresistible push of consumerism risks not only growth but survival.

DISCUSSION STARTERS

1. What did President Kennedy contribute to the consumerist movement?
2. What are the key federal agencies involved in consumerism?
3. What is Consumers Union?
4. How do companies typically handle the challenge of consumerism?
5. What is a consumer bill of rights?
6. What are typical consumerist objectives?
7. What is the office of the ombuds officer?
8. What is a bed bug letter?
9. Why must firms fear too many dissatisfied customers?
10. What can be learned from the Star Kist and Disney experiences in confronting increased consumer activism?

NOTES

1. Paul Burnham Finney, "Everyone Is Shouting the Q Word," Special Digest Advertising Section, *Newsweek* (December 10, 1990): 12.
2. Kathleen Deveny, "For Marketers, No Peeve Is Too Petty," *The Wall Street Journal* (November 14, 1990): B1.
3. "How Much More Does It Cost to Create a New Customer Compared to Keeping an Existing One?" *Public Relations Reporter* (May 30, 1988): 1.
4. Robert M. Cosenza and Jerry W. Wilson, "Managing Consumer Dissatisfaction: The Effective Use of the Corporate Written Response to Complaints," *Public Relations Quarterly* (Spring 1982): 17.
5. John R. Graham, "Words to Inspire Confidence," *Communication Briefings* (November 1988): 8.
6. "Star Kist Explains How Consumer Advocacy Inspired Its Decision for Policy Change," *Public Relations Reporter* (May 14, 1990): 4.
7. "Disney Pulls Doll Offensive to Homeless," *The Record* (December 15, 1990): A-5.

SUGGESTED READINGS

Communications Counselors. *Capital Contacts in Consumerism.* (Available from the author, 1701 K Street, NW, Washington, DC 20006.)

Connor, Richard, and Jeffrey Davidson. *Getting New Clients.* New York: Wiley, 1987.

Davidow, William H., and Bro Uttal. *Total Customer Service.* New York: Harper & Row, 1989.

TOP OF THE SHELF

Al Ries and Jack Trout. *The 22 Immutable Laws of Marketing.* New York: Harper Business, 1993.

Public relations professionals interested in the field of consumer relations owe it to themselves to consider *The 22 Immutable Laws of Marketing,* which turns conventional marketing wisdom on its head.

Al Ries and Jack Trout, iconoclastic marketers who have counseled hundreds of leading corporations, lay it on the line in a most untraditional way.

"Billions of dollars have been wasted on marketing," say the authors. "Many managers assume that a well-designed, well-executed, well-financed marketing program will work. It's not necessarily so. And you don't have to look further than IBM, General Motors, and Sears Roebuck to find examples."

Rather, say Ries and Trout, marketers should play straight with the consumer. Herewith, three "immutable laws":

1. **The law of candor** Tell consumers your problem, point out the negatives, and be honest with them if you want to look better in their eyes.
2. **The law of attributes** Too often companies attempt to emulate the leader. They must know what works, goes the rationale, so let's do something similar. Not good thinking.
3. **The law of success** Ego is the enemy of successful marketing. Objectivity is what's needed. When people become successful, they tend to be less objective. They often substitute their own judgment for what the consumer wants.

Public relations aspirants who wish to learn about perfecting their own consumer relations could gain much by reading this book.

DeCourcy Hinds, Michael. "Seeking Profits in Consumer Complaints." *The New York Times* (March 26, 1988). The author points out that competition necessitates keeping customers happy.

Donnelly, James H., Jr. *Close to the Customer: Management Tips from the Other Side of the Counter.* Homewood, IL: Business One Irwin, 1991.

Francese, Peter. *Capturing Consumers.* Ithaca, NY: American Demographics, 1989.

Hanan, Mack, and Peter Karp. *Customer Satisfaction.* New York: AMACOM, 1991.

Pertschuk, Michael. "The Role of Public Interest Groups in Setting the Public Agenda for the '90s." *Journal of Consumer Affairs* (Winter 1987): 171–182.

Rudd, Joel, and Vicki L. Buttolph. "Consumer Curriculum Materials: The First Content Analysis." *Journal of Consumer Affairs* (Summer 1987): 108–121. The researchers conclude that business-sponsored curriculum publications have more commercial and advertising content than do nonbusiness materials.

CASE STUDY

CRITICIZING WAL-MART'S "BUY AMERICA" PROGRAM

In the mid-1990s, no U.S. retailer was more successful than Wal-Mart, the Bentonville, Arkansas-based discount company started by the legendary Sam M. Walton.

Much of Wal-Mart's success evolved from a program its founder, affectionately known as "Mr. Sam," began in 1985. "Find products," he ordered his managers, "that American manufacturers have stopped producing because they couldn't compete with foreign imports." Walton's concern was translated into a letter to Wal-Mart's 3,000 domestic suppliers stating that between 1981 and 1984 an estimated 1.6 million American jobs were lost to imports. Said Mr. Sam, "Something can and must be done to reverse this very serious threat to our free enterprise system."

From this beginning, Wal-Mart initiated the "Buy America" program. This plan gave American manufacturers many of the same favorable terms and cooperation extended to foreign manufacturers. Specifically, Wal-Mart provided U.S. suppliers with long-term commitments and guaranteed orders, allowing American companies to commit to improved facilities and machinery and greater productivity in return for the security of ongoing orders.

The "Buy American" program was a great success for Wal-Mart, particularly in the area of positive public relations. No American retailer was more closely associated with America than Wal-Mart. And no individual was more beloved by his employees and the media than Mr. Sam.

Sam Walton died in 1992, shortly after receiving the Presidential Medal of Freedom from President Bush. That same year, Wal-Mart was voted among the top 10 companies in a national "Corporate Reputation Survey."

Then things began to change. Almost from the moment of Mr. Sam's death, the credibility of the company he had nurtured so assiduously, began to show serious signs of stress.

- Florida accused Wal-Mart of selling inferior "gray market" Seiko watches and of falsely telling customers that they carried Seiko warranties. (Gray market goods are those made abroad for sale abroad but imported into the United States without the manufacturer's consent and sold at discount prices.) Wal-Mart refused to comment on the allegations.
- New York State sued Wal-Mart for the reinstatement of a couple fired because they began a dating relationship. In doing so, they violated a Wal-Mart policy barring a married employee from dating another store employee. New York State's suit attempted to enjoin the company against further use of the policy.
- In California, American Indians threatened to boycott Wal-Mart after a developer announced plans to dig up an American Indian burial site in order to build a Wal-Mart store. Wal-Mart said it supported the preservation of "Indian culture" but kept a low profile on the controversy.
- Target Stores, Wal-Mart's chief competitor, accused its rival of false and misleading advertising in presenting Target's prices on specific items. Target harshly headlined its rebuttal ads "This Never Would Have Happened if Sam Walton Was Alive."

And then, in December 1992, Wal-Mart received the cruelest blow of all when NBC's *Dateline* reported that the company's heavily promoted "Buy America" program was not all Wal-Mart claimed it to be.

The report, broadcast to 14 million households, showed young children working for five cents an hour to produce Wal-Mart merchandise in Bangladesh, which has no child labor laws. The program also alleged that foreign-made merchandise was being sold under "Made in the USA" signs in Wal-Mart stores.

Wal-Mart CEO David Glass, the man who replaced Mr. Sam, was interviewed on the show and appeared, according to one media training manager, "ill prepared . . . like a rabbit caught in the headlights." Glass said he was unaware of any child exploitation by Wal-Mart suppliers. "To the best of my knowledge, we don't buy from any vendor who uses child labor," he asserted.

But when Glass was shown an on-air videotape of children in a cramped Bangladesh factory sewing Wal-Mart labels into jeans, a Wal-Mart public relations vice president stopped the NBC interview and CEO Glass hastened out of the room. NBC cameras recorded the entire scene.

Two weeks after the ill-fated NBC interview, *Dateline* was invited back to Wal-Mart headquarters to meet with President Glass. The Wal-Mart CEO said he had been "unprepared to answer questions about Wal-Mart's use of child labor in Bangladesh, but that now he was prepared." He said that he had sent someone from Arkansas to inspect the factory that NBC had told him about. His conclusion: "Wal-Mart could find no evidence of child labor."

Glass also said that his company had canceled its contract with a Hong Kong–based company being investigated for illegal shipments into the United States. Earlier, NBC had alleged that Wal-Mart allowed merchants to smuggle goods banned by U.S. law. In his first meeting with *Dateline*, Glass denied knowledge of Wal-Mart's dealings with the Hong Kong firm.

NBC noted in its report that America's First Family was a great booster of Wal-Mart. First Lady Hillary Clinton had been a member of Wal-Mart's board of directors for six years. "It's not likely that either one of the Clintons would approve of the kinds of things that we found" concluded the *Dateline* correspondent.

Wal-Mart's reaction to the critical NBC exposé was immediate and pointed. "The statements made in the program were inaccurate and misleading" concluded CEO Glass in a company-issued statement.

The company's public relations department acknowledged, however, that the firm had made some errors. "There was some mis-signing on some of our apparel racks—on some racks, apparel was sold out and imported merchandise inadvertently placed on racks topped with 'Made in America' signs," said a Wal-Mart spokesman.

The company was concerned enough about the *Dateline* piece to set up a toll-free consumer hotline. Wal-Mart reported that the day after the broadcast, 60 percent of the calls were "positive."

Wal-Mart also received strong support from its suppliers, who rushed to its defense with newspaper ads in national and local papers. Typical was a GE lighting ad headlined "We Support Wal-Mart's Buy America Program." The ad went on to say how "proud of its partnership with Wal-Mart" GE Lighting has been.

In all, about 100 suppliers bought ads in support of Wal-Mart. Later, it was suggested that Wal-Mart had asked suppliers to run ads and even offered appropriate copy. One apparent consequence of the advertising campaign was positive publicity in newspapers such as *USA Today*, where many of the supportive ads ran. Two *USA Today* follow-up stories were headlined "Wal-Mart Rebounds from Critical Report" and "Ad Support for Wal-Mart Swells."

Wal-Mart also communicated with its 475,000 employees—called "associates" by the company—through an in-house satellite network. Ads were posted on internal bulletin boards to make sure employees knew that the company was getting support from suppliers. Employees, too, were urged to check all merchandise displayed under "Made in the USA" labels.

Finally, in response to inquiries from concerned customers and others, Wal-Mart CEO David Glass responded personally with candid answers to the major NBC accusations.

When the dust settled, the company's stock price—which immediately after the broadcast had suffered a 2+ point drop—had rebounded. Last-minute pre-Christmas sale shopping at Wal-Mart also apparently was unaffected by the controversy. And a Wal-Mart spokesman concluded, "Consumers know what Wal-Mart is and what it stands for, and they saw through the transparency of the *Dateline* show, the allegations and the lies and the questionable sources."

Perhaps.

WAL★MART

WAL★MART STORES, INC.
CORPORATE OFFICES
BENTONVILLE, ARKANSAS 72716-0001

David Glass
President and
Chief Executive Officer
(501) 273-4198

February 10, 1993

Mr. Fraser P. Seitel, Managing Partner
Emerald Partners Communications Counselors
177 Main Street, Ste 215
Fort Lee, NJ 07024

Dear Mr. Seitel:

Thank you for the opportunity to respond directly to you regarding the allegations made against Wal-Mart by NBC News. We greatly appreciate your interest in taking the time to write to us and can clearly understand your concern. Needless to say, we were extremely disappointed with the report and the unethical, and terribly misleading and untruthful manner in which it was presented. I will attempt to address each issue.

Among the allegations was that Wal-Mart imports private label clothes made in factories employing child labor. Here are the facts: Wal-Mart does not condone nor have we ever knowingly purchased merchandise made with child labor in any country. Our purchase orders and Letters of Credit are stamped with that direction. If that should ever happen we will immediately cancel all outstanding orders with that firm. In the 11 months Wal-Mart has directly imported from Bangladesh, manufacturers have certified that no illegal child labor has ever been used in manufacturing our merchandise. We conducted a surprise visit by a Wal-Mart executive to ensure that is not happening. Our agent, who conducts regular inspections of the factories, also confirmed no illegal child labor is used. We feel very strongly about this and have initiated additional steps of control to see that it never happens.

We unequivocally deny we have ever engaged in any criminal scheme to transship or smuggle any garments from any foreign country or that we have ever been informed that our company is the subject of any such criminal investigation.

Regarding the allegation that Wal-Mart was responsible for putting a North Carolina manufacturer out of business - this is absolutely untrue! Here are the facts: Wal-Mart continued to support the troubled plant in an effort to keep it in business, including warehousing some of their merchandise at our cost and when the plant finally declared bankruptcy, Wal-Mart was left with unfilled orders. Furthermore, no replacement merchandise from the plant was ever purchased overseas - the knitting machines from the bankrupt plant were sold to a New Jersey manufacturer and are used today to make cardigan sweaters for Wal-Mart. These sweaters were previously imported.

Page 2

Finally, in response to the charge that imports have increased since Wal-Mart instituted its Buy American Program in 1985 - here are the facts: In 1985 when we began our Buy American Program we were seeing our imports rise dramatically - that's why we began our program; we felt we could make a difference and we have. In a letter to our vendor partners, Sam Walton said, "...our company is firmly committed to the philosophy of buying everything possible from suppliers who manufacture their products in the United States. We must insure that American manufacturers continue to be the entrepreneurs that provide the fuel that drives the economy..." Our commitment to that philosophy is stronger today than ever. We have converted hundreds of items that we previously bought overseas and have created tens of thousands of jobs in the United States as a result. The percent of sales of directly imported goods is, in fact, down from previous years. Those are the truthful facts that were ignored.

As reported in the news media, we have acted with haste to correct any real problems which we uncovered. I have already issued an apology to our customers because merchandise in some of our stores was signed incorrectly as "Made in U.S.A.," even though labels on each garment were clearly marked as imported items. We have also removed from sale a jacket whose label read, "Made in Bangladesh" yet shows an American flag. In both instances no intent was made to deceive our customers and steps have been taken to prevent a recurrence of the incorrect signing.

These are the solid facts to the allegations raised recently by NBC News.

Mr. Seitel, thank you for your letter and I assure you we remain more committed than ever to aggressively continue to set the example to all American companies to bring products and jobs home to the U.S.A. I hope this has answered any questions you may have had.

Sincerely,

David Glass

David Glass

DG/wpw

But another school of thought suggested that the *Dateline* criticism was fair warning to Wal-Mart that its pro-American/anti-international program, as well as its reputation for integrity—all carefully crafted over many years by its founder—would likely be subject to intense and unceasing scrutiny in the days and years ahead.

QUESTIONS

1. How would you assess Wal-Mart's handling of the initial interview with *Dateline*?
2. Was it wise for Wal-Mart to stop the on-camera interview with its CEO? What would you have advised the company to do instead?
3. Do you agree with the company's response to the NBC program?
4. What do you think of the supportive supplier ad program?
5. How would you advise Wal-Mart to manage its public relations relative to the "Buy America" program from now on?

For further information on the Wal-Mart case, see "The Corporate Reputation Survey," *Inside PR* (November 1992): 26; Kate Fitzgerald, "Target Accuses Wal-Mart in Ads," *Advertising Age* (March 29, 1993): 1, 50; Thomas C. Hayes, "Wal-Mart Disputes Report on Labor," *The New York Times* (December 24, 1993): D1, D4; and Gary Strauss, "Wal-Mart Rebounds from Critical Report," *USA Today* (December 24, 1992): 2B.

TIPS FROM THE TOP

DIANE PERLMUTTER

Diane Perlmutter is co-chief operating officer of the New York office of Burson-Marsteller, the world's largest public relations agency. She has created and managed multi-million-dollar programs in virtually every marketing discipline, including advertising, sales promotion, merchandising, incentives, and employee motivation. Prior to joining Burson-Marsteller, Ms. Perlmutter was vice president of advertising and campaign marketing at Avon Products. Ms. Perlmutter also teaches public relations and is a frequent lecturer on public relations topics.

How smart are consumers today?
Today's consumers are very smart, a combination of "street smart" and "educated." "Street smart" because they are exposed to an incredible array of products in stores, catalogs, and on television. Consumers have a strong sense of value; they know what is good. "Educated" because they can access a wide range of information from manufacturers, independent evaluators, and stores (e.g., unit pricing).

How enlightened are companies today?
Companies that are the most successful are the most enlightened. They range from giants like Johnson & Johnson and Xerox to entrepreneurs like Snapple and Ben & Jerry's.

What's the general state of consumer relations in the United States today?
Consumer relations are at an all-time high. And they keep improving every year as more companies make 800 numbers and other fast-response options available to their customers.

Which are the most responsive companies in dealing with consumers?
It's hard to single out the *most* responsive, but companies like GE, Gerber, and Cadillac are all doing an outstanding job.

What are the keys to organizing a successful consumer relations program?
The most successful are the most consumer-friendly. Their attributes can be summed up with the acronym FRIEND: Flexible, Responsive, Immediate, Educational, Need-driven and Dedicated.

How powerful is the consumer movement today?
The consumer movement is so powerful that it's really no longer a movement. It's a way of life.

How should a company react to criticism of its products by consumer advocates or the media?
While all companies dislike having their products criticized, they should base their reaction on three key elements: (1) source of criticism, (2) reason for criticism, (3) validity of criticism. There's no silver bullet; each scenario requires a different response.

What should a company do if its products are contaminated or sabotaged?
A company has a responsibility to ensure that its products do not create a health and safety risk for the consumer. The company's response should always be based on this.

What role is public relations likely to continue to play with consumer product companies?
Public relations will become an increasingly important communications tool in consumer products companies. In a world that is growing increasingly complex, public relations is the best communications vehicle to give consumers complicated information in a meaningful and understandable way.

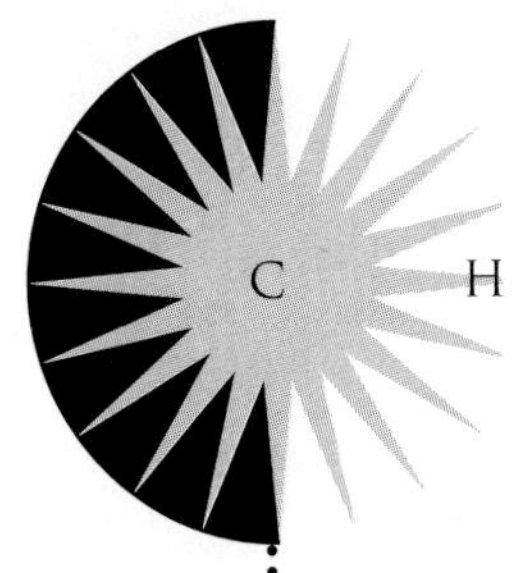

CHAPTER 16

GOVERNMENT

NOWHERE WAS THE IMMENSE POWER OF COMMUNICATIONS in government more amply demonstrated than in the presidential campaign of 1992.

As candidate Bill Clinton trudged into the pivotal primary State of New York, his campaign was in shambles. Charges against the presidential aspirant ranged from flip-flopping on positions to infidelity in his marriage. Candidate Clinton's standing in the polls was declining, and the Democrats were clearly worried. So they decided to do something radical.

They turned to "talk radio."

Specifically, candidate Clinton appeared solo one morning as the guest of an outrageous, fun-loving, well-informed radio morning man, Don Imus (Figure 16–1). Imus's playful but respectful treatment of the candidate coupled with Clinton's good-natured rebuttals not only made for good radio, it also convinced New York voters that the candidate wasn't such a bad guy after all.

Figure 16–1 Bill Clinton's interview with New York City radio personality Don Imus helped turn the tide in a flagging campaign. (*Courtesy of WFAN Radio*)

After his appearance on *Imus in the Morning*, Clinton won the New York primary handily, and the rest is history. Not surprisingly, Imus became a lifelong FOB (Friend of Bill).

Such is the power of communications in government as the nation approaches the year 2000.

PUBLIC RELATIONS IN GOVERNMENT

The growth of public relations work both *with* the government and *in* the government has exploded in recent years. Although it is difficult to categorize exactly how many public relations professionals are employed at the federal level, it's safe to assume that thousands of public relations–related jobs exist in the federal government and countless others in government at state and local levels. Thus, the field of government relations is a fertile one for public relations graduates.

Since 1970 some 20 new federal regulatory agencies have sprung up, ranging from the Environmental Protection Agency to the Consumer Product Safety Commission to the Department of Energy to the Department of Education to the Drug Enforcement Agency. Moreover, according to the Government Accounting Office (GAO), some 116 government agencies and programs now regulate business.

Little wonder that today, American business spends more time calling on, talking with, and lobbying government representatives on such generic issues as trade, interest rates, taxes, budget deficits, and all the other issues that concern individual industries and companies. Accordingly, organizations today continue to emphasize and expand their own government relations functions.

Beyond this, the nation's defense establishment offers some 3,000 public relations jobs in military and civilian positions. Indeed, with military service in the 1990s purely voluntary, the nation's defense machine must emphasize its public information, education, and recruiting efforts in order to maintain a sufficient military force. Thus, public relations opportunities in this realm of government work should expand as well.

Ironically, the public relations function has traditionally been something of a stepchild in the government. In 1913, Congress enacted the Gillett amendment, which almost barred the practice of public relations in government. The amendment stemmed from efforts by President Theodore Roosevelt to win public support for his programs through the use of a network of publicity experts. Congress, worried about the potential of this unlimited presidential persuasive power, passed an amendment stating: "Appropriated funds may not be used to pay a publicity expert unless specifically appropriated for that purpose."

Several years later, still leery of the president's power to influence legislation through communication, Congress passed the gag law, which prohibited "using any part of an appropriation for services, messages, or publications designed to influence any member of Congress in his attitude toward legislation or appropriations." Even today, no government worker may be employed in the practice of public relations. However, the government is flooded with public affairs experts, information officers, press secretaries, and communications specialists.

GOVERNMENT PRACTITIONERS

Most practitioners in government communicate the activities of the various agencies, commissions, and bureaus to the public. As consumer activist Ralph Nader has said, "In this nation, where the ultimate power is said to rest with the people, it is clear that a free and prompt flow of information from government to the people is essential."

It wasn't always as essential to form informational links between government officials and the public. In 1888, when there were 39 states in the Union and 330 members in the House of Representatives, the entire official Washington press corps consisted of 127 reporters. Today there are close to 4,000 full-time journalists covering the capital.

In 1990, the U.S. Office of Personnel Management reported nearly 15,000 public relations–related jobs in government. These consisted of nearly 4,000 in public affairs; 2,000 in writing and editing; 1,700 in technical writing and editing; 2,000 in visual information; 3,300 in foreign information; and 2,000 in editorial assistance.[1]

In 1986, the GAO responded to an inquiry by Senator William Proxmire requesting "how much federal executive agencies spend on public relations." The GAO reported that the 13 cabinet departments and 18 independent agencies spent about $337 million for public affairs activities during fiscal 1985, with almost 5,600 full-time employees assigned to public affairs duties. In addition, about $100 million was spent for congressional affairs activities, with almost 2,000 full-time employees assigned. Also, about $1.9 billion—that's $1.9 *billion*—was spent, primarily in the Department of Defense, "for certain public affairs–related activities not classified as public affairs." These included more than $65 million for military bands, $13 million for aerial teams,

$11 million for military museums, and more than $1 billion for advertising and printing regarding recruitment.[2]

UNITED STATES INFORMATION AGENCY

The most far-reaching of the federal government's public relations arms is the United States Information Agency (USIA), an independent foreign affairs agency within the executive branch. USIA maintains 205 posts in 128 countries, where it is known as the U.S. Information Service (USIS). The agency employs 8,500, most of whom are Americans working in Washington, DC, and overseas and almost 4,000 foreign nationals hired locally in countries abroad.

Under law, the purpose of USIA is to disseminate information abroad about the United States, its people, culture, and policies (Smith-Mundt Act of 1948) and to conduct educational and cultural exchanges between the United States and other countries (Fulbright-Hays Act of 1961). The director of USIA reports to the president and receives policy guidance from the secretary of state.

USIA's fiscal 1994 appropriation was a whopping $1.14 billion—a $200 million increase from the beginning of the decade.

In the 1990s, with democracy spreading throughout the globe, USIA's mission—"to support the national interest by conveying an understanding abroad of what the United States stands for"—has been modified to include five new challenges:

1. Build the intellectual and institutional foundations of democracy in societies throughout the world.
2. Support the "war on drugs" in producer and consumer countries.
3. Develop worldwide information programs to address environmental challenges.
4. Bring the truth to any society that fails to exercise free and open communication.
5. Advise the president on foreign public opinion considerations.[3]

Under the direction of such well-known media personalities as Edward R. Murrow, Carl Rowan, and Frank Shakespeare, the agency prospered. However, under the Reagan administration's director, Charles Z. Wick, USIA became an unsurpassed force in communicating America's message. One of Wick's innovations was WORLDNET, a 30-country satellite television network, dubbed the "jewel in the crown" of USIA communications techniques. Other USIA vehicles include the following:

1. **Radio** Voice of America has 111 transmitters, broadcasts in 42 languages, and reaches 120 million people in an average week. In addition to Voice of America, the USIA in 1985 began Radio Marti, in honor of José Marti, father of Cuban independence. Radio Marti's purpose is to broadcast to Cuba in Spanish and "tell the truth to the Cuban people."
2. **Film and television** USIA annually produces and acquires an extensive number of films and videocassettes for distribution in 125 countries.
3. **Media** About 25,000 words a day are radio-teletyped to 214 overseas posts for placement in the media.
4. **Publications** Overseas regional service centers publish 16 magazines in 18 languages and distribute pamphlets, leaflets, and posters to more than 100 countries.

5. **Exhibitions** USIA designs and manages about 35 major exhibits each year throughout the world, including Eastern European countries and the former Soviet Union.
6. **Libraries and books** USIA maintains or supports libraries in over 200 information centers and binational centers in more than 90 countries and assists publishers in distributing books overseas.
7. **Education** USIA is also active overseas in sponsoring educational programs through 111 binational centers where English is taught and in 11 language centers. Classes draw about 350,000 students annually.

GOVERNMENT BUREAUS

Nowhere has government public relations activity become more aggressive than in federal departments and regulatory agencies (Figure 16–2). Many agencies, in fact, have found that the quickest way to gain recognition is to increase their public relations aggressiveness.

The Federal Trade Commission (FTC), which columnist Jack Anderson once called a "sepulcher of official secrets," opened up in the late 1970s to become one of the most active government communicators. As a former FTC director of public information described the agency's attitude, "The basic premise underlying the commission's public information program is the public's inherent right to know what the FTC is doing."[4] When the FTC found a company's products wanting in standards of safety or quality, it often announced its complaint through a press conference. Although corporate critics branded this process "trial by press release," it helped transform the agency from a meek, mild-mannered bureau into an office with real teeth.

As noted, other government departments also have stepped up their public relations efforts. The Department of Defense has more than 1,000 people assigned to public relations–related work. In 1986, the Air Force alone answered about 35,000 letters from schoolchildren inquiring about this military branch.[5] The Department of Health and Human Services has a public affairs staff of 700 people. The departments of Agriculture, State, and Treasury each have communications staffs in excess of 400 people, and each spends more than $20 million per year in public relations–related activities.[6] Even the U.S. Central Intelligence Agency has three spokesmen. Out of how many CIA public relations people? Sorry, that's classified.

THE PRESIDENT

Despite early congressional efforts to limit the persuasive power of the nation's chief executive, the president today wields unprecedented public relations clout. Almost anything the president does or says makes news. The broadcast networks, daily newspapers, and national magazines follow his every move. His press secretary provides the White House press corps (a group of national reporters assigned to cover the president) with a constant flow of announcements supplemented by daily press briefings. Unlike many organizational press releases that seldom make it into print, many White House releases achieve national exposure.

Ronald Reagan was perhaps the most masterful presidential communicator in history. Reagan gained experience in the movies and on television, and even his most ardent critics agreed that he possessed a compelling stage presence. As America's presi-

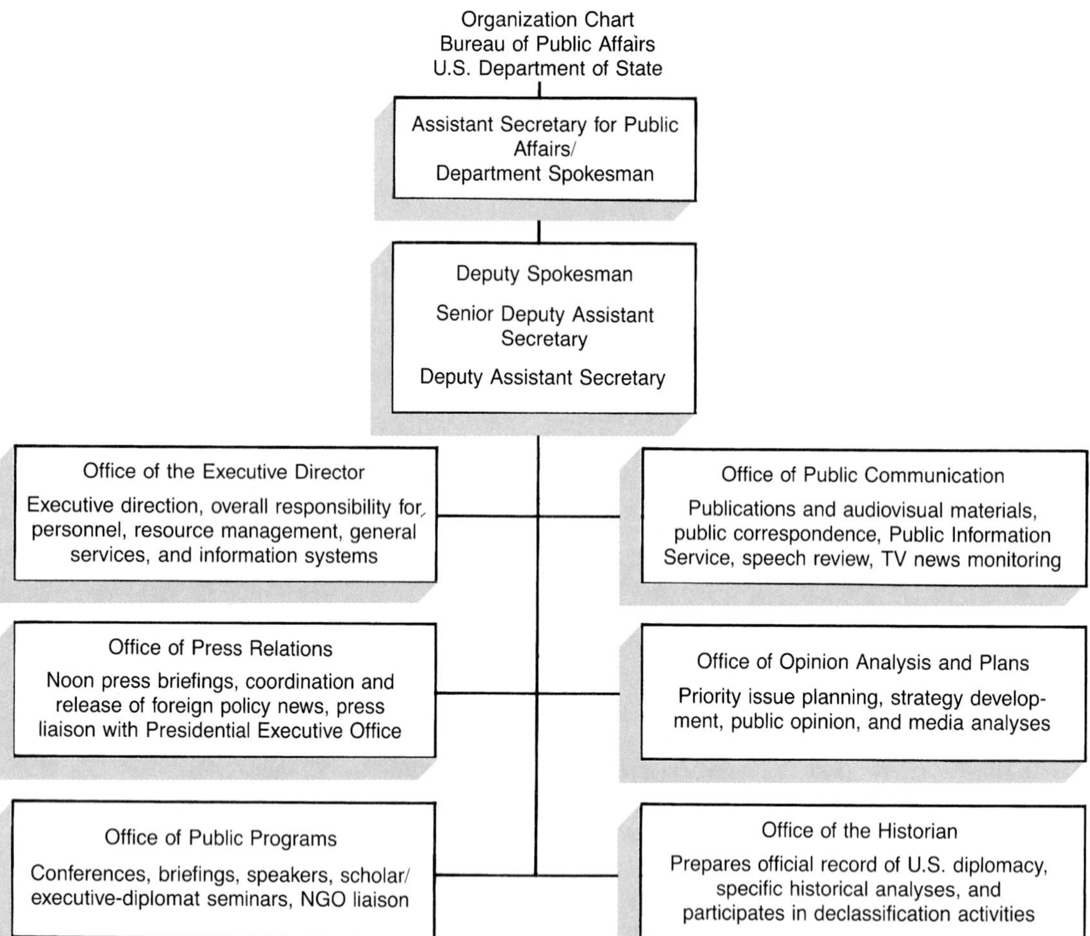

Figure 16–2 The Bureau of Public Affairs in the U.S. Department of State is typical of the public information mechanism in a federal department. The assistant secretary for public affairs in the State Department and in most other federal agencies reports directly to the secretary. (*Courtesy of United States Department of State*)

dent, he was truly the "Great Communicator." Reagan and his communications advisers followed seven principles in helping to "manage the news":

1. Plan ahead.
2. Stay on the offensive.
3. Control the flow of information.
4. Limit reporters' access to the president.
5. Talk about the issues *you* want to talk about.
6. Speak in one voice.
7. Repeat the same message many times.[7]

So coordinated was Reagan's effort to "get the right story out" that even in his greatest public relations test—the accusation at the end of his presidency that he and his aides shipped arms to Iran and funneled the payments to support Contra rebels in

Nicaragua, in defiance of the Congress—the president's "Teflon" image remained largely intact. The smears simply washed away.

George Bush was not as masterful as his predecessor in communicating with the American public. Indeed, Bush met his communications match in 1992, when Bill Clinton beat him soundly in the presidential race.

Clinton, learning from the disastrous presidential campaign of Democrat Michael Dukakis before him, organized a "media swat team" to beat back Republican allegations during the campaign. As soon as the Bush forces issued a charge against the Democrats, the Clinton "truth squad" rebutted the accusation.[8]

President Clinton, like Reagan before him, is a skilled communicator—particularly on a personal level. Using a technique mastered during the campaign, Clinton seeks to escape the confines of the "Washington Beltway" by staging "town meetings" throughout America to help promote health care and other programs. Clinton has also brought presidential politics into the satellite era by appearing on CNN's *Larry King Live* program and conducting presidential satellite media tours similar to the ones staged in the campaign.[9]

THE PRESIDENT'S PRESS SECRETARY

Some have called the job of presidential press secretary the second most difficult position in any administration. The press secretary is the chief public relations spokesperson for the administration. Like practitioners in private industry, the press secretary must communicate the policies and practices of the management (the president) to the public. Often, it is an impossible job.

In 1974, Gerald terHorst, President Ford's press secretary, quit after disagreeing with the pardon of former President Richard Nixon. Said terHorst, "A spokesman should feel in his heart and mind that the chief's decision is the right one, so that he can speak with a persuasiveness that stems from conviction."[10] A contrasting view of the press secretary's role was expressed by terHorst's replacement in the job, former NBC reporter Ron Nessen. Said Nessen, "A press secretary does not always have to agree with the president. His first loyalty is to the public, and he should not knowingly lie or mislead the press."[11] A third view of the proper role of the press secretary was offered by a former public relations professional and Nixon speechwriter who became a *New York Times* political columnist, William Safire:

> A good press secretary speaks up for the press to the president and speaks out for the president to the press. He makes his home in the pitted no-man's-land of an adversary relationship and is primarily an advocate, interpreter, and amplifier. He must be more the president's man than the press's. But he can be his own man as well.[12]

In recent years, the position of press secretary to the president has taken on increased responsibility and has attained a higher public profile. Jimmy Carter's press secretary, Jody Powell, for example, was among Carter's closest confidants and frequently advised the president on policy matters. Powell's successor as press secretary, James Brady, was seriously wounded in 1981 by a bullet aimed at President Reagan as they both departed from a Washington, DC, hotel. Although Brady was permanently paralyzed, he retained his title as presidential press secretary and returned for limited work at the White House.

Brady was then replaced by Larry Speakes, a former Hill & Knowlton executive, who was universally hailed by the media for his professionalism. During Reagan's second term, Speakes apparently was purposely kept in the dark by Reagan's military advisors planning an invasion of the island of Grenada. An upset Speakes later apologized to reporters for misleading them on the Grenada invasion.

Speakes was replaced by a low-key, trusted, and respected lifetime government public relations professional, Marlin Fitzwater. Fitzwater distinguished himself in the last two years of the Reagan presidency and in the subsequent administration of President Bush. Fitzwater, in turn, was replaced by another career political public relations professional, Dee Dee Myers. Myers was equally respected by the media and brought a refreshing perspective to her role as President Clinton's press secretary. (See the interview at the end of this chapter.)

Over the years, the number of reporters hounding the presidential press secretary—dubbed by some an imperial press corps—has grown from fewer than 300 reporters during President Kennedy's term to around 3,000 today. Salaries of $40,000 to $70,000, relatively rare in most newspaper offices in prior years, are today common in Washington bureaus. And TV network White House correspondents command six-figure incomes, with each major network assigning two or three correspondents to cover the White House simultaneously. Dealing with such a host of characters is no easy task. Perhaps Lyndon Johnson, the first chief executive to be labeled an imperial president by the Washington press corps, said it best when asked by a TV reporter what force or influence he thought had done the most to shape the nature of Washington policy. "You bastards," Johnson snapped.[13]

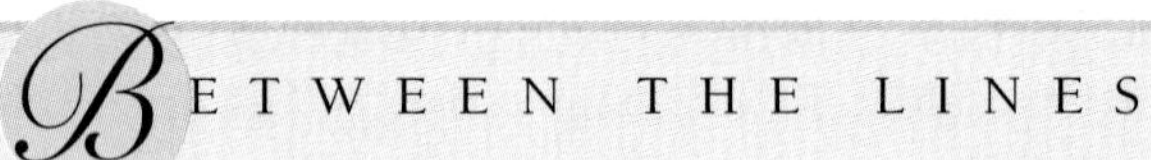

BUSH SPIN DOCTORS STEER OFF COURSE

The 1992 presidential campaign wasn't a memorable one for President George Bush.

Perhaps the candidate should have gotten the message early in the campaign, when Bush officials mistakenly faxed to reporters instructions intended for Republican operatives on "how to put the proper 'spin' on the president's debate performance against Bill Clinton." Said the fax:

> Call your local political reporter and give the spin. If there are any talk-radio shows on the air, call and praise the President's performance. Please use the talking points . . . all surrogates (should give) the same message."
>
> Later, you will receive "Letters to the Editor" points.

Among the "talking points" included in the fax were:

> Tonight was a clear win, a big win for the President. Bill Clinton came in cautious and weak . . . [and] failed to explain or defend his character problem. . . . On healthcare, legal reform, term limits, a balanced budget, education reform and crime, the President clearly bested Bill Clinton.

So much for modern communications technology.

LOBBYING THE GOVERNMENT

The business community, foundations, and philanthropic and quasi-public organizations have a common problem: dealing with government, particularly the mammoth federal bureaucracy. Because government has become so pervasive in organizational and individual life, the number of corporations and trade associations with government relations units has grown steadily in recent years.

Government relations people are primarily concerned with weighing the impact of impending legislation on the company, industry group, or client organization. Generally, a head office government relations staff complements staff members who represent the organization in Washington, DC, and state capitals. These representatives have several objectives:

1. To improve communications with government personnel and agencies.
2. To monitor legislators and regulatory agencies in areas affecting constituent operations.
3. To encourage constituent participation at all levels of government.
4. To influence legislation affecting the economy of the constituent's area, as well as its operations.
5. To advance awareness and understanding among lawmakers of the activities and operations of constituent organizations.

Carrying out these objectives requires knowing your way around the federal government and acquiring connections. A full-time Washington representative is often employed for these tasks.

To the uninitiated, Washington (or almost any state capital) can seem an incomprehensible maze. Consequently, organizations with an interest in government relations usually employ a professional representative, who may or may not be a registered lobbyist, whose responsibility, among other things, is to influence legislation. Lobbyists are required to comply with the federal Lobbying Act of 1947, which imposes certain reporting requirements on individuals or organizations that spend a significant amount of time or money attempting to influence members of Congress on legislation.

In fact, one need not register as a lobbyist in order to speak to a senator, congressional representative, or staff member about legislation. But a good lobbyist can earn the respect and trust of a legislator. Because of the need to analyze legislative proposals and deal with members of Congress, many lobbyists are lawyers with a strong Washington background. Lobbying ranks are filled with former administration officials and congressional members, who often turn immediately to lobbying when they move out of office.

Although lobbyists, at times, have been labeled everything from influence peddlers to fixers, such epithets are generally inaccurate and unfair. Today's lobbyist is more likely to be well informed in his or her field, furnishing Congress with facts and information. Indeed, the lobbyist's function is rooted in the First Amendment right of all citizens to petition government.

WHAT DO LOBBYISTS DO?

The number of lobbyists registered with the U.S. Senate increased from just over 3,000 in 1976 to well over 33,000 in 1990.[14] With the cost of lobbying efforts in the neighborhood of $100 million per year, lobbying has become big business.

But what exactly do lobbyists do?

In the spring of 1994, the Treasury Department issued a 30-page definition of lobbying that confounded most readers.[15] Among other decisions, the department ruled that anyone employed to "follow" federal or even state issues—say, by reading newspapers or magazines—is *not* engaged in lobbying. However, if the articles are clipped and filed as part of research intended to influence legislation, that the department ruled *is* lobbying.

The fact of the matter is, the essence of a lobbyist's job is to inform and persuade.

The contacts of lobbyists are important, but they must also have the right information available for the right legislator. The time to plant ideas with legislators is well before a bill is drawn up, and skillful lobbyists recognize that timing is critical in influencing legislation. The specific activities performed by individual lobbyists vary with the nature of the industry or group represented. Most take part in these activities:

1. **Fact finding** The government is an incredible storehouse of facts, statistics, economic data, opinions, and decisions that generally are available for the asking.
2. **Interpretation of government actions** A key function of the lobbyist is to interpret for management the significance of government events and the potential implications of pending legislation. Often a lobbyist predicts what can be expected to happen legislatively and recommends actions to deal with the expected outcome.
3. **Interpretation of company actions** Through almost daily contact with congressional members and staff assistants, a lobbyist conveys how a specific group feels about legislation. The lobbyist must be completely versed in the business of the client and the attitude of the organization toward governmental actions.
4. **Advocacy of a position** Beyond the presentation of facts, a lobbyist advocates positions on behalf of clients, both pro and con. Often, hitting a congressional representative early with a stand on pending legislation can mean getting a fair hearing for the client's position. Indeed, few congressional representatives have the time to study—or even read—every piece of legislation on which they are asked to vote. Therefore, they depend on lobbyists for information, especially on how the proposed legislation may affect their constituents.
5. **Publicity springboard** More news comes out of Washington than any other city in the world. It is the base for thousands of press, TV, radio, and magazine correspondents. This multiplicity of media makes it the ideal springboard for launching organizational publicity. The same holds true, to a lesser degree, in state capitals.
6. **Support of company sales** The government is one of the nation's largest purchasers of products. Lobbyists often serve as conduits through which sales are made. A lobbyist who is friendly with government personnel can serve as a valuable link for leads to company business.

In recent years, there has been no shortage of controversy surrounding former lobbyists entering the government and then allegedly assisting former clients. In 1994, Secretary of Commerce Ron Brown was accused of interceding in behalf of a Vietnamese businessman who formerly served as Brown's legal client. While the secretary dodged the bullet, the incident did little to enhance the reputation of the Clinton administration. Later in the Clinton presidency, White House adviser Howard Paster left to become chairman of Hill & Knowlton, the huge public relations firm. Although Paster did nothing wrong by accepting his new job, the furor over his appointment underscored the dilemma in the relationship of professional lobbyists to those being lobbied.

GRASS-ROOTS LOBBYING

Particularly effective recently has been the use of indirect, or grass-roots, lobbying (as opposed to conventional lobbying by paid agents). The main thrust of such lobbying is to mobilize local constituents of congressional members, together with the general public, to write, telephone, fax, or buttonhole members of Congress on legislation.

Grass-roots lobbying is a tactic that has been used most effectively by everyone from consumer advocates, such as Ralph Nader's organization and Common Cause, to President George Bush. In the early 1980s, a resurgence of citizens' activism, not seen since the 1960s, began to appear. Coalitions formed on both national and local levels on issues from arms to economics. Locally, tenants' organizations, neighborhood associations, and various other groups won significant concessions from government and corporate bodies.

The success of such grass-roots campaigns was not lost on big business. Business learned that grass-roots lobbying in the 1990s—applying pressure in the 50 states and the 435 congressional districts, from corporate headquarters to plant communities—lies at the heart of moving the powers in Washington. In one of the most successful campaigns in history, a massive grass-roots coalition beat back President's Clinton's energy tax in 1993. Constituents from all over the country—representing farmers, coal miners, aluminum manufacturers, the natural gas industry, home owners concerned about heating oil costs, and so on—wrote their congressional representatives and state legislators to pressure the White House. When the dust settled, the White House gave up on enacting a tax on the heat content of fuels.[16]

Whatever the objectives, grass-roots lobbying and lobbying in general are very much in vogue in the 1990s (Figure 16–3). Rare is the group not represented in Washington. The popcorn industry has its Popcorn Institute. The International Llama Association has its own lobbyists. Hunters have Safari Club International. Those against hunting have the Fund for Animals. Those opposed to increased packaging requirements have United We Resist Additional Packaging (UNWRAP). And all believe their lobbying efforts are most worthwhile.

POLITICAL ACTION COMMITTEES

The rise of political action committees (PACs) has been among the most controversial political developments in recent years. PACs grew in number from about 600 in 1974 to about 4,172 registered with the Federal Election Commission at the end of 1990. They contributed $159.3 million to candidates for the Senate and House of Representatives. Their influence on the political process is enormous.[17]

The increased influence of such groups on candidates is one reason why many people—including some legislators themselves—would like to see PACs severely curtailed or even banned. Indeed, in 1994, Congress severely limited what its members could accept in the form of trips and other niceties from the sponsors of PACs.

HEALING HEALTH CARE THROUGH COOPERATION NOT CONFRONTATION

An open letter to Government leaders and all Americans concerned about health-care reform:

As a physician, I am deeply concerned about the state of our nation's health-care system. It is sick — not terminally ill by any means — but under great stress from costs that have gone up too fast and from inadequate care for 37 million Americans who lack insurance.

Like any serious illness, leaving this one unattended would be irresponsible and self-destructive. It would threaten our people's physical health and our nation's economic strength.

But the problem is very complex, reflecting the diversity of our society. And in our eagerness to fix it, the worst thing would be to look for a quick fix. In this case, we need a search for truth, not for scapegoats.

"We need a search for truth, not for scapegoats."

Unfortunately, the truth has been lost twice in recent searches for scapegoats: last week when America's immunization crisis was blamed on the rising price of vaccines; and earlier, when the Senate Special Committee on Aging reported that we at Merck broke our pledge not to raise prices faster than inflation. In both of these cases, information that was essential to understanding the whole truth was left out.

The truth is: vaccine distribution, not cost, stands between our children and full immunization. It is misleading to ignore the Government's own findings of why so many children aren't being vaccinated. A 1991 report by the National Vaccine Advisory Committee cited 13 barriers to immunization, *none of which was the cost of vaccines*.

A separate study by the Centers for Disease Control said the Government's delivery system was missing many children in rural areas and inner cities — children whose shots are already provided free by the public health clinics.

Comparing today's price for complete immunization to that of 10 years ago misses the mark for other reasons too:

1) In 1988, the Federal Government added an excise tax onto the price of all pediatric vaccines to fund The Childhood Vaccine Injury Compensation Act.
2) As a benefit of new research, children are now being immunized with two additional vaccines to provide protection against two serious infections: Hib meningitis and hepatitis B.

Fully 80% of the increase in cost to vaccinate children was due to these two factors. Only 20% was due to price increases.

Merck is a world leader in children's vaccines, and, for the last two years, our price to the Federal Government for our M-M-R®II vaccine (Measles, Mumps, Rubella) has been unchanged. I think our vaccine that protects children from three potentially debilitating diseases provides outstanding value for the $10.89 per dose it costs the Federal Government. As the President has noted, every dollar invested in immunization saves $10 in avoidable health-care costs.

I would also like to address the Senate Committee's report that said Merck broke its pledge not to raise prices faster than inflation. We take this charge very seriously, because it questions Merck's most valuable asset — our integrity and corporate reputation.

The truth is: Merck kept its promise, and we will continue to do so.

Three years ago, we were the first pharmaceutical company to pledge not to raise our prices faster than inflation, calculated on a *weighted average* basis across our entire product line. We defined inflation as measured by the Consumer Price Index. And we have most definitely kept our pledge.

In 1992, for example, we didn't even recover inflation, because the end result of all our pricing actions — increases, rebates and discounts — was only a 2.7% increase. For the full three years, inflation in the United States averaged 4.0%, and our three-year price increases averaged 3.6%.

That's a far cry from how Merck was portrayed in the Senate Committee report. Unfortunately, the report focused on only 10 products rather than the entire 76 products in our line. This was misleading and unfair.

Like the Clinton Administration, Merck is sincere about improving health care — but the search for solutions must be honest and complete. Prescription drugs account for less than 7 cents of every health-care dollar. And good medicines save more money than they cost by keeping people out of hospitals, out of operating rooms, and out of nursing homes.

"Merck is committed to helping cure America's health-care ills."

I strongly encourage Government officials to work *with* companies like Merck — companies striving to solve our problems. We are participants in the health-care system. We have insights that we'd like to contribute to any discussion of health-care reform. What's more, we're eager to work with Government leaders and health-care providers to bring about meaningful changes that improve the lives of all Americans.

We are dedicated to improving health care. That's why Merck plowed back over $1.1 billion into research and development in 1992 in a tireless effort to conquer AIDS, cancer, Alzheimer's and other devastating diseases.

I want our leaders and all Americans to know that Merck is true to its word. We weren't named "America's Most Admired Corporation"* seven years in a row based on deceit and broken promises. We stand by our pledge, and we stand by the record.

Merck is committed to helping cure America's health-care ills. But to do so, we need unwavering cooperation from every American, both inside and outside of Government. Above all, we need dedication to the truth — the whole truth.

P. Roy Vagelos, M.D.
Chairman & Chief Executive Officer
Merck & Co., Inc.

MERCK

*Fortune magazine's annual Survey of Corporate Reputations

Figure 16–3 One way to reach government officials is to go over their heads to the ultimate authority: the American people. That's what Merck & Company did in 1994 on the burning national issue of health care. (*Courtesy of Merck & Co.*)

With just under 2,000 corporations, 750 associations, and 346 labor organizations sponsoring PACs, concern continues about the influence wielded by these committees. The evidence thus far is inconclusive. Although the number and size of PACs have increased, evidence of PAC-inspired indiscretions or illegalities has been minimal. Nonetheless, the furor over the heightened role of PACs in funding elections is bound to continue until campaign reform becomes reality.

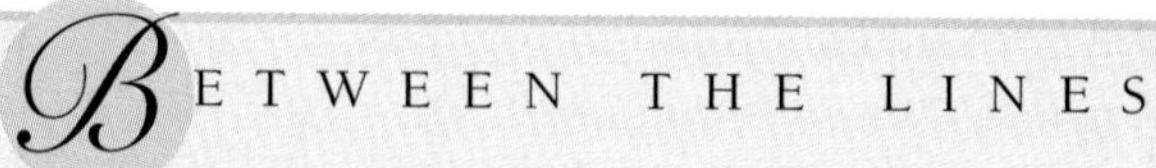

THE "BE" LIST OF GETTING THROUGH TO LEGISLATORS

Pat Choate, a veteran government relations professional at TRW Corporation, offered the following "be" list for anyone wishing to get through to legislators:

- **Be independent.** Policymakers value an independent view.
- **Be informed.** Government thrives on information. Timely facts, a deep knowledge of the subject, and specific examples are invaluable.
- **Be bipartisan.** Matters are more likely to be addressed on merit if approached in a bipartisan manner. Although it is necessary to be sensitive to political nuances, politics is best left to the politicians.
- **Be published.** Clear and cogent thinking, in articles and op-ed pieces, is noticed in Washington and at the statehouse.
- **Be broad-minded.** Don't peddle petty self-interest. Address the broader interests, and your counsel will be sought.
- **Be persistent.** A long-term, persistent commitment of time is mandatory in dealing with legislators.
- **Be practical.** Politicians value practical recommendations they can defend to their constituents.
- **Be honest.** Politicians and the press are skilled at spotting phonies. Honesty is the best policy. It works.

Source: Cindy Skrzycki, "Possible Leaders Abound in Business Community," *The Washington Post* (January 24, 1988): D-2.

DEALING WITH LOCAL GOVERNMENT

In 1980, Ronald Reagan rode to power on a platform of New Federalism, calling for a shift of political debate and public policy decisions to state and local levels. Thus, it became more important for public relations people to deal with local, state, and regional governments.

Dealing with such local entities, of course, differs considerably from dealing with the federal government. For example, opinion leaders in communities (those constituents with whom an organization might want to affiliate to influence public policy decisions) might include such sectors as local labor unions, teachers, civil service workers, and the like. Building a consensus among such diverse constituents is pure grassroots public relations.

The very nature of state and local issues makes it impossible to give one, all-encompassing blueprint for successful government relations strategies.

While the federal government's role—in wielding power and employing public relations professionals—is significant, state and local governments also are extremely important. Indeed, one viable route for entry-level public relations practitioners is through the local offices of city, county, regional, and state government officials.

In local government offices themselves, the need for public relations assistance is equally important. Local agencies deal directly—much more so than their counterparts in Washington—with individuals. State, county, and local officials must make themselves available for local media interviews, community forums and debates, and even door-to-door campaigning. In recent years, local and state officials have found that direct contact with constituents—often through call-in radio programs—is invaluable, not only in projecting an image, but also in keeping in touch with the voters.

Such officials, assigned to ensure the quality of local schools, the efficiency of local agencies, and the reliability of local fire and police departments, increasingly require smart and experienced public relations counsel. State and local information officer positions therefore have become valued and important posts for public relations graduates.

Getting Out the Vote—Literally

The stunning gubernatorial election victory of Christine Todd Whitman in New Jersey in 1993 was marred briefly at the start by the bizarre confession of Ed Rollins, her chief political strategist and campaign manager. After Ms. Whitman upset Governor Jim Florio by about 27,000 votes—less than 2 percent of the total—Rollins touched off a heated controversy and a string of lawsuits and investigations.

At a breakfast meeting in Washington, DC, shortly after Whitman's victory, Rollins told a group of reporters that Republicans had offered money to African-American ministers to prevent them from supporting the liberal Florio from their pulpits. Rollins also said that Republicans had paid likely Democratic voters to stay home on election day.

Later on, Rollins, whom most considered an experienced public relations hand, recanted his initial statements of voter suppression. But the damage had been done. Rollins's initial statements touched off a firestorm of anti-Whitman suspicion.

"Foul!" cried New Jersey Democrats. "Unfair!" screamed African-American leaders.

Complicating Ms. Whitman's problems were videotaped statements attributed to her own brother, who had replaced Rollins as campaign manager about a month before election day. In explaining how his sister had won the election, Webster B. Todd stated that the victory was "the result of getting out the vote on one side and voter sup—" he broke off at that point before resuming—"and keeping the vote down in other areas." Again, the Democrats screamed bloody murder.

All of which probably led newly elected Governor Whitman to ask, "With friends—and relatives—like these, who needs enemies?"

SUMMARY

The pervasive growth of government at all levels of society may not be welcome news for many people. However, government's growth has stimulated the need for increased public relations support and counsel.

The massive federal government bureaucracy, organized through individual agencies that seek to communicate with the public, is a vast repository for public relations jobs. The most powerful position in the land—that of president of the United States—has come to rely on public relations counsel to help maintain a positive public opinion of the office and the incumbent's handling of it.

On state and local levels, public relations expertise also has become a valued commodity. Local officials, too, attempt to describe their programs in the most effective manner.

In profit-making and nonprofit organizations alike, the need to communicate with various layers of government also is imperative. Government relations positions in industry, associations, labor unions, and nonprofit organizations have multiplied.

Like it or not, the growth of government in our society appears unstoppable. As a result, the need for public relations support in government relations will clearly continue to grow into the next century.

DISCUSSION STARTERS

1. Why is the public relations function regarded as something of a stepchild in government?
2. What is the primary function of the USIA?
3. What is meant by "trial by press release"?
4. Why was Ronald Reagan called the "Great Communicator"?
5. What is the function of the White House press secretary?
6. What are the objectives of government relations officers?
7. What are the primary functions of lobbyists?
8. What is meant by "grass-roots lobbying"?
9. What are the pros and cons of PACs?
10. What is President Clinton's strength as a communicator?

NOTES

1. Interview with Office of Communications, U.S. Office of Personnel Management, December 10, 1990.
2. "Public Affairs and Congressional Affairs Activities of Federal Agencies," U.S. General Accounting Office Report to the Honorable William Proxmire, United States Senate, February 1986.
3. "A Critical Article About Bruce Gelb," *Public Relations News* (June 25, 1990): 1.
4. David H. Buswell, "Trial by Press Release?" *NAM Reports* (January 17, 1972): 9–11.
5. "How the U.S. Air Force Communicates," *IABC Communication World* (May 1987): 14.
6. "Public Affairs and Congressional Affairs Activities of Federal Agencies," loc. cit.
7. Mark Hertsgaard, "Journalists Played Dead for Reagan—Will They Roll Over Again for Bush?" *Washington Journalism Review* (January–February 1989): 31.
8. Douglas Jehl and Thomas B. Rosenstiel, "Clinton Camp Orchestrates Effort at Message Control," *Los Angeles Times* (August 18, 1992): A1, A12.
9. Richard L. Berke, "Satellite Technology Allows Campaigns to Deliver Their Messages Unfiltered," *The New York Times* (October 22, 1992): A16.
10. Robert U. Brown, "Role of Press Secretary," *Editor & Publisher* (October 19, 1974): 40.
11. I. William Hill, "Nessen Lists Ways He Has Improved Press Relations," *Editor & Publisher* (April 10, 1975): 40.
12. William Safire, "One of Our Own," *The New York Times* (September 19, 1974): 43.
13. Michael J. Bennett, "The 'Imperial' Press Corps," *Public Relations Journal* (June 1982): 13.
14. "Number of Lobbyists Is on the Rise," *Jack O'Dwyer's Newsletter* (October 31, 1990): 7.
15. Robert D. Hershey, Jr., "In Very Fine Print the Treasury Defines a Lobbyist," *The New York Times* (May 11, 1994): A16.
16. Michael Wines, "Taxes' Demise Illustrate First Rule of Lobbying: Work, Work, Work," *The New York Times* (June 14, 1993): A1, A14.
17. Edward Zuckerman, *Almanac of Federal PACs: 1992* (Washington, DC: Amward Publications, 1992), IX.

SUGGESTED READINGS

Armstrong, Richard. *The Next Hurrah: The Changing Face of the American Political Process.* New York: Morrow, 1988.

How to Find Business Intelligence in Washington. Washington, DC: Washington Researchers Publishing Co., 1988.

TOP OF THE SHELF

Timothy E. Cook. *Making Laws and Making News: Media Strategies in the U.S. House of Representatives.* Washington, DC: The Brookings Institution, 1989.

Making Laws and Making News takes a penetrating look at how congressional media strategies are used to achieve policy goals and further political careers.

A political science teacher at Williams College in Massachusetts, Professor Cook dissects the sophisticated press operations of House members and how they use journalists to address particular issues, move a proposal along, and help them get reelected. Cook also looks at the roles of those who cover the Capitol—local reporters interested in interpreting legislators to small-town constituencies and journalists on the national beat. The press, he argues, wields influence by ultimately deciding what is newsworthy. If both press and politicians hold power, who manipulates whom? Cook sees the tug of war as a draw: "Each side holds important power—members of the House by controlling whether, when, where, and how to grant access; journalists by deciding whether, when, where, and how to pay attention."

Read *Making Laws and Making News* to understand why lawmakers seek publicity and how that need for exposure impacts legislation. Cook adeptly shows how two formidable institutions—the media and Congress—interact to shape the legislative agenda and define political thought.

Hudson, Howard Penn, and Mary Elizabeth Judson, eds. *Hudson's Washington News Media Contact Directory.* (Available from 2626 Pennsylvania Ave., NW, Washington, DC 20037.) This directory lists the Washington correspondents for major newspapers (by state or origin), news bureaus, foreign newspapers and news services, radio and TV networks (both domestic and foreign), magazines, specialized newsletters and periodicals, freelance writers, and photographic services.

Kern, Monague. *30-Second Politics: Political Advertising in the Eighties.* New York: Praeger, 1989.

Manheim, Jarol B. *All of the People, All of the Time: Strategic Communications and American Politics.* Armonk, NY.: M. E. Sharpe, 1991.

Manthorne, Joseph P. *Public Relations Tips in Small Business, the Arts, Education and Service Organizations.* Natick, MA: Manthorne Co., 1987 (48 Charles St.).

Napolitan, Joseph. "100 Things I Have Learned in 30 Years as a Political Consultant." (Available from Public Affairs Analysts, 342 Madison Ave., New York, NY 10173.) Paper for the 19th annual conference of the International Association of Political Consultants, November 1986.

National Directory of State Agencies 1987. (5161 River Rd., Bethesda, MD 20816).

Passarelli, Anne B. *Public Relations in Business, Government and Society: A Bibliographic Guide.* Engelwood, CO: Libraries Unlimited, 1989.

Public Affairs Council. *Leveraging State–Government Relations.* Washington, DC.: Public Affairs Council, 1990.
Smucker, Bob. *The Nonprofit Lobbying Guide.* San Francisco: Jossey-Bass, 1991.
Wittenberg, Ernest, and Elizabeth Wittenberg. *How to Win in Washington.* Cambridge, MA.: Basil Blackwell, 1990.

CASE STUDY

WHITEWATER

"Whitewater is not about cover-ups, it's about screw-ups."—David Gergen, White House Adviser

On April 22, 1994, more than two years after the name "Whitewater" first appeared in the public press, Hillary Clinton conducted a press conference to clear the air.

Sitting in a simple chair in front of a White House portrait of Abraham Lincoln, the First Lady gave a masterful performance, answering an hour's worth of reporters' questions about the ill-fated land deal known as Whitewater.

As effective as the First Lady's performance was, it also underscored the serious public relations crisis that the president and his associates had let Whitewater become.

For while Clintonian defenders, ranging from former U.S. Senator George McGovern to former Watergate lawyer Samuel Dash to humorist Garrison Keillor, bristled at what they claimed were "trumped-up charges that Whitewater was Bill Clinton's Watergate," the crisis was as serious as any impacting the Clinton presidency.

As proof, shortly before the First Lady's press conference, an emergency panel of public relations heavyweights—including Anne Wexler of the Wexler Group, Jody Powell of Powell/Tate, and Paul Costello of Edelman, Inc.—hurriedly formed the Back to Business Committee to defend the Clintons from Whitewater attacks.

"This was a political, not an ethical, situation," Mr. Costello said. "We wanted to provide perspective."

The background of the president's Whitewater investment and subsequent connection to a failed savings and loan institution was an intricate and complicated story. The story broke originally on the front page of *The New York Times* in March 1992 and was promptly ignored by the world.

The story may well have remained ignored had not one unfortunate incident befallen the Clinton administration.

Vince Foster, trusted Clinton confidante and personal attorney on such matters as Whitewater, shot himself in the head and was found dead in a Washington park near the Potomac River.

Thus were the floodgates of Whitewater unleashed for a critical press and a curious public.

While all the facts surrounding Whitewater may never be known, what is known is that at several key junctures, the Clinton public relations machinery fell asleep at the switch.

Consider the following:

As early as 1990, when then Governor Clinton faced stiff opposition in Arkansas, he released his tax returns for the previous 10 years. Curiously, he drew the line at 1980 even though he'd been governor in 1978–79. Tax returns for 1978–79 were conveniently not shared.

In 1992, during the presidential campaign, *The New York Times* asked how the Clintons could afford a $60,000 down payment on a house in 1980 when they'd both been earning much smaller salaries.

The answer, according to Mrs. Clinton, was that the money came from "savings and a gift from our parents." The Clinton campaign, meanwhile refused to release the 1978–79 returns, causing media mavens to wonder what they were hiding.

Later on, in 1994, when Whitewater re-emerged as a national issue after the Foster suicide, Clinton officials still refused to disclose pertinent data.

- White House Counsel Bernard Nussbaum removed Whitewater files from Mr. Foster's office after his death; people wondered what was being withheld.
- The White House initially refused to reveal how much of her own money Mrs. Clinton had used to make a miraculous $100,000 profit in the cattle futures market. People wondered what was being covered up.
- When Republicans called for a special investigator, the president first refused and then agreed to appoint a special counsel to investigate Whitewater. People wondered what he was shielding.

Meanwhile, Mrs. Clinton fared even worse.

Up to the time of Whitewater, the transformation of Hillary Clinton from obedient campaign spouse to White House policy dynamo was unprecedented in American political history.

In the first year of the Clinton presidency, no administration figure was more powerful and revered than the First Lady. Even Capitol Hill Republicans agreed that Hillary's health care testimony was pointed, poignant, and persuasive.

But when Whitewater struck, Hillary clammed up.

She ducked. She was unavailable. When she appeared in public at hospitals and schools, reporters were kept out of conversational range. When her good friends, Mr. Nussbaum and Justice Department attorney Webster Hubble, were forced to depart Washington, she uttered no public word.

Opined *New York Times* columnist Frank Rich, "Since she has the political capital, the firsthand knowledge, the poise and brains to answer many of the growing list of Whitewater questions, why not do so?"

Why not, indeed?

And then there were the president's spokespeople. Almost from the beginning, Whitewater was a study in spokesperson futility.

- George Stephanopoulos, the president's senior advisor, returned to Washington fresh from a New Year's 1994 ski holiday and declared on national television, "All of the pertinent papers in the Whitewater matter have been turned over to the Justice Department."

Wrong. In fact, no papers had been delivered.

It was left to Dee Dee Myers, the valiant White House press secretary, to correct Mr. Stephanopoulos's ill-timed remarks. The president's adviser, Ms. Myers suggested, had, in a phrase reminiscent of Nixonian Washington, "misspoken himself."

- Later on, the president's attorney, David Kendall, finally released the long-sought 1978–79 tax returns in what he called "a spirit of full cooperation and openness."

Well, sort of.

The returns reported Mrs. Clinton's windfall cattle futures profits, all right, but failed to include supporting records. The media screamed.

- Finally, in what may have been the most unfortunate example of "misspeaking oneself," Paul Begala, a longtime Clinton spokesman, purred to a Larry King national television audience, "Both Clintons, they just missed the '80s. These people are just not motivated by money."

Shortly thereafter, Mrs. Clinton's $100,000 cattle futures return on a $1,000 "investment" was revealed.

Perhaps the most unfortunate victim of Whitewater was public relations veteran David Gergen. Until Whitewater occurred, David Gergen was the unquestioned savior of the presidential image. The former Nixon-Ford-Reagan loyalist was recruited by President Clinton to turn around a reeling reputation.

Over the ensuing months, as the president's

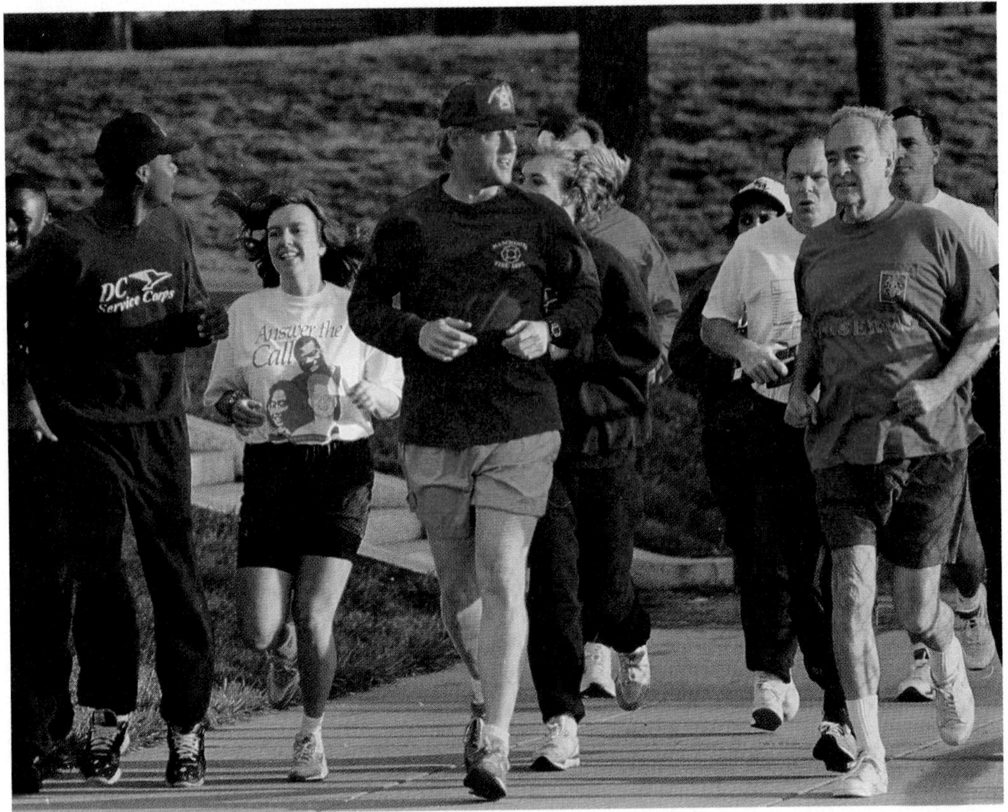

While President Clinton put up a good front during the Whitewater mess, including this effort in behalf of National Youth Service Day, he couldn't run away from the crisis. (*Courtesy of Padilla Speer Beardsley*)

popularity ascended, Gergen became the most prominent administration strategist and most visible presidential booster.

Then came Whitewater.

And counselor Gergen disappeared from the radar screen. He remained inexplicably invisible for weeks until the day *The New York Times* rousted him out for a front-page roasting.

"*With Boss Besieged, Gergen Finds Himself,*" clucked the *Times* headline.

Several weeks later, it was reported that adviser Gergen was on his way out of the administration and back to college (to teach at Duke). Yet another impeccable reputation had been drenched by Whitewater.

In the aftermath of the Whitewater saga, it was left to Leonard Garment, a close advisor to President Nixon during his Watergate trauma, to put the whole thing in perspective:

"In Watergate, there were two guys trying to get the Pulitzer, and in Whitewater there are roughly 50,000. Therefore, there has been an intensification by a very large factor of the pressure for disclosure . . . the creation of a mood of suspicion . . . and a generalized sense of outrage in Congress and the press at any attempts to withhold information."

In Whitewater, as in Watergate—and as in countless other crises afflicting countless other organizations—the best public relations remedy remained the oldest public relations bromide: "Whenever possible, tell the truth."

QUESTIONS

1. How would you characterize the Clintons' approach to disclosure with respect to Whitewater?
2. What was wrong with Mrs. Clinton's initial silence on Whitewater?
3. How would you assess Mr. Clinton's press conference in April 1994?
4. What lessons can be drawn from the missteps of the president's spokespeople?
5. What lessons can be drawn from the experiences of David Gergen?

For further information on Whitewater, see Richard L. Berke, "With Boss Besieged, Gergen Finds Himself," *The New York Times* (March 10, 1994): A1, A20; George J. Church and Michael Kramer, "Into the Line of Fire," *Time* (April 4, 1994): 20–26; Nancy Gibbs, "The Trials of Hillary,'" *Time* (March 21, 1994): 28–37; Frank Rich, "The Silent Partner," *The New York Times* (March 10, 1994): A23; William Safire, "The Whitewater Pulse," *The New York Times* (April 11, 1994): A24; and "Whitewater, Watergate," *The Wall Street Journal* (March 11, 1994): A12.

TIPS FROM THE TOP

DEE DEE MYERS

Dee Dee Myers was named press secretary and deputy assistant to President Bill Clinton upon his taking office in 1993. Ms. Myers was Clinton's press secretary during both the 1992 campaign and the presidential transition. Previously, she worked in Democratic politics at the state, local, and national levels. She served as campaign director for San Francisco Mayor Frank Jordan's 1991 campaign. She also worked as press secretary for former San Francisco Mayor Dianne Feinstein and Los Angeles Mayor Tom Bradley. She served in the 1988 presidential campaign of Governor Michael Dukakis and in the 1984 presidential campaign of Vice President Walter F. Mondale.

What is the primary mission of the president's press secretary?
The primary mission of the president's press secretary is to convey the president's policies, viewpoints, and statements to the media clearly and accurately so the public understands his decisions and his actions. At the same time, the press secretary must convey the press's point of view to the president and prepare him for potential questions or problems.

What is your greatest challenge as press secretary?
My greatest challenge as press secretary is to make sure that the press receives accurate information about what the president and the White House are doing and why.

With so many different issues facing the White House and the president, the press must rely on material from a number of places. There is a lot of potential for misinformation. It is very easy for things to be misconstrued by people with the best intentions. It is important that accurate information reaches the public, and an important part of my job is talking to the press corps and seeing that they receive the best possible information.

What is your daily routine?
Quite honestly, my "daily routine" is constantly changing, depending on the daily needs of the president, the press corps, and the White House. Generally, when I am not traveling with the president, I meet with the communications staff at 7:30 A.M. and the senior staff at 8:00 A.M. Then I meet informally with members of the White House briefing room sometime in the early afternoon. The rest of the day is generally filled with meetings, interviews, events, and phone calls from the press.

How would you describe your access to President Clinton?
The president is a very open and accessible person. He encourages openness among his staff and invites a number of viewpoints on a wide range of issues. It is one of his greatest qualities, and one which keeps him in touch with people and makes him such a great leader. I meet with the president several times a day to discuss the schedule, pending press events, and issues of the day.

What is the relationship between the administration and the media?
The relationship between the Clinton White House and the media has improved, though there are still some rough spots. The media have an important job to do, which they must and should take seriously. In doing their job, they must constantly analyze, synthesize, and evaluate information from a variety of different sources. Since we rely on them to convey the president's views, words, and actions to the American people, it is our job to make sure they get all of the facts correct. In doing our jobs, there can be a sort of back-and-forth exchange, which is not a sign of tension, but rather an effort on all parts to get the facts straight.

What are the most important attributes of a presidential press secretary?
The most important attributes of a presidential press secretary are, in my opinion, honesty, patience, the ability to say "I don't know"—and a darn good sense of humor.

What has been your toughest assignment as press secretary?
My toughest assignment as press secretary is preparing for the daily briefings. Being prepared to answer questions on a wide variety of topics in a fast-paced and constantly changing environment is, to say the least, challenging.

What is the most rewarding part of your job?
The most rewarding part of my job as press secretary to President Clinton is knowing that I have a role in making some of the administration's ideas to improve people's lives a reality. Passing the president's economic plan, which has helped to revive the economy and create jobs, the Family Medical Leave Act to allow persons to help a sick family member without the risk of losing their job—these are all great accomplishments. Being a part of these accomplishments has been very rewarding.

What advice would you give to someone aspiring to become a presidential press secretary?
Start with a genuine interest in politics and government. Find a candidate or public official you believe in. Be willing to do whatever it takes to get the job done. Add an interest in the news business and a real affection (most of the time!) for the press. Know that reporters are smart and experienced; many of them covered the beat before you came, and many will be there after you're gone. Never lie. Don't be afraid to say "I don't know"—and try to get the answer later. Don't take yourself too seriously, and never underestimate the value of a good sense of humor.

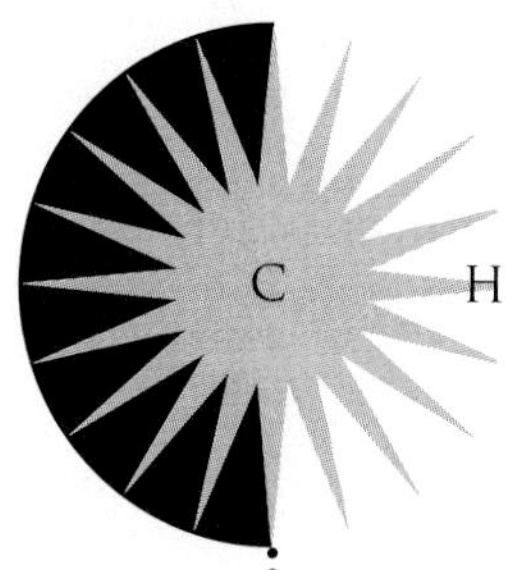

CHAPTER 17

INVESTORS

ECONOMICS, PEOPLE SAY, IS THE "DISMAL SCIENCE." MOST students wouldn't argue with that definition.

Nonetheless, someone also once said, "The business of America is business," and that, too, is true.

The point is that business dominates not only American society but societies around the world. Indeed, as the year 2000 approaches, the economies of the nations of the world are becoming inextricably intertwined.

A knowledge of business is therefore beneficial to any citizen. In public relations, business knowledge is becoming a necessity.

For one thing, most citizens—either through their own investments or through participation in pension funds, mutual funds, or profit-sharing plans—are shareholders. And in the 1990s, shareholders have become increasingly involved in the affairs of such venerable organizations as IBM, Westinghouse, Reebok, American Express, and others.[1]

For another thing, the field of financial public relations has become increasingly essential for public companies and therefore increasingly important for the practice of public relations.

INVESTOR RELATIONS

Financial relations—or investor relations or just IR—has been a growth area in public relations since the 1960s. Financial relations generally blends the skills of finance and writing with knowledge of the media, marketing, and, more recently, government because of its increased role in the capital markets.

Financial relations was born in the mid-1930s, shortly after the passage of the Securities Act of 1933 and the Securities Exchange Act of 1934, which attempted to protect the public from abuses in the issuance and sale of securities. Financial relations remained in relative obscurity, however, until the 1960s, when investors rushed to the stock market to strike their fortunes. Stock prices escalated, and IR enjoyed a heyday.

After a brief interruption in the 1970s, the investing public returned with a roar to the stock market in the 1980s. Then, in October 1987, a funny thing happened to the bull market—it crashed 500 points, sending stocks and investors tumbling back to reality.

The markets were resilient, though, and by the end of the 1980s, investors again were buying securities. The Wall Street scandals of the late 1980s—punctuated by the fines and jail terms levied against Ivan Boesky and Michael Milken—heightened the public's wariness of "Wall Street." (Which was also the title of a blockbuster Michael Douglas film that didn't help matters.)

Against this backdrop, the IR function has emerged in the 1990s as a senior-level position that helps plan, position, and market the perception of a company and justify the performance of its stock to the financial community and investors.[2]

IR combines the disciplines of finance and communications, as it portrays to current and future investors a company's financial performance and prospects. What distinguishes IR people from others in public relations are the specialized financial skills and experience required to communicate effectively with numbers-oriented audiences like individual and institutional investors and "buy-side" and "sell-side" stock market analysts (Figure 17–1).

ESSENCE OF IR

The 1990s has brought about a resurgence of interest among companies for people skilled in IR.

What exactly is IR?

Basically, it is the effort to narrow the gap between the perception of a company and the reality—in other words, helping the firms' securities reach their appropriate market price. To do this, IR professionals must encourage stockholders to hold company shares and persuade Wall Street financial analysts, banks, and mutual funds to take an interest.[3]

A company's stock price is its currency. Premium stock prices allow an organization to acquire others, whereas low stock prices encourage raids from competitors. If shares

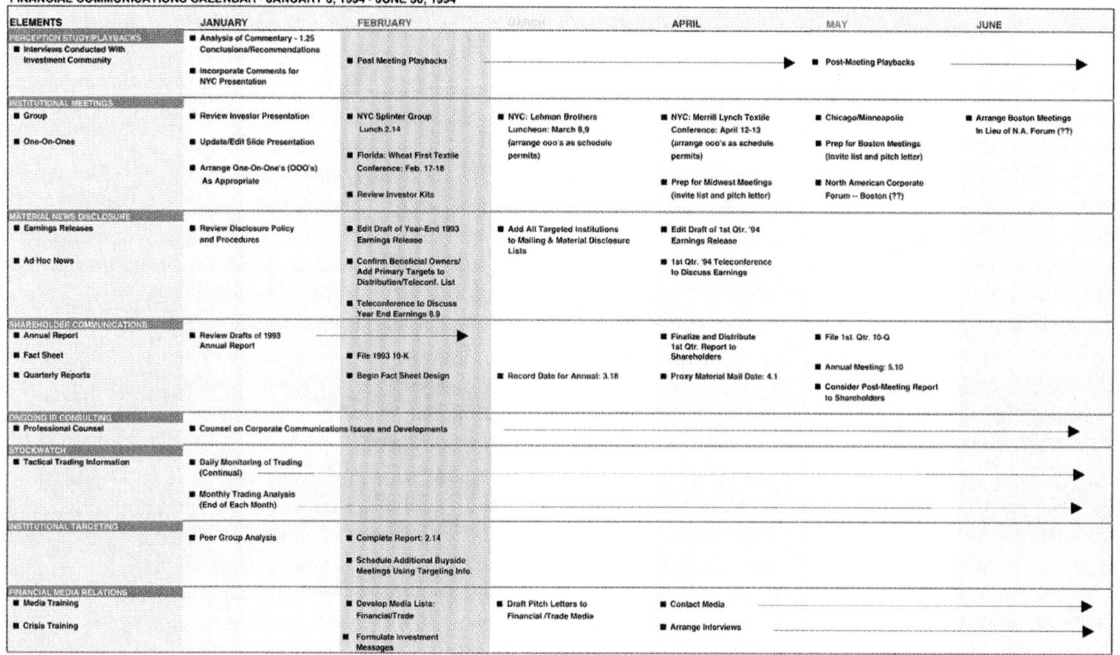

XYZ CORPORATION

FINANCIAL COMMUNICATIONS CALENDAR - JANUARY 3, 1994 - JUNE 30, 1994

ELEMENTS	JANUARY	FEBRUARY	MARCH	APRIL	MAY	JUNE
PERCEPTION STUDY/PLAYBACKS ■ Interviews Conducted With Investment Community	■ Analysis of Commentary - 1.25 Conclusions/Recommendations ■ Incorporate Comments for NYC Presentation	■ Post Meeting Playbacks			■ Post-Meeting Playbacks	
INSTITUTIONAL MEETINGS ■ Group ■ One-On-Ones	■ Review Investor Presentation ■ Update/Edit Slide Presentation ■ Arrange One-On-One's (OOO's) As Appropriate	■ NYC Splinter Group Lunch 2.14 ■ Florida: Wheat First Textile Conference: Feb. 17-18 ■ Review Investor Kits	■ NYC: Lehman Brothers Luncheon: March 8,9 (arrange ooo's as schedule permits)	■ NYC: Merrill Lynch Textile Conference: April 12-13 (arrange ooo's as schedule permits) ■ Prep for Midwest Meetings (invite list and pitch letter)	■ Chicago/Minneapolis ■ Prep for Boston Meetings (invite list and pitch letter) ■ North American Corporate Forum -- Boston (??)	■ Arrange Boston Meetings In Lieu of N.A. Forum (??)
MATERIAL NEWS DISCLOSURE ■ Earnings Releases ■ Ad Hoc News	■ Review Disclosure Policy and Procedures	■ Edit Draft of Year-End 1993 Earnings Release ■ Confirm Beneficial Owners/ Add Primary Targets to Distribution/Teleconf. List ■ Teleconference to Discuss Year End Earnings 8.9	■ Add All Targeted Institutions to Mailing & Material Disclosure Lists	■ Edit Draft of 1st Qtr. '94 Earnings Release ■ 1st Qtr. '94 Teleconference to Discuss Earnings		
SHAREHOLDER COMMUNICATIONS ■ Annual Report ■ Fact Sheet ■ Quarterly Reports	■ Review Drafts of 1993 Annual Report	■ File 1993 10-K ■ Begin Fact Sheet Design	■ Record Date for Annual: 3.18	■ Finalize and Distribute 1st Qtr. Report to Shareholders ■ Proxy Material Mail Date: 4.1	■ File 1st. Qtr. 10-Q ■ Annual Meeting: 5.10 ■ Consider Post-Meeting Report to Shareholders	
ONGOING IR CONSULTING ■ Professional Counsel	■ Counsel on Corporate Communications Issues and Developments					
STOCKWATCH ■ Tactical Trading Information	■ Daily Monitoring of Trading (Continual) ■ Monthly Trading Analysis (End of Each Month)					
INSTITUTIONAL TARGETING	■ Peer Group Analysis	■ Complete Report: 2.14 ■ Schedule Additional Buyside Meetings Using Targeting Info.				
FINANCIAL MEDIA RELATIONS ■ Media Training ■ Crisis Training		■ Develop Media Lists: Financial/Trade ■ Formulate Investment Messages	■ Draft Pitch Letters to Financial /Trade Media	■ Contact Media ■ Arrange Interviews		

Figure 17–1 IR, like any other aspect of public relations practice, begins with a plan. Typical elements include meetings with institutional buy-side analysts and brokerage firm sell-side analysts, as well as financial communications such as annual reports, fact sheets, quarterly reports, and financial media relations.

are fairly priced in relation to current or future expectations, the company has a better chance of raising money for future expansion. In any event, a strong shareholder base is necessary to support management's objectives.

A public company must communicate promptly and candidly any information, both good and bad, that may have an effect on its securities. Practitioners must see that shareholders receive such information fully, fairly, and quickly so that they can decide whether to buy, hold, or sell the company's securities.

The institutions and individuals who own the common stock of a company are, in effect, its owners. The shareholders, in person or by proxy, elect the board of directors, which in turn selects the officers who run the company. So, in theory at least, shareholders (who own the company) influence the operations of that company. In practice, corporate officers manage companies with relative independence. Nevertheless, shareholders constitute a critical public for any firm.

Why do investors buy a company's shares? The first requisite must be performance. A company that fails to perform can't expect good communications to sell its stock. On the other hand, a thoughtfully planned and executed financial communications program may materially enhance the reputation and therefore the market popularity of a company that performs well.

HOW IMPORTANT IS THE INDIVIDUAL INVESTOR?

Individual investors are a very important part of the New York Stock Exchange.

They are important because they provide capital for the growth of business and the economy. That means new jobs and a better quality of life in the communities in which we live.

They are important because they bring a diversity of investment goals and preferences. Their active participation adds significantly to the liquidity of the market—the ability to buy and sell shares at stable prices.

The NYSE demonstrates its commitment to the individual investor in many ways.

At the NYSE—and only at the NYSE—individual investors always get preferential treatment. Through an exclusive **NYSE Individual Investor Express Delivery Service,** individual investor orders get priority status over all other orders at all times. Even in periods of unusual activity, those orders go to the head of the line, in front of all others, including institutional and program trading orders.

America has a long history of individual investor involvement in business. In fact, one in five Americans directly owns stocks or shares of stock mutual funds. And the market they most often choose, and their funds most often choose, is the New York Stock Exchange.

The NYSE is dedicated to continuing that tradition and to making this market work for all investors.

When investors hold stock in NYSE-listed companies, they are sharing in a history of growth that outshines most other major investment vehicles. In the decade of the '80s, the compound rate of return on the Standard & Poor's 500 was 17.4%, compared with 10.6% for commercial real estate and 9.6% for money market funds.

When investors purchase NYSE-listed stock, they choose from 1,800 of the best U.S. and foreign businesses, companies with proven track records. They benefit from NYSE rules that ensure shareholder participation in corporate governance and full disclosure of corporate developments.

By placing orders on the NYSE, investors are assured of the best available price in a market that sets the standard for the world in terms of fairness, openness and liquidity. They are participating in a market that combines the most sophisticated technology and communications systems with the best professional judgment.

The NYSE provides the most meaningful market regulation in the world. Surveillance and enforcement activities include a close watch on industry sales practices. And NYSE arbitration procedures offer investors an efficient and inexpensive way to resolve any disputes with brokerage firms.

The NYSE's board of directors has approved a series of measures to address the problem of excess volatility in the market on both a short-term and a long-term basis.

Short-term measures include slowing the market down during hectic periods so that all investors can obtain information and participate equally in trading.

For the long term, the board created a blue-ribbon Panel on Market Volatility and Investor Confidence. Headed by General Motors Chairman Roger B. Smith, the panel has recommended added initiatives to maintain a strong market for all participants.

These are compelling reasons for individuals to invest in NYSE-listed stocks. And it is why they should be looking to invest for the long term, for their future and the future of their families.

The best way to begin is by sitting down and discussing investment goals with a broker who is registered and part of an NYSE-member organization. That means the investor is assured of dealing with a trained individual, qualified to provide advice and to serve the investor's needs with all the resources of a reputable firm.

At the New York Stock Exchange, concern for the individual investor will always be a priority.

NYSE

FOR THE BEST POSSIBLE PRICE, ASK YOUR BROKER TO TRADE NYSE-LISTED STOCKS ONLY ON THE NYSE.

Figure 17–2 The increased clout of institutional investors in the 1990s has caused concern about the diminished role of individual investors in the securities markets. This New York Stock Exchange ad illustrates what the world's largest stock exchange is doing to confront the issue. (*Courtesy of New York Stock Exchange*)

ORGANIZING THE PROGRAM

The most effective way to reach the investing public—individuals as well as institutions—is through a systematic program of financial relations, ordinarily managed by an IR director. Frequently, programs are bolstered by the involvement of a financial relations counseling firm (Figure 17–2).

Because most public companies perpetually compete for equity capital, an organized IR program is essential. IR has many audiences, including analysts who recommend the purchase and sale of securities, brokers, market makers who specialize in a stock, institutional and individual investors, the media, and even employees. All must receive direct communications but each has different needs.

The IR professional must be a good communicator and a good salesperson, knowledgeable in finance and accounting, conversant in the language of Wall Street, and outgoing. Almost 50 percent of IR executives surveyed in 1992 by the 2,350-member National Investor Relations Institute had backgrounds in finance and accounting or other corporate areas, up from 38 percent four years earlier. More than half of those surveyed reported directly to the chief financial officer or corporate treasurer rather than to the public relations department.[4] The rapidly changing practice of financial relations means that the IR director must be equally conversant in finance and communications. He or she also must be aware of recent Securities and Exchange Commission (SEC) rulings (see Appendix F).

OURCES OF INVESTOR INFORMATION

Investors receive corporate information from securities analysts, public media, and corporate communications vehicles such as annual and quarterly reports, fact books, and annual meetings.

SECURITIES ANALYSTS

Securities analysts greatly influence the buying habits of institutional investors and others. Today analysts are asked to follow an expanding number of companies, with the average analyst keeping tabs on as many as 40 firms. Frequently, analysts aren't able to evaluate a company that does not meet rigid criteria in terms of market value, capitalization, and trading volume. Additionally, many analysts today are young and less experienced, further complicating the role of the practitioner. Nevertheless, in financial relations, analysts are a key public and must be reached.

To reach analysts effectively, credible communications must play a major role. In that effort, a firm's management should be accessible; otherwise, a corporate message will likely fall on deaf ears, no matter how good a company's earnings record is. Good practitioners make sure that key analysts are heavily exposed to corporate management. In addition, analyst meetings, presentations, and field trips are most important. A luncheon appearance before the New York Society of Security Analysts, for example, can be a significant platform for reaching Wall Street. Company-sponsored meetings in leading cities can also serve to broaden interest in a company. Finally, inviting analysts to tour plants, visit headquarters, and meet corporate management on the firm's own turf is another way to introduce and educate analysts about a company and its leadership.

In recent years, analysts have been questioned on their objectivity in evaluating companies. The use of analysts to explain corporate decisions has become standard newspaper practice. But many times—particularly in securities underwritings and takeover situations—an analyst's firm also may serve as an adviser to a company. The use of analysts by the media to explain corporate decisions in such situations—especially when those comments may influence stockholders—is suspect.[5] Nonetheless, dealing with analysts on a regular basis is a hallmark of a solid IR program.

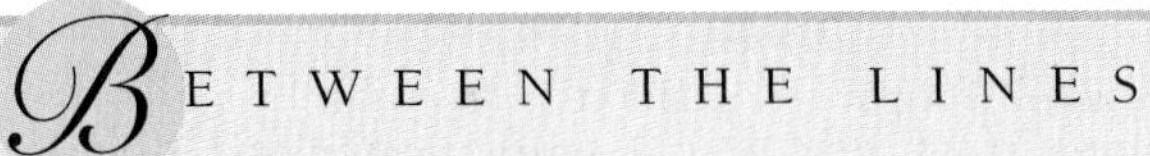

THE DONALD SNUFFS THE PEST

In the spring of 1990, when the financial empire of Donald Trump stood on shaky ground, the worst chapter in the history of IR was written.

When a little-known Philadelphia securities analyst named Marvin Roffman was quoted in *The Wall Street Journal* as questioning whether Trump's gaudy Atlantic City Taj Mahal casino would generate enough revenue to meet its $95 million debt service, The Donald, in effect, had Roffman fired.

Specifically, the morning after the article ran, Trump faxed a letter to the brokerage firm president threatening a lawsuit unless the firm agreed either to fire Roffman or to issue a letter of apology for his "outrageous" analysis. The firm caved in immediately and made Roffman sign a letter of apology. Muttered the firm's president, "We thought that in view of the fact that Trump was an influential person, he was due an apology."

A few days later, Roffman had second thoughts and retracted his apology. When he did, he was fired.

In the wake of the Trump–Roffman affair, investors correctly wondered how much they could trust other securities analysts if their firms were similarly chilled by threatened lawsuits. It's a good question.

P.S. Several months later, Mr. Roffman sued his former employer for improper dismissal. A few weeks after that, Mr. Trump renegotiated his Taj Mahal debt because he couldn't meet the interest payments.

P.P.S. In spring 1991, Mr. Roffman was awarded $750,000 by a three-member arbitration panel of the New York Stock Exchange. The award was paid by Mr. Roffman's former employer.

FINANCIAL PRESS

The stock exchanges insist that material corporate announcements must be released by the fastest available means. Ordinarily, this means that such information as top-management changes and dividend or earnings announcements must be disseminated by telephone, telegraph, or hand delivery to media outlets. Basically, companies are expected to release material information through the following channels:

1. **Major wire services**—Dow Jones & Company, Reuters Economic Service, Bloomberg Business Wire, or the Associated Press.
2. **Major New York City newspapers**—one or more of the New York City newspapers of general circulation that publish financial news, such as *The New York Times* and *The Wall Street Journal* (Figure 17–3).
3. **Statistical services**—particularly Standard & Poor's Corporation and Moody's Investor Service, which keep complete records on all publicly held companies.

IN ALL FAIRNESS, WE SAY FOUL.

Recently The Wall Street Journal devoted a good bit of space to an "exposé" of Dun & Bradstreet Business Credit Services.

In a nutshell, it was stated that D&B's data are inaccurate, outdated and skimpy, and that our methods for collection are suspect. In addition, it was alleged that we encourage our people to produce too many reports too quickly, that we rarely question data provided by the companies we report on, and that when problems do come to our attention, we're unresponsive.

Now, we'll be first to admit we're not perfect. Like every large database, ours contains errors. But to say that we ignore them, much less condone them, is irresponsible.

Over 60,000 customers rely on D&B business information for making millions of credit decisions every year. If things were even a tiny fraction as grim as The Journal suggests, the American economy would be in serious disarray.

The fact is, today's D&B information is far and away the best it has ever been and getting even better; it is the best available anywhere. Our investment in both human and technological resources is tremendous. We spend over $200,000,000 a year gathering and verifying fresh information, updating our files with more than 100,000,000 new data elements annually. We hire the best college graduates we possibly can, and we reward them with bonuses, not for quantity but for quality. Our quality-control standards are more exacting than ever, and our automated verifications are state-of-the-art.

We also ask the businesses we report on to review the reports for accuracy. Of the millions of reports we send out for review every year, fewer than 2% are returned for significant correction. And, of course, we correct them.

Even a casual reading of The Journal article reveals glaring inconsistencies and self-contradictions, but the biggest one is truly ironic: Dow Jones News Retrieval, a blood relative of The Wall Street Journal, sells large amounts of Dun & Bradstreet business information to its own customers.

If Dow Jones thinks our quality is so questionable, why do they accept money for it?

Which leads us to believe that the real issue raised by The Wall Street Journal isn't *caveat emptor*, but rather *caveat lector*.

"Let the reader beware."

Dun & Bradstreet Business Credit Services

DB a company of The Dun & Bradstreet Corporation

Figure 17–3 Perhaps no financial medium is as powerful as the daily *Wall Street Journal*. When a company is subject to a scathing first-page *Journal* article, it often fights back to reassure investors. Such was the case with this Dun & Bradstreet ad. (*Courtesy of Dun & Bradstreet Corporation*)

4. Private wire services—services such as PR News Wire and Business Wire, which guarantee, for a fee, that corporate news is carried promptly and reaches newspaper newsrooms and brokerage offices.

Achieving broad disclosure for a small company is not easy. A major corporation automatically attracts the attention of the financial community, but the smaller firm, in order to satisfy disclosure requirements, may have to use paid wire services and direct mailings to shareholders. For example, to make the Dow Jones wire, a firm's stock must be listed in the national or supplemental list of *The Wall Street Journal*. The burden of proof in conforming to disclosure requirements, however, rests squarely with the issuer, so a company must take appropriate measures to ensure that SEC requirements for prompt disclosure are met.

Positive media stories about a company offer substantial benefits. Investment community professionals read the trade press avidly. Consequently, strategically placed articles discussing technological innovations or effective strategies may boost a company in the eyes of security analysts, stockbrokers, and institutional portfolio managers.

In the 1990s, television is an important source for financial information. The nation's top financial show, *Wall Street Week*, has become an investor staple, reaching millions of viewers each week on the Public Broadcasting System (PBS). PBS also presents *The Nightly Business Report* each evening, to review the day's financial news. CNN has its own half-hour program, *Money Line*. The Consumer News and Business Channel (CNBC) provides round-the-clock financial news. CNBC, backed by the vast resources of the National Broadcasting Company, willingly absorbed early losses to establish a longer-term future in reporting financial news.

ORPORATE COMMUNICATIONS TOOLS

A company has numerous vehicles for financial communications at its disposal, including an annual report, quarterly reports, an annual meeting, and fact books.

THE ANNUAL REPORT

The annual report is a company's key financial communications tool. Many IR professionals swear by it. Others argue that the annual report is exaggerated in importance, contending that the ideal annual report might simply read:

> Dear Shareholder,
>
> We did well in 1994. Earnings and sales were up. Customers were happy and buying.
>
> Your dividend was increased. Thanks for purchasing our stock and not selling it.

Clearly, such brevity is not the trend. In fact, in the 1990s, annual reports have been pilloried as "grossly-overrated as a communications tool . . . over-designed and overwritten . . . too often intended to be read by the CEO and his senior executives and their families."[6]

This is too bad because corporate America spends $5 billion each year on the annual report. The average annual report costs a company about $3.52 per copy, is 44 pages in length, and entails an average printing of 129,000 copies.[7]

Although the individual elements and the general tone of annual reports change gradually over the years and among firms, most reports include a company description, letter to shareholders, financial review, explanation and analysis, management/marketing/issues discussion, and graphics.

- **Company description** This should include the company's name, its headquarters address, a description of its overall business, and a summary of its operations in both narrative and numerical form. Many firms begin their annual reports with a one-page, easily readable summary of financial highlights.
- **Letter to shareholders** This letter ordinarily incorporates a photo of the firm's chairperson and president. It covers these key areas: (1) an account of last year's achievements; (2) a discussion of both the general and the industry environment in which the company operated over the past year and will operate in the future; (3) a discussion of strategies for growth, the general operating philosophy for the future, and new product and capital spending plans; and (4) general targets for increased earnings and returns. In recent years, stimulated by the conversational shareholders' letters of legendary investor Warren Buffett, the Chairman's Letter has become more folksy. In 1993, for example, Disney Chairman Michael Eisner confided to his shareholders, "I am writing this letter on a plane the Sunday after Thanksgiving on my way to Houston with my wife and two of my sons, Breck and Anders, to see the Broadway tryout of *Beauty and the Beast.*" Such folksy letters typified the more "human" approach to shareholder communications in the 1990s.
- **Financial review** In light of the SEC's increasing demands for corporate disclosure, many companies have expanded financial reviews to encompass the data historically included in other reports, such as the 10-K. Financial reviews generally include multi-year summaries of such items as sales, cost of goods, operating costs, operating margin, expenses, capital expenditures, income taxes, and net earnings and such salient shareholder information as price/earnings ratios, debt ratios, return on assets, and return on equity.
- **Explanation and analysis** This complement to the financial review is a general discussion of the factors influencing the numbers in terms of earnings performance, operating income and expenses, asset growth, and other key financial indicators.
- **Management/marketing/issues discussion** The annual report's narrative section may be devoted to a general profile of key managers, an explanation of the company's markets or products, or essays detailing the company's view on emerging public issues.
- **Graphics** Photographs and charts are critical to the annual report. So, too, is an annual's cover, which should be warm, inviting, and even creative[8] (Figure 17–4). Most people have limited time to read a report, so a dynamic chart or striking photo may serve to draw readers into the annual's body copy. In recent years, criticism of the blandness, dullness, and sameness of annual reports has intensified.

QUARTERLY REPORTS

Quarterly reports or interim reports keep shareholders abreast of corporate developments between annual reports. In general, the SEC recommends that the quarterly report include comparative financial data for the most recent quarter and year-to-date

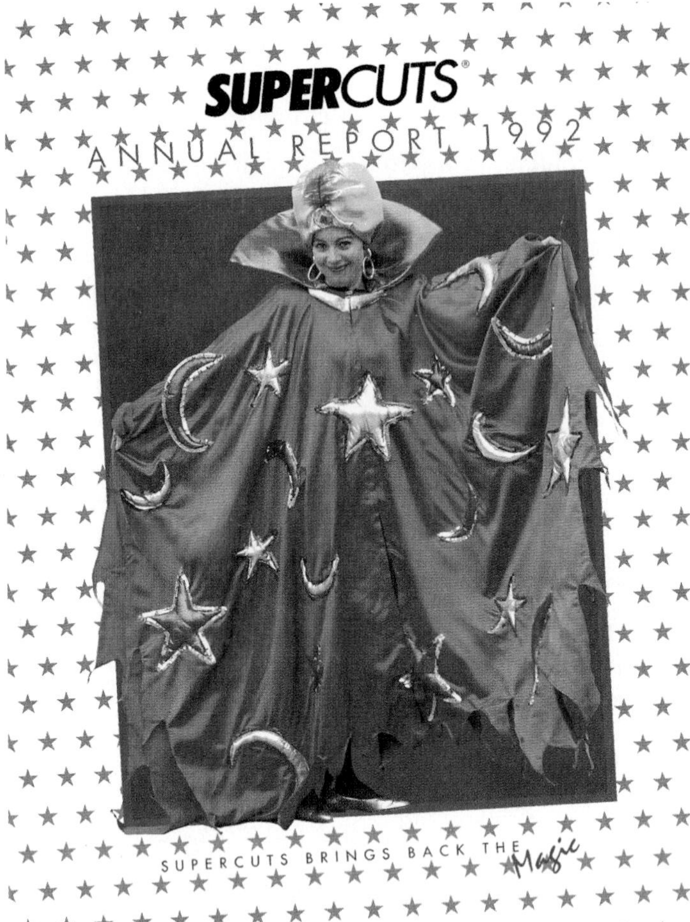

Figure 17–4 Annual reports in the 1990s have to be as provocative as possible to capture the attention of otherwise occupied shareholders. Rising to the challenge, Super Cuts chose this colorful presentation of its vice president of training and development for the cover of its 1992 annual. (*Courtesy of Super Cuts*)

for the current and preceding year. Such items as net sales, costs and expenses, gross and net income, assets, liabilities, net worth, and earnings per share should always be included. So, too, should a letter to the shareholders that analyzes the important developments during the quarter. In recent years, the SEC has been less rigorous in its quarterly report requirements, and some firms have cut back on expenses in producing such reports. McKesson Corporation, following publication of a summary annual report in 1987, went one step further by combining its quarterly report to shareholders with its employee magazine. The company reasoned that because many employees were also shareholders, combining the two publications could save money and be more all-encompassing.

ANNUAL MEETING

Once a year the management of public companies is required to meet with the shareholders in a forum. Occasionally, this annual "mating dance" inspires fear and trepidation among managers unused to the glare of public questioning and skepticism. Indeed, several annual meeting gadflies travel from annual meeting to annual meeting, probing management on unpleasant, difficult, and occasionally embarrassing subjects. The existence of these gadflies has led some managers to view the meeting with a degree of loathing.

Indeed some, including General Motors Chairman John Smale, argue that the annual meeting is a waste of time for corporate management and a waste of money for corporate stockholders.[9] When the gadflies take over, the annual meeting can become "an afternoon in hell" for an otherwise unflappable CEO. One notorious gadfly (who would sue your author if he mentioned her name) uses an outrageously priced "Annual Meeting Newsletter/Photo Album" as an, ahem, "inducement" for CEOs to escape harsh treatment at the annual meeting slugfest. Many CEOs willingly subscribe to the newsletter. Consequently, there are many who think the entire kabuki dance of the annual meeting is nutty.

Nonetheless, a well-planned, well-executed annual meeting can enable corporate managers to communicate effectively with investors (see Appendix G for an annual meeting checklist). Here are a few hints for organizing a successful meeting.

- **Management speeches** Beginning with short, punchy speeches from the chairman or president, or both, can establish the tone for the meeting. These speeches set an upbeat tempo for the rest of the meeting, emphasizing current developments and perhaps even announcing quarterly earnings or management changes.
- **Stockholder voting** Voting includes choosing directors and auditors and deciding on proposals presented by shareholders. Management's viewpoint on these proposals is spelled out in previously mailed proxy statements.
- **Question-and-answer sessions** The Q&A portion of the meeting is the reason that many stockholders attend. They like to see management in action, answering pertinent questions from the floor. How managers handle questions is thought to reflect their competence in running the company.

  Questions should be handled candidly, succinctly, and, whenever possible, in a light, nonthreatening manner. Most stockholders agree that the best meetings are those conducted in a friendly atmosphere. After all, stockholders own the business. A manager's light touch at an annual meeting may win over even the most skeptical stockholders.

For now, the annual meeting is still a corporate custom. Like any other communications tool, it should be actively managed to promote goodwill and further the positive perception of the company among its shareholders.

OTHER SPECIALIZED COMMUNICATIONS

Periodically, companies complement the traditional array of financial communications with specialized vehicles.

Investment Focus ... *Finding investment value in uncertain times and changing markets from the investment professionals at U.S. Trust*

U.S.TRUST

Vol.1, No.1 Monday, April 19,1993

FCC Ruling Could Actually Speed Cable's Evolution

The recent FCC announcement that it will establish benchmark prices for basic cable service should have little impact on the industry's exciting long-term prospects. In fact, according to U.S. Trust analyst Michael Hoover, the current weakness in these stocks presents some compelling investment opportunities.

Although uncertainty will persist until the FCC finalizes its regulations, all indications are that the new rates will cause a one-time 10% to 15% rollback in prices for basic cable. Moreover, these are not rate-of-return regulations; the FCC will regulate only top-line revenues. Cable operators will still be able to put through annual increases (probably at the rate of CPI plus some yet-to-be-determined amount).

In response to the ruling, cable operators are likely to accelerate their plans to expand their available channels (up to 500) to increase their non-regulated pay offerings — multichannel pay-per-view video, home transaction services, educational programs, interactive games and a host of others.

Time Warner is the core holding in the cable group, in Hoover's view. Expanded channel capacity entails a dramatic increase in demand for programming — a major plus for Time Warner's film, music and even publishing businesses. Time Warner is the world's largest manufacturer, manager and distributor of copyrights. Moreover, the company has the second largest portfolio of cable systems and is the dominant pay-TV player.

Comcast is also worth considering. Although largely a cable provider, the company does have cellular involvement — specifically its stake in Fleet Call, a major third-party provider of wireless service — which could offset any near-term negatives resulting from FCC regulations.

Paramount and Turner Broadcasting are possible beneficiaries of the trend toward greater demand for programming, but Hoover regards their stocks as fully valued and does not recommend their purchase.

HMOs Are at the Top of the Food Chain

Whatever the specific proposals of Hillary Rodham Clinton's health care task force, it is clear that health care in the U.S. will continue to grow — due to the aging of America, new technology and other factors. And higher-quality HMOs, in the view of U.S. Trust Analyst Robert Janis, should be among the long-term winners.

Managed competition, a likely proposal, would expand HMO membership. HMOs are not a panacea, but they are the best cost-effective solution. Employers, especially small employers, could join health insurance purchasing cooperatives (HIPCs) to gain pricing leverage in buying health care from HMOs or other providers.

CONTACT: ALLISON COOKE KELLOGG • 212-852-1127 • U.S. TRUST CORPORATION • 114 WEST 47TH STREET NEW YORK, NY 10036

Figure 17–5 U.S. Trust, a leading investment manager, issued a special biweekly "investment focus" mailer to interest journalists in its investment expertise. (*Courtesy of U.S. Trust*)

- **Fact books** Corporate fact books and fact sheets are statistical publications distributed primarily to securities analysts and institutional investors as supplements to the annual report. Their main value lies in giving a busy analyst a quick snapshot of a company's position and prospects.
- **Investors' guides** These mini fact books give a general corporate description and list leading products, office locations, and financial highlights. Such guides introduce a company and frequently contain tear-out cards for acquiring additional corporate information.
- **Private television packages** In addition to video annual reports and meetings, videocassette packages showing presentations by corporate officers can be shipped directly to portfolio managers and analysts around the country at a comparatively low cost. Video can extend and expand an executive's time and deliver the corporate story to a larger, more targeted financial public over a wider geographic area.

- **Dividend stuffers** Frequently, practitioners include management messages in dividend mailings. Shareholders tend to take seriously mailings that include checks; thus, these mailings help greatly in delivering the firm's ideas.
- **Publicity and advertising** Periodically, a company can reprint its income statement or balance sheet or even issue special media materials (Figure 17–5) to encourage a broad audience to find out more about the firm.
- **Special meetings** Some companies have taken the unusual step of organizing special meetings of interested publics, largely to reinspire investors to own the company's stock. The most famous gathering of this type was General Motors' extravagant and extraordinary exhibition in New York City in 1988 at a cost of $20 million. GM attracted 14,000 guests to the Waldorf-Astoria Hotel to show off present and future products. Although the event attracted its share of criticism, many believed that it was a sensible step to restabilize the company's declining image.

ACTIVIST SHAREHOLDERS

One emerging phenomenon of the mid-1990s is the emergence of shareholder activists. In an unprecedented wave of CEO firings, companies from American Express to IBM to Borden to General Motors, all found themselves besieged by shareholders unhappy with executive performance.

Said the departing chairman of Westinghouse after he was unseated by an irate shareholder group, "The entire market and structure in the United States relative to the relationship between shareholders and companies is changing."[10]

And so it is.

The nation's largest shareholder activist group is the California Public Employees Retirement System, or CALPERS. In the mid-1990s, CALPERS has begun stepping up the pressure on boards of directors of underperforming companies. "We want to see these companies turned around," said CALPERS' general counsel. And so, CALPERS published a list of more than a dozen companies it had targeted for action in shareholder proxy contests.[11]

The emerging shareholders' rights movement was born amid the takeover battles of the 1980s as shareholders became dismayed that corporations erected elaborate defenses to avoid being taken over and, in the process, froze out shareholders. As a consequence, in recent years, shareholders have focused on issues such as executive compensation and have taken management to task when earnings are inferior or management seems unresponsive to shareholders' concerns.[12]

This activist movement among shareholders will not end soon. The implications for IR professionals—who must deal skillfully with activist shareholders—are significant.

SUMMARY

The real bottom line in financial communications is improving corporate credibility. Investors show support only when they believe in a firm and its management. Doubletalk, fudging, and gobbledygook have no place in communicating with investors, who want to know all the news, the bad as well as the good, quickly and accurately. Because

Taking Both Sides in a Takeover Tussle

IR has become big business.

As a case in point, whenever a firm is involved in takeover or merger discussions, it hires, along with bankers and lawyers, outside IR specialists. One of the most savvy IR firms in the 1990s is New York City's Kekst & Company.

It wasn't surprising, therefore, when, in the fall of 1993, entertainment giants Paramount Communications and Viacom announced plans for a friendly merger, the two retained Kekst to spread the word. The situation quickly became complicated when another entertainment giant, QVC, made a hostile bid for Paramount, with a much larger potential payoff for Paramount shareholders.

Despite the seemingly better deal that Paramount's shareholders would have received from QVC, Kekst continued to help Viacom and Paramount in their attacks against their attacker.

Said the head of a shareholder rights advocacy group, "Rather than maximize shareholder value, they're thinking about preserving empires and perpetuating power and client relationships."

While Paramount and Viacom used different investment bankers and securities lawyers, both stayed with Kekst as their IR counsel. Said Kekst Chairman Gershon Kekst, "The firm's ethical conduct is beyond reproach. We take this integrity business very, very, seriously."

Nonetheless, many wondered, in light of Kekst's representation of the low bidder in the Paramount tussle, whether the firm was skating on thin conflict of interest ice.

corporate candor is the only path to credibility and respect, these general guidelines should be followed in communicating with the investment community:

1. **Be aggressive.** Aggressive companies don't necessarily acquire the reputation of being stock promoters. Companies today must compete vigorously for visibility. Analysts and investors want to stay informed. Therefore, aggressive communications, truthfully delivered, are the best kind.
2. **Promote success.** The record ordinarily does not speak for itself. Companies must communicate to investors an intelligent evaluation of their securities, competitive position, and market outlook.
3. **Meet despite bad news.** Companies should meet with investors in bad and good times; investors need constant communication. If there are problems within a firm, investors want to know what management is doing to solve them. Most of all, investors hate surprises.

4. **Go to investors; don't make them come to you.** Investors expect to be courted. Firms need to broaden investment ownership. Therefore, a company should volunteer information rather than make investors pry it loose.
5. **Enlist investors in the public policy area.** There are millions of stockholders in the United States today. The implications of even partially mobilizing this vast constituency are awesome. Historically, corporations have not sought out stockholder support for public policy viewpoints, which seems a tragic mistake. To accomplish meaningful legislative and regulatory reforms that favor free enterprise, all concerned parties—shareholders and management alike—must join the fight.

As the year 2000 approaches and corporate America continues to be restructured, financial markets become more global, and the trading of securities becomes a 24-hour process—largely due to the explosion in computer technology—IR will increase in importance. The best IR policy will continue to be one based on preserving and enhancing corporate credibility *all* the time.

DISCUSSION STARTERS

1. What was the significance to IR of the securities acts of 1933 and 1934?
2. What are the primary responsibilities in communicating to shareholders?
3. Why are securities analysts significant to a corporation?
4. What is required of companies in disseminating material news announcements?
5. How important is the annual report today?
6. What are the essential elements in the annual report's Letter to Shareholders?
7. What happens at an annual meeting?
8. What are some of the specialized communications that firms use to reach shareholders?
9. What are the duties of an IR officer in the face of a takeover attempt?
10. What is the key element in preserving an organization's credibility?

NOTES

1. James Kim, "Companies to Activists: Let's Make a Deal," *USA Today* (March 23, 1993): 1B–2B.
2. Robert E. Brown, "How Investor Relations Has Evolved," *Social Science Monitor* (August 1990): 1.
3. David Stahl, "Building an Investor Relations Program," *Savings and Community Banker* (April 1994): 34, 40.
4. Paul Sweeney, "Polishing the Tarnished Image of Investor Relations Executives," *The New York Times* (April 3, 1994): F5.
5. Paul Bernish, "Fighting a Takeover Battle in the Press," *Across the Board* (July–August 1989): 28.
6. "Annual Reports," *Inside PR* (October 1992): 25–26.
7. *Annual Report Production Cost Survey* (New York: Padilla Speer Beardsley, Inc., 1989).

8. Bey Freeman, "Special Report: Annual Reports," *IABC Focus* (March 1990): 1.
9. "GM's Smale Criticizes Annual Meetings," *Jack O'Dwyer's Newsletter* (May 4, 1994): 2.
10. "Shareholders at the Gate," *Inside PR* (March 1993): 22–23.
11. Veneeta Anand, "Shareholder Activists Will Keep Heckling Boards," *Investor's Business Daily* (January 29, 1993): 7.
12. Leslie Wayne, "Shareholders Exercise New Power with Nation's Biggest Companies," *The New York Times* (February 1, 1993): A1–A16.

TOP OF THE SHELF

Robert Slater, *Get Better or Get Beaten!* Homewood, IL.: Dow Jones Irwin, 1994.

The best way for a student to learn about business in the 1990s—with its downsizings and restructurings and reengineerings and cost cuttings—is to get things straight from the lion's mouth.

This book is subtitled *31 Leadership Secrets from GE's Jack Welch.* Welch, the chairman of General Electric Company, has been dubbed by friend and foe alike "Black Jack" for his decisive (some would say ruthless) corporate actions.

Welch is unequivocal in his philosophy of letting workers work and getting rid of them when they don't.

"Stop standing in the way of the people who work for you," lectures Welch. "They're a lot smarter than you probably are giving them credit for."

Welch goes on to suggest that "unleashing the energy and intelligence and raw ornery self-confidence of the American worker is the best way for any organization to get ahead." In other words, in the eyes of perhaps America's best-regarded business leader, the key to success is to "get in there and do it."

The downside in this leadership proclamation is that executives like Welch have little tolerance for excuses. "Forget about the 101 reasons why you failed and someone else succeeded," says the chairman. "Forget about arguing that life is unfair. Stop creating the impression that there is a conspiracy out there trying to get you."

Read this book, oh graduating senior . . . and be warned.

SUGGESTED READINGS

A.R.3: The Complete Annual Report & Corporate Image Planning Book. New York: Macmillan, 1988.

Casper, P. *The Corporate Annual Report and Corporate Identity Planning Book.* Chicago: Alexander Communications, 1987 (212 W. Superior 60610).

Corporate Annual Report Newsletter (407 S. Dearborn, Chicago, IL 60605).

Fowler, Elizabeth. "The Lure of Investor Relations." *The New York Times,* November 18, 1986. The writer sees IR as a growing career path. People are needed to help their employers by encouraging stockholders to hold on to shares and by persuading the financial industry and general public to take an interest in their firms.

Furlong, Carla. *Marketing Money.* Chicago: Probus, 1989.

Graves, Joseph. *Investor Relations Today.* Glen Ellyn, IL: Investor Relations Association, 1985 (364 Lorraine Ave. 60137).

Hogan, Bill. "The Asset Test." *Washington Journalism Review* (July 1985): 38–43.

Idea Bank for Annual Reports. New York: Corporate Shareholder Press, 1987 (271 Madison Ave., New York, NY 10016).

Investment Newsletters (Larimi Communications Associates, 5 W. 37th St., New York, NY 10018).

Investor Relations Almanac/Resource Directory. New York: Corporate Shareholder Press (271 Madison Ave., NY 10016).

Lewis, Richard A. *The Annual Report: A Tool to Achieve the CEO's Objectives.* New York: Corporate Annual Reports, 1987 (112 E. 31st Street, 10016).

Mahoney, William F. *Investor Relations: Professionals' Guide to Financial Marketing and Communications.* New York: New York Institute of Finance, 1990.

Marcus, Bruce W., and Sherwood L. Wallace. *Competing in the New Capital Markets: Investor Relations Strategies for the 1990s.* New York: Harper Business, 1991.

Nicholas, Donald. *The Handbook of Investor Relations.* Homewood, IL: Dow Jones-Irwin, 1988.

Powell, Joanna. "Institutional Investor." *Washington Journalism Review* (July 1985): 44–46.

Watt, Roop & Co. *Street Talk.* Cleveland, OH: Watt, Roop & Co. Watt, a public relations and marketing counseling firm, prepared this IR planning guide for companies that go public.

What Non-U.S. Companies Need to Know About Financial Disclosure in the United States. New York: Hill & Knowlton, 1989 (420 Lexington Ave. 10017).

Winter, Elmer L. *A Complete Guide to Preparing a Corporate Annual Report.* New York: Van Nostrand Reinhold, 1987.

CASE STUDY

ROGER AND HIM

For any major corporation, dealing with investors also means being sensitive to the big picture—particularly the way a company and its leaders are portrayed in public. The CEO is the organization's most pivotal spokesperson. How a CEO's strength, courage, and character are characterized may significantly influence an investor's decision to buy, hold, or sell a stock.

And so it was in the spring of 1990 that the nation's premier automobile company, General Motors, and its chairman, Roger Smith, became a source of national derision as they fumbled and bumbled in the face of an unabashedly biased, shoestring-budgeted movie entitled *Roger & Me.*

The $200,000 film was the brainchild of one Michael Moore, a chubby, left-leaning, independent producer born in Flint, Michigan—the town that was the subject of the film.

In his work, Moore portrayed GM and its officials as callous, remote, and unfair toward those who live in Flint—the city in which GM itself also was born.

The film's tone was revealed early when Moore began:

> Maybe I got this wrong, but I thought companies lay off people when they hit hard times. GM was the richest company in the world and was closing factories when it was making profits in the billions. GM chairman Roger Smith appeared to have a brilliant plan: First, close 11 factories in the United States, then open 11 in Mexico, where you pay the workers 70 cents an hour. Then use the money you save by building cars in Mexico to take over other companies, preferably high-tech firms and weapons manufacturers. Next, tell the union you're broke and they happily agree to give back a couple billion dollars in wage cuts. Take that money from the workers and eliminate their jobs by building more foreign factories.

The film got more vicious.

Complicating matters was GM's response to Moore. The company avoided the producer at every turn. The premise of the film, in fact, was Moore's futile attempt to track Smith down, to question him about GM plant closings in Flint.

Along the way, moviegoers witnessed the following:

- Flint's civic leaders pictured as buffoons, hatching one harebrained scheme after another in an attempt to spur economic development.

  In one scene, Flint's upper crust threw a "Great Gatsby" party, hiring unemployed GM workers as human statues to brighten the festivities.
- Flint portrayed as a city of abandoned buildings, boarded-up businesses, and impoverished people. One woman said she raised rabbits "for pets or meat" to supplement her Social Security check. In one charming scene, she obligingly clubs a rabbit into submission and then skins the cuddly creature on camera.

- Interviews with laid-off GM workers revealed desperation. One declared, "GM should get rid of Smith and all the other SOBs. I am sick and tired of the fat cats. Smith can't look an auto worker in the eye."

And neither, so it seemed, could the GM chairman.

The producer sought the chairman at the swank Grosse Point Yacht Club, the Detroit Athletic Club, and New York's Waldorf-Astoria. Moore was booted from each location.

He then attended GM's annual meeting, waiting patiently until all the stockholders had their say at mikes placed around the room. Then, just as he was about to fire a question at Smith, the GM chairman cut Moore off and declared the meeting closed. The last laugh, however, was on Roger. Moore's camera crew zeroed in on Smith and the other executives on the rostrum, who were heard congratulating themselves on how they dispensed with Moore.

Finally, the film producer and the chairman came face-to-face—at the annual GM Christmas party that Moore invaded. After Moore told Smith of the mass evictions of the poor people in

Flint, Smith responded, "GM did not evict them." He then refused Moore's coaxing to go to Flint. While the chairman partied, the scene was interrupted by yet another Flint family being thrown out of its home, Christmas tree and all, the day before Christmas Eve.

By the beginning of 1991, millions of film buffs had seen *Roger & Me.* The film—biased as it surely was—nonetheless was critically acclaimed and won numerous awards. Warner Brothers spent millions promoting the movie, and it became a box-office and video-store smash. Even Michael Moore became rich as a result, although he insisted on continuing to dress shabbily and wear a baseball cap.

In a written statement after the film's release, GM Chairman Smith said:

> I haven't seen the film, but from what I have read it does a great disservice to the community of Flint and the thousands of GM employees who are making a positive contribution to the city and to GM. How I personally feel is unimportant. It is unfortunate that people who have pride in their community and the products they build are subjected to public embarrassment at a time when they are producing some of the finest products in America.

GM's public relations executives defended their decision not to meet with Moore. They insisted that Moore would "have taken advantage of Smith" if they had agreed to a meeting. Even if Smith had agreed to give an interview, Moore would have found a way to make him look silly, the executives said.

Not only did GM refuse to meet with Moore, but even after the film's success, the company wouldn't budge. When Moore appeared on not one but two live Phil Donahue broadcasts from Flint, GM still refused to send a representative. Even worse, reports circulated that GM had asked its advertising agencies not to place commercials on television programs that featured Michael Moore.

At the end of 1990, Roger Smith, regarded by many as a fine executive and decent man, retired from GM. In his final interview as chairman, Smith told *The Wall Street Journal* that, while he regretted the movie and found it completely unfair and prejudiced, had he been faced with the same situation again, he wouldn't have altered GM's posture one bit.

QUESTIONS

1. How do you think *Roger & Me* portrayed the chairman of GM?
2. How do you think *Roger & Me* portrayed GM's public relations people?
3. Do you agree with GM's handling of Michael Moore?
4. Had you been the public relations director of GM, what would you have advised Chairman Smith to do?
5. Do you think *Roger & Me* will hurt GM's long-term image?

TIPS FROM THE TOP

CAROL SANGER

Carol Sanger is vice president of corporate communications for Federated Department Stores, Inc. Prior to joining Federated in 1984, Ms. Sanger was business editor of *The Cincinnati Enquirer.* A journalist and reporter, she also served as press secretary to U.S. Senator Birch Bayh of Indiana and special assistant to the U.S. secretary of transportation. She has received numerous honors in the fields of communications and journalism.

What is the essence of effective investor relations?
An open, two-way communications pipeline between the company and its key markets is essential to an effective IR program. Beyond the ability to channel the right information into the right external hands, an effective IR function needs to act as a filter and gauge for incoming data about the company and how it is being perceived in the financial marketplace. Because perception often is a more salient measure of reality than fact, the key is knowing and responding to what actually is out there in the markets. Yet, this often is the most difficult aspect of the job because what you must respond to is not necessarily what a company's management may want to acknowledge, much less address.

Can IR impact the price of a company's stock?
Perhaps in the short term it can. It certainly can be useful in helping to get your company's story out and prevent surprises, which—good or bad—the market never likes. Over the long haul, however, unless you have financial and operating performance to back you up, nothing an IR program can do will make a meaningful difference.

How important was public relations in the takeover of Federated?
Public relations, however, can influence perceptions among key internal and external audiences, and that factor can be of vital importance both during and in the aftermath of a corporate takeover. In the 1988 takeover of Federated Department Stores, for instance, an aggressive grass-roots public relations effort waged in the media, as well as at the community and state legislative levels, forced Campeau Corporation of Toronto to commit to maintaining Federated's corporate headquarters operations in Cincinnati. That decision clearly had a major impact on the local and state economy and on hundreds of lives that otherwise might have been uprooted.

How important is the annual report?
I'd like to say it is an important—or at least an effective—communications tool. That would help justify the innumerable hours, not to mention the cost, that go into producing it. But I honestly don't think it's either. Many companies began using the annual report as a marketing vehicle in the late 1960s, and this approach continued to evolve, so that each year's book was glossier, glitzier, and, not incidentally, costlier than the one before. Meanwhile, the editorial content has come to be viewed as less and less credible. There's an axiom that holds that more people read an annual report *before* it is published than after, and this is probably all too true. Still, if you are going to do a full-scale annual, remember that for many it is the only impression of your company that they will get. So it should tell the story you want to tell, even if only through color, photos, and headlines. It should reflect who you are and what you're doing, with more of a focus on the future than the past.

What distinguishes successful IR programs from unsuccessful ones?
Knowing your objective. If you don't know where you're going, you'll never get there. You'll just be wasting a lot of time and effort in the process and have nothing measurable to show for it in the end.

How do you view the emergence of women as a majority in public relations?
This question raises the specter of the "velvet ghetto," which suggests that once women are a majority in a field, its median level of compensation necessarily declines, along with its professional status. This, unfortunately, has been all too true in some fields in the past. Whether it will be as true in the future is debatable, but it definitely is a concern for today's public relations professional. A larger issue is the status assigned to the public relations profession overall. This has less to do with gender than it does with the expertise and legitimate professional credentials of individuals in the field. So long as public relations is an unregulated profession, in which all comers are free to enter and assign themselves professional standing at will, public relations will never attain the recognition or status of the licensed and regulated professions.

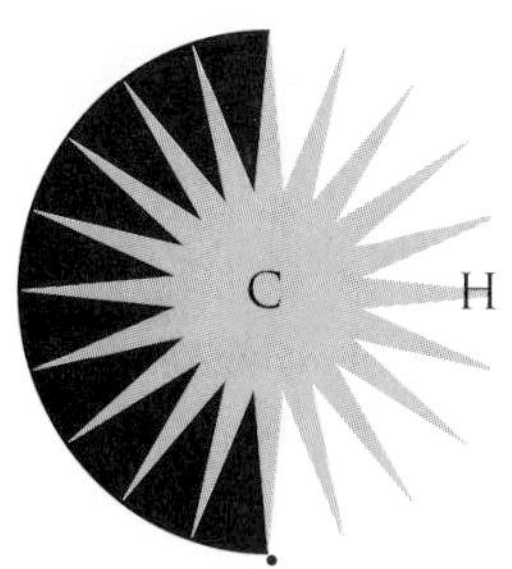

CHAPTER 18

PUBLIC RELATIONS AND THE LAW

A LAWYER, THE OLD SAW GOES, TELLS YOU WHAT YOU MUST do. A public relations professional, on the other hand, tells you what you should do. Therein lies the difference and the tension between the two functions.

A lawyer, correctly, must counsel the client on how best to perform in a court of law. A public relations professional must counsel a client on how to perform most effectively in another court—the court of public opinion.

There is a huge difference.

"Conclusions to be reached in a case will be induced only by evidence and argument in open court and not by outside influence, whether private talk or public print," proclaimed U.S. Supreme Court Justice Oliver Wendell Holmes in 1907. The esteemed justice obviously had no idea that approximately ninety years later, advances in technology would allow potential jurors throughout the community, as well as a worldwide audience, to view an incident on video dozens of times and listen to hundreds of commentators offer their opinions on a case before ever being invited to enter a courtroom.[1]

In recent years, defendants ranging from boxer Mike Tyson to singer Michael Jackson to millionaire mogul Leona Helmsley have found themselves judged guilty before ever entering a courtroom. So pervasive and powerful is communication in our society that public relations professionals increasingly have come to play a pivotal role in influencing public opinion, winning contested settlements, and generally affecting the outcome of legal issues.

PUBLIC RELATIONS AND THE LAW: AN UNEASY ALLIANCE

The legal and public relations professions have historically shared an uneasy alliance. Public relations practitioners must always understand the legal implications of any issue with which they become involved, and a firm's legal position must always be the first consideration.

From a legal point of view, normally the less an organization says prior to its day in court, the better. That way, the opposition can't gain any new ammunition that will become part of the public record. From a public relations standpoint, though, it may often make sense to go public early on, especially if the organization's integrity or credibility is being called into public question. Such different views are manifested in different advice. A smart general manager carefully weighs both legal and public relations counsel before making a decision.

It also should be noted that law and ethics are interrelated. The PRSA Code of Professional Standards (Appendix A) notes that many activities that are unethical are also illegal. However, there are instances where something is perfectly legal but unethical, and other instances in which things might be illegal but otherwise ethical. Thus, when a public relations professional reflects on what course to take in a particular situation, he or she must analyze not only the legal ramifications but also the ethical considerations.[2]

This chapter will examine the relationship between the law and public relations and the more prominent role the law plays in public relations practice. The discussion will not be all-encompassing. Rather, it will introduce the legal concerns of public relations professionals today: First Amendment considerations, insider trading, disclosure law, ethics law, privacy law, and copyright law—concerns that have become primary for public relations in the 1990s.

PUBLIC RELATIONS AND THE FIRST AMENDMENT

Any discussion of law and public relations should start with the First Amendment, which states: "Congress shall make no law . . . abridging the freedom of speech or the press." The First Amendment is the cornerstone of free speech in our society: what distinguishes America from many other nations.

The 1990s have seen a blizzard of First Amendment challenges.

- In the summer of 1990, North Carolina Senator Jesse Helms introduced an amendment to restrict the National Endowment for the Arts from funding "obscene" or "indecent" materials, defined as a host of antisocial acts (Figure 18–1).

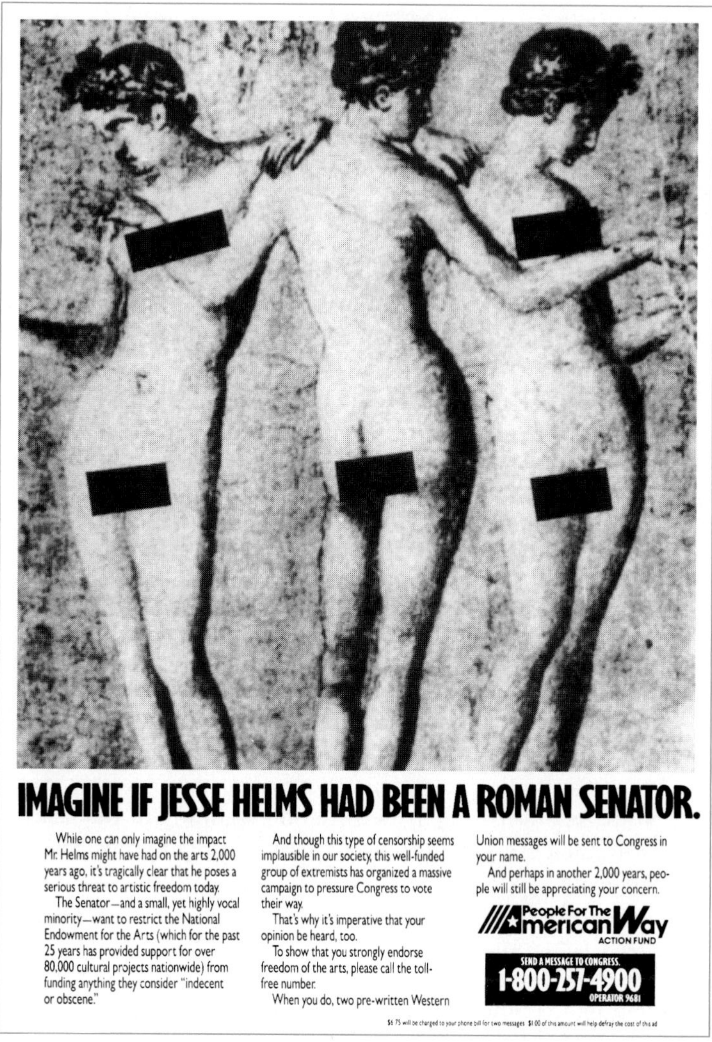

Figure 18–1 The arts community was chilled in 1990 by the attempts of Senator Jesse Helms to restrict federal funding from anything considered "indecent or obscene." *(Courtesy of People for the American Way)*

- That same summer, the rap group 2 Live Crew was arrested in Hollywood, Florida, when they sang tunes from their album "As Nasty as They Want To Be," whose sexual explicitness a federal judge ruled was obscene.
- In 1993, the Federal Communications Commission decided to delay deals totaling $170 million by the Infiniti Broadcasting Corporation because it employed foul-mouthed radio personality Howard Stern. As a result of Stern's scatological humor, Infiniti was fined well over $1 million by the FCC.[3]
- That same year, the Supreme Court reaffirmed its view that advertising is a form of speech protected by the First Amendment. The Court ruled that a city may not automatically exclude advertising brochures from the newspaper vending machines that it licenses for use on public property. The Court's ruling

reaffirmed the First Amendment protection of commercial speech.[4] In a landmark 1978 case, *First National Bank of Boston v. Belloti,* the Supreme Court struck down a Massachusetts law that permitted a business corporation to speak only on those issues "that materially affect its business, property or assets."[5]

- In the spring of 1994, television talk show host Phil Donahue was turned down on a First Amendment appeal to televise the execution of a willing condemned murderer.

As these recent skirmishes suggest, interpreting the First Amendment is no simple matter. One person's definition of obscenity may be another's definition of art. Interestingly, the case against 2 Live Crew ultimately was dismissed; as was the case against Infiniti; as was a celebrated case against the Cincinnati Contemporary Arts Center, which had exhibited a graphic retrospective on the effects of AIDS. Despite continuing challenges to the First Amendment, Americans continue to enjoy broad freedom of speech and expression. Because the First Amendment lies at the heart of the communications business, defending it is a front-line responsibility of the public relations profession.

PUBLIC RELATIONS AND INSIDER TRADING

Every public relations professional should know the laws that govern an organization. A practitioner in a hospital should have a general understanding of health care law. A practitioner working for a nonprofit organization should understand the laws that govern donors and recipients. A practitioner who works in a particular industry—chemicals, computers, sports—should understand the laws germane to that particular area.

Nowhere in public relations practice is an understanding of the law more important than in the area of financial disclosure. Every public company has an obligation to deal frankly, comprehensively, and immediately with any information that is considered material in a decision to buy, sell, or even hold the organization's securities. The Securities and Exchange Commission (SEC)—through a series of court cases, consent decrees, complaints, and comments over the years—has painted a general portrait of disclosure requirements for practitioners (see Appendix F), with which all practitioners in public companies should be familiar.

As mentioned in Chapter 17, the SEC's overriding concern is that all investors have an opportunity to learn about material information as promptly as possible. Through its general antifraud statute, Rule 10b-5 of the Securities and Exchange Act, the SEC strictly prohibits the dissemination of false or misleading information to investors. It also prohibits insider trading of securities on the basis of material information not disclosed to the public.

In recent years, the public has been shocked by a series of celebrated cases involving the use of insider information to amass illegal securities gains. The two most celebrated insider trading cases were those of Ivan Boesky and Michael Milken, Wall Street legends who were both slapped with nine-figure fines and jail terms. A host of their associates, equally guilty of insider trading violations, also were dispatched to the slammer.

Nor have journalists escaped the ignominy of insider trading convictions. The most famous case involved a *Wall Street Journal* reporter, R. Foster Winans, Jr., who was convicted in the summer of 1985 of illegally using his newspaper column in a get-rich-quick stock-trading scheme. Basically, Winans gave favorable opinions about companies in which a couple of his stockbroker friends had already invested heavily. The stocks then generally went up, the brokers and their clients profited handsomely, and Winans was sentenced to prison.

The Supreme Court, in 1987, upheld Winans's conviction for securities fraud by the narrowest of votes. In so doing, the Court reasoned that by "misappropriating information belonging to the *Journal*," Winans had violated the newspaper's intangible property rights. According to legal experts, this ruling has widespread implications for anyone with access to business information, including public relations professionals.

What the Supreme Court ruling means, in effect, is that an employer can adopt work rules or a code of ethics that can carry a criminal penalty. This may create problems for those, like public relations people, who share information with journalists; for whistleblowers, who could be threatened with prosecution for unauthorized disclosure of confidential information; or for anyone involved in the dissemination of sensitive company data.

PUBLIC RELATIONS AND DISCLOSURE LAW

Besides cracking down on insider trading, the SEC has challenged public relations firms on the accuracy of information they disseminate for clients. In 1982 the SEC issued a 95-page release, "Adoption of Integrated Disclosure System," which attempted to bring some order to the chaotic SEC requirements. Essentially, the document tried to make more uniform the instructions governing corporate disclosure of information. Today, in an environment of mergers, takeovers, consolidations, and the incessant rumors that circulate around them, a knowledge of disclosure law, a sensitivity to disclosure requirements, and a bias toward disclosing rather than withholding material information are important attributes of public relations officials.

PUBLIC RELATIONS AND ETHICS LAW

The laws regarding ethical misconduct in society have gotten quite a workout in recent years. Regrettably, public relations practitioners have, in several well-known cases, been at the center of the storm. In 1988, Lyn Nofziger, former White House political director and communications counselor, was sentenced to 90 days in prison and fined $30,000 for violating the Federal Ethics in Government Act, which forbids lobbying former contacts within one year of leaving the government. Also in 1988, former White House Deputy Chief of Staff Michael K. Deaver, another well-known public relations professional, was found guilty of perjury about his lobbying activities. He also faced a lengthy jail sentence and a serious fine. In response, Deaver railed against the "outrageousness of congressmen saying that I violated the public trust, when they go out and make all the money they want on speaking fees" paid for by special-interest groups.[6]

Deaver had a point. Some of the most powerful representatives in Congress—from House Ways and Means Chairman Dan Rostenkowski in 1994 to the 1990 "Keating Five" senators—were also called on the carpet and accused of violating government ethics laws.

The problems of Nofziger and Deaver called into question the role of lobbyists in government. As explained in Chapter 16, the activities of lobbyists have been closely watched by Congress since the imposition of the Lobbying Act of 1947. In recent years, however, the practice of lobbying has expanded greatly.

Complicating the lobbyist issue still further, foreign governments are particularly eager to retain savvy Washington insiders to guide them through the bureaucratic and congressional maze and polish their images in the United States. This was the problem Commerce Secretary Ron Brown confronted in 1994. Public relations counselors are strictly mandated by law to register the foreign entities they represent. However, in recent years, a number of representatives of foreign clients have been the subject of scandals and legal investigations.

The increasing number of government officials who resign to become play-for-pay lobbyists may indicate that those who govern and those who attempt to influence them will in the future be scrutinized more closely for how ethically they do business and how scrupulously they follow the law.

PUBLIC RELATIONS AND PRIVACY LAW

The laws that govern a person's privacy also have implications for the public relations profession. Privacy laws, particularly those that touch on libel and slander by the media, are curious indeed. When such alleged defamation involves a public figure, the laws get even more curious. Generally, the privacy of an ordinary citizen is protected under the law. A citizen in the limelight, however, has a more difficult problem, especially in proving defamation of character.

To prove such a charge, a public figure must show that the media acted with actual malice in its reporting. "Actual malice" in a public figure slander case means that statements have been published with the knowledge that they were false or with reckless disregard for whether the statements were false. In a landmark case in 1964, *New York Times v. Sullivan,* the Supreme Court nullified a libel award of $500,000 to an Alabama police official, holding that no damages could be awarded "in actions brought by public officials against critics of their official conduct" unless there was proof of "actual malice." And proving actual malice is difficult.

Several libel cases were particularly prominent.

- In 1992, *The Wall Street Journal* and its award-winning reporter Bryan Burrough were served with a $50 million libel suit by Harry L. Freeman, former executive vice president of American Express. The suit stemmed from the way Freeman was characterized in Burrough's book, *Vendetta: America Express and the Smearing of Edmund Safra* [7] (see the case study in Chapter 6).
- In 1993, writer Janet Malcolm was sued by Dr. Jeffrey M. Masson over charges that Malcolm fabricated quotations in her *New Yorker* magazine article, which defamed Dr. Masson. Jurors agreed that in several instances Ms. Malcolm acted with "reckless disregard" for the accuracy of the quotations and that Dr. Masson had indeed been damaged.[8]
- A decade earlier, in a landmark case, *The Washington Post* initially lost a $2 million suit after a federal jury decided that the newspaper had libeled William P. Tavoulareas when it alleged that he had used his position as president of Mobil Oil to further his son's career in a shipping business (Figure 18–2). The next year, a federal judge overturned the verdict against the *Post* because the article in question didn't contain "knowing lies or statements made in reckless disregard of the truth."

"It's a great commentary on our times when a jury finds for an oil company against a newspaper."

Frederick Taylor
Executive Editor, The Wall Street Journal
quoted in Newsweek, October 25, 1982

To avoid any misquotation, we wrote Mr. Taylor and asked him if the quote were accurate. His entire reply was the following: "I said it. And you can use it."

For several reasons, we think the statement reflects an astonishing degree of irresponsibility—particularly since Mr. Taylor is the Executive Editor of such a prestigious publication. Specifically—

ONE. The statement was made in reference to a unanimous verdict by a jury which found that *The Washington Post* and two reporters had libeled the President of Mobil. This was a personal suit, brought by him as an individual, which he totally paid for himself, to which Mobil was not a party. The jury did not "find for" Mobil. We seriously doubt that Mr. Taylor was unaware of this distinction. After all, his paper provided coverage of the case and clearly reported its private nature. It was an attempt to substitute a giant oil company as the Goliath attacking the "David-like" *Washington Post* (Some David!) It was an attempt to erase the fact that the issue in the case involved damage to an individual's reputation. No oil company was involved.

TWO. Even worse, the statement seems to betray a shocking bias. It appears to us that Mr. Taylor thinks oil companies are so venal, so inherently evil that no matter what injustices a newspaper might heap upon them, they should not prevail in a court of law before a jury.

Is Mr. Taylor suggesting that oil companies and their executives be stripped of their civil rights? Or that newspapers should be free to knowingly print false information about them? And, finally, should such behavior be immune from liability?

Mobil

Figure 18–2 The initial libel verdict against *The Washington Post* and in favor of the president of Mobil Oil and his son was chilling to journalists. In a three-column story, *The Wall Street Journal*'s executive editor, Frederick Taylor, blamed the verdict on growing public disenchantment with the press. Mobil almost immediately responded to Taylor's charge with this ad. (*Courtesy of Mobil Oil Corporation*)

Later, a federal appeals court reinstated the $2 million libel verdict against the *Post*. But later that year, the U.S. Court of Appeals of the District of Columbia agreed to reconsider the reinstatement. Finally, almost six years after the initial verdict, the Supreme Court ruled in favor of the *Post* by throwing out the Tavoulareas suit for lack of merit. A contrary ruling would have restricted the limits of investigative journalism and broadened the interpretation of defamation of character. Reporters breathed a sigh of relief at the decision.

- In another celebrated case in 1985, Israeli General Ariel Sharon brought a $50 million libel suit against *Time* magazine. It, too, ended without a libel verdict. However, once again, the jury criticized *Time* for negligent journalism in reporting Sharon's role in a massacre in a Palestinian refugee camp.
- In 1988, the Supreme Court threw out a suit brought by conservative televangelist/preacher Jerry Falwell against *Hustler* magazine, accusing the sex-oriented periodical with defaming his character in a fictitious liquor advertisement about his mother. Despite the grossness of the ad, the Supreme Court ruled that what was written was clearly a spoof of a public figure and that Falwell, therefore, didn't have a case.

What all these cases illustrate is a growing trend in society to challenge the media over their invasion of personal privacy. Although cases like these tend to confirm the rights of the media to report on public figures, in other cases—particularly those involving gossip-oriented tabloids—the courts have awarded settlements to celebrities who have been wronged.

PUBLIC RELATIONS AND COPYRIGHT LAW

One body of law that is particularly relevant to public relations professionals is copyright law and the protections it offers writers. Copyright law provides basic, automatic protection for writers, whether a manuscript is registered with the Copyright Office or even published. Under the Copyright Act of 1976, an "original work of authorship" has copyright protection from the moment the work is in fixed form. As soon as an article, short story, or book is put on paper or a computer disk or is spoken into a tape recorder, it is protected by copyright law. You created it, and you own it. What you sell to an editor isn't the article itself but the right to use the material.

Copyright protection exists for broad categories of works: literary works; musical works, including any accompanying words; dramatic works, including any accompanying music; pantomimes and choreographic works; pictorial, graphic, and sculptural works; motion pictures and other audiovisual works; and sound recordings. Copyright law gives the owner of the copyright the exclusive right to reproduce and authorize others to reproduce the work, prepare derivative works based on the copyrighted material, and perform and/or display the work publicly.[9] That's why Michael Jackson had to pay $47.5 million for the rights to the Beatles' compositions to the duly sworn representatives and heirs of John, Paul, George, and Ringo.

In 1989, the Supreme Court strengthened the copyright status of freelance artists and writers when it ruled that such professionals retain the right to copyright what they create "as long as they were not in a conventional employment relationship with the organization that commissioned their work."[10] The Court's revision of the copyright law set the stage for a wholesale reassessment of the ownership of billions of dollars in reproduction rights for computer programs, fiction and nonfiction writing, advertising copy, drawings, photographs, and so on.[11] As a result of the modification, public relations professionals must carefully document the authorization that has been secured for using freelance material. In other words, when engaging a freelance professional, public relations people must know the law.

Several categories of material are not eligible for copyright protection, such as titles and short slogans; works consisting entirely of information from common sources and public documents, such as calendars, lists, and tables; and speeches and performances that have not been fixed on paper or recorded. Work in the public domain—material that was never covered by copyright or for which the copyright has lapsed, material that lacks sufficient originality, and basic themes and plots—can't be protected by copyright.

Ideas cannot be protected either. This means that an old idea newly packaged is absolutely permissible, legal, and even recommended. Indeed, there are few truly new ideas in the world, only old ideas put together in new and different ways. So a public relations practitioner shouldn't be overly concerned with violating copyright laws when devising a campaign, program, or manuscript in support of a client's activity.

PUBLIC RELATIONS AND THE LEGAL PROFESSION

What has always been an uneasy alliance between lawyers and public relations professionals has today evolved into a relationship of grudging mutual respect. Lawyers, in fact, are making more use of public relations strategies than ever before.

By 1990, it was estimated that 75 percent of all major law firms used public relations consultants.[12] Lawyers and legal consultants attributed the increased use of public relations firms to heightened competition within the top tier of the legal profession. Many law firms have grown rapidly in the last decade and have to fight harder for clients and for top law school graduates. As a result, public relations has emerged as an important tool to get these firms' names circulated among clients, potential clients, and possible hires.

In 1984, the Supreme Court eased the ban on self-advertisement by lawyers. And while some lawyers are still reluctant to trumpet their capabilities, others are not. The leader of this ilk is Jacoby & Meyers, which, because of its pervasive national advertising, was derided by some as a "fast-food law firm."[13] But there was nothing funny about Jacoby & Meyers's client roster of 175,000 people and its $42 million business in 1989. For Jacoby & Meyers, advertising and publicity have paid very well indeed.

For their part, public relations counselors have become more open to lawyers and have relaxed the tensions that have existed between the two professions. One public relations practitioner offers this advice for working with lawyers:

1. **Become an equal partner with legal counsel.** At all times, maintain an overview of the legal cases before your organization or industry. Take the initiative with legal counsel to discuss those that you believe may have major public relations implications.
2. **Combat the legal no-comment syndrome.** Research cases in which an organization has publicly discussed issues without damage.

BETWEEN THE LINES

UNPLUGGING VANNA THE ROBOT

When glamorous game show letter turner Vanna White saw a videocassette recorder ad that showed a robot dressed just like her, blond wig and all, on a game show set that looked suspiciously like her *Wheel of Fortune,* she sued.

In 1994, the Supreme Court ruled that the real Vanna had the right to go to court to prove that the company behind "Vanna the Robot" stole her identity and violated her privacy.

Ms. White was in glittering company, as a host of celebrities in the 1990s invaded the courts to sue advertising agencies with misappropriating their look, their voice, and even their mannerisms in ads.

Figure 18–3 Vanna White. (*Courtesy of AP/Wide World Photos*)

The floodgates opened when singer Bette Midler won a $400,000 jury verdict in 1989 against the Young & Rubicam ad agency, which had created a Ford car ad using a Midler sound-alike. After Ms. Midler declined to appear in the ad, the agency hired the star's former backup singer, who belted out a sound-alike version of Ms. Midler's 1973 hit song "Do You Wanna Dance?"

In awarding Ms. Midler the verdict, the Federal Appeals Court ruled, "When a distinctive voice of a professional singer is widely known and deliberately imitated in order to sell a product, the sellers have appropriated what is not theirs." From that moment on, it was open season on all those advertising spokespersons who looked and sounded a little too much like "the real thing."

3. **Take the initiative in making announcements.** This will help manage the public perception of the issue. If an indictment is pending, consult the legal staff on the advisability of making statements—before you become a target.
4. **Research the background of the jury.** Past lists of jurors in a particular jurisdiction indicate occupations and other important demographic information.
5. **Winning may not be everything.** Outside law firms, trained in an adversarial mode and charging fees that depend on the size of the award, always want to "win." For legal counsel the stakes may also include a winning reputation, which helps to secure future cases. Public relations must bring a long-term perspective to strategic decisions.
6. **Beware of leaving a paper trail.** Any piece of paper that you create may end up in court. That includes desk calendars and notes to yourself. So be careful.[14]

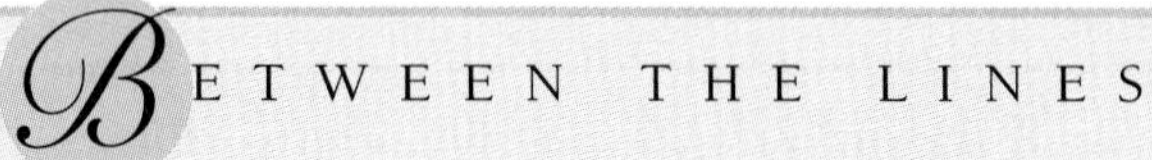

WHAT'S IN A SQUIGGLE?

People are curious about the tiny squiggles that appear above the names of certain company products or slogans.

They're trademarks.

A *trademark* is a kind of copyright that protects intellectual property. It gives one exclusive use of a particular word, name, symbol, or slogan—Kleenex®, Xerox®, and Coke®, for example. The squiggle ® indicates the mark you have registered with the U.S. Office of Patents and Trademarks.

A similar squiggle is called a *service mark*. This applies to an organization selling a service rather than a product—American Airlines' slogan, "Something Special in the Air,"℠ or the U.S. Army Reserve's slogan we used to chant, "Be All That You Can Be."℠

A similar squiggle,™, is the trademark symbol. (TM also stands for *transcendental meditation*, but that's another story completely.)

SUMMARY

As our society becomes more contentious, fractious, and litigious, public relations must become more concerned with the law. Indeed, public relations has already become involved with the law in many areas of communications beyond those already cited in this chapter.

- The Federal Communications Commission (FCC) ruled in 1987 that the Fairness Doctrine, the subject of years of debate among broadcasters and others, unconstitutionally restricted the First Amendment rights of broadcasters. The FCC said that broadcasters were no longer obligated to provide equal time for dissenting views. Congressional efforts to turn the doctrine into law were vetoed by President Reagan, but the debate may not be finished.
- The right of publicity has been challenged by the estates of deceased celebrities like Charlie Chaplin, W. C. Fields, Mae West, and the Marx brothers, whose likenesses have been portrayed in product advertisements without the permission of their heirs.
- In 1988, a federal jury found a cigarette manufacturer liable in the lung cancer death of a New Jersey woman because the company failed to warn of smoking's health risks before such warnings were required on cigarette packs in 1966. The verdict, which was upheld by the New Jersey Supreme Court in 1990, was hailed by antismoking advocates as the most important breakthrough since cigarette company advertising was forced off of television in 1971. With many similar antitobacco cases pending in the United States, it seems quite likely that advertised and publicized corporate claims will come under increased legal scrutiny, not only for cigarette manufacturers, but for all those who promote product and service claims.
- In 1993, the Supreme Court ruled that the rap group 2 Live Crew could release a vulgar rewrite of the old Roy Orbison hit "Pretty Woman," even though those who copyrighted the original material had refused permission. The Court ruled that the raunchy rappers were entitled to "fair use" of the material for the purpose of parody.

In addition to all of these legal areas, the public relations business itself increasingly is based on legal contracts: between agencies and clients, between employers and employees, between purchasers and vendors. All contracts—both written and oral—must be binding and enforceable.

In recent years, controversy in the field has erupted over noncompete clauses, in which former employees are prohibited, within certain time parameters, from working for a competitor or pitching a former account. Legal issues also have arisen over the postal laws that govern public relations people who disseminate materials through the mails. Add to these the blurring of the lines between public relations advice on the one hand and legal advice on the other, and it becomes clear that the connection between public relations and the law will intensify dramatically throughout the remainder of this decade and into the next century.

Nothing more clearly demonstrated the arrival of public relations to the legal profession than the appointment in 1993 of the first public relations director of the 370,000-member American Bar Association.

A Perfect Teen, a Grisly Crime, a Public Relations Disaster

Frank Dalton was the perfect teenager.

He earned A's in school. He played golf on the school team. He worked 35 hours each week in an after-school job. Little wonder that Frank Dalton was the unanimous choice for the 1993 Tacoma (Washington) Youth Hall of Fame.

But a strange thing happened to Frank Dalton. Right before the Youth Hall of Fame official ceremonies, it was revealed that the honoree was soon to stand trial for murdering his mother.

The situation started at the alternative school that young Dalton was required to attend while awaiting sentencing. In light of his excellent academic record and conscientiousness, a school worker nominated him for the Tacoma Youth Hall of Fame. He was accepted on his merits, with minimal fact checking. Only later were red-faced Tacoma city officials informed of their honoree's prior problems and imminent sentencing.

Tacoma's leaders pondered what to do. If they chose to withdraw the nomination, they would look like hypocrites. If they continued to allow the young man's induction, they were honoring a murderer. A lose/lose proposition.

At first, the city decided to defer its decision. Its dithering led to an enraged letter from the publisher of the *Tacoma Morning News Tribune*, a Hall of Fame sponsor. "The mishandling of this matter and related issues has removed my confidence in the staff's ability and willingness to run this program to standards justifying our involvement," huffed the publisher.

In ensuing days, the publicity drumbeat against the Youth Hall of Fame and its nomination standards was unending.

Finally, beneficently, the controversy ended when Frank Dalton withdrew his name from nomination. Wrote Dalton, "I am concerned that the attention to my case has the potential of diminishing this very real honor to the other young people who should be proud of this designation."

What would you have done had you been faced with the City of Tacoma's dilemma?

DISCUSSION STARTERS

1. What is the difference between a public relations professional's responsibility and a lawyer's responsibility?
2. What have been recent challenges to the First Amendment?
3. What is meant by the term *insider trading?*
4. What was the essence of the Foster Winans *Wall Street Journal* case?

5. What kinds of information *must* public companies disclose immediately?
6. What is meant by the legal term *actual malice* with respect to privacy law?
7. Whom does copyright law protect?
8. What group is protected by the most recent revisions in copyright law?
9. What is the attitude of law firms toward public relations counsel?
10. What general advice should a public relations professional consider in working with lawyers?

NOTES

1. "Guilty Until Proven Innocent?" *Inside PR* (August 1993): 41.
2. Gerhart L. Klein, *Public Relations Law: The Basics* (Mt. Laurel, NJ: Anne Klein and Associates, Inc., 1990), 1–2.
3. Edmund L. Andrews, "F.C.C. Delays Radio Deals by Howard Stern's Employer," *The New York Times* (December 31, 1993): A1, D2.
4. Linda Greenhouse, "Rights of Commercial Speech Affirmed," *The New York Times* (March 25, 1993): A7.
5. Stephen Wermiel, "U.S., State Officials Win Wider Leeway to Restrict Free Speech of Corporations," *The Wall Street Journal* (June 30, 1989): B6.
6. Evan Thomas and Thomas M. DeFrank, "Mike Deaver's Rise and Fall," *Newsweek* (March 23, 1987): 23.
7. Thomas K. Grose, "$50 Million Lawsuit Against WSJ and Burrough May Make Some Authors-to-Be Think Twice," *TFJR Report* (April 1992): 3.
8. Jane Gross, "Impasse Over Damages Over New Yorker Libel Case," *The New York Times* (June 4, 1993): A1.
9. Jay Stuller, "Your Guide to Copyright," *Writer's Digest* (June 1988): 29.
10. Linda Greenhouse, "Court Strengthens Copyright Status of Free-Lance Artists on Commission," *The New York Times* (June 6, 1989): A24.
11. Albert Scardino, "Copyright Ruling Opens a Costly Can of Worms," *The New York Times* (June 12, 1989): D12.
12. Ellen Joan Pollock, "Lawyers Are Cautiously Embracing PR Firms," *The Wall Street Journal* (March 14, 1990): B1.
13. Robyn Kelley, "Legal Beagles," *Spy* (August 1990): 74.
14. Lloyd Newman, "Litigation Public Relations: How to Work with Lawyers," *PR Reporter Tips and Tactics* (November 23, 1987): 2.

TOP OF THE SHELF

Gerhart L. Klein, *Public Relations Law: The Basics.* Mt. Laurel, NJ: Anne Klein and Associates, Inc., 1990.

Can public relations people tape their phone conversations? It depends. What constitutes defamation? Lots of things. To get some straight answers, consult *Public Relations Law,* which addresses the legal implications of public relations activities.

Gerhart Klein, a lawyer and seasoned public relations counselor, presents the legal issues practitioners need to check before performing their duties. In readable fashion, he covers the First Amendment, restrictions on free speech, copyright and trademark law, and financial disclosure. Of exceptional interest are his explanations of disclosure and "materiality," always murky areas for communicators. Klein also points out the pitfalls of contracts and of employing freelancers. If something's legal, it's also ethical, right? Not really. Klein cautions communicators to consider both issues when deciding what to do in certain situations.

Practitioners must be aware of the legal matters that affect their profession. While Klein's primer is no substitute for a lawyer's advice, *Public Relations Law* capably introduces practitioners to the legal ramifications of their actions.

SUGGESTED READINGS

Banta, William. *AIDS in the Workplace: Legal and Practical Answers.* Lexington, MA: Lexington Books, 1987.

Brown, Kathleen, and Joan Turner. *AIDS: Policies and Programs for the Workplace.* New York: Van Nostrand Reinhold, 1989.

Crisis Management: A Workbook for Survival. Belleville, NJ: Lempert Co., 1987.

Fink, Steven. *Crisis Management: Planning for the Inevitable.* New York: AMACOM, 1986.

Lerbinger, Otto. *Managing Corporate Crises: Strategies for Executives.* Boston: Barrington Press, 1986 (P.O. Box 291, Boston University Station 02215).

Meyers, Gerald. *When It Hits the Fan.* Scarborough, Ontario: New American Library of Canada Limited, 1987.

Nally, Margaret. *International Public Relations in Practice: Firsthand Experience of 14 Professionals.* Cambridge, MA: Kogan Page Limited, 1991.

New Principles for Public Companies After the Supreme Court Decision. Englewood Cliffs, NJ: Prentice-Hall, 1988.

Pinsdorf, Marion. *Communicating When Your Company Is Under Siege.* Lexington, MA: Lexington Books, 1986.

Posner, Ari. "The Culture of Plagiarism." *New Republic* (1988): 19.

The SEC, the Securities Market and Your Financial Communications. New York: Hill & Knowlton, 1991.

Walsh, Frank. *Public Relations and the Law.* New York: Institute for PR Research and Education, 1988.

What Non-U.S. Companies Need to Know About Financial Disclosure in the United States. New York: Hill & Knowlton, 1990.

Wouters, Joyce. *International Public Relations: How to Establish Your Company's Product.* New York: AMACOM, 1991.

CASE STUDY

BURNED BY THE MEDIA: GENERAL MOTORS EXTINGUISHES NBC

It is difficult now to believe that a proposal to send a camera crew to Indiana to tape an old car being pushed along a narrow road beside a corn field into an old truck fitted with igniters would be taken seriously.

> *Report of Inquiry Into Crash Demonstrations Broadcast on Dateline NBC November 17, 1992,* NBC Internal Report, Issued March 21, 1993

The estimated 17 million viewers of the November 17, 1992, *Dateline NBC* program couldn't help but be horrified as they observed a General Motors full-size pickup truck burst into flames after being hit broadside by a remote control–operated car. The clear conclusion for any viewer watching the debacle was that GM trucks were dangerous and ought to be taken off the road—immediately!

There was only one slight problem.

The NBC crash demonstration was a sham. The test was rigged. The segment was flawed from start to finish. And the reporting of NBC News was flatly fraudulent.

NBC News would have gotten away with its trickery had not GM struck back with a public relations vengeance unprecedented in American corporate history.

Immediately after the damaging NBC broadcast, GM embarked on a painstaking mission to research the facts of the NBC demonstration and expose the network's falsified report. But that effort would never have been seen had it not been for a lucky break—a call from a newsman who had discovered witnesses to the rigged demonstration on a rural road near Indianapolis.

Pete Pesterre, editor of *Popular Hot Rodding Magazine,* wrote an editorial criticizing the *Dateline NBC* story. Soon afterward, a reader of the magazine turned up a firefighter who had witnessed the filming of the crash and had filmed his own video of the incident.

Soon thereafter, GM obtained the firefighter's video. This proved to be the turning point in GM's efforts. The video clearly showed that the test was rigged. GM investigators located the trucks used in the staged crash. The investigators found the trucks at a salvage yard in Indiana and purchased them. In one of the pickups, a used model rocket engine was found.

Between the time the show aired in November 1992 and January 1993, four letters were sent to NBC by GM. They received no adequate response. GM then threatened suit. NBC continued to state that the story, according to NBC News President Michael Gartner, "was entirely accurate." In February 1993, GM filed a lawsuit against the National Broadcasting Company, charging that *Dateline NBC* had rigged the crash. GM also immediately went into crisis mode.

GM's crisis communications program was managed by two members of its recently reorganized communications staff—William J. O'Neill, then director of communications for GM's North American Operations (NAO), and Edward S. Lechtzin, director of legal and safety issues for the NAO communications staff. O'Neill, in fact, had agreed that GM would participate in the original *Dateline NBC* program but hadn't been told during the interview session about NBC's taped test. O'Neill and Lechtzin spearheaded a unique public relations team that also included three GM attorneys and two engineers.

The public relations professionals, attorneys, and engineers together provided a nucleus that could make key decisions quickly and authoritatively.

Lechtzin's boss, GM General Counsel Harry J. Pearce, was selected to face off with the media. At the center of the group's public relations offensive would be a press conference, conducted by Pearce, to lay bare the NBC deception. Further, the GM crisis communications team made a conscious decision to target television as the key medium to deliver GM's strongest message that it had been wronged and wasn't going to take it.

GOING TO WAR WITH NBC

Given the old adage "Don't pick a fight with the guy who buys ink by the barrel," a large number of "crisis communications consultants" wondered aloud during the days before the Pearce press conference if GM was doing the right thing.

At GM, there was never any doubt that the NBC deception should be publicized—as widely as possible. Briefed during an inaugural event for President Clinton, GM President Jack Smith told his public relations executives, "Don't overplay it, but do what's right."

During the three-week period between the tip and the press conference, the group pulling together the case against NBC was asked only two questions: (1) Do we have enough information? (2) Are we doing the right thing? No presentations. No briefing books. No background meetings. No groups of 15 to 20 people in a room trying to decide what was right. It was left to the small crisis task force to select the right strategy.

Harry Pearce was scheduled to take the stage in the GM showroom at 1 P.M. on February 8, 1993. Only one question remained: How would the media react?

THE PEARCE PRESS CONFERENCE

From the moment Harry Pearce strode on stage until the time he concluded more than two hours later, the assembled media personnel—numbering nearly 150 journalists and 25 camera crews—were mesmerized.

"What I'm about to share with you should shock the conscience of every member of your profession and mine, and I believe the American people as well," Pearce began, speaking to an uncommonly quiet media audience. "I will not allow the good men and women of General Motors and the thousands of independent businesses who sell our products and whose livelihood depends upon our products to suffer the consequences of NBC's irresponsible conduct transmitted via the airwaves throughout this great nation in the November *Dateline* program. GM has been irreparably damaged and we are going to defend ourselves."[1]

Courtesy of General Motors

For the next two hours, speaking without notes, Pearce systematically shredded any vestiges of defense that NBC might have had. The media audience was transfixed. There was no rushing to phones to call in the story, no shuffling of papers or sighs of boredom. The only sound that interrupted Pearce's devastating dissection of NBC was the intermittent click of camera shutters. Pearce was a skilled trial lawyer weaving a two-hour summation.

The GM attorney concluded by reading a brief statement issued earlier in the day by NBC in which the network said, "We feel that our use of those demonstrations was accurate and responsible." His reply was a challenge of the kind that a good lawyer gives to a jury—in this case, the assembled reporters and thousands of others watching the broadcast.

"Well, you decide that one," Pearce said. "And that's going to prove your mettle within your own profession. It's sometimes most difficult to police abuse in one's own profession."

THE CRASH DEMONSTRATION

At the heart of the Pearce press conference was a repeat of NBC's 55-second crash demonstration within a 16-minute broadcast segment. Using videotape, Pearce demonstrated that the segment was flawed from start to finish. It loaded the evidence to prove that GM's full-size C/K pickup trucks, equipped with so-called side-saddle fuel tanks, had a fatal flaw that in a high-speed side impact collision caused them to rupture and spew burning gasoline. The clear implication was that the trucks were unsafe.

However, no source—not even the internal report generated by NBC after the affair—fully explained what the crashes of two aged Citations being pushed into the sides of two Chevy pickups were supposed to prove. They certainly didn't prove the trucks were dangerous. If anything, the performance of the two old trucks—hit at speeds of 39 and 48 miles per hour, respectively—was superb. The only fire generated, as Pearce showed the reporters, was a 15-second grass fire caused by gasoline spewing from an overfilled filler tube after an ill-fitting gas cap came off on impact.

Careful editing from three views left the impression of a conflagration. As NBC's own investigative report indicated:

> We believe that the combined effect of the shot from the bullet car and the slow motion film creates an impression that the flames are about to consume the cabin of the truck. These images in the edited tape convey an impression quite different from what people saw at the scene. The fire was small, it did not consume the cabin of the truck, and it did not last long.[2]

Although the subsequent filmed truck crash resulted in no holocaust, the program, coupled with a well-orchestrated campaign by the plaintiff's attorneys, helped build public pressure that led the National Highway Traffic Safety Administration (NHTSA) to open an investigation into the safety of GM's trucks just one month later.

THE NBC RETRACTION

GM's historic news conference literally brought NBC News to its knees.

On the day following Pearce's performance, NBC initiated a negotiating session with the company that lasted for 12 hours. GM would accept nothing less from NBC than a full public retraction of its prior broadcast.

And on February 9, 1993, a day after the news conference, that is precisely what NBC did. *Dateline NBC* coanchors Jane Pauley and Stone Phillips read a four-minute, on-air retraction that put the blame for the bogus broadcast squarely at NBC's door and apologized to GM.

In the aftermath, three *Dateline* producers were fired, the on-air reporter was demoted and reassigned, and ultimately, NBC News President Gartner resigned in humiliation. NBC agreed to reimburse GM the roughly $2 million it had spent in a three-week period investigating the false report. In exchange, GM agreed to drop the defamation suit it had filed against NBC.

For its part, GM was spared years of costly litigation over its suit. The company also was quickly able to put to rest what could have been a nightmarish visual every time GM trucks were mentioned on the evening news.

The cloak-and-dagger story on how GM put its case together remains tantalizingly vague.

Nonetheless, what is clear was that in a single day, with a single press conference, GM successfully transformed the pickup truck story from a sensationalized and slanted media feeding frenzy into a serious question of journalistic ethics and integrity.

GM Communications Director O'Neill was blunt in his assessment: "I quite honestly wanted this to happen and I was glad it did happen, because I think these people purposely lied and misrepresented the facts and knew they were doing it. I do not think there is any room for that in this business."[3]

THE AFTERMATH

After NBC's stunning *mea culpa,* GM increased its public relations offensive to counter concerns about the safety of its trucks.

It sought to show that the plaintiff's bar—the trial lawyers—had a vested financial interest in nurturing the idea that the trucks were dangerous. Another group was the so-called safety

Courtesy of General Motors

experts, cited by NBC and others, who either were financed by the plaintiff's attorneys or served as expert witnesses in mounting legal action against the company.

In the same scrupulous way it had dissected NBC's case, GM systematically discredited the credentials and objectivity of the so-called safety experts.

Apparently galvanized by the publicity, the NHTSA demanded—even before it had completed its own investigation—that GM voluntarily recall its pickup trucks. The company refused. In April 1993, GM sponsored two two-hour shirt-sleeve briefings by Pearce with key members of the media, explaining why the company wouldn't recall its trucks and why NHTSA's conclusions were flawed. Interestingly, television representatives were not invited to these sessions because it was felt that the medium could only "enflame the situation further."

In subsequent months, the GM–NBC News controversy received lengthy coverage in newspapers and magazines. In most, NBC fared poorly. Summarized one journalist:

> An investigation of past network auto-safety coverage reveals that both CBS and ABC have run the same sorts of material facts about the tests and relied on the same dubious experts with the same ties to plaintiff's bar.[4]

The Executive Summary of NBC's internal report concluded, "The story of this ill-fated crash demonstration and its aftermath is rather a story of lapsed judgment—serious lapses—by persons generally well-intentioned and well-qualified. And it is a story of a breakdown in the system for correction and compliance that every organization, including a news organization and network, needs."[5]

One could add that it is also a story that may never have been told had it not been for a gutsy, unyielding public relations initiative by an organization that refused to be dealt with unfairly.

QUESTIONS

1. What other options did GM have in addition to going public in the wake of the *Dateline NBC* report?
2. What was the downside risk for GM of being so public in its response?
3. Do you agree with GM's strategy on sending its general counsel to confront the media?
4. Do you agree with GM's decision not to invite television to its media briefings after the initial Pearce press conference?
5. In terms of reputation/credibility, what do you think its response to the *Dateline NBC* broadcast meant to GM?

1. General Motors press conference transcript, Detroit, February 8, 1993.
2. "NBC Internal Report of Inquiry Into Crash Demonstrations Broadcast on *Dateline NBC,* November 17, 1992," issued March 21, 1993.
3. Catherine Gates, "NBC Learns a Lesson," *Public Relations Quarterly* (Winter 1993–1994): 42.
4. "It Didn't Start with 'Dateline NBC,'" *National Review* (June 21, 1993): 41.
5. "Report of Inquiry Into Crash Demonstrations Broadcast on *Dateline NBC,* November 17, 1992," Issued March 21, 1993, p. 8.

TIPS FROM THE TOP

HARRY J. PEARCE

Harry Pearce, an executive vice president in charge of all corporate staffs at General Motors, was the automaker's general counsel at the time of the *Dateline NBC* affair in 1992 and 1993. He also is responsible for GM Hughes Electronic Corporation and Electronic Data Systems Corporation.

He also is a member of GM's President's Council. Mr. Pearce's extensive legal background prior to joining GM included service as staff judge advocate in the Air Force and service as a municipal judge and police commissioner in Bismarck, North Dakota. Mr. Pearce served as GM's chief spokesman in the *Dateline NBC* crisis.

What were the relative contributions of public relations and law to GM's handling of the *Dateline NBC* issue?

GM's handling of the *Dateline NBC* issue was unique because the traditional distinctions between the purely legal and public relations lines got blurred. Dedicating key disciplines to a single team allowed each member the ability to focus on the same goal, and the individual contributions of the members became irrelevant.

Because of the litigation aspect of the pickup truck issue, there were some technical issues that only an attorney could address. However, in the larger challenge presented by NBC and the likely media coverage of the dispute, the common goal eliminated a lot of the traditional boundaries between lawyers, engineers, and public relations experts.

What was your objective in going after NBC?

The common goal was at once simple and critical. GM needed to create an environment where facts—not shrill and rhetorical sound bites or sensational video footage—would prevail. In simple terms, we had to neutralize the rhetoric with hard facts, and we needed to shock the media so that it would listen to our message. We knew that we had solid evidence that the *Dateline NBC* segment had crossed the ethical boundaries. And we knew that we had the right facts about the safety of our pickup trucks. We needed to create a climate where that became more, rather than less, important.

Once the facts about NBC's irresponsible conduct were clear to us, the question was really quite easy to answer. The lawsuit was necessary to preserve our legal rights. We then had to ask: "How do we best communicate the truth about the inaccuracies and deception NBC perpetrated against GM and the American people?" It would have been wrong to let the *Dateline NBC* segment go unchallenged. It was obviously a high-stakes decision to go as public as we did, but when you operate on the principle that you are going to do what's right, it really isn't difficult to understand what needs to be done once you have the facts.

How would you characterize the journalistic ethics in the *Dateline* case?
In retrospect, NBC was probably shell-shocked because, as gross as we revealed the segment to be, I'd bet there are dozens of other examples of TV news programs that exhibited a similar bias. The difference in this case was that we were able to obtain the hard physical evidence of the deception—and it was one that we felt the American public would understand. Frankly, the work their so-called experts did was so sloppy, and the technical advice they got was so incompetent, that it made our job easy once we knew where to look.

The "ethics" of what *Dateline* did, and failed to do, are manifest throughout the 16-minute segment itself. Though some at the network once would have liked to hide behind a facade that the show was fair except for the "rigged rocket" segment, the fact is that it was biased from start to finish. It was evident that *Dateline* had already decided the trucks were unsafe before even starting to film the segment, and relied heavily on plaintiff attorneys and a family ready to go to trial for much of its input. There was never an attempt to present an objective look at the issue—just to provide sensational footage and grieving parents to gain rating points.

How important is the practice of public relations for a company like GM?
Public relations is a critical function, but we need to be clear how we at GM view this role. These folks aren't just mouthpieces.

We will ultimately succeed or fail in any endeavor based on the quality of our products and services. That's as it should be. The role for PR at GM is to help communicate the facts effectively on any given situation. It sounds simple, but when you commit yourself as a company to being straightforward with employees, the public, and the media, you eliminate a lot of unnecessary complication.

What should be the relationship between public relations and law?
We live in an age when instant communications and sound bites are a way of life, so the link between the law and public relations is both obvious and unavoidable. However, corporations don't often try to win their cases in the media, as do plaintiff attorneys and industry critics. We simply try to neutralize the bombastic

rhetoric and distortions to create an environment where the facts can become the focus of the discussion. That's all we ever wanted, and we believe GM was able to achieve that environment in the truck issue.

However, given the media's love of sensationalism and the willingness of members of the legal profession to exploit it, there is a temptation on the part of some on our side of the fence to engage in the same tactics. It's a temptation that both the public relations and legal staffs have to resist.

How would you compare the ethical principles of a lawyer to those of a public relations professional?
In general, the legal duties of a lawyer to a client and to the profession are much higher than the legal or ethical duty of a public relations person. While there is no Code of Professional Responsibility, with the associated legal consequences, for a member of the public relations profession who fails to follow specific ethical guidelines, PR professionals do have a Code of Ethics administered by the Public Relations Society of America. It is strict and brings with it consequences for inappropriate actions.

In practical terms, all GM PR professionals must conduct themselves by the highest ethical standards. We will not compromise integrity at GM, and our PR staff is the public face of credibility.

How would you characterize the shift in GM's public relations strategy in recent years?
It's probably a fair criticism of GM that we've tended to hold back and avoid taking very aggressive public positions when we were unfairly attacked in the press. Maybe it's a function of our history of being the biggest target for such abuse.

However, it makes no sense to us to let false reports and inaccurate statements about our products go unchallenged. We don't seek an unfair advantage with the media, but we fervently believe that GM is entitled to fair treatment. If that means we must be aggressive to get the facts out, so be it.

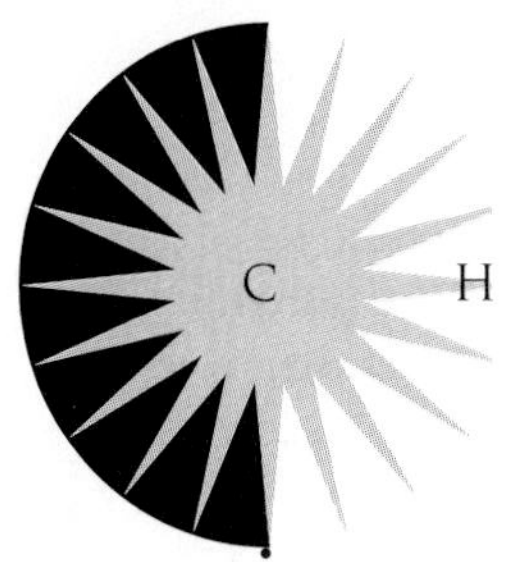

CHAPTER 19

Managing Crisis and Opportunity

WHEN PUBLIC RELATIONS PROFESSIONALS ARE ASKED WHAT subject they want covered in mid-career seminars, "crisis communications" invariably heads the list. Some scholars suggest that any self-respecting introductory public relations text should contain an *entire chapter* devoted to crisis management. (Sorry, scholars!) Indeed, many of the legendary case studies in this book—from the *Exxon Valdez* tanker oil spill to the Whitewater political scandal to the Tylenol murders discussed at the end of this chapter—concern public relations crises.

Helping to manage both crisis and opportunity is the ultimate assignment for a public relations professional. Smart managements value public relations advice in developing an organization's response not only to crises but to public issues in general. Hundreds of American companies, in fact, have created executive posts for "issues managers," whose task is to help the organization define and deal with the political, economic, and social issues that affect it.

The list of such issues—and of the crises they often evoke—is unending.

In the 1990s, society is flooded with front-burner issues that effect individuals and organizations. From abortion to AIDS, from discrimination to downsizing, from environmentalism to energy conservation, the domain of issues management has become increasingly important for public relations professionals (Figure 19–1).

ISSUES MANAGEMENT

The process of issues management has been around for two decades. The term was coined in 1976 by W. Howard Chase, who defined it this way:

> Issues management is the capacity to understand, mobilize, coordinate, and direct all strategic and policy planning functions, and all public affairs/public relations skills, toward achievement of one objective: meaningful participation in creation of public policy that affects personal and institutional destiny.[1]

As the Chase/Jones management process model in Figure 19–2 illustrates, issues management is a five-step process that (1) *identifies* issues with which the organization must be concerned, (2) *analyzes* and delimits each issue with respect to its impact on constituent publics, (3) *displays* the various strategic options available to the organization, (4) *implements* an action program to communicate the organization's views and influence perception on the issue, and (5) *evaluates* its program in terms of reaching organizational goals.

Many suggest that the term *issues management* is another way of saying that the most important public relations skill is "counseling management." Others suggest that issues management is another way of saying "reputation management"—orchestrating the process whose goal is to help preserve markets, reduce risk, create opportunities, and manage image as an organizational asset for the benefit of both an organization and its primary shareholders.[2]

In specific terms, issues management encompasses the following elements:

- **Anticipate emerging issues** Normally, the issues management process anticipates issues 18 months to 3 years away. Therefore, it is neither crisis planning nor postcrisis planning, but rather precrisis planning. In other words, issues management deals with an issue that will hit the organization a year later, thus distinguishing the practice from the normal crisis planning aspects of public relations.
- **Selectively identify issues** An organization can influence only a few issues at a time. Therefore, a good issues management process will select several—perhaps 5 to 10—specific priority issues with which to deal. In this way, issues management can focus on the most important issues affecting the organization.
- **Deal with opportunities and vulnerabilities** Most issues, anticipated well in advance, offer both opportunities and vulnerabilities for organizations. For example, in assessing promised federal budget cuts, an insurance company might anticipate that less money will mean fewer people driving and therefore fewer accident claims. This would mark an opportunity. On the other hand,

If you can't do a thing about the way you look, call us.

Beauty is only skin deep. But if you're a battered woman, your bruises go straight to the heart. And you can make up, but it never lasts. You're not alone. One out of every two women in America will be abused by a man who says he loves her. You deserve our help. So do your kids. Call Rose Brooks' 24-hour crisis line at **861-6100**. Because you can't keep turning the other cheek.

Figure 19–1 In the 1990s, hospitals and health care institutions accelerated communications appeals to the public to deal with individual crises. (*Courtesy of Rose Brooks for Battered Women and Their Children*)

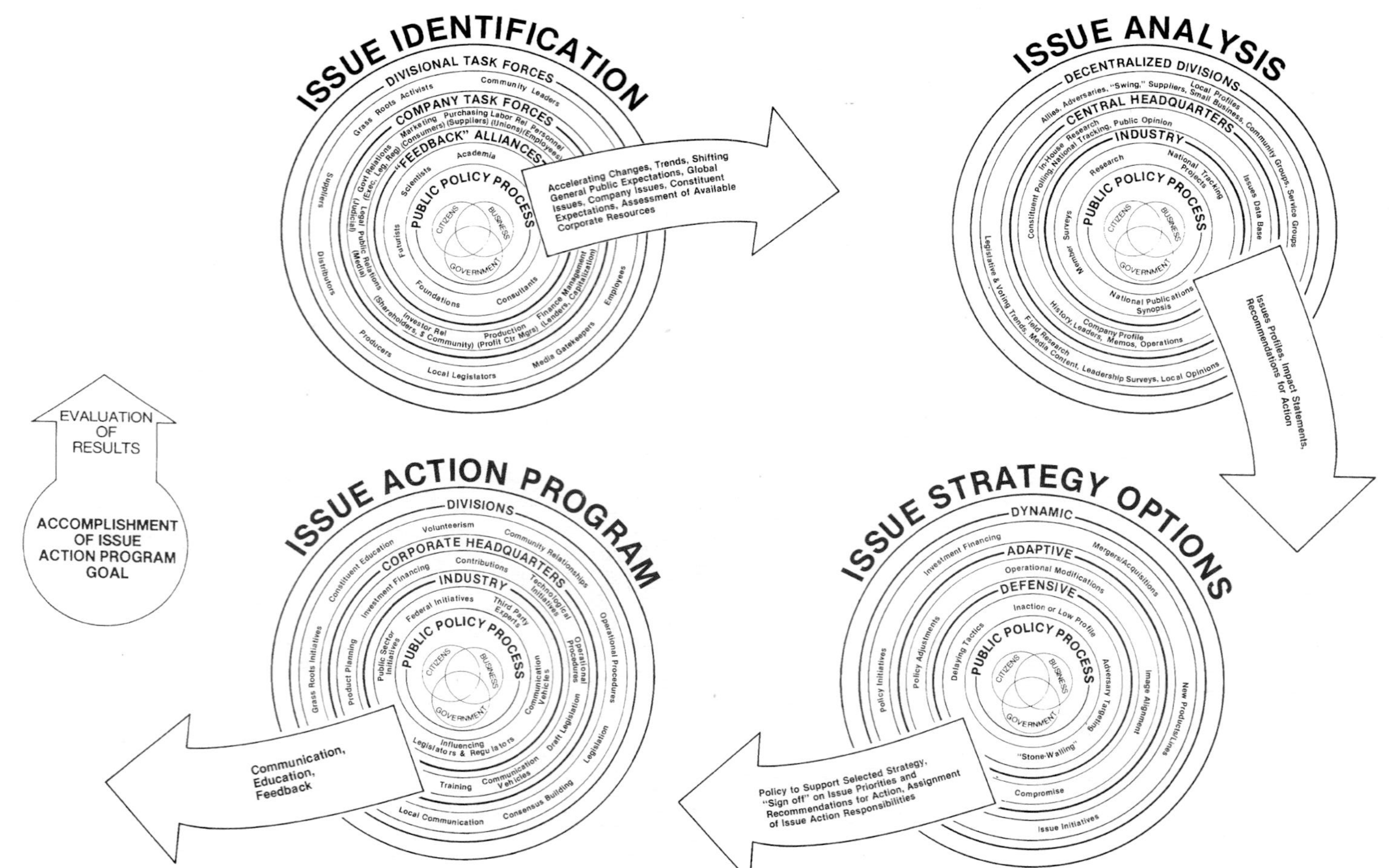

Figure 19–2 A pioneer in the field of issues management, W. Howard Chase, along with Barrie L. Jones, developed this model for predicting the effect of internal and external environmental changes on the performance of the overall corporate system. The model itself assigns decision-making authority and evaluation of issues manager performance. *(Courtesy of Issue Action Publications)*

those cuts might mean that more people are unable to pay their premiums. This, clearly, is a vulnerability that a sharp company should anticipate well in advance.

- **Plan from the outside in** The external environment—not internal strategies—dictates the selection of priority issues. This differs from the normal strategic planning approach, which, to a large degree, is driven by internal strengths and objectives. Issues management is very much driven by external factors.
- **Profit-line orientation** Although many people tend to look at issues management as anticipating crises, its real purpose should be to defend the organization in the light of external factors, as well as to enhance the firm's business by seizing imminent opportunities.
- **Action timetable** Just as the issues management process must identify emerging issues and set them in order, it must propose policy, programs, and an implementation timetable to deal with those issues. Action is the key to an effective issues management process.
- **Dealing from the top** Just as a public relations department is powerless without the confidence and respect of top management, the issues management process must operate with the support of the chief executive. The chief executive's personal sanction is critical to the acceptance and conduct of issues management within a firm.

The Mouse That Poured

Product tampering can be among the most serious crises with which an organization is faced. The key in any crisis is to act decisively and quickly.

In July 1988, an unemployed Jacksonville, Florida, construction worker, James Harvey, angry over a traffic accident involving a Coors beer truck, called the Coors Consumer Hotline to complain that he had found a mouse in his beer can.

When Coors got the hotline call, it sent two headquarters consumer affairs people the next day to placate Harvey with $1,500, in exchange for the canned mouse. Harvey refused the offer and tried to raise the ante first to $35,000, and then $50,000, for the mouse and the can. Coors refused.

Several days later, after shopping the story around to local TV stations, Harvey struck pay dirt. Gannett-owned WTLV-TV aired a 6 o'clock piece on the local man who felt "something against my mouth while drinking beer." Harvey and a camera crew took the can to the local Board of Health, where the mouse was exposed—on camera.

Reports of the mouse being poured out of a 16-ounce Coors can reached Coors public relations officials in Colorado, who then reported the dilemma to top management.

Coors wasted no time. It insisted that lab tests be conducted immediately on the mouse. The subsequent tests revealed two crucial facts:

- First, the mouse had died about a week before the tests, but the can had been sealed at the Coors brewery a full three months earlier.
- Second, the mouse hadn't drowned, but rather had wounds that indicated it had been stuffed through the can's pop-top opening.

Despite the clear implication of tampering, Coors couldn't keep the film footage off the airwaves. Mouse-in-the-can film aired 72 times in Jacksonville alone, where the local Coors distributor lost more than $250,000 in sales and probably much more in public image.

It was little consolation to Coors that four months to the day after the original story aired, Harvey was exposed as a fraud, arrested, and jailed for attempted extortion.

How would you assess Coors's handling of this crisis?

IMPLEMENTING ISSUES MANAGEMENT

In a typical organization, the tactical implementation of issues management tends to consist of four specific job tasks:

1. **Identifying issues and trends** Issue identification can be accomplished through traditional research techniques, as well as through more informal methods. Organizations are most concerned about issues that affect their own residential area. For example, in 1990, when Southern California's sunny skies were steadily threatened by increasingly significant doses of smog, the Unocal Corporation, a Los Angeles–based oil company, seized the initiative. Unocal announced an innovative program, called SCRAP, in which it promised to spend more than $5 million to eliminate 6 million pounds of air pollution by paying for and scrapping 7,000 old cars. Thanks to SCRAP, in four months California rid its highways of 8,376 gas-guzzling pollution machines. And Unocal won millions of dollars in goodwill[3] (Figure 19–3).

   One way to keep informed about what is being said about a company, industry, or issue is to subscribe to issues-oriented publications of every political persuasion—from *Mother Jones* and *The Village Voice* on the far left to the Liberty Lobby's *Spotlight* on the far right and everything else in between.
2. **Evaluating issue impact and setting priorities** Evaluation and analysis may be handled by issues committees within an organization. Committees can set priorities for issues management action. At the Upjohn Company, for example, a senior policy committee—composed of managers in each of the firm's major divisions, as well as public affairs and legal staff members—meets quarterly to set issues priorities.

Unocal Corporation
1201 West 5th Street, P.O. Box 7600
Los Angeles, California 90051

UNOCAL 76

News Release

Contact: Barry Lane 213/977-7601
Jim Bray 213/977-5390
Jeff Callender 213/977-7208

FOR IMMEDIATE RELEASE

Los Angeles, May 10 -- The end of the road is already in sight for more than 2,500 of the 7,000 model year 1970 or older cars Unocal has promised to junk through its SCRAP project.

As part of its South Coast Recycled Auto Program announced last month to fight air pollution in the Los Angeles basin, Unocal has pledged to remove 7,000 1970 or older cars from Southern California freeways. Beginning June 1, the company will pay $700 for each vehicle.

Since the program was announced April 26, Unocal has made appointments to accept autos from more than 2,500 prospective sellers. The cars, which pollute 15 to 30 times more than new models, will be crushed and shredded, and the metal recycled.

The response by sellers to a toll-free telephone number (800-866-2251) was so heavy it prompted telephone company intervention and required the installation of numerous additional lines, according to Richard J. Stegemeier, chairman, president and chief executive officer.

MORE...

-2-

"We were swamped with calls," Stegemeier said. "We couldn't answer the phones fast enough. We're well on our way to reaching the 7,000-car mark and taking millions of pounds of pollutants out of our air permanently."

The 7,000 vehicles Unocal will scrap are estimated to emit 6 million pounds of carbon monoxide, reactive organic gases and nitrogen oxides annually, according to Stegemeier. Among automobiles, 1970 or older cars are the worst polluters on the road.

Other companies also think the program is a good idea. T. J. Rodgers, president and chief executive officer of Cypress Semiconductor, San Jose, Calif., sent Stegemeier a note and a check for $700.

"What a great idea!" Rodgers wrote. "The employees of Cypress Semiconductor and I would like you to buy and bury one for us, too."

The program is part of a three-point Unocal offensive against vehicle emissions. They cause at least 60 percent of the basin's smog, according to the California Air Resources Board.

Besides SCRAP, the other programs are Smog-Fighter, which offers free smog checks and low-emission tune-ups to owners of 1974 and older vehicles, and Protech Patrol, in which emergency vehicles will offer free service to motorists stranded on freeways.

-30-

May 10, 1990

Figure 19–3 Unocal's campaign in the spring of 1990 to rid the Los Angeles Basin of millions of pounds of air pollution was an outstanding example of managing a public relations opportunity. (*Courtesy of Unocal Corporation*)

3. **Establishing a company position** Establishing a position can be a formal process. After the Upjohn senior policy committee has met and decided on issues, Upjohn's public affairs staff prepares policy statements on each topic. At PPG Industries, individual issues managers prepare position papers for executive review on topics of direct concern.
4. **Designing company action and response to achieve results** The best-organized companies for issues management orchestrate integrated responses to achieve results. Typically, organizations may coordinate their Washington offices, state lobbying operations, management speeches, advertising messages, and employee communications to their point of view (Figure 19–4).

GROWTH OF RISK COMMUNICATION

In the 1990s, issues management has taken a back seat to *risk communication*. Risk communication is basically the process of taking scientific data related to health and environmental hazards and presenting them to a lay audience in a manner that is both understandable and meaningful.[4]

In Defense of a Little Virginity

a message from Focus on the Family

The federal government has spent almost $3 billion of our taxes since 1970 to promote contraceptives and "safe sex" among our teenagers. Isn't it time we asked, ***What have we gotten for our money?*** *These are the facts:*

- The federal Centers for Disease Control estimate that there are now 1 million cases of HIV infection nationwide.[1]
- 1 in 100 students coming to the University of Texas health center now carries the deadly virus.[2]
- The rate of heterosexual HIV transmission has increased 44% since September 1989.[3]
- Sexually transmitted diseases (STDs) infect 3 million teenagers annually.[4]
- 63% of all STD cases occur among persons less than 25 years of age.[5]
- 1 million new cases of pelvic inflammatory disease occur annually.[6]
- 1.3 million new cases of gonorrhea occur annually[7]; strains of gonorrhea have developed that are resistant to penicillin.
- Syphilis is at a 40-year high, with 134,000 new infections per year.[8]
- 500,000 new cases of herpes occur annually[9]; it is estimated that 16.4% of the U.S. population ages 15-74 is infected, totaling more than 25 million Americans — among certain groups, the infection rate is as high as 60%.[10]
- 4 million cases of chlamydia occur annually[11]; 10-30% of 15- to19-year-olds are infected.[12]
- There are now 24 million cases of human papilloma virus (HPV), with a higher prevalence among teens.[13]

To date, over 20 different and dangerous sexually transmitted diseases are rampant among the young. Add to that the problems associated with promiscuous behavior: infertility, abortions and infected newborns. The cost of this epidemic is staggering, both in human suffering and in expense to society; yet epidemiologists tell us we've only seen the beginning.

Incredibly, the "safe-sex" gurus and condom promoters who got us into this mess are still determining our policy regarding adolescent sexuality. Their ideas have failed, and it is time to rethink their bankrupt policies.

How long has it been since you've heard anyone tell teenagers why it is to *their* advantage to remain virgins until married? The facts are being withheld from them, with tragic consequences. Unless we come to terms with the sickness that stalks a generation of Americans, teen promiscuity will continue, and millions of kids . . . thinking they are protected . . . will suffer for the rest of their lives. Many will die of AIDS.

There is only one safe way to remain healthy in the midst of a sexual revolution. It is to abstain from intercourse until marriage, and then wed and be faithful to an uninfected partner. It is a concept that was widely endorsed in society until the 1960s. Since then, a "better idea" has come along . . . one that now threatens the entire human family.

Inevitable questions are raised whenever abstinence is proposed. It's time we gave some clear answers:

Why, apart from moral considerations, do you think teenagers should be taught to abstain from sex until marriage?

No other approach to the epidemic of sexually transmitted diseases will work. The so-called "safe-sex" solution is a disaster in the making. Condoms can fail at least 15.7 percent of the time annually in preventing pregnancy.[14] They fail 36.3 percent of the time annually in preventing pregnancy among young, unmarried minority women.[15] In a study of homosexual men, the *British Medical Journal* reported the failure rate due to slippage and breakage to be 26 percent.[16] Given these findings, it is obvious why we have a word for people who rely on condoms as a means of birth control. We call them . . . "parents."

Remembering that a woman can conceive only one or two days per month, we can only guess how high the failure rate for condoms must be in preventing disease, which can be transmitted 365 days per year! If the devices are not used properly, or if they slip just once, viruses and bacteria are exchanged and the disease process begins. One mistake after 500 "protected" episodes is all it takes to contract a sexually transmitted disease. The damage is done in a single moment when rational thought is overridden by passion.

Those who would depend on so insecure a method must use it properly on *every* occasion, and even then a high failure rate is brought about by factors beyond their control. The young victim who is told by his elders that this little latex device is "safe" may not know he is risking lifelong pain and even death for so brief a window of pleasure. What a burden to place on an immature mind and body!

Then we must recognize that there are other differences between pregnancy prevention and disease prevention. HIV is 1/25th the width of sperm,[17] and can pass easily through even the smallest gaps in condoms. Researchers studying surgical gloves made out of latex, the same material in condoms, found "channels of 5 microns that penetrated the entire thickness of the glove."[18] HIV measures .1 microns.[19] Given these findings, what rational, informed person would trust his or her very life to such flimsy armor?

This surely explains why not one of 800 sexologists at a conference a few years ago raised a hand when asked if they would trust a thin rubber sheath to protect them during intercourse with a known HIV-infected person.[20] Who could blame them? They're not crazy, after all. And yet they're perfectly willing to tell our kids that "safe sex" is within reach and that they can sleep around with impunity.

There is only one way to protect ourselves from the deadly diseases that lie in wait. It is abstinence before marriage, then marriage and mutual fidelity for life to an uninfected partner. Anything less is potentially suicidal.

That position is simply NOT realistic today. It's an unworkable solution: Kids will NOT implement it.

Some will. Some won't. It's still the only answer. But let's talk about an "unworkable solution" of the first order. Since 1970, the federal government has spent nearly $3 billion to promote contraception and "safe sex." This year alone, 450 million of your tax dollars will go down that drain![21] (Compared with less than $8 million for abstinence programs, which Sen. Teddy Kennedy and company have sought repeatedly to eliminate altogether.) Isn't it time we ask what we've gotten for our money? After 22 years and nearly $3 billion, some 58 percent of teenage girls under 18 still did not use contraception during their first intercourse.[22] Furthermore, teenagers tend to keep having unprotected intercourse for a full year, on average, before starting any kind of contraception.[23] That is the success ratio of the experts who call abstinence "unrealistic" and "unworkable."

Even if we spent another $50 billion to promote condom usage, most teenagers would still not use them consistently and properly. The nature of human beings and the passion of the act simply do not lend themselves to a disciplined response in young romantics.

But if you knew a teenager was going to have intercourse, wouldn't you teach him or her about proper condom usage?

No, because that approach has an unintended consequence. The process of recommending condom usage to teenagers inevitably conveys five dangerous ideas: (1) that "safe sex" is achievable; (2) that everybody is doing it; (3) that responsible adults expect them to do it; (4) that it's a good thing; and (5) that their peers know they know these things, breeding promiscuity. Those are very destructive messages to give our kids.

Furthermore, Planned Parenthood's own data show that the number one reason teenagers engage in intercourse is peer pressure![24] Therefore, anything we do to imply that "everybody is doing it" results in more . . . not fewer . . . people who give the game a try. Condom distribution programs do not reduce the number of kids exposed to disease . . . they radically increase it!

Want proof of that fact? Since the federal government began its major contraception program in 1970, unwed pregnancies have increased 87 percent among 15- to 19-year-olds.[25] Likewise, abortions among teens rose 67 percent;[26] unwed births went up 61 percent.[27] And venereal disease has infected a generation of young people. Nice job, sex counselors. Good thinking, senators and congressmen. Nice nap, America.

Having made a blunder that now threatens the human family, one would think the designers would be backtracking and apologizing for their miscalculations. Instead, they continue to lobby Congress and corporate America for more money. Given the misinformation extant on this subject, they'll probably get it.

But if you were a parent and knew that your son or daughter was having sex, wouldn't you rather he or she used a condom?

How much risk is acceptable when you're talking about your teenager's life? One study of married couples in which one partner was infected with HIV found that 17% of the partners using condoms for protection still caught the virus within a year and a half.[28] Telling our teens to "reduce their risk" to one in six (17%) is not much better than advocating Russian roulette. Both are fatal, eventually. The difference is that with a gun, death is quicker. Suppose your son or daughter were joining an 18-month skydiving club of six members. If you knew that one of their parachutes would definitely fail, would you recommend that they simply buckle the chutes tighter? Certainly not. You would say, "Please don't jump. Your life is at stake!" How could a loving parent do less?

Kids won't listen to the abstinence message. You're just wasting your breath to try to sell them a notion like that.

It is a popular myth that teenagers are incapable of understanding that it is in their best interest to save themselves until marriage. Almost 65 percent of all high school females under 18 are virgins.[29]

A few years ago in Lexington, Ky., a youth event was held that featured no sports contest, no rock groups—just an ex-convict named Harold Morris talking about abstinence, among other subjects. The coliseum seated 18,000 people, but 26,000 teenagers showed up! Eventually, more than 2,000 stood outside the packed auditorium and listened over a hastily prepared public address system. Who says kids won't listen to this time-honored message?

Even teens who have been sexually active can choose to stop. This is often called "secondary virginity," a good concept that conveys the idea that kids can start over. One young girl recently wrote Ann Landers to say she wished she had kept her virginity, signing the letter, "Sorry I didn't and wish I could take it back." As responsible adults we need to tell her that even though she can't go back, she can go forward. She can regain her self-respect and protect her health, because it's never too late to start saying "no" to premarital sex.

Even though the safe-sex advocates predominate in educational circles, are there no positive examples of abstinence-based programs for kids?

Thankfully, some excellent programs have been developed. Spokane-based *Teen-Aid* and Chicago's *Southwest Parents Committee* are good examples. So are *Next Generation* in Maryland, *Choices* in California and *Respect Inc.* in Illinois. Other curricula such as *Facing Reality; Sex Respect; Me, My World, My Future; Reasonable Reasons to Wait; Sex, Love & Choices; F.A.C.T.S.* etc., are all abstinence-themed programs to help kids make good sexual decisions.

A good curriculum for inner-city youth is Elayne Bennett's *Best Friends Program*. This successful "mentoring" project helps adolescents in Washington, D.C. graduate from high school and remain abstinent. In five years, not one female has become pregnant while in the *Best Friends Program!*

Establishing and nurturing abstinence ideas with kids, however, can be like spitting into the wind. Not because they won't listen, because most will. But pro-abstinence messages are drowned out in a sea of toxic teen-sex-is-inevitable-use-a-condom propaganda from "safe-sex" professionals.

You place major responsibility on those who have told adolescents that sexual expression is their right as long as they do it "properly." Who else has contributed to the epidemic?

The entertainment industry must certainly share the blame, including television producers. It is interesting in this context that all four networks and the cable television entities are wringing their hands about this terrible epidemic of AIDS. They profess to be very concerned about those who are infected with sexually transmitted diseases, and perhaps they are sincere. However, TV executives and movie moguls have contributed mightily to the existence of this plague. For decades, they have depicted teens and young adults climbing in and out of each other's beds like so many sexual robots. Only the nerds were shown to be chaste, and they were too stupid or ugly to find partners.

Of course, the beautiful young actors in those steamy dramas never faced any consequences for their sexual indulgence. No one ever came down with herpes, or syphilis, or chlamydia, or pelvic inflammatory disease, or infertility, or AIDS, or genital warts, or cervical cancer. No patients were ever told by a physician that there was no cure for their disease or that they would have to deal with the pain for the rest of their lives. No one ever heard that genital cancers associated with the human papilloma virus (HPV) kill more women than AIDS,[30] or that strains of gonorrhea are now resistant to penicillin.[31]

No, there was no downside. It all looked like so much fun. But what a price we are paying now for the lies we have been told.

The government has also contributed to this crisis and continues to exacerbate the problem. For example, a current brochure from the federal Centers for Disease Control and the City of New York is entitled, "Teens Have the Right," and is apparently intended to free adolescents from adult authority. Inside are the six declarations that make up a "Teenager's Bill of Rights," as follows:

- I have the right to think for myself.
- I have the right to decide whether to have sex and who[m] to have it with.
- I have the right to use protection when I have sex.
- I have the right to buy and use condoms.
- I have the right to express myself.
- I have the right to ask for help if I need it.

Under this final item (the right to ask for help) is a list of organizations and phone numbers that readers are encouraged to call. The philosophy that governs several of the organizations reflects the homosexual agenda, which includes recruitment of the young and vigorous promotion of a teen's right to sexual expression.

Your tax dollars at work!

Surely there are other Americans who recognize the danger now threatening a generation of our best and brightest. It is time to speak up for an old-fashioned value called virginity. *Now, more than ever, virtue is a necessity.*

If you agree with Focus on the Family that it is time for a new approach to adolescent sexuality, tear out this ad and save it. Take it to your next school board meeting. Send it to your congressman or senator. Distribute copies to the PTA. And by all means, share it with your teenagers. Begin to promote abstinence before marriage as the *only* healthy way to survive this worldwide epidemic.

Please use the coupon below to obtain a valuable booklet on abstinence. There is no charge for it. However, your support is requested for an upcoming TV program for teenagers on this important topic. Your comments are also solicited.

FOCUS ON THE FAMILY ®

Yes! I want to support a national television broadcast on abstinence and help Focus on the Family reach out to America's kids.

☐ Please send me ________ copies of the booklet, "Teaching Your Kids to Say 'No' to Sex." (Up to 10: FREE — More than 10: 35¢ each*) LF213 $________

☐ Please send me ______ copies of this ad. (Up to 10: FREE — More than 10: 25¢ each*) FX273 $________

☐ I am enclosing a tax-deductible gift of $________ 2DEXAP

Your Name ________________
Address ________________
City ________________ State ______ Zip ________
Phone ________________

Please make check payable to Focus on the Family. Clip this reply form and send it along with your tax-deductible donation to: Focus on the Family, Colorado Springs, CO 80995-0001
Or call 1-719-633-6287

*suggested donation

Data Sources:

Figure 19–4 As a complement to its national religious broadcasts, the group Focus on the Family sponsored this ad in response to such developments as the public school distribution of condoms. This ad was placed in more than 900 newspapers across the country and translated into six languages in seven foreign countries. (*Courtesy of Focus on the Family*)

Models of risk communication have been developed based on the position that "perception is reality"—a concept that has been part of public relations for years. Indeed, the disciplines of risk communication and public relations have much in common. Risk communication deals with a high level of emotion. Fear, confusion, frustration, and anger are common feelings in dealing with environmental issues. For example, in 1994, when the tobacco industry was charged with withholding scientific data linking cigarette smoking to cancer, the public was outraged (Figure 19–5).

Tobacco is an addictive drug — as addictive as heroin.*
Tobacco addiction is America's leading cause of preventable death.*

How do they live with themselves?

Si Newhouse
He could voluntarily refuse to push tobacco in his magazines, as many major magazines do. But he hasn't. His magazines probably do more to make smoking seem attractive and sophisticated — what every young person wants to be — than any others. *Fortune* puts his net worth at $5 billion.

Rupert Murdoch
Tobacco advertising is banned on TV, so tobacco companies go after kids in Murdoch's *TV Guide*. He could say no. He's worth $3 billion.

Larry Tisch
As the man who controls Lorillard Tobacco, he could ask Congress to halt all tobacco advertising and promotion. The tobacco companies would save $4 billion a year. That's $4 billion more annual profit for their shareholders — in the short run. In the long run, fewer kids would be enticed to replace smokers who die or quit. But is that bad? *Fortune* says Tisch is a billionaire.

Henry Kravis
Since his company, RJR, began using a cartoon character to push Camels, Camel's share of the teen and pre-teen market has jumped from 1% to 32%. He could become a health hero by joining with Tisch in asking Congress to ban all tobacco promotion — and boost the industry bottom line by $4 billion. Judging from the *Forbes* 400 list, he can afford this risk. He's worth half a billion.

Michael Miles
Miles runs Philip Morris. Who'd have more reason to want a total ad ban than the shareholders of Philip Morris? Marlboro smokers wouldn't quit buying Marlboros just because the advertising stopped; yet Philip Morris could quit spending all those billions trying to defend its market share. Miles — who himself quit smoking long ago — made $5 million last year.

Like most people who profit from the sale of addictive, unhealthy substances, these men have the good sense not to use those substances themselves. Not one of them smokes cigarettes.

Si, Rupert, Larry, Henry, Mike: If you'll agree it's crazy for a society to *promote* its leading cause of preventable death, and stop doing it, we'll take out an ad **twice as big** honoring you and saying thanks. There's no greater contribution you could make to America's health.

*U.S. Surgeon General

STAT *Stop Teenage Addiction to Tobacco*
NATIONAL OFFICE 511 East Columbus Avenue, Springfield, MA 01105 (413) 732-STAT

For a free book, KIDS SAY DON'T SMOKE, send four 29-cent stamps. If you can help us pay for more ads like this, we'd appreciate it!

Figure 19–5 Led by the Federal Trade Commission, the tobacco industry was besieged in the mid-1990s. So, too, was anyone even remotely related to the industry. (*Courtesy of Stop Teenage Addiction to Tobacco*)

Occasionally—even often—intense emotion flows from a lack of knowledge and understanding about the science that underlies societal risk. Therefore, frequent and forceful communication is necessary to inform, educate, and even dampen emotion. The first rule in responding to a perceived public risk is to take the matter seriously. After this, according to risk management expert William Adams, seven steps are helpful in planning a risk communication program:

1. Recognize risk communication as part of a larger risk management program and understand that the whole program is based on politics, power, and controversial issues.
2. Encourage management to join the "communications loop," and help train them to deal effectively with the news media.
3. Develop credible outside experts to act as news sources for journalists.
4. Become an in-house expert in your own area of risk to enhance your credibility with journalists.
5. Approach the news media with solid facts and figures *before* they approach you. Verify the veracity of your data.
6. Research perceptions of your organization by the media and other publics to gauge credibility and help determine if your messages will be believable.
7. Understand your target audiences and how the news media can help you communicate effectively.[5]

Like any other area of public relations, risk communication depends basically on an organization's actions. In the long run, deeds, not words, are what count in communicating risk.

MANAGING IN A CRISIS

The most significant test for any organization comes when it is hit by a major accident or disaster. How it handles itself in the midst of a crisis may influence how it is perceived for years to come. Poor handling of events with the magnitude of NASA's shuttle disaster, Tylenol's capsule poisoning, or Union Carbide's Bhopal tragedy not only can cripple an organization's reputation but also can cause it enormous monetary loss. It is essential, therefore, that such emergencies be managed intelligently and forthrightly with the news media, employees, and the community at large.

As any organization unfortunate enough to experience a crisis recognizes, when the crisis strikes, seven instant warning signs invariably appear:

1. **Surprise** When a crisis breaks out, it's usually unexpected. Often, it's a natural disaster—a tornado or hurricane. Sometimes, it's a human-made disaster—robbery, embezzlement, or large loss. Frequently, the first a public relations professional learns of such an event is when the media call and demand to know what immediate action will be taken.
2. **Insufficient information** Many things happen at once. Rumors fly. Wire services want to know why the company's stock is falling. It's difficult to get a grip on everything that's happening.

3. **Escalating events** The crisis expands. The Stock Exchange wants to know what's going on. Will the organization issue a statement? Are the rumors true? While rumors run rampant, truthful information is difficult to obtain. You want to respond in an orderly manner, but events are unfolding too quickly. This is what Johnson & Johnson experienced as the reports of deaths from Tylenol kept rising.
4. **Loss of control** The unfortunate natural outgrowth of escalating events is that too many things are happening simultaneously. Erroneous stories hit the wires, then the newsstands, and then the airwaves. As in the case of the Coors mouse in the can, rampant rumors can't easily be controlled.
5. **Increased outside scrutiny** The media, stockbrokers, talk-show hosts, and the public in general feed on rumors. "Helpful" politicians and observers of all stripes comment on what's going on. The media want responses. Investors demand answers. Customers must know what's going on.
6. **Siege mentality** The organization, understandably, feels surrounded. Lawyers counsel, "Anything we say will be held against us." The easiest thing to do is to say nothing. But does that make sense?
7. **Panic** With the walls caving in and with leaks too numerous to plug, a sense of panic pervades. In such an environment, it is difficult to convince management to take immediate action and to communicate what's going on.[6]

OMMUNICATING IN A CRISIS

The key communications principle in dealing with a crisis is not to clam up when disaster strikes. The most effective crisis communicators are those who provide prompt, frank, and full information to the media in the eye of the storm. Invariably, the first inclination of executives is to say, "Let's wait until all the facts are in." But as President Carter's press secretary, Jody Powell, used to say, "Bad news is a lot like fish. It doesn't get better with age." In saying nothing, an organization is perceived as already having made a decision. That angers the media and compounds the problem. On the other hand, inexperienced spokespersons, speculating nervously or using emotionally charged language, are even worse.

Most public relations professionals consider the cardinal rule for communications during a crisis to be

TELL IT ALL AND TELL IT FAST!

As a general rule, when information gets out quickly, rumors are stopped and nerves are calmed. There is nothing complicated about the goals of crisis management. They are (1) terminate the crisis quickly; (2) limit the damage; and (3) restore credibility.[7]

Among the most important steps in crisis management is planning. The natural enemy of prior planning is the "it can't happen here" mentality. This is essentially what happened when NASA suffered its calamitous explosion of the *Challenger* in 1986. The organization, huge and resourceful as it was, nonetheless stood powerless in the face of an unprecedented disaster.

When crisis hits, the organization must assess its communications—particularly in evaluating media requests—by answering the following questions:

1. **What do we gain by participating?** If you have absolutely nothing to gain from an interview, then don't give one. Period.
2. **What are the risks?** The answer is based on your level of comfort with the medium, who the interviewer is, the amount of preparation time available to you, legal liability, and how much the organization loses if the story is told without the interview.
3. **Can we get our message across?** Will this particular medium allow us to deliver our message clearly to the public?
4. **Is this audience worth it?** Often, a particular television program or newspaper may not be germane to the specific audience the organization needs to reach.
5. **How will management react?** An important variable in assessing whether to appear is the potential reaction of top management. In the final analysis, you have to explain your recommendation or action to them.
6. **Does your legal liability outweigh the public interest?** This is seldom the case, although company lawyers often disagree.
7. **Is there a better way?** This is a key question. If an uncontrolled media interview can be avoided, do so. However, reaching pertinent publics through the press is often the best way to communicate in a crisis.[8]

In the final analysis, communicating in a crisis depends on a rigorous analysis of the risks versus the benefits of going public. Communicating effectively also depends on the judgment and experience of the public relations professional. Every call is a close one, and there is no guarantee that the organization will benefit, no matter what course is chosen. One thing is clear: Helping to navigate the organization through the shoals of a crisis is the ultimate test of a public relations professional.

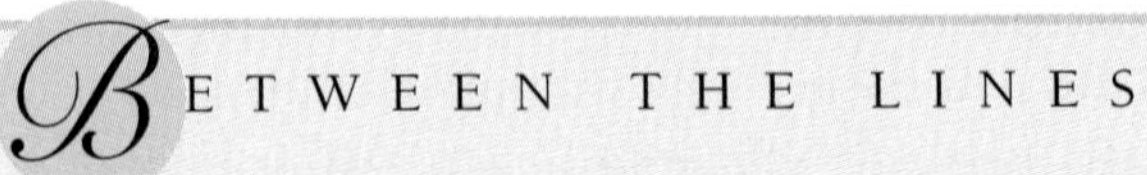

THE LESSONS OF VALDEZ

Remember the *Exxon Valdez* case discussed in Chapter 3? Since you've probably already dissected it thoroughly, it won't matter if we divulge here, courtesy of crisis expert Tim Wallace, how Exxon *should* have handled the situation.

1. **Develop a clear, straightforward position.** In a crisis, you can't appear to waffle. You must remain flexible enough to respond to changing developments, but you must also stick to your underlying position. Exxon's seemed to waver.
2. **Involve top management.** Management must not only be involved, it must also *appear* to be involved. In Exxon's case, from all reports, Chairman Lawrence Rawl was involved with the Gulf of Valdez solutions every step of the way. But that's not how it appeared in public. Rather, he was perceived as distant from the crisis. And Exxon suffered.

3. **Activate third-party support.** This support may come from Wall Street analysts, independent engineers, technology experts, or legal authorities. Any objective party with credentials can help your case.
4. **Establish an on-site presence.** The chairman of Union Carbide flew to Bhopal, India, in 1984, when a Carbide plant explosion killed thousands. His trip at least showed corporate concern. When Chairman Rawl explained that he "had better things to do" than fly to Valdez, Exxon effectively lost the public relations battle.
5. **Centralize communications.** In any crisis, a communications point person should be appointed and a support team established. It is the point person's job—and his or hers alone—to state the organization's position.
6. **Cooperate with the media.** In a crisis, journalists are repugnant; they're obnoxious; they'll stoop to any level to get the story. But don't take it personally. Treat the media as friendly adversaries and explain your side of the crisis. Making them enemies will only exacerbate tensions.
7. **Don't ignore employees.** Keeping employees informed helps ensure that the organization's business proceeds as normally as possible. Employees are your greatest ally. Don't keep them in the dark.

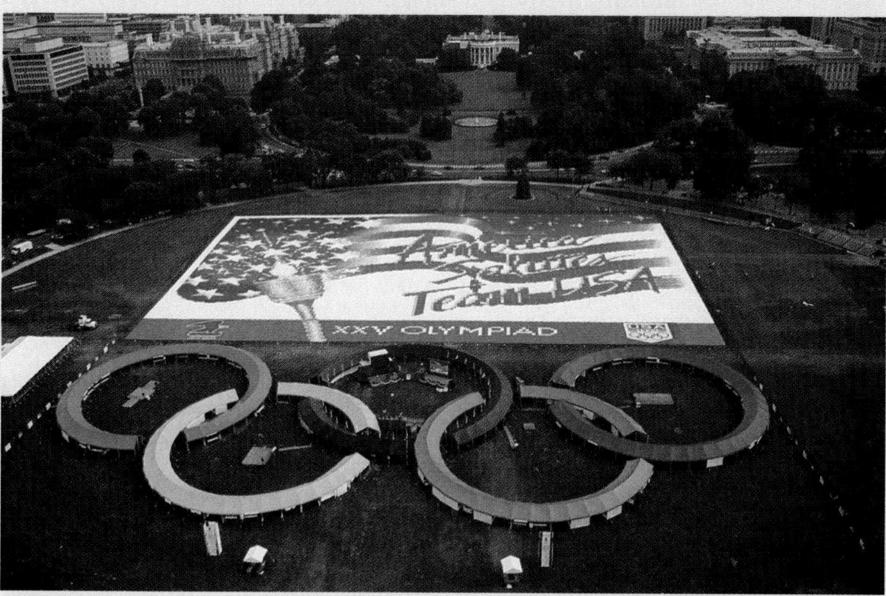

Figure 19–6 One way to head off crises is to emphasize opportunities that build goodwill. Such was the case in 1992 when the U.S. Postal Service presented the U.S. Olympic Team with a 522-by-348 foot postcard signed by nearly three quarters of a million Americans. The check, displayed on the Ellipse near the White House, was accompanied by a real check for $519,608 collected mostly in $1 donations from Americans during Olympic Spirit Week. (*Courtesy of the U.S. Postal Service*)

8. **Keep the crisis in perspective.** Often management underreacts at the start of a crisis and overreacts when it builds. The prevailing wisdom seems to be "Just because we're paranoid doesn't mean they're not out to get us!" Avoid hunkering down. Exxon made this mistake, and it cost them dearly.
9. **Begin positioning the organization for the time when the crisis is over.** Concentrate on communicating the steps that the organization will take to deal with the crisis. Admit blame if it's due. But then quickly focus on what you are doing now rather than on what went wrong.
10. **Continuously monitor and evaluate the process.** Survey, survey, survey. Take the pulse of your employees, customers, suppliers, distributors, investors, and, if appropriate, the general public. Determine whether your messages are getting through. Constantly check to see which aspects of the program are working and which are not. Adjust accordingly.

SUMMARY

Although prevention remains the best insurance for any organization, crisis management has become one of the most revered skills in the practice of public relations. Organizations of every variety are faced, sooner or later, with a crisis. Nor are crises limited by geographical boundaries. Japan, in recent years, has suffered a rash of major crises and handled them in uniquely Japanese fashion. (When a Japan Air Lines jet crashed, killing more than 500 people, the airline's president resigned after traveling across the country personally to express his apologies to the families of the victims.)

The issues that confront society—from energy and the environment to health and nutrition, to corporate social responsibility and minority rights—will not soon abate. Indeed, issues such as AIDS have gripped society to such a degree that no organization can be silent on the topic (Figure 19–7).

All of this suggests that experienced and knowledgeable crisis managers, who can skillfully navigate and effectively communicate, turning crisis into opportunity, will be valuable resources for organizations into the next century. In the years ahead, few challenges will be more significant for public relations professionals than helping to manage crisis.

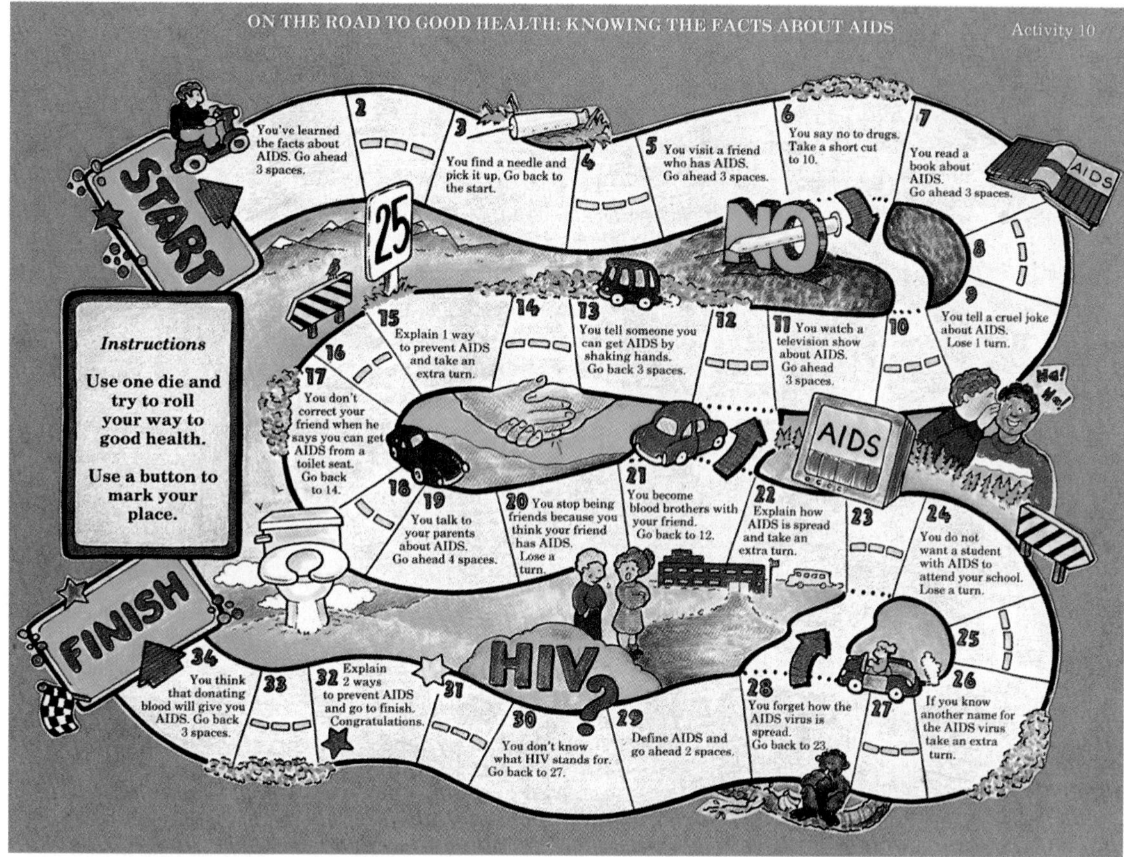

Figure 19–7 Canadian Life and Health Insurance companies teamed up with the Canadian Public Health Association to produce Canada's first AIDS teaching resource for fifth- and sixth-grade students. The package included a student booklet, teacher's guide, word games, and quizzes about the deadly disease. (*Courtesy of Canadian Life and Health Insurance Inc.*)

DISCUSSION STARTERS

1. What is meant by the term *issues management?*
2. How can an organization influence the development of an issue in society?
3. What are the general steps in implementing an issues management program?
4. What are the usual stages that an organization experiences in a crisis?
5. What is the cardinal rule for communicating in a crisis?
6. What are the keys to successful crisis communication?
7. What is the meaning of the term *reputation management?*
8. What steps should be followed in enhancing reputation management?
9. Contrast the way Coors handled its mouse crisis with the way Pepsi handled its syringe crisis.
10. What are likely to be the flashpoint issues in the 1990s?

NOTES

1. "Issues Management Conference—A Special Report," *Corporate Public Issues* 7, no. 23 (December 1, 1982): 1–2.
2. Kerry Tucker and Glen Broom, "Managing Issues Acts as Bridge to Strategic Planning," *Public Relations Journal* (November 1993): 38.
3. Michael Lev, "Give Me Your Tired, Your Rusty . . ." *The New York Times*, October 6, 1990, D1.
4. Jeffrey P. Julin, "Is 'PR' a Risk to Effective Risk Communication?" *IABC Communication World* (October 1993): 14–15.
5. William C. Adams, "Strategic Advice in Handling Risk," presented during the Business, Environmental Issues and Risk Conference, Washington, DC, November 12, 1992.
6. Fraser P. Seitel, "Communicating in Crisis," *United States Banker* (December 1990): 49.
7. Tim Wallace, "Crisis Management: Practical Tips on Restoring Trust," *The Journal of Private Sector Policy* (November 1991): 14.
8. Martin Arnold, "Crisis Communication," *IABC Communication World* (June 1989): 44.

TOP OF THE SHELF

Jack A. Gottschalk, editor. *Crisis Response: Inside Stories on Managing Image Under Siege*. Detroit: Visible Press, 1993.

This unique volume contains 25 firsthand accounts of crises recounted by those involved in the situations.

Crises are divided into three broad areas: business calamities, consumer troubles, and human tragedies. All contain invaluable lessons about managing in a crisis.

As contributing editor Kurt Stocker says, "The right response to a crisis for one organization may be the exact opposite of the right response for another." Indeed, there is never one right answer in dealing with a crisis. Each response is as unique as the organization involved.

The crises included in this book—from environmental mishaps, such as the "Meltdown on Three Mile Island" and "The Exxon Valdez Paradox," to great human tragedies, such as "Disaster at Lockerbie" and "Massacre at My Lai"—offer many valuable insights.

This book takes a sophisticated look at both capturing the reality and the cost of crises without attempting to provide simplistic solutions. Reading about what others did when placed in the catbird seat of crisis will add greatly to the crisis management expertise of students and practitioners. It is worth the voyage.

SUGGESTED READINGS

Bernstein, Alan. *Emergency Public Relations Manual*, 3rd ed. Highland Park, NJ: Pase, 1988 (P.O. Box 1299 08904).

Blakey, H. Allen. *Environmental Communications and Public Relations Handbook.* Rockville, MD: Government Institute, 1989 (966 Hungerford Dr. 20850).

Bogue, Donald. *The Population of the United States: Historical Trends and Future Projections.* Ithaca, NY: American Demographics, 1988 (P.O. Box 68 14851).

Brown, Kathleen, and Joan Turner. *AIDS: Policies and Programs for the Workplace.* New York: Van Nostrand Reinhold, 1989.

Buchholz, Rogene. *Business Environment and Public Policy: Implications for Management.* Englewood Cliffs, NJ: Prentice-Hall, 1989.

Ciabattari, Jane. *Winning Moves: How to Survive (and Manage) a Corporate Shakeup.* New York: Rawson Associates, 1988 (866 Third Ave. 10022).

Clarke, Lee. *Acceptable Risk? Making Decisions in a Toxic Environment.* Berkeley: University of California Press, 1989.

Cook, Timothy E. *Making Laws and Making News.* Washington, DC: The Brookings Institution, 1989.

Covello, Vincent T., David B. McCallum, and Maria T. Pavlov, eds. *Effective Risk Communication: The Role and Responsibility of Government and Nongovernment Organizations.* New York: Plenum Press, 1989.

Covello, Vincent T., Peter M. Sandman, and Paul Slovic. *Risk Communication, Risk Statistics, and Risk Comparisons: A Manual for Plant Managers.* Washington, DC: Chemical Manufacturers Association, 1988.

Dennis, Everette E., ed.-in-chief. "Covering the Environment." *Gannett Center Journal*, Vol. 4, No. 3 (Summer 1990).

E. Bruce Harrison Co., Inc., eds. *Environmental Communication and Public Relations Handbook.* Rockville, MD: Government Institutes, Inc., 1988.

Federal Register. (Available from Superintendent of Documents, U.S. Government Printing Office, Washington, DC 20402.) The *Federal Register* provides a method of tracking rules and regulations from government agencies and keeping abreast of changes.

Ferguson, M. A., J. M. Valenti, and G. Melwani. "Communicating with Risk Takers: A Public Relations Perspective." *Public Relations Research Annual*, Vol. 3. Hillsdale, NJ: Erlbaum, 1993.

Food, Pesticides and the Question of Risk. Handbook. Wilmington, DE: ICI Americas, Inc., 1989.

The Fundamentals of Issue Management. Monograph. (Available from Public Affairs Council, 1220 16th St. NW, Washington, DC 20036.)

Hadden, S. G. *A Citizen's Right to Know: Risk Communication and Public Policy.* Boulder, CO: Westview Press, 1988.

Health, Robert. *Strategic Issues Management.* San Francisco: Jossey-Bass, 1988.

Holmes, Paul A., ed. "Risk Communication: Outrage Causes Misperception." *Inside PR* New York (September 1992): 2.

Howard, Carole M. "Managing Media Relations for Environmental Issues." *Public Relations Quarterly* (Summer 1988).

"It Can Happen to Anyone in a Few Short Seconds." *PR Week* (April 18–24, 1988): 10, 11.

Janis, Irving L. *Crucial Decisions: Leadership in Policy Making and Crisis Management.* New York: Free Press, 1988.

Lerbinger, Otto. *Managing Corporate Crises: Strategies for Executives.* Boston: Barrington Press, 1986.

Merriam, John, and Joel Makower. *Trend Watching.* New York: AMACOM, 1988.

Murphy, Priscilla. "Using Games as a Model for Crisis Communications." *Public Relations Review* (*Winter 1987*): 19–28.

National Research Council. *Improving Risk Communication.* Washington, DC: National Academy Press, 1989.

O'Dwyer, Jack, ed. *Jack O'Dwyer's Newsletter.* Weekly newsletter. (271 Madison Ave., New York, NY 10016).

PR Reporter. Weekly newsletter. (Box 600, Exeter, NH 03833).

Prato, Lou. *Covering the Environmental Beat.* Washington, DC: RTNDA/Media Institute, Environmental Reporting Forum, 1991.

Public Relations Review. Quarterly. (Available from the Foundation for Public Relations Research and Education, University of Maryland College of Journalism, College Park, MD 20742.)

Rautenberg, Steven. "Crisis Public Relations in the Age of Apology: From Chernobyl to Monongahela." Address to the American Bankers Association Security and Planning Conference, Orlando, FL, January 28, 1988.

Sandman, Peter M. "Addressing Skepticism About Responsible Care." Washington, DC: Chemical Manufacturers Association, March 1991.

Sandman, Peter M. *Risk = Hazard + Outrage: A Formula for Effective Risk Communication.* Akron, OH: American Industrial Hygiene Association, 1991.

Sauerhaft, Stan, and Chris Atkins. *Image Wars.* New York: Wiley, 1989.

Shrader-Frechette, K. S. *Risk and Rationality: Philosophical Foundations for Populist Reforms.* Berkeley: University of California Press, 1991.

For close to 100 years, Johnson & Johnson Company (J&J) of New Brunswick, NJ, was the epitome of a well-managed, highly profitable, and tight-lipped consumer products manufacturer.

ROUND I

That image changed on the morning of September 30, 1982, when J&J faced as devastating a public relations problem as had confronted any company in history. That morning, J&J's management learned that its premier product, extra-strength Tylenol, had been used as a murder weapon to kill three people. In the days that followed, another three people died from swallowing Tylenol capsules loaded with cyanide. And although all the cyanide deaths occurred in Chicago, reports from other parts of the country also implicated extra-strength Tylenol capsules in illnesses of various sorts. These latter reports were later proved to be unfounded, but J&J and its Tylenol-producing subsidiary, McNeil Consumer Products Company, found themselves at the center of a public relations trauma the likes of which few companies had ever experienced.

Tylenol had been an astoundingly profitable product for J&J. At the time of the Tylenol murders, the product held 35 percent of the $1 billion analgesic market. It contributed an estimated 7 percent to J&J's worldwide sales and almost 20 percent to its profits. Throughout the years, J&J had not been—and hadn't needed to be—a particularly high-profile company. Its chairman, James E. Burke, who had been with the company for almost 30 years, had never appeared on television and had rarely participated in print interviews.

J&J's management, understandably, was caught totally by surprise when the news hit. Initially, J&J had no facts and, indeed, got much of its information from the media calls that inundated the firm from the beginning. The company recognized that it needed the media to get out as much information to the public as quickly as possible to prevent a panic. Therefore, almost immediately, J&J made a key decision: to open its doors to the media.

On the second day of the crisis, J&J discovered that an earlier statement that no cyanide was used on its premises was wrong. The company didn't hesitate. Its public relations department quickly announced that the earlier information had been false. Even though the reversal embarrassed the company briefly, J&J's openness was hailed and made up for any damage to its credibility.

Early on in the crisis, the company was largely convinced that the poisonings had not occurred at any of its plants. Nonetheless, J&J recalled an entire lot of 93,000 bottles of extra-strength Tylenol associated with the reported murders. In the process, it telegrammed warnings to doctors, hospitals, and distributors, at a cost of half a million dollars. McNeil also suspended all Tylenol advertising to reduce attention to the product.

By the second day, the company was convinced that the tampering had taken place during Chicago distribution and not in the manufacturing process. Therefore, a total Tylenol recall did not seem obligatory. Chairman Burke himself leaned toward immediately recalling all extra-strength Tylenol capsules, but after consulting with the Federal Bureau of Investigation, he decided not to do so. The FBI was worried that a precipitous recall would encourage copycat poisoning attempts. Nonetheless, five days later, when a copycat strychnine poisoning occurred in California, J&J did recall all extra-strength Tylenol capsules—31 million bottles—at a cost of over $100 million.

Although the company knew it had done nothing wrong, J&J resisted the temptation to disclaim any possible connection between its product and the murders. Rather, while moving quickly to trace the lot numbers of the poisoned packages, it also posted a $100,000 reward for the killer. Through advertisements promising to exchange capsules for tablets, through thousands of letters to the trade, and through statements to the media, the company hoped to put the incident into proper perspective.

At the same time, J&J commissioned a nationwide opinion survey to assess the consumer implications of the Tylenol poisonings. The good news was that 87 percent of Tylenol users surveyed said they realized that the maker of Tylenol was not responsible for the deaths. The bad news was that although a high percentage didn't blame Tylenol, 61 percent still said they were not likely to buy extra-strength Tylenol capsules in the future. In other words, even though most consumers knew the deaths weren't Tylenol's fault, they still feared using the product.

But Chairman Burke and J&J weren't about to knuckle under to the deranged saboteur or saboteurs who had poisoned their product. Despite predictions of the imminent demise of extra-strength Tylenol, J&J decided to relaunch the product in a new triple-safety-sealed, tamper-resistant package (Figure 19–8). Many on Wall Street and in the marketing community were stunned by J&J's bold decision.

But so confident was J&J's management that it launched an all-out media blitz to make sure that people understood its commitment. Chairman Burke appeared on the widely watched Phil Donahue network television program and skillfully handled 60 minutes of intense public ques-

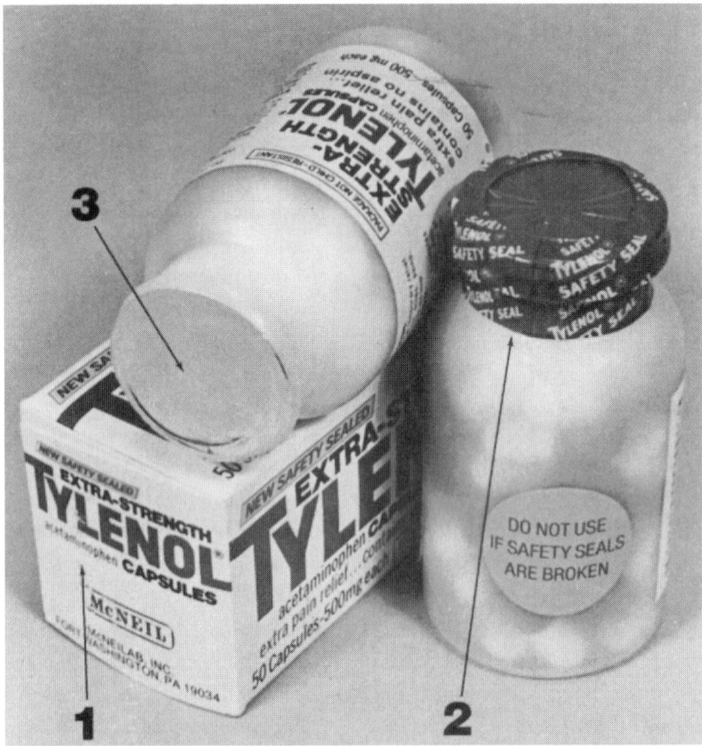

Figure 19–8 The triple-safety-sealed, tamper-resistant package for Tylenol capsules had (1) glued flaps on the outer box, (2) a tight plastic neck seal, and (3) a strong inner foil seal over the mouth of the bottle. A bright yellow label on the bottle was imprinted with a red warning: "Do not use if safety seals are broken." As it turned out, all these precautions didn't work. (*Courtesy of Johnson & Johnson*)

tioning. The investigative news program *60 Minutes*—the scourge of corporate America—was invited by J&J to film its executive strategy sessions to prepare for the new launch. When the program was aired, reporter Mike Wallace concluded that although Wall Street had been ready at first to write off the company, it was now "hedging its bets because of J&J's stunning campaign of facts, money, the media, and truth."

Finally, on November 11, 1982, less than two months after the murders, J&J's management held an elaborate video press conference in New York City, beamed to additional locations around the country, to introduce the new extra-strength Tylenol package. Said J&J's chairman to the media,

> It is our job at Johnson & Johnson to ensure the survival of Tylenol, and we are pledged to do this. While we consider this crime an assault on society, we are nevertheless ready to fulfill our responsibility, which includes paying the price of this heinous crime. But I urge you not to make Tylenol the scapegoat.

In the days and months that followed Burke's news conference, it became clear that Tylenol

Our Credo

We believe our first responsibility is to the doctors, nurses and patients,
to mothers and all others who use our products and services.
In meeting their needs everything we do must be of high quality.
We must constantly strive to reduce our costs
in order to maintain reasonable prices.
Customers' orders must be serviced promptly and accurately.
Our suppliers and distributors must have an opportunity
to make a fair profit.

We are responsible to our employees,
the men and women who work with us throughout the world.
Everyone must be considered as an individual.
We must respect their dignity and recognize their merit.
They must have a sense of security in their jobs.
Compensation must be fair and adequate,
and working conditions clean, orderly and safe.
Employees must feel free to make suggestions and complaints.
There must be equal opportunity for employment, development
and advancement for those qualified.
We must provide competent management,
and their actions must be just and ethical.

We are responsible to the communities in which we live and work
and to the world community as well.
We must be good citizens — support good works and charities
and bear our fair share of taxes.
We must encourage civic improvements and better health and education.
We must maintain in good order
the property we are privileged to use,
protecting the environment and natural resources.

Our final responsibility is to our stockholders.
Business must make a sound profit.
We must experiment with new ideas.
Research must be carried on, innovative programs developed
and mistakes paid for.
New equipment must be purchased, new facilities provided
and new products launched.
Reserves must be created to provide for adverse times.
When we operate according to these principles,
the stockholders should realize a fair return.

Johnson & Johnson

Figure 19–9 *(Courtesy of Johnson & Johnson)*

would not become a scapegoat. In fact, by the beginning of 1983, Tylenol had recaptured an astounding 95 percent of its prior market share. Morale at the company, according to its chairman, was "higher than in years" (Figure 19–9). The euphoria lasted until February 1986, when, unbelievably, tragedy struck again.

ROUND II

Late in the evening of February 10, 1986, news reports began to circulate that a woman had died in Yonkers, New York, after taking poisoned capsules of extra-strength Tylenol. The nightmare for J&J began anew.

A special message from the makers of TYLENOL® products.

If you have TYLENOL capsules, we'll replace them with TYLENOL caplets.

And we'll do it at our expense.

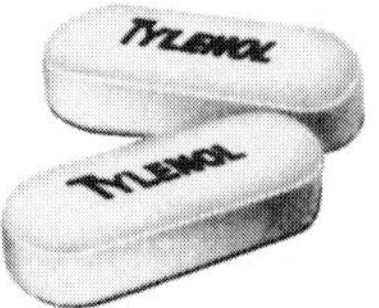

As you know, there has been a tragic event. A small number of Extra-Strength TYLENOL® Capsules in one isolated area in New York have been criminally tampered with.

This was an outrageous act which damages all of us.

Both federal and local authorities have established that it was only capsules that were tampered with.

In order to prevent any further capsule tampering, we have removed all our capsules from your retailers' shelves. This includes Regular and Extra-Strength TYLENOL capsules, CO-TYLENOL® capsules, Maximum-Strength TYLENOL® Sinus Medication capsules, Extra-Strength SINE-AID® capsules, and DIMENSYN® Menstrual Relief capsules.

And Johnson & Johnson's McNeil Consumer Products Company has decided to cease the manufacture, sale, and distribution of **all** capsule forms of over-the-counter medicines.

If you're a regular capsule user, you may be wondering what to use instead. That's why we'd like you to try TYLENOL caplets.

The caplet is a solid form of TYLENOL pain reliever, which research has proven is the form most preferred by consumers. Unlike tablets, it is specially shaped and coated for easy, comfortable swallowing. And the caplet delivers a full extra-strength dose quickly and effectively.

So, if you have any TYLENOL Capsules in your home, do one of the following:

1. Return the bottles with the unused portion to us, together with your name and address on the form below. And we'll replace your TYLENOL capsules with TYLENOL Caplets (or tablets, if you prefer). We'll also refund your postage. Or...

2. If you prefer, you can receive a cash refund for the unused capsules by sending the bottle to us along with a letter requesting the refund.

We are taking this step because, for the past 25 years, over 100 million Americans have made TYLENOL products a trusted part of their health care.

We're continuing to do everything we can to keep your trust.

Send to:
TYLENOL® Capsule Exchange
P.O. Box 2000
Maple Plain, MN 55348
Please send my coupon for free replacement caplets or tablets to:
Please print
Name ______
Address ______
City ______
State ______ Zip ______
Offer expires May 1, 1986

Figure 19–10 *(Courtesy of Johnson & Johnson)*

Once again, the company sprang into action. Chairman Burke addressed reporters at a news conference a day after the incident. A phone survey found that the public didn't blame the company. However, with the discovery of other poisoned Tylenol capsules two days later, the nightmare intensified. The company recorded 15,000 toll-free calls at its Tylenol hotline. And, once again, production of Tylenol capsules was halted. "I'm heartsick," Burke told the press. "We didn't believe it could happen again, and nobody else did either."

This time, although Tylenol earned some 13 percent of the company's net profits, the firm decided once and for all to cease production of its over-the-counter medications in capsule form. It offered to replace all unused Tylenol capsules with new Tylenol caplets, a solid form of medication that was less tamper-prone (Figure 19–10). This time the withdrawal of its capsules cost J&J upward of $150 million after taxes.

And, once again, in the face of tragedy, the company and its chairman received high marks. As President Reagan said at a White House reception two weeks after the crisis hit, "Jim Burke of Johnson & Johnson, you have our deepest appreciation for living up to the highest ideals of corporate responsibility and grace under pressure."*

*For further information on the first round of Tylenol murders, see Jerry Knight, "Tylenol's Maker Shows How to Respond to Crisis," *The Washington Post* (October 11, 1982): 1; Thomas Moore, "The Fight to Save Tylenol," *Fortune* (November 29, 1982): 48; Michael Waldholz, "Tylenol Regains Most of No. 1 Market Share, Amazing Doomsayers," *The Wall Street Journal* (December 24, 1982): 1, 19; and *60 Minutes*, CBS-TV, December 19, 1982.

For further information on the second round of Tylenol murders, see Irvin Molotsky, "Tylenol Maker Hopeful on Solving Poisoning Case," *The New York Times* (February 20, 1986); Steven Prokesch, "A Leader in a Crisis," *The New York Times* (February 19, 1986): B4; Michael Waldholz, "For Tylenol's Manufacturer, the Dilemma Is to Be Aggressive—But Not Appear Pushy," *The Wall Street Journal* (February 20, 1986): 27; and "Tylenol II: How a Company Responds to a Calamity," *U.S. News & World Report* (February 24, 1986): 49.

QUESTIONS

1. What might have been the consequences if J&J had decided to "tough out" the first reports of Tylenol-related deaths and not recall the product?
2. What other public relations options did J&J have in responding to the first round of Tylenol murders?
3. Do you think the company made a wise decision by reintroducing extra-strength Tylenol?
4. In light of the response of other companies not to move precipitously when faced with a crisis, do you think J&J should have acted so quickly to remove the Tylenol product when the second round of Tylenol murders occurred in 1986?
5. What specific lessons can be derived from the way in which J&J handled the public relations aspects of these tragedies?

TIPS FROM THE TOP

DOFF MEYER

Doff Meyer has had over 20 years of experience in public relations and corporate communications in both the profit and nonprofit sectors. She began her career with the Boston Repertory Theatre as director of publicity. Since 1989, Ms. Meyer has operated her own corporate communications consulting practice, Doff Meyer Communications. Her roster of clients includes American Guaranty Corporation, Bankers Trust Company, the Global Settlement Fund, the Palmieri Company, Quality Care Systems, and Regis Retirement Plan Services.

What advice do you give a client in crisis?
I advise four things off the top:

1. Let the public know and understand what the problem is and how it might affect them. *Are they in any danger?*
2. Explain what you are doing to solve the problem or to minimize any risk that the problem might cause. *Tell them what you are doing and what they should be doing.*
3. Explain the cause of the problem. *What do you know and how did you find it out?*
4. Do something about the problem. *Demonstrate that you are managing the crisis.*

How do you influence public opinion about a client?
Once we've identified the messages and image the company and its principals should convey, we decide on the most appropriate and effective methods to communicate those messages to the people who need to hear them.

Determining an appropriate image for a client is always our first step. We usually go through a rigorous research phase with any new client, during which we learn everything we can about the client's business and products or services, as well as the market for the products and the competition. We try to identify the product's key attributes at the same time that we identify the marketplace's perceptions of its needs. When we've hit on which attributes of the product intersect with the stated needs of the market, we've got the core of our message.

What are the keys to a positive counselor–client relationship?
Honesty and commitment. These two attributes are the keys to a positive counselor–client relationship.

Let's start with commitment. A good PR counselor has to understand a client's needs, believe in the client's potential for success, and truly root for that success. As a counselor, you really are part of the client's team, so you must be a classic team player, doing your best to contribute to the success for which your client will rightfully claim the glory.

Honesty is also vitally important. A client may have lofty visions of front-page stories and network interviews. These visions may be totally devoid of reality. I once walked into a new client's office and stated matter-of-factly that the client's expectations—in terms of specific media placements and timing of a campaign—were unrealistic and, in my view, unachievable. It was not an easy conversation, but it was an honest one. He appreciated that and listened to my counsel. And, I'm happy to report, he's still a client.

How difficult is the competition today for a small public relations agency?
There's lots of competition, especially in a large metropolitan area like New York. But there is also a lot of opportunity. Many corporations have downsized or eliminated their internal communications and public affairs departments. They haven't, however, eliminated the need to engage the public. So, they're outsourcing. Small agencies, with their streamlined structure and flexibility, can step into these situations quickly.

What are the chances for an entrepreneur in public relations today?
An entrepreneur in public relations stands as good a chance for success as an entrepreneur in any business today, which is to say that most will fail or move on, but some will enjoy great success. First, one has to know his or her own market. It's unlikely that the same person could offer expert PR counsel to a media celebrity, a business manager in a highly technical financial discipline, and a toy manufacturer. While these cases have some similarities, there are specialties to each niche that only someone with experience in that particular market could know. So, focusing on one or two niches, which you really understand, is one way to build business and respect.

Second, an entrepreneur should understand what kind of business he or she wants to run. What types of clients will you work best with? What types of products or services or people interest you and will capture your imagination?

Third, an entrepreneur must believe in his or her ability to provide a high-quality service to clients. If *you* don't think you offer a better product, no one else will.

Finally, you have to be willing to work hard. Starting a business and keeping it healthy are demanding tasks.

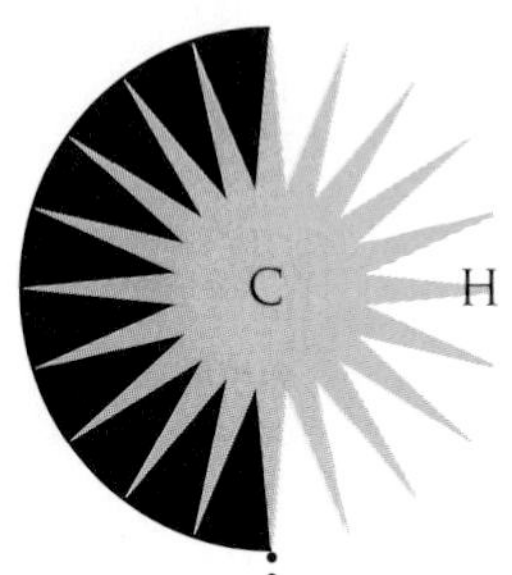

CHAPTER 20

THE FUTURE

IN ITS "REPORT AND RECOMMENDATIONS," THE SECOND TASK Force on the Stature and Role of Public Relations, released by the Public Relations Society of America in 1993, concluded:

> Public relations will either become recognized as an indispensable key to all organizations' viability or it will be relegated to merely carrying out a range of useful techniques. There is evidence that since 1980, while the field has grown greatly in number of practitioners, the majority of additions have been at the tactical level.[1]

Therein lies the difficulty in which public relations finds itself as we approach the year 2000. On the one hand, the ability of individuals and organizations to communicate has never been more critical. On the other hand, the mergers, consolidations, takeovers, and downsizings that have ravaged America and the world have taken a heavy toll on the ranks of public relations professionals.[2]

The challenge, then, for all who practice public relations in the years ahead is to seize the tremendous opportunities that accompany the emerging issues of the day.

Public relations is faced with all of the challenges associated with an increasingly popular field. The practice is "hot," and many want to enter it. However, as noted, with the recession and cutbacks of the 1990s, fewer public relations positions are available.

In addition, as management becomes more aware of the role of public relations, its performance expectations of the practice become higher. Thus, the standards to which public relations professionals are held will also increase. Finally, because access to top management is a coveted role and public relations is generally granted that access, key public relations positions will be sought eagerly by managers outside the public relations discipline. This is yet another key challenge that confronts public relations professionals.

A SOCIETY IN FLUX

Undeniably, the people who practice public relations today must be better than those who came before them. Institutions today operate in a pressure-cooker environment and must keep several steps ahead of the rapid pace of social, economic, and political change. The environment is being shaped by many factors.

- **Economic globalization** This is affecting all organizations, even nonmultinational companies. Competition will intensify, and so will communications, making it easier to communicate around the world but much more difficult to be heard. Public relations has become a growth industry around the world.
- **Shifting public opinion** Sudden shifts in public opinion are being ignited by instantaneous communications, challenging the ability of communicators to respond to fast-moving events.
- **Aging of society** Households headed by people over 55 are the fastest-growing segment of the consumer market in America, and this group controls an increasing percentage of all personal income.
- **Downsizing** With downsizing, companies are continuing to pare overhead and trim staff to become more competitive. The effect on business and employee morale is profound, and the need for good internal communications is critical.
- **Corporate responsibility** This buzzword of the 1960s and 1970s, which all but disappeared in the 1980s, has resurfaced in the 1990s. This is especially true as organizations eliminate jobs and as legal and ethical questions arise on issues from AIDS to corporate democracy to proper treatment of the environment (Figure 20–1).
- **Technology** The emerging "information highway" that will link television, telephones, and databases is a potential gold mine for public relations professionals, who can help consumers navigate their way through the many electronic offerings.[3] In addition, the emergence of on-line data sources, facts on demand, computer software programs, and CD-ROM disks is revolutionizing the way public relations practitioners target their messages (Figure 20–2).

Coupled with these factors is a society that seems incapable of curbing its voracious appetite for costly litigation. No product or service area is immune from potential suit.

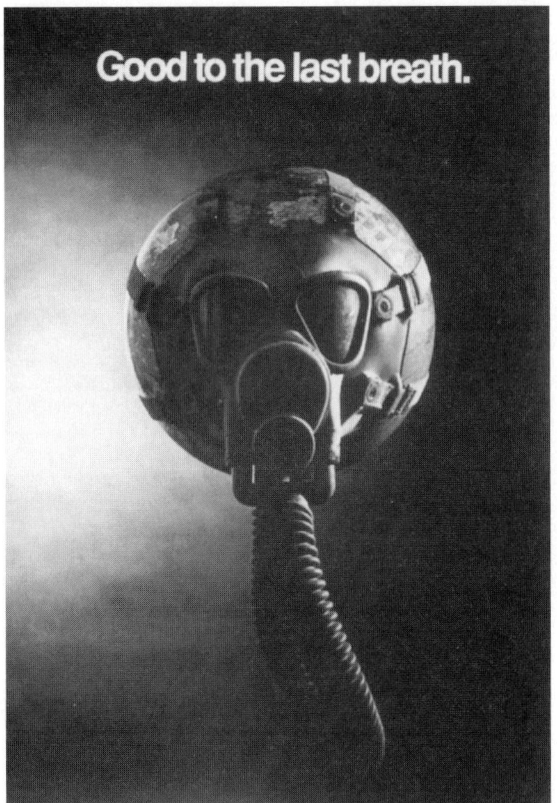

Figure 20–1 In 1990, according to a Louis Harris poll, many Americans rated a "clean environment more important than a satisfactory sex life." Society's renewed concern with the environment, symbolized by this original poster for the first Earth Day two decades ago, is a front-burner public relations issue in the 1990s. (*Photographed by Don Brewster of Lieber Brewster Corporate Design, New York City. The designer-photographer team of Robert Leydenfrost and Don Brewster created the poster as a public service for the Port Authority of New York and New Jersey.*)

And bigness is back in vogue, with mergers not only among huge industrial corporations, but also among hospitals, banks, media companies, and others. Yet, at the same time, a growing body of opinion sees big business as a threat, especially because it has become more active politically. Product stewardship, an idea that holds a manufacturer responsible for products in perpetuity, is gaining advocacy.[4] Additionally, consumers are demanding greater accountability from all institutions, as well as higher standards of ethical conduct.

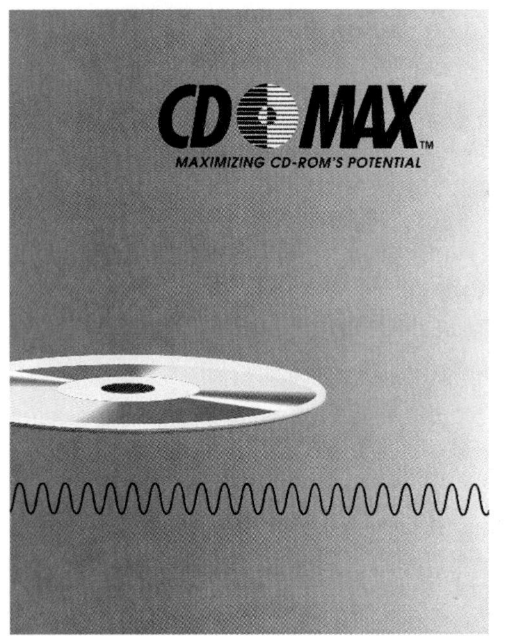

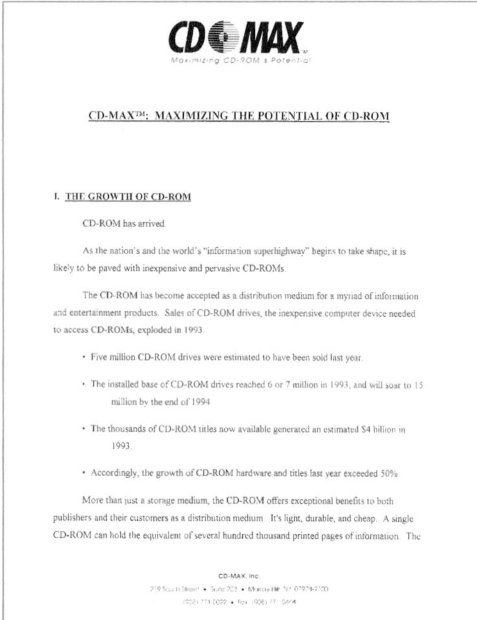

CD MAX
Maximizing CD-ROM's Potential

CD-MAX™: MAXIMIZING THE POTENTIAL OF CD-ROM

I. THE GROWTH OF CD-ROM

CD-ROM has arrived.

As the nation's and the world's "information superhighway" begins to take shape, it is likely to be paved with inexpensive and pervasive CD-ROMs.

The CD-ROM has become accepted as a distribution medium for a myriad of information and entertainment products. Sales of CD-ROM drives, the inexpensive computer device needed to access CD-ROMs, exploded in 1993.

- Five million CD-ROM drives were estimated to have been sold last year.
- The installed base of CD-ROM drives reached 6 or 7 million in 1993, and will soar to 15 million by the end of 1994.
- The thousands of CD-ROM titles now available generated an estimated $4 billion in 1993.
- Accordingly, the growth of CD-ROM hardware and titles last year exceeded 50%.

More than just a storage medium, the CD-ROM offers exceptional benefits to both publishers and their customers as a distribution medium. It's light, durable, and cheap. A single CD-ROM can hold the equivalent of several hundred thousand printed pages of information. The

CD-MAX, Inc.

Figure 20–2 Maximizing the potential of CD-ROMs is one of the significant challenges that confronts the public relations profession as society approaches the year 2000. (*Courtesy of CD-MAX*)

In the face of all these changes, it is understandable that management today is giving greater attention than ever before to the public's opinions of its organization and to public relations professionals who can help deal with those opinions.

PUBLIC RELATIONS CHALLENGES FOR THE YEAR 2000

As the significance of the practice of public relations intensifies, so will the challenges confronting the public relations profession. The challenges will be worldwide, just as the field itself has become worldwide. The power of communication, especially global communication, will no longer be an American domain. Among the significant challenges confronting public relations professionals will be these:

- **Need for tailored approaches** Demographic changes will affect the way professionals communicate. Public relations practitioners will have to target messages across cultural lines to special groups within the population. This will involve narrowcasting, as opposed to broadcasting. With the mass media, as noted, playing a less important role in the 1990s, more emphasis will be required on personalized, tailored approaches.

- **Development of new media** As technology continues to advance, new and exotic forms of information dissemination will evolve. These media will capture public attention in the most creative ways—talking billboards, blimps, in-flight headsets, and myriad others. Public relations will have to be equally creative to keep up with the new media and harness them for persuasive purposes.
- **Increased specialization** Public relations professionals will have to be much more than a conduit between an organization and the public. They will have to be much more fully informed about company policy and activities. They will have to be specialists—experts in dealing with, for example, the media, consumers, and investors—possessing the sophisticated writing ability that management demands.
- **Results orientation** The growth of research to measure and evaluate public relations results will continue. Public relations professionals must find ways to improve their measurement capability and justify their performance—that is, the results of their actions—to management.
- **Creativity** Innovation in the 1990s will be at a premium. Management will expect public relations people to provide creative approaches to organizational problems, thoughtful programs for overcoming or avoiding trouble, and novel ideas for getting attention. This will be particularly true in the increased need for marketing support by public relations professionals. The public relations department must be the storehouse of creativity in the organization.
- **Decreased sexism** Women are becoming more dominant in public relations. Their numbers are increasing, and the salary gap with men is decreasing. While women have not yet achieved parity in salary, power, or recognition, the gap may be eliminated by the year 2000.
- **Increased globalization** The globalization of public relations will accelerate for three reasons in the 1990s. First, U.S. and international companies will increasingly recognize the potential of overseas expansion. Second, media globalization will mandate that stories be told worldwide and not kept within national borders. Third, more countries will realize the benefits of professional public relations assistance.
- **Technology** Public relations professionals, as noted, will be blessed with an expanding array of technological tools to cope with the speed and impact of rapid, more global communications. Professionals must be aware of and master the technology described in the next section, if the field is to continue to develop.[5]

PUBLIC RELATIONS GOES GLOBAL

According to some public relations professionals, as we approach the year 2000, no emerging trend will be more important for the field than that of globalization. Says the former chairman of Hill & Knowlton, "Clearly, there are great challenges for us ahead in public relations to tell the true story of global competition and our new world economic order. And that story must be told accurately, objectively, clinically, if we are to stave off a return to trade barriers and to regionalized economic wars."[6]

BETWEEN THE LINES

PUBLIC RELATIONS AND TECHNOLOGY

by John R. Ward
President, Branyon–Ward & Ward

Computer technology, as a pervasive tool of information management, has made a noiseless infusion into the way we do business. For many, becoming a part of the quiet revolution that is changing the way business is viewing and using information has occurred by accident.

The proliferation of products—word processors, computers, cellular phones, facsimile machines, e-mail, video news releases, audiotext, and informational networking—usually leads to the adoption of one, and then another, and another. While print for the public relations person has long been the communication vehicle of choice, particularly where the role is viewed as publicity, the stage on which we perform is experiencing a continuous change of scenery in the form of new computer technology.

The capture, manipulation, transmission, and use of information has become a critical function in public relations. Clever use of available technology will help a business gain efficiency, improve quality, and lead the field.

We're involved in computer technology integration whether we like it or not. As microchip processing power, denser storage, and faster retrieval illuminate the hardware scene, the software follows right behind, turning the computer into a television, a telephone, a moving map, and an illustrator's canvas, replaying video images and music, organizing databases, and coordinating activities across time and space in real time. Access to information reveals a new way to look at the past, to manage the present, and to envision the future—with a few keystrokes.

Tunnel vision of a single discipline has become obsolete. Not only will the emerging technologies be a concern, but the merging of diverse technologies must be learned and understood. In similar fashion, the clear delineation between disciplines of public relations, marketing, and information management will become blurred. New questions will be the fuel of the communications engine. On the one hand, everything seems possible; on the other, for mostly economic reasons, it is clear that everything cannot be realized. The role of the communicator will be to identify what is *worthwhile* to be done as the future unfolds.

The culture is becoming one of "doing" as old ideas die and new ones give birth in the most unsuspecting environments. This means using the technology of the day but implies combining diverse technologies in new ways.

Even though everything appears possible, many things won't be worth doing; the individual practitioner makes that decision. It becomes necessary to know how to decide, without ambiguity, what is worth doing in order to use technology strategically.

But when almost everyone has access to the same sources of information and data, where is the power or the advantage? How information and data are *used* and *presented* becomes a creative opportunity to lead and differentiate.

For example, Geographical Information Systems (GIS) allows the presentation of multidimensional maps to graphically represent relationships important to effective communication with different publics. Maps of the entire world are available on four CD ROMS. Most businesses have a geographical component, whether in land, money, housing, health care, research, defense, crime, law, taxes, or products and services. Relationships between a company's databases and the geography of the business can be seen visually. Over 100 layers of different data can be selected for display. Suppose there was a critical situation and you needed to know the location of emergency vehicles, local media sources, hospitals, and government facilities. "What if?" scenarios or analyses could be quickly and easily reviewed to determine the best course of action. Or you might simply want to map your priority audiences.

The interrelationship of GIS with management information systems (MIS) and global positioning systems (GPS) is another interesting hybrid of technologies. The military defense system of satellites provides time and positioning data continuously, like a 24-hour news broadcast. Such technology can support or refute the position of antagonistic publics. You are in a position to advise management as never before. The ever-increasing power of technology and the available mix of communication pathways will astound the most conservative planner.

Wireless communication from geostationary communications satellites will permit direct mobile phone-to-satellite communication worldwide. You will have the freedom to communicate with anyone, anytime, anywhere. Such communications, however, place a responsibility on the user to control the data that matter. It will not be enough to be a "me too" innovator. The public relations person will be the command center for the flow of information, with little or no lag time between what people discover and when or how they respond to an event. As the interconnectivity of communication networks grows, so must the ability of the communicator to see the relationships between different technologies and how they can serve business needs—ideas that the communicator must have the vision to understand.

The task, then, is not to acquire the knowledge and use of technology by accident. The task is to do it on purpose.

Major political shifts throughout the world, coupled with the rapidity of worldwide communications, have focused new attention on public relations in the 1990s. The collapse of communism, the coming together of European economies, and the outbreak of democracy everywhere from East Germany to South Africa have brought the global role of public relations into a new spotlight.

CANADA

Canadian public relations is the rival of American practice in terms of its level of acceptance, respect, sophistication, and maturity. The Canadian Public Relations Society, formed in 1948, is extremely active. Canada differs from the United States in the aggressiveness of its public relations practice. While most communications programs, activities, and theories appear, on the surface, to be the same as in the United States, Canadian communications—particularly internal communications—is still some years behind those of its southern neighbor.[7]

LATIN AMERICA

In Latin America the scene is more chaotic. The field is most highly developed in Mexico, where public relations practice began in the 1930s. Mexican schools of higher learning also teach public relations. The passage of the North American Free Trade Agreement (NAFTA) in 1993 means increasing opportunities for U.S.–Mexican trade and therefore for public relations growth. In the other countries of Latin America, public relations is less well developed. However, the rebounding economies of Argentina, Brazil, Chile, and Venezuela, in particular, indicate clearly that Latin American public relations will grow in the later 1990s and beyond.

THE NEW EUROPE

Privatization and the synthesis of the European Community into a more unified bloc have spurred increased public relations action in many European countries. For example, public relations has experienced tremendous growth in Great Britain. The largest U.K.-based public relations operation is one of the world's largest independent agencies, the Shandwick Group.

Recent surveys indicate that the public relations issues germane to the United States also are prominent in Europe. Among them, global competition, government regulation, environmental issues, and new technology head the list.[8]

As European organizations pay increased attention to their reputations and how they are perceived, public relations is certain to be at the forefront of European commercial concern in the years ahead.

ASIA

Although public relations has evolved slowly in Asia, in the 1990s Asian public relations is experiencing sharp growth.[9]

In Japan, the public relations profession was established after World War II. Although the Japanese take a low-key approach to public relations work—especially self-advocacy—the field is growing, particularly as the media—six major national newspapers and four national networks—become more aggressive in investigating a proliferation of national scandals. Japanese public relations differs markedly from that of the West. For example, Keiretsu business associations—which bring together individual firms—operate with enormous influence as intermediaries in arranging press events. In the 1990s, television in general and talk shows in particular have become increasingly popular in Japan.

Elsewhere in Asia, public relations also has begun to take root. Korea has an active public relations community, as do Singapore and Taiwan. In China, after a number of false starts—the opening of McDonald's outlets in Beijing and Guangzhou, as well as other American corporate fixtures—there are indications that communications in China will be a growing business as the new century approaches.

Finally, as Vietnam rejoins the world community, opportunities for public relations work there also will emerge. Indeed, a major U.S. business and trade mission to Hanoi in 1993 suggested the public relations potential of a newly rediscovered Vietnam.

EASTERN EUROPE

There are 370 million consumers in recently democratized Eastern Europe. The prospects for public relations expansion are enticing.

- More than 80 percent of all Eastern Europeans watch television daily. Nearly 100 percent watch several times a week.
- In Hungary, about 20 percent of the population have TV sets connected to satellite dishes.
- In Poland, 13 percent of the population report owning VCRs.
- In Hungary, Serbia, and Croatia, about two-thirds of the population read newspapers daily.[10]

Typical of the growing importance of public relations is the burgeoning public relations workload in Russia. AT&T, Intel, Coca-Cola, and many other companies are already ensconced there. Large American public relations firms have also set up bases. PR Newswire, in combination with the news agency TASS, distributes news releases from U.S. companies to locations in the Commonwealth of Independent States. Releases are translated into Russian and reach 40 newspapers in Moscow alone.

AUSTRALIA

The 1988 International Public Relations Association Conference in Melbourne was indicative of the rapid advance of the public relations practice "down under." The Public Relations Institute of Australia is an extremely active organization and the practice is widespread, particularly in the country's two commercial centers, Melbourne and Sydney.

MIDDLE EAST

While the public relations profession is less active in the Middle East, the power of public relations is well known and understood. Indeed, during the 1990 invasion of Kuwait, Iraq's leader, Saddam Hussein, was quick to harness the world's communications apparatus to spread his views. The Kuwaitis, as noted, responded by hiring Hill & Knowlton to represent the country in an appeal for American support. Even in countries as traditional as Saudi Arabia, public relations work has begun to carry increased significance.[11]

AFRICA

In Africa, too, the practice of public relations is growing. In 1990, the largest public relations meeting in the history of the continent was held in Abuja, Nigeria, with 1,000 attendees from 25 countries. In 1994, as a result of an extensive worldwide communications and public relations campaign, Nelson R. Mandela was elected the first democratically elected president of the nation of South Africa (Figure 20–3). Africa, too, has discovered the power of public relations.

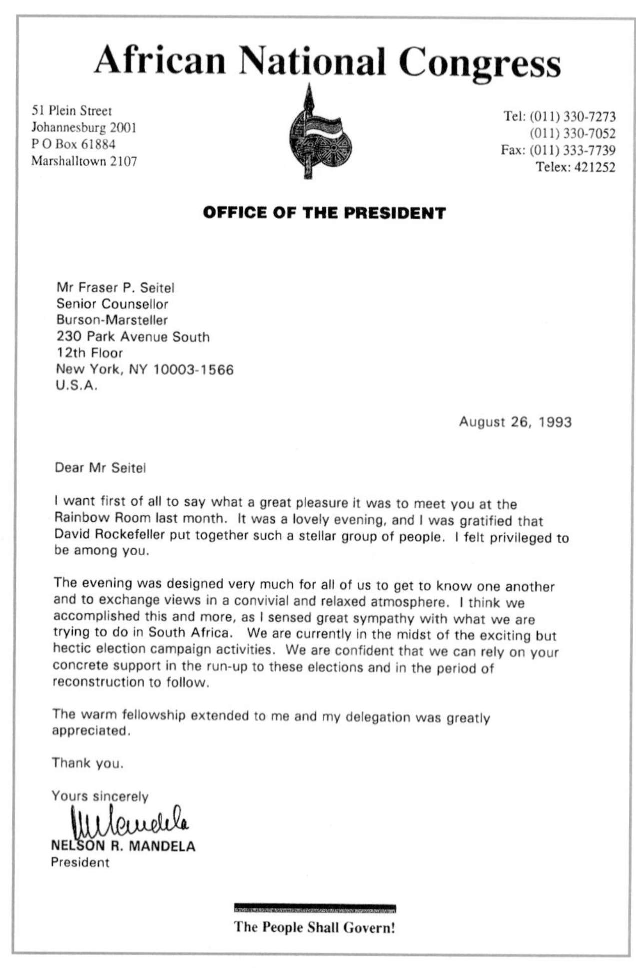

African National Congress

51 Plein Street
Johannesburg 2001
P O Box 61884
Marshalltown 2107

Tel: (011) 330-7273
(011) 330-7052
Fax: (011) 333-7739
Telex: 421252

OFFICE OF THE PRESIDENT

Mr Fraser P. Seitel
Senior Counsellor
Burson-Marsteller
230 Park Avenue South
12th Floor
New York, NY 10003-1566
U.S.A.

August 26, 1993

Dear Mr Seitel

I want first of all to say what a great pleasure it was to meet you at the Rainbow Room last month. It was a lovely evening, and I was gratified that David Rockefeller put together such a stellar group of people. I felt privileged to be among you.

The evening was designed very much for all of us to get to know one another and to exchange views in a convivial and relaxed atmosphere. I think we accomplished this and more, as I sensed great sympathy with what we are trying to do in South Africa. We are currently in the midst of the exciting but hectic election campaign activities. We are confident that we can rely on your concrete support in the run-up to these elections and in the period of reconstruction to follow.

The warm fellowship extended to me and my delegation was greatly appreciated.

Thank you.

Yours sincerely

NELSON R. MANDELA
President

The People Shall Govern!

Figure 20–3 A worldwide communications campaign for sympathy and support fueled the dramatic sea change in South Africa when Nelson R. Mandela became the first democratically elected president of that nation in the spring of 1994.

Brushing Away a Dark Blot

Colgate-Palmolive is one of the most savvy international conglomerates. Colgate's toothpaste, shampoo, detergent, and other household and hygiene products account for more than $6 billion in worldwide sales.

However, when Colgate purchased 50 percent of the Hawley & Hazel Company in Hong Kong in 1985, it had no idea of the international controversy the union would spark. Hawley & Hazel marketed "Darkie," the best-selling toothpaste brand in several Asian countries. Darkie toothpaste was identifiable in Asia by the picture of a minstrel in black face on the package. The minstrel became part of the product's package design in the 1920s, after the then CEO of Hawley & Hazel saw American singer Al Jolson and thought his wide, white, toothy smile would make an excellent logo.

And for many years, it did—until the union with Colgate-Palmolive brought intense criticism from religious groups and others, not only for the depiction of the minstrel, but also for using the name Darkie.

In 1986, three Roman Catholic groups filed a shareholder petition demanding that Colgate-Palmolive change the Darkie name and logotype.

Michigan Congressman John Conyers joined the fracas when he learned about Darkie while traveling in Taiwan in 1988.

Colgate responded by conducting extensive consumer studies and considering hundreds of alternatives. Because Darkie accounted for nearly all of Hawley & Hazel's business, with a market share ranging from 20 to 70 percent in Hong Kong, Malaysia, Singapore, Taiwan, and Thailand, the company feared a false step.

Finally, in 1989, Colgate Chairman Ruben Mark announced the toothpaste would be renamed Darlie, and the logotype would become a portrait of a man of ambiguous race wearing a silk top hat, tuxedo, and bow tie. Said Mr. Mark, "It's just plain wrong. It's just offensive. The morally right thing dictated that we must change. What we have to do is find a way to change that is least damaging to the economic interests of our partners."

Under the agreement, Colgate-Palmolive agreed to pay for all redesign and repackaging costs and for the added advertising costs involved in the changeover. It also said it would reimburse Hawley & Hazel for any loss in profits caused by customer confusion over the change to Darlie.

How do you think Colgate-Palmolive handled this controversy?

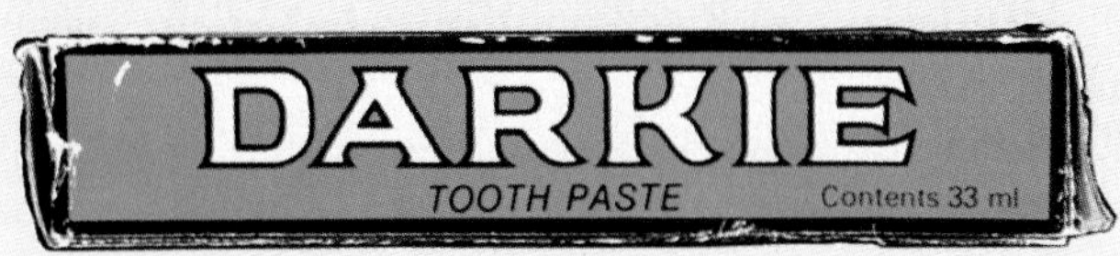

BETWEEN THE LINES

WHEN IN ROME . . .

Communicating overseas can be a tricky business. Words, mannerisms, figures of speech, customs—all are different in other countries.

- In Latin America, *no* is almost a dirty word in polite society. Not wanting to give a flatly negative answer to a friend or colleague, Latin Americans customarily say "Yes" or "Of course."
- *Yes* in Japanese means "Yes, I hear what you say," but it doesn't necessarily mean "Yes, I agree."
- In Bulgaria, a nod means no and a shake of the head means yes.
- In Italy, if you don't use your hands in an animated fashion in conversation, you are perceived as a bore.
- Arabs point or beckon in summoning dogs, so they don't appreciate that gesture for people.
- Japanese humor is overt; slapstick humor is popular. A subtle approach in communications just doesn't work.

And then there is the minefield of fast-food communications in other countries.

- When Burger King opened its first restaurant in London, employees found the floor littered with pickles. The English, you see, don't care for pickles on their burgers.
- Pizza Hut found that one of the best-selling items in its Far Eastern restaurants was seaweed pizza.
- Employees of the 515 Kentucky Fried Chicken restaurants in Japan take time off to pray for the souls of dead chickens.
- Wendy's International removed the "hot stuffed" baked potato description from its British menu when it found the expression had a most improper connotation in the United Kingdom.

COUNSELING TOP MANAGEMENT

No challenge for public relations professionals in the 1990s is more important than counseling senior management. Top managers in companies, hospitals, associations, governments, educational institutions, and most other organizations need counsel because, as they say, "It's lonely at the top."

Public relations people in the years ahead must be willing and eager to provide a counseling role to management. Accomplishing such a task will depend on the following characteristics:

1. **Intimate knowledge of the institution** A public relations professional may be an excellent communicator, but without knowledge of the industry or institution represented, his or her ultimate value will be limited.
2. **Access to and respect for management** The public relations professional who acquires the respect of top management is a powerful force in an organization. Respect comes only from exposure. Thus, it is essential that the public relations professional have ready access to the most senior managers in an organization.
3. **Access to an intelligence network** Public relations professionals need their own intelligence network to give them the unvarnished truth about programs and projects. If the executive vice-president is an idiot, if the employee incentive program isn't working, or if the chairman's speech was terrible, the public relations professional must be able to tap a team of candid employees who will tell the truth, so that the practitioner can tell the unvarnished truth to top management—unexpurgated, uncensored, between the eyes.
4. **Familiarity with the reporter on the beat** A public relations professional, no matter how high up in an organization, should keep in touch with the reporters and analysts who follow the organization. Valuable information can be gleaned from such observers and can be most helpful to top management.
5. **Solid skills base** The most competent public relations counselors don't just give orders, they demonstrate skills. They are generally good writers who don't mind pitching in to complete a job competently. In public relations, communications competence is a prerequisite for counseling competence.
6. **Propensity toward action** In working for top management, results and performance are all that count. Certainly, planning and setting strategies are critical aspects of public relations. But practitioners, especially those who counsel management, must be inclined toward action. They must be doers. That's what management demands.
7. **Knowledge of the law** Public relations work today confronts legal issues: privacy, copyright, lobbying, and securities laws, broadcasting regulations, and so on. Although public relations professionals need not be trained lawyers, they must at least be conversant in the general concepts of the law in order to counsel management effectively and to deal with legal counselors.
8. **Strong sense of integrity and confidence** As noted in Chapter 5, public relations professionals must be the ethical conscience of organizations. Their motives and methods must be above reproach. It's also important that public relations counselors demonstrate confidence in their own positions and abilities. They must surround themselves with the highest-caliber performers to enhance the status of the public relations function within the organization.
9. **Contentment with anonymity** Public relations counselors must understand that they are exactly that: counselors to top management. It is the chief who delivers the speeches, charts the strategies, and makes the decisions. And it is the chief, too, who derives the credit. Public relations counselors must remain in the background and should try to stay anonymous. Today, with newspapers demanding the names of spokespersons, with some public relations practitioners attaining national celebrity status, and with the field itself becoming more and more prominent, the challenge of anonymity becomes increasingly more difficult.[12]

MERGING ISSUES IN PUBLIC RELATIONS

The issues that concern public relations professionals vary from organization to organization and from industry to industry. Nonetheless, several issues concern all practitioners, especially as the field continues to grow in respect and improve its credibility.

PUBLIC RELATIONS EDUCATION

For public relations to continue to prosper, a solid educational foundation for public relations students must be in place. Today's practitioner has two key stakes in public relations education: future employees and the profession itself.

Over the last few years, the Public Relations Society of America and other organizations have focused on the formal education of public relations students. In 1987, a design for undergraduate public relations education was authored by the Public Relations Division of the Association for Education in Journalism and Mass Communication, the Educator's Section of PRSA, and PRSA itself.[13] Among the highlights of the report were these findings and recommendations:

- Two subjects tied for the highest ratings by practitioners and educators: English (within general education) and an internship/practicum/work-study program (within public relations education).
- It is recommended that public relations students, especially those planning to enter the corporate or agency world, give strong consideration to business as their secondary area of study.
- The traditional arts and sciences remain the solid basis for the undergraduate education of public relations students, essential to their professional functioning in a complex society.

The report indicated strong agreement between practitioners and educators on what the content of undergraduate public relations education should be. Basically, strong emphasis was placed on communications studies, public relations principles and practices, and ethics. The report further concluded that the growing cooperation and relationships among professionals in the practice of public relations and in education should be nurtured and strengthened, to benefit today's students of the field.

WOMEN IN PUBLIC RELATIONS

Another issue of concern in the field is the aforementioned impact of the increasing percentage of women in public relations and business communications. In 1980, women accounted for only 10 percent of the public relations population. Today that number is well over 50 percent.[14] Many practitioners express concern that public relations could become a "velvet ghetto," populated almost entirely by women. The expansion of women in public relations is not surprising. Women account for up to 65 percent of all journalism graduates in the United States.

One of the most comprehensive studies of this issue was launched in 1986 by the International Association of Business Communicators. Its results indicated that women are increasingly filling the role of communications technicians rather than managers. As a result, women are being paid less than men, with gender being the strongest predictor of salary. Among its conclusions, the report found that the situation does not appear to be improving. Instead, men are turning to other professions or are positioning themselves in the most highly paid areas within the field, such as communications management.

Despite this, changes should arrive soon—perhaps by the end of this decade. Clearly, more women will enter top management jobs, not only in public relations but in many other fields. Some predict the 1990s will be the "Decade of Women in Leadership Positions." Two who do are John Naisbitt and Patricia Aburdene, coauthors of *Megatrends 2000,* who point to the following:

- Women already hold 39 percent of the 14 million U.S. executive, administrative, and management jobs, according to the Bureau of Labor Statistics—nearly double the figure of two decades ago.
- More than half of all officers, managers, and professionals in the nation's 50 largest commercial banks are women.
- More than one-third of Procter & Gamble's marketing executives are women. At the Gannett Company, almost 40 percent of the managers, professionals, technicians, and sales force are women. At Apple Computer, the numbers are similar.
- Of today's MBA degree recipients, 33 percent are women. Women now earn 13 times more engineering degrees than they did 15 years ago.
- In 1966, fewer than 7 percent of M.D. degrees were granted to women. Today the number is 33 percent. In 1966, women were awarded 3 percent of all law degrees. Today, 40 percent of all law degrees are granted to women.
- Women are starting their own businesses at twice the rate of men.[15]

In light of these data, the emergence of women as leaders in the public relations field is inevitable by the year 2000.

EXTERNAL CHALLENGES

Inevitably, as public relations has enhanced its role in society and increased its respect within organizations, the field itself has attracted others—lawyers, accountants, personnel managers, and general managers of varying backgrounds. Because the public relations executive of an organization is usually close to top management and because access is power in an organization, the role occupied by public relations has become a coveted one. In the 1990s, incursions into public relations by others in an organization are apt to intensify, thereby increasing the pressure on public relations practitioners to use their special expertise and unique experience to reinforce their prominent positions in the organizational hierarchy.

One antidote for the incursion into the field by others is for public relations professionals to become well versed in the multiplying array of issues that concern organizations and the public. The issues that capture public attention are diverse and rapidly changing. This suggests that the truly successful practitioner in the years ahead must stay abreast of the changing issues that dominate public discourse (Figures 20–4, 20–5).

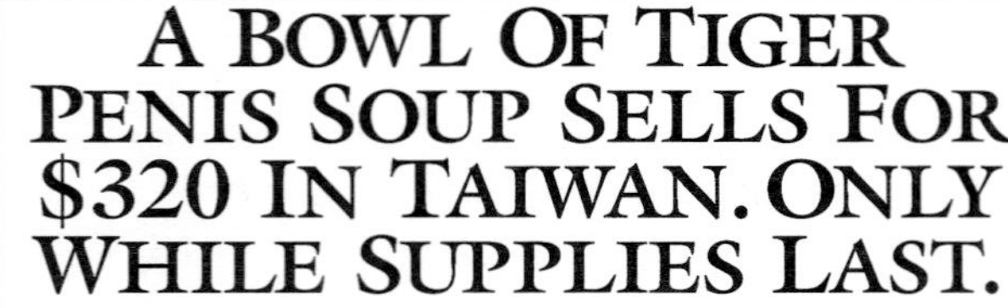

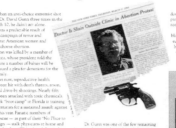

Figures 20–4, 20–5 Among the most influential—and controversial—public issues advocates in the 1990s is the Public Media Center, a nonprofit ad agency based in San Francisco. PMC is responsible for some of the most riveting issues ads of the day. (*Courtesy of the Public Media Center*)

BETWEEN THE LINES

A GLOSSARY FOR THE 1990S

Like it or not, getting along as a public relations professional in the 1990s demands a working knowledge of the vocabulary common to the age group that dominates our society: teenagers. Here's a taste of teen terminology in the 1990s.

Abusak: Elevator music, a blend of "abuse" and "Muzak."
Airmail: Garbage thrown out the window.
Arbuckle: Dingbat.
Bad: Good. (A term that keeps hanging on.)
Bail: Either to cut a class or to put something down, as in "bail that."
Biscuit: Easy.
Bogus: Phoney. Bad (as in "bad," not good.)
Brainiac: Intelligent student.
Buff: Muscular, tough.
Bust a move: Try it. Go for it.
Cheesehead: A jerk. Also known as cheese meister.
Clydesdale: A stud, a good-lookin' guy.
Daddylac: An expensive car that has been given to a young driver by his or her parents.
Death: To be very appealing, to die for.
Def: Outstanding, terrific.
Dexter: Nerd.
Homeboy/Homegirl: Friendly term of address for someone of the same neighborhood or school.
Lame: State of boredom, nerdy.
Sick: Good, awesome.
Tamale time: Embarrassment.
Waldo: Out of it.
Woof: To brag.

Even with this cursory introduction to 1990s terminology, a professional should be able to avoid tamale time when asked, "Who's that def Clydesdale in the Daddylac?" Just don't woof about knowing the answer.

IMPLICATIONS FOR BEGINNERS

The reality of a more respected and, therefore, more competitive public relations profession has numerous implications for people just starting out in the field. Although competition for public relations positions is stiff, experience is the great equalizer, and smart beginners can optimize their potential for employment by getting a jump on the competition through early experience. How?

BETWEEN THE LINES

ALL IS NOT WON . . .

"Ethnic cleansing. It's got a nice ring to it. Let's find out who's doing their P.R."

Figure 20–6 Even in the 1990s, public relations still suffers an image problem. To wit, this cynical view in response to the 1994 Serbian attack on Muslims in Croatia. (*Drawing by Ziegler; © 1992, The New Yorker Magazine, Inc.*)

- By becoming involved with and active in student public relations organizations
- By securing—through faculty or others—part-time employment that uses the skills important in public relations work
- By attending professional meetings in the community, learning about public relations activities, and meeting public relations practitioners who might prove to be valuable contacts later on

- By seizing every opportunity, from informal internships to voluntary work for nonprofit associations or political candidates to service on the school newspaper to merchandising in-class projects to local merchants

The key to finding and securing a job in public relations is experience. So, rather than bemoan the "catch 22" reality of a field in which you must have worked first in order to land a job, full-time students should use their college days to begin to acquire working knowledge in public relations. That way, when they look for that first job, they already have experience.

BETWEEN THE LINES

. . . BUT ALL IS NOT LOST

Just when you think the deck is stacked against you and your profession, something happens to rekindle your enthusiasm.

Behold the public relations blunder of the year.

Figure 20–7 In the spring of 1994, a roving photographer caught President Clinton's White House director of administration red-handed, apparently using the presidential helicopter to wedge in a round of golf at taxpayers' expense. As a dutiful U.S. Marine saluted the departing duffers and screams of "Choppergate" rose in the land, all of us employed in the practice of public relations were reassured once again that ours is a profession that will never become obsolete. (*Courtesy of AP/Wide World Photos*)

SUMMARY

Most professions undergo constant change, but few experience more critical or frequent change than public relations. In the 1990s, practitioners have been introduced to a tidal wave of primary concerns: consumerism, environmentalism, government relations, and public policy forecasting. Areas of public relations opportunity have shifted from marketing publicity to financial relations to employee communications to public issues management. Steadily, the field has expanded its horizons and increased its influence.

As the year 2000 approaches, public relations stands at the threshold of its golden age. To get there, however, public relations professionals must exhibit certain qualities; among them are the following:

- **Professionalism** Practitioners must recognize that every time someone in public relations is accused of bending the truth, all in the practice suffer. The cardinal rule must always be: "Tell the truth."

  Being professional also means standing for something. At base, public relations people are *professional communicators*. Communications standards therefore must remain high, and practitioners must take pride in the communications products for which they are responsible.
- **Generalized specialization** The old notion that people in public relations must be generalists rather than specialists simply won't wash in the year 2000. As noted, the competition today is ferocious. Public relations people must have an edge to differentiate themselves from others. Clearly, a solid general base of communications knowledge is still obligatory for public relations work. But at the same time, it has become more urgent today to master a specialty—to become conversant in and knowledgeable about a specific aspect of public relations work—investor relations, government relations, or speechwriting, for example—or about a particular industry—such as computers, health care, sports, or the arts. Public relations people must become generalized specialists.
- **Guts** Public relations people also must be willing to stand up for what they stand for. Too often, public relations managers are posturers rather than practitioners, politicians rather than professionals, corporate lapdogs rather than leaders. Such faint-hearted communications counsel won't be sufficient in the year 2000. As top management gets better, public relations must also improve its standing.
- **Ethics** The public relations professional must be the most ethical individual in the organization. Public relations must be the conscience of the corporation, the standard bearer for honor and ethics and integrity. Public relations people therefore should *never* compromise their values. The first question the public relations professional must ask is, "Are we doing the right thing?" Few others in the organization will ever pose this question.
- **Leadership** Finally, public relations professionals must be leaders. To accomplish this, they must have the vision, courage, character to lead themselves, their organizations, and their profession into the next golden century.

DISCUSSION STARTERS

1. What evidence can you point to to indicate the increased stature of public relations practice?
2. What factors are shaping the environment of the 1990s?
3. What are the primary challenges for public relations in the 1990s?
4. What are the skills requisite for counseling management in the 1990s?
5. How should a public relations professional regard anonymity?
6. What are the pressing issues in public relations education?
7. What is the outlook for women in public relations?
8. How important is technological knowledge for public relations practitioners?
9. What is the key challenge for entry-level public relations professionals in the 1990s?
10. What is the outlook for public relations practice?

NOTES

1. "Report and Recommendations of the Second Task Force on Stature and Role of Public Relations," Public Relations Society of America, November 1991, released by the PRSA board of directors in August 1993.
2. Remarks by Fraser P. Seitel at Sixth Annual Harold Burson Distinguished Lecturer, Raymond Simon Institute for Public Relations, Utica College–Syracuse University, April 1, 1992.
3. "PR to Help Map Trip Down the 'Information Highway,'" *O'Dwyer's PR Services Report* (January 1994): 1.
4. Joseph Nolan, "To Gain a Good Reputation," *Across the Board* (October 1985): 36.
5. Dirk C. Gibson, "Future Trends in Public Relations," *Social Science Monitor* (February 1990): 1–3.
6. "H&K Chief Cites Six Trends That Will Change the Face of PR," *PR News* (May 4, 1992): 1.
7. Roger Feather, "Internal Communications in Canada," *IABC Communications World* (December 1990): 37.
8. Susan Fry Bovet, "Trends in the 'New' Europe," *Public Relations Journal* (September 1993): 19.
9. Monique El Faizy, "It's No Occident PR Firms Fill Asian Void," *Crain's New York Business* (April 12, 1993): 13.
10. Ray Hiebert, "Special Report: Communication in Eastern Europe," *Social Science Monitor* (November 1990): 1.
11. Abdulrahman H. Al-Enad, "Values of Public Relations Conduct in Saudi Arabia," *Public Relations Review* (Summer 1992): 213.
12. Fraser Seitel, "Staying There," *United States Banker* (May 1989): 67, 69.
13. "The Design for Undergraduate Public Relations Education," study cosponsored by the Public Relations Division of the Association for Education in Journalism and Mass Communications, the Public Relations Society of America, and the Educators Section of PRSA (1987): 1.
14. David M. Dozier and Glen M. Broom, "Evolution of the Managerial Role in Public Relations," paper presented at the Association for Education in Journalism and Mass Communications convention, August 1993.
15. John Naisbitt and Patricia Aburdene, *Megatrends 2000* (New York: William Morrow, 1990), 224–225.

TOP OF THE SHELF

Scott M. Cutlip, Allen H. Center, and Glenn M. Broom.
Effective Public Relations, 7th ed. Englewood Cliffs,
NJ: Prentice-Hall, 1994.

The pioneer of public relations textbooks, *Effective Public Relations* still offers the most comprehensive and detailed look at the field.

This book's strength is its breadth. From providing solid instruction in public relations planning to explaining the nature of the profession and its role as a management function to discussing the skills required to become a successful practitioner, *Effective Public Relations* offers sound grounding in the field.

Particularly helpful are its extensive treatment of the historical origins of public relations, organizational settings within the field, and the theoretical underpinnings of communication and public opinion. Equally relevant is the book's extensive treatment of public relations as a management process.

Effective Public Relations, written by three veteran public relations professors, offers wide coverage of the traditional view of the field. It is a most worthwhile resource.

SUGGESTED READINGS

Basye, Dale. "Why Is PR a Dumping Ground?" *Across the Board* (September 1994): 48–49.

Bogue, Donald. *The Population of the United States: Historical Trends and Future Projections*. Ithaca, NY: American Demographics, 1988.

Brody, E. W. *Communication Tomorrow: New Audiences, New Technologies*. Westport, CT: Praeger, 1990.

Brody, E. W., ed. *New Technology and Public Relations: On to the Future*. Sarasota, FL: Institute for Public Relations and Education, 1992.

Careers in Public Relations. (Available from the Public Relations Society of America, 845 Third Ave., New York, NY 10022.)

Cavusgil, Tamer, and Michael R. Czinkota. *International Perspective on Trade Promotion and Assistance*. Westport, CT: Greenwood Press, 1990.

Design for Public Relations Education. (Available from the Public Relations Society of America, 845 Third Ave., New York, NY 10022.)

Dilenschneider, Robert L. "What's Ahead for Public Relations: Problems or Progress?" *Public Relations Quarterly* (Fall 1987): 5–8.

Drucker, Peter F. *The New Realities*. New York: Harper & Row, 1989.

Drucker, Peter F. *Managing for the Future: The 1990s and Beyond*. New York: Nal-Dutton, 1992.

European Public Affairs Directory, 1992. Bristol, PA: International Publications Services, 1992.

Futurist. (Available from World Future Society, 4916 St. Elmo Ave., Washington, DC 20014.) This bimonthly journal includes forecasts, trends, and ideas about the future on all topics.

International Directory of Business Information Sources. Chicago: Probus, 1991.

Naisbitt, John, and Patricia Aburdene. *Megatrends 2000*. New York: William Morrow, 1990.

Ruch, William V. *International Handbook of Corporate Communication*. Jefferson, NC: McFarland & Company, 1989.

"Sixth Annual Review and Forecast of Public Relations Trends." *Cantor Commentary* (January 1988) (171 Madison Ave., New York, NY 10016).

"A Wild Plunge into the Future." *Cantor Commentary* (October 1987) (171 Madison Ave., New York, NY 10016).

CASE STUDY

"SAY IT AIN'T SO O. (J.)"

Without question, the public relations event of the decade was the tragic double homicide case in 1994 involving football legend and media superstar O.J. Simpson.

The public was stunned when it was reported in June that Simpson's former wife and a male friend were found murdered at her Brentwood, California home and that a beloved O.J. was the accused murderer.

Simpson's dramatic fall from grace was as devastating and riveting a public spectacle as any in America since Lee Harvey Oswald was gunned down in full view of millions of American TV viewers.

Indeed, 95 million Americans—67% of all households—watched live television news coverage of the low-speed chase involving Simpson and the Los Angeles Police Department. That chase earned CNN its highest ratings since the 1991 Clarence Thomas hearings.

The matter of The People v. O.J. Simpson introduced a new set of bare knuckles ground rules for public relations professionals, particularly those involved with national crises.

DUELING ATTORNEYS

On one side stood the defense team, led by Robert L. Shapiro, trying to generate national sympathy and support for a fallen icon. On the other side stood the prosecution, led by Los Angeles District Attorney Gil Garcetti, trying to generate a national sense of outrage over the issue of domestic violence.

In the Simpson criminal case, it was the prosecution team which broke quickly from the starting blocks and then was joined by the defense.

D.A. Garcetti set the tone early by immediately telling a press conference of Simpson's disappearance after charges were filed against him. Shortly thereafter, the D.A. followed with another press conference to declare that Simpson was the "sole murderer" and that "the investigation does not indicate that anyone else was involved."

Garcetti, whose department had been stung with several major court defeats in recent years, propelled his public profile with appearances on all major networks and in numerous national TV news and talk shows.

The defense team was just slightly less aggressive in stating its client's case and inferring his innocence. When it was reported that a "bloody ski mask" had been found at the crime scene, Shapiro, an expert in using cameras in the courtroom, demanded the right to examine the evidence. This forced the prosecution to reveal sheepishly, live on CNN, "There is no ski mask."

Figure 20–8 O.J. Simpson, as he appeared in a mugshot subsequent to his arrest in Los Angeles on two counts of murder. (*Courtesy of A.P./Wide World Photos*)

LEADING WITH SYMPATHY

Shapiro sought immediately to portray his client as a troubled, confused, kind-hearted hero, who inexplicably had wound up in a bad scrape.

"He's been very, very, depressed," the lawyer recounted to reporters after Simpson's arraignment. "He wished me a happy Father's Day. He told me to spend time with my boys. Then he stated to cry and said, 'I wish I could spend Father's Day with my kids.' "

The clear message of Shapiro's statements was that rather than viewing his client as an alleged cold-blooded murderer, the public should view O.J. with empathy and understanding.

SEIZING THE "SPIN CYCLE"

One reason Michael Dukakis was beaten so soundly for president in 1988 was that he failed to answer Bush campaign accusations within "news cycles"—those half-day intervals on which the electronic news, in particular, is based. Dukakis was forced to play "catch up"—confronting his adversaries' claims after they had gone unchallenged on the evening news. Four years later, Dukakis' Democratic successor made no such mistake.

Candidate Bill Clinton created a public relations "spin control swat team" to shoot down any 1992 campaign allegation as soon as the charge was made. So, too, were both sides in the Simpson case ready to pounce on breaking news for their own "spin" purposes.

Immediately after Shapiro's statements about a "forlorn O.J.," Deputy District Attorney Marcia Clark lashed out at yet another press conference, "We should not forget the fact that we have two victims who were brutally slain, two young people whose lives stretched out before them."

No sooner had Ms. Clark spoken than Mr. Shapiro countered, asserting to reporters that prosecutors were slow in making available to him, as required by law, the basic outline of their case against Simpson. "To make any comment on a case before arraignment undermines our system of fair play and fundamental justice," Shapiro huffed.

LEAKING STRATEGICALLY

Chief Prosecutor Garcetti summarized his challenge thusly, "It's hard to get all 12 jurors with you in any case, but when you're up against a celebrity—I didn't say hero—like O.J. Simpson, it may be two, three times more difficult."

To combat the possibility of growing support for such a beloved figure,—and therefore the likelihood of a "hung jury"—selective leaks, often from "sources close to the investigation," began to emerge.

- A golf course observer was reported as revealing an enraged Simpson screaming at an associate the day of the murders.
- A motorist was reported as viewing a disturbed Simpson yelling loudly, while driving alone the night of the murders.
- A shop dealer was reported as revealing that Simpson had purchased a 15-inch knife that fit the description of the murder weapon.

Each of these unsubstantiated leaks, condemned by the defense, helped tear down the perception of "O.J. Simpson as hero."

EXUDING CONFIDENCE

From the get-go in the Simpson case, both sides expressed confidence in the outcome. Garcetti told one news conference that the evidence he had compiled would establish "beyond the necessary burden of proof" that Simpson was guilty of murder.

On the other side, Simpson's first attorney, Howard Weitzman, initially suggested that, at the time of the killings, his client was either on his way to Los Angeles International Airport or already there to catch a flight to Chicago.

Backtracking a bit from this earlier statement, new attorney Shapiro conceded that his client might have been at the murder scene at the time of the murders, but that he flatly "wasn't guilty." Simpson wrote an "open letter to the public" which also reiterated this claim of innocence.

LINING UP YOUR ALLIES

The Simpson side also produced numerous "character witnesses" willing to appear on the air and in print to corroborate the "veracity" of the accused.

Such corroboration was particularly important in accommodating the voracious appetites of the numerous news magazine shows—"20/20," "Dateline NBC," "Eye-to-Eye," as well as the slightly sleazier "Inside Story," "A Current Affair," "Hard Copy," and other tabloid programs.

In the Simpson case, within hours of the cell door slamming shut behind O.J., the parade of "character witnesses"—from past football playing buddies to current girlfriends—flooded the airwaves to testify to the "goodness" of their fallen friend.

BLASTING YOUR ADVERSARIES

The Simpson case underscored that crisis public relations is no place for the faint of heart.

Part of the challenge was to keep opponents off balance by constantly belittling what they claimed to be the case. When Garcetti fumed publicly about Simpson's first reneging on an agreement to turn himself in and then taking off on a 60-mile police chase, Shapiro argued that his client wasn't running from the police at all, but rather making his way to the fresh grave of his ex-wife, where he intended to take his own life.

When the prosecution charged Simpson's long-time friend Al Cowlings with aiding and abetting his friend's flight from justice, Shapiro retorted that Cowlings had thwarted Simpson's suicide plan. "Thank God Al Cowlings talked him out of that and encouraged him to return home," Shapiro said.

LINKING WITH A LARGER CAUSE

Also in the Simpson case, the prosecution tried to "elevate" the issues in their case to a broader level of concern. The "larger issue," according to the District Attorney, was wife beating, of which Simpson had been found guilty several years earlier.

In the wake of the Simpson murder case, the media were flooded with discussions of the subject of spousal abuse. Several state legislators, in fact, used the nationally televised Simpson hearings to spur legislation regarding spousal abuse in their states.

Defense Attorney Shapiro made no bones about his use of public relations techniques to win the day for O.J. Shapiro suggested in a booklet he prepared on the media, "The publicity objective is to portray the client in the most favorable light."

Many others voiced concern about the blatant use of publicity to influence court verdicts. One expert, Carole Gorney of Lehigh University, said, "There need to be limitations on what can be said publicly in a pre-trial environment. I neither see the need for, nor do I think it is ethically correct to seek such pre-trial publicity."

Indeed, after the release of police recordings on which Simpson was heard screaming and cursing at his former wife, D.A. Garcetti called another press conference to halt any additional information being made public "in the interest of justice to Mr. Simpson."

Defense Attorney Shapiro echoed that sentiment, "In America we have the presumption of innocence, not the assumption of guilt. There has been so much speculation that has gone on across the country that it is time to turn this matter to the system of justice where it belongs."

And in time, the justice system would decide the fate of O.J. Simpson. Nonetheless, as the case continued to titillate the vast majority of the American public, no one could deny the impact on the O.J. affair of the practice of public relations.

QUESTION

1. How would you characterize the "public relations ethics" in the case of O.J. Simpson?

TIPS FROM THE TOP

JEAN CARDWELL

Jean Cardwell is president of Cardwell Enterprises, an executive recruitment and management consulting firm headquartered in Chicago. Before starting her company 20 years ago, Cardwell—who recruits only corporate communications, public relations and public affairs, financial, and investor relations professionals for *Fortune* 500 companies and major agencies—worked on the "other side of the fence" as senior vice president–communications for New York City–based management consultant J. D. Stefek. She speaks and lectures frequently on strategies for and careers in the communications business.

How difficult is it to find work in public relations today?
I wish I could say it's easy, but, with even experienced professionals on the street because of this economy, I can't gloss over the truth. In part, the difficulty in job seeking arises from professionals in other businesses—lawyers, accountants, and the like—who discover public relations and decide that they can do communications.

What advice do you give students entering the field?
Take any job—please! Seriously, start practicing the profession before you graduate. Apply for internships. Work for your college newspaper or for a television or radio station. Volunteer for community work requiring public relations skills. And write, write, write. I've seen all too many professionals who, when faced with pencil and paper or the blinking computer cursor, just can't string two intelligible sentences together. Ironic, isn't it, that they call themselves communicators?

What are the best public relations entry points for a college graduate?
If you're a journalism major, probably a newspaper position—anywhere. A public relations major might find the best opportunities in the nonprofit world.

Should a graduate try corporate or agency work?
I'm biased toward starting a career in agencies. Why? Because it teaches organizational abilities and time management skills—juggling the demands of a number of clients who all want their work done yesterday. In the big multinational firms, the graduate will also be exposed to a variety of industries and techniques that all but the largest corporations can't duplicate. Finally, you'll learn the business from an entrepreneurial viewpoint—an invaluable experience for furthering a professional career.

Where are the best opportunities today in public relations?
Probably the hottest specialty in the field right now, and for some time to come, is media relations. And please don't assume that that's synonymous with schmoozing the press. Far from it. The ideal candidate is one who can counsel top management about the possible communications impact of decisions, who can foresee issues and trends, who can help position the firm in the vagaries of public opinion, and who then, yes, works with the media to help communicate corporate goals. A mouthful, to be sure, but a talent much in demand.

Next is the cry for experienced financial communications professionals. Then, close behind, marketing public relations.

What industries today present the best opportunities?
Any industry in crisis. Because nowhere else will you learn so much so fast. One prime example right now—the airlines.

Many of my colleagues consider health care a tremendous opportunity. I disagree. From my perspective, it's financial services and consumer products, industries that offer the most challenging—and, often, most creative—opportunities.

How do you go about finding a job?

I detest the word *networking* because it's been overused and abused. But, no doubt about it, people give jobs to people they know—or have been referred to. The key to successful networking is to have a genuine interest in the people you're meeting, to remember their names, their hobbies, their kids' occupations.

Networking also means talking to your uncles and aunts, next-door neighbors, doctors, and lawyers about your aspirations. Ask people for advice; everyone loves to be a "Dear Ann." Rule number one: You never know where leads will come from.

Another idea: Create your own job. I've been counseling pros for years to target a company with no communications department, write the CEO/president/owner or vice president of marketing a compelling letter about the benefits of public relations—and then sell the function. No, it's not necessarily easy, but then neither is job hunting.

What qualities distinguish a successful job seeker?
There are three qualities that will distinguish a successful job seeker: (1) being a good, versatile writer; (2) reading everything from *The Wall Street Journal* to your local city magazine; and (3) retaining relevant information and learning about the business of business, not only about the business of public relations. Sure, the ability to get along with a diverse bunch of personalities helps, but never, ever say that you entered the field because "you like people." Today's top professionals have succeeded because they're creative and assertive, have good instincts, understand a variety of industries, communicate well, know how to manage, delegate, and counsel. They're "people persons" only in the fact that they can figure out how to work with all kinds of people, and do so with genuine respect and trust.

APPENDICES

APPENDIX A

CODE OF PROFESSIONAL STANDARDS FOR THE PRACTICE OF PUBLIC RELATIONS

Public Relations Society of America

This code was adopted by the Assembly of the Public Relations Society of America (PRSA) in 1988. It replaces a Code of Ethics in force since 1950 and revised in 1954, 1959, 1963, 1977, and 1983.

On November 12, 1988, PRSA's Assembly approved a revision of the Society's code for the following reasons:

1. To make the language clearer and more understandable—hence easier to apply and to follow.
   As Elias "Buck" Buchwald, APR, chairman of the Board of Ethics and Professional Standards, explained to the Assembly, the revision introduced no substantive changes to the code; it merely clarified and strengthened the language.

2. To help advance the unification of the public relations profession—part of PRSA's mission.
   The PRSA code's revision was based on the Code of the North American Public Relations Council, an organization of 13-member groups, including PRSA. Eight of the 13 have now revised their own codes in accordance with the NAPRC code—an important step toward unification.
   Code interpretations, as published on pages 17–20 of the 1988–1989 Register, remain in effect. However, the Board of Ethics and Professional Standards is in the process of revising and updating them.

Declaration of Principles

Members of the Public Relations Society of America base their professional principles on the fundamental value and dignity of the individual, holding that the free exercise of human rights, especially freedom of speech, freedom of assembly, and freedom of the press, is essential to the practice of public relations.

In serving the interests of clients and employers, we dedicate ourselves to the goals of better communication, understanding, and cooperation among the diverse individuals, groups, and institutions of society, and of equal opportunity of employment in the public relations profession.

We pledge:

To conduct ourselves professionally, with truth, accuracy, fairness, and responsibility to the public;

To improve our individual competence and advance the knowledge and proficiency of the profession through continuing research and education;

And to adhere to the articles of the Code of Professional Standards for the Practice of Public Relations as adopted by the governing Assembly of the Society.

Code of Professional Standards for the Practice of Public Relations

These articles have been adopted by the Public Relations Society of America to promote and maintain high standards of public service and ethical conduct among its members.

1. A member shall conduct his or her professional life in accord with the **public interest.**
2. A member shall exemplify high standards of **honesty and integrity** while carrying out dual obligations to a client or employer and to the democratic process.
3. A member shall **deal fairly** with the public, with past or present clients or employers, and with fellow practitioners, giving due respect to the ideal of free inquiry and to the opinions of others.
4. A member shall adhere to the highest standards of **accuracy and truth,** avoiding extravagant claims or unfair comparisons and giving credit for ideas and words borrowed from others.
5. A member shall not knowingly disseminate **false or misleading information** and shall act promptly to correct erroneous communications for which he or she is responsible.
6. A member shall not engage in any practice which has the purpose of **corrupting** the integrity of channels of communications or the processes of government.
7. A member shall be prepared to **identify publicly** the name of the client or employer on whose behalf any public communication is made.
8. A member shall not use any individual or organization professing to serve or represent an announced cause, or professing to be independent or unbiased, but actually serving another or **undisclosed interest.**
9. A member shall not **guarantee the achievement** of specified results beyond the member's direct control.
10. A member shall **not represent conflicting** or competing interests without the express consent of those concerned, given after a full disclosure of the facts.
11. A member shall not place himself or herself in a position where the member's **personal interest is or may be in conflict** with an obligation to an employer or client, or others, without full disclosure of such interests to all involved.
12. A member shall **not accept fees, commissions, gifts, or any other consideration** from anyone except clients or employers for whom services are performed without their express consent, given after full disclosure of the facts.
13. A member shall scrupulously safeguard

the **confidences and privacy rights** of present, former, and prospective clients or employers.

14. A member shall not intentionally **damage the professional reputation** or practice of another practitioner.
15. If a member has evidence that another member has been guilty of unethical, illegal, or unfair practices, including those in violation of this Code, the member is obligated to present the information promptly to the proper authorities of the Society for action in accordance with the procedure set forth in Article XII of the Bylaws.
16. A member called as a witness in a proceeding for enforcement of this Code is obligated to appear, unless excused for sufficient reason by the judicial panel.
17. A member shall, as soon as possible, sever relations with any organization or individual if such relationship requires conduct contrary to the articles of this Code.

INTERNATIONAL CODE OF ETHICS

CODE OF ATHENS

English Version

adopted by IPRA General Assembly at Athens on 12 May 1965 and modified at Tehran on 17 April 1968

CONSIDERING that all Member countries of the United Nations Organisation have agreed to abide by its Charter which reaffirms "its faith in fundamental human rights, in the dignity and worth of the human person" and that having regard to the very nature of their profession, Public Relations practitioners in these countries should undertake to ascertain and observe the principles set out in this Charter;

CONSIDERING that, apart from "rights", human beings have not only physical or material needs but also intellectual, moral and social needs, and that their rights are of real benefit to them only in so far as these needs are essentially met:

CONSIDERING that, in the course of their professional duties and depending on how these duties are performed, Public Relations practitioners can substantially help to meet these intellectual, moral and social needs:

And lastly, CONSIDERING that the use of techniques enabling them to come simultaneously into contact with millions of people gives Public Relations practitioners a power that has to be restrained by the observance of a strict moral code.

On all these grounds, the undersigned Public Relations Associations hereby declare that they accept as their moral charter the principles of the following Code of Ethics, and that if, in the light of evidence submitted to the Council, a member of these associations should be found to have infringed this Code in the course of his professional duties, he will be deemed to be guilty of serious misconduct calling for an appropriate penalty.

Accordingly, each Member of these Associations:

SHALL ENDEAVOUR

1 To contribute to the achievement of the moral and cultural conditions enabling human beings to reach their full stature and enjoy the indefeasible rights to which they are entitled under the "Universal Declaration of Human Rights";

2 To establish communication patterns and channels which, by fostering the free flow of essential information, will make each member of the society in which he lives feel that he is being kept informed, and also give him an awareness of his own personal involvement and responsibility, and of his solidarity with other members;

3 To bear in mind that, because of the relationship between his profession and the public, his conduct – even in private – will have an impact on the way in which the profession as a whole is appraised;

4 To respect, in the course of his professional duties, the moral principles and rules of the "Universal Declaration of Human Rights";

5 To pay due regard to, and uphold, human dignity, and to recognise the right of each individual to judge for himself;

6 To encourage the moral, psychological and intellectual conditions for dialogue in its true sense, and to recognise the right of the parties involved to state their case and express their views;

SHALL UNDERTAKE

7 To conduct himself always and in all circumstances in such a manner as to deserve and secure the confidence of those with whom he comes into contact;

8 To act, in all circumstances, in such a manner as to take account of the respective interests of the parties involved: both the interests of the organisation which he serves and the interests of the publics concerned;

9 To carry out his duties with integrity, avoiding language likely to lead to ambiguity or misunderstanding, and to maintain loyalty to his clients or employers, whether past or present;

SHALL REFRAIN FROM

10 Subordinating the truth to other requirements;

11 Circulating information which is not based on established and ascertainable facts;

12 Taking part in any venture or undertaking which is unethical or dishonest or capable of impairing human dignity and integrity;

13 Using any "manipulative" methods or techniques designed to create subconscious motivations which the individual cannot control of his own free will and so cannot be held accountable for the action taken on them.

APPENDIX

ADVERTISING EFFECTIVENESS TRACKING STUDY

CONTEMPORARY MARKETING RESEARCH INC.
1270 Broadway
New York, NY 10001

#6-1-107
February 1986

ADVERTISING EFFECTIVENESS TRACKING STUDY
MAIN QUESTIONNAIRE

Card 1
(11-17Z)

RESPONDENT'S NAME: ______________________________

1a. Today I am interested in obtaining your opinions of financial institutions. To begin with, I'd like you to tell me the names of all the financial institutions you have heard of. (DO NOT READ LIST. RECORD FIRST INSTITUTION MENTIONED SEPARATELY FROM ALL OTHERS UNDER "FIRST MENTION.") (PROBE:) Any others? (RECORD BELOW UNDER "OTHERS.")

1b. Now, thinking only of banks in the New York area, what (other) banks have you heard of (RECORD BELOW UNDER "OTHERS.")

2. And what financial institutions, including banks, have you seen or heard advertised within the past 3 months? (DO NOT READ LIST. RECORD BELOW UNDER Q.2.)

3. FOR EACH ASTERISKED INSTITUTION LISTED BELOW AND NOT MENTIONED IN Q.1a/1b OR Q.2, ASK:

   Have you ever heard of (NAME)? (RECORD BELOW UNDER Q.3.)

4. FOR EACH ASTERISKED INSTITUTION CIRCLED IN Q.1a/1b OR Q.3 AND NOT CIRCLED IN Q.2, ASK:

   Have you seen or heard advertising for (NAME) within the past 3 months? (RECORD BELOW UNDER Q.4.)

	Q. 1a/1b AWARE OF		Q.2	Q.3	Q.4
	FIRST MENTION (18)	OTHERS (21)	AWARE ADVTG. (24)	AWARE OF (AIDED)	AWARE ADVTG. (AIDED)
Anchor Savings Bank	1	1	1		
Apple Savings Bank	2	2	2		
Astoria Federal Savings	3	3	3		
Bank of Commerce	4	4	4		
Bank of New York	5	5	5		
Bankers Trust	6	6	6		

Card 1

	Q. 1a/1b AWARE OF		Q.2	Q.3	Q.4
	FIRST MENTION	OTHERS	AWARE ADVTG.	AWARE OF (AIDED)	AWARE ADVTG. (AIDED)
	(18)	(21)	(24)		
Barclays Bank	7	7	7		
Bowery Savings Bank	8	8	8		
*Chase Manhattan Bank	9	9	9	9 (27)	9 (29)
*Chemical Bank	0	0	0	0	0
*Citibank	X	X	X	X	X
Crossland Savings Bank	Y	Y	Y		
*Dean Witter	1 (19)	1 (22)	1 (25)	1 (28)	1 (30)
Dime Savings Bank	2	2	2		
Dollar Dry Dock Savings Bank	3	3	3		
*Dreyfus	4	4	4	4	4
Emigrant Savings Bank	5	5	5		
European American Bank	6	6	6		
Fidelity	7	7	7		
Goldome Savings Bank	8	8	8		
*Manufacturer's Hanover Trust	9	9	9	9	9
*Marine Midland Bank	0	0	0	0	0
*Merrill Lynch	X	X	X	X	X
*National Westminster Bank	Y	Y	Y	Y	Y
Prudential Bache	1 (20)	1 (23)	1 (26)		
Shearson-Lehman	2	2	2		
Other (SPECIFY):					
________________	X	X	X		
________________					
________________					

REFER BACK TO Q.2 AND 4. IF RESPONDENT IS AWARE OF ADVERTISING FOR CHASE MANHATTAN BANK IN Q.2 OR Q.4, ASK Q.5a. OTHERWISE, SKIP TO Q.6.

5a. Today we are asking different people about different banks. In your case, we'd like to talk about Chase Manhattan Bank. You just mentioned that you remember seeing or hearing advertising for Chase Manhattan Bank. Please tell me everything you remember seeing or hearing in the advertising. (PROBE FOR SPECIFICS) What else?

____ (31)

____ (32)

____ (33)

____ (34)

____ (35)

Card 1

5b. And where did you see or hear advertising for Chase Manhattan Bank? (Do NOT READ LIST) (MORE THAN ONE ANSWER MAY BE GIVEN).

	(36)
Television	1
Radio	2
Newspaper	3
Magazine	4
Billboard	5
Other (SPECIFY): ____________	X

6. Different banks use different slogans. (START WITH THE X'D QUESTION BELOW AND CONTINUE UNTIL ALL FOUR QUESTIONS (Q.6a-6d) HAVE BEEN ASKED.)

START:
(√) 6a. What slogan or statement do you associate with Chase Manhattan Bank? (DO NOT READ LIST)

	(37)
Chase. The Experience Shows	1
You Have a Friend at Chase	2
Ideas You Can Bank On	3
The Chase Is On	4
Other (SPECIFY) ____________	X

____

____

( ) 6b. What slogan does Chemical Bank use? (DO NOT READ LIST)

	(38)
The Chemistry's Just Right at Chemical	1
Other (SPECIFY) X	

(√) 6c. What slogan or statement do you associate with Citibank? (DO NOT READ LIST)

	(39)
It's Your Citi	1
The Citi Never Sleeps	2
Other (SPECIFY)______ X	

____

____

( ) 6d. What slogan does Manufacturer's Hanover Trust use? (DO NOT READ LIST)

	(40)
The Financial Source. Worldwide	1
We Realize Your Potential	2
Other (SPECIFY) ______________________	X

____

____

Card 1

7. Now, I'd like to know how likely you yourself are to consider banking at several different banks in the future. For each bank I read, please tell me whether you would definitely consider banking there, probably consider banking there, might or might not consider banking there, probably not consider banking there or definitely not consider banking there in the future. Now, how likely are you to consider banking at (READ X'D BANK) in the future? (REPEAT SCALE IF NECESSARY. OBTAIN A RATING FOR EACH BANK.)

START:	( )	( )	( )	(√)
	CHASE MANHATTAN BANK	CHEMICAL BANK	CITIBANK	MANU-FACTURER'S HANOVER TRUST
Definitely Consider Banking There	5 (41)	5 (42)	5 (43)	5 (44)
Probably Consider Banking There	4	4	4	4
Might Or Might Not Consider Banking There	3	3	3	3
Probably Not Consider Banking There	2	2	2	2
Definitely Not Consider Banking There	1	1	1	1
(DO NOT READ)→(Currently Bank There)	X	X	X	X
			(45-1)	

8a. Now, I'd like you to rate one bank on a series of statements—Chase Manhattan Bank. If you have never banked there, please base your answers on what you know about this bank and your perceptions of it. After I read each statement, please tell me whether you agree completely, agree somewhat, neither agree nor disagree, disagree somewhat or disagree completely that this statement describes Chase Manhattan Bank. (START WITH X'D STATEMENT AND CONTINUE UNTIL ALL ARE RATED.)

START HERE:	AGREE COM-PLETELY	AGREE SOME-WHAT	NEITHER AGREE NOR DISAGREE	DISAGREE SOME-WHAT	DISAGREE COM-PLETELY
[ ] Is Responsive to Your Needs	5	4	3	2	1 (46)
[ ] Offers High Quality Accounts and Services	5	4	3	2	1 (47)
[ ] Deals With Its Customers on a Personalized Level	5	4	3	2	1 (48)
[ ] Helps Make Banking Easier	5	4	3	2	1 (49)
[ ] Has Bank Personnel That Are Concerned About You	5	4	3	2	1 (50)
[ ] Designs Accounts to Meet Your Special Needs	5	4	3	2	1 (51)
[ ] Is Responsive to Community Needs	5	4	3	2	1 (52)
[ ] Makes It Easy to Open an IRA Account	5	4	3	2	1 (53)
[ ] Has a Full Range of Banking and Investment Services	5	4	3	2	1 (54)
[ ] Is a Bank Where You Want to Have Most of Your Accounts	5	4	3	2	1 (55)

Card 1

START HERE:	AGREE COM-PLETELY	AGREE SOME-WHAT	NEITHER AGREE NOR DISAGREE	DISAGREE SOME-WHAT	DISAGREE COM-PLETELY
[ ] Has Bank Personnel That Are Experienced	5	4	3	2	1 (56)
[ ] Has Innovative Accounts and Services	5	4	3	2	1 (57)
[ ] Understands Your Banking Needs	5	4	3	2	1 (58)
[ ] Has Branches That Are Pleasant to Bank In	5	4	3	2	1 (59)
[ ] Has Accounts to Help People Just Starting Out	5	4	3	2	1 (60)
[ ] Continuously Develops Services to Meet Your Needs	5	4	3	2	1 (61)
[ ] Has Bank Personnel That Are Friendly and Courteous	5	4	3	2	1 (62)
[ ] Has Accounts and Services That Are Right for You	5	4	3	2	1 (63)
[√] Puts Customers' Needs First	5	4	3	2	1 (64)
[ ] Is a Modern, Up-to-Date Bank	5	4	3	2	1 (65)

END CARD 1

LEADING MEDIA DIRECTORIES

When public relations professionals are asked which media directories they use most often, their answers are as varied as the tasks their firms perform. Publishers have carved such precise market niches for their wares that direct comparison of one directory to another is usually inappropriate. A comprehensive list of media directories begins on this page. Directories are listed by category and then alphabetically. Another list provides complete names and addresses of the publishers cited.

Directories

Newspapers

E&P International Yearbook. Annual list of U.S. and Canadian daily newspaper personnel and other data. $60. **Editor & Publisher.**

Family Page Directory. $60 for two editions printed at six-month intervals. Contains information about home, cooking, and family interest sections of newspapers. **Public Relations Plus.**

Media Alerts. Data on 200 major dailies as well as 1,900 magazines. $155. **Bacon's.**

National Directory of Community Newspapers. Listings on newspapers serving smaller communities. $35. **American Newspaper Representatives.**

Publicity Checker, Volume 2: Newspapers. $155 when purchased with Volume 1 on magazines. Two volumes list over 7,500 publications. **Bacon's.**

Working Press of the Nation, Volume I: Newspapers. Part of a $260 five-volume set with 25,000 publicity outlets. **National Research Bureau.**

1988 News Bureaus in the U.S. $133. **Larimi.**

Magazines

Media Alerts. Data on 1,900 magazines and 200 major daily newspapers. $155. **Bacon's.**

National Directory of Magazines. Lists basic information on 1,300 magazines in the United States and Canada. $125. **Oxbridge.**

Publicity Checker, Volume 1. Part of a two-volume set (for magazines and newspapers) with over 7,500 listings. $155 for both volumes. **Bacon's.**

Standard Periodical Directory. Has 60,000 titles with 50 fields of data per title, divided into 250 subject areas. $295. **Oxbridge.**

Working Press of the Nation, Volume 2: Magazines. Part of a $260 five-volume set with data on 25,000 publicity outlets. **National Research Bureau.**

Television

Cable Contacts Yearbook. Lists all cable systems. $184. **Larimi.**

Radio-TV Directory. Over 1,300 TV stations and 9,000 radio stations. $155. **Bacon's.**

Talk Show Selects. Identifies talk show contacts nationwide for both TV and radio. Emphasizes network and syndication programs. $185. **Broadcast Interview.**

Television Contacts. Updated extensive listings. $233. **Larimi.**

TV News. Guide to news directors and assignment editors. $172. **Larimi.**

TV Publicity Outlets. Two editions are printed at six-month intervals. $159.50. **Public Relations Plus.**

Working Press of the Nation, Volume 3: TV and Radio. Part of a $260 five-volume set with 25,000 publicity outlets. **National Research Bureau.**

Radio

National Radio Publicity Outlets. Two editions are printed at six-month intervals. $159.50 for both. **Public Relations Plus.**

Radio Contacts. Extensive, updated listings. $239. **Larimi.**

Radio-TV Directory. Over 9,000 radio and 1,300 TV stations. $155. **Bacon's.**

Talk Show Selects. Identifies both radio and TV talk show contacts nationwide. Emphasis is on syndicated and network programs. $185. **Broadcast Interview.**

Working Press of the Nation, Volume 3. Includes both radio and TV. Part of a five-volume $260 set that contains data on 25,000 publicity outlets. **National Research Bureau.**

Newsletters

Directory of Newsletters. Has 13,500 newsletters in the United States and Canada. Publications are divided into 168 categories. $125. **Oxbridge.**

The Newsletter Yearbook Directory. Lists worldwide newsletters available by subscription. $60. **Newsletter Clearinghouse.**

Newsletters Directory. Guide to more than 8,000 subscription, membership and free newsletters. $140. **Gale Research.**

1988 Investment Newsletters. Lists over 1,000 newsletters. $160. **Larimi.**

Regional

Burrelle's Media Directories. Regional directories for New York State ($85), New Jersey ($70), Pennsylvania ($38), New England ($95), Connecticut ($32), Maine ($25), New Hampshire ($25), Massachusetts ($44), Rhode Island ($25), Vermont ($25), and Greater Boston ($29). **Burrelle's.**

Metro California Media. Detailed listing of California media. $89.50 includes semiannual revised edition. **Public Relations Plus.**

Minnesota Non-Metro Media Directory. Guide to the media in the Twin Cities region. $90. **Publicity Central.**

New York Publicity Outlets. Media within a 50-mile radius of New York City. $89.50 includes the semiannual revised edition. **Public Relations Plus.**

New York TV Directory. Lists producers, directors, and others active in the New York market. Published annually. $15. **National Academy.**

Vermont Media Directory. TV, radio, newspaper, and magazine listings. $99. **Kelliher.**

Washington News Media. Detailed listings of wire services, newspapers, magazines, radio-TV, and foreign correspondents. $99. **Hudson's.**

1988 Media Guide and Membership Direc-

tory. Chicago media outlets. $75. **Publicity Club of Chicago.**

International

International Literary Market Place. $85. **R. R. Bowker.**

International Media Guide. Publishers of *Newspapers Worldwide* and *Consumer Magazines Worldwide.* A four-volume set covers business and professional publications for Asia/Pacific; Middle East and Africa; Latin America; and Europe. Each volume sells for $100. **International Media Guide.**

International Publicity Checker. Lists 10,000 Western European business, trade, and technical magazines and 1,000 national and regional newspapers. $165. **Bacon's.**

Ulrich's International Periodicals Directory. Lists 70,730 periodicals in 542 subject areas in two volumes. Over 40,000 entries from the previous edition have been updated. $159.95. **Ulrich's.**

United Kingdom

Benn's Media Directory. Available in two books, one for the United Kingdom and the other for international listings. Each is $95; both are $160. Published by Benn Business Information Services. **Nichols.**

Bowdens Media Directory. Updated three times annually, with complete media listings. **Bowdens.**

Editors Media Directories. Series of directories covering journalists, features, and profiles. **Editors.**

Hollis Press and Public Relations Annual. Over 18,000 organizations in the public relations industry, with a full range of media. $36. **Hollis.**

PIMS United Kingdom Financial Directory. Detailed listings. $300 annually or $90 for a single copy. **PIMS U.S.A.**

PIMS United Kingdom Media Directory. Provides detailed access to the total range of U.K. media. $390 annually, $220 quarterly, or $90 for a single issue. **PIMS U.S.A.**

Willing's Press Guide. Extensive U.K. media listings. $105 plus $5 shipping. Published by Thomas Skinner Directories. **Business Press International.**

Canada

Matthews List. Contains 3,600 media throughout Canada. Updated three times annually. $130 per year. **Publicorp.**

Australia

Margaret Gee's Media Guide. Lists 2,400 Australian media. Updated three times annually. $100. **Margaret Gee.**

Japan

Publishers in English in Japan. Media selection for English-speaking readers. Published by Japan Publications Guide Service. **Pacific Subscription Service.**

Africa

African Book World and Press. Lists over 4,000 publishers. The latest edition is 1983. $78. **K. G. Saur.**

Specialists

Business and Financial News Media. Print, electronic, syndicated columns, and individual writers. $85. **Larriston.**

Business and Technical Media. Available on paper and floppy disk, at $200 total for both. **Ron Gold.**

Computer Industry Almanac. Extensive industry data, as well as a publications directory. $49.50 hardcover; $29.95 softcover. **Computer Industry Almanac.**

Directory of the College Student Press in America. Has 5,000 student newspapers and magazines on 3,600 campuses. $75. **Oxbridge.**

Encyclopedia of Association Periodicals. Three-volume directory sells for $150; individual volumes sell for $60. Vol. I: business and finance. Vol. II: science and medicine. Vol. III: social sciences and education. **Gale Research.**

Medical and Science News Media. Specialized listings with major news contacts. $85. **Larriston.**

Medical Press List. Available on paper and floppy disk at a combination price of $125. **Ron Gold.**

Nelson's Directory of Investment Research. Contact information and areas of specialization for over 3,000 security analysts. $259. **W. R. Nelson.**

TIA International Travel News Directory. Comprehensive travel media listings. $35. **Travel Industry Association.**

Travel, Leisure and Entertainment News Media. Major nationwide contacts. $85. **Larriston.**

1988 College/Alumni/Military Publications. Over 1,150 publications in these three fields. $87. **Larimi.**

Working Press of the Nation, Volume 5. Internal Publications Directory. Describes house organs published primarily for distribution inside companies. Part of a five-volume library selling for $250. **National Research Bureau.**

Ethnic

Black Media in America. $50. **Hall Co.**

Burrelle's Special Directories. Directories of Black, Latino, and women's media are covered in three volumes at $50 each. **Burrelle's.**

Hispanic Media, U.S.A. Provides a narrative description of Spanish-language media. Includes newspapers, radio, and TV stations. $75 plus $1.50 handling. **The Media Institute.**

General

Business Publications Rates and Data. Monthly directory of magazines and newspapers categorized by field. $398 for 12 monthly issues, or $194 for one copy. **Standard Rate and Data Service.**

Directory of Directories. More than 10,000 entries in two volumes. $195. **Gale Research.**

Gale Directory of Publications. Annual directory to newspapers, magazines, journals, and related publications. $135. **Gale.**

Gebbie All-In-One Directory. Comprehensive listings of all media. $79.25. **Gebbie Press.**

Market Guide. Has data on population, income, households, and retail sales for markets around the nation. $70. **E&P.**

Print Media Editorial Calendars. Lists 12-month editorial calendars for 4,200 trades, 1,700 newspapers, 1,500 consumer magazines, and 400 farm publications. $195. **Standard Rate and Data Service.**

Experts and Writers

Directory of Experts, Authorities and Spokespersons. Access to over 3,569 experts. $19.95 plus $3.50 shipping. Can be ordered on Rolodex cards for $165. **Broadcast Interview.**

1988 Syndicated Columnists. Over 1,400 columnists listed. $157. **Larimi.**

Syndicate Directory. Lists syndicated features by classification and by-lines, as well as how material is furnished. $6. **E&P.**

Working Press of the Nation, Volume 4: Feature Writer and Photographer Directory. Part of a five-volume set selling for $260. **National Research Bureau.**

Directory Publishers

Publishers of media directories are presented in alphabetical order in the list that follows.

American Newspaper Representatives
12 South Sixth St., Ste. 520
Minneapolis, MN 55402
612/332-8686
National Directory of Community Newspapers

Bacon's PR and Media Information Systems
332 S. Michigan Ave.
Chicago, IL 60604
800/621-0561
International Publicity Checker
Media Alerts
Publicity Checker
Radio-TV Directory

Bowden's Information Services
624 King Street West
Toronto ON M5V 2X9, Canada
416/860-0794
Bowden's Media Directory

Broadcast Interview Source
2500 Wisconsin Ave., NW
Suite 930
Washington, DC 20007
202/333-4904
Directory of Experts
Talk Show Selects

Burrelle's Press Clipping Service
75 East Northfield Ave.
Livingston, NJ 07039
201/992-6600
Regional Media Directories

Computer Industry Almanac
8111 LBJ Freeway, 13th floor
Dallas, TX 75251-1313
214/231-8735
Computer Industry Almanac

Editor and Publisher
11 West 19th St.
New York, NY 10011
212/675-4380
E&P International Yearbook
Market Guide
Syndicate Directory

Editors Media Directories
9/10 Great Sutton St.
London EC1 VOBX England
Editors Media Directories

Gale Research
Book Tower
Detroit, MI 48226
313/961-2242
Directory of Directories
Directory of Publications
Encyclopedia of Association Periodicals
Newsletters Directory

Gebbie Press
Box 1000
New Paltz, NY 12561
914/255-7560
Gebbie All-In-One Directory

Hollis Directories
Contact House
Sunbury-on-Thames
Middlesex TW16 5HG, England
Hollis Press and Public Relations Annual

International Media Guide Enterprises
22 Elizabeth St.
South Norwalk, CT 06856
203/853-7880
International Media Guide

Kelliher/Samets
130 South Willard St.
Burlington, VT 05401
802/862-8261
Vermont Media Directory

Larimi Communications Associates
5 West 37th St.
New York, NY 10018
800/634-4020
212/819-9310
Cable Contacts Yearbook
1988 News Bureaus in the U.S.
Radio Contacts
Television Contacts
TV News

Larriston Communications
P.O. Box 20229
New York, NY 10025
212/864-0150
Business and Financial News Media
Medical and Science News Media
Travel, Leisure and Entertainment News Media

Margaret Gee Media Group
384 Flinders Lane
Melbourne, Victoria 3000 Australia
Information Australia
Margaret Gee's Media Guide

The Media Institute
3017 M Street
Washington, DC 20007
202/298-7512
Hispanic Media, U.S.A.

National Academy of Television
Arts and Sciences
New York Chapter
110 West 57th St.
New York, NY 10019
212/765-2450
New York TV Directory

National Research Bureau
310 S. Michigan Ave.
Chicago, IL 60604
312/663-5580
Working Press of the Nation

W. R. Nelson Co.
1 Gateway Plaza
Port Chester, NY 10573
914/937-8400
Nelson's Directory of Investment Research

Newsletter Clearinghouse
44 W. Market St.
P.O. Box 311
Rhinebeck, NY 12572
914/876-2081
Hudson's Washington News Media
Newsletter Yearbook Directory

Nichols Publishing
P.O. Box 96
New York, NY 10024
212/580-8079
Benn's Media Directory

Oxbridge Communications
150 Fifth Ave.
New York, NY 10011
212/741-0231
National Directory of Magazines
Standard Periodical Directory

Pacific Subscription Service
P.O. Box 811
FDR Station
New York, NY 10150
212/929-1629
Publishers in English in Japan

PIMS U.S.A.
1133 Broadway
New York, NY 10010
212/645-5112
United Kingdom Financial Directory
United Kingdom Media Directory

Public Relations Plus
P.O. Drawer 1197
New Milford, CT 06776
203/354-9361
All TV Publicity Outlets
Metro California Media
National Radio Publicity Outlets
New York Publicity Outlets
The Family Page Directory

Publicity Club of Chicago
1441 Shermer Rd. (#110)
Northbrook, IL 60062
1988 Media Guide
Publicity Club of Chicago Membership Directory

Publicorp Communications
Box 1029
Pointe Claire PQ
W9S 4H9 Canada
Matthews List

Reed Business Publishing
205 E. 42nd St., Ste. 1705
New York, NY 10017
212/867-2080
Willing's Press Guide

Ron Gold, N.A.
1341 Ocean Ave. (#366)
Santa Monica, CA 90401
213/399-7938
Business and Technical Media
Medical Press List

R. R. Bowker
245 West 17th St.
New York, NY 10011
212/645-9700
Ulrich's International Periodicals Directory

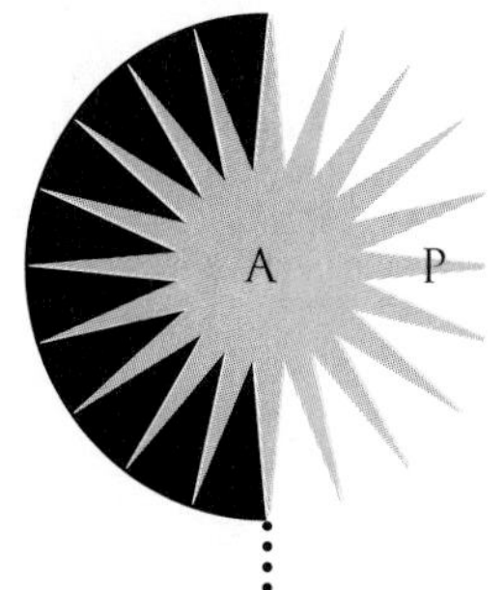

A P P E N D I X **D**

AUDIOVISUAL SUPPORTS

Material	*Advantages*	*Limitations*
Slide series A form of projected audiovisual materials easy to prepare with any 35mm camera	1. Prepared with any 35mm camera for most uses 2. Requires only filming, with processing and mounting by film laboratory 3. Colorful, realistic reproductions of original subjects 4. Easily revised, updated, handled, stored, and rearranged 5. Can be combined with taped narration for greater effectiveness 6. May be played through remote control presentation	1. Requires some skill in photography 2. Requires special equipment for close-up photography and copying 3. Prone to get out of sequence and be projected incorrectly
Filmstrips Closely related to slides, but instead of being mounted as separate pictures, remains uncut as a continuous strip	1. Compact, easily handled, and always in proper sequence 2. Can be supplemented with captions or recordings 3. Inexpensive when quantity reproduction is required 4. Projected with simple, lightweight equipment 5. Projection rate controlled by presenter	1. Relatively difficult to prepare locally 2. Requires film laboratory service to convert slides to filmstrip form 3. In permanent sequence and therefore cannot be rearranged or revised
Overhead transparencies A popular form of locally prepared materials, requiring an overhead projector for presentation	1. Can present information in systematic, developmental sequences 2. Simple-to-operate projector with presentation rate controlled by presenter 3. Requires limited planning 4. Can be prepared by a variety of simple, inexpensive methods	1. Requires special equipment, facilities, and skills for more advanced preparation methods 2. May be cumbersome and lack finesse of more remote processes

APPENDIX E

Guide to Video/Satellite Terms

People in the video field use a number of terms that may be unfamiliar to PR professionals. *O'Dwyer's PR Services Report* presents a glossary of key terms as a service to its readers.

Actuality: The voices of people involved in a news story. Also called a *sound cut* or *sound bite*.

ADI: Area of Dominant Influence is Arbitron Rating Company's geographic market designation that defines each TV market based on measurable viewing patterns.

Assignment Editor: Newsperson who is responsible for assigning stories to reporters and camera crews.

Audience Reach: The estimated number of viewers for a specific station or show based on the number of TV households.

Background Package: The hard copy or background materials that are often sent to journalists prior to an interview via satellite. May include press releases, videocassette, etc.

Betacam: Form of videotape with a higher resolution quality than its forerunner, 3/4-inch U-Matic. More commonly used worldwide because of its high picture quality.

Bridge: Words that connect one piece of narration or sound bite to another.

B-roll: Usually an unedited version of the same visuals without narration, which permits stations to edit and air the footage using their own announcers to create the feeling that the material was gathered and is being presented by their own news bureau.

C-band: A term identifying satellite services; literally, the 6/4 GHz portion of the spectrum. Like AM and FM on radio bands.

Character Generator: Electronic equipment used to produce supers (lettering) over video.

Chromakey: The electronic placement of pictures behind the person on camera.

Conversion: Process of changing video footage from one format to another.

Cover Footage: Video shot used to cover or replace the pictures of the interviewer and interviewee while their voices are being heard.

Cue Card: A large, hand-lettered card that contains copy usually held next to the camera lens by floor personnel.

Cutaway: A shot used to avoid a jump cut.

Degauss: To wipe or clean audio or videotape electronically before reusing.

Depth of Field: The range in which objects will appear in focus.

Digital Still Store: Also called *electronic still store system* or *ESS;* device that takes a single video frame from any video source and stores it in digital form on a disk.

Digital Video Effects: Also called *DVE;* visual effects produced by devices that change normal video signals into digital (numerical) information.

Dissolve: Special video effect that slowly replaces one image on the screen with another.

DMA: Designated Market Area, a viewing region defined by Nielsen Media Research.

Downlink: Retransmission of a signal from a satellite down to earth for reception by ground stations.

Dub: To copy or record audio or video material.

Dub Master: First-generation copy of the original tape master.

Eng Crew: Electronic news-gathering crew, usually one camera person and one audio technician, with portable, self-contained, and largely automated video equipment.

Establishing Shot: A wide shot of a scene, usually used at the beginning of a story to orient viewers to the location of the story.

Evergreens: TV stories with an indefinite "shelf life"; updated material that can be used at any time. Also known as *features*.

Gain: Volume of an audio or video signal.

Ground Station: The originators and receivers of satellite transmissions. Also known as *earth stations*.

Hard Copy: A cassette copy of video material.

Hard Lead: A lead that includes the most important information in the first sentence.

IFB: Interrupted Feedback System, a small earpiece worn by the talent that carries program sound or instructions from the director or producer.

Indie: Independent, as in independent producer or independent TV station, the former not affiliated with a major studio, the latter not affiliated or owned by a network.

Insert Studio: Small studio used for interviews or shoots.

Jump-cut: An erratic movement of a head that results when video is edited internally to eliminate some of the speaker's words.

Keeper: Usable tape.

Ku-band: A term identifying satellite services in the 11–24 GHz portion of the spectrum.

Live Shot: A live, or videotaped as live, interactive interview with a video signal transmitted via satellite and audio carried on telephone lines.

Live-on-tape: A satellite interview taped for playback in a later broadcast. Also called *taped-as-live*.

Medium Shot: Camera shot that shows about half of a person's body. Also called a *waist shot*.

Mix Minus: Prevents interview subjects from hearing their own voices echoing back to them on the IFB line from the station conducting the interview.

Montage: A series of audio or video segments edited together. Used frequently in reaction or "person on the street" interviews.

Moray: Video disturbance caused by objects being videotaped. Jewelry and clothing colors are two common causes.

Multiscreen Presentations: Video, slide, or film presentations in which TV screens are "stacked" and used to present the entire image that would normally appear on one screen.

Natsot: Abbreviation for *natural sound,* background sound recorded on tape during a shoot. Also called *ambience*.

O/C: Abbreviation of "on camera."

Off-line Editing: Editing process for producing videotape workprints not intended for broadcast. The workprint information is then fed into the on-line (system for production of the release master tape).

On-line Editing: A master editing system using high-quality videotape recorders for high-band release master tapes.

On-location Shot: Represents a production in which the camera is brought to the scene. Also known as *field shoot*.

Origination Site: Term indicating where a satellite transmission will originate.

Package: A news story that includes an interview, narration, and cover footage.

Pan: Camera moving in a horizontal position.

Postproduction: Any production activity that occurs after production, including announcer recording, editing, and sound mixing.

Preproduction: Any production activity that takes place before a production, including scripting and location survey.

Pre-roll: To start a videotape and let it roll for a few seconds before it is put in the playback or record mode in order to give the electronic system time to stabilize.

Production Line: Line between the director of the live shot and the producer at the TV station receiving the satellite transmission.

Receive Site: Term indicating where a satellite transmission is being fed.

Reversal: A shot of the interviewer looking at the person being interviewed, used as a cutaway.

Satellite Coordinates: Designation for fixing the location of a satellite, for uplinking and downlinking satellite signals. Like latitude and longitude.

Satellite Media Tour: A series of interviews, via satellite, by journalists, with representatives of business or organizations. The spokesperson, in a fixed location, is interviewed by journalists anywhere in the world who have access to satellite downlink facilities. Also called *satellite tour* and *satellite press tour.*

Scroll: Horizontal or vertical movement of word supers either up or across the TV screen.

Segue: Smooth flow from one topic to another.

Slate: Names on billboard.

Soft Lead: A lead in which the most important information is not given immediately.

Soft-out: A satellite or studio booking with an option to go past the scheduled end time.

Sot: Abbreviation for "sound on tape" used to indicate the use of videotape with sound, usually a sound bite.

Sound Bite or Cut: Portion of a statement or interview that is included in a packaged news story.

Space Segment: The actual time-slot booked on a satellite. Also called a *window.*

Squeeze Frame: Reducing a picture on camera until it takes up only part of the screen. Also known as *squeeze zoom.*

Super: Short for *superimposing* lettering over graphics or video. Most commonly used to give the names and titles of interview subjects while on screen. Also known as *font.*

Tag: Sentence or two used to end a story or introduce a second part in a multipart series.

Tight Shot: Close-up camera shot of an individual or object.

Time-coding: The recording of the time of day on the edge of the videotape as it is being shot to assist the editing process.

Time-in: The specific time when a window begins.

Time-out: The specific time when a window ends—usually very firm, as another window or interview is scheduled to follow immediately.

Transponder: Equipment on a satellite, including a receiver, transmitter, and antennae, forming a channel or link between two earth stations.

Two-shot: Camera shot of two people.

Two-way Audio: Audio signals between the interviewer and the spokesperson being interviewed so that the interviewer and spokesperson can hear each other.

Upcut: The loss of words at the beginning of the videotape.

VNR: Stands for *video news release,* which may be transmitted to stations by satellite or sent via videocassette. Usually used for soft news and runs about 90 seconds.

V/O: Abbreviation for *voice-over,* the term used to indicate that the announcer's voice is being heard over the video for cover footage.

VTR: Videotape recorder.

APPENDIX F

CORPORATE REPORTING REQUIREMENTS

Periodically, the Hill & Knowlton public relations firm updates this compilation of "Disclosure and Filing Requirements for Public Companies." It details the specific requirements of the various exchanges as well as the Securities and Exchange Commission.

Disclosure Requirements

Reporting Required for:	Securities and Exchange Commission	New York Stock Exchange	American Stock Exchange	National Association of Securities Dealers	Generally Recommended Publicity Practice, All Companies
Accounting: Change in Auditors	Form 8-K; if principal accountant (or accountant for a subsidiary) resigns, declines to be reelected, or is dismissed or if another is engaged. Disclose date of resignation, details of disagreement (any adverse opinions, disclaimers of opinion, or qualifications of opinion occurring during the audits of the two most recent fiscal years), comment letters to SEC by former accountant on whether he agrees with the company's statements in the 8-K. See also Regulations S-K, Item 304.	Prompt notice to Exchange, 8-K when filed.	Prompt notification of Listing Representative, prior to filing of 8-K, *and* must state reason for change (Listing Form SD-1, Item 1a).	Prompt notification concurrently with press disclosure (company must file 8-K with SEC, and information may be material enough to warrant trading halt. See NASD Schedule D). Contact NASD's Market Surveillance Section at (202) 728-8187, preferably before public release and when in doubt about "material information." (NASD Schedule D.) Promptly confirm in writing all oral communications to NASD. If public release made after 5:30 p.m. Eastern Standard Time, notify	Press release desirable at time of filing 8-K if differences are major. Consider clear statement in annual report or elsewhere on independence of auditors, including their reporting relationship to Board's audit committee; state company policy on rotation/nonrotation of auditors periodically.

Reporting Required for:	Securities and Exchange Commission	New York Stock Exchange	American Stock Exchange	National Association of Securities Dealers	Generally Recommended Publicity Practice, All Companies
				NASD by 9:30 a.m. the following trading day. (NASD Schedule D).	
Annual (or Special) Meeting of Stockholders	10-Q following meeting, including date of meeting, name of each director elected, summary of other matters voted on.	Five copies of all proxy material sent to shareholders filed with Exchange not later than date material sent to any shareholder. Ten days' advance notice of record date or closing transfer books to Exchange. The notice should state the purpose(s) for which the record date has been fixed. Preferably, notice should be given by TWX (TWX No. 710-581-2801); or, if by telephone, promptly confirmed by TWX, telegram, or letter.	Six copies of all material sent to shareholders should be sent to the Securities Division as soon as mailed to shareholders (Listing Form SD-1, Item 13). Other requirements same as for NYSE (Listing Form SD-1, Item 1H for notice regarding record date).	File 10-Q concurrently with SEC filing.	Press release at time of meeting. Competition for news space minimizes public coverage except on actively contested issues. Check NYSE schedules for competing meetings. Recommended wide distribution of post-meeting report to shareholders.
Annual Report to Shareholders: Contents	Requirements listed under Rule 14a-3 of the 1934 Act. They include audited balance sheets for two most recent fiscal years; audited income statements and changes in financial position for each of three most recent fiscal years; management's discussion and analysis of financial condition and results of financial operations; brief description of general nature and scope of the business; industry segment information; company directors and officers; stock price and dividends. SEC encourages "freedom of management expression."	Include in annual report principal office's address; directors' and officers' names; audit committee and other committee members; trustees, transfer agents, and registrars; numbers of employees and shareholders (*NYSE Company Manual* Section 203.01). Also include the number of shares of stock issuable under outstanding options at the beginning of the year; separate totals of changes in the number of shares of its stock under option resulting from issuance,	Annual report must contain: balance sheets, income statements, and statements of changes in financial position. Financial statements should be prepared in accordance with generally accepted accounting principles, and SEC Regulation S-X.	No specific requirements, but NASD receives 10-K.	Check printed annual report and appropriate news release to ensure that they conform to information reported on Form 10-K. News releases necessary if annual report contains previously undisclosed material information. Trend is to consider report a marketing tool.

Reporting Required for:	Securities and Exchange Commission	New York Stock Exchange	American Stock Exchange	National Association of Securities Dealers	Generally Recommended Publicity Practice, All Companies
		exercise, expiration, or cancellation of options; and the number of shares issuable under outstanding options at the close of the year, the number of unoptioned shares available at the beginning and at the close of the year for the granting of options under an option plan, and any changes in the price of outstanding options, through cancellation and reissuance or otherwise, except price changes resulting from the normal operation of antidilution provisions of the options (NYSE Listing Agreement, Section 901.01).			
Annual Report to Shareholders: Time and Distribution	Annual report to shareholders must precede or accompany delivery of proxy material. State law notice requirements govern the timing of proxy material mailing prior to annual meeting. Form 10-K must be filed within 90 days of close of year.	Published and submitted to shareholders at least 15 days before annual meeting but no later than three months after close of fiscal year. Four copies to Exchange together with advice as to the date of mailing to shareholders. PROMPTEST POSSIBLE ISSUANCE URGED. Recommend release of audited figures as soon as available.	Published and submitted to shareholders at least 15 days before annual meeting but no later than four months after close of fiscal year. PROMPTEST POSSIBLE ISSUANCE URGED. Recommend release of audited figures as soon as available. Six copies of the report to be filed with the Securities division of the Exchange (Listing Form SD-1, Item 17).	File 10-K concurrently with SEC filing.	Financial information should be released as soon as available; second release at time printed report is issued if report contains other material information. NYSE and AMEX urge broad distribution of report—including distribution to statistical services—so that company information is available for "ready public reference."
Annual Report: Form 10-K	Required by Section 13 or 15(d) of Securities Exchange Act of 1934 on Form 10-K. To be filed with SEC no later than 90 days	Four copies must be filed with Exchange concurrently with SEC filing; also provide notice to Exchange as to date	Three copies must be filed with Exchange concurrently with SEC filing. (*See Company Guide*, pp. 12-2.)	File 10-K concurrently with SEC filing.	Publicity usually not necessary unless 10-K contains previously unreported material information.

Reporting Required for:	Securities and Exchange Commission	New York Stock Exchange	American Stock Exchange	National Association of Securities Dealers	Generally Recommended Publicity Practice, All Companies
	after close of fiscal year. (Some schedules may be filed 120 days thereafter.) Extensive incorporation by reference from annual report to shareholders and from proxy statement now make integration of Form 10-K and report to shareholders more practical (see general instructions G and H of Form 10-K).	mailed to shareholders. (*NYSE Company Manual* Sections 203.01 and 204.04).			
Cash Dividends (see Stock Split)	All issuers of publicly traded securities are required to give notice of dividend declarations pursuant to Rule 10B-17. Over-the-counter companies must provide the NASD with advance notice of record date for subsequent dissemination to investors, extending comparable stock exchange requirements to OTC market. Failure to comply places issuer in violation of Section 10(b) of the Securities Exchange Act of 1934.	Prompt notice to Exchange and immediate publicity required for *any* action related to a dividend, including omission or postponement of dividend at customary time. The NYSE prefers that it be given notice by TWX (TWX No. 710-581-2801) or by telephone promptly confirmed by TWX, telegram, or letter. Ten days' advance notice of record date. NYSE manual implies announcement of management intention prior to formal board action may be required in case of a "leak" or rumor. *Notice regarding declaration of a cash dividend should include* declaration date; record date(s) for closing or reopening transfer books (or any other	Same as NYSE. Notification to Exchange by telephone or telegram, with confirmation by letter (Listing Form SD-1, Item 1g).	Prompt notification 10 days before record date. File one copy of 10b-17 Report (included in "Reporting Requirements for NASDAQ Companies") with officer's signature.	Prepare publicity in advance and release immediately by a designated officer on word of declaration. Publicity especially important when dividend rate changes. Statement of dividend policy now common in annual reports. Statements of "intention" to take dividend policy now common in annual reports. Statements of "intention" to take dividend action also becoming common.

Reporting Required for:	Securities and Exchange Commission	New York Stock Exchange	American Stock Exchange	National Association of Securities Dealers	Generally Recommended Publicity Practice, All Companies
		meaningful dates); per share amount of tax to be with-held with respect to the dividend, description of tax, net after-tax fee share dividend; any conditions upon which payment of dividend hinges.			
Earnings	Form 10-Q required within 45 days of close of each of first three fiscal quarters. Include information outlined in 10-Q plus a narrative management analysis in form outlined in Form S-K, Item 303. Summary of quarterly results for two years in "unaudited" annual report footnote. Form 10-K required to report full year's earnings.	Quarterly. Publicity required. No fourth quarter statement is required, though items of unusual or nonrecurring nature should be reflected in the company's interim earnings statements.	Quarterly. Should be published within 45 days after end of the first, second, and third fiscal quarters. (No statement is required for the fourth quarter, since that period is covered by the annual report.) Five copies of release should be sent to the Exchange. Press release must be sent to one or more New York City newspapers regularly publishing financial news and to one or more of the national newswires.	Prompt notification and press disclosure if earnings are unusual. File 10-Q and 10-K concurrently with SEC filings.	Immediate publicity; do not hold data until printed quarterly report is published and mailed. Release no later than 10-Q filing; annual results as soon as available. Information in news release must be consistent with 10-Q. Breakout of current quarter results together with year-to-date totals desirable in second, third, and fourth quarter releases.
Legal Proceedings	Form 10-Q at start or termination of proceedings and in any quarter when material development occurs (generally damage claims in excess of 10% of current assets); also any suit against company by an officer, director, or major stockholder. See Regulation S-K, Item 103. See also appendix entry entitled "environmental matters."	No notice to NYSE required unless proceeding bears on ownership, dividends, interest, or principal of listed securities, or start of receivership bankruptcy, or reorganization proceedings.	"Significant litigation." Public disclosure if material. Prompt notice to Exchange.	Prompt notification and public disclosure if material or if company must file report with SEC.	Public disclosure recommended if outcome of legal proceeding could have material effect on company and news of proceeding has not already become public. Court filings now commonly distributed to key business media with or without press release.
Merger: Acquisition or Disposition of Assets	Form 8-K if company acquires or disposes of a significant (10% of total assets or whole subsidiary)	Form 8-K filed (where assets acquired). Immediate public disclosure. Prompt notice	Form 8-K if filed, for acquisition or disposition of assets. Immediate public disclosure.	Prompt notification and public disclosure (8-K filed with SEC).	Exchange policy requires immediate announcement as soon as confidential

Reporting Required for:	Securities and Exchange Commission	New York Stock Exchange	American Stock Exchange	National Association of Securities Dealers	Generally Recommended Publicity Practice, All Companies
	amount of assets or business other than in normal course of business. Proxy soliciting material or registration statement may also be required. Check application of Rule 145 (b) of Securities Act of 1933, to any such transaction involving exchange of stock (see also Tender Offers).	to Exchange where assets disposed of.			disclosures relating to such important matters are made to "outsiders" (i.e., other than "top management" and their individual confidential "advisers"). Immediate publicity, especially when assets consist of an entire product line, division, operating unit, or a "substantial" part of the business.
Merger: Commenting on Unusual Market Activity	After SEC ruling in *In re Carnation*, and appeals court decision in *Levinson, et al., v. Basic Industries*, company can state "no comment" about merger discussions when stock shows unusual market activity. However, if company comments in response to Exchange or regulatory inquiry, it must do so truthfully and acknowledge that merger discussions are taking place.	Prepare to make immediate public announcement concerning unusual market activity from merger negotiations. Immediate, candid public statement concerning state of negotiations or development of corporate plans, if rumors are correct or there are developments. Make statement as soon as disclosure made to outsiders (from business appraisals, financing arrangements, market surveys, etc.). Public statements should be definite regarding price, ratio, timing, any other pertinent information necessary to evaluation. Should include disclosures made to outsiders (*NYSE Company Manual*, Sections 202.01 and .03).	Promptly and publicly disseminate previously undisclosed information contained in any "leak" that resulted in market action. If company unable to determine cause of market action, Exchange may suggest that company issue "no news" release stating that there have been no undisclosed recent developments affecting the company that would account for unusual market activity. Company need not issue public announcement at each stage of merger negotiations, but may await agreement in principle on specific terms or point at which negotiations stabilize. However, publicly release announcement setting forth facts to clarify rumor or report containing material information. (See *Company Guide*, p. 4-7 to 4-8.)	Prompt notification and public disclosure if material or if company must file report with SEC.	Either issue "no comment" statement or explain reason for market activity known to company. Comment asserting that company is "unaware of any reason" to explain market activity is a comment. If company knows the reason for market activity but denies its awareness, it has made a false comment and is probably liable.

Reporting Required for:	Securities and Exchange Commission	New York Stock Exchange	American Stock Exchange	National Association of Securities Dealers	Generally Recommended Publicity Practice, All Companies
Projection: Forecast or Estimate of Earnings	See Reg. S-K General Policy (b). SEC policy encourages use of projections of future economic performance that have "a reasonable basis" and are presented in an appropriate format. Obligation to correct promptly when facts change. Should not discontinue or resume projections without clear explanation of action.	Immediate public disclosure when news goes beyond insiders and their confidential advisers.	Exchange warns against "unwarranted promotional disclosure," including premature announcements of products, and interviews with analysts and financial writers which would unduly influence market activity.	Prompt notification and public disclosure if material (NASD Schedule D).	Projections should be either avoided altogether or widely circulated, with all assumptions stated. Projections by others may require correction by company if wrong but widely believed. Once having made projection, issuer has obligation to update it promptly if assumptions prove wrong. Press releases and other communications should include all information necessary to an understanding of the projection. Legal counsel should be consulted.
Stock Split, Stock Dividend, or Other Change in Capitalization	10-Q required for increase or decrease if exceeds 5% of amount of securities of the class previously outstanding. Notice to NASD or exchange 10 days before record date under Securities Exchange Act's antifraud provisions.	Exchange suggests preliminary discussion. Immediate public disclosure and Exchange notification. Issuance of new shares requires prior listing approval. Either "telephone alert" procedure should be followed or, preferably, wire by TWX. Separate confirmation letter to Exchange. Company's notice to Exchange should indicate brokers' and nominees' requirements and date by which they must notify disbursing agent of full and fractional share requirements. Exchange will publicize this in its *Weekly Bulletin* or special circulars.	Immediate public disclosure and Exchange notification. Issuance of new shares requires prior listing approval. Treatment of fractional shares must be announced.	Prompt notification and public disclosure 10 days before record date. File one copy of 10b-17 Report (included in "Reporting Requirements for NASDAQ Companies") with officer's signature. File 10-Q concurrently with SEC filing.	Immediate publicity as soon as proposal becomes known to outsiders, whether formally voted or not. Discuss early whether to describe transaction as a split, dividend, or both and use terminology consistently.

Reporting Required for:	Securities and Exchange Commission	New York Stock Exchange	American Stock Exchange	National Association of Securities Dealers	Generally Recommended Publicity Practice, All Companies
		Notice regarding stock dividend, split, or distribution should include: ratio of stock dividend or split; record date for holders entitled to receive distribution; conditions upon which transaction hinges; date for mailing of certificates for additional shares.			
Tender Offer	Conduct and published remarks of all parties governed by Sections 13(d), 13(e), 14(d), 14(e) of the 1934 Act and regulations thereunder. Schedule 14D-1 disclosure required of raider. Target required to file Schedule 14D-9 for any solicitation or recommendation to security holders. (See also *Hart-Scott-Rodino* requirements.)	Consult Exchange Stock List Department in advance. Immediate publicity and notice to Exchange. Deliver offering material to Exchange no later than distribution date to shareholders. Consult Exchange when terms of tender at variance with Exchange principles regarding tender offers.	Consult Exchange Securities Division in advance. Immediate publicity and notice to Exchange.	Prompt notification and public disclosure (NASD Schedule D).	Massive publicity effort required; should not be attempted without thorough familiarity with current rules and constant consultation with counsel. Neither raider nor target should comment publicly until necessary SEC filings have been made. "Stop, look, listen" letter permitted under Rule 14D-9(e).

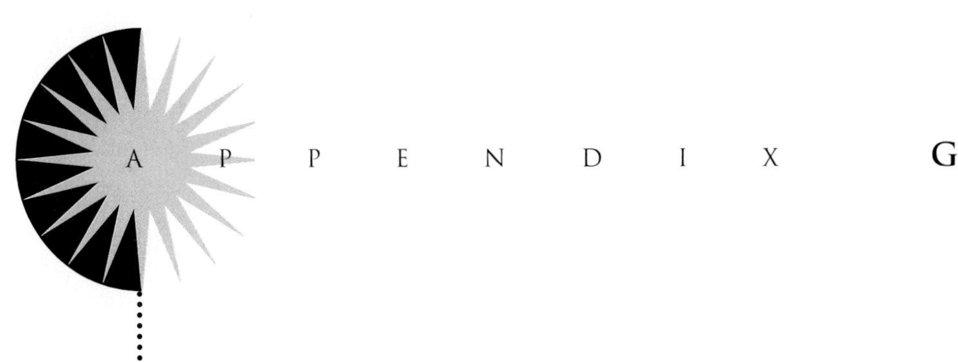

ANNUAL MEETING CHECKLIST

By Frank Widder

The following annual shareholder's meeting checklist can be adapted to serve as a "preflight" plan for almost any major meeting.

I. Meeting announcement
   A. Shareholder's proxy statement and general notice
   B. Investment houses', major brokers', and institutional investors' notice and invitation
   C. Financial media invitations
   D. Employee notice of meeting
   E. Guests

   Follow-up (by phone or in person)
   A. Investor relations contacts with major shareholders to determine participation, major areas of interest, potential problems
   B. Major investment houses involved with company
   C. Local financial press
   D. Guest relations

II. Management announcement
   A. Notify all key management personnel to make sure they will be there and arrange alternates for those who cannot make it
   B. Notify all members of the board to determine their ability to make the meeting
   C. Arrange flight times and book hotel in advance; guarantee arrival if necessary

III. Management coaching
   A. Draft basic list of shareholders' problems and questions
   B. Arrange meeting with CEO and chairman to prepare answers, with key staff and legal department to run down answers, and practice those answers
   C. Review and practice management speeches

IV. Presentation materials
   A. Review orders for graphs and slides, compare with financial review speech
   B. Screen any films
   C. Review displays

V. Agenda: order of presentations with approximate running times (in minutes)
   A. Introduction—chairman calls meeting to order and introduces board and management (4:00)
   B. Opening comments by chairman and review of overall activities of company (6:00)
   C. President's message (with visuals) (15:00)
   D. Financial report by vice president, finance (with slide highlights) (5:00)
   E. Film (20:00)
   F. Present proposals in proxy (limit each shareholder to one statement per issue; hand out ballots to shareholders at beginning) (20:00)
   G. Voting, collect ballots (3:00)
   H. General discussion (limit shareholders to one question each) (30:00)
   I. Announce voting results (3:00)
   J. Present company awards of appreciation (2:00)
   K. Adjournment (1:00)—total: 1 hour, 49 minutes

   Agenda allows 20 additional minutes for discussion or for more questions during presentation of proposals. Final agenda will be printed and passed out by ushers at meeting.

VI. Site preparation
   A. Staff
      1. Electrician, lighting, and sound equipment specialists on hand from 8 A.M. to 5 P.M.
      2. Supervisor of custodial, security, and equipment staffs
      3. Walkie-talkie communications network with equipment staff
      4. Waiters for lounge
      5. Caterers for lounge
   B. Parking
      1. Traffic direction displays at parking lot entrances
      2. Parking attendants directing traffic to proper area
      3. Signs pointing to meeting entrance in parking lot
   C. Entrance/reception
      1. Reception tables with pencils and guest roster
      2. Receptionists to staff tables and answer questions about facilities (need to be briefed beforehand)
      3. Well-marked rest areas and signs indicating meeting area
      4. Unarmed security guards to control crowd and provide protection
      5. Armed security guards located in discrete areas of meeting room
      6. Name tags for all representatives of company
   D. Display area
      1. Displays set up along walls, to avoid impeding foot traffic, and checked for operation 24 hours in advance
      2. Representatives to staff each booth and be prepared for questions about display
      3. Tables to display necessary financial information—annual report, 10-K, proxy statement, quarterlies
   E. Lounge area
      1. Adequate seating for participants, guests
      2. Breakfast/luncheon tables

F. Meeting areas
   1. Sound, lighting, video checks
   2. Sound mikes for all stage participants
   3. Additional speakers for amplification
   4. Alternate hookup in case of failures—sound, lighting, and video; alternate film in case of breakage
   5. Large screen for slide and film
   6. Slide and film projectors for presentation
   7. Audio and lighting mixers
   8. Portable, remote mikes with long cords for audience questions
   9. Tape recorder hookup to record proceedings

G. Construction
   1. Podium constructed high enough for everyone to have direct view of all participants
   2. Area blocked off for board and management to view film
   3. Area blocked off for lighting and sound equipment
   4. Exits properly marked
   5. Access to podium and all chairs necessary for seating board and management
   6. Logo prominently displayed and lighted above podium

H. Staff
   1. Ushers with flashlights at all entrances for seating
   2. Security at far corners of room
   3. Backstage technicians for sound emergencies
   4. Remote mike monitors on both aisles or front and back of room
   5. Photographer to shoot proceedings, displays, and key presentations

I. Stage seating arrangements
   1. Podium in middle, chairs to either side
   2. Arrange board members in tenure order
   3. Management in hierarchy order
   4. Chairman sits on board side
   5. President on management side
   6. Nameplates for all participants on podium
   7. Glasses, water, ashtrays

J. Shareholder seating
   1. First-come basis
   2. Areas roped off for invited shareholders and guests
   3. Areas roped off for film viewing by participants
   4. Special area for members not represented on stage—public accountants, special staff, guests

VII. Final run-through

A. Day prior to meeting, complete mock session of annual report, with key principals and timing of presentation—including possible questions and responses

B. Review slide show and cues four hours before meeting

C. Check screening room communications to begin film; make sure time is allowed to clear stage

D. Make sure award is ready for presentation

E. Hand out scripts to key participants and technical people

VIII. Day of meeting

A. Review with supervisor to ensure that all technical checks are okay

B. See that all displays are up and working

C. Contact board and management people to check for emergencies in transportation; arrange backup accommodations if necessary
D. Sit-down breakfast with key participants to go over agenda and cover any last-minute questions
E. Go to convention center, check in with supervisor, security head, parking attendant; ensure that copies of scripts are placed at podium
F. Greet participants and guide to lounge
G. Wait for shareholders and investors, media; be available for questions and arrange interviews
H. Sit down and wait
I. Guide participants, guests to luncheon in lounge; make sure bar is set up
J. Have a drink—and good night

APPENDIX H

ON-LINE DATABASES

Particularly important for public relations research are on-line databases, which store vast quantities of information on current and historical subjects. Some of the major service information vendors available to public relations practitioners are described here.

CD Plus Technologies
333 Seventh Avenue
4th Floor
New York, NY 10001

For over a decade, this service has supplied a large number of databases, with primary emphasis on medical, engineering, educational, and business-oriented information. Price structure varies according to the type of service selected. The Open Access Plan has an annual password fee of $80, a per connect-hour charge of between $10 and $139, depending on the service, and a telecommunications charge of about $12.

DIALCOM Services, Inc.
2560 N. First Street
P.O. Box 49019
San Jose, CA 95161-9019
800-872-7654

DIALCOM, begun in 1970, was purchased by MCI. It offers gateways to databases such as UPI, the Official Airline Guide, and the Bureau of National Affairs. It also offers gateway services to other on-line vendors, which enable customers to access databases offered on Dow Jones News/Retrieval Service, BRS, and DIALOG. The fee structure is based on the number of hours used, not the databases accessed. Costs for accessing the gateway services are based on the rates charged by other vendors. The service operates 24 hours a day, seven days a week.

DIALOG Information Services, Inc.
Lockheed Corporation
3460 Hillview Avenue
Palo Alto, CA 94304
800-334-2564

DIALOG was started as a commercial venture in 1972 by the Lockheed Corporation. It is one of the largest on-line services, offering nearly 400 databases that range from business and economics to science and technology. DIALOG charges a $295 initiation fee, $100 of which can be applied to future use, and has a wide variation in connect-hour cost. Each database has a set hourly cost, ranging from $30 to $300. DIALOG is available 24 hours a day, seven days a week.

Dow Jones News/Retrieval
P.O. Box 300
Princeton, NJ 08543
800-522-3567

This is part of Dow Jones and Company, publisher of *The Wall Street Journal.* More than 60 databases are offered, primarily relating to business and economics, financial and investment services, and general news and information. *The Wall Street Journal* is available in summary form, as well as in its entirety. The fee structure for companies is complex. For individuals, costs start with a $29.95 sign-up fee and an $18 annual service fee that kicks in after the first year. Then fees range from $.50 to $2.85 per minute for prime time and from $0.08 to $0.60 per minute for nonprime time. The service is available 24 hours a day.

Facts on File
460 Park Avenue South
New York, NY 10016
212-683-2244

Facts on File summarizes information daily from leading U.S. and foreign periodicals, the publications of Commerce Clearing House, *Congressional Quarterly, Congressional Record, State Department Bulletin,* presidential documents, and official press releases. Subject areas are as diverse as the news of the day. The annual subscription fee is $680.

Find/SVP
625 Avenue of the Americas
New York, NY 10011
212/645-4500

Find/SVP provides quick consulting and research services by telephone for decision makers as a primary information resource to small and medium-sized companies and as a supplemental service to larger corporations that maintain in-house research and information centers. It has access to more than 3,000 on-line databases, 2,000 periodical subscriptions, tens of thousands of subject company and company files, hundreds of directories and reference works, dozens of cabinets of microfiche, and extensive CD-ROM sources. Its activities are organized into ten consultant teams: (1) business/financial, (2) consumer products, (3) technical/industrial, (4) human resources/employee benefits, (5) document services, (6) accounting/tax, (7) legal, (8) health care, (9) society and media, and (10) PC help. Hourly rates range from $40 to $175, depending on the complexity of the request. Retainers of $500 to $1,500, plus out-of-pocket expenses, entitle unlimited use. Find/SVP promises that "in most cases, you'll have your answer in less than 48 hours from the time you call."

LEXIS and NEXIS
Mead Data Central
9443 Springboro Pike
P.O. Box 933
Dayton, OH 45401
800-227-4908

LEXIS and NEXIS are two of the information services provided by this division of Mead Corporation. LEXIS is a legal information database containing the full text of case law from state, federal, and international courts; state and federal regulations; and other legal records. NEXIS is a full-text database containing 750 major newspapers, magazines, and newsletters. In 1988, a group of media in the NEXIS databank was organized as the Advertising and Public Relations Library, including news wires and communications-oriented publications. The fee structure is complex, but the range of costs varies from $6 to $50 for the search and $35 per hour for connect charges. Both services are available 24 hours a day on weekdays and all weekend, except from 2 A.M. to 10 A.M. Sunday.

NewsNet, Inc.
945 Haverford Road
Bryn Mawr, PA 19010
800-345-1301

NewsNet was started in 1982 by Independent Publications. It offers primarily newsletters and wire services. There are more than 400 specialized business newsletters and wire services covering more than 35 industries, including telecommunications, publishing, broadcasting, electronics and computers, energy, investment, accounting, and taxation. Prices range from $24 to more than $100 an hour, depending on the newsletter being accessed. There is also a monthly minimum charge of $15. NewsNet is available 24 hours a day.

INDEX